BIG TEN
FOOTBALL

Since 1895

Books by John D. McCallum

The Encyclopedia of World Boxing Champions
The World Heavyweight Boxing Championship: A History
Ty Cobb
The Tiger Wore Spikes
We Remember Rockne
College Football, U.S.A.
This Was Football
Dumb Dan
Boxing Fans' Almanac
Everest Diary
Going Their Way
That Kelly Family
Six Roads from Abilene
The Story of Dan Lyons, S.J.
Not by Bread Alone
Scooper
How You Can Play Little League Baseball
The Gladiators and other books . . .

John D. McCallum

BIG TEN FOOTBALL

Since 1895

Chilton Book Company
RADNOR, PENNSYLVANIA

Copyright © 1976 by John D. McCallum

First Edition   *All Rights Reserved*

Published in Radnor, Pa., by Chilton Book Company
and simultaneously in Don Mills, Ont., Canada
by Thomas Nelson & Sons, Ltd.

Designed by Anne Churchman

Manufactured in the United States of America

Library of Congress Catalogue Card Number: 76-28579
ISBN Number: 0-8019-6396-6

Acknowledgments

Pictures courtesy of the universities of
Michigan, Ohio State, Iowa, Michigan State,
Minnesota, Northwestern, Indiana, Illinois,
Wisconsin, and Purdue.

1 2 3 4 5 6 7 8 9 0   5 4 3 2 1 0 9 8 7 6

To

F. Peavey Heffelfinger,

**Long-time friend extraordinary—
a Yale man who grew up in
big ten country**

Contents

The First

80

Years

And Then There Were Ten
1895–1920

History is not clear on the question, but the origin of football has been traced as far back as 478 B.C. Some claim that it all started when Julius Caesar came upon Teutonic tribesmen kicking and throwing and running with an oval-shaped ball in what vaguely resembled a game of football. Closer inspection revealed, however, that it wasn't a ball at all they were playing with—it was the freshly severed head of an enemy soldier. Boys will be boys.

Since the cruel days of the cestus, football has become a geographical, historical, and social event, and sometimes all three. Ever since the founding of the Big Ten Conference in 1895, every Midwesterner has had *somebody* he especially likes to see beaten. During the week of their game, Ohio State feels about Michigan the way Army feels about Navy. Beneath the breast of every Indiana tuba player, it has been said, lies a hatred for Purdue. Turn a Minnesota man around three times and he'll stagger straight to Ann Arbor with a couple of buckets of maroon and gold paint, if the green and white of Michigan State hasn't already beaten him there. Give a Wisconsin supporter two drinks and he'll bet all the cheese he's got that the Badgers will whip Illinois.

Tradition and rivalry are words that belong almost exclusively to the vernacular of college football, right in there with Grange, Zuppke, Hurry-Up, Stagg, Bronko, The Horse, Harmon, Chick, Eckie, and all that kind of thing. Old as

the two words are, they are irreplaceable, for it is what they suggest that specifically separates the college game from that of the professionals. Sophisticates, with their double drag-outs and their post-and-gos, may not like it, but college football *is* Michigan playing Minnesota for the Little Brown Jug, a street brawl in downtown Columbus the night before the Buckeyes play the Wolverines, and Illinois students stealing the Northwestern mascot.

There are many types of rivalries, all of which help any college season keep its hip pads up. There are intrastate border, crosstown and interservice rivalries. These are natural rivalries. The most common are the intrastate variety. In the Midwest, any football-minded boy of six can name the most noteworthy of all of the types: Purdue–Indiana, Purdue–Notre Dame, Michigan–Michigan State, Minnesota–Wisconsin, Illinois–Northwestern, Iowa–Indiana, and Ohio State vs. anybody.

One august rivalry, Michigan–Minnesota, is not so easy to understand. Geography certainly could not have had much to do with it. Ann Arbor is closer to Nashville, Tennessee than it is to Minneapolis. If you want the truth, the Michigan–Minnesota traditional for the Little Brown Jug began quite by accident, although there is probably behind it some seed of the Midwestern ethic, a mutual fondness for wheat fields, silos, or duck hunting, perhaps.

At any rate, the Little Brown Jug, which is neither little nor brown and never was, has become football's best-known *objet d'art,* because Michigan and Minnesota have played a lot of big games and turned out hordes of good teams.

The jug, which is two-and-a-half feet tall, was originally an old gray plaster crock that Fielding H. Yost of Michigan carried around so that his legions could drink fresh Ann Arbor spring water as they went around beating everybody 100 to 0. The tradition of Minnesota and Michigan playing for the jug began with one of the most exotic upsets in collegiate football history. It happened in 1903. That season Michigan, with Willie Heston carrying the ball to immortality, arrived in Minneapolis in the midst of a memorable streak. The Wolverines had won 29 straight games, and had scored 1,631 points—56 per game—to a total of 12 points for their opponents.

One of football's significant innovations took place that day. Minnesota used a seven-man defensive line for the first time, with the other four players forming an early-day rendition of the umbrella secondary. Prior to this, all defenses had been nine-man lines with so little passing to guard against, and Willie Heston had always been long gone every time he cracked through the first barrier. Minnesota's defense was designed to give Heston two walls to get through. He never did. The game was played on old Northrup Field and the Golden Gophers clawed their way to a 6–6 tie.

Hurry-Up Yost was in such a hurry to whisk his boys out of town after the upset that they forgot the crock of water. The oversight led to the immediate joke among Minnesota Swedes: *"Jost* left his *yug."* So the Gophers kept the jug and sent word back to Michigan that the Wolverines would have to win it back. They have been fighting over it ever since. If the rivalry has improved with age, so has the jug. It is now painted maroon (for Minnesota) and blue (for Michigan), and the scores of all the games are on it, including a recent string of eight Michigan victories in a row.

Over the span of years, the Big Ten has played some of the best college football in the country. Out in the cornbelt they grow them tougher and stronger and bigger.

In his Civil War *Memoirs,* General William T. Sherman pointed out that while the Southerners usually beat the Easterners on the battlefield, it was the hard-bitten farm boys from the Middle West who broke the back of the Confederacy.

"Our cornbelt pioneers had not forgotten how to use their legs," General Sherman said. "They could really march."

The motorcar age doesn't seem to atrophy those Midwestern legs, either, as witness the number of Top Ten teams and the All-Americans that come out of the Big Ten year after year. When writing a history of the Conference, one automatically goes back to the particulars surrounding its origin. The year was 1895. James H. Smart, President of Pur-

Willie Heston (top center of photo) gains 15 yards in the historic 1903 Little Brown Jug game against Minnesota. The checkerboard markings extended over the entire field and allowed the ball-carrier to roam any place beyond the scrimmage line, providing he ran five yards outside of the spot where the ball was centered. Because of the griddle-like lines, sports writers started calling a playing field "the gridiron."

W. W. (Pudge) Heffelfinger (back row, fifth from left) was still in high school in Minneapolis when he played for the 1887 Minnesota football team. The following year, Heffelfinger went on to Yale, where he became a three-time All-American guard and Hall of Famer. Alf Pillsbury, later the flour company tycoon, is pictured in bottom row, fourth from left.

due, invited six other college presidents from the Midwest to meet with him in Chicago to talk about control of intercollegiate athletics. And so they came, the presidents of Minnesota, Wisconsin, Illinois, Northwestern, Michigan, and University of Chicago.

"Gentlemen," President Smart told the meeting, "the problems are awesome."

Indeed they were. There were no rules of eligibility, and no organization to draw up or enforce any. Colleges commonly bolstered their teams with raw-boned recruits not even enrolled in school. In 1890, for example, Michigan had seven players on the football varsity who were not even in school. Tramp athletes played for as many as three and four different schools—without bothering to enroll! Some coaches even inserted themselves in their lineups. The late Pudge Heffelfinger, legendary Yale All-American guard in 1889–90–91, confessed to me in 1954 while we were collaborating on a book that he was still a senior in high school when the University of Minnesota recruited him to play in the line for the Gophers in 1887.

"It was not unusual for a man to play for eight or so years for the same school," Pudge said. "No one thought anything of it. Everyone was doing it."

The meeting of presidents was held on January 11, 1895, at the Palmer House and included President Angell of Michigan, President Rogers of Northwestern, President Northrop of Minnesota, President Draper of Illinois, President Adams of Wisconsin, President Harper of Chicago, and President Smart. The conference lasted for one day, and from it came the formal designation of the "Intercollegiate Conference of Faculty Representatives," the forerunner of the Western Conference, or Big Ten as it is called today. The seven presidents at the first meeting established the first set of rules:

1. Each college and university which has not already done so shall appoint a committee on college athletics which shall take general supervision of all athletic matters in the respective college or university, and which shall have all responsibility of enforcing the college or university rules regarding athletics and all intercollegiate sports.

2. No one shall participate in any game or athletic sport unless he be a bona fide student doing full work in a regular or special course as defined in the curriculum of his college; and no person who has participated in any match game as a member of any college team shall be permitted to participate in any game as a member of another college team, until he has been a matriculate in said college under the above conditions for a period of six months. This

rule shall not apply to students who, having graduated at one college, shall enter another college for professional or graduate study.

3. No person shall be admitted to any intercollegiate contest who receives any gift, remuneration or pay for his services on the college team.

4. Any student of any institution who shall be pursuing a regularly prescribed resident graduate course within such institution, whether for an advanced degree or in one of its professional schools, may be permitted to play for the period of the minimum number of years required for securing the graduate or professional degree for which he is a candidate.

5. No person who has been employed in training a college team for intercollegiate contests shall be allowed to participate in any intercollegiate contest as a member of any team which he has trained, and no professional athlete or person who has ever been a member of a professional team shall play at any intercollegiate contest.

6. No student shall play in any game under an assumed name.

7. No student shall be permitted to participate in any intercollegiate contest who is found by the faculty to be delinquent in his studies.

8. All games shall be played on grounds either owned by or under the immediate control of one or both of the colleges participating in the contest, and all games shall be played under student management and not under the patronage or control of any other corporation, association or private individual.

9. The election of managers and captains of teams in each college shall be subject to the approval of its committee on athletics.

10. College teams shall not engage in games with professional teams nor with those representing so-called athletic clubs.

11. Before every intercollegiate contest a list of men proposing to play shall be presented by each team or teams to the other or others, certifying that all the members are entitled to play under conditions of the rules adopted, such certificate to be signed by the registrar or secretary of the college or university. It shall be the duty of the captain to enforce this rule.

12. We call upon the expert managers of football teams to so revise the rules as to reduce the liability to injury to a minimum.

In the years to come, these rules would be amplified, reconsidered, strengthened, softened, praised, jeered, ignored, and followed religiously.

A year later, each school agreed to send a faculty representative back to Chicago as the second step toward a new concept of intercollegiate athletic supervision, by the *faculty*, not the athletic department. The University of Chicago went even further. In 1892, it had already elevated Amos Alonzo Stagg, who had been a teammate of Pudge Heffelfinger's at Yale, to faculty status. And so in 1896, Stagg, coach and director of athletics, attended the second meeting in Chicago as a *faculty* representative.

The group agreed to convene twice a year as a permanent body and to accept other schools in the Midwest who felt about athletic control as they did: That is, each member would police itself as well as each other. Every collegiate conference that followed was founded upon this Western Conference philosophy.

Caspar Whitney, famous sports writer of the day, wrote: "The most notable clearing of the atmosphere is to be seen in the West. Football—indeed, *all* Midwestern college sports—was very near total extinction because of a rampant professional spirit that had ranged throughout nearly all the universities, leaving corruption in its wake. The meeting last winter in Chicago marked the beginning of a new and clarified era in Western collegiate sport."

Because the men of Yale got the jump on football, they were almost always Eastern and National football champions between the years 1872 and 1910. For this reason it was logical that Yale men would go out into the world carrying football to all parts of America. So deeply rooted was the Blue in the evolutionary scheme of the modern game, that Harry Mehre, coach of Georgia, was heard to remark many years later, "I would rather beat any team in the country than Yale. For to me and most of us, Yale *means* American football."

Fielding Yost said much the same thing.

"Yale and Walter Camp *are* football," Hurry-Up said. "Yale was the first to have the true feel of the game, a game which means spirit, body contact, and team play, all the finest elements of competition. Many others have come along since, but it was Yale that set the earlier pace."

Knute Rockne was asked one time to reveal where his famous Notre Dame shift came from.

"Where everything else in football came from," Rock said. "Yale. All football comes from Yale."

It was not totally unexpected, then, that a

Yale man, Pudge Heffelfinger, would show up in Minneapolis, his home town, to coach the Golden Gophers in 1895. In the one year he coached the Maroon and Gold, his record was 7–3–0. Perhaps more noteworthy about Heffelfinger that year, however, was the November 12th exhibition game he played in at Pittsburgh. The Allegheny Athletic Association paid him $500 to play against the Pittsburgh Athletic Club—the first recorded case of an athlete being paid openly to play football. Pudge earned his money, too. Late in the game, he scooped up a fumble and ran it back for the winning touchdown.

At Minnesota, Pudge stressed line play. In 10 games, only 54 points were scored against the Gophers. Five opponents were shut out.

"The secret to line play is your stance," Pudge told his recruits. "Both on attack and defense you have to stand more or less erect, knees bent in a slight crouch, body leaning forward from the hips, legs spread about three feet part, left foot advanced when playing left guard. Hit your man with a shoulder lunge on attack and use your hands to start his head in the direction you want to move him, when we are on defense. A man's body must go where his head goes. Don't get down on one or both knees. A man is no good on his knees. Nobody would have heard of me at Yale if Walter Camp had made me take it kneeling down. Our Yale linemen had their heads up where they could see what was happening across the neutral zone. We never went down unless we had to. We whipped underneath our opponents from that half-crouch something like the way a hammer thrower pivots his body on the release.

"Now, some of these younger coaches say it can't be done that way. They say you'll end up on your backs. My only answer to that is that I've played against the best, and nobody has put me on my back yet. It's method, not muscle, that will give you the jump on linemen. So stay on your feet. When you're up on your feet you are in position to get into enemy territory fast. You can't do that so quickly if you're down on your knees. From a semi-standing stance you can look the defense formation over, or size up the enemy grouping on attack. By watching the ball closely, you can detect the slightest flexing of the opposing center's hands—the tip-off that he's going to snap

it—and in this way time your charge with the ball. Our old Yale line always charged on the ball. Our linemen were strong and fast rather than big and ponderous.

"What happens to a boxer who bores in blindly with his head down? He gets his ears knocked off. He can't ward off blows which he doesn't see coming. Well, the same thing goes for a football lineman. I never kept my head down. I wanted to see what was coming, and be up on my feet where I could deliver. If you're up against a much better man, then you can fall down and grab legs; but stay on your feet as long as you can. They tell me I'd be mousetrapped if I charged fast today with my legs driving. Boloney! I'd have my eyes open and fight off the mousetrapper before he got me. I never made a blind charge. I drove in toward the pressure point and mussed things up before the interference could form. If you hit 'em first you catch 'em off balance. My old coach, Walter Camp, used to tell us on defense: 'Let 'em have two yards.' To which I'd reply, 'No, sir, not two inches!'

"On offense, a running guard can get out much quicker from a stand-by stance to lead interference. A standing line helps screen the ball-carrier. I should know something about this because I originated line interference. That's right, I was the first to drop out of the line and spearhead the play. It happened five years ago in the Yale–Penn game. Penn had a good team and expected to hold us to a close score. But the guard stunt panicked them. I'd pivot out of the line, take three strides to the right, and then turn in ahead of Lee McClung, our great ball-carrier, outside the defensive tackle. If you hit the spot on the dot you're bound to make yardage. We made plenty against Penn. I got a perfect blocking angle on either the end or defensive back, and McClung had a clear path to the safety man. He was the first ball-carrier I've ever seen to use the cutback after breaking through the line."

In my Heffelfinger notes I find what Pudge called a "Strategy Chart." Here you see how the model play-caller, circa 1895, plotted his attack according to position on the field:

0–10. This is the last ditch zone. Take no chances. Kick on first down. A fumble here may cost you the game.

10–30. May try strong running play first—but kick on second or third down. Never pass unless score calls for drastic measures. Hang on to ball. Take no chances on blocked punt or fumble.

30–40. Sweeps, wide runs, long gain plays—but never risk loss of ball. Kick on second or third down.

40–50. Long passes on first, second or third down, preferably second and third. Wide sweeps and off-tackle plays are good here. Do not use best plays here. Save them for surprises.

50–40. Offensive territory. Press hard. Use mousetraps, sneaks, spinners, etc. Punt out of bounds on last try. Take a chance.

40–20. Use all tricks in your bag. Scoring passes, reverse and fake reverses, spinners. Save your best tricks for this zone.

20–10. Stay in the middle of the field. Use strongest running plays and best passes. Aim at opponent's weak spots—if little hope for touchdowns—try placekick, or dropkick.

10–0. Point blank zone. Going tough. Defense compressed. If power plays gain three yards, repeat. If stopped, pull out trick play—avoid wide end runs until last down. Intensive power drive on each play.

Go-go-Gophers!

Northwestern halfbacks Jesse Van Doozer, left, and Al Potter catapulted the new Western Conference to national heights in 1896.

Placekicker Neil Snow and holder Bill Cunningham, stars of the late 1890s, were Michigan's first All-Americans.

Even in the 1890s the Midwest was on the way toward establishing a Big Four of its own—Chicago, Michigan, Wisconsin, and Minnesota—to rival the East Coast's Big Three—Yale, Harvard, and Princeton. Well before the arrival of Hurry-Up Yost in 1901, Michigan was turning out strong football teams. One of them went East in 1895 and held mighty Harvard to a field goal, a respectable showing despite the fact that Michigan failed to score. Wisconsin, too, suited up strong elevens and barely lost by a touchdown to Yale. Make no bones about it, formidable football was on the rise in the heartland.

Wisconsin won the first two Western Conference titles—in 1896 and 1897—and stayed near the top for most of the league's first decade, as did Chicago, Minnesota, and Michigan. This was no great surprise, since these were the sectional leaders even before the Conference was founded.

Around Madison, Wisconsin, everybody's

Saturday's hero was Pat O'Dea. The great kicking star from Australia had a kick like a kangaroo. For four years Badger Pat displayed a ravishing style that America never knew before and may never know again. What he left in the record books should keep his name alive as long as football is played.

In 1896, O'Dea made his college debut in a night game against Pop Warner's champion Carlisle Indians. He sent a 50-yard "punted forward pass" to Judge Ike Carroll who, from an "outside" start, was eligible to and able to fall on the ball at the goal and roll over for the score. The Indians, who never saw the football because it went high over the girders holding the lights, refused to believe what had happened.

Against Minnesota, in 1897, in his first game against the team that had been treating Wisconsin badly, O'Dea got cornered, let the ball loose on the run and dropkicked 40 yards through the uprights. Dad Moulton, later a Stanford track coach, then a trainer, dropped his water bucket in amazement on the sideline. An astonished Minnesota team, from that moment on, was kicked to death, 39–0.

Against Chicago, a "championship game," Pat dropped over two 40-yard field goals and punted Chicago to submission, 28–0, much as Joe Paglia punted California into helplessness in a classic exhibition 37 years later.

In 1897, against Beloit, a team that was tough, O'Dea was supposed to let his Badger teammates do the work. The team couldn't do it, so O'Dea dropped over two dropkicks, only to get a bawling out from Coach Phil King. The final score was 10–0, field goals counting 5 points each in those days.

In 1898 Northwestern was a team supposed to whale the dickens out of Wisconsin, known as the famous "kindergarten" team of those days, since it included only one veteran besides Pat. O'Dea had a disagreement with alumni representatives, who wanted to bring more help and Pat is said to have been nettled going into the game. Afer running two plays, he dropped back, took two steps, and dropkicked the ball 63 yards through the bars, the world record. The ball went over the tops of the uprights, and 20 yards on to hit the fence surrounding the field. The score at the finish: Wisconsin 48, Northwestern 0!

The Wisconsin game against Illinois in 1899

Pat O'Dea, Wisconsin 1896–1899, was the greatest punter and dropkicker in college football during his era.

was another tough one. A 20-mile wind blew across the field, while, 55 yards from the goal posts, O'Dea prepared for a placekick. "What are you doing?" the referee wanted to know, after Pat had made a fair catch. "What do you think?" O'Dea replied. "I think you're nuts," the ref said, "if you're trying to score against this wind."

Bill Juneau held the ball. Pat lined up so as to kick almost for the righthand corner of the field. One step and he kicked, with the crowd spellbound. The ball sailed directly for the corner, then finally, as the wind caught it, swerved back to the left, and floated straight through the middle of the bars—an almost impossible stunt.

Against Michigan, in 1899, with the press commenting freely on the proposition that the Wolverines had to stop O'Dea, Pat gave them a 35-yard dropkick score to start with, and a long curve punt, which the Michigan safety dropped, allowing a Wisconsin man to pick it up for a touchdown, all in the first half. Later, O'Dea was forced out of the only college game in which he did not play the full 60 minutes. After the game, the Michigan center was quoted in one newspaper as saying, "We could have won if we had gotten O'Dea out sooner."

In the Minnesota game in 1899, after two plays O'Dea got the ball and started on an end sweep. Gil Dobie—that's right, Gloomy Gil—cornered him. O'Dea bluffed going wide and Dobie prepared to nail him. Suddenly, O'Dea sidestepped Dobie's lunge and dropkicked the ball *over* Gil's head—55 yards through the air, and through the bars.

Once, in a tight spot, Paul Trat, the Wisconsin halfback, had the ball and was in a tangle when a touchdown was needed. So Pat O'Dea picked Trat up out of the jam and carried him, football and all, over the goal. "No, Paul wasn't so big," O'Dea said afterward. "He was just a little over six feet and 170 pounds."

Speaking of trick plays, Heffelfinger once told me about an odd play at the turn of the century that Columbia used to run. They called it the "hurdle" play and the central figure was Harold Weekes. It was his specialty, poor fellow. Weekes would get the ball some five yards behind his front line, which was all pinched in tight, and he'd get off to a running start, and using the back of his center—a fellow with the name of "Bessy" Bruce—he'd go off like a diver from a springboard, trying to launch himself into space. His ends would come around and push him if he was in danger of toppling back. It was like trying to scale a mountain sometimes if the opposition bunched up on him.

In 1902, in the Princeton game, the Tigers came up with a defense against Weekes: they got a guy named Dana Kafer and they hurdled him the same time Weekes was coming over the top; they met in midflight, and both were carried off in pieces.

Those were the days!

In 1899, Indiana and Iowa joined the Western Conference, and that year for the first time the name "Big Nine" broke into public print. Chicago won its first football championship under Amos Alonzo Stagg, who arrived on the campus in 1892 when the squad numbered only 13 players; he himself played the first two years. "The game was too young and weak," he explained, "for such a situation to be thought particularly unusual." Chicago's first game against a college team, Northwestern, resulted in a scoreless tie and gate receipts of

$22.65. The University of Chicago was endowed by America's richest millionaire, John D. Rockefeller, and early cash flow of Rockefeller dollars was so slow that Coach Stagg had to go into his own pocket to rent a dressing room for practice.

With wedge, mass, and mass momentum plays predominating, the game was so rough anything went, short of murder. The last game Stagg played in, against Purdue in 1893, got so bad that the district attorney for Tippecanoe County strode onto the field and threatened indictments for assault and battery.

Amidst the brawling, Stagg's integrity still managed to shine forth, and he was even invited to officiate games in which Chicago played. On one of these assignments he rushed to the Chicago dressing room as soon as the half was over and gave the only mercenary fight talk of his career. "Boys," he said, "you've got to win! John D. Rockefeller is in the stands!"

From these hardy beginnings, Stagg brought Chicago football to national stature. Before the turn of the century, the Maroon won the Con-

Fullback Clarence Herschberger, Chicago 1898, here shown, and Michigan's center William Cunningham, were the first two stars from the Big Ten to make the All-American team.

ference championship in 1896 and 1899. Walter Kennedy, of Albion, Michigan, was the captain and quarterback of the 1899 squad. He had great admiration for Coach Stagg.

"We were lucky to have played at Chicago at the same time as the Old Man was there," said Kennedy some years ago. "I think every member of our 1899 squad agrees with me. No one could have spent four years in personal contact with Stagg without absorbing some of his sterling ideas of right and wrong. While few of us have achieved his high plane of life, we all came under his influence, and it is not beyond the realms of the imagination that some of us are enjoying life today because of the things outside of football that he taught us.

"That was some Chicago team, 1899. We played 18 games and won them all except for two ties with Iowa and Penn. We rolled over Notre Dame, 23–6, and smothered Purdue (44–0), Northwestern (76–0), Minnesota (29–0), and Wisconsin (17–0), among others. We scored a total of 500 points against a mere 28.

"In the 5-to-5 tie with Pennsylvania, we should have won easily. I lost it by wanting to make a touchdown through All-American Truxton Hare, one of the best linemen in history. With the ball only a yard from their goal, Hare challenged us by spreading wide from his position at guard. Foolishly I accepted his challenge and threw Frank Slaker at him. Nine times out of 10 Frank would have gone through Hare or any other lineman for a yard, but something slipped and we lost our big chance to score.

"It is interesting to us oldtimers to note the changes 30 years have made in football. I think it is a better game for the players now, and more exciting to the fans, but at the same time, I still have a feeling of pride of having been able to play 30 years ago, for the game then surely required more physical stamina than it does now. In 1899, we played 18 games, compared to the six to eight games they play now. The halves then were 45 minutes with a 10-minute intermission, against the present four 15-minute quarters and a 15-minute rest between halves. Now the huddle system of giving signals prevails, cutting down materially the number of plays. Then we not only gave signals as rapidly as possible, trying to get the plays off before the other team got lined up, but often series plays were used, one signal

meaning three or four plays, which were snapped into as rapidly as the team could line up.

"In spite of the old system of bruising play, when it was not only legitimate but good football to smash into the kicker after every punt, when officials were not very strict in enforcing the rules against roughness, when five yards in three attempts gave a first down, Chicago in 1899 used 14 men in enough games to earn them letters, and two of these were substitutes. Yea, verily, there were giants in those days.

"Chicago and Wisconsin came down to the final game of the '99 season, December 9, undefeated. With the Conference championship at stake, the game was played at Madison and several special trains were needed to carry all our Chicago fans who wanted to see the game, giving the Badgers the largest crowd in its history up to that time. There was a lot of betting on the contest and when the first train load of Chicago rooters reached Madison the odds went 2-to-1 on Wisconsin. The local rooters were afraid they couldn't get their money up. The second train load from Chicago brought the betting even and the third changed it to 2-to-1 on Chicago.

"The game itself is history. We won, 17–0, and our goal was never in serious danger, although Pat O'Dea came near kicking a goal from a free catch near the sideline from 55 yards away. O'Dea's punts were so hurried by the charging of our Frank Slaker, Jimmy Henry and the rest of the line, in a special formation Coach Stagg devised, that Wisconsin didn't come down the field very far, but how they did rise in the air. I believe Billy Eldridge caught every one, and they were hard to catch. Ralph Hamill couldn't see well enough to get them. 'There are always *two* balls coming down,' he said, 'and I can't tell which one to go after.' But Ralph could see well enough to run interference and he played a whale of a game.

"Frank Slaker and Jimmy Henry were the stalwarts of our attack, ably assisted by Fred Feil going around from tackle, with Jimmy Sheldon pushing from behind, and John Webb and Billy Eldridge in similar roles from the other side. Linemen could carry the ball in those days, and pushing and pulling the ball-carrier was legal. Clipping, hacking, tackling

Amos Alonzo Stagg teams played their home games at University of Chicago stadium in 1904. This picture was taken during the Chicago–Wisconsin game.

below the knees, smashing the kicker, slugging, hurdling and a few other tricks were still permitted. It was raw-meat football. Almost every decision the referee made caused arguments. Our line from tackle to tackle didn't look or act tough, but no other line ever started anything that our Feil, Ahlswede, Speed, Flanagan and John Webb didn't finish. They played the whole season without substitutes. Wisconsin couldn't budge them.

"Beating Wisconsin gave Chicago its first undisputed league championship, and we all

Mrs. Amos Alonzo Stagg drove "Old Double-A" around the practice field in his electric car as he continued to coach while recovering from an injury sustained during a previous practice session. Coach Stagg frequently got out and demonstrated blocking and tackling tactics to his Chicago players. He was still coaching football at 88.

got new sweaters and gold footballs. What a season! What a team! What a coach! Three solid months from the first to the last game. Practice from three until dark, five days a week and often signal-practice indoors after dinner. An old wood floor gymnasium to dress in, with no place to dry our clothes, and an inside rubbing room with a door laid across two wooden horses for a rubbing table. As for headgear, some guys wore knitted caps to protect their ears, but nothing else. Helmets were out. We simply let our hair grow long and pulled it through a turtleneck sweater. We wore very little padding. It was a rough game." It was also a very confusing game. Some people have never been able to figure it out.

The late Tom O'Reilly, writer, used to tell about these cowboys who lived on a ranch in west Texas 150 miles from a town of any size. Not one of these cowhands had ever seen a football game before. They had read about Heffelfinger and O'Dea and Stagg and Hinkey and other big names of the era in old newspapers but they couldn't figure out the difference between a halfback and an offside or anything else about the game, and they were curious.

One day they heard that a football game had been scheduled in the town 150 miles from their ranch. Obviously they all couldn't go so they pooled up their money and drew lots and one cowboy, named Ike, was chosen. He was to get on his horse and ride the 150 miles and see the football game. Then he was to get on his horse and ride back and tell the others all about it.

The cowboys were gathered at the gate when Ike came riding back. They swarmed around him when he dismounted.

"What was it like, Ike?" they wanted to know. "How was it played? Was it exciting?"

"Quiet down," Ike told them, and then he launched into his story. "Fellers, this football is a caution. All I gotta do is tell yuh how the gol-dang thing started off. They's a bunch of fellers in funny rig out on this here field. They's a guy in a cook's outfit totin' a pig bladder that's been blowed up and kivvered all around with cowhide. Well, these fellers all spreads out over the field and the cook puts the bladder on the ground and then one feller comes a-runnin' and kicks that bladder a helluva kick, clean up in the air.

"When it comes down they put it on the ground again. Then one great big feller walks up to the bladder and bends over like as if he's gonna pick it up. He hardly no more'n gits his hands on it when a little feller comes creepin' up behind him, all bent over, and this little feller gits closer and all of a sudden the little feller bites that big feller right square on the butt and it turns into the gol-dangest fight you ever saw in yore life!"

Some years ago, I took an Englishman to see his first American football game. Army was playing Navy in Philadelphia. Afterward, he wrote to friends back in London about the experience:

"A hundred thousand Americans swarmed into this huge stadium to see the Army Academy vs. the Navy Academy in what they call a 'real old-fashioned American football game.' Boy cheerleaders from the services pranced in front of the crowd waving megaphones and inciting yells like 'A-R-M-Y, *Army*,' or 'N-A-V-Y, *Navy*.' Meanwhile, a free fight seemed to be going on in the center of the stadium. Twenty-two enormous young men in crash helmets were locked in deadly struggle for an oval football. They wore spiked—*cleated* is the word Americans use—shoes, strange ginger shorts which cling closely to the thighs and end abruptly just below the knee, and padded jerseys, black and gold for the Army, navy blue for the Navy. They needed those pads, and the crash helmets.

"The object of the game seems to be to pass the ball to some unfortunate player, and then for everyone else to fall on him. One of the rules is he must never let go of the ball. So he goes down with a crash. The only thing that moves play toward the goal posts seems to be the instinct of self-preservation of the man with the ball. He runs as far as he can before he is maimed or killed by the other players. The program seemed sinister. It gave the names of the 11 men of each team. It then gave a list of 25 *substitutes* for each team.

"First casualty went to Navy. Horrified, I watched a student dash across the field with two buckets in his hands. But not, as I thought, to mop up the blood. He avoided the prostrate player and was besieged by the rest of the team. The buckets held towels and water for the players still alive. Six times during the game the buckets are rushed out. If a team asks for them more often it is penalized. Casualties are dealt with by a doctor, who rushes out with a black bag, and by the umpires and stretcher bearers, if they are needed.

"American football is played in four quarters, not two halves like ours. Each team has the ball for four turns. If by that time they have not got to the goal line the other side takes over. Before each try the team which has the ball goes into a huddle while the captain decides who shall be the next victim to receive the ball—and the subsequent assaults.

"You can assault your opponent any way at all except by *clipping* the back of his legs. That, my American friend tells me, is liable to break them. Favorite method of attack seems to be: (1) Springing like a tiger at the man's throat, or (2) just shoving so that sheer weight crushes him down. The attacker must keep one foot on the ground as he tackles. After the tackle he is usually all on the ground.

"The Navy lost, 38 points to nil. As the average weight of the Army was about 16 stone, I felt sorry for the Navy, whose top weight was a mere 13 stone. Bands played and the goat mascot paraded with the donkey mascot of the Army. On the Tube coming to my hotel there was strange jargon all around. 'He got smeared' seemed to mean literally that a player was rolled into the earth. 'Bullet pass' also had a literal meaning. It meant that a ball was thrown at a man so hard it knocked him down. It was a favorite pass. But the 100,000 Yankees had had a good time—and so had I."

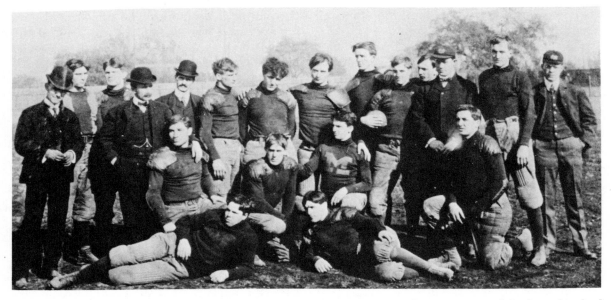

The 1901 Michigan Wolverines, pictured here, scored 550 points to their opponents' 0, then thrashed Stanford, 49–0, on New Year's Day, 1902, in the first Tournament of Roses game at Pasadena. Standing, left to right: 1. unidentified, 2. Sweeley, 3. Shorts, 4. Fitzpatrick, trainer, 5. Baird, athletic director, 6. Herrnstein, 7. Gregory, 8. McGugin, 9. unidentified, 10. Captain White, 11. Redden, 12. coach F. H. Yost, 13. Neil Snow, 14. manager Carfts. Middle row, from left: Wilson, Graver, Weeks, unidentified. On ground, from left: Willie Heston and Redner.

In 1900, Michigan and Iowa, both unbeaten in Western Conference competition, and losers only once outside of it, shared the championship. For the next five years, the Wolverines would go with the lease, while the Hawkeyes wouldn't be back knocking on the door again for more than 20 years.

The following season, it was Michigan again, winning 11 straight games. The other big team in the Conference was Wisconsin, with a 9–0–0 record. The 1901 Michigan team scored 550 points to its opponents' 0, then thrashed Stanford, 49–0, on New Year's Day, 1902, in the first Tournament of Roses game at

Michigan players all decked out in what the well-dressed collegians wore in 1902. The Wolverines were on a sightseeing tour of Pasadena before the Rose Bowl game.

Pasadena, California, 1902, where Michigan bombed Stanford, 49–0, in the first Rose Bowl game. Tournament of Roses officials were so embarrassed by the score they did not renew football competition for 14 years. Picture shows the opening kickoff of the contest in 1902.

Arriving at Ann Arbor in 1901, a young Fielding H. Yost came prepared with a football tucked under one arm.

Pasadena. The classic was not renewed for 14 years. Some claimed the Midwesterners didn't wish to waste their time on such inadequate opposition and some said the Westerners didn't wish to stick their necks out for other possible slaughters. The truth lies somewhere in between, with the added factor that the Tournament of Roses officials at Pasadena became somewhat disenchanted with football as part of their New Year's Day celebration after what Fielding Harris Yost's juggernaut did to poor old Stanford. So what did they substitute for football? *Professional chariot racing!*

"Hurry up" was his battle cry, and Hurry Up was his nickname, and when he first came to Michigan at 30, Yost already had a wide reputation. He had developed a state championship team in his first coaching job, Ohio Wesleyan in 1897; it tied Michigan and beat Ohio State, 6–0, for its only victory over O.S.U. in history. To see the country, Yost coached Nebraska in 1898, and Kansas in 1899, winning Missouri Valley titles. Missouri wanted him to do the same for her in 1900, but he decided in favor of Stanford, where he produced another state champion with a 7–2–0 record.

Fielding H. Yost's first five Michigan teams, 1901 through 1905, played 56 games without a loss until beaten at Chicago in 1905 by a score of 2 to 0. They averaged 50 points a game and were known as the "point-a-minute" teams. The star back was Willie Heston, All-American in 1903 and 1904, and an automatic member of

any all-time team in the era before the forward pass, if not after. Heston, 5–8 and 184 pounds, was born in Galesburg, Illinois, but his family moved to Grants Pass, Oregon; he attended San Jose State with plans to become a teacher.

In those days, football was still an infant. Eligibility and recruiting standards were loose or nonexistent. Yost himself had played at three schools—Ohio Northern, three years at West Virginia, and Lafayette—on his way to earning a law degree. So after Heston graduated from San Jose, Coach Yost talked him out of teaching and into coming to Michigan to study law.

When Yost needed a player to keep his juggernaut moving, he just reached out and grabbed one. In 1904, he was short a good tackle, so he talked Tom Smull, football captain at Ohio Northern, into transferring to Ann Arbor, where he starred for two years and got his engineering degree. Yost didn't care where or how he got players, just so they were good *students*—and could hit and tackle and block.

Yost had only two major recruiting failures. One was the decision of quarterback Walter Eckersall to attend Chicago. The other was a

Willie Heston was the most famous member of the crushing 1901–1904 "Point-a-Minute" teams that scored 2,326 points in 40 games. Left halfback Heston personally scored 71 touchdowns.

Walter Eckersall was just a little squirt, but the Chicago quarterback was an All-American in 1904–05–06.

There was nothing halfway about Yost. You either loved him or hated him. As he grew into an elder statesman and Michigan became known as "Champions of the West," the increasing popularity of football forced the colleges to police their own recruiting and subsidizing, and Yost became a staunch disciple of pure amateurism. Those who liked him said, "He ranks high as a preacher and practicer of the highest morality in sport. He has developed from a rough, fighting coach to an idealist, and is living proof of what football can do as a moral force." His detractors said, "Yost was a schemer. He did much to establish Michigan as the political and football power of the Big Ten. He was a sanctimonious man who preached a good line, then did what was necessary to win. For a long time he had the only really well-manned squad in the Big Ten, but when Stagg and Minnesota's Dr. Henry L. Williams began to give him trouble, he ran out of the Big Ten and turned eastward for his opponents. During the years that Yost was out of the Conference, Dr. Williams had his best Gopher teams and would have played him flat even."

From 1907 through 1914, Michigan dropped out of the Big Ten and operated as an independent; the reason was an argument on institutional control of athletics. Chicago won the league's first five-game championship, led by end Harlan (Pat) Page, the first nine-letterman in the Conference's history. At Minnesota, Dr. Henry Williams became the first college coach to use a flanker in connection with the forward pass, and George Capron, the

challenge Wisconsin had posed by using as its mascot a live badger. Yost decided that Michigan must have a live wolverine, and after a hunt that would have done credit to Frank Buck, he rounded up 10 wild animals. They were all so vicious, however, he had to give them away to zoos. One of them, Biff, was given to the campus zoo, and became the Michigan mascot. Biff could not be brought to Ferry Field, however, and Yost regarded the experiment as a personal defeat.

Hall of Famer Germany Scultz, far left, is shown here working out with the 1905 Michigan backfield. That's quarterback Fred Norcross handing off to Tom Hammond.

Wally Steffen, later a federal judge, was another All-American quarterback who learned his skills under Amos Alonzo Stagg at Chicago. In leading the Maroon to the Big Ten title in 1908, Steffen was the first player to use the forward pass as a fake, resulting in a sprint through a hole in the line.

Gophers' great dropkicker, scored 75 percent of the team's points that season. The big name at Ann Arbor was Adolph (Germany) Schulz, All-American center and first truly Hall of Fame lineman from the Midwest.

Quarterback Wally Steffen, the first ball-handler to use the pass as a feint, was the apple of Stagg's eye in 1908 as Chicago repeated as champion of the Western Conference. He was sensational as he ran wild against Minnesota in a 29–0 romp that decided the title. Steffen's sleight-of-hand faking was made all the more potent by his two ends, Pat Page and John Schommer, the league's first pair of pass-catchers of star quality.

While Michigan sat it out, Minnesota dominated Big Nine football in 1909, 1910, and 1911. The 1909 edition was quarterbacked by John McGovern, its first All-American. At 5–5 and 155 pounds, he was the smallest All-American signal-caller since Chicago's Walter Eckersall, at 140 pounds, won the honor in 1904–05–06. McGovern's size belied his big heart. He battled tough Wisconsin for 60 full minutes with a broken collar bone in 1909.

Illinois played seven games in 1910 and won them all. The Illini also won the league crown, based largely on the fact that Minnesota played only two Conference games,

winning them both but losing to Michigan 6–0 in a nonleague matchup.

The most dramatic innovation in 1910 was Dr. Henry Williams' "Minnesota Shift," which revolutionized football by having all backs at both ends spring into different positions just before the ball was hiked, thus confusing the defense.

Meanwhile, Stagg, always alert, was taking advantage of a new 1910 ruling which, for the first time, allowed the quarterback to run anywhere with the ball. Formerly, the quarterback had to run at least five yards left or right of the center. Stagg taught his own quarterback, Norm Paine, to fake to the fullback or halfback, then whirl around and into the line over center or guard. It was the first quarterback spinner and eventually led to all sorts of bedevilment for the defense to figure out.

College football was changing on all fronts

At 5-foot-5 one of the shortest All-Americans in football history, quarterback John McGovern ran, kicked, and played defense for the 1909 Minnesota Gophers.

One of the finest squads in the early days was the 1912 Wisconsin Badgers. Nine members were picked on the *Chicago Tribune's* All-Conference team. The coach was Bill Juneau, here seated, left. Elected to the National Football Hall of Fame from this bunch was tackle Butts Butler, fourth row, second from right.

now. At Oak Park High School in Chicago, they were talking about a new concept of football offense fashioned by a pint-sized young mentor named Bob Zuppke. Zup dropped his guards back to protect his forward passer, widening the attack even more.

After Minnesota rolled to its third straight unbeaten football season in 1911, the Wisconsin Badgers, who had tied the Gophers 6–6 in 1911, piled up 246 points to 29 in seven games to win the Conference crown in 1912. The undefeated Cardinal and White goes down in history as one of the greatest elevens in league annals. The Chicago *Tribune* was so impressed by the Badgers it named nine members to its All-Conference team, including tackle Butts Butler, the school's first All-American lineman. The other eight were tackle Ed Samp, ends Ed Hoeffel and Hod Ofstie, guards Max Gelein and Ray Keeler, quarterback Eddie Gillette, halfback John Van Riper, and fullback Al Tanberg. Efforts were made to match Wisconsin against undefeated Harvard in a postseason national champion-

ship contest, but the Madison officials said no.

The year 1913 was memorable for several reasons:

1. Another great Stagg team went undefeated, won the Conference championship, laid claim to national honors. The stars were Captain Nels Norgren, halfback, and Paul (Shorty) Des Jardiens, All-American center.

2. Jesse Hawley's Iowa Hawkeyes scored 310 points in seven games, the most by a Conference team since football was revised in 1906, and except for a 6–0 loss to ultimate champion Chicago, came just this far from earning the brass ring.

3. Bob Zuppke was named head coach at Illinois. Many Old Grads pinched their noses over the appointment. "It's a sad day for Illinois when the best the school can do is give the job to a high school coach who has never even played college ball, himself."

4. Ohio State University joined the Conference.

5. Wayne Woodrow Hayes was born.

The Buckeyes were the last team to be admitted to the Big Ten and not only was it the baby brother in the lodge, but it had previously taken more than its share of horrendous shellackings from such gridiron giants as Oberlin, Western Reserve, Case, Wittenberg, Kenyon, and even Ohio Medical College. What's more, the struggling Buckeyes had never, never beaten Michigan. In one stretch of 11 straight games the Wolverines had outscored them, 311 to 12, and had also handed Ohio State its worst clobbering in history, 86–0, in 1902.

Three factors turned Ohio State shame into towering pride. Admission to the Big Ten and the arrival in 1913 of Dr. John W. Wilce, a 25-year-old physician from Wisconsin who had played football for the Badgers and who said, sure, he'd try to rescue the Buckeye football program but with the stipulation he be allowed to practice medicine on the side.

Sawed-off Bob Zuppke wasted little time making his presence felt in the Western Conference. In 1914, his second year, he developed what he later picked as "my greatest Illinois team of my career—better, even, than the Red Grange teams of 1923–24–25." Zuppke said that the 1914 Illini's diversification in talent enabled him to give it a more complex offense than any of his later teams. Next to Grange, he considered quarterback George (Potsy) Clark and halfback Harold Pogue of that team his greatest players.

From 1913 through 1919, the pigskin pigments in Illini Blue and Gold ran rich for Zuppke, and he used them well. In those seven years, Illinois won two Big Ten titles outright, tied for one, and finished second once. The 1914 and 1915 teams were undefeated; in 1914, the Illini had a good claim on the national championship.

"The 1914 squad had everything," Zup said one time. *"Everything!* They were adventurers, boys who played football out of sheer love of competition. They gloried in a tough fight. They had the fastest pickup of any team I ever saw. Snap! The team, as a unit, was off like a shot when that ball was passed from center. They were chatterboxes, they talked it up all through the game—all through the week— with their fire and zest and drive. Those boys couldn't eat after a game; they'd play themselves out so.

"Our backfield of Potsy Clark, Hal Pogue, Bart Macomber and Gene Schobinger averaged only 146 pounds. In fact, the whole team

The 1914 Illinois football squad, Coach Bob Zuppke's first national champions. Here pictured, front row, left: Rue, Wagner, Watson, captain Chapman, Schobinger, Armstrong. Second row, left: Graves, Clark, Pogue, coach Zuppke, Nelson, Stewart, Macomber. Back row, left: assistant coach Lindgren, M. Petty, Madsen, Glimstedt (trainer), Squier, Derby, manager Rayburn.

suited up at about 174 pounds per man. We had one big boy, Stewart, who weighed 214 but could he run. All the line had speed— Squier, Graves, Armstrong, Petty, Chapman, Watson, and Stewart. The team could rise to any situation. In 1914, Chicago, the big power in the Midwest, year in and year out, led us 7 to 0 at the half. They were tough, especially that fellow Des Jardiens. On one play he stood on his two-yard line to punt and the ball rolled out of bounds on our *one*. Our kickout only went to our own 18 and they scored from there. After the half, Potsy Clark, the greatest quarterback I ever saw, came back out and took the kickoff and ran through the whole Chicago team to put us on the scoreboard. The team then went on to score its usual three touchdowns and we won, 20–7.

"There's a little story behind our victory over Minnesota in 1914. We had a 14–0 lead late in the last quarter and I pulled nine of my regulars out of the game. Minnesota went to the air and scored immediately. A few minutes later they had the ball again and marched straight down the field on another passing barrage. I didn't waste any time putting my regulars back into the game. Pogue usually played safety, but before he went back in I told him to take an 'up' position in the secondary and grab one of those passes.

"As the next play started, I was busy giving instructions to another substitute and wasn't watching the field of play. Then I heard a roar and looked up just in time to see Pogue running like blazes toward the Minnesota goal 60 yards away. He scored and we won, 21–7. Pogue had intercepted Minnesota's first pass after the regulars returned to the field. That's what I like, a man who obeys orders."

In 1915, Illinois and Minnesota shared the Conference championship. Pogue injured his ankle and missed most of the season, and Potsy Clark broke his jaw and was forced to play wearing an iron mask. Other key men suffered hurts and spent time on the bench during important games. Yet the Illini rode down bad luck and came up to the Minnesota game deadlocked for the league lead with the Gophers.

"The contest ended in a 6–6 tie," Zuppke recalled. "One of the stars for Minnesota was 'Galloping' Sprafka who got loose for a long run. I protested that he'd stepped out of bounds and during the argument I said to him,

'You know darned well you went out of bounds!' Sprafka was indignant. 'I was not out of bounds!' he snapped. *'I only had one foot out!'* Incidentally, Bernie Bierman was one of the Minnesota backs that day."

Zuppke's all-time upset was the 14–9 defeat of Minnesota at Minneapolis in 1916, the year Ohio State sprung Chick Harley on the Conference and won the championship. Illinois began the season with a solid eleven, but injuries cut the regulars down one by one. Even at full strength, however, the Illini would have been given sparse chance against Dr. Henry Williams' Gophers. Minnesota was loaded. It had run up scores of 67–0 against Iowa; 81–0 against South Dakota, which later lost to Notre Dame by the close score of 6–0; 47–7 against North Dakota; and 41–7 against South Dakota State.

Minnesota had beaten its first four opponents by a total of 241 to 14 and would beat its last two, Wisconsin and Chicago, 54–0 and 49–0. It was favored to do the same thing to Illinois. Ring Lardner picked the Gophers by seven touchdowns in his *Chicago Tribune* column.

The Minnesota attack was headed by Joe (Galloping) Sprafka and Hal Hensen at halfbacks, Pudge Wyman at fullback, Shorty Long at quarterback, and team captain Bert Baston, two-time All-American end.

The week before the game, Zuppke scrimmaged his players furiously. "We're supposed to be killed Saturday," he told them, "so we might as well have the satisfaction of killing ourselves rather than letting Minnesota do it."

When the team arrived in Minneapolis on Friday afternoon, Zuppke suspended training rules. "Go out on the town and relax," he advised the team, "but be in bed by midnight."

It was not easy to relax. Even the bellhops at the hotel where Illinois was staying were laying 20 to 1 on Minnesota to win in a romp, and 10 to 1 that the visitors wouldn't even get on the scoreboard.

Before the game, Zuppke took his players into the dressing room for last-minute instructions.

"Today," he told them, "I want you to have some fun. I don't care if they run a hundred points up on you, have fun. Now I want to tell you something. I've had this great team scouted. On the first play, Sprafka will get the ball. I want all eleven men to tackle him. On the second play Wyman will get the ball. I want all eleven men to tackle him. On the third play, Hansen will get the ball. All eleven tackle him."

"But, coach," one of the Illini piped up, "what if the ball goes back to somebody else?"

"Then I'll tackle him myself," Zuppke said. "I am Louis the Fourteenth, and you are my court! *After us the deluge!*"

The meaning of the phrase went over the players' heads, but it sounded good. They responded with a loud cheer and tumbled out the door.

Illinois, as planned, kicked off a flat ball that Minnesota fumbled around in its end zone before bringing it back to the 5. The Gophers were tense, feeling the pressure. Then, as Zuppke had predicted, Sprafka, Wyman, and Hansen tried straight bucks into the line and were smeared, forcing a punt. The Illini lined up in a complicated spread on their first play and quarterback Bart Macomber passed to Sternaman for 25 yards. Running plays quickly carried the ball down to the Minnesota 5. The rattled Gophers went offside. Macomber sneaked over from the 1 and kicked the point.

On the kickoff, Sprafka brought the ball back to his 30, from where Minnesota backs pounded out 15 more yards. Then came one of the key plays of the game. Wyman's pass intended for Baston was intercepted by left end Ren Kraft, who ran it back 50 yards for a touchdown, and Macomber again kicked the extra point. Now Illinois led, 14–0. Minnesota was confused, frustrated.

In the second half, the Gophers stormed back to score nine points, and they kept throwing in fresh troops in the last quarter, testing the Illini reserve. Macomber later confessed that he never acted more than he did in those final 10 minutes.

"I kept tying my shoes, breaking string on my shoulder pads, losing my helmet, deliberately fouling up signals," he said. "But we managed to hang on to win."

Illinois 14, Minnesota 9.

Chick Harley was the center of life in Columbus during the years 1916–1919. Harley was a hometown boy who had played high school football almost in the shadow of Ohio Field. He had accumulated an enormous fan club in Columbus even before he appeared in a college game. The late James Thurber, author, always claimed that Harley did more than

After only three years in the Big Ten, Ohio State won its first Conference championship with this squad in 1916. Star of the team was Chick Harley, shown here in second row, fifth from left.

In 1917, Ohio State won its second title in a row as Pete Stinchcomb, here shown, moved up to take his place alongside the great Chick Harley. In his first varsity game, Stinchcomb scored three touchdowns against Northwestern.

This was what George Halas, later founder and owner of the Chicago Bears, looked like as end on the 1918 Illinois eleven.

anyone to transform the attitude that the city had toward its state university. Aside from being the state capital, Columbus was a flat, nondescript farm town years ago. When you read of early Ohio State athletics it was impossible not to feel that its citizens were heartily ashamed of the poor, struggling school on the outskirts of town. In those days the big sports

Illinois, 1919 national champions. Back row, left, coach Zuppke, Bob Fletcher, Walquist, Koch, Schlaudeman, Smith, Lindgren. Middle row, left, Bullock, Simmons (manager), Mohr, Crangle, Olander, E. Sternaman, Ralph Fletcher, Lovejoy. Front row, left, Reichle, O. Petty, Applegran, captain Kopp, Depler, Lifvendahl, Ingwersen, Carney.

events in town were the baseball and football games between Columbus East High School and Columbus North or Columbus General. High school games often drew bigger crowds than college games. Thurber went to East High and was the president of the senior class, and George Bellows, the famous painter, played basketball and baseball at Central High. Bob Thurber, brother of James, captained the East High basketball team.

But it was Charles Wesley (Chick) Harley who really won over Columbus for Ohio State University. He went into the university determined to live up to the fantastic reputation he had earned in high school.

With Harley at halfback, Ohio State did not lose a game in 1916 on its way to its first Big Ten football championship in history. The Buckeyes repeated as champions in 1917, the year Michigan returned to the league and placed eighth.

Harley served in the Army in 1918 but returned in time to take the Buckeyes through an all-but-unbeaten season in 1919. With the Big Ten championship at stake, Ohio State led Illinois, 7–6, with only five minutes left on the clock. Suddenly, the Illini intercepted a Harley pass and marched from their 20 to Ohio's 20 on passes from quarterback Laurie Walquist to ace end Chuck Carney. Now there were only eight seconds left, just time enough for a field goal try. Ralph Fletcher, Illinois' regular placekicker, was sidelined by injury, but his brother Bob, who never had attempted a field goal in a game, bounced off the bench and was sent in to try to win the game.

"The kick was perfect," James Thurber was saying many years later. "That final 9 to 7 score reduced our Ohio State faithful to a most pitiable condition."

And so ended the second decade of the century.

The Golden Age:

The 1920s

The Golden Age extended over the bonanza years from 1920 to 1930. The war was over and the world practically overnight turned into a spiralling, dizzy, mad, whirling planet of play. It was an era of superlatives. Everything that was done right was done more right and bigger than ever. The same applied to everything that was done wrong. Hoodlums no longer fought each other with stones and bats. Now they took each other for a one-way ride in an automobile.

It was an age of exaggeration. Men who had been casual drinkers now had to get drunk. Women were not satisfied with the role of attracting the male to marriage and making a home for him. They had to be his equal on the public forum, in politics and in bed. It was a time of Public Enemy No. 1, too, and giants of the underworld like Owney Madden, Dutch Schultz, Al Capone, and Johnny Torrio became as well known as stars of the silent screen. A smart man saved his money and acquired $25,000; a clever one played the market and had a million. Automobiles were being made bigger and faster, traffic lanes were appearing on streets and highways, and more car accidents inspired the invention of safety bumpers. Trains were running between New York and Chicago in 18 hours. In defiance of law, men made alcohol in cellar distilleries, bottled beer and sold it with an eye against a slot in the door. Young ladies cut their hair, shortened their dresses, drank gin, and read Dr. Warner Fabian's *Flaming Youth*.

There were flagpole sitters, cross-country walkers, and a loud lady named Texas Guinan saw patrons tip a band leader a hundred dollars to play "Ain't She Sweet." Women played Mah-jong and Junior could play "Poet and Peasant" by pumping the pedals of a player piano. Air mail flights began from New York to San Francisco, Admiral Richard E. Byrd navigated the first plane trip over the North Pole, and a lanky, thin-faced young pilot named Lindbergh thrilled the world by flying his little monoplane, nonstop, from Long Island to Paris. An insurance company booklet described Moses as "one of the greatest salesmen and real-estate promoters that ever lived," and Jesus Christ was called "the founder of modern business."

It has been described as the era of wonderful nonsense, and nowhere was the hysteria more boisterous or the screaming louder than in sports. Throwing off its bush-league trappings, sports suddenly erupted in the 1920s as big business and lavish entertainment. This was the decade that witnessed the first million-dollar fight and World Series, that made stadiums which accommodated 100,000 spectators for a football game appear inadequate, that spawned sprawling country clubs where golf and tennis were practiced with a fervor verging on religious zeal, that spread a red carpet for men with swift and strong and skillful muscles.

This was, indeed, the Golden Age of Sport,

and the times produced more vital, vibrant performers than any other decade in the chronicles of athletics. Every sport had a dominant personality who attracted and held public attention, for this was the era of Ty Cobb, still slashing into third, his spikes aglimmer; Babe Ruth standing at the plate on his thin, matchstick ankles, slowly waving his bludgeon like a cobra poised to strike; Big Bill Tilden banging his unreturnable cannonball service across the net; Bobby Jones, waving to cheering thousands—after winning the golf championships of Britain—as he received a ticker-tape reception down Broadway, an event previously reserved only for visiting royalty and transatlantic aviators; the death wagons roaring around the Indianapolis speedway track at 125 miles per hour; Paavo Nurmi dog-trotting around the running track in a steady, devastating assault upon Time.

No other period has called forth so many aliases: the Roaring Twenties, the Golden Twenties, the Dry Decade, the Era of Excess, the Era of Wonderful Nonsense, the Jazz Age. It was the last big spree between World Wars, marking a national rite of passage, a maudlin farewell to the innocence and hope of a childhood now irrevocably gone. And it was more than just a coincidence that when this age found its poet, F. Scott Fitzgerald would write longingly of the pads worn for a day on the football fields of Princeton.

The decade was largely gold and cheering crowds and gallant heroes. College football dressed itself in spangles and tinsel, and came a-swinging into the campus stadiums on a white steed behind the booming ballyhoo band. An age in quest of heroes looked to the gridiron and saw Rockne and Gipp, the Four Horsemen, the Galloping Ghost, Wrong-Way Riegels, Friedman and Oosterbaan, Wonder Teams, Aubrey Devine Teams, Praying Colonels, the Team of Destiny, Ramblers and Nomads, Nagurski and Nevers, Kaw and Pfann, Red Cagle, and Little Boy Blue. Time was to make legendary these glory figures, and as they came and went there was through the 10-year period the dominating and ever-growing figure of Rockne, the Notre Dame coach. The little man with the crinkled nose, the bright eyes, and the crisp, staccato manner of talking—on the radio, in the newspapers, in the movies, on the field—was everywhere.

Schools received publicity either because they used the Rockne system or because they didn't. Graduates from his teams dotted the country in coaching positions, spreading his gospel. A coincidence—a football-mad nation, postwar, halcyon days, money days—and Knute Kenneth Rockne. From 1920 to 1930, his Fighting Irish lost but 11 games while winning 93, and unlike Michigan's juggernaut, they ranged from coast to coast, flinging their passes into the damp air of the Atlantic Seaboard or the clear blue of the Pacific Slope. They made Pittsburgh and Atlanta and Philadelphia their way stations, looked in on Baltimore, and New York with its "subway alumni" was their second home. And always out in front of them, guiding, shouting, encouraging, leaving his lasting imprint—Rockne.

It was just an accident that took Rock to South Bend. Born in Norway but raised in Chicago, he was so poor that he had to go to work after high school in order to get money for college. He had his mind set somewhat vaguely on the University of Illinois but agreed to tag after a couple of schoolboy buddies to Notre Dame, even though he was a Protestant. He quickly fell in love with Notre Dame. He loved it beneath the golden dome and college was easy for him. His freshman marks averaged 98.3. They were 91.3 as a sophomore, 90 as a junior and 92.5 as a senior, including 10 perfect grades of 100.

Rock applied that brilliant mind to football and he was always one full season ahead of the rules committee. He'd devise something novel, such as his Notre Dame shift, and the authorities would clamp a restriction on it. So Rock would dream up something else. He was usually one season ahead of the opposition, too.

Everybody wanted to see Rockne's teams play. No other school matched his dominance over an individual conference as he did over the Western Conference. His record against Big Ten teams between the years 1920–1930 was 23 wins, 2 losses, 1 tie. Only Iowa and Wisconsin defeated him, and Minnesota got a tie. He beat Indiana seven times, Michigan State twice, Northwestern six times, Minnesota twice, Wisconsin twice, and Purdue four times. Significantly, such powers as Michigan, Ohio State, Illinois, and Chicago refused to even play Notre Dame. Rockne wanted in the Big Ten, but those close to Notre Dame swore that the religious question kept the Irish out.

Coincidentally, the 1920 game between Notre Dame and Northwestern spawned the most romantic episode in the history of college football, when George Gipp got off a sick bed to play against the Wildcats at Evanston. A cold-edged wind blustered across the icy field, chilling Gipp to the bone. In an age of no wonder drugs, he died of pneumonia a fortnight later, on December 14, 1920, at the age of 25.

The story of George Gipp did not end there. In 1928, Notre Dame traveled to New York to play Army at Yankee Stadium. The Cadets were loaded. They had talent, depth—and Red Cagle. Oddsmakers made the Army a heavy favorite, but the so-so, twice-beaten Irish fought savagely to a 0–0 halftime tie.

Playing tackle for Notre Dame that day was Ted Twomey, 6–1 and 205 pounds, who several years ago told me what happened inside the Irish dressing room as the players waited for Rockne to come in.

"Rock waited for us all to settle before he made his appearance, and then he walked in and in a very slow, serious voice he said, 'Boys, I want to tell you a story,'" recalled Twomey. "Rock confessed that he never thought he'd probably have to tell us the story, but the time had come to tell it. He asked all of us to gather around this rubbing table and listen. We got up from our benches and surrounded the table.

"Now Rock started talking. That harsh staccato was gone now. His voice was soft, almost pleading, and very paternal. He leaned down over this rubbing table, talking about George Gipp, and he was so dramatic, so convincing that you could almost see the Gipper lying on that table, dying. I was clumped with Tim Moynihan and Eddie Collins and Jack Cannon and Moon Mullins and Bucky O'Connor and Freddie Miller and Frank Carideo and all the rest of the guys and the Gipper was on that table, I tell you, trying to speak. *Talking through Rock.*

"Rock told us, 'It was eight years ago, and there I was, up at the hospital with Gipp and Gipp was really passing away, right in front of my eyes. There wasn't much time left. Gipp

motioned to me and said, "Rock, can you hear me?"'—Rock bent his head a little closer to that rubbing table for dramatic effect, and the deathly white face of George Gipp suddenly reappeared in my imagination—and Rock said, '"Yes, George, I can hear you." And George said, "Rock, it's not so tough to go. I've no complaint. It's all right. I'm not afraid." His eyes then brightened in a frame of pallor. "Some day, Rock," he said, "when the team's up against it; when things are wrong and the breaks are beating the boys—tell them to go in there with all they've got and win just one for the Gipper. I don't know where I'll be then, Rock. But I'll know about it, and I'll be happy."' Rock quietly straightened up and looked around the room, studying our faces. We were all sobbing. Then he said, 'All right, boys, let's go get them! *This is that game!*'

"The rest is history. In the second half, Army didn't know it but they were playing against 12 men, our starting team—and the spirit of George Gipp. The final score was Notre Dame 12, Army 6. Somewhere up there in the heavens, George Gipp must have been very happy."

Inside the Big Ten, Ohio State and Illinois had dominated football every year from 1916 through 1920, but now it was Iowa's turn. The Hawkeyes had called on a Yale man, Howard Jones, to build them a winning program and he responded with perfect records in 1921 and 1922. The 1921 eleven was the first team to upset Notre Dame in three years.

Some of the most famous players developed in the Big Ten played on those two Iowa teams. They included All-Americans Aubrey Devine, Gordon Locke, Duke Slater, and Leland Parkin.

"The 1921 team had no weaknesses," Devine said some years ago when asked about the Hawkeyes. "The power of Locke driving behind Slater was the main strong point. As the defense shifted to meet this, I was able to run and pass successfully from the single wing formation we used.

"The boys on the team were strictly Iowa. That is, they were all born and raised in the state. I doubt if in the history of the Big Ten or any other sectional conference there has ever been a championship team all natives of the state in which the school was located. I also doubt if there has been such a team that pos-

Hall of Famer Gordon Locke crashes into the end zone to score the winning touchdown for Iowa in a 10–7 victory over Notre Dame in 1921. Note bareheaded Duke Slater, another of the Hawkeyes' Hall of Famers. Duke scoffed at headguards. At right rear here is Eddie Anderson, Notre Dame end who later became a prominent physician and head coach at Iowa during the Nile Kinnick years.

sessed the durability of this one, as proven by the fact that only one man in the entire season was removed from the game for injuries. That was Gordon Locke in the Notre Dame game. He had battered his head against the Irish line so hard that he became slightly confused and wanted to whip the whole Notre Dame team. It happened in the third quarter after he had scored the only Iowa touchdown and had given the vaunted Irish a lesson in line plunging they still remember. All players except Locke played 60 minutes of that game.

"In the conference games we played Illinois first and there were no substitutions, all starters playing 60 minutes. The Purdue game was next and was played in a sea of water and mud. All Iowa starters played 60 minutes except Locke, who played 30 minutes, and Shuttleworth, who was taken out with 10 minutes to go.

"The third conference game was against Minnesota at Minneapolis. All players played the full game except Locke, who was taken out of the game in the third quarter when the score was 28–0, and myself as the game was drawing to a close. It was the most thrilling moment of my career as the packed homecoming Minnesota stands stood up and deafened my ears until I was well on the way to the dressing room. I had given my greatest exhibition, having carried the ball from scrimmage 175 yards, passed 125 yards, and returned punts and kickoffs and intercepted passes 200 yards for a total of 500 yards. I had scored 29 points and passed for 12 more, and although I was proud of my achievement, the whole-hearted sportsmanship of the Minnesota fans in the face of a 41–7 defeat left me with the feeling that their demonstration was quite as unusual and more commendable than my own.

"We went back to Iowa City and the next Saturday played our homecoming game against Indiana. This was the last home game for four of us seniors who had never lost a game in Iowa City.

"We completed the season undefeated and untied by beating Northwestern, 14 to 0. All first-team members played the entire 60 minutes.

"Another unusual thing about the 1921 team I should mention was that only two men, Locke and myself, ever touched the ball on offense, except on the receiving end of forward passes. The first string included Max Kadesky at left end, who was a better defensive player than Lester Belding but Les at right end was a greater pass-catcher. George Thompson at left tackle equalled the great Duke Slater at right tackle defensively, though Duke deserved All-American recognition because of his powerful, unmatched offensive charge.

"Coach Howard Jones was a persistent, aggressive driver who pushed himself as hard as he did the team. He lacked imagination and

Howard Jones, later of University of Southern California fame, first brought out his highly successful shift in 1921 at Iowa and the Hawkeyes won the Big Ten championship.

creative ability but he had the good sense to recognize genuine ability in his players when he saw it. He was also able to separate a good idea from a bad one. These assets together with his ability to perfect and improve what he had made him a successful coach. His personal life was one of marital sorrow of which he said very little but which caused deep lines in his face and an inner nervousness which he tried to hide. His only interests outside football were bridge, trout fishing, and golf. He coached by demonstration rather than lectures. He applied a raw, direct psychological approach rather than methods of indirection. It seemed to work for him in getting us up for important games. He was unique in that no one else could do or has done so much with his system and methods as he did."

Up at Ann Arbor, Phil Bartelme, who had served as athletic director since 1909, suddenly resigned his position at Michigan in 1921, and Fielding Yost agreed to double as both athletic director and football coach for a single salary.

The Wolverines had not won a Conference championship in 16 years, but 5–9, 158-pound Harry Kipke, a high school sensation from Lansing, was well on the way to changing all that. Kipke could run, pass, punt and catch,

and he was joined by Doug Roby and Bernie Kirk, a brilliant athlete who had transferred from Notre Dame. Iowa won the crown in 1921, but Michigan, with a 5–1–1 record, was not far from being a serious contender the following season.

Down at Columbus, Ohio State had just built a mammoth new football stadium, the largest west of Yale Bowl, and the Buckeyes invited Michigan to help them dedicate it. Some 72,500 partisans showed up to watch the Bucks crush the Wolverines for the fourth straight year—but Michigan didn't follow the script. The visitors moved to an early 3–0 lead when Paul Goebel blocked a punt and then kicked a 28-yard field goal. In the second quarter, Irwin Uteritz, the Michigan quarterback, took the snap from center on the Ohio State 34, started to his right, and faked a handoff to the end coming around. Harry Kipke, who was also fading right from his tailback position, suddenly whirled to the left and took a short shovel pass. Two defenders reversed their charge, but too late. Kipke was two steps in front of them and on into the end zone. As he

One of the great spot-punters of all time, Harry Kipke, All-American halfback at Michigan in 1922, won a total of nine letters in three sports—football, basketball, and baseball. Later, as head coach, his Michigan football teams won the Conference championship in 1930, 1931, 1932, and 1933.

hit the goal line, he turned to one of the officials and said, "Well, the place is *really* dedicated now!" The scoring play was Yost's famous "Old 83," but Kipke was not finished dedicating the stadium. In the third quarter he intercepted a pass and ran 45 yards for another touchdown. Late in the game, Kipke put another three points on the scoreboard by intercepting another pass, returning it to the Ohio State 37, where he dropkicked a field goal to make the final score, Michigan 19, Ohio State 0.

"Kipke," Walter Camp said after the game, "you're the greatest punter I've ever seen."

Kipke, on 11 punts, had merely kicked the first two into the end zone, but the next nine sailed out of bounds inside Ohio State's 8-yard line. He averaged 47 yards per kick.

The Michigan machine rolled along Saturday after Saturday. It blanked Illinois, 24–0, as Bernie Kirk ran 80 yards for one of the touchdowns. They smashed Michigan State, 63–0, got past Wisconsin, 13–6, and accentuated the positive by beating Minnesota, 16–7, in the final game. A scoreless tie against Vanderbilt was the only blemish on an otherwise perfect record. In this way Michigan had its first piece of the Big Ten title since 1906, sharing the top place with Iowa. Kipke and Goebel were named on Camp's All-American team, and Kirk on the second team. Shortly after the season, Kirk was badly hurt in an auto wreck, meningitis set in, and five days later he died.

While Iowa and Michigan locked in a tie for the championship, another Big Ten member, Chicago, was a party in one of college football's most unforgettable games in history. Allison Danzig ranked it with the Yale–Army contest of 1929, Southern California vs. Notre Dame in 1931, and Notre Dame vs. Ohio State in 1935.

Chicago's opponent in 1922 was hopelessly outclassed Princeton, coached by Bill Roper. The Tigers were being called the "Team of Destiny" by the romanticists because they could not, would not lose, no matter how desperate their plight. They won three games on field goals or extra points. Ken Smith's kicking toe and a strong Princeton defense were the major tangibles that made the Tigers winners Saturday after Saturday.

"We were truly a team of destiny," remarked the late Charlie Caldwell, a halfback on the team who went on to win fame as football coach at Princeton. "Every Saturday the odds-makers picked us to lose and we won, even though we weren't much on offense. We had no blocking. We couldn't make a first down at times if we had to. We had no forward passing to speak of. We played a 7–1–2–1 defense all the time and I was the linebacker. I played wingback on offense, but we never ran reverses. I carried the ball once all season and had more actual playing time than anyone else on the team. Our offense consisted of the best plays other teams used. Roper felt that football was 90 percent fight and all the rest was 10 percent. He was a great psychologist. He would use anything to advantage. He was wonderful talking to the team. He was a Princetonian and would tell us that if we had a Princeton jersey on and the other team didn't, we had it licked."

Princeton came down to the Chicago game imbued with the spirit of Johnny Poe, who years ago had coined the memorable phrase, "A team that won't be beat can't be beat." Since a team often takes on the characteristics of its coach, Coach Roper's elevens were seldom machine-like but always opportunistic. Inside the enemy's 10-yard line where so many attacks bog down, the Tigers cultivated the habit of scoring.

The game marked the first time in history that a Princeton football team had come to the Midwest, and they were 3 to 1 underdogs in the betting. Amos Alonzo Stagg, as much a part of the University of Chicago as the maroon he had himself chosen for the college color, had fashioned a stone-cracking steamroller which hit an opposing line with the force of a runaway truck.

Princeton grads from every Midwestern city and black-earth farmland flocked to the Midway that October afternoon, prepared to tear their lungs out in a lost cause. They came to Chicago praying for a miracle, but fully expecting to see the burgundy-jerseyed giants go like a steamroller over Bill Roper's cagey eleven.

Stagg Field, with its inadequate 40,000 seats, had been sold out weeks in advance. Not even standing room could be bought for what Midwesterners were convinced would be a Waterloo for the once Napoleonic East. The

Princeton players were perhaps the only persons at Stagg Field who didn't anticipate being sacrificed to make a Chicago holiday. Roper, a disciple of suggestion, had fed his athletes recurrent doses of psychology.

As the Tigers spread out over Stagg Field, how huge the Chicago players looked to them in their form-fitting deep maroon jerseys. What swank figures they cut in their tailor-made uniforms. It might have been some crack platoon of the prewar Prussian guard, stepping out smartly for parade. The warriors from Old Nassau, shoddy, unkempt as always, presented a sloppy contrast. In their tattered, dirt-begrimed jerseys, their patched moleskins varying in hue from faded green to sweat-stained brown, and their motley assortment of helmets, the Tigers looked as if they had stepped from the pages of *Huckleberry Finn.*

It seems to be a Princeton tradition that football players should have a hard-boiled look. Perhaps the Poes, with their contempt for "putting on the dog," set this disheveled fashion. In this showdown on Stagg Field it was the supposedly rough and ready Middlewest that held fast to the Beau Brummel tradition.

A whistle shrilled and the slaughter began. The game wasn't two minutes old before the veriest tyro understood that the smallish Tiger linemen couldn't stop Chicago's pile-driving mass on tackle. Rat-tat-tat! As a pneumatic riveter drives home a red-hot bolt, so did the burly Maroon backs sledge a path through the physically overmatched tackles from New Jersey. There was no iron worker's "dolly bar" to buck up that weakening Tiger line against the thrust of the Chicago riveters.

Sixty yards downfield moved the Maroon phalanx for all the world like a blood-red caterpillar crawling along a dark-green leaf. Princeton's forwards had never faced such relentless power. They were shoved contemptuously aside as if they were pygmies. "Thus it is that a mastiff handles a yapping terrier," wrote one reporter in the language of the day. And before the raccoon-coated grads could sample their hip flasks, Chicago was over for the first touchdown. What matter if the extra point was missed? Who cared?

Confident in their strength, the Chicago players were annoyed rather than worried when Princeton leaped ahead with a surprising touchdown at the start of the second quar-

ter. A far-flung Tiger pass caught the Maroon secondaries sound asleep. They awoke to find the ball on their 7-yard line. Princeton punched it over for a touchdown in four lunges. A 2-yard penalty enabled Nassau to eke out the distance. The goal was kicked: Princeton 7, Chicago 6.

"Let's go!" shouted Tiny Lewis, the hulking Chicago captain. "Go, Chicago!" echoed the Midway cheering section.

Chicago went! Sliding inside the Tiger tackles, bulling their way through center, the mulberry-jerseyed backs ate up the chalk marks. John Thomas, sinewed like an Andalusian bull, hammered Princeton's groggy line to a pulp. It was "Thomas five yards—Thomas six yards—Thomas five yards," and when Thomas began to wobble a bit, Stagg sent in Zorn. From Princeton's standpoint, this was a change for the worse. "Zorn seven yards through guard—Zorn eight yards inside tackle," droned the announcer. A Princeton fan shouted, "Take out Zorn and put back Thomas!" Before the laughter died away, Chicago had its second touchdown. Again the goal was missed. Who gave a damn? The score was 12 to 7, wasn't it? Chicago was riding high now, with more points to come.

Those points were not long coming. Near the end of the third quarter the Maroon tank crunched its way across the Princeton goal line for the third and last time. Once again the try-for-point fizzled. But who cared? Nobody at that moment. But those three failures to convert were soon to plague Chicagoans as Job was never tortured by all his flock of boils. Those three points were to spell the difference between an unsatisfying tie and a heartbreaking defeat.

The teams changed ends of the field to start the last 15 minutes of the game. Chicago punted deep to little Johnny Gorman, who caught the ball in the shadow of his own goal posts and, swirling quickly, essayed a daring lateral pass to Jack Cleaves. A stony-hearted referee ruled that the ball had been thrown forward. Princeton was penalized back to her own 2-yard line.

Now came the all-or-nothing play that confounded Chicago and changed the course of football destiny. Conservative strategy called for Princeton to punt out from behind her goal line. Had she done so, Chicago most surely would have won. Consider how gloomy was Princeton's position, pinned against her goal posts, and trailing 7 to 18 with scarcely 12 minutes to play.

It was a time for drastic measures, and swaggering, insolent little Johnny Gorman was the chap to stake everything on one throw of the dice.

"Kick formation, Cleaves back!" barked quarterback Gorman in the huddle. Watching nervously from the sideline, Coach Roper saw Gorman whisper in Cleaves' ear as the Tigers lined up. Johnny and Jack had been schoolmates at Mercersburg and were noted for improvising plays under pressure, for concocting schemes that were not in "the book."

"Block that punt!" chanted the Chicago cheering section. Scenting another touchdown, the Maroons tried desperately to obey their fans. They stormed through blindly, arms flailing the air for the kick that never came. Cool as an iced shad, Cleaves faked a punt, pivoted to his right, and arched a long pass toward the east sideline. Running on the wings of the dank Lake Michigan wind, Johnny Gorman kept his rendezvous with that flying ball. He picked it out of the air with his fingertips and darted to midfield before the Chicago safety man nailed him. There was nothing gentle about that tackle. They had to carry Johnny off the field.

Princeton was forced to kick—and then luck smiled on Old Nassau when Chicago in turn had to punt. The substitute center for Chicago made a crazy snap to Zorn, striking him on the shoulder and caroming straight into the arms of Howard Gray, Princeton's alert end. Gray didn't have to break his stride. He clutched the ball and raced 43 yards across the Chicago goal. The try for point was good and now the score was Chicago 18, Princeton 14, with six minutes to play.

That gift touchdown "hopped up" the Tigers as a shot of dope energizes a cocaine addict. The Princeton backfield suddenly became whirling dervishes, unstoppable berserkers, and its line started to open big gaps in the defense. A shrewdly masked pass completed Chicago's breakdown, placing the ball on her own 7 yard line. The Maroon braced for the attack. Three Tiger lunges left the ball still 3 yards short of the end zone.

Over on the Princeton bench things were stirring. Burly Crum, nicknamed "Maud" because of his mule-like "kick" on close plunges, pleaded with Bill Roper to send him in.

"Fourth down—three yards to go—two minutes to play!" cried Crum. "I can score that touchdown, Coach, give me a chance! *Please.*"

Roper heeded Crum's plea. It was a hunch. "All right, go in!"

Crum went—and didn't stop going until he had knifed across the Chicago goal. The placekick was good and now Princeton led, 21–18. That's what the scoreboard read, but the Maroon didn't intend it to be final. From the cedar closet where they had kept their cleverly designed passing attack wrapped up in moth balls, they dug up the neglected forward pass. The air was full of footballs, and every one of them came to rest in the arms of Maroon jerseys.

It was what Stagg had been waiting for. At halftime he had begged his quarterback to use the pass more. "They've tightened up their line defense, so throw the ball!" he had ordered. Now, with seconds ticking away, with defeat mocking them, his young men finally went to the air. That flurry of Chicago passes devoured distance. Strohmeier caught the final pass on Princeton's 6-yard line. Only 30 seconds to play—and the Chicago quarterback suddenly switched back to his old ground attack. *Whang!* Two yards inside tackle. *Bam!* Two yards through center. Once more came the thud of colliding bodies and only a yard separated the ball from the last chalk mark. Fourth down—a yard to go—a second to play!

Lonny Stagg gritted his teeth. How many times had he warned his quarterback that a straight line is not the shortest distance between two points on a football field?

Bill Roper turned his eyes away from the field. Behind the big Maroon line John Thomas crouched for the plunge that meant victory or defeat. His sweat-stained face was haggard, the corners of his mouth were drawn down in a scowl. Facing him, the Princeton forwards dug their cleats into the turf. Wingate, the peppery Tiger substitute quarterback, stormed to and fro behind his linemen, slapping one on the back, kicking another, exhorting them to hold. From the stadium above came a staccato babel: "Hurry, Chicago!"

Every Tiger knew intuitively that Chicago

Illinois, 1923 national champions. Back row, left, assistant coach Lindgren, assistant coach Bearg, trainer Bullock. Third row, left, manager Podlesak, Umnus, Brown, Roberts, Slimmer, coach Zuppke. Second row, left, Oakes, Crawford, Red Grange, Britton, H. Hall, McIlwain, Coutchie. Front row, left, Schultz, Richards, Miller, Green, captain McMillen, R. Hall, Rokusek, Muhl.

would stake its last play on a straight center buck, and the Princeton line massed for the charge. The defensive backs, disregarding their exposed flanks, converged toward the middle, blanketing the Maroon wave.

For a heart-stopping second it seemed as if Thomas' leather helmet projected across the line. Then he collapsed in a welter of black and orange—a few scant inches from the whitewashed stripe. Nobody heard the whistle, so deafening was the roar that went up from the crowd. Final score: Princeton 21, Chicago 18. And so it stands.

Ironically, that magnificent Princeton goal line stand could very well have had a different ending. During the previous winter, as a member of the rules committee, Lonny Stagg sponsored legislation to prevent the transmission of information from the bench to the playing field by a substitute.

In those final, wild seconds of the Princeton game, Fritz Crisler, Stagg's assistant, pleaded with him to send his son, a substitute quarterback, into the game with orders to pass.

"With Princeton massed to stop Thomas," cried Crisler, "the end zone is wide open. He can win the game for us."

Lonny Stagg only shook his head.

"No," he said. "I have to live with my conscience. Let the boys work it out for themselves."

Iowa, undefeated in 1921 and 1922, and with a solid claim on the 1922 national title, began its defeatless string with the fifth game in 1920 and extended it to the fourth game of 1923. The victory-snapper was a 9–6 loss to Illinois. Earl Britton's passes to Red Grange, then a sophomore, and Grange's running brought the Illini touchdown, and Britton placekicked the winning field goal from the 47-yard line. Grange, who held the ball, called it his greatest thrill.

When Howard Jones left Iowa after the 1923 season, to coach one year at Duke before going to Southern California, there was a rumor, and not without foundation, that Knute Rockne of Notre Dame seriously considered accepting the job at Iowa City.

The name Red Grange and his pseudonyms—The Galloping Ghost and The Wheaton Iceman—soon became household words. Old No. 77 made Jack Dempsey move over. He put college football ahead of boxing as the Golden Age picked up momentum. He also made some of the football stadiums obsolete; they couldn't handle the crowds. He made people buy more radios: how could you wait until Sunday morning to find out what deeds Red Grange had performed on Saturday? He was "The Galloping Ghost" and he made the sports historians torture their portables without mercy.

Nobody seemed quite able to describe the elusive halfback. The sports writers of the day were torn, strangely, between references to fire, ice, superman, and the supernatural. "A streak of fire, a breath of flame," wrote Grantland Rice. "The Wheaton Iceman," said another. "He is three or four men and a horse rolled into one," said Damon Runyon. Bob Zuppke never did learn to pronounce Red's last name correctly. The best he could do was "Grainch."

The first time Grange and Zuppke met was at a state Interscholastics track meet in Champaign in May of Red's senior year in high school.

"I'd just got through broad jumping when Zup came over," Grange recalled one time. "He said: 'Is your name *Grainche*?' That's the way he always pronounced my name. I said, 'Yes,' and he said, 'Where are you going to college?' I said, 'I don't know.' He put his arm around my shoulders and he said, 'I hope here. You may have a chance to make the team here.' That was the greatest moment I'd know."

That September, Grange arrived at Champaign with a battered second-hand trunk, one suit, a couple of pairs of trousers, and a sweater. He had been working for four summers on an ice wagon in Wheaton, and his one luxury now was to pledge Zeta Psi fraternity.

One day, the members lined up the pledges in the living room of the fraternity house. Red wanted to go out for basketball and track, but they started to point around the room and say, "You go out for cheerleader. You go out for football manager. You go out for the band." When they came to Red they said, "You go out for football."

That very afternoon Red went over to the gymnasium and he was late. He looked out the window, and it looked like Zuppke had 300 freshman candidates out for football. Red went back to the frat house and told one of the seniors, "I can't go out for football. I'll never make that team." So Johnny Hawks—that was the senior's name—lined Red up near the wall,

with his head down, and hit him a hell of a wallop with a big paddle. Johnny hit Red so hard that the force of it made a dent in the wall, where Red's head took a piece of plaster out roughly the size of a half-dollar.

Johnny Hawks was from Goshen, Indiana, and many years later at a reunion, Red said to him, "Damn you, Johnny. If it wasn't for you I'd never have gone out for football." Johnny got a big kick out of that.

That No. 77, the most famous number in football, how did Grange first get it?

"It was just handed to me my sophomore year," Red said. "When you're a sophomore you don't ask for anything. I guess anybody who has a number and does all right with it gets a little superstitious, and I guess that began against Nebraska in my first varsity game."

The game that started Grange to national fame was the 1923 Nebraska game. The previous year the Cornhuskers had beaten Notre Dame and they were to beat "The Four Horsemen" later that same season. In the first quarter Grange sprinted 35 yards for a touchdown. In the second quarter he ran 60 yards for another. In the third period he scored again on a 12-yard burst, and Illinois won, 24–7. The next day, over Walter Eckersall's story in the Chicago *Tribune*, the headline read: GRANGE SPRINTS TO FAME.

From the Nebraska game, Illinois went to an undefeated season. Against Butler, Grange scored twice. Against Iowa he scored the only touchdown as Illinois won, 9–6. In the first quarter against Northwestern he intercepted a pass and ran it back 90 yards to score the first of his three touchdowns. He made the lone touchdown against Chicago and did the same against Ohio State, this time from 34 yards out, in the last game of the season.

"All Grange can do is run," Fielding Yost was quoted as saying.

"Yes," Bob Zuppke said, "and all Galli-Curci can do is sing."

Grange's greatest day came on October 18, 1924, in his junior year against Michigan. The Wolverines were undefeated in 20 games, and for months the nation's football fans had been waiting for this meeting. The University of Illinois also chose that day to dedicate its brand new $1,700,000 Memorial Stadium. The largest crowd up to that time ever to see a foot-

The University of Illinois built a huge stadium to hold the crowds that wanted to see the sensational Red Grange play. Here 67,000 partisans packed Memorial Stadium on October 18, 1924—dedication day—as the Illini blasted Michigan, 39–14.

ball game in the Midwest—67,000—were in the stands as Michigan kicked off. Grange waited on the goal line, with Wally McIlwain, whom Zuppke was to call "the greatest open-field blocker of all time" on his right, Harry Hall, the Illinois quarterback on his left, and Britton in front of him. Michigan tried to kick to McIlwain, but as the ball came down, Grange moved over. He caught it on the 5-yard line and McIlwain turned and took out the first Michigan man. Britton cut down the next one, and Grange was underway. He started to his left, reversed his field to avoid one man and then, cutting back again to the left, ran diagonally across the field through the oncoming Michigan players. At the Michigan 40 yard line he was in the clear and went on in to score

standing up. Michigan never recovered. In less than 12 minutes Grange scored three more touchdowns, from 67, 56, and 44 yards out, and Zuppke took him out to rest him. In the third quarter he re-entered the game and circled right end for 15 yards and another touchdown. In the last period he passed for another, and Illinois won, 39–14. In summary, he had handled the ball 20 times, gained 402 yards, scored five touchdowns and had a part in a sixth. Amos Alonzo Stagg later called it "the most spectacular single-handed performance ever made in a major game."

Grange once picked the Chicago game, three weeks later at Stagg Field, as his toughest college contest. Some 40,000 spectators filled the stands and, outside the walls,

Red Grange's running style was to start wide, cut back, then cut back again, carving a big S on the field. He had 9.8 hundred-yard-dash speed, excellent balance, change-of-pace, and the uncanny ability to see tacklers coming from the sides.

scalpers were getting $100 a ticket. Chicago led, 14–0, in the second quarter, when Grange, carrying the ball six times and throwing three completed passes,covered 75 yards for the first score. Chicago then increased its lead to 21–7, and Grange made it 21–14, carrying nine times and catching two passes. In the third quarter he ran 80 yards through a barrier of Chicago tacklers, and the game ended 21–21.

When Grange started his senior year, Illinois had lost seven starters by graduation and Harry Hall because of a broken collarbone. Zuppke shifted Grange to quarterback, and Illinois lost to Nebraska, Iowa and Michigan, and barely beat Butler before they played Pennsylvania in Philadelphia, on October 31, 1925. The Quakers had been considered the champions of the East in 1924, and they had now beaten Brown, Yale, and Chicago, among others, and, although Grange's amazing feats in the Midwest had been widely reported for two years in Eastern papers, most of the 65,000 spectators and the East Coast press had to be convinced.

George Trevor, famous football editor-reporter for the New York *Sun*, was one of those who had to be convinced. Many years later, at his home in Portchester, New York, I sat in his living room and listened to him recount that cloudy afternoon at Franklin Field.

"For two years," George said, "we effete Easterners had been fed up on the fabulous tales of Grange's exploits, so we came prepared to be disillusioned. Nobody could be that good! Eager to cooperate in making Grange's debut in the East a fizzle, our Pennsylvania pals had turned the fire hose on Franklin Field all night in an effort to abet the puny efforts of reluctant nature. It had been spitting rain intermittently all morning, but not enough to stop a Gazelle, let alone a Grange. The fire department really did the job—or so Penn fans hoped.

"Fiery little Bob Zuppke, the marine artist-coach, turned purple when he saw that marshy field. And he cussed in the Germanic version of *Oski-Wowow!* Zup could handle oaths like a Prussian drill sergeant. He liked to say, 'I build my football teams out of mass and fire, just as an oil painter arranges his pigments on canvas.' In Grange, Zuppke had the hottest, brightest bolt of kinetic energy ever to flash across a football field. Picture, if you can, a tall

Harold (Red) Grange and coach Bob Zuppke of Illinois helped lift college football into the big time in 1923-24-25.

Greyhound of a boy, with hair the color of a Turner sunset, the rhythm of a Pavlova, and two speeds—fast and faster. That was Red Grange.

"I remember that an eerie feeling of suspense hung over Penn's sky-top pressbox, that eagle's perch so aptly christened 'Thrombosis Terrace' by Red Smith. We had come down from New York to see a natural phenomenon, and we writers experienced that spine-tingling anticipation which is a prelude to witnessing the supernatural. Would Mr. Grange let us down? That was the silent question on everybody's mind.

"Following Penn's kickoff, Illinois put the ball in play on its own 24-yard line. Grange back. No quibbling, no fooling around. The ball was hiked to Red. He slithered off tackle like a gigantic fiddler crab, broke suddenly to the outside through the muddy going, swept the Penn flank, cut back to midfield distancing all pursuers, and fled for the goal line. Not a hand was laid on him during this 76-yard trip to the end zone.

" 'Ring the fire bells!' somebody shouted. 'This guy's gonna burn the joint down!'

"That was the first of three spectacular touchdowns Red scored. I remember he chalked one up on Zuppke's pet flea-flicker play, a forward pass down the middle alley to Charlie Kassel, the end, who tossed a wide Rugby lateral to Red who stormed on the outside. Illinois won, 24–2, with Red getting credit for a total of 363 yards in 36 tries, scoring three times, and setting up another.

"In addition to blinding speed, a baffling change of pace, a lethal straight arm—a weapon seldom seen anymore—a tricky cross step, and an evasive hip motion, Grange had what doctors call psychosomatic perception— that is, the ability to sense the presence of unseen hazards. This amounts to peripheral vision, which is best explained by the common expression: 'He has eyes in the back of his head.' In other words, Grange could visualize the entire pattern of the field at one glance. Even while he was eluding a given tackler, he could sense the approach of another and was already figuring out ways to give him the slip.

"That catalogue of football virtues reminds me of Coach John McEwan's description of his flawless University of Oregon fullback, John Kitzmiller. 'Kitz could do all eight things expected of a great back perfectly,' McEwan once told me. 'In fact, the kid had only one weakness—he couldn't *read!*'

"The impact left upon me by my first glimpse of Red Grange was so overwhelming that I sat motionless in the pressbox for 20 minutes after the game unable to write a line. Around me I heard the ripping sound of paper as stories were torn out of typewriters and tossed to the floor. *This is just too big for me,* seemed to be the consensus of hardened reporters. For the first time in years of reporting football, we were all at a loss for words.

"Time has a way of restoring perspective, and to skeptics of the younger generation Grange may be just another back, but if Red wasn't outstanding as a passer or kicker I'll string along with Bob Zuppke and his Galli-Curci simile: '*Mein Gott,* how that guy could dance!' "

In 1975, Larry Keith, writing in *Sports Illustrated,* ventured the opinion that today's college ball-carriers are faster, stronger, bigger and longer lasting than at any time in the past.

"They confound more defenses, accumulate more records and inspire more clichés," Keith wrote. "Of the 10 leading ground-gainers of all time, five were on display in 1975—Ohio State's Archie Griffin, Pitt's Tony Dorsett, Oklahoma's Joe Washington, Kentucky's Sonny Collins and Wisconsin's Bill Marek. A 100-yard-per-game average is now as commonplace as a four-minute mile: a record 28 players topped that in '75 . . . Red Grange, Tom Harmon, Glenn Davis, Hopalong Cassady and Jim Brown never gained 1,000 yards in a season, a routine event nowadays . . . Professional scouts are calling the current senior class the best they have ever seen, and the junior class at least as good . . ."

Not everyone agrees that today's stars are the best ever, of course. They point out that the times have made the man, that today's players are different, not necessarily better, because the game is different. Glenn Davis, Mr. Outside of Army's vaunted Blanchard-Davis one-two punch of the World War II era, said, "There is no way you can compare a player today against a player of the past."

"The greatest backs 10, 20, 30 years ago would be great now, too," added Alabama's Bear Bryant.

Tommy Harmon, Michigan's Heisman Trophy winner in 1940, agreed.

"A thousand yards would have been nothing for Red Grange, Glenn Davis or Jay Berwanger," Harmon said. "Give a guy like Grange the football 40 times under two-platoon rules and he'd kill you. He might be running yet."

The Grange Era saw Illinois and Michigan tie for the Big Ten championship in 1923; Chicago won it in 1924 despite 3 ties, and the Wolverines stood alone in 1925. Chicago's victory marked the beginning of the end for the great Stagg teams there. In fact, the Maroon never won the title again. Michigan, unbeaten in 1922 and 1923, lingered in fourth place in 1924, and George Little, coach of the Wolverines that one season while Fielding Yost confined himself to athletic administration work, blamed Red Grange for a 6–2–0 record.

In 1954, George and I used to spend our summer weekends together at a resort down on the Jersey coast, and then, 30 years after the Ghost had played, the memory of Grange made George toss in his sleep.

"Grange practically wrecked us single-handed," George told me. "As he and his Illinois teammates swamped us, 39 to 14, I stood in front of our bench and said to myself, 'Oh, oh, there goes our season.' Thank God, my kids were not quitters. They went on to win four out of our last five games, held Wisconsin, Minnesota and Northwestern scoreless, and gave up only 6 points to Ohio State. I had a great little quarterback in Bennie Friedman. In fact, he was too good. The following year he came back to haunt me. I had gone from Michigan to Wisconsin in 1925 as head coach and as the record shows, I left Ann Arbor a year too early. I should have waited until Bennie was gone. In my first season at Madison, we lost only one game—to Michigan, 21 to 0. Bennie figured in all the touchdowns. On the very first play of the game he pitched to Bruce Gregory for a touchdown. In those days, the team that had been scored upon had the choice of kicking or receiving, and we chose to kick. So on the very first scrimmage play, Bennie tucked the ball under his arm and scored on a play that registered 65 yards. Then to impress upon us who was boss, Bennie passed again for the third touchdown. It was a nightmare."

Fielding Yost, who had overruled his doctors and came back for two more seasons as head coach, called his 1925 eleven the "best ever" at Michigan, superior even to his celebrated Point-a-Minute Teams of 1901–1905. The 1925 Wolverines had their traditionally stingy defense, even more unyielding than usual, and they outscored their eight opponents, 227 to 3. In their two Bennies—Friedman and Oosterbaan—they had one of the greatest passing combinations in history. Friedman was a brilliant quarterback, a dangerous runner, and an expert field-goal kicker, as well as an alert pass defender. Oosterbaan was an uncanny receiver with a knack of filtering through an opposing secondary and making acrobatic catches. His defensive finesse heralded him as one of the two or three top ends of all time.

To go with Bennie F. and Benny O., Yost had an array of agile, opportunistic linemen and a bevy of versatile backs. No one on the team weighed more than 200 pounds, but no

Michigan's Benny Friedman, left, and Bennie Oosterbaan remain the only passing combination in college football history to be named All-American two years in a row, 1925–26.

Big Ten team has since matched their defensive record.

The defense really came into its own against Illinois. In the same stadium where they had been embarrassed a year earlier, the Wolverines, bolstered by some brilliant sophomores, held Red Grange to 64 yards in 21 carries. In the 1924 game, he had made more than that the first time he got his hands on the ball. A steady rain helped to slow Red down, but it also handicapped Friedman's passing attack. Bennie managed to placekick a field goal, however, and that was the way the game ended, 3–0, Michigan. Oosterbaan, though only a sophomore, played an inspired game, continually forcing Grange to run inside tackle, where he was smothered.

Incredibly, the team that Yost called his best lost a game in 1925. For five days preceding the Northwestern game it rained cats and dogs. Soldier Field became a quagmire. The playing conditions virtually neutralized the Friedman-to-Oosterbaan aerial circus. Rushing was also futile. Michigan gained a total of 35 yards, Northwestern 28. Early in the contest, the Wildcats recovered a Michigan fumble, kicked a field goal, then purposely gave up a safety to allow better field position and hang on to win by the baseball score of 3 to 2. That one-point difference was just enough for Dartmouth and Alabama to claim the mythical national championship.

George Little's Wisconsin team finished in a second-place tie with Northwestern in the 1925 Conference standings. The Wildcats were 5–2–0 on the season going into the final Saturday against Notre Dame. The Irish hadn't lost a game at South Bend in 20 years, but midway through this one it seemed certain the record would be broken. To the surprise of everybody, Northwestern led at halftime, 10 to 0. The story of what took place in the Notre Dame dressing room during the half remains a classic. Joe Boland, who later became well-known as the radio broadcaster of the Notre Dame games, was the first-string left tackle on that 1925 Irish eleven.

"I remember walking back to the locker room, up in the northwest corner of the old field house," Joe recalled once. "All of us wondered what Rock would say for the way we had been playing. It was not exactly the best performance of our careers. We flopped down in the room and waited for him. We kept looking at the door expecting him to come bursting through any minute. But he did not show. Finally, the three-minute warning came and still no Rockne. Then he walked in. He was fuming. When he was that mad, the cords stood out in his neck and he bit off the words so that every one of them hurt. 'The Fighting Irish!' he snapped in a voice that curled your shoulder pads. 'BAH!' He let that sink in for a moment, then, 'Well, you'll be able to tell your grandchildren you're the first Notre Dame team that ever quit.' He turned to Hunk Anderson, the assistant coach, and said, 'You take 'em, Hunk. I'm through with them.' Then he walked out the door.

"I don't remember how we got through the door, but I remember that Rome Dugan was standing behind it and he got flattened against the wall. We went out there and took the kickoff and slammed 75 yards for a touchdown. Didn't use a pass or an end run. Enright and Christy Flanagan just socked tackle and guard until we went over. When they kicked to us again, we pounded another 78 yards for the second touchdown of the third quarter. At the end of the game, that's the way it stood, 13 to 10. Earlier, I kept looking over at the bench for

Rock, but he was nowhere in sight. He had hidden himself up in the stands. But towards the end of the game he showed up, crouching on the sidelines, twiddling that cigar just as if nothing had happened."

Which was how Knute Rockne tricked the Irish into beating Northwestern with the shortest fight talk on record.

The year 1925 was also the year that the poll business had its origin. And as you might have guessed, good old Rock had a hand in that, too. What occurred was this. A teacher of economics at the University of Illinois named Frank G. Dickinson was a football buff who privately enjoyed rating all of the teams in the country by his own mathematical formula. He happened to mention this in the classroom one day and a student on the back row who was sports editor of the *Daily Illini* wrote a story about it. The story came to the attention of a Chicago clothing manufacturer named Jack Rissman, another buff, who decided he would like to use Dickinson's ratings to select the top team in the Western Conference each year— they didn't all play each other—so that he could present a trophy to the winner. When Knute Rockne heard about this, he invited both Professor Dickinson and Rissman to lunch at South Bend and said, "Why don't you make it a *national* trophy that Notre Dame will have a chance to win?" Never one to miss out on a good thing, Rock also persuaded Dickinson and Rissman to predate the whole thing a year so that the 1924 "Four Horsemen, Seven Mules" Notre Dame team could be the first genuinely "official" national champion. That was actually how football polls began, and how the Fighting Irish won their first national crown—at lunch!

Professor Dickinson's system was quite simple. Once the season was over, he divided all teams into two categories—those that won more games than they lost, and those that didn't. Then he gave points for wins over teams in the first division and fewer points for wins over teams in the second division. Quality of schedule was not a factor but the number of games played was, except for postseason bowls. Still, the Dickinson rating system was accepted by fans as the most authoritative until the late 1930s, when there was a rash of other polls.

At Wisconsin, in 1926, it was a testy, frustrated atmosphere which George Little braved. His mandate was clear, total, unqualified. He was supposed to win the Big Ten championship, and the victims en route were supposed to include not only the No. 1 and No. 2 traditional rivals, Chicago and Minnesota, but Michigan and Iowa as well. He had failed to deliver the Big Ten title in 1925 and he had not beaten Minnesota and Michigan. He knew he would have to do better than that to hang on. He already had an able staff of assistants in Tom Lieb, Irv Uteritz, Edliff (Butch) Slaughter, Guy Sundt, and Glenn Holmes. Lieb was a former Notre Dame tackle who would later assist Rockne. Uteritz, a brainy fellow, had won All-American mention as the 1922 Michigan quarterback. Slaughter had been an All-American Michigan guard in 1924. Sundt, Wisconsin captain in 1921, later became athletic director and track coach. Holmes coached the freshmen and later carried on the winning tradition at Oak Park High School in Illinois by Bob Zuppke, and by his immediate successor Glenn Thistlethwaite, who moved up to Northwestern.

Coach Little figured he could help himself by bringing Earl (Red) Blaik in to coach the ends and also help with the scouting. Blaik wanted to help George out if he could, and he promised him he would talk it over with his father. Red pointed out to his dad that he would be at Madison for only two months, beginning September 15, and then he would return home and help out with the family business. The idea did not overplease Blaik senior, but he didn't stand in Red's way. He said it might even help Red get rid of some of his restlessness. So, after Labor Day, Red Blaik packed a bag and went up to Madison. He lived at the University Club and received a $1,500 salary, listed as "expenses."

"We had a 5–2–1 record, 3–2–1 in the Conference," Colonel Blaik recalled. "Michigan and Northwestern, each 5–0, finished first. We were outclassed by another Friedman-Oosterbaan team, 37–0. We beat Chicago, 14–7; Iowa, 20–10; Indiana, 27–7; and tied Purdue, 0–0. The game that deprived us of a clear claim on second place in the Conference and probably brought the end of George Little as head coach was the defeat by Minnesota at Wisconsin's Camp Randall Stadium.

Rotund Dr. Clarence W. Spears headed up the Minnesota football coaching corps in 1925–1929. With a profile like this, little wonder he was called "Fats."

"The year before, a 12–12 tie with the Gophers at Minneapolis had been such a wild affair that it threatened a rupture of the series. Dr. Clarence W. (Fats) Spears, the Minnesota coach and later coach at Wisconsin, taught strictly Spartan football, which he had first learned as an All-American guard at Dartmouth under Major Frank W. Cavanaugh. Dr. Spears was a smart, articulate man, ostensibly cold, yet I later knew him to possess a warmth he revealed to a few. He probably gave his warm side a brief airing after our 1926 game. We had no license to win the game, yet we were sorely distressed over losing it and with strong reason. We never did make a first down, yet we got 10 points. We scored our touchdown peculiarly. Herb Joesting, the Minnesota fullback, fumbled and the ball bounced away crazily and ended up hopping into the hands of our end, Jeff Burrus, who was far from the origin of the play. Burrus, who was anything but fast, managed to beat everybody to the Minnesota goal line 85 yards away. Our field goal was a placement from the 40-yard line by Butch Leitl.

"Minnesota, which wound up with something like 18 first downs, would still have lost, 10–9, except that with four minutes to go, Mally Nydahl, the Gopher right halfback, returned Barnum's longest punt of the day for 60 yards and a touchdown. The final score was Minnesota 16, Wisconsin 10.

"From this bitter disappointment, we rallied well to defeat Burt Ingwersen's Iowa team, which had one of the best cutback runners I ever saw in Nick (Cowboy) Kutch. We then went down to Chicago, to finish the season with Mr. Amos Alonzo Stagg's team. There had been a heavy storm, and snow was banked along the sidelines and behind the end zone. I was eager to meet Mr. Stagg, and during pregame practice managed to strike up a conversation with him. I asked him how he felt before a big game, and he replied, 'I never worry about football. I just take the attitude: Let the better team win.'

"Mr. Stagg's philosophy seemed to be belied by his obvious emotions in front of his bench as the game unrolled. We scored twice in the first quarter and went on to win, 14–7. Chicago rallied in the third quarter on a pass from Wally Marks to Kyle Anderson. The Maroon completed 11 of 28 passes for 184 yards, something special for those days.

"My wife Merle was watching the game with Helen Little, George's wife. George had told Helen she should never pray for victory, because it was wrong to be bothering God about football when He had so many other more important petitions to consider. Helen got around this by praying, 'God give them sense,' and included George.

"We won, 14–7, but if God gave us the sense to do it, he apparently continued to withhold any from the obstreperous segments of Wisconsin die-hards. The defeat by Minnesota prompted many to write letters to Coach Little. George would have been far better off to ignore them, but he was the type to try to mold the opinions of others to coincide with his own, instead of adopting the view that you are not going to change them, so why bother! He delegated me to answer most of these letters. Since I was representing George, my replies bore no relation to my thoughts.

"The Madison papers also were taking a dyspeptic view of George's coaching, which upset him. He definitely wasn't fired, however, although it is logical to assume that he

Coach Glen Thistlethwaite built Northwestern teams in 1925 and 1926 almost as tough as his name was to spell. Here he talks to Moon Baker, his 1926 All-American halfback. A loss to Notre Dame was all that kept the Wildcats from winning the national championship that season.

would eventually have been forced to give up the football job. Anyhow, that winter, he informed the athletic board that he was stepping out of coaching and would concentrate on being athletic director. He also recommended and had appointed as his successor Glenn Thistlethwaite, who had lifted Northwestern to the top of the Big Ten, yet was eager to leave Evanston.

"Thistlethwaite lasted five years, the longest of any Wisconsin coach from 1903 till 1941, but he could not deliver a championship either. So George Little's removing himself from the football job did not materially affect Wisconsin's football fortunes."

In 1926, a dogfight developed among Michigan, Ohio State, and Northwestern for the Big Ten title. In the next-to-last game of the season, Michigan, 3–0–0 in the Conference, traveled to Columbus to play Ohio State, 2–0–0. Though trailing the Wolverines in the standings, the Bucks hadn't lost a game all season, while the team from Ann Arbor had lost once, to Navy.

A record crowd of 90,411 watched Ohio State shock Michigan with 10 points in the first 12 minutes. When Michigan took a timeout, Wally Weber said to Bennie Oosterbaan, "At this rate they're going to drub us by 40 points." And Bennie's face reddened and he said,

The 1926 Wildcats were the first Northwestern footballers to roll through a Big Ten schedule unbeaten, marred only by a last-minute 6–0 nonleague loss to Notre Dame. Stars of the team were All-American nominees, *clockwise*, back Ralph (Moon) Baker, fullback Tiny Lewis, tackle Bob Johnson, and end Waldo Fisher.

"Dammit, Wally, we haven't even had the ball yet!"

When Michigan did get the ball, Bennie Friedman fired a bullet to Oosterbaan on State's 21. Then going into a placekick formation, he hit Oosterbaan again, this time for a touchdown.

There were only 30 seconds left in the half when Michigan again went into a placekick formation. As the Wolverines took their positions, Oosterbaan paused a moment, then hurried over and whispered something to Friedman.

"Fake, fake, watch Oosterbaan!" cried the once-stung Buckeyes as Oosterbaan returned to his position on the flank. The ball rested at an angle on the Ohio State 43-yard line, and as the holder, Lou Gilbert, took the snap from center and placed the ball down, Friedman, without the normal pressure of a charging Ohio State line, sailed it through the uprights to tie the score, 10–10. When asked later what

he had said to Friedman, Oosterbaan confessed, "I merely asked him if he didn't think that was an awfully long way to kick a football."

Michigan got its big break in the fourth quarter when Sid Dewey recovered an Ohio State fumble on the Buckeye 6-yard line. Three straight running plays failed to move the ball, then Friedman lobbed a pass over the middle to Leo Hoffman for a touchdown, converted the extra point, and now Michigan led, 17–10.

The Bucks fought to the very end. Driving from their own end of the field, they managed to forge their way to the Michigan 6, where fullback Marty Karow exploded across the goal to make the score 16–17. Now the pressure was all on Myers Clark, the Ohio State placekicker. The Ohio State cheer leaders, who had been exploding from the ground like human jumping jacks after that last touchdown, suddenly grew gravely quiet and watched with everyone else as Clark prepared to try to tie the game. It was on him now, on him and on the holder.

The Buckeyes were tired. They had played their hearts out for 59½ minutes. Let's not die here now, the Columbus fans were thinking. "All right, Clark!" they shouted. "Let's make it!" They were thinking, We drove all this way—80 yards—and we should make this big point good. Let's make this one, last point. "You linemen!" they shouted. "Block!"

It had all come down to this one kick. The Bucks broke from the huddle now and walked slowly up to the line of scrimmage. The referee's whistle blew and the two lines braced themselves.

Under his breath, Coach John Wilce was saying, Don't reach for the ball and hit it too high, Clark. Don't squirt it to either side. Plant that right foot straight and lock the right ankle and . . .

Wilce saw the center snap the ball. He saw the holder catch it and turn the ball as he placed it down. The two lines rose, struggling, and Clark took steps and his foot came forward. The ball rose, up and over Michigan arms. There was a moment then while the ball was in flight, and the crowd silent, not a cry, not a word, waiting, a moment when everything stood still or seemed to, and you could almost feel the hope in everyone as they wished the ball over the crossbar. The kick was high enough, but then at the very last second it swerved to the right, and without even looking up you could tell by the sigh of the Ohio State spectators it had missed.

Wilce felt empty. He wanted to die. He was not alone. Groans filled the air. Wilce looked up at the scoreboard and it was all up there:

"Michigan 17, Ohio State 16."

Fifty years later, Michigan historians still refer to that contest as "one of the two most dramatic victories ever recorded by the Wolverines."

The second most dramatic was played at Minneapolis the following Saturday, with the Little Brown Jug at stake. The Minnesota winter had moved in early, and the field was frozen. Coach Fielding Yost surveyed the field on Friday, saw it was covered with hay to guard against the ice, and ordered his players to run through a special practice drill to test the turf.

The contest marked the second time the two teams had met that season. Michigan won the first game, 20–0, at Ann Arbor.

Bennie Friedman had doubts about playing Minnesota twice in one season, and his fears appeared justified when the Gophers went ahead in the second quarter and led at halftime, 6–0. Minnesota's relentless ground attack continued bending the Michigan defense in the third and part of the fourth quarters, but could not cross the goal line. Yost's strategy was to wait for a break. It finally came late in the game as the Gophers had a first-and-10 on their own 40. The ball was snapped—and suddenly it was thrashing around in the Minnesota backfield. Oosterbaan smashed in from his end position, scooped up the ball, and was off for the races. The play was good for 60 yards and a touchdown.

Now the pressure was on Bennie Friedman, instead of on Myers Clark. The game hinged on the conversion.

"Com'on, Bennie!" Yost shouted. "You can do it!"

Tension hung like heavy fog over the stadium. The predominantly Minneapolis crowd was quiet now. Everybody was standing, their hearts pounding, as they watched Friedman line up his placekick. Slowly he took two steps back and, head down, faced the goal posts, waiting for the snap back. Those muscular arms hung loosely at his sides. His jersey was covered with sweat and grime, a testimony to having played the whole game. A long murmur ran around the stadium. You could almost hear the silent prayers, the pleas from the small contingent of Michigan fans, encouraging him, helping him all they could. No one was sitting now. Seven days ago all the pressure had been on Ohio State's Myers Clark—and he had failed. Now it was on Bennie Friedman.

The ball was snapped. The holder set it up nice and pretty. Bennie stepped forward and dug his toe viciously into the ball. The ball tumbled high and forward. It wavered for just an instant in the wind, and then curved toward the center of the goal posts. For a split second there was no signal from the referee—and then he suddenly flung his hands upward.

The riot was on. The Michigan players swarmed all over Friedman, doing strange dances and hugging and shouting. Those back on the bench poured out onto the field and shook his hand and patted him on the back, and you could tell by the wide grin on Bennie's face that that was a supreme moment of his life.

Final score: Michigan 7, Minnesota 6.

Michigan thus shared the Big Ten title with Northwestern—the fourth championship for the Wolverines in five years. And the two Bennies, Friedman and Oosterbaan, became the first passing combination in history to make the All-American team two years in a row.

For Fielding Yost, he had coached his last Michigan football team. In a quarter century at the helm, his teams had won 165 games, lost 29, tied 10. Fifteen times they fought for the Western Conference championship, and 10 of those times they won or shared it. His coaching career at Michigan shaped up almost like bookends: He came into the league with four straight winners, and he left with four out of five winners.

Though they groped around in the bottom half of the Big Ten standings (6th-place tie with Northwestern), the Ohio State Buckeyes' one bright spot in 1927 was tackle Leo Raskowski, All-American.

The years 1927–28 were all Illinois, after popping up from deep in the league standings (6th) in 1926. The secret to Bob Zuppke's success was that he adjusted his formations from year to year, according to the available personnel. The 1927 Illini were led by Russ Crain, guard; Al Nowack, tackle; and halfback Jud Timm. By now, Red Grange had graduated, but he was familiar with the players.

"It was not a big team," Red recalled. "Fritz Humbert was the biggest man in the backfield at 166 pounds. But they were a hard-working bunch and except for a 12–12 nonconference tie with Iowa State, they marched through the league unbeaten and untied. My kid brother, Garland, played end on that team and I was proud of him.

"Look at the weights of that little backfield: Stuessy, 156 pounds; Blair French, 148; Jud Timm, 164; Frank Walker, 154; Doug Mills, 148; and Humbert, 166. They had fire, rhythm and harmony, however, and they mopped up. In the line, Butch Nowack, big and powerful, made plenty of room for the ball-carriers to run. So did Russ Crain. As the 1927 season progressed, the name Lou Muegge kept popping up in the papers. He was a tackle and made the starting team against physical odds. They called him 'Step-and-a-half' Muegge because a boyhood disability gave him sort of a step-and-a-half gait. But he had a great, sunny disposition, a winning attitude, and he believed in the power of his body so much the coaches couldn't keep him out of the lineup.

"The 1927 team was captained by the greatest center ever to play for Zup, Bob Reitsch. He was flanked on one side by Russ Crain, whom Grantland Rice named as an All-American guard, and on the other by tough Bill McClure. Hickman, Wolgast, Jolley and my brother, Gardie, were the ends. 'Peanuts' Schultz and Lou Gordon also played a lot of football for the team. Gordon was the finest Jewish athlete Zup ever coached. He came out for football in 1926 and failed to make the freshman team, but became a sensation on the varsity. He and Weitz made their side of the line impregnable. Gordon received honorable mention on many All-American selections. He later played pro ball for the Green Bay Packers.

"The 1927 Illinois champions were called 'the team of nobodies, from nowhere,' because

National champions from Illinois, 1927. The Illini finished first in the Big Ten with 5–0–0 record, but were tied by Iowa State, 12–12, in a non-Conference game to finish with an overall 7–0–1 record. Pictured, front row, left: Humbert, Deimling, Crane, Walker, Perkins, captain Reitsch, French, Muegge, McClure, Schultz. Second row, left: Nelson, Mitterwalner, Nowack, Timm, G. Grange, Mills, Stewart, Short, Wietz. Third row, left: Burdick, Grable, Marriner, Gordon, Jolley, D'Ambrosia, Richman, Wolgast. Back row, left: Stuessy, Rokusek, Kline, Lindgren, Olander, Bullock, manager Grimes, coach Zuppke.

they weren't conceded a chance of winning the title prior to the opening game. Northwestern, under Dick Hanley, had a fine eleven and were favored over Illinois in the first game, but the 'nobodies' came 'out of nowhere' to upset the Wildcats, 7 to 6. Jolley scored on a forward pass from Stuessy to win and from that point on, Illinois bowled over Michigan, Iowa, Chicago and Ohio State, scoring a combined total of 56 points against only one touchdown in the four contests. Dick Hanley later said that the Illini in '27 had the greatest team speed of any college team he had ever seen. The squad was nicely balanced with sophomores, juniors, and seniors. According to Zup, an exceptionally well-balanced varsity would have four seniors, four juniors, and three sophomores. He figured the seniors would contribute experience and poise, the juniors, zest; and the sophomores, high hopes."

Zuppke, himself, was once quoted as saying that division by classes had the advantage of overlapping, or carrying material over into the next season. He said that the ideal division of a football team would be to have a 50–50 division of experienced men of ability and new men with latent talent.

"The beginners learn by imitating the older stars," Zup explained. "It is easy to learn how to play football through the eye; it is far more difficult to learn by the ear, by being *told* how to do things. And, incidentally, try and carry a boy with a sense of humor on the team. You might find him among the scrubs. We've carried many a scrub with us on trips, without expecting to use him, merely because his contagious cheerfulness offsets the 'Gloomy Guses' on the squad."

Minnesota finished second and third in 1927–28 in Big Ten standings. The coach was Clarence Wiley Spears, better known as Fat, Cupid, and Doc. He had the face of a cherub, and the body of a gorilla. He stood 5–7 and weighed about 236. Spears was an All-American guard at Dartmouth in 1914 and 1915 and could run like the wind. As a player and coach, he thought of football primarily as a game of condition and contact.

Dick Cullum, long-time Minneapolis

Tribune sports columnist, remembers Doc Spears as a driving, crackdown type of coach.

"He'd have been too tough on the field for today's football," Dick said. "But he was a warm man with his players, excepting at practice. The good players loved him, the rest did not."

Ken Haycraft, All-American end, was one of the "good" players.

"My viewpoint of Doc probably differs from others because I first went out for football at Minnesota in 1925, when Doc first arrived in Minneapolis and issued an invitation to anyone interested in going out for the team," Ken told me recently. "He said, 'You don't need to know football, we'll teach you if you have the desire to play.' What a far cry that was from today's scholarship or no-play situation. I'd never even been in a scrimmage in high school, but I did want to play football in college. So my older brother, Jolly Haycraft, and I reported to Fall practice.

"The first day out, I was in a scrimmage at tackle—I weighed only 162 as a freshman—and I spent the rest of the season gaining experience by scrimmaging against the varsity daily, until a knee injury sidelined me for a while. When the knee healed, Doc assigned me a brand new uniform and a jersey with a number on it and told me I was going with the team to Ann Arbor for the Michigan game. We had two tackles out with injuries and Doc said I was now a second-string tackle. Fortunately, I did not get into the game. Doc told me that since it was the last game of the season—and because Michigan was beating us, 35–0—he had decided to hold me out so I'd still have three years of varsity eligibility remaining. One minute of play would have cost me a whole year's competition.

"The next Fall, I was out early for practice. For the first week, Doc experimented with me at guard, but when I finished third in a squad footrace, he shifted me to end. Five minutes against North Dakota, 10 minutes against Notre Dame, and thereafter I was the starting left end for Minnesota for the next three years, culminated by being selected by Grantland Rice and others as left end on the 1928 All-American team.

"Perhaps because of my inexperience, I never thought I knew more than the coach in the four years I played for Doc Spears. And I

can truthfully say that he never said a mean or sarcastic word to me. He was known as a hard driver, a fierce taskmaster—and, granted, he was surely both—but he was also a good psychologist. At the half in the Notre Dame field house in 1927—final score was 7–7—while we rested and waited for Doc to give us his analysis of what went wrong—we trailed 0–7 as Notre Dame scored against our second team—we suddenly heard a loud voice rising and falling from someplace beyond an inner partition. We all became quiet as it dawned on us that we were hearing Rockne's famous between-halves fight talk to the Irish. When Rockne had finished with his GO! GO! GO!, Doc Spears turned to us and said: 'That goes for you, too! Now go back out there and play ball!' That was all the talk he made that day.

"I'm sure Doc made mistakes in his analysis of individuals, and I know he made life miserable for several, as my brother Jolly was one of his favorite targets, but to this day Jolly admires and respects the memory of Doc as a coach and a man and still speaks very highly of him.

"Our 1927 team (undefeated) has had a reunion every five years since 1957. There is a strong bond of fellowship between the players who played under Doc and who, in Doc's words, 'brought Minnesota back to its rightful place in the sun,' at the top of the Big Ten."

Because of the bruising (but clean) type of football Doc Spears insisted on, Big Ten teams shied away from scheduling Minnesota. In 1925 the Gophers had only three Conference games, with Michigan, Iowa, and Wisconsin, when a minimum of four was required to qualify for the championship.

"You may beat Minnesota," said Dr. John Wilce, of Ohio State, "but the next week you can't beat anybody."

At the 1926 winter meeting, only Wisconsin, Iowa, and Michigan agreed to play the Gophers again. Fielding Yost solved the problem by signing to play Minnesota twice.

Doc Spears always picked the 1927 team as his best at Minnesota. The Gophers were undefeated but tied by Indiana, 14–14, and Notre Dame, 7–7. A sophomore from International Falls, Bronko Nagurski, appeared in the Minnesota lineup. "When I asked him what position he played," said Spears, "he replied, 'All of them.'" Bronko proved himself so right that

Bronko Nagurski was one of the most devastating runners in football history. An All-American fullback, tackle, and end, Minnesota lost only four games during the Nagurski years, 1927–1929. When Red Grange was asked recently to describe Bronko in terms of modern stars, Old 77 replied, "He played offense like Larry Csonka and defense like Dick Butkus."

after his senior season, when Grantland Rice asked Doc where he should place Bronko on his All-American team, Doc replied seriously, "Just pick your first 10 men and then put Nagurski in any spot that's left." Nagurski was used mainly at tackle and fullback by Spears, although Doc always maintained that end would have been the ideal position for him.

I once asked Pudge Heffelfinger to give me his analysis of Nagurski, and the all-time All-American guard said, "He reminded me of a wise old mule in a pasture with a bunch of horses. The mule may look dumb, but he sees everything out of the corner of his eye. Nagurski could play any position on a football team up to the hilt. Doc Spears used him at fullback a lot because of his line-smashing power, but I think he was even greater at tackle. You never caught Bronko down on his knees, with his nose scraping turf. Nagurski

was bigger and stronger than I ever was. More important, he knew how to apply his strength. I'd rate him as the greatest of post-World War I players—equally good at fullback or tackle or end. What a full-time end he would have made, with his speed and crashing power. Nagurski probably had more leg drive than even Ernie Nevers. It was nothing for Nag to carry three or four tacklers along with him."

George Trevor, who loved creating legends with his facile pen, often told of the time Nagurski exploded across the Indiana goal line with such momentum that he crashed into the concrete wall beyond the end zone. Doc Spears called him to the bench for a rest.

"How's their line?" Doc wanted to know.

Bronko, still somewhat punchy from the crash, shook his head.

"Weak at right tackle," he was supposed to have replied, "but that linebacker on the short side is sure built *solid!*"

In 1927, Minnesota went down to Notre Dame for a game. A blizzard struck. Knute Rockne respected the Gophers so much he did not start his second line, which was his habit. Spears, meanwhile, started his second team, so the Irish could count on no psychological or chemical edge. Nagurski forced and recovered a fumble deep in Notre Dame territory. After two smashes at the line, Herb Joesting, the Minnesota fullback, passed to Len Walsh for

Quarterback Fred Hovde supplied the 1927–28 Minnesota Gophers with plenty of candlepower. He went on to become a Rhodes Scholar and President of Purdue University.

the touchdown. Late in the game, Notre Dame tied it on a 20-yard run by halfback Christy Flanagan. It ended, 7–7. The next week Notre Dame was beaten by Army, 18–0.

Doc Spears' biggest upset and probably Nagurski's single greatest game came in a 6–0 upset at Wisconsin in 1928. Joesting, an All-American, and other key players were sidelined with injuries. Nagurski, wearing a special brace on his back, was put in Joesting's place at fullback. Wisconsin had heard that Nagurski was injured and wouldn't play, and they were rattled when he showed up in a new position and began ripping holes in their line. Nag recovered a fumble on the Badger 17 and in six straight shots scored the game's only touchdown. Late in the last quarter, Bo Cuisinier, speedy Wisconsin back, caught a pass and headed for the goal line, but Nagurski caught up with him and brought him down on the 8-yard line.

"I wasn't sure where Bronk was on the play," Cuisinier said, "but I expected if he tackled me, he'd at least knock me forward a few yards. But instead he grabbed me by the shoulder, thrust one big leg between mine, and yanked me backward. I couldn't budge."

During Nagurski's three varsity seasons at Minnesota, the Gophers won 18 games, lost 4, tied 2. They outscored opponents 572 to 126. The four defeats were by Iowa (7–6) and Northwestern (10–9) in 1928, and by Michigan (7–6) and Iowa (9–7) in 1929—a 5-point spread for the four contests.

Doc Spears quit Minnesota for University of Oregon in 1929. He had been feuding with the Minnesota athletic director, Fred Leuhring, accusing him of pinching pennies. But it was Dr. Lotus D. Coffman, the college president, who really got under Doc's skin. In 1927, Illinois had a conference record of 5–0–0, while Minnesota's was 3–0–1. On a percentage basis both teams were all even, but Illinois had the better-looking record. Spears, however, thought this was no reason for President Coffman to send a telegram to Illinois, conceding. He never did get over this burn and finally resigned as football coach in 1929.

While Doc Spears was leaving Minneapolis in a huff, Michigan State, an independent, took steps to strengthen its football program by hiring Jimmy Crowley. If Sleepy Jim had not

Meeting at football coaches convention in 1927 were Knute Rockne, Northwestern Athletic Director Tug Wilson (later Big Ten Commissioner), and Dick Hanley, Northwestern football coach.

been one of the Four Horsemen, if he had gone to a school less glamorous than Notre Dame, if he had played under less of an immortal than Knute Rockne, if he had, in fact, been only an ordinary player, he still could not have missed becoming the superior coach that he was at Michigan State from 1929 through 1932. Crowley's record at East Lansing—27 wins, 11 defeats, 3 ties—was the best there since the days of John Macklin before World War I. The Spartans under Crowley could score points. In the four seasons he coached them they put 908 points up on the scoreboard against 261.

How did a Notre Dame man end up coaching at Michigan State?

"I owed the job to Rockne," Crowley told me. "I spent 1928 working for the Coca-Cola Company in Pittsburgh, and in June of '29 I received a wire from Ralph Young asking me to come to East Lansing for an interview. Harry Kipke, who coached the Spartans in 1928, had just been asked to take the head job at Michigan, his alma mater, and suddenly Michigan State was without a football coach. I had never been a head coach before and football was still very much in my blood, so I drove over to East Lansing to talk to Ralph. When I got there, Ralph, who was the director of athletics, informed me that he had been contacted by Rockne recommending me for the position. The result was that I quit my job at Coca-Cola and went back to college football—and I owed it all to Rock.

Only four years after graduation from Notre Dame, where he had been one of Knute Rockne's fabled "Four Horsemen," Jim Crowley was hired by Michigan State as head football coach in 1929.

One of the central figures in the temporary suspension of Iowa from the Big Ten in 1929 was star halfback Oran Pape. Conference officials charged that he and his running mate, All-American Willis Glassgow, had received irregular financial aid. It marked the only time in history that a school was kicked out of the league. The suspension held for only nine months, however.

"For the record, every player on our 1924 team at Notre Dame—that is, the starting eleven and many of the reserve players—got coaching jobs after they graduated. They were all jobs at very fine universities, too. The point I want to make is that they were all arranged by our old coach, Rockne."

Everything that it takes to be a great football coach Jimmy Crowley had in abundance. He was a natural leader, inspiring talker, busy recruiter, shrewd psychologist, sportsmanlike image, and manipulator of the golden key of football: defense. His Michigan State attack, especially with the backfield of Alton Kircher, Bob Monnett, Abe Eliowitz and Bernie McNutt, was brilliant and explosive. With them he upset Fordham at the Polo Grounds, 19–13, in 1932 and established himself as successor to the ailing Major Cavanaugh, who died in 1933.

After a drought of 30 years, Purdue finally won the Big Ten football championship in 1929. Jimmy Phelan, a Rockne man, built his

A central figure in the temporary ousting of Iowa from the Big Ten in 1929 was All-American halfback and league MVP Willis Glassgow. The Hawkeyes were caught giving Glassgow and running mate Oran Pape irregular financial aid.

team around Ralph (Pest) Welch, a triple-threat halfback; three-sport star Glen Harmeson, quarterback; and Red Sleight, a sharp, mobile tackle. On their way to the Black and Gold's first undefeated season in history, they shut out Chicago, Wisconsin, Iowa and Indiana, and drubbed Michigan, 30–16, for a perfect 5–0–0 record in the Conference. They also bowled over the Kansas Aggies, DePauw, and Mississippi. The victory over Michigan was Purdue's first over the Wolverines since 1892.

Seven players from the Big Ten were virtually unanimous All-Americans in 1929. They included Welch and Sleight of Purdue; Nagurski, Minnesota; end Wes Fesler, Ohio State, for the second straight year; Billy Glasgow, all-around back from Iowa; Hank Anderson, guard, Northwestern; and Lou Gordon, the vicious Illinois tackle.

Never before had the Big Ten contributed as many authentic All-Americans to the all-star squad as it did in 1929.

All-around halfback Ralph (Pest) Welch led the 1929 Purdue Boilermakers to the school's first undisputed Big Ten championship. Welch was the first Purdue gridder to make All-American.

Hard Times
and the Age of Reason
The 1930s

The extravagant, ebullient treatment that typified sportswriting of the 1920s vanished abruptly before breadlines and bankruptcies and bank holidays that were the evidences of a social revolution in the 1930s. Journalistically, a sense of the fitness of things tempered the writing that appeared with increasing frequency on the sport pages.

For the first time, the men who reported sport began to suggest that some of the heroes had feet, as well as heads, of clay. Restraint brought mature objectivity and critical examination of methods and motives. The boys no longer were naive and they were not given to supporting promotions merely for the sake of boosting the business. Their growing prestige gave them a feeling of responsibility and they commenced to expose rascals and denounce skulduggery.

Better pay and play in the paper brought more intelligent, well-rounded writers into the field. The overlapping of seasons and the expanding popularity of all sports gradually eliminated the specialists who were equipped to cover only one game. Budgets that were reduced during the Depression no longer could afford the luxury of one-shot experts who went into hiding after their seasons were completed.

Smaller staffs called for men who could go from baseball to football to boxing or track or basketball, with a side excursion into other fields, without drawing a deep breath. The reporting of technical aspects of the several games did not seemingly suffer from this constant rotation of assignments. Indeed, the readers were fed more precise and illuminating information than ever before.

Stories were shorter and demanded sounder craftsmanship since all the elements of reporting now were incorporated in one concise piece. The man who padded his copy with ringing, elaborate phrases that often collapsed under the sheer weight of words no longer was regarded as the fellow to be followed. The leaders were the men who wrote simply and compactly and did not neglect to include in their leads the winner of the ball game.

Perhaps the most important trend to appear during the 1930s was the gradual swing toward professional sport. The backbone of the sport pages always had been major league baseball, boxing, and racing, but during the 1920s college football made claims on space that pushed practically all other news out of the sport section. A forthright appraisal of the ideals and alleged lily-white purity of college teams turned many men to the out-and-out pros, with their refreshing frankness and higher caliber of performance.

In Big Ten football, most of the attention was focused on four schools during the so-called "Age of Reason." Northwestern tied for

The Michigan Hestons. Papa Willie shows sons Jack, left, and Willie, Jr., how he gripped football when he was the star of Fielding H. Yost's vaunted "Point-a-Minute" teams. Jack lettered for the Wolverines in 1929–30, and brother Willie in 1931–32–33.

the championship in 1930 and 1931, and won it outright in 1936; Michigan shared the crown in 1930 and 1931, and won it outright in 1932 and 1933; Minnesota was champion in 1934, tied with Ohio State in 1935, and stood alone at the top in 1937 and 1938; Ohio State was co-winner in 1935, won the title outright in 1939, and finished second four times.

The big names in coaching were Dick Hanley, Fritz Crisler, Bernie Bierman, and Francis Schmidt.

Like all superior college teams, Northwestern's of 1930 and 1931 were assembled not by chance. A two-week coaching school at Northwestern attracted as many as 480 high school coaches and the contacts Coach Hanley made with them enabled him to enrich his recruiting. The class that entered Northwestern in 1928 formed the nucleus of the back-to-back champions. There were 125 freshmen, for example, and 36 of them were All-State high school players. Only 16 of the original 125 proved to be important players, but that was enough.

Northwestern under Hanley used the Warner double-wing attack, and each year after the season, Dick would visit Pop in Palo Alto for days of football talk. It was in 1931 that the defense began to catch up with the double wing, as defenses ultimately catch up with any offense.

The Wildcats were 5–1–0 in the league in 1931, and Hanley, who could dip into psychology with the best of them, had a lot to do with a triumph over Minnesota. As the teams left the field at halftime with the Gophers leading, 14–7, Dick was forced to incite his team to anger by his dressing-room oratory.

"Gentlemen," he told them, "and I call you this because you have been playing such polite football, people play this game for diverse reasons. Some wish to be popular at tea parties. Some hope for a better job some day. Some wish to prove that they are *men*.

"Why you play football I cannot say, but today this team is becoming immortal. At halftime you've become the first football team in Northwestern history to be booed off the field by your classmates, your schoolmates, your brothers. I ask you to go back on that field and show these people that you are men, not quitters. We were supposed to be favorites today, but the referee told me on the way in here that Minnesota has chosen to begin the second half by *kicking off*. That's an insult to you. They are saying, 'Take the ball on the kickoff—you can't go any place with it, anyway.' So I want you to go back out there and run that kickoff right down their backs!"

The Wildcats, feeling the goad of pride, did exactly that. All-American Pug Rentner caught the ball and behind some punishing downfield blocking and with lightning speed ran it back 95 yards for a touchdown. The extra point was wide, so the Gophers still led, 14–13. That's the way the score stood until late in the last quarter, when Ollie Olson passed to end Dick Fencl, who lateraled to Jakie Sullivan, and Jakie sped 55 yards across the goal line. Two more long-gainers quickly added two more touchdowns. Olson scored one and Rentner got another on a punt return and Northwestern won going away, 32–14.

The honeymoon lasted only two years at Northwestern, and Hanley finally left Evanston after lean seasons in 1932–33–34, in which the Wildcats won a total of only seven games. The 1933 team logged a peculiar record: it scored 25 points in its only victory, over Indiana, and failed to score in its seven other games. Yet, it gained two upset scoreless ties, with a Bierman Minnesota team and the first of Stanford's famous "Vow Boy" Rose Bowl eleven.

Life also went from bad to worse for Bob Zuppke. After the 1929 season, when his material fell off, Illinois was in the Big Ten second division much of the time. He talked then of the bad in football, as he saw it.

"They tell me that I should go around kissing babies and talking to mothers of poor boys to persuade them to send their sons to Illinois," he said. "And they say this is one of the duties of a modern coach. I told them that if that was the duty of a modern coach, then I wasn't capable of being a modern coach."

In his last 12 seasons, 1930–1941, Zup had a fair team in 1933 (5–3–0) and a very good 1934 team (7–1–0). A 7–3 loss to Wisconsin in 1934 cost him a chance to tie Minnesota for the Conference title. He had one big upset left, against Michigan in 1939, 16–7.

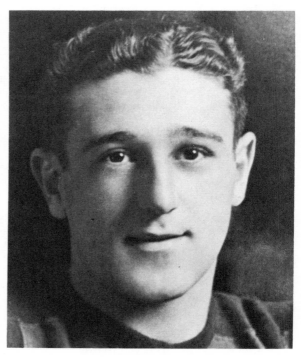

Harry Newman stood only 5-foot-8 and weighed 170 pounds, but he was the unforgettable quarterback and national passing leader of Michigan's 1932 undefeated national champions. He was named college football's MVP in 1932.

An accomplished painter, Bob Zuppke was called "the Rembrandt of the Prairies" by fellow coaches. "A painting is a creation and so is a football team," the Illinois coach often said. "Just as an artist creates a picture on a canvas, a football coach creates a mobile image out of an array of raw physical masses. Just as paintings are made up of dabs and swabs of different pigments, so football compositions are an orderly conglomeration of different types of men in motion."

At Ann Arbor, Harry Kipke, an All-American halfback at Michigan in 1922, and considered the best punter in the country, gave fans of the Maize and Blue plenty to cheer about. In one four-year span, 1930–1933, his teams won 31 games, lost 1, and tied 3, and scored a total of 546 points to 81 in the 35 games. A 20–7 loss to Ohio State in 1931 was their only defeat, leaving them in a three-way tie with Northwestern and Purdue for the championship.

In 15 of 20 games, the Michigan goal line stood uncrossed, in 1,200 minutes of football against big, strapping college squads that stressed power tactics.

"A great defense is a great offense," Kipke often said. "Perhaps it is elementary, but if they can't score, they can't beat you. During one stretch of 30 games, our opponents often had the ball sixty percent of the time. When the defense is strong and positive there's an actual advantage in letting the other side strain and struggle. This permits you to conserve your own weapons, and when the right moment comes and you strike back on offense, the opposition doesn't know what to look for. But a more important reason lies in the fact that when the other team has the ball, you have the chance to gain a big piece of ground by picking up a fumble, blocking a kick, or rushing a kick. Most big coaches opened the preseason with a hunt for two tackles, but at Michigan I always looked for a center. We regarded our center as the most valuable single defensive unit on the team. Perhaps that accounted for the list of All-Americans we had at center after World War I."

One of those centers was Gerald Ford, winner of the team's 1934 MVP award. How good a football player was President Ford? Will Perry, the Sports Information Director at Michigan, looked up the record in his files and sent me the following data:

"Ford was not a captain, not an All-American. He was a reserve on two national championship teams, 1932–1933, and a starter

Future President Jerry Ford shows you the linebacking stance that gained him Michigan's MVP award in 1934.

on the 1934 team which won only 1 out of 8 games. He played behind a two-time All-American center, Chuck Bernard, his sophomore and junior years. Bennie Oosterbaan, an assistant coach then, said Ford could have started at another line position, but the center position was so critical he was kept there.

"Jerry Ford knew he faced a challenge in 1934. The scouting reports by the Michigan coaches left little doubt that Minnesota would be the finest team the Wolverines would play that season. Ford stood 6–2 and weighed 198 and as center-linebacker he was expected to help contain the running of All-American Pug Lund and Stan Kostka, a sophomore sensation at fullback. Ford had played on Michigan's two national championship teams of 1932 and 1933, but now in his senior year the Wolverines were struggling with just one victory in four games. The Gophers, headed straight for the Big Ten title, were 4- to 5-touchdown favorites.

"Ford and the Michigan defense managed somehow to hold Minnesota to a scoreless tie in the first half, but Lund, Kostka and their teammates roared back in the last 30 minutes to win, 34–0."

Recently, I asked Pug Lund to comment on Ford as a football player.

"Jerry was a pretty hard-nosed linebacker," Pug said, "and as a center his passbacks were accurate and consistent and what more can you say about a *good* center?"

When President Ford moved into the White House, Pug sent him a telegram: "Anyone who could bring down someone as *elusive* as me *deserves* to be President."

Norris Dean played the whole Michigan-Georgia Tech game at tackle against Ford. "Ford was a tough player and knocked me down more than I did him, but I know I got him, too," Dean recalled.

Jay Berwanger, University of Chicago's All-American halfback and winner of the first Heisman Trophy in 1935, knows the story behind the tiny scar Ford wears on his cheek. "He says he got it from the heel of my football shoe when he tried to tackle me in 1934," Berwanger said. "I'm sure I ran over him more than once." Chicago 27, Michigan 0.

John Theodore ran right over Ford to score the winning touchdown for Illinois to beat Michigan, 7–6, in 1934. "Jerry actually

Triple-threat All-American Jay Berwanger on his way to his second touchdown against Michigan in 1934. Chicago 27, Wolverines 0. In 1935, Berwanger became the first player to win the Heisman Trophy.

stopped me about a foot short of the goal," Theodore said, "but the referee called it a touchdown."

In summer of 1975, Pug Lund and President Ford played golf together in Minneapolis.

"We had a great time," Pug told me. "As partners we won and I beat him in our individual game. Along the way we talked a great deal about our college football days; about our teammates and the Michigan–Minnesota games involved. Both of us won the MVP at our respective schools in 1934, and then we were teammates in the East–West Shrine Game at San Francisco, and in the All-Star Game against the Chicago Bears in 1935. The Bears beat us, 5–0, on a rainy night."

Minnesota teams spoke loudly for Bernie Bierman. From 1932 through 1941, the Golden Gophers won 64, lost 11, tied 5. They were undefeated five times, won six Big Ten titles (1934, 1935, 1937, 1938, 1940, 1941), and were national champions four times (1934, 1936, 1940 and 1941).

A 28-game defeatless string, the last 21 of

For those who played under him at Minnesota in the 1930s and 1940s, Bernie Bierman made football a stern, challenging task. As a player and coach he gave the game everything. To Bierman, it was inconceivable that any player wouldn't be willing to sacrifice anything, take anything, to work and win for the Golden Gophers.

them victories, was broken, 6–0, on Northwestern's muddy field in 1936. A 15-yard roughness penalty on Ed Widseth, the Gophers' star left tackle, set up a 1-yard scoring plunge by fullback Steve Toth. That contest cost Minnesota the Conference crown, but it was still ranked No. 1 in the nation.

After he quit coaching, Bierman called the 1934 Minnesota team the best he ever turned out.

"It had great spirit and poise," he said. "It was two deep and in some positions three deep without falloff. It was very well coordinated and this came to some extent from uniform speed. We had no real fast man in the backfield and no real slow one in the line. Glen Seidel at quarterback did a great job running the offense, and Pug Lund, captain and left half, gave it great spirit; so did guard Billy Bevan, who was the last Minnesota player not to wear a helmet."

Other linemen included All-American Frank (Butch) Larson, Bob Tenner, and John Romig, ends; Dick Smith, Phil Bengston, and Ed Widseth, tackles; Milt Bruhn, Vern Oech, and Bud Wilkinson, guards; and Dale Rennebohm and Bud Svendsen, centers. Besides Seidel and Lund in the backfield, there were Babe LeVoir and Art Clarkson, halfbacks, and Sheldon Beise and Stanislaus (the Hammer) Kostka at fullback.

"It was the greatest team I ever saw or coached against," said Harry Kipke, speaking for the majority. "Why, their *reserves* could have beaten almost any team in the country."

"We were a strong running team," Pug Lund told me in 1975. "Operating from the single wing, we seldom passed. The forward pass wasn't the weapon it is today. We stressed fundamentals—blocking, swiftness, hard tackling. We simply dominated our opponents and wore them down. I was left halfback at tailback and handled the ball on almost every play. We had three players on Grantland Rice's All-American team. Granny said at the time that he could have named nearly our whole starting lineup. Our backs averaged about 190 and our line, quick and durable, scaled out around 215 to 220 per man. As the team's punter, I did not kick 'em long, but I did have a success story for banging 'em inside the 10-yard line.

"We played rock-'em-sock-'em football. We put six men on the line and had the ends crashing. They really tailed in there. We never monkeyed around with a lot of defense. We played 6–3–2 or 6–2–2–1 defense and never varied it much, like over-shifting. Bierman emphasized the charge, the defensive charge. He had our guys really popping out of there.

"In my junior year, 1933, we didn't lose any games but we had four ties. We were the team to beat. Opposing coaches tried funny things

University of Minnesota's 1934 undefeated national champions.

on defense to try and stop us. That previous summer, Bernie worked out a blocking system whereby our linemen, regardless of the defensive stationing, knew exactly which man to block no matter what play we called. That was the sign of a good coach. Line play today has gotten super sophisticated with this specialty-team business, but back in 1933 any change from the orthodox was brand new and gave us a big advantage.

"We played bruising schedules. Every game was a killer. There were no soft spots, no set-ups. I suppose the Depression had something to do with it. We were all hungry. We had to work hard to survive, to get an education, and football was just part of it. We were all Jack Dempseys in football suits, with plenty of blood-lust and desperate for success. We had no opportunity to be prima-donnas.

"Our big games were with Michigan, Wisconsin and Iowa. They were always on our schedule. Dating back to 1907, we hadn't beaten Michigan until 1934, my senior year, and Jerry Ford played center for them. That was the turning point. After that, Bierman beat the Wolverines regularly.

"Unlike Rockne, Bierman was not a great halftime orator. He was firm, reserved, very low-key. It was out of character for him to display any emotionalism. If he wanted to get us up he'd have one of his assistants, Sig Harris or Bert Baston, give us that emotional, rah-rah motivation. But at practice, Bernie was the boss. He never used profanity, but when he dressed you down you sure knew where you stood with him."

One of the biggest and best-played games of the decade was when Minnesota played Pitt at Pittsburgh in 1934, the first time the Gophers had ever gone East. The year before, in Minneapolis, they had beaten the Panthers, 7–3, but Pitt brushed it off as a fluke. Although this second meeting was played early in the season, October 20, its outcome, as expected, stood up in determining the national championship. By winning, 13–7, Minnesota finished No. 1; by losing, Pitt finished No. 2. Each won the rest of its games; neither was hard-pressed.

Pug Lund played in the second Pitt game minus the little finger on his left hand.

"I first broke the finger pole-vaulting," Pug told me. "The fracture forced the joint to

Bud Wilkinson played outstanding guard for Bernie Bierman in 1934 and 1935 and in his senior year was shifted to quarterback, where he led Minnesota to the national championship in the first year of the AP poll.

stiffen and gave me a lot of trouble. In that first win over Pitt, in 1933, the finger picked a helluva time to pop out of the socket. At the start of the second half, Pitt kicked off and the ball came to me with a crazy spin on it. I caught the ball and damned if all that spinning didn't knock my finger out of joint. As I was running the ball back with it tucked in here, I reached over and pulled the joint back in place before any Pitt tacklers got to me, not breaking stride once. In fact, I almost broke into the clear, too. I got up to the 20 as it was—and still managed to pop that knuckle back in place.

"At spring practice the next year, I hit head-on into somebody's helmet and shattered two more joints of the little finger. I finally had to have it amputated and played my senior season with only four fingers on that hand."

The second Pitt game found the Gophers

trailing, 7–0, at halftime. The Panthers scored on a 64-yard play in which fullback Izzy Weinstock plunged for nine yards, then lateraled off to halfback Mike Nicksick who went the rest of the way for the touchdown. In the Minnesota dressing room at the half, Bierman opened and closed his speech in five words: "Two touchdowns will win it." That's all he said. The Gophers came back out and scored two touchdowns. Both scores produced a significant clinic for assaying Bierman football, power with precision, yes, but well-conceived, multiple-ballhandling plays and use of the forward pass judiciously. Minnesota passed three times and completed two of them, the second for the winning touchdown.

Both touchdowns were set up through hard inside blasting by Kostka alternating with Lund. Despite his 230 pounds, Kostka could start quick and veer at top speed. After his line-wrecking had driven the Gophers to the Pitt 22, Seidel called on a reverse to Alphonse who went around Pitt's right side behind sharp blocking all the way.

A fumbled punt soon after, by safety man Bobby LaRue, punchy from steady pounding, was recovered by Butch Larson on the Pitt 45. That was the big break of the game. Kostka went thrashing and smashing through the Panther defense again and drove to the 18. Then on fourth down and short yardage, Kostka, faking a blast into the line, handed the ball off to Seidel, who pivoted and pitched out to Lund, who faked an end sweep, stopped and passed to Tenner, the left end. Tenner cut diagonally across the Pitt secondary and took the ball without breaking stride to score the touchdown.

In 1954, Bierman gave me his prescription for winning football games.

"My system—call it the Minnesota system if you wish—was based upon 12 rather simple fundamental rules. They were flexible enough to be adapted to any style of attack. Here they are: (1) No boy will play good football unless he enjoys the game and gives his best on every play. (2) To play the best, a boy must be in good physical condition and have adequate rest before a game. (3) A boy who places personal glory and success above the best interests of the team is a liability rather than an asset. (4) A large, fairly well-developed squad is more desirable than a team composed of a few stars and a group of mediocre, undeveloped talent. (5) A single-wing formation with appropriate and seasonal variations seems most desirable for our offense needs. (6) We like to shift, but we can and have played from a set formation. (7) We believe in a rather large number of plays and sometimes put in special plays for certain opponents. (8) We believe that fundamentals such as blocking, charging, tackling and ball-carrying, to mention only a few, are more important than plays themselves. (9) We lean to an aggressive six-man line on defense. (10) We favor a calm, determined team rather than one keyed up to a hysterical pitch for a game. (11) Speed is an essential component of a sound style of play. (12) Players develop through hard work over a comparatively long period rather than from short intensive drives during the heat of a Fall campaign.

"That last rule probably was the heart of major college football when I coached at Minnesota, for despite the talk of the *good old days*, the game has become infinitely more exacting and precise since my retirement. Despite the storybooks, there is no such thing any more as the flash who drives through for the winning touchdown in the first game he enters. Every lad you see on successive Saturdays during the season is the product of weeks and months of rigid, painstaking training. Some lads take until their senior year in college to blossom and others don't live up to their full potential until they have been in professional football some years after graduation.

"Why did I put so much emphasis on blocking, tackling and the running game? Well, it was the potential ability of the Midwestern lads to block so powerfully which first tempted me to stress the running game as a major part of the Minnesota attack shortly after I arrived in Minneapolis from Tulane in 1932. Under another set of circumstances and blessed with a different type of material, I'd probably have favored the forward pass or the lateral. As a matter of fact, one season at Tulane I did develop an offense that featured the quick-kick and received wide publicity for its success. I had boys, though, who could handle that specialty and made it click.

"But my boys at Minnesota, once they acquired the knack, loved to block mostly and they fit in perfectly with my scheme of things.

It was not uncommon during the season to walk onto the practice field and see my players, in twos and threes, or even alone, taking daily stints at the blocking dummies, entirely on their own time without a word from the coaching staff. There was really nothing mysterious about the way we blocked; open-field blocking in particular. It was really no more difficult than tackling. At Minnesota, we made blocking practice as painless as possible, although the real polishing called for bodily contact, 'live bait,' Fritz Crisler called it. We started by using dummies. Behind each dummy was a teammate to give the blockers the feel of throwing their weight against what approximated an opponent. The coaches by this method got an idea of the force with which blockers smack the opposition. We were rather fond of having our boys drive at the dummies hard enough to bowl over their teammates who had the backstop assignment. In other words, blocking in practice was no different from a regular game. The fundamentals were acquired in this manner, next came the timing, the rhythm, which was a slow and tedious process that pitted man against man. Eventually, our kids got the knack of the trick and wore it like a suit of old clothes.

"If you followed the daily newspapers back in the 1930's and early 1940's, you saw where I loved to win. Of course I loved winning. In your search of rare specimens, try digging up someday a football coach who doesn't want to win all of his games. If you found one who didn't, I'm certain his fellow coaches would ship him off to a psychiatrist as a mental case."

Probably the greatest single clinical play in Bierman's dynasty was an extemporaneous lateral of a punt that brought victory when a scoreless tie seemed imminent. Bud Wilkinson played outstanding guard for Bierman in 1934 and 1935 and the following year was shifted to quarterback, where again he stood out. He engineered the beginning of the remarkable play. Dick Cullum was there and described it this way in the Minneapolis *Times*:

"There were 68 seconds to play . . . Nebraska had the ball on its 43-yard line . . . Sam Francis, Nebraska's best kicker, had been removed in favor of sophomore Ron Douglas. He punted a short, high one to Wilkinson on Minnesota's 28. Wilkinson caught the ball near the sideline, and took the first step to the inside and backwards, drawing all the tacklers toward him.

"It was not until one of them had him by one leg that he let the ball go. Uram caught it on the 25-yard line and ran through a broken field 75 yards to a touchdown. It was unquestionably one of football's finest plays. Bierman called it the most perfectly executed spur-of-the-moment play ever to come to his attention. He also insisted that every man used the maximum of good judgment in clearing the way for Uram, who himself used perfect judgment in setting his pace and choosing his course. At one stage, every Nebraska player was on his back. This phenomenal and brilliant play decided a very tough ball game, 7–0, in the final minute."

On defense, Bierman's Minnesota teams were nearly impregnable. In three games, 1938–39–40, Tommy Harmon, Michigan's famed No. 98, failed to get into the Gophers' end zone. Of the five defeats incurred by Fritz Crisler's Michigan teams, 1938–39–40–41, four came from Minnesota.

The headline rivalry of Bierman's pre-World War II years, however, was with Lynn O. (Pappy) Waldorf's Northwestern teams from 1935 through 1941. Minnesota won four, Northwestern three. The Minnesota margins were 21–13, 7–0, 13–12, 8–7; Northwestern's margins were 6–0, 6–3, 14–7. Total points were Gophers 59, Wildcats 58.

Bud Wilkinson, who went on to become the winningest coach of his time, in 1936 won the Big Ten Medal as outstanding scholar-athlete. One of his classmates was Otis Dypwick, later best man at Bud's wedding.

"It used to gripe the heck out of me in class," Otis told me. "Bud, a super all-around athlete, would go on football or hockey trips and I'd take notes in class for him and he'd get A in the subject while I got a C. Because his success as football coach at Oklahoma so overshadowed the rest of his career, people forgot that Bud was one of the greatest goalies in the history of college hockey. In school, Bud was a tall, handsome guy and plenty smart and very versatile. He could have lettered in three or four varsity sports—baseball, golf, football and hockey. He was a running guard for Bierman, before switching to quarterback when we ran out of quarterbacks in his senior year. He led

Three last-quarter touchdowns brought underdog Notre Dame from behind to stun powerful Ohio State, 18–13, in 1935 in what has often been called "the greatest game in history."

us to the national championship in 1936, the first year of the AP poll."

Wilkinson said the switch from guard to quarterback was not too difficult. "Minnesota ran from a single wing and the quarterback was the blocking back," Bud said. Even so, with just one season under his belt, he was named the College All-Star team's quarterback and led the collegians to their first victory over the Green Bay Packers, 7–0.

Later, as a coach, Wilkinson said he acquired most of his technical knowledge of football from Bierman. He also learned the importance of physical fitness in Bernie's ultra-physical methods.

"The best way to attain superb physical condition is to punish yourself in practice after you are already dead tired," Bud explained. "In other words, run those windsprints, hit that dummy, again and again and again. There's nothing new about this concept. I learned it myself, the hard way, at Minnesota. I'll never forget it as long as I live. It was a cold, raw day and we were practicing in the field house. Coach Bierman had us running windsprints. We'd run, then stop, then he'd have us run again, and again and again. It was torture. But I have another clear memory, too. It was of the game on the very next Saturday. We beat Iowa, 52–6."

Bob Geigengack, Yale's outstanding track coach, was at Iowa Pre-Flight with Wilkinson in 1943. Bud was just one of a very large staff of famous sports names there, but Geigengack never forgot a remark by Moon Mullins,

former Notre Dame star under Rockne, which Bob later found to be prophetic.

"We used to hold clinics at Iowa Pre-Flight," Geigengack recalled, "and going home from one of these one night, Moon said to me: 'Bob, any time you are in a civilian capacity and an opportunity comes up to recommend that youngster, Bud Wilkinson, don't hesitate to do so, because I believe he will some day be established as the finest football brain in the United States.' It certainly turned out that way, and I often wonder how Moon Mullins could have known so far in advance."

One of the most exciting last-ditch rallies in college football history occurred at Columbus on November 2, 1935, in a game between Ohio State and Notre Dame. Trailing 13 to 0 at the end of the third quarter after being manhandled in fearful fashion for the first 45 minutes by 220-pound Gomer Jones and his giant teammates, the Irish looked to be so hopelessly beaten that no one among the 81,000 spectators conceded them the barest ghost of a chance. The fact that Notre Dame had five times missed scoring opportunities left its supporters with a feeling of utter frustration.

Then the impossible started to unfold. In the space of only several minutes, with the clock ticking off precious seconds in the gathering dusk and threatening to save the game for the Buckeyes, a team that had appeared so irretrievably doomed struck twice through the air to draw within one point of the Bucks, 12–13.

Andy Pilney was plainly the hero for Notre

Dame. With his pinpoint passing and his swirling, fearless running from scrimmage and punt returns, he was virtually a One-Man Gang as he saved the day for the Irish and stole the show from Joe Williams, the sensational sophomore for Ohio State.

Less than a minute remained to play in the game when halfback Pilney dropped back to pass, saw no receiver in the clear, so he tucked the ball under his arm and started picking his way downfield 10, 15, 20, 25—32 yards to the Ohio State 19. Pilney collapsed under the weight of three tacklers and when the traffic cleared he remained motionless on the ground. For what seemed like an eternity the heart of the Notre Dame attack did not move. An ambulance arrived on the scene. The Notre Dame rooters went calm as death as they saw their star driven away to the hospital. With him went their dreams for victory—or so it seemed.

Now there was time enough for only one more play. Now the crowd was standing up solidly, row after row, going wild. The tension was building up to fever pitch. Could the Irish come all the way back? Did they have 19 yards left in their offense? Up in the pressbox, the sports writers, packed like sardines, were pounding out their stories play-by-play and the radio announcers were hoarse and excited, maybe worse than anyone else there. And now Bill Shakespeare was down on the field, walking out of the Notre Dame huddle as play resumed, his back wet and dark where the sweat had soaked through, his helmet shoved down tight on his head. You wondered if he was nervous out there. Grown Notre Dame fans were seen to grab their thumbs and say a short, silent prayer for him. They were almost afraid to look.

Notre Dame's ball, first and 10 on the Ohio State 19-yard line, the Bucks leading, 13 to 12, and time enough for only this play.

The signals were called. Shakespeare shifted with his teammates, into the slot. The ball was his. Shakespeare backpedaled, looking, looking for a receiver in the open. His blockers swept to the right, sucking the defenders along with them, while over on the left, in the end zone, far from any company, stood Wayne Millner, waiting for the ball. The ball rode high from Shakespeare's palm as he released his throw. The blur of the ball assumed shape. It came to Millner's hands and he felt the old elation, and he heard the deafening noise break from the Notre Dame cheering section as he hauled the ball in and hugged it to his chest for six more points. It was wonderful and beautiful and impossible, but there it was: Notre Dame 18, Ohio State 13.

The riot was on. Notre Dame players had their arms around each other and were hugging the breath out of each other. Grown people on the Notre Dame side were doing strange dances on the seats and kissing and crying. And out on the field the Irish swarmed all over Millner and Shakespeare. They poured from the bench and around their heroes and all of them were shaking their hands and trying to pat their backs, and you could tell by the wide grins on their faces that this was the supreme moment of their lives.

As it happened, a lot of youngsters who were there learned rather early in life that the result of a college football game can sometimes be more important than wars and depressions and wind storms. But for some it would not be too clear why grown men would sit for two hours after the game was over, and with mist in their eyes use some funny language and take swigs out of those little silver-looking bottles in their pockets. "Cough medicine," the kids were told, but when they, themselves, coughed they were told by the older men that they didn't need any.

Thus the team that Ohio State fans thought invincible had lost, 18 to 13; their national championship dreams had come to an end. They could lay most of the blame on Andy Pilney, the substitute halfback from Chicago who, incidentally, had suffered no more than a torn ligament in his leg while traveling those 32 yards to set up the winning touchdown.

To fully appreciate Pilney's role in the victory, consider his accomplishments: It was his 28-yard runback of Kabealo's punt, after two skillful kicks out of bounds by Shakespeare, that started his team on the path to victory on the final play of the third quarter. That put the ball on the Ohio State 12-yard line and then Pilney's pass to Gaul took it down to the 1, from where Millner punched it over. Two minutes after Stilley missed the extra point, Pilney was on the move again. From his own 46 he carried and threw the ball 53 more yards, hurling three passes to Layden and Zwers for another 36 yards to the Ohio State 1. But the

Irish failed to score as Karcher recovered Millner's fumble in the end zone for a touchback.

A minute later, Jumpin' Joe Williams broke loose on a 23-yard reverse around left end to put the Buckeyes on their own 43, with the clock ticking on. Notre Dame's chances looked dim indeed. But the Irish defense stiffened, forcing Kabealo to punt out of bounds on the Notre Dame 22. There Pilney went back into action again. In an attempt to stop the Notre Dame passing attack, Ohio State changed from the eight-man line and seven-man line with a diamond defense, and it dropped back defenders in a futile effort to intercept the ball. But Pilney was red-hot. He connected on three passes and caught one himself to account for 75 of the 78 yards as Notre Dame marched to another touchdown.

Trailing 12-13 after Fromhart missed the placement, and with hardly more than a minute left in the game, Notre Dame kicked off short, hoping to recover the ball, and failed to pounce on it. But fighting like fury, they tack-

Ohio State's wide open, high-scoring attack in the mid-1930s earned coach Francis Schmidt the nickname of "Close-The-Gates-of-Mercy-Schmidt." In the seven seasons he coached at Columbus, 1934–1940, the Buckeyes won or shared the Big Ten championship twice and finished second three times.

led Beltz so hard on the first scrimmage that he fumbled the ball at midfield and Notre Dame recovered. Here was a final reprieve. There were only about 50 seconds left now. Pilney then bowed out of the game with his 32-yard run to set up the winning points.

Two years later, Notre Dame again figured in a major upset of the Big Ten champions. The victim this time was Minnesota. Notre Dame had a spotty record, going into the game. They had beaten Drake and Navy, but a scoreless tie with Illinois and a loss to Carnegie Tech had the bettors favoring the Gophers by three touchdowns, even though Minnesota had lost to Nebraska, 14–9, three weeks earlier.

But the Gophers were high for the Irish after trouncing Michigan, 39–6, and on the bus taking them to Memorial Stadium in Minneapolis from the Lowry Hotel in St. Paul where they were staying, the Notre Dame players rode in silence, remembering the terrors that local papers predicted were in store for them. At the moment of deepest gloom, a noisy procession of Minnesota fans passed them. Bringing up the rear was another bus marked "The Golden Gopher Special," and it carried the Minnesota football team. Then with a rush and a roar, accompanied by the symphony of horns and raucous shouts, the Gophers bolted past in clouds of dust and smoke.

No one on the Notre Dame bus spoke for a moment. All eyes focused glumly on the tailend of the gaily decorated Minnesota bus. Finally, Chuck Sweeney, who played end for the Irish, spoke up. "That's the last time Minnesota will pass us today." Notre Dame 7, Minnesota 6.

After 1933, Illinois could finish no higher than sixth in the Conference under Zuppke, but he did have one big upset left, against Michigan in 1939. Tommy Harmon, then a junior, was at the peak of his fantastic career for the Wolverines. Michigan was undefeated, had lost only one game in Harmon's varsity career, to Minnesota, 7–6, in 1938. Illinois had lost four out of four, and was considered to have as much of a chance as its 1916 predecessor against Minnesota. Michigan was coached by the sagacious Herbert O. (Fritz) Crisler, but Fritz let himself be quoted that Harmon was a better back than Red Grange.

Zuppke seized on it. The week of the game, he never stopped repeating the Crisler quote. "So, Crisler says Harmon is better than Grange," he told his players. "Did you read it? Harmon is better than Grange." He worked on a defense built around seven-man and six-man fronts and a secondary rotating into the side where Michigan was strong after its deploy. And all week long to everybody he met, Zup kept saying, "Crisler says Harmon is better than Grange."

The upshot was that Illinois roundly stopped Harmon and won the game, 16–7. Zuppke then went back to his study of philosophy and painting, which he loved as dearly as football.

From the fiery Yost to the urbane, suave Fritz Crisler, was a cycle in Michigan football, yet both had the ability to dramatize themselves while organizing victorious regimes. Crisler's spinner-cycle offense was perhaps the most eye-catching ever seen in football. It required meticulous execution, with hairbreadth timing and flawless faking. One misstep, a clumsy hand, and the smooth mechanism was shattered. Such a complicated attack could not be taught to ordinary kids, but, then, Michigan under Crisler did not have ordinary players. They were usually tops.

If the Midwest ever had a counterpart to Red Grange it was Tommy Harmon. In total yardage gained over a three-year span (1938–40), Harmon barely missed Grange's record. Tommy generated more power than Red, but was less elusive than Grange.

Against Pennsylvania in 1939, Harmon virtually duplicated Grange's climax running heroics of 1925. On one play Penn had Tommy pinned against the sidelines, deep in Michigan territory. But like Houdini, he somehow escaped from this trap and powered his way through tacklers to score the decisive touchdown.

Harmon had a theatrical personality and was well aware of his own importance. His roomate, Bob Ingalls, tried to keep Tommy from getting a swelled head. When Harmon reached the field late for practice one afternoon, Ingalls sang out: "Everybody make a low bow, please. Here comes the Michigan football team."

During the 1938 Northwestern game, Ralph

Fritz, the giant Michigan tackle, whispered confidentially to his Wildcat rival across the scrimmage line: "Kid, I don't mind telling you, we've just called Harmon's signal over your position. I don't know what you're going to do, but I'm goin' to get the hell out of here."

Perhaps the poorest exhibition a Michigan football team ever gave under Crisler was its 15–13 narrow-squeak victory over a weak Yale team in 1938 at New Haven. Late in the contest, Yale was leading, 13–9, when Bob Brooks, the Eli tackle, nearly blocked Regeczi's fourth-down punt from the Michigan 15-yard line. The ball glanced off Regeczi's foot, giving Yale possession deep in Michigan territory. This big break apparently clinched the game—until it was discovered that Brooks had bumped into the Michigan punter, exacting a harsh penalty from the referee. Now Michigan had a first down, plus five yards. The Wolverines promptly marched 80 yards to victory. Thus did a fine individual play cost the weaker team the ball game.

During halftime that day, Crisler distributed paper and pencils to his sluggish athletes in the dressing room. A master of sarcasm, Fritz announced: "I want all you fellows to write

Old 98, Tommy Harmon, scores for Michigan against Iowa in 1939. Michigan 27, Iowa 7.

your alibis now, explaining how you happened to lose this game. Our alumni will want to know."

Crisler arrived at Ann Arbor in 1938 concurrent with Harmon's sophomore year, and for the next three seasons the Wolverines logged a 19–4–1 record, with three of the defeats administered by Bierman's Minnesota teams, two of them 7–6. Fumbles and other misadventures prevented Harmon from ever scoring against the Gophers, but that represented about his only failure. Before he retired his famous No. 98, Harmon scored three touchdowns against Ohio State to bring his three-year total to 33; Red Grange scored 31 in four fewer games. A fusion of exceptional speed, power, and deception, Harmon carried the ball 399 times for 2,151 yards, an average just shy

Superb blocking quarterback Forest Evashevski paved the way for Tommy Harmon's sensational runs at Michigan in 1938–39–40. Twenty-two years later, Evy's son, Forest J. Evashevski, Jr., lettered in football for the Wolverines (1962–63–64). Evy, Sr., later went on to coaching greatness at Washington State and Iowa.

of six yards. He completed 101 of 233 passes for 1,346 yards and 16 touchdowns. He averaged 38 yards punting, and placekicked 33 extra points and two field goals. Like Grange, his favorite running maneuver was the cutback over tackle, going to either side.

When Michigan first offered the head football-coaching job to Crisler, he thought his terms were so far out of line that they would be unacceptable. He was surprised when the officials at Ann Arbor said yes to his request for a $15,000-a-year salary, more money than any coach ever made in the Middle West up to then. He also demanded that he be allowed to pick his own assistant coaches—the men who are largely responsible for the head man's tactical success on the field. And he insisted on, and got, assurance that Fielding H. Yost would not interfere in the football program, as well as the promise that he would be appointed athletic director when Yost reached the retirement age of 70 in 1942.

Yost's dominating influence at Michigan for almost 40 years was actually the deterrent that made Crisler hesitate to accept the job. A strong, commanding personality, Yost was the power behind the three football coaches who succeeded him after 1926 and he made certain that they played his kind of football and followed his policies.

Yost, fighting Crisler's appointment, tried to see that the job went to George Veenker, one of his old boys who became athletic director at Iowa State College. The alumni angle, as usual, was dragged in by the heels. There was a lingering resentment among old Wolverines against any Chicago man. In the dim, dark ages, remember, Stagg's 1905 team broke Michigan's remarkable undefeated streak of 56 consecutive games by winning, 2–0, and that game still rankled in aged bosoms at Ann Arbor. No one had to brief Crisler on all the implications of the job, while Yost still occupied the front office; and Fritz demanded that the old man clearly understand he was to be the boss.

Michigan acceded to every condition because it had a peculiar public relations job which only Crisler could handle. Michigan always has had higher academic standards than any other school in the Big Ten, with the exception of Chicago when the Maroon was in the league. To matriculate at Ann Arbor, a high school student during the Crisler years, as now, must have "done work appreciably higher than the average." In practical application, this meant a student had to be in the upper third of his class with an overall average of 83 to 85 percent. Such rigorous requirements eliminated many outstanding athletes.

Another factor complicating life for Crisler at Michigan was the nature of the alumni, who made up a more cosmopolitan group than the alumni of most Midwest colleges. The majority lived outside the state, and they didn't leap off tall buildings when the team happened to lose a game. They'd become aroused at a protracted slump, as they did when Harry Kipke had four straight bad seasons, but, in the main, their attitude toward football was pretty sane. There were exceptions, of course, but Michigan's lily-white purity kept them in line.

Dr. Ralph Aigler, who was dean of the law school and Michigan's Big Ten faculty representative, was an indefatigable bird dog in tracking down skulduggery and sly evasions of the amateur code.

An uncompromising attitude toward football tramps taking snap courses in dendrology and music appreciation began to have the inevitable result on the football field at Ann Arbor. Michigan authorities realized that a new approach, a gimmick, had to be found for tapping sources of material, and Crisler, with his talent for organization and applying the techniques of big business to football, had the answer.

Crisler began operating a unique correspondence school for high school coaches in need of big league advice. The coach who wanted a new play to win a big game, didn't know what defense to use against a certain offense, had a morale problem with his players, needed pointers in conditioning a squad or wanted a once-over-lightly in general strategy, could have his questions solved by writing to Crisler. He corresponded with more than 200 coaches in Michigan and the surrounding area, and the pay-off was obvious. In return for services rendered, coaches were expected to steer likely prospects to Ann Arbor.

Crisler also organized clinics. Each year, at the end of spring practice, all high school coaches and players were invited to attend the classes, in which he freely demonstrated his plays and methods. Between 1,200 and 1,500 attended the clinics, and Crisler kept no secrets from his audience.

"The coach who draws diagrams full of confusing X's and arrows, and who spouts a lot of doubletalk, is a phony," Crisler said. "There's no harm in telling coaches everything you've got, as long as you don't let them know when you're going to use it."

When you talk about Midwest football coaches of the Thirties, the name Charlie Bachman inevitably comes up. Michigan State was glad to hire him as Jimmy Crowley's successor in 1933 when Sleepy Jim left East Lansing for Fordham.

Bachman didn't disappoint the Spartans. Until he arrived, they had beaten Michigan only twice in 28 games: 12–7 in 1913 and 24–0 in 1915. Bachman's teams beat the Wolverines four in a row, 1934–37, a feat later tied by Biggie Munn and Duffy Daugherty, but at the time so totally unprecedented as to evoke hysteria. It should be added that even though Bachman's first Michigan State team—or Michigan Aggies in those days—lost to Michigan, 20–6, it scored a touchdown on the Wolverines for the first time since 1918.

In the 1934 victory, 16–0, which broke an 18-year drought, the only sophomore to start for the Spartans was left tackle Howard Zindel, later Chairman of the Department of Poultry Science.

"Charlie was all football and no nonsense," Dr. Zindel recalled some years later. "He was alert to new teaching techniques. He not only told us how to do it, but being a big rugged man, he showed us how."

It is doubtful any other coach who ever lived was more seriously dedicated to football than Bachman. His strong, rugged face suggested a German U-boat commander's, and it was no facade. Charlie was a tough-fibered man, physically and mentally.

When he was only 27 and a neophyte coach at Northwestern, Bachman was matched against Fielding Yost. Michigan won the game, 16–13. Bachman believed that Yost had violated a tenet of sportsmanship, having to do with an eligible man catching the ball out of bounds, and after the game he invaded Yost's dressing room and dressed him down for it.

"I'll have you thrown out of here," Yost shouted.

"Nobody will throw me out of here," Bachman said calmly. "I came in on my own and I'll go out on my own."

He did, too.

Bachman's teams were always well pre-pared in all phases of football. In his 28 years of coaching, they had kicks blocked only twice.

The most rewarding football years for Bachman had to be from 1934 through 1937, when Michigan State not only beat Michigan four in a row but put together records of 8–1–0, 6–2–0, 6–1–2, and 8–2–0, for a total of 28–6–2. Unbeaten seasons were frustrated in 1934 by Syracuse, 10–0, and in 1936 by Marquette, 13–7. Those were the years of John Pingel and Sid Wagner and the Orange Bowl (Auburn 6, Michigan State O). Bachman, like Crowley be-fore him, was building Michigan State up to the level where it could legitimately claim strength worthy of being taken into the Big Ten in 1953.

Bachman's dead seriousness was in sharp contrast to Crowley's personality. Jimmy's na-tive humor often served as an anodyne to the worry, a safety valve to the tension that ac-companied a white-hot competitive pride. In 1938, he compared notes with Harry Stuhl-dreher, his old Four Horseman teammate at Notre Dame, who was preparing the Wiscon-sin Badgers for a big game against the Pittsburgh Panthers. Stuhldreher, who was given to violent dreams during the football season, told Crowley that he had experienced his worst nightmare yet. It was built around Marshall Goldberg, Pitt's All-American back, a solid runner, blocker and defender. Crowley, whose Fordham Rams had lost to the Panthers earlier in the season, 24–13, listened quietly.

"He had broken through our defense and was in the open, streaking for a touchdown," Harry told Jimmy, reliving the horror of his Goldberg dream, "when I couldn't stand it any longer. In my nightmare I leaped off the bench to tackle him. In reality, I sprang off my bed and hit the damned radiator. And that's how I got this black eye."

"Never mind the shiner," said Crowley im-patiently. "Did you stop Goldberg?"

One of the most talked-about coaches in the nation in the 1930's was Francis A. Schmidt of Ohio State, dubbed "Close-the-Gates-of-Mercy" Schmidt because of the way his Buck-eyes got touchdowns in bunches. In the seven years (1934–1940) Francis the First was at Co-lumbus, Ohio State won 39 games, lost 16, tied 1; won or shared the Big Ten championship twice, and was runnerup three times. The re-cord included four straight, heady, lopsided victories over Michigan, 1934, 1935, 1936, and 1937.

Jerry Brondfield, the Buckeye historian, has described Schmidt as "the zaniest, maddest, most imaginative football coach ever to hit the Big Ten, and the record still holds." It was Schmidt who launched Ohio State's modern era of football eminence. A World War I bayonet drill instructor with a loud, raucous and colorful approach to the English language, he had a genius for football offense. In his first season at Ohio State he amazed the opposition by trotting out—in the same game—the single wing, double wing, short punt and, for the first time ever seen, the I formation. He displayed reverses, double reverses, and spinners. The Bucks were the most lateral-pass conscious team within memory. His backs threw laterals,

In 1938, all-around halfback John Pingel earned a niche for himself in the Michigan State Hall of Fame by becoming the third first-team All-American in Spartan football history.

and then laterals off of laterals downfield. It was not uncommon for three men to handle the ball in the backfield.

"Schmidt was a bow-tied, tobacco-chewing, hawk-faced, white-haired, profane practitioner of the football arts—modern football's first roaring madman on the practice field and the sidelines," Bronfield said, "and so completely zonked out on football that legend ties him to the greatest football story of the Twentieth Century. So caught up was he in his diagrams and charts that there was hardly a waking moment when he wasn't furiously scratching away at them. He took his car into a filling station for an oil change but stayed right in the car while the mechanics hoisted it high above the subterranean oil pit to do their work. Immersed in his X's and O's, he simply forgot where he was. For some reason he decided to get out of the car, still concentrating on his diagram. He opened the door on the driver's side and stepped out into the void, which ended eight feet south of him in the pit. He later refused to explain the limp which he carried with him to practice that day."

The Schmidt overall record at Ohio State read like this:

1934......7–1–0
1935......7–1–0   (Co-Champions)
1936......5–3–0
1937......6–2–0
1938......4–3–1
1939......6–2–0   (Champions)
1940......4–4–0

The 1939 champion Bucks were big and fast. Their ace was quarterback Don Scott, 6–1 and 205 pounds, who called signals, led the Big Ten in punting, placekicked, ran with the ball, passed for touchdowns, and was a bear on defense. Rounding out the backfield were Jim Strausbaugh, a swift, picture runner at left half; Frank Zadworney, a vicious blocker and power runner on reverses; and Jimmy Langhurst, a speedy, smashing fullback. The big men in the line included Captain Steve Andrako, center; tackles Bob Thornton and Charley Maag; and Esco Sarkkinen, flashy end.

Ohio State opened the season with impressive triumphs over Missouri and Northwestern. When they came from behind to upset Minnesota, 23–20, the pollsters began touting them for national honors. Then came Cornell, the best of the Ivy League but no match for Ohio State. Or so the experts figured.

What happened to the Buckeyes that day was much the same thing that happened to them in the Notre Dame game of 1935. In both instances they met with shocking defeat after it had appeared that they would win in a rout.

For most of the first 20 minutes Cornell was baffled by the ever-changing Ohio State attack. It had to shift into a different defense practically every play. The Bucks took the ball on their 14 and went all the way, 86 yards, in 19 straight running plays. Not a pass was thrown. It was Strausbaugh, Zadworney, Scott, and Langhurst slashing off tackle, skirting the end, smashing the middle, and reversing from a formation that was never the same for two plays in a row as they shifted into single wing, double wing, and spread alignments. At the start of the second quarter they went 72 yards for another touchdown, with Scott bulling across for the score. Muttered one Chicago writer: "The East doesn't belong on the same field with the Big Ten."

And then, in almost the next instant, a Cornell halfback broke into the clear through State's left tackle, set flight down the sideline, and with the shrieks of 50,000 Columbus partisans crying, "Stop him! Stop him!" 159-pound Pop Scholl raced 79 yards across the goal line. Hardly had the stricken crowd recovered its composure when the Big Red struck again. This time it was Swifty Borhman, substitute wingback, who had the ball, taking a pass from Scholl and scoring on a 63-yard play.

Ohio State never quite got over the shock. Something happened to the Buckeyes' confidence. The courage, skill, and intelligence of Cornell in striking twice with a single play to tie all that Ohio State had gained through long, grinding marches, had a psychological effect that turned the contest around. In the third quarter, Cornell drove 34 yards for a third touchdown, and it stopped State's only other sustained march—for 53 yards—at the 10, as big Nick Drahos smothered Scott's attempt to pass. The Ithacans also broke up the Bucks' one other scoring threat, in the fourth period, as Scholl intercepted a pass; and they sealed the victory with Drahos' field goal after Landsberg had smashed through the short side for 41 yards.

All-American Nile Kinnick crosses the Notre Dame goal line in a 1939 thriller to tie the score, then on the next play dropkicked the extra point to win the game for Iowa, 7–6.

While the 23–14 defeat galled Schmidt, he was able to pick up his Buckeyes for three straight shutout victories in the Big Ten to go into the final Saturday of competition leading Iowa for first place in the standings. Michigan was out of it following a pair of midseason upset losses to Illinois and Minnesota. The Bucks (5–0–0) led Iowa (4–1–0) by a game. Going into the final Saturday, a victory for Iowa and a loss for Ohio State would earn the Hawkeyes a half-share in the championship. Michigan did its part, beating State, 21–14, but Iowa was tied by Northwestern, 7–7, and had to settle for second place. It was OSU's fourth full claim to the Big Ten title since joining the Conference in 1913.

They were heralded by the romanticists as "the team of destiny," the 1939 Hawkeyes. This was a bunch of Iowans who had come from nowhere, with no expectations, to beat Notre Dame, South Dakota, Indiana, Wisconsin, Purdue, and Minnesota. Coached by the imaginative Dr. Eddie Anderson, who had compiled so superior a record at Holy Cross, they lost only to Michigan, 27–7, with the great Tommy Harmon–Forest Evashevski clicking beautifully for the Wolverines.

In Nile Kinnick the 1939 Hawkeyes had their most famous player in history—winner of the Heisman, Maxwell, Walter Camp, and other trophies, including the *Chicago Tribune* silver football; voted the most valuable player

of the Big Ten; and named on just about everybody's All-American team. After playing only half the game in Iowa's opener with South Dakota, Kinnick proceeded to play 402 minutes out of a possible 420 in the final seven major games, including successive 60-minute stints against Indiana, Michigan, Wisconsin,

In 1939, Nile Kinnick, shown here with his Iowa coach, Dr. Eddie Anderson, won the Heisman, Maxwell, and Camp Trophies as the No. 1 college player in America.

Purdue, Notre Dame, and Minnesota. He passed for two touchdowns in the fourth quarter to defeat Minnesota, and scored the winning touchdown against Notre Dame.

The job done by Dr. Eddie Anderson and his aides created tremendous enthusiasm among Iowa fans after years of adversity—from 1930 until 1938 the Hawkeyes had won just 22 of 72 games, with 16 of those 22 victories coming at the expense of inferior opposition—and Dr. Anderson was voted Coach of the Year in the national poll of coaches.

The so-called Age of Reason ended with President Robert Maynard Hutchins renouncing the University of Chicago's pursuit of big-time athletics. The Maroon thus dropped out of football after finishing the 1939 season tied with Wisconsin in last place, turning the Big Ten into the Big Nine. That's the way it stood until 1953, when Michigan State began play and the Western Conference of Faculty Representatives (the group's proper name) became the Big Ten once more.

College Football Goes to War:
The 1940s

In 1940 and 1941, Bernie Bierman, before exchanging his grey sweatshirt for a Marine suit and marching off to war, built Minnesota two more championship teams. Both had perfect records and were ranked No. 1 in the AP poll. Of the two squads, Bierman picked the 1941 edition as his best, right up there alongside his powerful 1934 bunch.

"I believe our 1941 team was potentially as great a team as the 1934 eleven," Bierman said. "The line was probably even better and the backfield could be more potent when all the men were in good shape. But we were rather short of backfield reserves and were handicapped most of the season by a run of backfield injuries which cut down our effectiveness greatly in some of the games. Bruce Smith was the key backfield man, but he was injured during a considerable portion of the season. Bill Daley furnished the real power. This team made much use of the running pass.

"The 1940 team was a young team that struggled through in fine style. We had a young, hustling line and a great pair of halfbacks in George Franck and Bruce Smith."

The Golden Gophers were in trouble in a number of their games and had to come from behind to win six of them. Franck went 98 yards for a touchdown on a kickoff return after Washington had led, 13–10. The Huskies later fumbled on Minnesota's 5-yard line. Ohio State was stopped on the Gophers' 1-yard line.

Michigan led by 6–0 and then blocked a Minnesota punt to recover the ball on the 3. It failed on its chance to score a second touchdown when Tommy Harmon was stopped and then threw a pass which was intercepted for a touchback. Minnesota then put the ball in play on their 20, and on the first scrimmage Bruce Smith went 80 yards to score.

Northwestern was rugged opposition for the Gophers both years, the margin of victory being one point each time. To pull out of the 1941 game Minnesota had to "pull a fast one." Behind by 7–2 in the second half, the Gophers sprang a play without shifting or calling signals. Little Bud Higgins went around his own right end and ran half the length of the field to score. Minnesota 8, Northwestern 7.

"It became famous as the *talking play,*" Bierman said. "It'd probably be illegal now, but in 1941 the ball was considered in play as soon as the referee placed it. If the ball was run out of bounds or downed between the sidelines and the hash mark it was put back in play at the hash mark. The hash marks were about 15 yards from the sidelines. The play was designed to follow immediately after the ball was run to the far side of the field requiring the referee to put it in play at the 15-yard hash mark. While he was placing it down, our players stood to the wide side nonchalantly but motionless and onside. Soon as the referee put it down, our center flicked the ball back to

69

Captain of the 1941 Minnesota National Champions was tailback Bruce Smith, winner of the Heisman Trophy whose ability to make the big play game after game earned him the reputation as the "Game Breaker."

Teaming up with the great Bruce Smith in the 1940 Minnesota backfield was All-American halfback George Franck.

little Bud Higgins and he was off to the races, with our whole team blocking for him. In practice that season, we probably ran the play no more than six or seven times, but we had it ready whenever we might need it. Against Northwestern we needed it."

Fullback Bob Sweiger was the one who set up the play.

"I was playing right half at the time and ran the ball between the out-of-bounds line and the 15-yard stripe," Sweiger recalled. "After I lugged the ball our team didn't move. In the meantime, I purposely picked an argument with one of the Wildcats and soon his teammates gathered around. Then Gene Flick, our center, shouted at me, 'Come on, Bob, let's go!' I waited for the ref to place the ball down on the hash mark . . ."

Flick picks up the story:

"I waited for the referee to put the ball down

but when Sweiger got into that argument the Northwestern guy punched him in the gut and Sweiger tore into him. I thought Bob was going to destroy the whole play so I got him out of there. Then I put my leg right around the ref's leg and flicked the ball back to Higgins. The whole maneuver was built around the rule not requiring the ball to be snapped between the center's legs but it had to be hiked in one continuous motion. Northwestern claimed the play was illegal but we'd warned the officials before the game we might use it and they ruled for us. It won the game for us. Later, I ran into the Northwestern line coach at preflight school in North Carolina during the war and went out for his football team. I reminded him of that center snap against the Wildcats in 1941 and he shook his head and snapped, 'That was an illegal play and you know it.' And I said, 'How do you know? You didn't even see it.'"

The most famous modern contest for the Little Brown Jug came in 1940. Both Minnesota and Michigan were overstocked with stars.

The Wolverines had Tom Harmon, of course, who was busy breaking some of Red Grange's records. He would win the Heisman Trophy. Michigan also had four others who either were or would be All-Americans, one of them the noted blocking back Forest Evashevski. Michigan was undefeated in five games and went into Minneapolis, together with 15 train cars of fans, as the No. 1 team. But Minnesota was just as undefeated, ranked No. 2 and had its own lineup of All-Americans, including tailback Bruce Smith, who would be the Heisman winner a year later, and sophomore Bill Daley, who would lend a footnote to the Minnesota–Michigan series by becoming a *Michigan* All-American in 1943 when he wound up at Ann Arbor through the fortunes of World War II and a naval training program.

There was only one thing wrong with what could have been a historic game. A heavy rain storm turned the Minnesota stadium into a quagmire. This hurt Michigan the most, for Harmon, who was fast and fancy, was slowed down to the speed of an arthritic race horse. He had a poor afternoon, slipping and sloshing around and missing an extra point that still irritates him. He did pass for the touchdown that gave Michigan a 6–0 lead, but later on Bruce Smith, on a surprise reverse play, waded 80

Dave Nelson, Michigan's crackerjack quarterback of 1941, went on to become one of the leading innovators of modern football as the Delaware coach.

yards for a touchdown and the Golden Gophers became the national champions, 7–6. Poor Old 98 still had a chance to win the game when he drove the Wolverines down to Minnesota's goal line in the last quarter. There, however, with a hole opened up for him wide enough to drive a truck through, Harmon slipped in the mud.

"I can still see the hole," Harmon will tell you. "It's bigger than a room, but I just can't get there."

Harmon had better luck against Ohio State, however. The Bucks dropped three in a row while he was in the Michigan backfield. The 1940 game was particularly irritating to Francis Schmidt as Harmon ran for three touchdowns, raising his career total to 33 and breaking Red Grange's record. He also passed for two. The 40–0 clobbering was the worst suffered by Ohio State since it had entered football's big time.

Some claim the defeat cost Schmidt his job. He knew the Ohio State Athletic Board was debating his future. Francis was the sort of coach who would rather die than be fired, so he handed in his resignation before the Board could act. When news photographers came around for goodbye pictures, Schmidt, bitter, told them sarcastically, "You guys have dozens of my pictures in your files. Just dig out one of them and use it. And while you're at it, just caption it, 'Rest in peace.'"

Three years later, at Idaho, Francis Schmidt suffered a heart attack and died. Some say of a broken heart.

When Schmidt packed his bags in Columbus and went West to Moscow, Idaho, Ohio State signed youthful Paul E. Brown as his successor. Brown was being hailed around the state as the colossus of Ohio prep school football. In the years between 1935 and 1940, his Massillon Tigers had won six straight state championships and had gone 56 games in a row without defeat, with 51 consecutive wins in the streak. The Tigers averaged 40 points a game, against 2.8 for opponents.

The Bucks' new football coach was just 32 years old. Starting salary, $7,000.

In his first season at Columbus, he lost only in an upset to a Northwestern team led by Otto Graham. He tied Michigan and was on his way. The next year, 1942, he installed the T

When Paul Brown first started coaching, in 1931, Herbert Hoover was still in the White House. Ten years later, he brought his single wing, short punt, and new-fangled T to Ohio State and ran up a 15–2–1 record in his first two seasons, including the national championship in 1942. After World War II, he led Cleveland to NFL titles in 1950, 1954 and 1955 and took over the newly organized Cincinnati Bengals in 1967. All told, his 41-year coaching record included 351 victories, 133 losses, and 16 ties. He finally retired in 1975.

All-American end Bob Shaw caught a lot of the passes that helped Ohio State and Coach Paul Brown win 9 of 10 games in 1942 to cop the Big Ten and national championships.

formation, the first Big Ten coach to do so, and won the national championship with a team of all juniors and sophomores. His 1943 edition might have been his best, except that by 1943 his players had gone away to war, most of them never to play football again. Brown thus had a poor season in 1943, using a strange amalgam of wartime material. The next year, he, too, was gone from Columbus, having volunteered for military duty and been assigned as head football coach of the powerful, star-studded Great Lakes Naval Training team in Chicago.

The big war years, 1943–44, were the years that the colleges called upon Grantland Rice's kind of athletes to man their football squads: "the youngster, the collegian, the boy, the scrub, who all but burst his lungs and broke his butt trying to put *his* team across . . . " It was a period of the 17- and 18-year-olds as Big Ten football players went into the armed forces by the hundreds. Freshmen were made eligible for varsity competition, and boys not yet of draft age, or 18-year-olds not yet called up, filled out squads that rostered 4-F's plus seasoned athletes assigned to a campus which had special naval training programs.

Michigan and Purdue landed some talented football players out of the service grab bag as stars from other schools were sent to campuses which formerly were their fiercest enemies. Which was how Minnesota's Bill Daley and Wisconsin's Elroy (Crazy Legs) Hirsch and Jack Wink happened to turn up in Maize and Blue colors. Meanwhile, Illinois' All-

All-American tackle Chuck Csuri was one of the big reasons why Paul Brown's 1942 Ohio State Buckeyes finished No. 1 in the polls.

Due to war-time transfer obligations, former Minnesota star Herb Hein switched to Northwestern in 1943 and developed into an All-American end.

American guard Alex Agase went to Purdue and Northwestern got Minnesota's Herm Frickey, Herb Hein and Jerry Carle. Ohio State, Iowa, Illinois, and Wisconsin, with no naval training program, had to make do with teenagers and military rejects. Predictably, the battle between the Haves and Have-nots resulted in Michigan and Purdue tying for the 1943 Big Ten championship with 6–0–0 league records. Overall, the Boilermakers won nine straight games, their first undefeated season since 1929, and only the second in their Conference history. Much of their offensive load was carried by Tony Butkovich, hard-running fullback, who in only four games against Ohio State, Illinois, Wisconsin, and Iowa broke the Conference scoring record with 13 touchdowns. He later died in the war. Other star members of the team were Alex Agase, halfback Boris Dimancheff, and guard Dick Barwegan.

With Daley and Hirsch leading the attack, the Michigan ball-carriers operated behind a powerful line, led by tackle Merv Pregulman, and won every game but one. Notre Dame's great quarterback, Angelo Bertelli, passed

Elroy (Crazy-Legs) Hirsch starred for both Wisconsin (1942) and Michigan (1943) as an All-American, Hall of Fame halfback, and then made All-Pro as a pass-catching end.

them dizzy, 35–12, on the way to the national championship.

Northwestern missed by one game sharing in the 1943 Conference title. Despite a 27–7 defeat by Michigan, Otto Graham had his finest college season and was named All-American.

The talk of the league was Bob (Hunchy) Hoernschemeyer, an 18-year-old Indiana freshman halfback, playing under wartime eligibility rules, who amazed the nation by leading the Big Ten in total offense, 873 yards, breaking the old rushing and passing records previously held by Tom Harmon and Otto Graham.

The weirdest game in the nation that season was at Columbus between Ohio State and Illinois. The contest supposedly ended in a tie, 26–26, with the Bucks on the Illini 35-yard line. Everybody started to go home. Both teams were in their dressing rooms when they were suddenly called back onto the field.

In an era preceding the T formation (1941–42–43), halfback Otto Graham was the triple-threat in Pappy Waldorf's single wing offense at Northwestern. At 6-feet-1 and 190 pounds, this is the way he looked as a sophomore.

"The game's not over," the referee informed them. "Illinois was off-side on that last play. The game cannot end on a penalty. There's still six seconds left to play."

The crowd, filing from the stadium, was astonished to see the teams lining up for one final play. Several of the linemen actually wore only sweat socks on their feet, so unexpected was this ending. Then John Stungis, an 18-year-old freshman quarterback who had never kicked a field goal in his life, swung his foot and the ball wobbled toward the crossbar 35 yards away. The startled network radio announcer who had been reporting the game forgot he was still on the air and screamed, "The son of a bitch made it!" They say he blew out radio tubes from Boston to Bremerton, Washington. The final score was 29–26, Ohio State, in what they still call "the fifth quarter victory."

Paul Brown's replacement in 1944 was Carroll Widdoes, one of his assistant coaches at Ohio State. Widdoes was an overnight sensation. Using the same sort of subpar material he'd inherited from Brown—teenagers and 4-F upperclassmen and medical trainees—Widdoes won nine straight games. One of those victories was over Great Lakes and Paul Brown! The star of the team was a dental student named Les Horvath, a Mr. All-Everything in the backfield. Horvath merely grabbed off the Heisman Trophy, and Widdoes was acclaimed Coach of the Year. That was the first time in history that the two major awards went to the same school. Besides Horvath, Ohio State also placed end Jack Dugger, tackle Bill Willis, and guard Bill Hackett on the All-American team, the largest contingent yet named from one Big Ten school. Other league stars picked on the various all-star selections were Buddy Young (Illinois), Ralph Serpico (Illinois), John Tavener (Indiana), Boris Dimancheff (Purdue), and Jug Girard (Wisconsin).

Down at Bloomington, Indiana was beginning to flex its muscles. The 1944 Hoosiers lost to Illinois, Minnesota, and Ohio State, but they ranked high in national polls and scored more points (292) than any Indiana football team in history. In his eleventh season at Bloomington, A. N. (Bo) McMillin, was just one year away from giving the Hoosiers what they'd waited 50 years for—a Big Ten football championship.

Ohio State dental student Les Horvath, 5–11 and 172 pounds, passed, punted, and ran the Buckeyes to an undefeated Conference championship in 1944 on his way to winning the Heisman Trophy.

Track star Buddy Young was converted to halfback at Illinois in 1944 and sprinted his way right into the National Football Hall of Fame on the strength of his sensational breakaway running.

The ogre of college football of the war years, of course, was Army, coached by Red Blaik, former assistant at Wisconsin. A lot of folk call him the most successful football coach in the history of our service academies. His teams won national championships in 1944, 1945, and 1946. This is known as the "Blanchard-Davis Era." Fritz Crisler said that in his more than 30 years of playing and teaching football, he had never before seen two such stars as Doc Blanchard and Glenn Davis in one backfield.

"Illinois had its Red Grange, Michigan had its Tom Harmon, Stanford had its Ernie Nevers, Notre Dame had its George Gipp, Washington had its George Wilson, but Army boasted *two* super ball carriers," Crisler said. "In my book, Blanchard and Davis comprised the finest one-two punch in football history."

In 1944, Army romped over Notre Dame, 59–0, the worst defeat in Irish history. The Cadets scored several of their touchdowns on pass interceptions.

"Army was dangerous every time Notre Dame had the ball," cracked the late Tom Meany.

For those who brushed Army aside as a lucky football team, Coach Blaik had a stock answer: "In football I seldom leave anything to chance. I maintain that it isn't luck if the bounce of the ball goes against you. If you kick it properly, it will bounce correctly. It isn't luck if a Statue of Liberty play fools you. If you play your position as it should be played, it won't fool you. I tell my men that inches make a champion—and the champion makes his own luck."

Preparing his teams for a game, Colonel Blaik never left anything to chance. "At West Point," he told me, "we had about 20 basic offensive plays, with variations. In addition, we had other plays devised to capitalize special weaknesses or to run against special defenses. In spring practice, we scrimmaged the basic plays more than a *hundred* times apiece. When the squad turned out in the fall we started over, because the players were rusty. So we scrimmaged the plays a hundred more times or so. Throughout the season we continued to use contact work to keep the players sharp. You don't develop good teeth by eating mush. You don't keep a blocker sharp by giving him theory and letting him go through the motions in dummy."

Red Blaik told me that of all the national

honors he earned as a football coach, his proudest achievement was the fact that 24 of his former assistant coaches became head coaches, and 33 of his players made the All-American team. One of those assistant mentors, of course, was—Vincent Thomas Lombardi!

With the growing success of Fritz Crisler at Michigan in the 1940s, Charlie Bachman's record against the Wolverines dimmed as his Spartans lost seven in a row to them. The last two defeats, in 1945 and 1946, saw Michigan State badly outgunned, 40–0 and 55–7. Bachman, whose contract would be running out on July 1, 1947, agreed with his detractors who believed he should step down. In accepting the coach's resignation, President Hannah said: "I checked the record again today. Bach's teams have played 95 major games, at least what I consider major games. I've crossed off all the Waynes and Albions and Illinois Wesleyans. He's won 57, tied 7, and lost 37. He's taught good, hard, clean football here and has never, in any way, either personally or with his teams, done anything to embarrass the institution."

Charlie Bachman was 54 when he left Michigan State and coaching.

In 1945, Carroll Widdoes slipped a bit. He was upset by Purdue, 35–13, picked up steam again to whip Minnesota and end Bernie Bierman's 21-game winning streak, and went into the Michigan finale with a good chance to repeat as Big Ten champion. But the Wolverines hung on to win, 7–3, and after the game Widdoes surprised everybody by handing in his resignation.

With great candor, he explained, "I've had two years of this big-time pressure cooker. I want out."

Widdoes then recommended that Paul Bixler, his assistant, be named head coach. Bixler thus became the fourth football coach in seven years at Columbus. He did all right, too, losing only two of his first eight games, but then he made the mistake of losing to Michigan, 58–6, at *Columbus*, to end both the season and his career at Ohio State. The following year he was coaching at Colgate.

In his preseason capsule of the Big Ten teams in 1945, George Trevor, writing in the

Amos Alonzo Stagg and Tug Wilson, the Northwestern athletic director who became Big Ten commissioner in 1945.

New York Sun, bunched Ohio State, Minnesota, Michigan, and Purdue as the hottest contenders for the championship, "with Indiana, Wisconsin, Northwestern, and Iowa straggling among the also-rans." Pinned down, George said he would have to go along with Ohio State. "The Buckeyes," he said, "paced by such savage linemen as Bill Hackett, Warren Amling, and John Thomas, might repeat their 1944 triumph, even though Oliver Cline is no Les Horvath at lugging leather. As for mighty Minnesota, with Bernie Bierman back from the war, the Gophers may return to their old proud place at the peak. Red Williams is a great broken-field runner, and backs Hockey Mealey, Vic Kulbitski and Merland Kispert are there to help him. Beware the Gophers! Michigan will also be up there, as usual, spearheaded by plunger John Weisenburger and blocker Joe Ponsetto, but the Wolverines 'asked for it' when they scheduled Army and Navy."

Three months later, Trevor summed up the league race this way: "Coach Bo McMillin's 'pore little Indiana boys' finally achieved an age-old ambition of winning the Big Ten Conference Title. Michigan's youthful Wolverines finished a good second, with Ohio State third. And mighty Minnesota? They skidded into the Western Conference cellar."

Bernie Bierman's failure was imputed to several causes. One was that he failed to adjust to meet the changes made in the game by rules liberalization, especially in free substitution, and the T formation.

"Bernie is too much of an introvert to change," one of his old players charged.

Except for a few T plays and an abortive triple-wing deploy, Bierman did adhere to his old power blueprints. But he probably could have continued to win with them, just as old-line Neyland football won at Tennessee. The difference was material. Minnesota simply had not regained prewar standards. Even so, Bierman, from 1945 through 1950, won more games than he lost. But he had set a standard, much higher than that before World War II. And that was to become his undoing.

Indiana and Michigan battled right down to the final Saturday before settling the 1945 title. The Hoosiers could cinch it with a victory over Purdue at Bloomington in their annual Old Oaken Bucket clash. Jesse Ambramson was there for the New York *Herald Tribune*, November 24, and this was his postgame report:

"The Old Oaken Bucket was filled to the brim today with joy such as Indiana University never has known before. Bo McMillin's 'pore little boys,' who live on the wrong side of the Western Conference tracks, up and smashed Purdue, 26 to 0, with four touchdowns in the second half, completing the first undefeated season in Hoosier history and winning the Big Ten championship for the first time after 46 years of trying.

"Indiana cleared all objectives in magnificent style and left no shred of doubt among the jam-packed 27,000 spectators in Memorial Stadium that justice had been done. The best team on the Central Plains from the opening gun was the best team and the only undefeated Western team at the end as the Hoosiers made it nine victories with one early-season tie in 10 starts.

"After a scoreless first half in which the hard-bitten, hard-hitting veteran Indiana eleven outgained the Boilermakers, but not by enough to break them down, the down-state Hoosiers tore the game apart with two touchdowns in each of the third and fourth quarters.

"Big Pete Pihos, coming back from Europe to take over the fullback portfolio, although he had been an All-Conference end two and three years ago, scored both third-period touchdowns from inside a yard, the first on the end of a 77-yard march on the seventh play culminating a 77-yard parade overland and

through the air, the second on one buck after Ted Kluszewski, Indiana end, had picked an airline fumble out of Ed Cody's hands at point-blank range." (Kluszewski later became the great slugging first baseman of the Cincinnati Reds.)

"That was more than enough for this rugged Hoosier bunch whose main asset all season has been its terrific defense. But the Hoosiers, watching the signal-calling Pihos carried off with a back injury on the first play of the fourth quarter, would not let Purdue up.

"Ben Raimondi, quarterback from Erasmus Hall, Brooklyn, took over the field direction, and Ben likes to pass. He pitched two touchdown passes, covering 7 yards and 2, to Kluszewski and Louis Mihajkovich, substitute end, completing running and passing raids of 65 and 33 yards. Charley Armstrong place-kicked the important first conversion and another after the fourth.

"Alvin Nugent (Bo) McMillin, the little white-haired Southern gentleman carried off in triumph on the shoulders of his 'pore little boys,' now 'pore' no more, had his greatest thrill since he quarterbacked the Praying Colonels of Centre College to a famous victory over Harvard nearly a quarter-century ago. The coach's dream of an undefeated team came to him for the first time since his 1925 Geneva eleven won 'em all. In his 12th year he found the rainbow. Not that he needed it, for he has just received another 10-year contract, and can and will stay here for life.

"All the 11 Hoosier starters who played with virtually no relief until the game was won were equal heroes. George Taliaferro, black freshman left half from Gary, Indiana, contributed 100 yards running, caught the pass setting up the first touchdown and got off a 48-yard punt from deep in his end zone late in the first half—the only time Indiana was in a hole. Pihos bucked for 50 yards, and right halfback Mel Groomes gained 68 yards and was impeccable on defense and in blocking. Raimondi completed seven of 11 passes for all Indiana's aerial gains.

"Colonel Bo wouldn't have been in character without cooking up something special for the big day. This time it was a cockeyed defense, with four men on the line of scrimmage and four backers up. Russ Deal, acting captain and tackle, played right end. Howard Brown, guard, played left end. The ostensible backers-up, Pihos and John Cannady, plugged the tackle holes, playing a yard back, and the ends, Kluszewski and Bob Ravensburg, deployed two yards back, protecting the outside. John Goldsberry, tackle, and Joe Sowinski, guard, operated as defensive guards, solidifying the middle.

"This rock-ribbed 202-pound line was impenetrable against the rushes of Bill Canfield and Cody, the leading Conference ground-gainers. Purdue never penetrated the Indiana 35-yard line under its own power. But late in the second quarter it got to the 20-yard line by recovering Taliaferro's fumble. The Boilermakers couldn't make a yard, then a fourth-down pass by Bob DeMoss was intercepted by Taliaferro in the second zone.

"After the game, Cecil Isbell, Purdue coach, paraphrasing John L. Sullivan's immortal words, could have said, 'I'm glad it was a Hoosier team.'"

Red Blaik gives you an idea of what Michigan had in 1945.

"With the first elements of its later great teams of 1946 and '47, the Wolverines defeated Great Lakes and finished second in the Big Ten with a 5–1 record," Colonel Blaik recalled. "They lost only to Indiana, 13–7.

"My Army team played Michigan at Yankee Stadium before a 70,000 sellout, and it may have been our most interesting game of the year. The Wolverines were young, but they were talented, spirited and, like all Fritz Crisler teams, precise, deceptive, diversified, and colorful on the attack.

"Michigan never would have been able to make the fight of it she did, however, had not Crisler taken advantage of unlimited substitution, permitted by the rules since 1941, to use separate units, or close to it, on offense and defense. This kept fresh men in action, which cut down the edge of superior personnel. It also emphasized the incontrovertible principle that there are always more boys on a squad who can play the game better one way, offensively or defensively, than there are those who can play it both ways.

"What I saw that day in Michigan's separate units for offense and defense stayed with me and was to exert a salutary effect on Army football soon after the Blanchard-Davis era.

"Michigan fought flashily and spiritedly, but Blanchard and Davis, helped by McWilliams, gradually cut them to pieces with long runs and we won, 28–7."

Halfway through the decade, practically every heretofore single wing coach was switching to the modern T with man in motion. Therefore, I found a talk I had with Charley Caldwell at Princeton particularly interesting. After experimenting with the new T craze, Coach Caldwell, who went on to win 30 of 31 games in one streak, quickly junked it in favor of the bread-and-butter single wing. He laughed at self-styled experts who argued that the single wing represented old-style football, while the T was the only way to go.

"It depends upon whose single wing or T it is," Caldwell said. "The single wing, as I use it, is a complex and elaborate system involving power, deception, perfect timing and multiple threats from different sides. It has more variations than the T. Our basic off-tackle play on a direct pass and buck-lateral series has 13 variations. Not the least asset of the single wing is that it lends itself to control of the ball. In one of our big games, there were 137 plays. We had the ball for 101. When our opponents came in pressing, to stop the steady attack, we went outside or passed them silly. When they drew back a little, we resumed the inside and reverse plays.

"Coaches who tell you they use this system or that system because of the nature of their material is nonsense. If you have the material for the T, you have the material for the single wing. They're going to the T because they are afraid of the alumni, who insist on a more fan-pleasing, wide-open game. It's a case of economics. They have to sell tickets to fill those big stadiums."

Caldwell said he would take the single wing over the T when it came to passing tactics.

"The T quarterback takes the ball from center, swings back faking a pitch-out and runs back farther to pass," he explained. "He gets little opportunity to spot anyone except the primary receiver.

"The single wing passer is always looking forward, watching developments and spotting secondary receivers in case the primary one is covered. He doesn't commit himself to pass until the last second, and defending backs cannot give undivided attention to potential

Gangway for the 1946 championship Illinois backfield. On New Year's Day, 1947, quarterback Perry Moss (left), right halfback Dwight Eddleman, fullback Russ Steger, and left half Art Dufelmeier led the way in a 45–14 rout of UCLA in the Rose Bowl.

receivers until he does. Many times the play continues as a ground attack."

Listening to Charley Caldwell I had to wonder why so many coaches were switching to the modern T with man-in-motion.

"They had modern football at its best all the while," Charley said. "All they had to do was embellish it."

Though Michigan generally was regarded as potentially the strongest team in the Western Conference in 1946, Illinois finally won the championship via a 13–9 victory over the Wolverines. It was the first Illini title since 1928. Perry Moss, granted an extra year of eligibility after returning from the war, combined his own signal-calling, passing, and running with that of star halfbacks Buddy Young and Julie Rykovich to win six out of seven Conference games. Alex Agase, Ike Owens, and sophomore Jim Valek bolstered the line. *Agase?* That's right. He is the only man in history to hopscotch back and forth three times between two schools and make All-American all three years—Illinois in 1942, Purdue in 1943, and Illinois in 1946.

Illinois had lost to Notre Dame, the national champions, 26–6, on the second Saturday of the season, and midway through the campaign was upset by Indiana, 14–7, and it was the Michigan game which really made the season for the Illini and put them in the national news. To protect a 13–9 lead in the fourth quarter the Orange and Blue fought off the Wolverines inside its 10-yard line four times in the last 12 minutes to win the game.

On January 1, 1947, Illinois smothered highly touted UCLA, 45–14, to inaugurate the new Big Ten–Pacific Coast Rose Bowl pact.

Ray Eliot, who replaced Bob Zuppke in 1942, had a style reminiscent of Knute Rockne. He was admired for his oratory. Like Rock, his harangues were "like champagne from a battered oil can." He could really stir up the blood and put fight in the Fighting Illini. A true fireball, Eliot's rapid-fire, staccato delivery appealed to young emotions, almost spiritual in style.

"There are three facets of the football mind," Ray told a coaches' clinic a few years ago. "One, *courage.* Courage to throw your bodies around on the field of play. In football, it's *contact* courage. You gotta hit, men. You gotta him 'em hard. You can't flinch. Can you do something about courage? *Of course*, you can! If you'll work at it. Of course, you can. If you don't have courage, then we'll do something about it. Talk to yourself. Give yourself some beliefs. Put something in your spine that should be there. Teach yourself to be a *man*, and not a coward. Teach yourself not to duck your head. *Courage*.

"The second thing is *game intelligence*. Smartness on the field. Game intelligence. How to handle yourself out there. Smartness—not just in calling plays—but smartness in attacking the problem facing you. The problem of getting your man out of the play, and not just beating your heads. Game intelligence, the same as law intelligence, medical intelligence, business intelligence. Smartness on the field—and smartness *off* the field. Taking good care of your lives. Doing the things you gotta do to be a better man.

"But the most important thing of all is a simple old thing called *common sense*. The proper state of mind. And by the proper state of mind I mean that dynamic something that comes into your hearts and souls and says I can, I will, I must; that regardless of odds . . . *regardless of odds* . . regardless of what the odds may be, I will get the job done. The will to win, gentlemen. The will to succeed.

"Let me tell you about the war years at Illinois. We weren't blessed with a Navy program, nothing like that a-tall. Anybody who could *breathe* could play at our place. As long as the pulse was beating, we had him.

"I'll never forget the summer of '43. This young chap walked into my office—139-pound halfback Eddie Bray—and Eddie said, 'I wanna play Big Ten football.' Well, I took one look at him and said to myself, 'Whew, we've really gone to the bottom of the barrel now.' But if I had to pick my all-time backfield, sir, I hasten to say that little Eddie Bray would be my left halfback, because in four years of Big Ten football he averaged 7.1-yards per carry on the ground. And while he wasn't a speed demon and couldn't make the track team—and while he wasn't a big boy—he had a heart as big as this room. He had a never-say-die spirit. He could block ya' and he could tackle ya'. *The will to succeed*, that says it all about him.

"I was particularly proud of our 1944 team at Illinois. We gave out 27 letters that season, and 21 of them went to 17-year-old boys; when they became 18 they were gone to war. Two of the remaining six letters went to 16-year-old

boys. And *that* team, sir, led the United States of America in yards gained. They had nine touchdowns taken away from them during the course of the season, and had three of those touchdowns stuck we'd have been National Champions. Oh, you think we played a soft schedule, huh? Well, we played seven Big Ten schools, and we played Great Lakes Naval Station. And let me tell you about Great Lakes, because Paul Brown, then the coach there, must have stopped every monster of 270 pounds that came into the Naval Station and put a football suit on him. I swear to God I never saw so many monsters in my life. They were so big they couldn't play a six-man line, they had to play a five-man line to fit between the sidelines. All-Pro tackles, All-American, All-This and All-That. We had a kid from our school on that Great Lakes team, an All-American tackle, and he was playing *third* team there. Whooh! That Paul Brown was an organizer, I'll tell ya'. Hmmph! Bray, a 139-pounder at left half for me. Ed McGovern, a 138-pounder at right half. And a snarling, 168-pound devil from Collinsville at fullback.

"In those days, I always led my boys onto the field—we always walked hand-and-hand, because after all, I was responsible for those kids, they were away from home. Well, we loosened up in the end zone, then went back into our dressing room and had a cup of tea and talked over our strategy. I said to my boys, 'How many of you kids are willing to play this game?' And the whole 27 stood up. I was really proud of Young America that day. Well, sir, we went back onto the field and at the end of the first half we were in front, 19–6. We couldn't hold on, though, and had to settle for a 26–26 tie. The numbers were 26–26 up on that scoreboard, and 19 seconds left. Suddenly, Mr. Mello, the All-American from Notre Dame, broke into the open with the ball and started making tracks for our goal line. The only man between him and the winning touchdown was this kid Bray. When I saw those two bodies coming close together, I really wondered what I was going to say to Eddie's mother at the funeral. But I looked up just in time to see one of the greatest tackles I ever saw or heard on a football field in my life, when Eddie Bray put those bony little old shoulders into the oncoming, piston-like legs of Mr. Mello. He picked him up and laid him back the way he was coming from, and then sat on him until the clock ran out.

"So I ask you, sir, what did the job there? Bones and muscles? Bray's biceps were no bigger than my thumbs. He could have done like so many guys do in games and avoided the runner head-on. He could have dived along the turf and made it look like the old college try, dauntless with courage. You've ducked things in the game of life, too, don't you know? You duck 'em. Sure, you do. That kid Bray never ducked his responsibility, though. He met the problem head-on. He didn't say, oh, why did you put me here? He asked no quarter. He just wanted to sock that guy and he brought him down. And what brought him down? Bones and muscles? No, sir, a *heart*. A *big* heart. A desire. A will. A never-say-die spirit. Regardless of odds . . . *regardless of odds* . . . he got the job done. Big heart. You'll see it on our gridirons all your lives.

"Let me tell you about Alex Agase. He went to Evanston High School and couldn't even make a letter. Could . . . not . . . make . . . a . . . letter. He came to us and was a three-time All-American. All-American three years in a row. He must have been big, huh? Well, the heaviest he ever weighed was 189 pounds. Then he must have been fast. In a wind sprint with seven guards each night he finished seventh. Well, he must have been strong as hell; he holds the dubious distinction in physical education at Illinois of being able to chin himself three times. Oh, yes, he had agility, he had quickness, but, baby, most of all, he had *heart*. Oh, did he have heart. Oh, he had one, sir. What a great leader. During the war, he was a Marine and right in the middle of it I received a letter from him. It went something like this: 'Dear Coach—I didn't think I'd ever be carried off a field in my life. But I got it down here. Nineteen of us went out and only two returned . . .' I'll skip the sordid details, but the letter went on: 'All I'm waiting for, Coach, is one thing. Daily I'm praying for that moment when I get back at the enemy. Nothing will ever beat us, sir. *Nothing* will ever beat us—because nothing can beat the spirit of the United States Marine Corps.' *Spirit! Spirit!* The will to win.

"Do you remember a guy named Lincoln? Abraham, that is. You've heard of him, haven't you? Quite a man. I wonder how well you know him. I have a bust of Lincoln on my desk, and every time the going gets rough for me and I sit at that desk, he looks at me with a twinkle in his eye and he tells me something. You know what he tells me? He says, 'Ray, remember now, I tried 27 times to be elected to public office. *Twenty-seven times I tried to be something.* And I failed 25 times!' Did you ever stop to think of that guy at the end of the fifth time he failed? Why, he couldn't have been our President. I wonder how many of you in this room could fail five times and say I'm licked, I'm no good, they don't want me? Or could you go on and fail 10 times, and still with chin high and a smile on your face go out and conquer and believe in yourselves. I wonder how many of you can fail 25 times and still believe in yourselves enough to emerge triumphant? Now do you know Mr. Lincoln a little better?

"It's like Bing Crosby once said to me: 'Sing with your mouth? No, Ray, you sing with your heart.' Did you ever hear him sing 'White Christmas'? Did you ever hear him sing 'Silent Night'? From the *heart* of the man.

"The great paintings of the world done by a man's bones and muscles—yes, educated bones and muscles—but all from the *heart* of a man. *Heart*. You who lack the heart, you who have lost the spirit and hope, you who have lost self-confidence—you are *dead*, sir. You are done. You must have heart.

"It takes me back to 1939, when a little band of kids at Illinois had to meet the most powerful juggernaut in America. I mean, the University of Michigan team that had five All-Americans on it. There was Harmon at tailback, Westfall at fullback, Frutig at left end, Ingalls at center, and Evashevski at blocking back. The year before they were among the Top Ten teams in America, and here they are in '39 with the same group of men. Oh, what a powerful bunch of men. And Illinois? We had no All-Americans. We were a bunch of babies. We had one good leader, a kid named Mel Brewer, our captain. A really fine football player. What had Michigan done? Well, they had beaten Michigan State (26–13), Iowa (27–7), Chicago (85–0), and Yale (27–7). And what did we do in our first four games? Well, in our first game we tied Bradley, 0–0. In the second game we lost to California by 20-some points. Indiana beat us in the third game, and in the fourth game

Northwestern drubbed us. To make matters worse, the Monday before the Michigan game we lost the services of Captain Brewer, our inspiration, our leader, who was called home because of the death of his mother.

"It was the custom in those days to take the boys to the Champaign Country Club on the eve of all home games and feed and bed them and Coach Zuppke would talk to them. So at 8 o'clock sharp that night, as the boys sat around in easy chairs in front of a big roaring fireplace fire, with no light in the room except that from burning logs, Zup reviewed our game plan for the next day. All of a sudden a door opened from the far end of the room, and Capt. Brewer came in silently and joined his teammates sitting on the floor. Zup saw who it was and walked over and offered the boy beautiful, fatherly condolences. As Zup turned to go back to the center of the room, Captain Brewer stood up; and in a voice filled with emotion, he said, 'Fellas, my sister and my daddy join me in saying thanks to you for your beautiful flowers and telegrams.' Then his voice became almost raspy as he said, 'If you feel the way I do right now—and I didn't travel 250 miles here for nothing—if you feel the way I do we will go out there and beat the hell out of Michigan tomorrow.' He sat down on the floor again and you should have seen the faces of his teammates. I wish you could have seen them, I wish you could have been there. *Electricity*. It filled the room. The feeling, the intensity. Tears streamed down young faces. Zup saw it, and he knew anything else he said would only be anti-climatic, so he stopped and dismissed them. Normally, it was hard to get the players into bed by 10 o'clock, but on this night they were all tucked in at five minutes past nine— and nobody asked them to be there. As I walked down a long line of cots I couldn't believe my eyes. No talking, no horsing around, no noise—just kids staring quietly at the ceiling. The only words spoken were when I reached to switch off the light, and they said, 'Goodnight, Coach.' I turned and went on home. I knew something had to happen.

"The next afternoon, just as we got ready to dash onto the field, Michigan's student manager handed me a note addressed to Mel Brewer, who told me to open it for him and read it to the team. It said, 'Dear Mel, we at Michigan send our condolences to you on the loss of your Mom. We hope you are back in time to play against us because we wouldn't want to play against a weakened team . . . ' It was signed by the entire Michigan team and coaching staff. Sportsmanship at its highest.

"We went out into the stadium and loosened up, then returned to the dressing room, where something happened I'd never seen before. As Coach Zuppke called off the names of each starter, everybody else in the room rose to his feet and gave that guy a tremendous ovation and charged him with the responsibilities of the day. I was the last guy in the room to say goodbye to the eleven starters as they went past me. They usually came up and said don't worry, we'll take care of it, but this time they never said a word. You know the rest of the story. That day, one of the greatest upsets in the history of the Big Ten took place as our kids whipped the finest college team in America, 16–7. And the guy who started us off by kicking a field goal was—Captain Brewer, who'd never before kicked a field goal in his life. Many times, since then, Tom Harmon told me he was never hit so hard and so often as he was that afternoon. 'I played pro ball, I played in the Big Ten, I played everywhere,' Tom said, 'but I was never hit so hard as your kids hit me.' Before coming to Champaign that day, Harmon averaged 165 yards a game, but after the game with us, he walked out of the stadium minus-19 yards.

"That's what I mean by heart. The 1939 Illini—the same team that had been tied by Bradley—the same team that lost to California, Indiana, and Northwestern—it was the same Orange and Blue spangles, the same eyes, ears, teeth, arms, and legs—the same abilities, the same skills, the same speeds—*but not the same men, sir, because now it came from their hearts*. The will to succeed, that's what beat Michigan that day. As one poet wrote, it's all in the state of mind. With due respect to the O's and X's, that is the beginning and the end and the in-between of football."

The year was 1947 and George Trevor, in his annual preview of college football, wrote in the *New York Sun* that Notre Dame, in a class by itself, would go through the season undefeated and win the mythical national championship. "That Notre Dame line has no equal in the entire country," he said. "Thus the Irish will get sweet revenge on Army, now that the once invincible Cadets have been cut down to size by the graduation of Blanchard, Davis and Tucker."

But, George, what about the Big Ten race?

"Michigan should nose out Illinois for the championship and go to the Rose Bowl," Trevor wrote. "The Wolverines last appeared at Pasadena in 1902, with Yost's point-a-minute team. Illinois, with many of its Rose Bowl victors in harness, will battle Michigan savagely. Ohio State, Minnesota, Iowa, Indiana and Northwestern look next best in the Conference."

Fritz Crisler wanted one more undefeated team before retiring. After 17 seasons of coaching he had accomplished just about everything in his Master Plan—except to go to the Rose Bowl and win the national championship. Now, in 1947, he went for broke.

Crisler had actually begun to build his last great team three years before it ever came to its senior year. The 17- and 18-year-old freshmen who broke in during the war years had gained invaluable experience. They were joined in 1946 by a host of returning servicemen and the next season by a handful of very talented sophomores. The team represented the full bloom of Crisler's platoon system. His offense averaged 195 pounds and was fast and flexible; his defense, big, agile, with excellent pursuit.

The man who made the offense move was quarterback Howard Yerges, son of the old Ohio State signal-caller whose 1919 Bucks, with Chick Harley, were the first ever to beat Michigan. Yerges junior had a computer mind and seemed to know each man's assignment on every play and precisely the right moment to baffle a defense.

Bob Chappuis, an Air Corps veteran who had been shot down in Italy, was No. 1 at the all-important tailback position. He had been on the varsity in 1942 and was familiar with Crisler's attack. The biggest man in the backfield at 184 pounds, Bob was a strong runner and pinpoint passer.

Chalmers (Bump) Elliott, later the Michigan coach, was at the other halfback post, and brother Pete Elliott, later coach at Illinois, was the second-string quarterback. Their father once served as assistant coach at Northwestern. Bump weighed only 168 and played for Purdue during the war. He was the ideal

Michigan's 1947 Dream Backfield, left to right: wingback Bump Elliott, quarterback Howard Yerges, fullback Jack Weisenburger, and tailback Bob Chappuis.

wingback in the Crisler system, probably the most versatile player on the entire squad.

Jack Weisenburger, the fullback, manned possibly the most important position of all. In Michigan's version of the single wing, the ball was generally centered directly to Weisenburger, who then set in motion the tricky spinner cycle. He whirled and either handed the ball to the tailback or wingback, or kept it himself and plunged into the line or slipped it to the quarterback. Jack was small for a fullback, 178 pounds, but as a former tailback he was quick enough to slide around either end for good yardage. At deception he was a magician, masking his ball-handling so deftly that even the Michigan coaches could not be certain which of his colleagues had received the ball. This craftiness was the distinguishing feature of the whole backfield. Few backfields have ever functioned so smoothly together.

The Wolverines operated from seven different formations and turned loose a fantastic array of full spinners, half spinners, buck laterals, reverses, end arounds, and quick openers, on many of which three and even four men handled the ball.

Michigan rolled over opponents in the manner of a bulldozer. A good Michigan State team was obliterated, 55–0. Pittsburgh suffered its worst defeat in history, 69–0. Stanford and Northwestern were buried, 49–13 and 49–21. Only Minnesota, playing an inspired game, with its huge line led by Leo Nomellini and Clayton Tonnemaker, and a tough Illinois team, succeeded in holding down the score. Michigan beat the Gophers, 13–6, and the Illini, 14–7, and then swept on to crush Indiana (35–0), Wisconsin (40–6), and Ohio State (21–0).

Michigan scored a total of 345 points, the most a Big Ten team had compiled since the turn of the century, and allowed nine opponents only 53.

All that remained now was for this collection of "chrome-plated, hand-tooled specialists," as *Time* Magazine had called them, to play Southern California, losers only to Notre Dame, 38–7, in the Rose Bowl on New Year's Day.

In 1902, Michigan had beaten Stanford, 49–0. Now, 46 years later, Michigan trounced the Trojans 49–0! The Wolverines were in a rut!

Michigan No. 1 in the national poll? "It'd be a sacrilege to mention any other college team in the same breath with Michigan," Red Smith said.

Thus ended the Fritz Crisler Era at Michigan. He had what he wanted—a Rose Bowl victory and the national championship—and he felt it was time to step down as head football coach to devote all his energies to the job of athletic director.

Bennie Oosterbaan, who had served as Crisler's assistant, became the new coach, and the all-time, All-American end picked up where Fritz had left off and won Big Ten championships in 1948, 1949, and 1950. In 1948, he inherited an almost intact defense, but graduation had wiped out the great offensive unit of 1947. Bennie quickly made Pete Elliott his starting quarterback and made Tom Peterson his fullback. Then he installed Chuck Ortmann and Leo Koceski, a couple of sophomores, at the important tailback and wingback positions. Ortmann was a perfect choice to succeed All-American Bob Chappuis. He could pass and run and blended splendidly with versatile Koceski, who caught passes and specialized in taking the handoff on key reverse plays.

Michigan rolled through its nine-game schedule without defeat or tie to register a second straight perfect season and another national championship. They were not as flamboyant on offense as the 1947 Wolverines, but they still managed to outscore their rivals, 252 points to 44. Having played for Fielding Yost, Oosterbaan had a deep appreciation of defensive football. In the game that meant the Big Ten championship, Northwestern's strong team was shut out, 28–0, and finished second with a 5–1–0 record. However, because of the Big Ten–Pacific Coast Conference pact that stipulated no team could play twice in succession in the Rose Bowl, Pappy Waldorf's Wildcats got to go to Pasadena, where they beat California, 20–14. A member of that team was Frosty Westering, a sophomore reserve end who is now a successful head coach at Pacific Lutheran University, Tacoma, Washington. Frosty gives you a sampling of what it meant to play for a Big Ten team:

"I was raised in Iowa, the heart of Big Ten country, in the era of Nile Kinnick," Westering told me recently. "Those of us who grew up in the Midwest lived for the day when we'd be old enough to play in the Western Conference. In those days, a player would go into the game and stay there. There was very little substitution. Because of the one-platoons, recruiting wasn't so intense as it is now. College scouts and recruiters looked for a different type of player. Football was a power game and they preferred hard-nosed players. It was a way of life. Midwesterners identify with a *rugged* history—a people who were forced to withstand severe winters, sweltering summers, hard work—an endless battle for survival. This harsh background is reflected in the Big Ten's style of play.

"Football started changing in the Forties. Teams began gambling more, particularly on defense. Heretofore, so much had been standardized defense: the old 7-man line, or a 6-2-2-1, or an occasional 5-man line, and that was about it. Then defenses started gambling, such as the mini-automatic systems and the things that began showing up in the late 1940's.

"Another change was the size of the players. They were getting bigger. The little guy was being squeezed out. There were a few little guys in uniform, but not many. Still, the big man then was not the big man of today. A big man then was a 6-foot-1, 200-pounder; the kind of guy who did a lot of hitting, the name of the game. I'm not saying they hit harder then, because they didn't; football today is at its highest level. But football was probably more dangerous 35 years ago. There were no face masks, no face bars. In my own case, I broke my nose *three* times, and lost several front teeth, requiring a bridge I wear today.

"On the question of attitude, I think the players of the 1940's were more docile than now. They seldom questioned the coach's commands. They accepted orders pretty much face-value. When given an order, you went ahead and did it. In some ways, I think there was more *team* feeling. And yet the team feeling of today is better in other ways, because the kids now are self-starters, not forced-starters. I think there was more fear in the old days among the players, not a fear of body contact on the field, but a fear of authority. There was a different kind of coach-player closeness—the coaches lacked the warmth you see

among the coaches today. The oldtimers were more like Marine drill sergeants. They made you feel as though you were being punished if you didn't win. I think the punishment idea is gone now, though some coaches feel we should go back to the strict discipline theory. Maybe the answer is something in between.

"Bob Voigts coached our Northwestern team in the 1949 Rose Bowl game. He was from the old school, firm, silent, commanded respect, though was fair. He insisted on good grades in the classroom. The academic standards at Northwestern always have been high. We had counselors who regularly checked our marks to make sure we were passing. I don't remember very many ineligible players.

"The biggest change in football since our Rose Bowl team has been the defense. As I said, the defense has changed tremendously, with different types of secondary coverages, changing of alignments, and all that. The coaches have probably gone as far as they can. They'll probably have to change the rules before you see anything new in football. Actually, you can go back all the way to Rockne and you'll discover the things we are doing now

Alex Sarkisian, a terrific center, was another reason why Northwestern finished a strong second in the Big Ten in 1948 and then went to the Rose Bowl when Michigan stayed home on the no-repeat ruling.

Halfback Ed Tunnicliff got loose on a 50-yard dash in the final minute of play for Northwestern to beat California in the 1949 Rose Bowl game, 20–14.

were just as sound then. I really think football travels in cycles. I think the coaches like today's game so much because the rules allow a team to operate like a well-oiled machine. You've got all the offense, the defense, the specialists, more kids get to play. If you didn't have to scholarship so many boys to man platoon-football, we'd have the *perfect* game.

"How many of that 1948 Northwestern team could play today? I think most of them. I really do. Some of them would play defense, some offense, and some would be specialists.

"I don't know what happened to us at Northwestern in 1949. We had all our seniors back from the Rose Bowl team, yet won only four games. We had a bad case of senioritis; so many guys came off that Rose Bowl squad and just couldn't put it all together. We were supposed to be one of the strong teams in the Big Ten and beat only Purdue, Michigan, Colgate and Illinois. It showed the power of the Conference. Year in and year out, dating back to 1895, I have to believe that the best college football played in America has been played by the Big Ten."

At the end of the 1948 season, Harry Stuhldreher lost his job at Wisconsin. The best the old Four Horseman could do at Madison in

13 years was to finish second twice, 1942 and 1947. Much of the time his Badgers placed below fourth position. When it was all over, Mary Stuhldreher, his wife, described the pressure that cost Harry his job.

"Our 1947 season got off to a good start with a win over Purdue and a tie with Indiana," she recalled. "Then we lost to California, 48–7, and the wolves began to howl. There were two phone calls, one facetious—'Was Harry at the game, and did he know what the score was?' and one nasty—'A fine coaching job. Why don't you quit?' Then our son Peter, 10, came home from school with a bloody nose. Some kid had told him that Harry was a lousy coach, and that made Peter mad. 'You see,' he told us, 'I kinda like my dad.'

"It is not easy to be a losing coach's wife. Even the townspeople of Madison were outspoken and inconsiderate. I didn't relish their candid contempt, but I understood it. Wisconsin was their school, Wisconsin wasn't winning, and they were feeling let down.

"I went uptown to shop one day, and a salesgirl said, 'Sorry, madam, it's my lunch hour,' and walked away.

"'You didn't eat much breakfast,' I said. 'It's just 10 o'clock.'

"'Someone else will take care of you,' she said.

"The girl who finally waited on me said, 'Don't mind her. Her busband's family is from Iowa, and they've been giving her a riding about our team.'

"I went for the locksmith to open a desk drawer. 'What's the matter?' he asked. 'Harry got his strategy locked inside?' I went to a tea, and a faculty wife said to me, 'This talk about your husband reminds me of a football game. I keep wondering who's going to win, and who's going to lose.'

"For a long while, I enjoyed being a football coach's wife. I could take the criticism—until 1946. After that it got pretty rough. Harry was accused of racial prejudice. There was talk of dissension on the team. The movement to oust my husband built up steam. I took it, but I didn't like it. Mine was not an isolated experience, however, Much the same thing happened to Mrs. Eddie Anderson at Iowa, and Mrs. Wesley Fesler at Ohio State. They watched their husbands tossed on the frying pan, too. I guess it bothered Mrs. Fesler the

most—she lost weight, and their children refused to go to school. Columbus, Ohio, is not a
very comfortable place to live for a football
coach's family when he finishes ninth in the
Big Ten."

Wes Fesler, the most versatile and popular
athlete in Ohio State history, had been brought
in to replace Paul Bixler in 1947 and wound up
dead last in the league. His record for the season was 2–6–1. But such was his charisma that
nobody in authority let out a peep. He moved
up to fourth in 1948 with an overall record of
6–3–0, and in 1949 when the Ohio State
placekicker got a second chance at a point-
after-touchdown because Michigan was
offside, the Buckeyes got a tie with the Wolverines and went to the Rose Bowl, where
they beat California by a field goal, 17–14.

In spite of his second 6–3–0 record in three
years, and a second-place tie with Wisconsin,
Fesler shocked Ohio State supporters by up
and quitting in 1950. For more than a year he
had been privately brooding over major college football: its pandering to teenage high
school athletes and their parents; the whole
recruiting rat race; the hypocrisy and the rampant hanky-panky.

"To hell with intersectional games," he said.
"Let's control our own methods and destinies
and play a complete Big Ten round-robin
schedule."

It was too late to stop the world and get off,
however. There was no way to turn back the
decades of Midwest chauvinism, the fervor of
Ohio State fans for national recognition. A lot
of Buckeye bred-in-the-bone fans suddenly
turned against Fesler. He couldn't believe the
vicious phone calls or the hateful mail he received because of his stand. He was almost
nauseated when his wife was subjected to
abuse, and he knew that any love he had for
football, Ohio State brand, had come apart. He
suffered severe headaches and couldn't sleep.
So Wes Fesler, a truly class guy, quit. He just
up and quit. One more ghost in the graveyard
of Ohio State football coaches.

Waiting in the wings was Wayne Woodrow
Hayes—with the toughest hide of all.

No matter how successful a coach may be,
every coach eventually reaches a point where
a lot of people want somebody else. Bernie
Bierman, for instance. His 10-year record at
Minnesota prior to World War II was un-

equaled. Yet, after finishing third in the Big
Ten in 1947, 1948 and 1949, there came a day
following a seventh-place finish in 1950 when
he was no longer wanted. Some 14 years later,
from the home he retired to in Laguna Hills,
California, Bierman recalled that he was hung
in effigy and there were signs that read, "Bye,
Bye, Bernie."

"I was saddened," Bierman said. "I had to
be after all those years, and it took me a while
to come back. But I know how fickle a fan can
be. Every coach thinks about what might happen to him if he starts losing."

"It's a game for madmen," Vince Lombardi
used to say. He meant that coaching football
was more than enough to drive a man mad.

A Bierman legend was that he never shed a
tear, shouted, raged, or dropped a player from
his squad. Dale Warner, a halfback for him in
the late Forties, told me that Bernie was the
most organized man he had ever been around.

"And that's how he coached," testified
Warner, a successful businessman in Minneapolis today. "Every minute was organized.
Every day of practice, he gave us a sheet of
paper outlining exactly what we were going to
do. After every game we played, he showed us
what we did on *every* play, position by position. He and his staff spent all day Sunday reviewing each game, so that by Monday afternoon practice they were ready for us. We were
awed by Bierman, respectful. Many of his
players were walk-ons. I was a walk-on from
St. Paul. They gave me a uniform and I worked
my way on to the squad from there. But that's
all gone now. You rarely hear of walk-ons
anymore. It's very professional now. Too bad.
I think they overlook some good prospects that
way.

"The worst part of the year was late August
and early September, during those preseason
workouts, when everybody tried to make the
team. We'd start each practice in the morning
and the lights had to be turned on before we
went home. No one knew who was going to
make the squad and Bernie drove us hard.

"During the dog days of Summer, Bernie
kept in touch with each of us by mail regularly.
He told us to run a lot, play touch football, and
lots of soccer. He wrote to us weekly. He especially wanted to know about our weight, what
our last-semester grades were, things like that.
Without good grades, he banished you off the

Minnesota's Leo Nomellini was a great tackle, an All-American in 1948 and 1949, who later starred for the San Francisco 49ers.

and only get a yard or so, ever, and he'd always get the stuffing popped out of him. In college, we had a lot of fun with Leo. He kept us loose."

In many ways the highlight of the 1949 season came at Ann Arbor on October 7, when Army played Michigan. The Wolverines, who tied Ohio State for the Big Ten championship with a 4–1–1 league record, went into that game with a proud 25-game winning streak that had begun back in 1946. They were indeed a shining target and since they were the third game on Army's schedule, the Cadets were able to prepare for them almost from the end of the previous season.

"We studied films of their games until we felt we knew their strong and weak points and their habits, collectively and individually, in any given situation," Colonel Red Blaik re-

squad. The conference lost some good athletes because of poor marks—and they'd go play in the Big Eight. The Big Eight would take them.

"I played on the same squad with Bud Grant and Leo Nomellini. Bud won nine letters at Minnesota and was the Philadelphia Eagles' No. 1 draft pick. In his first nine years as head coach of the Minnesota Vikings, he took them to the Division playoffs seven times. He was that kind of football player. As for Leo, he was a great tackle, All-American in 1948 and '49. He later played with the San Francisco 49ers and used to run the ball as a fullback every once in a while. Frankie Albert, the 49er quarterback, knew that Leo's idol was Bronko Nagurski, the old Minnesota fullback. So in the huddle, if things were going all right, Frankie would call the 31-wedge, and he'd say, 'Nomo, you run it.' And Leo would run it

Bud Grant, here shown, and Gordy Soltau gave Bernie Bierman two of the finest ends in college football in 1949. Grant won nine letters at Minnesota and was the Philadelphia Eagles' No. 1 draft pick.

Clayton Tonnemaker was All-American center in the great Minnesota line of 1949, along with such great names as Nomellini, Grant, and Soltau, yet the Gophers had to settle for third place in the final league standings behind co-champions Michigan and Ohio State.

Bob, in at quarter. Bob had looked good throwing touchdown passes in our opening victories against Davidson and Penn State. I finally decided, however, that he did not have sufficient experience for the spot. Kuckhahn's powerful charges set up our first score and he went over from the seven for the third marker that clinched a tremendous 21–7 victory. 'A West Pointer Looked West,' said one headline, and that was no overstatement. We had been looking West at Michigan for a long time."

Four straight Big Ten triumphs in the Rose Bowl made West Coast football the laughing stock of the sporting world. Northwestern and Ohio State victories were the final straw. In the January 1, 1949, game, California had been unbeaten, while the Wildcats had been whipped twice, by Notre Dame and Michigan. Northwestern had finished no better than second in the Big Ten. The Pacific Coast Conference truly held all of the trump cards, but the Big Ten won again—with its *second* best team.

A similar situation existed on New Year's Day, 1950. California had rolled over all 10 of its opponents. Ohio State, although tying for the Conference title, was no better than the third strongest team in the Big Ten. The Buckeyes had been snowed under by Minnesota, 27–0, and they were lucky to tie Michigan, 7–7. To make matters worse, Ohio also tied Southern California, 13–13, and the Trojans were only the No. 4 team in the Pacific Coast Conference. Under such circumstances, the pressure was on California to beat Ohio State, or be laughed right off the football map.

The Golden Bears were favored, but not by much. Against mutual opponents, California and Ohio State were almost square. Cal beat Southern California, 16–10, and Wisconsin, 35–20. Ohio State tied USC, 13–13, but defeated Wisconsin, 21–0. Both teams were weak on defense. Most experts agreed that the breaks would decide the game. For once they were right. At the end, a field goal made the difference for the Buckeyes.

Afterward, there was a lot of fuss in Los Angeles about the PCC's inability to beat the Big Ten in the Rose Bowl. Some cry-babies urged the West Coast to withdraw from the pact with the Big Ten. L. H. Gregory, the fiery columnist of *The Oregonian* at Portland, shot down that proposal fast.

called. "We boiled down a huge amount of information to essentials, in order to parcel it out to our platoons within the relatively restricted time they were available. We sent the Cadets into the game thoroughly briefed on what must be done and how it could be done.

"For example, Michigan's players were tall with high centers of gravity. We exploited that fact by blocking them so low we got underneath their natural forearm or hand charge. Our success in this maneuver had a profound effect on the game, psychologically as well as physically. We drummed into our quarterback, Arnold Galiffa, a sequence of plays we felt sure would work, in such a way he could not possibly forget them. This paid off also, for we struck them fiercely at the beginning and rolled them back on a 10-play, 89-yard drive, which Galiffa generaled impeccably.

"The week of the game, an aggravation to Gil Stephenson's leg forced us to move Karl Kuckhahn from defensive linebacker to offensive fullback. For a time I even considered shifting Galiffa to fullback and putting my son,

"When you have lost four in a row to the Big Ten," he asked me at the time, "is *that* the time to talk about pulling out and de-emphasizing football? Apparently in the faculty view it might be. But if the PCC does pull out of the Rose Bowl with the Big Ten, you well know it will be a faculty matter, not one of the athletic department's. I hope to gosh the entire country joins in jumping on the old boys for this defeatist, quitting attitude. But you know the kind of intellects that run the faculty side of Pacific Coast Conference football!"

The Fierce Fifties:
1950

For shocks and surprises, 1950 was one of the greatest football seasons in modern times. Notre Dame, the perennial preseason favorite nationally, finished the year with a humble 4–4–1 record. Mighty Army was derailed as Coach Red Blaik's express-train runners were ganged by Navy's wreckers in their annual service school showdown. Other big powers like Southern Methodist, Vanderbilt, and Ohio State, which started the season with such promise, hit the skids hard along the way.

Of the three major unbeaten, untied squads that emerged from regular season play, only Princeton survived New Year's Day—maybe only because the Tigers kept up a traditional policy of avoiding postseason games. On the Western Conference bowl front, thrice-beaten, once-tied Michigan got past California in the Rose Bowl, 14 to 6, on January 1, 1951, at Pasadena, to make it five in a row over the Pacific Coast since the two leagues started their exclusive pact in 1947.

Three teams were in contention for the championship right up to the last day of the schedule in the Western Conference. Ohio State, which had pulverized five straight opponents via a 230-point scoring rampage after being upset by SMU, 32–27, in the season opener, suddenly lost to Illinois, 14–7, going into the final weekend to set up the three-way dogfight. The possibilities were mind-boggling as the Illini met Northwestern, and

Michigan played the Buckeyes at Columbus. Jerry Brondfield, an alumnus of Ohio State who once wrote sports for my old company, NEA, saw the game.

"The Buckeyes needed only a win over Michigan to go to the Rose Bowl," Jerry remembered. "Michigan wasn't much to shout about. They'd been tied by Minnesota and dumped by Army, Michigan State, not yet a league member, and Illinois. It was a spotty record and a spotty team whose only redeeming features were two exceptionally fine backs, Chuck Ortmann and Don Dufek, and a terrific tackle, Allen Wahl. They also had a fine end in Lowell Perry and a very good center named Tony Momsen, whose brother, Bob, incidentally, was a starting guard in the Ohio State line."

Meanwhile, the Buckeyes were sizzling. The Illinois defeat had left them in a savage mood. They couldn't wait to take it out on arch rival Michigan.

The day before the game, snow started falling all over Ohio. Nobody paid much attention to it at first, but by evening there was no let-up. Battered by gale-force winds, snow drifts were hip-high in places. All through the night it snowed. By Saturday morning the temperature had dropped to 3 degrees above zero—and still the snow came.

"The drifts were four and five feet high in some places," Brondfield recalled. "Ohio

Stadium was really something to see. Somewhere, beneath tons and tons of snow was the tarpaulin covering the field—and it was frozen stiff. Stranded on highways throughout central Ohio were thousands of automobiles headed for Columbus and the game. All public transportation—plane, train, bus and taxi—had been shut down tight. Columbus was a sealed city.

"Despite road conditions, more than 50,000 of the 80,000 ticket-holders got through to the stadium and swept all that snow off the seats to find their numbers. But one question remained: Would there be a game. Fritz Crisler of Michigan and Dick Larkins of Ohio State, the two athletic directors, talked to coaches Bennie Oosterbaan and Wes Fesler and then went into a huddle. Fesler later confessed he didn't think anybody should be forced to play under such horrible conditions. It was finally decided, however, to play the game."

What followed was not precisely football as taught by the Old Masters. Hindered by the blizzard, deception, ball-handling and trap-

Vic Janowicz, 5-foot-9, 185 pounds, was Ohio State's Mr. All-Everything in 1950 as he ran, passed, punted, and placekicked the Buckeyes into second place in the Big Ten standings, while winning the Heisman Trophy for himself.

Versatile Chuck Ortmann punted 24 times for 723 yards in the famous 1950 "Blizzard Bowl" against Ohio State and was a vital factor in leading Michigan to the Big Ten title that season.

blocking were forgotten. Linemen were lucky to even make contact on their blocks. The ball-carriers had to go it alone, minus traction. The game soon developed into a kicking duel. Chuck Ortmann, the Michigan tailback, punted the ball 24 times, the most ever in a Big Ten game, and All-American Vic Janowicz kicked 21 times for Ohio State. Most of their punts were on third down, several on second down, and even a few on first down—hoping the snow-blinded receivers would not be able to see the ball or bobble it if they tried for it.

From whistle to gun, Michigan gained 27 yards and never made a first down. Ohio State got three first downs. Janowicz carried the ball 19 times for a net loss of 9 yards. Michigan's longest gain was a 6-yard skid around end by Ortmann. Eighteen passes were thrown by both teams. Michigan didn't complete a one, Ohio State only 3.

The Buckeyes scored first, on a 27-yard field goal by Janowicz late in the first quarter. Michigan closed the gap to 3–2 on a safety in the second period. Then, with 40 seconds remaining in the first half, the Wolverines forced the Buckeyes to punt from the 4-yard line on third down. The ball was snapped to Janowicz, and blurred, blue fingers got to him just as he swung his leg. The ball bounded off the charging Wolverine and back into the end zone. Suddenly, 22 bodies were diving into snowbanks all over the place, looking frantically for the ball. Tony Momsen, the big center, found it first and Michigan had a touchdown. That ended the scoring for the day. Final score: Michigan 9, Ohio State 3.

It was one of the weirdest games in the history of the Conference. Chuck Ortmann later told me about Leo Koceski, who held option on the other wingback position in the Michigan backfield that day. Ortmann played the entire 60 minutes and held the safety assignment on defense.

"Coach Oosterbaan always stressed to us safety men never to take our eyes off the ball," Chuck recollected. "Well, there I was, peering through that blinding gale of snow flurries trying to find that blamed football, when suddenly I heard the sharp clatter of cleats bearing down on top of me. I glanced down momentarily to see these four linemen in Ohio State jerseys coming up fast to pounce on me. Just then, the ball struck by hands and bounded away. I looked sharply to my right and saw Koceski there. The ball rolled about five paces in his direction—and stopped dead in a snow drift. 'Okay, Leo,' I yelled at him, 'you take it!' Leo was no dummy. 'Nuts!' he shouted back at me, 'you fumbled it—take it yourself!'"

Koceski kept Michigan spirits high. He was always good for a laugh. On the train going to Columbus, Coach Oosterbaan found Leo talking to Momsen in Polish.

"What's going on here?" the coach wanted to know.

"Well," Koceski explained, "I hear that Janowicz sometimes calls signals in Polish to confuse opponents and that he has taught his

One of the nine stars from the Big Ten who earned All-American recognition in 1950 was Northwestern's end Don Stonesifer, who led the conference in pass catches and, against Minnesota, set a single-game record for receptions with 13.

teammates certain numbers and phrases. Since Tony here calls the signals for us on defense, I think it would help for him to know Polish. So I'm teaching him the language."

"Leo, you don't really think you can teach Tony enough Polish to help in such a short time, do you?"

"What's the matter with you, coach?" Koceski asked. "You think we're dumb?"

While Michigan was knocking off Ohio State in the Snow Bowl—Wes Fesler later resigned as Buckeye coach for what he said were "personal reasons," but some fans claimed it was because "he just can't live with that blocked punt against Michigan"—Northwestern roared out of obscurity to make sure that the Wolverines got the Rose Bowl bid by upsetting their traditional rivals from Illinois, 14–7.

All told, it was some season. Even the cellar teams had their little fun. Minnesota, with Coach Bernie Bierman on the way out, tied Michigan, 7–7, earlier in the year, while both Indiana (3–5–1) and Purdue (2–7) deflated Frank Leahy's balloon at Notre Dame. For the

Irish, it was a case of too much preseason publicity, too much Western Conference spirit, and too little depth. They were even tied by Iowa (3–5–1).

Meanwhile, over in the Independents, Michigan State, which would begin Big Ten play in 1953, reigned supreme, with only a 34–7 loss to Maryland marring an otherwise unblemished record.

Looking back 25 years, Red Blaik said some time ago that he would have to rate that 1950 Michigan bunch as "a good team," despite its three losses and a tie. One of the defeats was to Blaik's Black Knights of Army, 26–7, on October 2, even though the Wolverines had gone into the contest 3–1, 13-point favorites.

"No outcome that fall caused greater shock," Colonel Blaik said. "It was basically an offensive-possession victory. We tore into them like wildcats. Our quick line rolled theirs back. With Vann as pilot, Bell, Uebel, and Mike Zeigler slashed and stabbed on short, medium, and long-gainers in an impressive show of infantry. It was a hot muggy day, I remember, but we thrived on it. Bell scored twice, on 10- and 48-yard runs. Their only score came on a second-period 46-yard pass. Although it was a fine team effort, we derived special satisfaction from the work of Mike Zeigler and Ski Ordway. Zeigler spent much of the summer in the hospital with a back injury that threatened to finish his football career. Ordway was one of that legion who overcame limited talent by desire. Ski was an offensive center as a plebe and yearling in the dark days of '51 and '52. Ordway's sixty-minute job against Michigan was a principal reason why we made our best defensive showing of the year. That same day we beat Michigan was also memorable for several of my former assistant coaches, Stu Holcomb and Murray Warmath. Stu's Purdue team upset Notre Dame, 27–14, to end a 13-game Irish streak, and Murray's Minnesota ran over Pittsburgh, 46–7. Our victory over Michigan was our fifth straight against them."

Some people considered it startling that Vic Janowicz won the Heisman Trophy in 1950. To do it, he had to beat out Kyle Rote, Reds Bagnell of Penn, who won the Maxwell Trophy, Babe Parilli of Kentucky, who won the Walter Camp Trophy, Bobby Reynolds of Nebraska, Johnny Bright of Drake, and such

linemen as Bud McFadin of Texas, who won the Rockne Trophy, Les Richter of California, Bob Gain of Kentucky, and Dan Foldberg of Army. Reynolds ran for 1,300 yards. Parilli passed for 1,600 yards and 23 touchdowns. Bagnell ran and passed for 1,600 yards and 14 touchdowns. Bright ran and passed for 2,400 yards and 30 touchdowns. But Reynolds was a sophomore and Bright and Parilli were juniors.

But Janowicz was only a junior, too. And the Buckeyes were just average during the Janowicz years. His personal statistics were not much better. The season he won the Heisman, he ran for only 314 yards, less than a 3-yard average, and he passed for 561 yards. He caught only one pass and intercepted only one. Two-platoon football was officially installed that season, but he did play a lot on defense. He punted for less than a 38-yard average. But he was tough, a big-play guy. He had a 50-yard pass against Pitt and a 61-yard punt return against Iowa. He blasted the opening kickoff into the end zone against the Hawkeyes. On the first play, an Iowa back fumbled; Vic recovered and ran 11 yards for a touchdown. The next time he got his hands on the ball he ran that punt back to score. Iowa fumbled again, Ohio State recovered, and Vic threw a 12-yard pass for another score. He passed for three more touchdowns and kicked 10 extra points in 11 tries as Ohio State rolled over Iowa, 83–21.

Helping to seal the Heisman for Janowicz was Ohio State's 41–7 rout of Pitt, in which Vic scored a touchdown, kicked two field goals, and threw four touchdown passes.

The Heisman Award already had been voted Janowicz when Ohio State ended its season against Michigan. "Winning the Heisman was a surprise," Vic confessed many years later. "I had to beat out Kyle Rote and Reds Bagnell. I later became friendly with Reds and he often visited me in Columbus. I'd call him No. 3 and he'd call me No. 1. The Heisman, incidentally, was the first award I ever won. I was lucky to be one of the rare ones to win it as a junior because I would never have won it as a senior, when I ran for only 376 yards, passed for 74 more and scored only one touchdown. We lost 5 of 9 games and I did not even finish in the Top 10 of the Heisman voting. Actually, I had no real chance to repeat. I'd had a fantastic year under a great coach, Wes Fesler, as a junior, but a new coach, Woody Hayes, came along my senior season, and with him came a new system. I didn't fit into his plans; he put aside passing, and it wasn't the greatest of years for me or the team."

Testifying to the calibre of competition in the Big Ten, no fewer than 10 stalwarts earned All-American recognition in 1950: Janowicz, Momsen, and center Bob McCullough, Ohio State; Don Stonesifer, the magnificent Northwestern end who topped the conference in pass receptions and whose 13 against Minnesota broke the Big Ten's single-game record; versatile Dorne Dibble, the Michigan State wingback; Sonny Grandelius, Michigan State's great halfback; Al Wahl, powerful tackle from Michigan; tackle Al Tate and guard Bob Vohaska, heart and soul of the Illinois line; and defensive halfback star Ed Withers of Wisconsin.

Though overlooked by the All-America pollsters, Wisconsin's John Coatta and Minnesota's Don Roedel got in their licks, too. Coatta's .642 percentage for pass completions established a Big Ten record, and Roedel, a guard, doubled as the busiest punter in league annals with 56 kicks in six conference games.

1951

Except for new faces and new tricks, football in the Big Ten was a carbon copy of what it had been in 1950, one of the closest races in the Conference's long and illustrious history. The championship battle went right down to the wire, with Illinois, led by Tommy O'Connell's passing and Rex Smith's catches, finally bumping Northwestern, 3–0, to qualify for an invitation to the Rose Bowl, where it stomped Stanford, 40–7.

Three of the Illini's five conference victories were won by the total margin of 14 points. Ray Eliot believed that his philosophy of "the proper state of mind" was the difference.

Looking back on 1951, he said, "When you can get the boys in the proper state of mind, you've got a winner. I'm thinking now of a game we played at Champaign against Wisconsin. The Badgers outweighed us 21 pounds per man. I had a young linebacker named Chuck Boyle. D'you know how much one yard is? Thirty-six inches, three feet—the shortest darn thing, yet the longest when you're trying to get the football into the end zone. One yard.

Quarterback Tommy O'Connell took charge of the attack and guard Chuck Studley the defense while leading Illinois to the 1951 Big Ten championship. Tommygun Tommy completed 108 passes out of 191 attempts for 1,308 yards to establish a new league record.

Johnny Coatta took his Wisconsin team back into the huddle, and as Johnny was about to enter the huddle, that kid Boyle of mine, 187 pounds and meaner than a boot full of bob wire, shouted at him, 'Hey, Johnny, send Ameche at me!' *Send Ameche at me.* Can you just see the audacity of that little feller? Hell, most of us would have wished Alan Ameche had gone North someplace. Do you get the impact of the situation, sir? Do you get the impact? *Send Ameche at me.* Seventy-thousand people looking at us, one yard away from something big. And Johnny Coatta sent Ameche at Boyle—and Chuck nailed him for a three-yard loss. And when the four downs were over, instead of the ball crossing the goal, it rested on the six-yard line.

"Sir, one yard from the winning of the game. One yard from the Big Ten championship. One yard from the Rose Bowl championship. One yard from success or failure. One yard from distinction or nothing. And in this game of life you play, that well could be one inch; or not turning the right corner, or not having the guts to open the right door; or pitying yourself by saying I can't go on. One yard—yes, how can I do it? One yard from being somebody."

For the second straight year, Wisconsin was a stout challenger all the way. Michigan, Ohio

State, and Purdue, which won four out of five league games, got in their licks, too.

The only flaw in an otherwise perfect season for Illinois was at Columbus in mid-November when the Scarlet and Grey held them to a scoreless tie. That set the stage for the final game at Northwestern, seven days later, where Sam Rebecca placekicked Illinois into the Rose Bowl from the 26-yard line for a 3–0 triumph.

All-American John Karras, All-American Chuck Boerio, fullback Bill Tate (5.6-yard rushing average), and quarterback O'Connel (62 completions of 120 pass attempts) were the big weapons for the Illini. The split T formation made a tremendous impression upon Big Ten coaches in 1951, especially upon those at Ohio State, Iowa, and Michigan State. A big, flamboyant reader of von Clausewitz and Emerson's essays named Wayne Woodrow Hayes had replaced Wes Fesler at Columbus. He inherited good material, including Vic Janowicz, but it was not to be Ohio State's year.

Northwestern (2–4 in the conference) made it two in a row over a good Navy eleven, 16–7. Which provoked Eddie Erdelatz, the Annapolis coach, to point out how difficult it is to be a football coach at Crabtown. He is torn between two responsibilities: the Navy brass and academicians on one side, and his football policies on the other. "After all," Erdelatz told me after losing to Northwestern, "the primary mission of the Naval Academy is to develop Midshipmen morally, mentally and physically and to imbue them with the highest ideals of duty, honor and loyalty in order to provide graduates who are dedicated to a career of Naval Service and have potential for future development in mind and character to assume the highest responsibilities of command, citizenship and government. Yet despite all of the restrictions imposed upon our athletes, we're expected to win for Navy."

Eddie Erdelatz won most of the time. In nine seasons at Annapolis (1950–1958), he won 48 games, lost 26, tied 8; twelve of those defeats coming in his first two seasons, while he was still getting the Navy football program reorganized and firmed up. He was 5–3–1 against Army, and he won his only two bowl games. What was his secret? "Hard work," he told me. "Hard, *frustrating* work."

One day, Larry Merchant, then of the Philadelphia *Daily News,* sat talking with Eddie in the coach's office. Larry casually turned to Eddie and said, "Coach, would you like to discuss the problems of coaching at a Service school?" Erdelatz, just as casually, said, "*On* record or *off* the record?" Larry replied, "Everything I do is *on* the record." Smiling, Erdelatz said, "Everything at Annapolis is great." Then, after a short pause, added, "Now, do you want me to talk *off* the record?" End of interview.

Though they were still two years away from Big Ten football competition, the Spartans of Michigan State already had begun their Golden Age of Football. In 1951, they won nine straight games and finished second to Tennessee in the national polls. This was the first Michigan State team to finish with a perfect

Don Coleman, 180 pounds, was the lightest regular tackle in the Big Ten in 1951, yet he was so talented that he made the National Football Hall of Fame and saw his jersey number retired at Michigan State.

Michigan State partisans picked this 88-yard touchdown romp by Dick Panin on the first offensive play in a 1951 contest against Notre Dame as one of the most spectacular runs in Spartan history. State won, 35–0.

record since 1913. Among their victims were Michigan (25–0), Ohio State (24–20), and Notre Dame (35–0).

Coach Biggie Munn was the first to admit that the Spartans' 9–0 record was misleading.

"We had to come from behind or break through a tie late in the game in six of the nine games," he said. "We got into trouble time after time and then had the resourcefulness and perhaps good luck, too, to come on and win. It was a team of opportunists, a hot and cold bunch that had a tough time putting a complete good game together. One exception was the Notre Dame game in which I got 60 solid minutes of football out of my players. More typical was the Ohio State game, in which we trailed, 20–10, with only 10 minutes left to play, and still we came on to win, 24–20. The clincher was one of the most dramatic touchdowns I ever saw. With about two minutes remaining, Tom Yewcic, our sophomore left halfback, was sent into the game with one express play in mind. We had to score and score quickly. The key play came after a decoy play was run off, and Yewcic fired a long, long pass from the one sideline diagonally across the field to Al Dorow on the other. Al took the ball on the 11 and ran it across the goal line. The play covered 28 yards. Even then Dorow had to elude three Ohio State tacklers to score."

The undefeated Spartans, although not yet

Fullback Bill Reichardt was the Big Ten's Most Valuable Player in 1951, despite the fact Iowa finished dead last in the standings.

officially a Big Ten member, equalled Ohio State's record of four All-American choices in 1951, as the various pickers named Dorow, end Bob Carey, safety Jim Ellis, and Don Coleman, the great tackle who promptly had his No. 78 retired after earning the title as "the finest lineman in Michigan State history."

Other Big Ten stars with the "All-American"

Wisconsin quarterback John Coatta was the Big Ten's leading passer in both 1950 and 1951.

Speedy halfback Johnny Karras, of Illinois, was one of nine Conference stars to gain places on the various 1951 All-American selections.

stamp on them included halfback Johnny Karras and the ball-hawking Al Brosky of Illinois; ends Lowell Perry (Michigan), Leo Sugar (Purdue), Pat O'Donahue (Wisconsin), and Hal Faverty (Wisconsin)—the largest contingent ever selected from one conference at the same position; and Bill Reichardt (Iowa), the hard-smashing fullback.

Down at Madison, they were also talking about a bull-like young freshman named Alan Ameche. He was the first yearling in history to lead the Big Ten in rushing (774 yards, a 5.3 average). Before he was through, they'd be calling him The Horse.

Outside the conference, debates were heating up about the future of college football. At New Haven, Connecticut, Robert A. Hall, Yale's progressive athletic director, gave me 15 ways that the game should be de-emphasized. The list included (1) the abolishment of athletic scholarships, (2) the elimination of organized practice out of season, and (3) no more postseason games between college teams.

The movement against "pressure football" at the college-president level definitely was under way.

"The superstructure of college athletics may be full of termites," Bob Hall told me, "but the base is sound. All the colleges have to do is get back on an athletics-for-all policy, and quit wasting football receipts on athletic scholarships. Countless boys who had athletic scholarships became fine, upstanding citizens, but a free ride because the boy is a star athlete puts emphasis where it very definitely should not be. This stuff about helping a poor boy is a lot of bunk. If a boy wants an education badly enough, he can find a way to get it."

Meanwhile, the Pacific Coast Conference (now PAC-8) was advocating two moves: Ending out-of-season practice and the exclusion of the two-platoon system. Bob Hall said he

Gangway for Alan (The Horse) Ameche. Seen here tearing the Purdue line apart, the 6-foot, 215-pound Wisconsin fullback should have won the Heisman Trophy in his sophomore or junior year, but had to wait until he was a senior to get it. In four years on the Badger varsity, 1951–1954, Ameche played 55 minutes a game most games. He averaged nearly 5 yards per carry and scored a total of 25 touchdowns.

could go along with the PCC on both counts. "But," he wanted to know, "why doesn't it also put an end to New Year's Day Bowl games between college teams? I realize that post-season games serve worthy community and charitable purposes, but I object to coaches being rated according to how many teams they've put in a Bowl. The coach's prestige depends entirely on his ability to land his team in a Bowl. To accomplish this, he has to re-cruit, and that costs money. Then he simply has to make a Bowl to pay the bill."

Bob Hall wasn't saying he would outlaw Bowl games. He would merely alter their character, so as not to upset the academic applecart. He approved of the Christmas Shrine East-West and North-South All-Star games for crippled children in San Francisco and Miami. They were between seniors from many teams and played during the holiday va-cation. "But I consider it a shame that outright promotions involving college teams knock the charity games out of the traditional New Year's Day date," Hall said. "Maybe the various Bowls should arrange similar All-Star matches, or engage professional teams. Anything, as long as they leave college football alone."

1952

Prior to the opening of the 1952 season, NEA sent me out to the Midwest to size the teams up. In my dispatch back to the New York office, I wrote:

Wisconsin and Illinois are the top choices in the Western Conference. Michigan State, which joins the Big 10 in football next year, and Notre Dame shape up as the best of the Independents.

Handicappers tell you to circle Oct. 4 on the calendar. Wisconsin and Illinois, the defending champion, collide that early in what visionaries flatly declare will be the championship game.

The Illini grabbed this one a year ago, and though Ray Eliot's agents are super-charged again the Bad-gers boast a psychological weapon. Illinois, win or lose, can't go to the Rose Bowl, a factor which has been known to hurt Big 10 teams. Wisconsin holds a convincing trump card in Alan Ameche, a human pile-driver who opens up gaps big enough for Primo Carnera to wade through. With the Madison Mad-man operating behind a rugged and resolute line, Coach Ivy Williamson blends his infantry attack with Jerry Witt, a slippery-snake-hipped halfback.

The Badgers line up against Ohio State a week after entertaining Illinois, and this could mean

trouble. Vic Janowicz is gone, but the Buckeyes have Johnny Borton, a sophomore, and Tony Cur-cillo to inject life in 1951's punchless machine, now accustomed to the T.

Purdue retains 29 king-size veterans from last year's team, which finished second. Dale Samuels, the whiz-bang quarterback who has accounted for 17 touchdowns via the air, sparks the attack. Given a full head of steam, the Boilermakers might catch the Pasadena Special.

Bennie Oosterbaan, grand vizier at Michigan, has entrusted Duncan MacDonald, a clever sophomore quarterback, with air and ground operations.

Paul (Duz) Giel most certainly lived up to his nickname at Minnesota last season. The unadver-tised soph smashes ground-gaining records, punts and plays defense. But it takes more than a one-man gang to get to the Rose Bowl.

Northwestern expects to be stronger than it has been since it romped to the Rose Bowl four years ago, but, then, everybody else is better, too. Bernie Crimmins, the old Notre Damer, inherits a tight first team at Indiana, but lacks depth. Iowa losses were especially heavy and new coach Forest Evashevski is starting from scratch. No doubt he'll wish he was back at Washington State before the season is over.

Biggie Munn is grooming another powerhouse at Michigan State. The Spartans, lavishly stocked at all key positions, are taking dead aim at another na-tional championship. They figure to extend their unbeaten skein from 15 to 24. Men to watch are backfield veterans Tom Yewcic and Capt. McAuliffe and Paul Dekker . . .

In the very first weekend of Conference competition, Indiana lost to Ohio State, 33 to 13. Bernie Crimmins was asked if he thought the Hoosiers would win any of their remaining games.

"Yes and no," replied the new Indiana coach.

"What do you mean, yes and no?" he was asked.

"Yes, I think we will, but no, we won't."

The Hoosiers managed to scramble to a 2–7 record.

After blasting Indiana, Woody Hayes ex-perienced troubles of his own at Columbus. It seems that Coach Hayes committed the unfor-givable sin of losing to Purdue, 21–14, in Ohio State's second game of the season. That old familiar cry—Goodbye, Woody!—shook the housetops around Columbus. It was time for action. Hayes had lost to Purdue and there was nothing to do but can the coach.

"Give him another chance," someone said.

"Sure," cried the wolves, "we'll give him another chance—at another school."

But then the Buckeyes popped up like a jack-in-the-box and belted touted Wisconsin, 23–14, and life around town was considerably brighter for Woody again—until Iowa came along and upset the Scarlet and Grey, 8 to 0. Compounding the defeat was the fact that the Hawkeyes installed the split T only five days before the game. "Perhaps it isn't a bad idea to junk your offense after each game for a new one," cracked Iowa Coach Forest Evashevski.

Around the league, Wisconsin and Purdue shared the Big Ten title in 1952, the first time the Badgers finished at the top since 1912. Wisconsin then received the Rose Bowl assignment on the strength of its superior overall record (6–2–1 vs. 4–3–2). At Pasadena, Southern California won, 7–0.

The big honors in the nation went to Michigan State. For the second season in a row, the Spartans had a perfect 9–0 record and finished No. 1 in both news service polls.

After losing to Michigan State, 48–6, perhaps Texas A & M's Coach Ray George summed up the Spartans best: "It isn't so much what their first and second teams do to you—but the third, fourth and fifth teams simply kill you!"

Biggie Munn's troops got the job done innumerable ways. There was the single wing, the double wing, the straight T, winged T, split T, short punt, and several random variations that Coach Munn had put together. They did it with a pony backfield behind a light, inexperienced line. The biggest man in the backfield was captain McAuliffe at 190 pounds, and Jim Neal's 215 pounds were the heaviest in the line. Yet the Spartans seldom were in trouble.

"Only twice were we seriously threatened," Coach Munn said later. "In our second game of the season, against Oregon State, we needed another chance on a penalty when we missed a field goal attempt with seven seconds left, but Gene Lekenta made the second chance good with two seconds left on the clock. Later, against Purdue, we needed an interception to protect our 14–7 lead in the fourth quarter. Otherwise, we rolled along pretty well on our way to the National title."

Coaches who scouted the 1952 Spartans called them the finest college football squad they had ever seen. Roy Simmons, who had been with Syracuse since his quarterbacking days (1922–23–24), said the splendid Illinois defense units of 1951 might have been comparable to those of the 1952 Spartans, but not the offensive platoons.

"You ought to give the Michigan State players a saliva test," Simmons said. Ben Schwartzwalder, the head coach at Syracuse, joined in. "There may be more formidable personnel on other college teams," Ben said, "but as a combination the Spartans can't go wrong. I have never set eyes on a stronger college team." Michigan State manhandled Syracuse, 48 to 7. "The Spartans aren't going to be softened up any when they join the Big Ten with full stature next year," Schwartzwalder added. "Our boys ate with them after our game, and their seniors admitted that the sophomores are better because they have more speed. The only difference between the three offensive and defensive platoons is game experience. Munn has 22 backs and they all run and hang back of interference until they see daylight. The ends and linemen were running backs in high school, too, so run right along with them."

The highly complex Munn system required lots of candlepower behind the horsepower to move the football. "Our offense lines up in an unbalanced T," explained Munn at the time. "The play can go off from there, or the team may shift into the single wing, left or right. The system incorporates the split T, double wing, winged T, the buck lateral, and some other things. Basically, the blocking assignments don't change with the varied backfield patterns, but that only adds to the other side's confusion."

In Munn's hyped and complex system, football was no longer a Broadway for the scholastic jerk. The accent on split-second timing and thinking under conditions that put the premium on physical violence was no longer a pastime for a dunce. "You don't advance the ball by sheer weight of numbers in platoon football," Munn said. "Fresh players are constantly flooding the field. Mental and physical coordination is the answer. Football today is a game of chess at high speed. Dullards only mess up the works."

Thirteen members of the 1952 Spartans were B students. Johnny Wilson, the defensive left halfback, was a Rhodes Scholarship candidate as a journalism undergraduate. It was good to see the emphasis on the books instead of the bucks for a change.

Just how scientific football had become was brought home to me when I put a stopwatch on the Spartans and their opponents. I discovered that the ball was generally in action only 12 minutes. The other 48 minutes were spent calling signals, talking things over in the huddle, and otherwise gathering up steam to put the ball in play. Subsequently, each side was on the move only six minutes. Incredible? Not by Lynn Waldorf's calculations. By now, Pappy Waldorf was coaching at California, and thinking about how much the game had changed since he got into the business, he said, "Most teams are in possession of the ball only 13 times during an entire game. Top-flight teams, of course, are able to hold the ball longer than six minutes of actual play, but the run-o'-the-mill teams don't exceed that total. When I was at Northwestern and we played Notre Dame in 1946, the Irish held on to the ball for 12½ minutes in the second quarter. During that spell, they ran off 23 plays, drove down to our one-yard line, and yet failed to punch it across. That's what I call ball-control."

Brigadier General Robert Neyland was another clock-watcher. He demanded precision and split-second timing. The Tennessee coach was known to order a certain play to be run in practice 500 times prior to using it in a game. Before the Alabama game in 1952, Neyland detailed one of his assistants to sit in the stands and clock the 'Bama punter in practice. The idea was to record the time it took the kicker to get off his punts. After 10 punts, the assistant discovered that half of them were timed in 2.2 seconds, the other half in 2.3. Armed with this information, Neyland immediately organized a punt-blocking formation which would send one of his linemen into the Alabama punter's path at precisely 2.3 seconds. "If he takes 2.3 seconds on any kick in the game, he's a dead duck," Neyland declared. Alabama's first kick was 2.3. Tennessee defenders blocked it, setting up a touchdown, and the Volunteers went on to win, 20–0. That was generating a lot of mileage out of the Pappy Waldorf figures.

Don McAuliffe, Frank Kush, and Dick Tamburo represented Michigan State in the 1952 All-American sweepstakes. Six other Big Ten stars joined them: Paul Giel (Minnesota and Conference MVP), Mike Takacs (Ohio State, guard), Bernie Flowers (Purdue, end), Joe Collier (Northwestern, end), Dave Suminski (Wisconsin, tackle), and Don Voss (Wisconsin, end). Biggie Munn was named Coach of the Year.

Back in New York, after Harry Grayson, Murray Olderman, and I had picked our annual NEA All-American team, the letters started pouring in. "After the All-America squads come the All-America squawks," growled Sports Editor Grayson. Typical of the letters we received was this one from Harry E. Kidd, Sports Editor of *The Daily Gazette* of Sterling, Illinois:

I don't know whether a guy is nuts to try picking an All-America team, but I guess if you are nuts it might help. Perhaps I'm nuts, but I don't go in for all-star picks. You hurt too many boys, who because of circumstances are not named. I realize you cannot name them all, but I'd rather pass it all up than hurt even one, and in a nation-wide pick, you certainly hurt plenty of them. Besides, many people are ready to cut your heart out.

Personally, I was interested in Max Schmaling, Purdue fullback from Sterling High. Midwest newspapers and commentators repeatedly said he had not received the publicity he deserved. Going into Purdue's final game with Indiana, Schmaling was third in Big Ten yardage, but one yard short of Ted Kress, the Michigan halfback, at 443 to 442. He has been a workhorse. Schmaling from the start was billed as being of All-America caliber, and he lived up to the billing despite the fact that he was not given the opportunity to score when he repeatedly carried the ball to within the 10 and even the 5-yard line. Yet not even Honorable Mention. How unfair can a picker be? And how about Tommy O'Connell, the Illinois quarterback, who broke Western Conference passing records (306 yards on 22 completions out of 34 against Iowa)? Also John Ryan, receiver of most of Tommy's passes, along with Rex Smith?

Despite the fact that football was well into the platoon era in 1952, one national slick-paper magazine was still coming out with only one single-platoon All-American team. Proof that this tended to stress tackling linemen was the fact that six of its seven were primarily defensive men. Three of the backs were strictly attackers. The fourth was best known for scoring touchdowns.

In reply to Harry E. Kidd, Sports Editor Grayson wrote: "I agree that the supply of All-America football candidates far exceeds the demand even with the positions now doubled to 22. But even if the selectors were naming 222, there still wouldn't be enough places to satisfy everybody. But, then, I guess nobody will ever succeed in making All-America teams unpopular with the customers."

While there were arguments aplenty over the All-American business, nobody challenged the longest run of the season. That occurred during the Penn–Penn State frosh game. Penn State scored and then kicked the extra point. Grasping the ball as it dropped into the end zone bleachers was a small boy, about as big as 30 cents worth of steak. He was last seen disappearing over the fence.

1953

After nearly a decade of two-platooning and super-specialization, the year 1953 saw the sudden return of one-platoon football, although in a somewhat modified form. Football fans seemed to enjoy watching the players prove that they could block as well as tackle, or vice versa, and if there was any deterioration in the quality of play it was not visible to the untutored eye. In fact, 1953 was notable for its number of close, exciting games and there were a gratifying number of upsets. However, over the full course of the season, the strong teams established their strength and the weak fell by the wayside. Despite fears to the contrary, the return to two-way player operation did not seriously upset the natural balance of power. At the end of the season, even the viewers-with-alarm seemed to be softening in their opposition to restricted substitution. With the players more familiar with double-duty assignments and talent-rich squads employing alternate two-way units, performance improved steadily.

Some coaches, however, were divided on the question of going back to the single platoon. Red Blaik, who had been so successful with pure two-platoon at West Point during the 1940s, was dead set against the changeover.

"My fellow coaches fail year after year to get the rules committee to accept their recommendations for unlimited substitution because the faculty people, who appoint and control the rules committee, go on record against it," Colonel Blaik said at the time. "One of the main arguments of the faculty people is that two-platoon ball would require more players. Why, then, in making their pitch, have not the coaches precluded that argument by concurrently proposing that a rule be adopted preventing more than 36 players to suit up for a game? No coach is going to recruit a man he can't suit up, be it even, as old Herman Hickman used to say, three-platoon ball, with the third platoon to go to class."

On the other side, Brigadier General Bob Neyland said he was positive that the return to one-platoon football was just what the fans ordered. The former Tennessee coach was on the committee that abolished the two-platoon system.

"On the day before we went into our meeting," Neyland told me, "the waitress at breakfast, knowing we were on the rules committee, said she hoped we did something about the two-platoon system. Later, I was riding in a taxicab, and the driver remarked that he hoped we would abolish the two-platoon. And then at lunch, the hostess at the hotel said she hoped we did something about the two-platoon. Some coaches may have objected, but I knew how the fans felt."

For every coach's pitch against the new deal, there were players with perfect rebuttals.

"If you're in shape, you play both ways without getting tired," said Johnny Lujack, the 1947 Heisman winner who did it for Notre Dame. "The backs have little to do on most defensive plays, so get a rest when the other side has the ball. Offensively, linemen often don't do much more than lunge at opponents, particularly when the play is going to the opposite side. So they rest when you have the ball."

Bruce Bosley, the West Virginia guard, and halfback Don Miller of Southern Methodist liked the idea that now it was every man for himself all the way down the line. They stressed the fact that the athlete in good condition is freer from injuries.

George Timberlake, Southern California lineman, said that if he were a fan he would be more interested in watching players who could do everything. And Don Fullam, the Navy end, felt the main improvement was that the fans would now have a chance to become better acquainted with the players. "It will be a lot easier to follow the lineups instead of having to unscramble a mass of players every time the ball changes hands," Midshipman Fullam said. "Teamwork, the real purpose of football, has finally been restored. In the two-platoon system, it was hard to get the feeling of genuine teamwork because the units were so completely separate during practice."

At NEA, we surveyed the players in the Big Ten, and of the more than a hundred we contacted, a whopping 73 percent agreed they got as much or more pleasure from playing under single-platoon rules. "Limited substitution brings the game back to the players," one big Minnesota tackle told me. "It injects an individual-against-individual element. Guys who like physical contact will especially get a big bang out of the new rule."

Some teams were able to adjust to the single-platoon faster than others. One of these was unbeaten Maryland, named No. 1 in both major news service polls. The selection of the Terrapins brought anguished howls from Notre Dame fans. In fairness, the Irish probably had at least an equal claim to the mythical national title. Their season-ending tie with Iowa, however, caused them to lose out to Maryland in both the AP and UP voting.

It was a great year for Big Ten football. Three conference members—Michigan State, Illinois, and Iowa—finished in the Top Ten. The Hawkeyes made a big score in the balloting with their 14–14 tie of the Irish, who went into the contest unbeaten. The pressures of keeping a 31-game victory streak alive imposed a crushing strain upon Frank Leahy. He had collapsed during halftime of the Georgia Tech game, and doctors were pleading with him to give up coaching. The Iowa game marked the end of Leahy's career, one of the most successful in all history, and his players vowed to send him out in a blaze of glory. Leading the way was Johnny Lattner, the 1953 Heisman winner who did just about everything—run, pass, catch passes, and kick. His forte was making the big interception or tackle when it was most needed. A flawless 60-minute performer, he bore a striking similarity to Johnny Lujack.

But against Iowa, it appeared the unbeaten Notre Dame string was about to be broken. The Hawkeyes led by a touchdown with time running out in the first half. A Notre Dame player feigned injury, thus enabling the Irish to gain a few precious seconds. They used them well, tying the score. Then in the final moments of the fourth quarter, after Iowa had fought back to regain the lead, the identical situation arose again, and the Irish managed to salvage a tie with the furious Hawkeyes.

The tactics used by Notre Dame in deliberately faking injuries provoked national resentment. The Irish were criticized for poor sportsmanship. But the score stood: Iowa 14, Notre Dame 14.

The Big Ten Conference race narrowed down to a tie between Michigan State and Illinois, both with 5–1 league records, but the Spartans got to go to the Rose Bowl in their first official season in the Conference because the Illini had been out to Pasadena two years previously and the last-to-go rule gave the invitation to Michigan State. Either team would have made a superior representative. Ray Eliot's squad led the Big Ten in scoring, first downs, rushing, and total yards gained. Two great sophomore halfbacks—J. C. Caroline and Mickey Bates—were the workhorses in the backfield. Caroline led the league in rushing, Bates in scoring.

What about Michigan State?

"The key to our 8 and 1 record and 28 to 20 victory over UCLA in the Rose Bowl was the remarkable adjustment my players made to one-platoon football," Biggie Munn said. "For three years, we had been strictly a two-platoon team. Except for a few third-team subs, there wasn't a man who reported for football in 1953 who had played both offense and defense in college. Here was a terrific challenge for our coaches and players alike. Fellows like Captain Don Dohoney, LeRoy Bolden, Billy Wells, Tom Yewcic, Larry Fowler, Jim Neal, Evan Slonac and Ellis Duckett, established stars under the two-platoon system, had to start all over again with the lowliest sophomores in learning the game all over again.

"I think Dohoney was the best example of how well the boys made the switch from two-platoon football. Don was one of the great defensive ends in the nation as a soph and junior. Suddenly he was being asked to play offensive end, too, something he had worked at but little in high school. He'd never played a minute of offense in college. Yet he made the adjustment so well and so quickly that he won All-American honors.

"The main strength of our 1953 team was a tremendous desire to win and the ability it engendered to come back from seeming defeat. The team did this on several occasions, the most notable example being in the Texas Christian game, in which we were behind by 19–7 late in the third period, and the Rose Bowl game, in which we were down to UCLA by 14–0 before starting to move. Another strength was balance and depth in material, particularly in the backfield. Our 'pony backfield' was, I think, one of the finest units that ever played for a college team. Anyone of the four—Bolden, Wells, Yewcic, Slonac—could blow a ball game wide open, and one or more usually did so."

As Coach Munn pointed out, it was no one-day job in the development of a two-way football player in 1953. Ron Drzewiecki, for example, stressed the frustration he had learning how to block. Against Cincinnati that season, the Marquette halfback threw what he thought was a terrific block.

"How'd you like that block?" he asked his quarterback, returning to the huddle.

"Great," replied the signal-caller, "but you were supposed to *carry* the ball on that play!"

The Big Ten was handsomely represented on the various All-America's in 1953, with Michigan State once more leading the way with three: Don Dohoney, end; LeRoy Bolden, halfback; and Larry Fowler, tackle. Paul Giel was again named at halfback from Minnesota, and for the second straight season won the Conference MVP award. He barely lost out to Johnny Lattner for the Heisman Trophy. Dale Warner, a teammate, told me recently in Minneapolis that, in his opinion, Giel was the greatest football player in Gopher history.

"Keep in mind," Dale said, "that Paul had no team to help him very much. He did it all practically on his own, whereas Bruce Smith, for example, had a super bunch behind him. I think his greatest game in college was against Michigan, in 1953. We beat them, 22–0, and all he did was handle the ball a record 53 times, gain 112 yards on the ground, complete 13 of 18 passes for another 169 yards, score 2 touchdowns and pass for another. In his last season, he called signals, averaged more than a

Paul Giel topped off a brilliant collegiate career at Minnesota in 1953 by earning All-American honors in both football and baseball. Drafted by the Chicago Bears, he turned down George Halas' offer to sign with the New York baseball Giants.

hundred yards per game, was a one-man gang. He stands alone in the annals of Minnesota football."

While Minnesota had its Paul Giel, Wisconsin had its Alan Ameche, who, in 1953, ran for more than 900 yards as a junior. He was another of those college workhorses who played 55 minutes a game most games. A 6-foot, 215-pounder, he was a powerful, pile-driving fullback who ran almost straight up, and with good speed. It was a peculiar running style—something of an upright galloping stride with knees pumping, arms flailing and nothing but moving muscle to grab. With his head up and his neck straight, he looked as if he would be easy to hit. In fact, one pro scout watching him run at Wisconsin, said, "He'd get killed if he ever tried that with the pros." It never happened in the Big Ten, though, because, strong and unexpectedly quick, Ameche could cut away, move in hard, change direction, and take punishment. Style had nothing to do with any of this. Ameche's running reminded many football people of Frankie Sinkwich. Ameche had that same duck-walk running motion, that wide-braced footing that kept him from getting knocked over easily. And he could "run up," that is, gather himself at the last moment before crunching into the line or jarring against a linebacker. Where most fullbacks banged into a defense head first, Ameche put his body behind one of his good-sized shoulders and rammed. In slow motion, it looked like a fellow pushing against a jammed door.

There were some things his coaches might have changed about Ameche's style, but because he seemed to be able to handle himself anyway, they decided to leave him alone. What probably bothered them more than anything else about his running was his footwork. The Wisconsin attack was quick and precise. Every step of a play was predetermined and clocked. But Ameche, with his big feet, would overstep in his moves toward the line. Going off tackle, for example, where the fullback was supposed to make his cut with his rear foot and then, in three steps, be at the line, Ameche would cut with his front foot and get to the line in four steps. Badger coaches weren't too fussy about it, though. Instead of forcing him to cut with that rear foot, they just lined him up a step closer to the line. That way, they were able to maintain their close timing and Ameche was able to keep his unorthodox running habit.

Wisconsin was smack in the middle of the Conference dog fight until the very last hour of the season, when Minnesota battled Ameche and the Badgers to a 21–21 tie, costing them one-third share of the championship.

Other all-stars from the Big Ten were J. C. Caroline, Joe Collier (Northwestern, end), and Jerry Hilgenberg (Iowa, center). Hilgenberg was the first Hawkeye to receive All-American recognition since 1940.

1954

In its second season of two-platoon football after a long spell of two-way specialization, college football offered another season of thrills, upsets, and glowing performances. Fans, players, and most coaches agreed that the game benefitted from the reinstated requirements that a varsity hero should block as well as tackle. A year older now, the athletes obviously discharged their dual responsibilities with greater efficiency.

There was a hung jury as to the top team of 1954. Ohio State, with its first perfect record (9–0) since 1944, was the No. 1 choice in the Associated Press poll. UCLA received the nod in the United Press balloting. The Uclans and Oklahoma, everybody's third choice, were also undefeated. Notre Dame, Navy, Mississippi, Army, Arkansas, Wisconsin, and Maryland rounded out the nation's Top Ten.

Alan Ameche, the Wisconsin fullback, won the Heisman Trophy and was generally acclaimed Player of the Year. This despite the fact that he was hobbled by an injury and gained less than 700 yards as a senior. In three seasons at Madison, however, "The Horse" galloped for a total of 3,212 yards, a national record at the time. He averaged almost 5 yards a carry and scored 25 touchdowns. His Heisman was clearly a career reward. Sixteen times he ran for 100 yards or more in games. Once, against Minnesota, he ran for more than 200 yards, including a run of 42 yards. He also had runs of 41, 43, 47, 54, and 64 yards in his career, sometimes running right over tacklers. A linebacker on defense, he had 14 unassisted tackles against Penn State as a junior to demonstrate how well-rounded he was.

For the first time since 1944, Ohio State won undisputed claim to the Big Ten championship and was the first to win seven Conference games since Lonnie Stagg's 1913 Chicago champions played their entire schedule in the league.

The Buckeyes' perfect season was totally unanticipated. In the preseason ratings they had been completely ignored in one forecast, were rated 20th in a second, 15th in a third, and 10th in a fourth. The rivalry between Ohio State and UCLA extended to their coaches in the Coach of the Year race. When the votes were counted up, Red Sanders was first and Woody Hayes second.

The achievement of the 1954 Buckeyes was all the greater when you considered that they lost three times in 1953. From the failure of 1953 they grew into one of the finest teams in Ohio State history. In his fourth year at Columbus, Woody's offense was keyed to a former local high school star who reminded Ohio State alumni of Chick Harley. What Howard "Hopalong" Cassady had in common with Chick was the ability to turn a game around on one play. Twice he did this in 1954 to snatch victory from defeat.

In the Wisconsin game the unbeaten Badgers and their crushing fullback, Alan Ameche, led 7 to 3 and were pounding on the Ohio State door for 6 more points. Cassady, however, intercepted a pass on his 12-yard line and ran it all the way back for the go-ahead touchdown. This sudden reversal destroyed the Badgers' composure and the Buckeyes went on to win by 17 points.

In the finale against Michigan, Cassady ran 60 yards after Ohio State had made a magnificent goal line stand late in the game. His sprint set up the touchdown that broke a deadlock and gave Ohio State a perfect season.

Fans and journalists criticized Hayes for lack of imagination in his offense. The scornful phrase of the day was "three yards and a cloud of dust," but those who had to defend against

With a football tucked under one arm, Howard (Hopalong) Cassady could fly like the wind. He sparked Ohio State to the national championship in 1954, then led the Buckeyes to a second straight unbeaten Conference championship in 1955 as he became the league's fourth player to win the Heisman Trophy. His own son, Craig, starred as an open-side defensive halfback for the 1975 champion Bucks.

the Ohio State bulldozer gave it grudging respect. Hayes liked to batter opponents with his fullbacks moving behind devastating blocking. In Jim Parker he had one of the all-time great guards, and whenever a vital yard was needed, the backs followed him and always got it. The running quarterback was another hallmark of the Ohio State offense. There was little need to pass, Hayes believed, as long as the ball could be moved on the ground. The strategy bored the spectators but it won football games.

The Legend of Woody Hayes was just starting to grow now. He made his first contentious headlines in his first Rose Bowl appearance on New Year's Day against Southern California. To begin with, it had rained heavily just before the contest, and the field was uncommonly soggy by Pasadena standards. "And it's not going to get any better," Woody growled, "with those two marching bands prancing around on it. Let's keep them off the grass."

Rose Bowl officials weren't sure they had heard him correctly? How was that again, Coach?

"Listen," Woody told them, "millions of people saw them on television this morning during your Rose Parade, so who cares if they don't strut their stuff on the football field at halftime? The field is already ankle-deep in mud. Let's save what's left for the football players."

Bandsmen from both Ohio State and Southern California were shocked. They had worked for a month polishing up their acts. The hell with Woody Hayes! Woody was overruled.

There was even more commotion several hours later when Woody tangled with Pacific Coast sports writers. He had previously angered them during the pregame practice period by forbidding them to talk to his players. Then to their frustration he refused to let the writers interview the Buckeyes after they smashed the Trojans, 20 to 7. "Nobody talks to my kids," was the Woody Hayes philosophy. Equally odious, as far as the reporters were concerned, Woody kept them waiting 20 minutes for the traditional postgame interview. When he finally walked into the pressroom, he dropped another bomb.

"There are at least four or five teams in the Big Ten that could have whipped your Trojans today," he told them.

The West Coast press corps was outraged. That goddamn Woody Hayes! Such a lousy winner! Downgrading the Pacific Coast schools that way!! Mr. Hayes had launched his career as the most unpopular coach ever to visit Los Angeles. Paul Zimmerman, the football writer for the New York *Post*, pretty well summed up everybody's attitude toward Woody in this fashion: "I sustain two views of him," Paul said. "One is of Woody as a football coach, and one as a man whom I as a writer would have to cover on my job. I know how Woody Hayes coaches football, and if I were a young player I'd give my left testicle to play for him. But I also know his general opinion of the press, and as a sports writer you couldn't pay me enough to cover him on a regular basis."

When he came right down to it, Woody Hayes didn't give a damn what the writers thought of him—and he didn't give a damn what anybody thought about his not giving a damn. That, he figured, took care of that.

All-American tight end Ron Kramer of Michigan demonstrated his pass-catching finesse in 1954 with this game-winning circus snare against Iowa. The Wolverines won, 14–13.

Both Hopalong Cassady and Alan "The Horse" Ameche were unanimous All-Americans in 1954; ditto Cal Jones (Iowa, guard), Art Walker (Michigan, tackle), Tom Bettis (Purdue, guard), and Bob McNamara (Minnesota, halfback).

Two new Big Ten scoring records were registered as Iowa's Eddie Vincent dashed 96 yards for the longest touchdown from scrimmage, and Billy Lowe, of Wisconsin, intercepted an Iowa pass and ran it back 98 yards for a touchdown.

1955

The 1955 Ohio State squad started out as though it was to be as much of a disappointment as the 1954 crew had been a surprise. It lost to Stanford in its second game, 6 to 0, and then to Duke on the fourth Saturday, 20–14, but at the end of the season the Buckeyes were Big Ten champions for the second straight season and No. 6 in the national polls. Hopalong Cassady won the Heisman, the third Ohio State player to get it, and Woody Hayes finished third behind Duffy Daugherty of Michigan State and Oklahoma's Bud Wilkinson in the poll for Coach of the Year.

Ohio State, to win the Conference championship, shut out favored Michigan, 17 to 0, in its last game of the season. The Wolverines had whipped a powerful Army eleven and plastered the only defeat of the year on Michigan State, conqueror of Notre Dame. Michigan had faltered badly against Illinois, 25–6, but they were still expected to beat the Buckeyes and win the Big Ten title and go to the Rose Bowl. Instead, they were badly outplayed, and the defeat, the first on their own field at the hands of Ohio State since 1937, cost them the championship and the trip to Pasadena. Ohio State, according to the Pacific Coast–Big Ten pact, was not eligible to play in the Rose Bowl two years in a row, so Michigan State was chosen to go.

My old friend, the late Joe Sheehan, of *The New York Times*, went out to Ann Arbor to cover the Ohio State vs. Michigan contest, and in his dispatch back to his newspaper called it "a weird game that almost wound up in a free-for-all." He guessed it would be a long time before anybody forgot it.

"Ohio State scored four times in three different ways, and each score was marked by some unusual incident," Joe wrote. "The Buckeyes broke the ice in the second period with a 23-yard field goal by Fred Kriss. His kick struck the left upright and caromed over the crossbar. On the third play of the fourth quarter the remarkable Hopalong Cassady slashed over from 2 yards out. He lost the ball by a fumble as he crossed the goal, but over Michigan's heated protests the touchdown was allowed. Shortly after, Ohio State was credited with a safety when Michigan completed a forward pass for a 5-yard loss. Aurelius Thomas tackled Terry Barr, the receiver of the boomerang toss, in the Michigan end zone. Within a minute the Buckeyes bagged their second touchdown on a 1-yard plunge by Don Vicic after successive penalties for unnecessary roughness and unsportsmanlike conduct had been called against Michigan.

"For the rest of the game there might just as well not have been a football. Virtually everyone on either side was too busy taking pot shots at each other to pay any attention to it. Jubilant Ohio State fans who had left the stands occasionally joined the fun. Official red foul markers were flying two, three, and four at a clip. The game was close to not being completed at all.

"Ohio State's bulldozing line, led by 250-pound Jim Parker, overpowered the Wolverines on offense and overwhelmed them on defense. The Buckeyes, disdaining the forward pass, rolled up 21 first downs to 5 and outgained Michigan from scrimmage, 337 to 109. Whereas Ohio State was almost continually threatening, the Wolverines crossed midfield only once, in the last minute, and on a penalty at that."

On his way to the Heisman, Howard Cassady led all Conference rushers with 711 yards, a 6-yard average, and was leading scorer with 11 touchdowns and 66 points. He led in kickoff returns with an average of nearly 30 yards per return. He also excelled on defense. In a backfield that fumbled the ball only 0.8 times per game were halfbacks Jerry Harkrader and Jim Roseboro, and fullbacks Don Vicic and Galen Cisco. They gave Cassady plenty of help.

A second-week loss to Michigan slightly tarnished Michigan State's early dreams in 1955, but the Spartans came on the rest of the way to go undefeated and nip UCLA in the Rose Bowl, 17 to 14. Duffy Daugherty, in his second year at East Lansing, was an unanimous choice for Coach of the Year, and he gave much credit for the Spartans' success to his quarterback, passing star Earl Morrall, and to his all-purpose guard, Captain Carl Nystrom. Both were All-Americans, along with two teammates, fullback Gerry Planutis and tackle Norm Masters.

Earl Morrall, who later starred in the pros, was a meticulous ball-handler even as a collegian. He often spoke of the advantages of peripheral vision, "a type of split vision," he called it. "Let's say you run a pass play," he'd say. "Once you're back in the pocket here's what you *should* see: you see your short receiver, the number three man, and you see how he is going, then you pick up the long man to see if the defensive safety's got him covered, then back to the three man, and you *go* to him, unless the linebackers are in his zone, in which case you throw out into the right flat to your swing man, the safety valve. Then you have the man going down from the eight hole 10 yards on the left and buttonhooking, so that actually you have four possible receivers in an arc of 180 degrees, and since you've only got two, maybe three, seconds to pick one of those people out you can see how helpful a wide angle of vision can be. The angle seems to widen with experience. When you start out in football and don't know quite where to look, it's as thin as a flashlight beam. Pass patterns are set up to help you see your receivers fast. Your primary receivers are usually on a direct line of sight from you."

Morrall's qualities of leadership were those of the squad leader. He was easy-going and you could joke with him. His attitude toward football was quite gypsylike, emotional, impassioned, yet sometimes haphazard, a trait which marked his play as well—it often seemed scrambled and styleless, the play breaking down all around him, so that in the din from the stands quarterback Morrall scampered about like a chicken under pursuit; and yet he would somehow extricate himself—finding his way to the line of scrimmage, or getting off a successful pass from his shoetops while being flipped down on his back. He was a very exciting quarterback to watch, though it was difficult to sit comfortably and feel confidence in his attack, which seemed improvised out of turmoil.

Go into Morrall's mind, however, and you discovered a lot of football player. "The quarterback has to remember the things *not* to do, so that you don't tip the play," he'd tell you. "The defense is always looking for little things that will help them. A good lineman can tell from seeing how much pressure the man down opposite him has on his fingertips whether he's going to charge or pull. If he's got his weight forward on his fingers, they'll show pale, and that means he's going to charge."

After college, Morrall teamed up with Hopalong Cassady on the Detroit Lions. In a game at Baltimore they were behind 8 to 3 with not much time to go. "I threw a pass to Howard," Morrall said. "He got it all right and ran *bam!* into a goal post, which bounced him back out about four yards, and then he went in the end zone again, rubberlegged, like a guy with the shakes. I ran up to him with my hand out to grab his—it was a great effort of Cassady's—and he wandered right past me, just dazed. He didn't know where he was or what he'd done. It sort of took the pleasure out of it for him. They told him about scoring the touchdown. He was sitting on the bench, and when his head cleared, he'd say, 'Tell me again, tell me how I caught it.'"

Woody Hayes, at the end of the 1955 season, said Cassady was the greatest football player he had ever seen. "You can compare him with Red Grange," Woody said. "He was *defensed* in every game, yet they couldn't keep him from getting 125 yards every game. He was a great blocker and, as for defense, don't throw the ball unless you want him to come up with it. He played 55 minutes every game. We didn't have much to relieve him. We did not have nearly the depth and experience of 1954, but our victory over Michigan was a sounder one."

In four years at Ohio State, Cassady scored 222 points on 37 touchdowns to break the school record of 201 set by Chick Harley in 1919.

Two superlative performances went into Big Ten books in 1955, as Len Dawson, Purdue's crackerjack junior quarterback, established a new Conference record with a 95-yard scoring pass to Erich Barnes against Northwestern; while Minnesota's big fullback, Kevin Kleberg, averaged 44.2 yards on 25 kicks to break the punting record.

Dawson played brilliantly despite a hairline fracture of his right thumb. He had a cast made for the thumb that could be slipped on and off.

"When I played weak safety on defense, I put it on," Len said, "and when I was on offense I removed it so that I could throw the ball. Even at that, I could only throw short passes. Fortunately, I had Lamar Lundy, who was 6'7" as a target. All I had to do was get the ball up in the air and he'd catch it."

Dawson led the Boilermakers in pass completions, total offense, and did the punting. Purdue finished fourth in the Conference with a 4–2–1 record. During the Dawson years, they also beat Notre Dame two out of three times.

"At Purdue," Dawson said, "we had two major rivalries. One was Notre Dame and the other Indiana. I had wondered how and why Notre Dame and Purdue had become such intense rivals, other than the fact that they are both located in the same state. I found out when I arrived at Purdue that we had many Catholic boys on our team from the Chicago area where they have a fine parochial school system. A lot of the players from the Chicago area would go to Notre Dame. Several players on our squad had picked Notre Dame as their first choice, but because of the heavy enrollment from Chicago, Notre Dame couldn't take them all and they were turned down. Being rejected was enough to fire up some of those guys so that they liked nothing better than beating Notre Dame.

"Our Old Oaken Bucket game with Indiana was also a real big deal. The 1955 contest was quite unusual. The game was played at Bloomington and we wound up beating them by the baseball score of 6 to 4. It was a terrific battle if for no other reason that I scored all four points for –Indiana. Twice I was tackled in our end zone, once intentionally. With less than a minute left on the clock, we were backed up against our goal and in a punting situation. Coach Stu Holcomb told me to run around in the end zone. I had never done it before, nor had I even heard of it being done. I was averaging only about 30 yards on my punts and I didn't kick very well under pressure. Coach Holcomb didn't want to take a chance that we couldn't cover a punt. There was that danger of running it back for a touchdown, or getting close enough for a field goal. So I ran around in the end zone, gave up 2 points on a safety, and in doing so killed about 15 seconds. We kicked off, and Milt Campbell, the great Indiana back who later starred in the deca-thlon in the Olympic Games, almost ran it all the way back for a touchdown. He scooted right past me, but four of our guys finally hit him and brought him down and we held In-diana long enough to win the game."

The following year, Len Dawson was the No. 1 draft choice of the Pittsburgh Steelers.

The year 1955 was noteworthy for other rea-sons, too. It was the season, for instance, that Ray Nitschke began his varsity career at Il-linois. Twenty years later, football commen-tators would be calling him "the greatest mid-dle linebacker in pro football history." Fifteen years with the Green Bay Packers and an un-precedented five world championships, Nitschke was called "the meanest man in foot-ball," a living legend on a legendary team. But what about Ray Nitschke, sophomore?

"I was a real selfish guy who didn't have much love for anything or anybody when I first arrived at Illinois," Nitschke said. "I worried about myself. I stayed away from people. I wasn't really prepared for college. I was on a football scholarship, a full ride, but it took me a year just to learn how to study in college. I'd been a big shot in high school, but in a big school like Illinois I was just another face in the crowd. That took some getting used to.

"I had hoped to play quarterback, but Ray Eliot had other plans for me. He had only one fullback, Danny Wile, and he needed a backup man. So in 1955, Coach Eliot called me into his office and said, 'Ray, what's it going to be: second-string quarterback or first-string fullback?' I said 'Coach, I'd rather be the first-string quarterback.' But Coach Eliot said I was no better than a third-team quarterback, be-hind Hiles Stout and Em Lindbeck, and he flatly announced I was being moved to fullback. I was so disappointed that I just sat there in his office and *cried*. Me—Ray Nitschke—the *meanest man in football!*

"Since we had to play both ways in 1955, and because the fullback was a linebacker on defense, I thus became a linebacker at 200 pounds.

"Some of the sports writers picked us to win the Big Ten in 1955, but Ohio State beat us,

Earl Morrall, who went on to star in the pros, was a meticulous ball-handling quarterback even as a col-legian. He showed that his qualities of leadership were those of the squad leader as he led Michigan State to 17–14 victory over UCLA in the Rose Bowl on New Year's Day, 1956.

27–12, to stop all that talk. A charley horse kept me out of both the Ohio State and Minnesota games, but I was ready for the Michigan State game. That gave me a chance to chase Earl Morrall, who demonstrated a lot of class even then. They beat us, 19 to 14."

It was a frustrating season for sophomore Nitschke and Illinois. Instead of winning the Big Ten championship, they wound up with a 5–3–1 record overall and 3–3–1 in the Confer-ence. Their one big bright spot was a 25–6 triumph over heavily favored Michigan, which was the worst beating the Wolverines had taken from the Illini since Red Grange helped whip them, 39–14, in 1924. At one point, Michigan tried four straight passes from the Illinois 16-yard line and missed them all. For the afternoon, Illinois' pass defense held Michigan to 3 completions out of 22 attempts.

Even then, Ray Nitschke demonstrated tremendous pride. He felt he was going to be the best man in college football at his position, and each Saturday afternoon he set out to prove it. On defense, he seemed to spend all his time roaming around enemy backfields; he had his arms around the ball-carrier so often they should have been engaged. Nitschke stopped just about everybody who cracked the line of scrimmage; he stopped them in the middle, on the left, on the right, everywhere.

To understand the anger festering inside Nitschke, you had to understand his circumstances. He didn't have an easy childhood in suburban Chicago. He grew up without any luxuries, without anybody ever coming close to spoiling him.

"You know," he confessed one time, "once, when I was a little kid, someone gave me a ride in a Lincoln. Ever since then I've dreamed of owning one. I never thought I would."

You would have sworn that Mr. Nitschke was ready to bawl.

I don't suppose any ball-carrier who ever ran against him in the Big Ten or the pros would believe that.

1956

College football continued its resurgence in 1956, reaching new heights of interest. Fans who heretofore had become disaffected because of the dehumanizing effects of the automation that crept in under the push-button, two-platoon system, once more valued the entertainment return of weekend visits to the campus.

The codists who defied football's ground rules again declined to tamper seriously with the precepts of what once more was an absorbing game, in which players, with their individual strengths and weaknesses, repossessed the spotlight. One-platoon football, requiring a player to block as well as tackle, had restored warmth and personality to the game that was lacking under the two-platoon system, in which individuality was sacrificed at the altar of cold, efficient specialization.

The transitional fall-off in skilled execution that accompanied the return to two-way play no longer was evident. By now, a whole varsity generation had become adjusted to playing on defense as well as offense and the level of performance was high. Most of the coaches who

Best interior lineman in college football in 1956 was Ohio State guard Jim Parker, winner of the Outland Trophy.

had opposed the restoration of one-platoon football had also become reconciled. Those sufficiently endowed with material still could maneuver by using alternate two-way team units.

On the national scene, Oklahoma made the 1956 season special by bowling over 10 opponents to extend a four-year winning streak to 40 games—the longest victory string put together by a college eleven. Coach Bud Wilkinson's Sooners, devastatingly resourceful on attack and fiercely resistant on defense, again were proclaimed the nation's No. 1 college team and set a rushing record with an average of 391 yards per game.

Tennessee, unbeaten during the regular season, but upended by Baylor, 13 to 7, in the Sugar Bowl, won No. 2 ranking. Other leaders were Iowa, undisputed Big Ten champion for the first time since 1921 and Rose Bowl winner over Oregon State, 35–19; Georgia Tech, beaten only by Tennessee and a Gator Bowl victor over Pittsburgh, and Texas A & M, the undefeated, once-tied champion of the Southwest Conference.

Iowa surprised the experts in 1956 by winning the Big Ten championship, culminated by a 35–19 triumph over Oregon State in the Rose Bowl. Two of Coach Forest Evashevski's key players were Kenny Ploen, left, pin-point passer and master of the keeper play, and pass-catching end Frank Gilliam. All-American Ploen won the league's MVP award in 1956.

Thirty-four years between Conference crowns was a long, long time for Iowa fans to wait, but once Coach Forest Evashevski got the habit he couldn't be stopped. During the next five seasons, the Hawkeyes won three Big Ten titles and two Rose Bowl games. With adept passing from quarterback Ken Ploen, behind a large, agile line, Iowa was the most exciting wing T team in the country. They missed a perfect season by the slim margin of a field goal when Michigan nipped them, 17–14. On the way to the championship, however, they beat Purdue, 21–20. Len Dawson was the Purdue quarterback.

"We had it all figured out how to defense Iowa because Kenny Ploen, their quarterback, used to stagger his feet," Dawson said. "That is, when he took the snap his left foot would be in front of his right foot or his right foot was in front of his left. If his right foot was back, that meant they were going to the right side. He'd pivot that way, and vice versa. Our linebackers were calling out signals and moving when they saw the position of the quarterback's feet, and we were gearing our entire defense against them by the direction of Ploen's foot. But we still didn't beat them, because I was the goat. We tied the score, 20 to 20, and I missed the extra point. The year before, I made it and we tied them, 21–21.

"But the week prior to that 1956 contest, Evashevski held secret sessions at Iowa. He was an adviser with the Wilson Sporting Goods Company and had his name on a football. Everybody else in the Big Ten used the Spalding J5B. But when we went to Iowa we had to use the Wilson ball. When they came to Purdue to play, we figured they'd have to use the Spalding J5B, giving us an advantage. But Evashevski was crafty. He brought his own Wilson ball with him so when they got possession of the ball they'd exchange it for one of their own. Our coaches were infuriated.

"Iowa came out with a double-wing reverse in the game, and I was always the free safety away from the flow of action. They pulled the double reverse and used it to score all 21 of their points in the first half. We adjusted to the ploy in the second half and shut them out, while we were tying the score. And then I missed the extra point."

There was plenty of glory for Evashevski and his Hawkeyes. Evy, himself, finished high in the Coach of the Year voting, Alex Karras was an All-American tackle, Kenny Ploen won the Big Ten's MVP award, and the team was No. 3 in the nation's Top Ten.

Karras was by far the toughest tackle in the league. Playing against him was like playing a chess game. If you tried to pop him, he'd beat you like a stepchild. You had to be thinking all the time. You had to be thinking about the move he beat you with the year before. You had to remember that everything with him was a countermove.

"You spend a lot of time thinking about

Alex," an opponent remarked. "He eats break-fast with you, goes to the john with you, brushes your teeth with you. You think about him every minute, how difficult he is to cut off on the inside, how he likes the outside on a pass rush, how he just loves to hit the quarter-back."

Karras had four or five different, effective moves and he got so he could use all of them. One of his moves was a little hop and a skip to the outside. He actually hopped, and it looked funny, but it worked. He charged to the out-side maybe 90 percent of the time, but oppo-nents couldn't overadjust because he liked to change up and come to the inside with a real strong move, doubly hard to stop because they didn't expect it.

"You learned through experience never to bad-mouth Alex," said Jerry Kramer, who saw lots of Karras in pro ball. "The best example I can remember was Dan Grimm, a pretty good kid. Dan filled in for me one time when I was hurt and we played Detroit and he handled Alex very well. After the game, Grimm told some sports writer that Alex wasn't as tough as he thought he was. 'He didn't show me many moves,' Dan said. The quote appeared in the paper. The kid didn't know that Alex was play-ing with a pulled groin muscle. The next time we faced the Lions, Alex ate Grimm up. He tore the kid's helmet off, knocked him down, chewed him up and spat him out. After one vicious attack, Alex looked at the kid and growled, 'How do you like those moves, ass-face?'"

Karras' outward appearance was belying. He was the type of player you never thought was ready. But with the ball in the air, he was dynamite. He had everything: instinct, size, ability, the "moves of a ballet dancer, *dainty*," in the words of Jerry Kramer. "One of the nicknames for him was 'Tippy-toes,'" Jerry said. "That's hard to believe—I mean, the fel-low standing still looks like he's sunk in the ground. But then he takes one step and you can spot that he's all springs and coils inside."

Karras' description of himself was, "I'm nothing but a poor, fat Greek kid out of Gary, Indiana." His pugnacious playing style in-spired football fans to christen him the "Mad Duck." He looked like a morose troll. His vis-ion was so myopic that he once mistakenly slugged his own brother during a game. After he made the All-American team, a teammate observed: "Success has not turned Alex's head, because his neck is too short for any-thing to turn it."

At Michigan State, Duffy Daugherty, in his third season at East Lansing, was the only Big Ten coach annually confronted with a triple demand: Beat Michigan, beat Notre Dame, and win the Conference championship. In 1956, he did the first two—9 to 0 over Michi-gan, and 47–14 over Notre Dame—but he finished in a tie with Ohio State for fourth place in the Big Ten (4 wins, 2 losses), and was 7–2 overall.

Duffy, by now, had become the court jester of college football. He had the face and man-ners of a friar not averse to a friendly joust with quarterstaves, followed by a tankard of ale; a cop with a trick nightstick full of lollipops, or a South Boston politician who had survived the kitchens of a thousand wakes. His wit was con-tagious. Against Notre Dame at South Bend, Duffy warned his players that the tradition-steeped Irish would return for the second half ablaze with the spirit of Knute Rockne and George Gipp, the fabled halfback who died in 1920. So after John Matsko, the Spartan center, made a questionable hike and Notre Dame re-covered the resultant fumble, he said to Daugherty: "It wasn't our fault. When I tried to center the ball, it wouldn't go right. It was like somebody was holding it." And halfback Clarence Peaks piped up, "Maybe Gipp was reaching up."

"Let's not be sacrilegious," Duffy said. "Let's just say that Gipp was reaching *down*."

1957

College football's longest winning streak on record came to an end on November 16, 1957, when Notre Dame upset Oklahoma, 7 to 0. The Sooners had rolled up 47 straight triumphs over a five-year span.

There was another hung jury when it came time to pick the No. 1 team in the nation. The AP poll favored Auburn, while Ohio State im-pressed the UP selection panel. Woody Hayes was acclaimed as Coach of the Year by his fel-lows of the American Football Coaches Asso-ciation, and John David Crow of Texas A&M won the Heisman Trophy.

Other top college teams were Michigan State, Navy, Iowa, Mississippi, Rice, Texas A&M, Oklahoma, and Notre Dame.

Ohio State opened the season losing to Texas Christian, 18–14, and ended the year with a 10–7 victory over Oregon in the Rose Bowl. In between, they defeated Washington, Illinois, Indiana, Wisconsin, Northwestern, Purdue, Iowa, and Michigan.

Second-place Michigan State lost only to Purdue, 20–13. They beat Michigan (35–6) and Notre Dame (34–6) by almost identical scores.

Alex Karras, an All-American repeater and winner of the Outland Trophy as the best interior lineman in the nation, was a big reason why Iowa had a 7–1–1 record. The ponderous tackle then moved on to professional football without first earning his degree.

"I was at Iowa only two terms," Karras cracked. "Truman's and Eisenhower's. Seriously, I was the nuttiest kid alive. I had all the hangups. I loved to play football and get drunk. I didn't feel comfortable doing anything else."

There are innumerable tales about Karras as a college man. Some are fact, some fiction. Most of them are fiction.

"There's not much truth to a lot of the crazy stories you hear about Alex when he was at Iowa," commented his old coach, Forest Evashevski. "Sometimes I think he went to a different school and played under different coaches."

Iowa's Alex Karras twice won All-American honors and in 1957 added the Outland Trophy to his list of awards as best interior lineman in college football.

Karras will tell you, quite frankly, that there was no love lost between himself and Evashevski. Alex says he once challenged the coach to a fist-fight. Evy demurred.

"I could've licked him, too," Alex says, remembering the incident.

"Perhaps his attitude is based on resentment for the way I goaded him," Evashevski said. "I can't pretend I was easy on him. It hurt him not to get his letter in his sophomore year. Maybe I invited his antipathy by riding him until he lived up to his potential. He could have remained fat and sassy and coasted aimlessly through life if I hadn't laid down the law. Actually, I had complete respect for him as a football player. He was a fine player. That part of him I understood."

Karras was supposed to have established some restrictions of his own while at Iowa. According to reports, he would play football in his junior and senior years only if Evashevski stopped riding him.

"Completely false," Evashevski corrected. "No player of mine ever laid down conditions to me. He played only under *my* terms. As head coach, I could not have operated under such conditions, a player telling me what to do. It never happened."

The Hawkeyes made history, headlines, and hot debate all season. They were still unbeaten at mid-year and the Michigan game at Ann Arbor loomed just ahead. Iowa had not beaten the Wolverines in 11 straight meetings. No one had to tell the Hawks what was at stake. In the last 30 minutes they fought back with two touchdowns to tie the score, 21–21, and then, with only three minutes remaining to play, Iowa got the ball. Evashevski ordered his team to run the ball exclusively. "Score if you can, but don't pass," he told them. Every Big Ten team except Ohio State had lost at least once and if Iowa could come away from Michigan with at least a tie they could retain the Conference championship by beating the Buckeyes in the final game of the season. So the Hawkeyes stayed on the ground and ran out the clock. The game ended in a tie and Evashevski was loudly criticized for his conservative strategy.

The following Saturday, Iowa swamped Minnesota, 44–20, and in doing so established a new Big Ten ground-gaining record of 535 yards. This led up to the showdown with Ohio State at Columbus.

Late in the fourth quarter, Iowa was in front, 13 to 10. With time running out, Ohio State got the ball on their own 32, where Frank Kremblas, the quarterback, began feeding the ball to his big sophomore fullback, 215-pound Bob White. On five straight plunges—inside tackle, up the middle, over guard—White carried the ball down to the Iowa 10-yard line. Then it was halfback Dick LeBeau for two. Now back to White again, down to the 3—and then on into the end zone on the very next play. Bob White had simply packed the ball seven out of eight times for 66 of the 68 yards which brought Ohio State the Big Ten crown and another trip to Pasadena. Ironically, that was the only touchdown that White scored in 1957.

At the end of the season, there were a number of coaching changes around the country. Bear Bryant moved from Texas A & M to Alabama, Jack Curtice from Utah to Stanford, Jack Mitchell from Arkansas to Kansas, Dan Devine from Arizona State to Missouri, just to name a few. The football world was saddened by the death of Charlie Caldwell, who had done so much to put Princeton back on the football map.

It was the Rules Committee that provided the headline news of the interim report. At their annual 1957–58 winter meeting, the game's legislators came up with several shockers. Altering scoring values that had stood unchanged since 1912, they decided to award two points for conversion by running or passing. They also set the 3-yard line as the new take-off point for the conversion try. They liberalized the substitution rule to an extent that two platoon operation again was possible. They tightened the blocking rules, so as to permit only hand or arm to be brought into play. They changed the kickoff rule and made various other revisions.

These rule changes were bound to lend controversial spice to the 1958 season.

1958

Football, as predicted months in advance, had one of its more intriguing seasons in 1958. It was a year marked by the first change in scoring values since 1912: the award by the colleges of two points for conversions by running or passing. It was also a year enriched by Army's introduction of the "lonely end" attack and by Louisiana State's use of a novel three-

platoon system in which a two-way "White" team was supported by offensive and defensive units dubbed "Go" team and "Chinese Bandits."

It was a year that saw the breakup of the old Pacific Coast Conference, and the cancellation of the PCC–Big Ten Rose Bowl pact.

Going into 1958, college football was all shook up over the two-point conversion change, but initial opposition dwindled as it became evident that the new rule spiced a previously dull play and generally livened matters. The result was that the season had many competitive highlights. Louisiana State, the only unbeaten, untied major team, was acclaimed national champion by both news service polls. In recognition of his team's superlative performance and his new concept of three alternating units—a starting two-way eleven and relief offense and defensive teams—LSU's Paul Dietzel won the Coach of the Year award. The perfect record was the first ever for the Tigers.

Army, also unbeaten but once-tied, was another headliner with its "lonely end" formation, in which the flanker remained aloof from the huddle.

One of the provocative football questions of 1958 was, "How does the 'lonely end' know what play Army will run?" The "lonely end" was a colorful aspect of the exciting new attack Earl Blaik conceived for the Cadets as an antidote to stacked defenses. Technically, Army's set-up was an unbalanced-line wing T with the strong side end flanked. The gimmick was that the wide end remained completely aloof. While his teammates huddled, he went directly to his outpost. This unorthodox procedure was noted by a vigilant press corps as soon as Army unveiled the formation in a first-game rout of South Carolina. The attack was immediately dubbed "lonely end" and Bill Carpenter was nicknamed "Lonesome George" in recognition of his title role.

Despite diligent inspection by enemy scouts and much public speculation, the "lonely end" mystery remained unsolved until Blaik broke silence after the season was over.

"The position of the quarterback's feet tells the end what the play is," Red said. "It's really very simple."

Opponents, however, found the "lonely end" attack insolubly complex. Carpenter's isolation spread the defense, opening the gates for Army's swift runners and creating passing opportunities that Army cashed in to an extent that it led the nation in aerial yardage.

Meanwhile, members of the Big Ten Conference dominated the list of Top Ten teams of 1958: Iowa finished No. 2, Wisconsin No. 6, and Ohio State No. 7. Randy Duncan (Iowa), Bob White (Ohio State), and Sammy Williams (Michigan State) represented the Conference on the All-American first team.

Leading Iowa to its second Big Ten title in three seasons, quarterback Duncan was the most talked-about Hawkeye since Nile Kinnick won the Heisman. Handy Randy, 6-foot tall and 180 pounds, put it all together in 1958. He was second in the Heisman balloting, won the Conference MVP, led the nation in pass percentage and yards gained passing, tied for first in touchdown passes with 12, was second in total offense, and established a Big Ten career record of 24 touchdown passes.

Duncan had three great ends to pass to: Curt Merz, Don Norton, and Bob Prescott. The first-string tackles were John Burroughs and Mac Lewis, the guards were Gary Grouwinkel and Don Shipanik, while Don Suchy started at center. In charge of the running game were halfbacks Willie Fleming, Bob Jauch, Bob Jeter, and Kevin Furlong. Team captain John

Unanimous All-American quarterback Randy Duncan sparked Iowa to the 1958 league title on his way to finishing second in the annual Heisman Trophy balloting.

Nocera and Don Horn provided explosive power at fullback. Everything did not come up roses for Iowa on the way to Pasadena. After beating Texas Christian, 17 to 0, in the season opener, the Hawkeyes were outhustled by a surprisingly solid Air Force Academy eleven and barely hung on for a 13–13 tie. "We needed that sobering experience to set us right," Coach Evashevski remarked later. "We'd never have won the Big Ten championship if we had won from the Air Force."

Indiana, Wisconsin, Northwestern, Michigan and Minnesota fell like toy soldiers before the Hawkeyes faced Ohio State at Iowa City in what Woody Hayes later called "the greatest game of offensive football I've ever been in." It was the last Conference contest of the season for Iowa—they had already cinched the championship—and they were heavily favored. The Buckeyes had lost to Northwestern and been tied by Wisconsin and Purdue.

The game was a donneybrook from start to finish. It was 7–7 at the end of the first quarter, 21–21 at halftime, and 28–28 after 45 minutes. Then in a burst of ground fire, Ohio State came up with 10 points and pulled the game out, 38–28, for Iowa's only loss of the year. Between them, Ohio State and Iowa piled up a grand total of 889 yards passing and rushing, with the Buckeyes getting 462 of them.

The following Saturday, Iowa took its frustration out on Notre Dame via a 31–21 victory, with Duncan throwing two touchdown passes. They ended the season with a smashing 38–12 triumph over California in the Rose Bowl on the strength of 516 total yards. Bob Jeter personally accounted for 194 yards, a new Rose Bowl record.

While the AP and UP were picking Louisiana State, the Football Writers Association of America waited until after the bowl games to name Iowa winner of the Grantland Rice Trophy, symbolic of the country's No. 1 college football team.

"That's only as it should be," commented Ike Armstrong, Director of Athletics at Minnesota. "Iowa is the best team I've ever seen in the Big Ten."

The Hawkeyes merely led the Conference in scoring, rushing, passing, pass-completion average, first downs, and total yards gained. Randy Duncan won the Walter Camp Trophy as the best back in the nation.

Judy Klemesrud, who went on to write for the *New York Times*, remembers those years of the Iowa Rose Bowl teams. As an Iowa coed, she remembers that she used to hang out at the Iowa Memorial Union and watch the athletes play cards, drink Cokes, and act rowdy.

"They were so sexy in their black leather jackets with the golden I's over their hearts," she recalled recently. "I even went on a few picnics with some of them, until I read in the campus newspaper that six of the star football players had been expelled for gang-banging a coed at a picnic along the Iowa River. After that, I worshiped them from afar."

Boys will be boys!

1959

College football, acutely aware of professional football's growing appeal, widened their goal posts in 1959 from 18 feet 6 inches to 23 feet 4 inches to encourage field goal kicking. The major college placekickers responded by booting the unprecedented total of 192 field goals out of 380 attempts. Randy Sims of Texas A&M kicked one from 52 yards, the longest by a collegian since 1941.

College officials also added a "wild card" substitution rule permitting each team to send in one player without charge whenever the clock was stopped. This gave the college game greater scope for specialization and made it easier to pass instructions to quarterbacks and defensive signal-callers.

The 1959 campaign was distinguished by Syracuse's sweep of the major honors, after being ignored in preseason ratings. Ben Schwartzwalder's mighty Orange eleven, almost irresistible on attack and almost immovable on defense, rolled over 10 regular-season opponents for its first perfect record in history, then polished off Texas, 23–14, in the Cotton Bowl. Many experts hailed Syracuse as the best-rounded varsity football team of the postwar era and "Old Ben" Schwartzwalder was named Coach of the Year. Three of his stars—guard Roger Davis, and Fred Mautino, and tackle Bob Yates—were tapped by the All-American selection committee. Billy Cannon, Louisiana State's fleet 208-pound, 6-foot-1 halfback, won the Heisman Trophy.

Trailing Syracuse in the Top Ten were Mississippi, Louisiana State, Texas, Georgia, Wisconsin, Texas Christian, Washington, Arkansas, and Alabama. Oklahoma suffered its first loss in its conference since 1946 but still won the championship for the 12th year in a row.

In the wake of Army's spectacular 1958 success with its "lonely end" attack, there was a generally greater emphasis on flanker set-ups that lent themselves to open play and passing. But the most significant technical development was the rediscovery of the field goal as a scoring weapon.

For the first time in years, the Big Ten failed to produce a super team. Defending champion Iowa fell to 6th place in the standings, while Wisconsin won the title despite two defeats on its Conference record. Coach Milt Bruhn simply took advantage of an off-year for the other nine teams. League schools, for example, lost a combined total of 39 games.

During the regular season, the Badgers lost to Purdue, 21 to 0, and to Illinois, 9 to 6, yet qualified to represent the Big Ten in the Rose Bowl against high-scoring Washington, a Husky eleven that had been upset only once, by Southern California.

The Huskies were coached by young, tough, dedicated Jim Owens, another of Bud Wilkinson's boys at Oklahoma, who kept his mouth shut and worked hard. After two years of building up fan interest in a team that didn't play well on the road—hell, it didn't even play well in practice—Owens began putting it all together. He turned a one-eyed fullback, Bob Schloredt, into an All-American quarterback. He took the castoffs and culls from other recruiters, and he put together a team that actually won. Sometimes they won close—oh, so close—and one Seattle cartoonist dubbed them "Hairbreadth Husky."

Washington was ranked No. 7 in the national poll, right behind No. 6 Wisconsin, but John Thompson, the Husky press agent, told Emmett Watson, Seattle newspaper columnist, that he had that certain feeling when it came time to speculate on the outcome of the Rose Bowl game. "We're going to win this one," Thompson said. Watson began calling some people he knew who took bets. You could get Washington and 10 points. Watson got quite a bit of Wisconsin money.

"And on that one, glorious New Year's Day in Pasadena, the air turned red," remembers Emmett Watson. "Washington dismembered Wisconsin, 44 to 8, and no press agent since

DAN LANPHEAR   DALE HACKBART   HENRY DERLETH   JERRY STALCUP

Four important reasons why Wisconsin won the 1959 Big Ten championship: left, tackle Dan Lanphear, quarterback Dale Hackbart, end Henry Derleth, and guard Jerry Stalcup.

has had trouble selling Washington as a big draw and national news.''

Individual stars of the year were All-Americans Dan Lanphear (Wisconsin), Bill Burrell (Illinois), and Ron Burton (Northwestern).

Michigan State, 0–5–1 in Conference standings in 1958, bounced back with a 4–2–0 record in 1959 to place second. One of those victories was a one-sided 34–8 triumph over Michigan, a rivalry fraught with tension. A few days before the game the Spartans' practice was interrupted when a sheriff's car, with siren screeching, pulled up alongside the field. A deputy stepped out and approached with handcuffs.

"A theft has been reported," he told Coach Duffy Daugherty. "There's evidence that the guilty man is one of your players."

Duffy dropped his head. He was plainly embarrassed. Then he braced his shoulders and pointed to Ed McLucas, the big tackle.

"There's your man, deputy," Duffy said. The deputy seized McLucas, slapped the cuffs on him, and pushed him toward the car.

"Officer, this is Michigan week!" pleaded Lou Agase, an assistant coach. "You can't take McLucas! We need him!"

The arresting officer was adamant. Agase doubled up his fists as if to punch the deputy.

"If you don't behave I'll arrest you, too!" snarled the lawman. "Now, stand back."

By this time the frightened McLucas had found his voice.

"Just tell me one thing," he asked. *"What did I do?"*

"Mr. Daugherty says you've been stealing cereal from the training table to take home to your children."

That broke up the gag—and some of the pre-Michigan game tension. The culprit? Hugh Duffy Daugherty!

"Life without work is insipid, and life without fun and relaxation is deadening," Duffy said.

The esprit of his squads reflected the rapport between the coach and his athletes. He would interrupt a hot September practice to treat the players to soft drinks or reward a good session by cutting it short to send the boys for a swim. If it happened to be September 8th, his birthday, the players often surprised him by wheeling a cake onto the field bearing a caricature of Duffy's face, in the school colors of green and white.

Duffy's light-hearted touch did not dilute discipline, however. At Ann Arbor, during the Michigan contest, he sent in a sub with instructions to quarterback Dean Look to call a sweep. Dean, a favorite of the coach's, disre-

garded orders and called a roll-out pass. It went for 60 yards and a touchdown. Look trotted to the bench, a self-satisfied smile on his face. Duffy gave him a good tongue-lashing and benched him for the rest of the game.

A land-grant school with a wide diversity of courses, Michigan State was tailored to Duffy's philosophy that a poor boy who was an ordinary student but was an extraordinary athlete should be given the chance for an education if he wanted one.

"As for Phi Beta Kappas," Duffy grinned, "I could have been one myself if I had made better grades."

At Michigan State, court jester Duffy Daugherty was the only Big Ten coach annually confronted with a triple demand: beat Michigan, beat Notre Dame—and win the Conference championship.

Space Age:
The 1960s

College football entered a new era in more ways than one with the arrival of the Sixties, and in the ensuing decade the sport enjoyed its greatest growth in history. College attendance increased from 20,403,000 to nearly 30,000,000, or approximately seven times faster than that of the preceding decade.

The Space Age was also here.

On the 1969 afternoon that Apollo 12 was swinging toward lunar orbit, James Stewart-Gordon, the writer, was in the nerve center of the NASA complex, the inner computer chamber where each tick of each astronaut's heart and the performance of each tiny part of their hurtling spacecraft was recorded and studied by experts. Stewart-Gordon sidled up to an off-duty scientific brain and glanced at his tiny TV screen, expecting to see the astronauts tensely soaring through space. He, instead, saw a football field on which the Dallas Cowboys were ripping off yardage against the Washington Redskins. James Stewart-Gordon tapped the technocrat on his shoulder and asked, "What about the astronauts?"

Plainly annoyed by this intrusion, the scientist held his temper while carefully considering the question.

"If they want the score," he replied finally, "they're just going to have to wait until halftime."

And so it went through the sonic Sixties.

1960

College football's bursting vitality in 1959 continued on through the 1960 national schedule. There were great teams, great players, blazing competition, big crowds—and one significant rule change: The "wild card" substitute rule of 1959 was liberalized to allow each team to make one free substitution between successive downs, even when the clock was running. This helped the coaches get specialists into action, call out quarterbacks for consultation, and to send in plays to suit the situation.

The greater freedom in the use of specialists stimulated additional offensive enterprise, along the lines of the various flanker formations inspired by the 1958 success of Red Blaik's "lonely end" formation at Army. It also permitted limited platooning of offensive and defensive units, without lowering the bars entirely to outright two-platooning, which remained distasteful to many devotees of college football.

Under the impetus of the 1959 rules change that widened the goal posts from 18 feet 6 inches to 23 feet 4 inches, while leaving them on the backline of the end zone, the field goal continued to regain importance as a scoring and strategical factor in the colleges. A record total of 224 field goals was recorded in major games. They decided 38 games.

The Team of the Year was Minnesota. The

Golden Gophers rose from last place in the Big Ten in 1959 to a tie (5–1–0) with Iowa for the 1960 crown, were ranked No. 1 nationally in both the AP and UPI polls, and won the MacArthur Bowl, given by the National Football Foundation and Hall of Fame. They lost to a superb Washington team in the Rose Bowl, 17 to 7, but losing to the Huskies from Seattle was nothing to be embarrassed about. The Big Five, or Athletic Association of Western Universities, champions had gained tremendous prestige by their 44–8 Rose Bowl triumph over Wisconsin the year before, the first Pacific Coast success against the Big Ten since 1953, and all 11 starters were back for 1960, including All-American Bob Schloredt, their one-eyed quarterback, and two honor-bound lineman, Kurt Gegner and Chuck Allen. The Huskies were a solid team, well-manned at all positions and deep in reserves.

If there was any doubt about the toughness of Big Ten football, it could be dispelled by the final listing of the Top Ten teams: Minnesota finished No. 1, Iowa was No. 2, and Ohio State No. 8. Tom Brown, the Minnesota guard, and Bob Ferguson, Ohio State's swift ball-carrier, were both acclaimed first-team All-Americans.

For leading Minnesota out of the wilderness, Murray Warmath was named Coach of the Year. (In the 18 years Warmath coached the Gophers, 1954–1972, he sent 57 players to the NFL. "He had the reputation among the pros that when one of his boys reported to the NFL, he was ready to play," said Otis Dypwick. "They didn't have to first spend a year or two getting him ready for professional competition.")

Forest Evashevski, winner of 8 out of 9 games, shocked the coaching fraternity by calling it quits at Iowa. His announcement reminded Dave Stidolph, who had been Evashevski's Sports Information Director at Washington State University in 1950–1951, of an incident involving Evy before his first game at WSU.

"I had arranged for Evy to address an Alumni party at Portland, Oregon," Stidolph said. "He had come down with a cold and was in a lousy mood. His message to Cougar Alumni was hard-nosed. He warned them not to interfere in his coaching affairs at Pullman, and then for good measure signed off by say-

For leading Minnesota out of the wilderness in 1960, Murray Warmath was named Coach of the Year. The Gophers ranked No. 1 nationally in both the AP and UPI polls. In the 18 years he coached Minnesota, Warmath sent an estimated 57 players to the National Football League.

ing, 'Just remember, I don't have to coach football for a living. I have a wealthy father-in-law back in Michigan.' He emphasized that more than once. In those days, I doubled as stringer for INS, and I walked over to the INS office in Portland and told the sports editor about Evashevski's threat to quit at WSU if the alumni got in his way; and about not needing to coach because he was the son-in-law of Prentice Brown, Chairman of the Board of Detroit Edison and former U.S. Senator. The story was sent out on the wire. Next morning, I heard a roar from Evy's hotel suite. He had just received a wire from his daddy-in-law: 'Treat the Washington State alumni with much more respect,' it read. 'I don't have near the money you think I do.'"

The biggest Saturday of the 1960 Big Ten schedule was November 5. That's when Iowa and Minnesota locked horns for the championship. The Hawkeyes went into the contest ranked No. 1 in the nation, while the Gophers

A big factor in Minnesota's title-sharing team of 1960 was Tom Brown, the Gophers' talented guard who was All-American and the Conference MVP. Though they lost to Washington in the Rose Bowl, 17–7, the Gophers finished No. 1 in the national polls at the end of the year.

were No. 2. Both teams were unbeaten. Coach Murray Warmath was especially impressed with the pregame tension surrounding the showdown.

"I remember the pep rally we had on the mall in front of Northrop Auditorium Friday noon before the game," Murray said. "More than 10,000 people attended. Pregame jitters were unbelievable."

This was reflected on the field the next day.

"There was so much emotion that both teams were sloppy early in the game and lost the ball on fumbles," Warmath said.

Tom Brown, All-American guard, gave Minnesota its first break leading to a first-quarter touchdown. He busted the Iowa center so hard on a fourth down punting situation that the ball sailed over the kicker's head, giving the Gophers the ball on the Iowa 14-yard line. Three plays later Sandy Stephens, a daring, running-passing quarterback, lateralled to halfback Bill Munsey who fought his way into the end zone.

In the second period Iowa took a Stephens punt and drove to the Minnesota 5 in 12 plays for a second-and-goal situation. An incomplete pass made it third and goal. On the next play, Tom Brown cut up the guard hole as Bill Di-Cindio, the Iowa guard, was pulling and knocked him into the backfield and nailed the quarterback for a big 6-yard loss. That forced the Hawkeyes to settle for a field goal by Tom Moore.

Minnesota held a 7–3 halftime lead.

Iowa roared back in the third quarter to take the lead, 10–7, when Wilburn Hollis scored on a 20-yard run up the middle on a trap play to cap a 55-yard drive in six plays. But then the Gophers marched right back on their very next series of downs and drove 81 yards in 11 plays to take the lead again, 13–10. Early in the fourth quarter, fullback Roger Hagberg, who carried the ball 15 times in the game for 103 yards, broke loose for 42 yards on an inside maneuver and made it 20 to 10. Minnesota scored again minutes later when tackle Bobby Bell recovered a fumble on the Iowa 19 and four plays later Jim Rogers punched into the

Big man in the 1960 Iowa line was All-American guard Mark Manders.

All-American halfback Larry Ferguson paced the 1960 Iowa attack to a 5–1–0 Conference record and a tie with Minnesota for the championship.

held on to the No. 1 ranking to earn the right to play in the Rose Bowl for the first time in Minnesota history.

The Minnesota–Purdue game produced plenty of hard-hitting. Midway in the battle, Coach Warmath noticed that Bobby Bell's mouth was bleeding profusely. He beckoned his big tackle to the bench. After wiping the blood off Bobby's face, Murray saw that one of the boy's front teeth was broken in two.

"What happened to your tooth?" Warmath wanted to know.

"I swallowed it, Coach."

"Swallowed it!"

"Yes," Bobby Bell said. "You don't think it will bite me again, do ya?"

Two years later, Mr. Bell won the Outland Trophy as the best interior lineman in America.

By now, the legend of Woody Hayes was in full flower. Since coming into the Conference, he had three championships to his credit, with a fourth waiting for him in 1961. But as for 1960, it was a season of disappointment, with the Bucks going down to defeat at the hands of Purdue (24–21) and Iowa (35–12), which was the most one-sided shellacking absorbed by Woody since Illinois trounced Ohio State, 41–20, in 1953.

Woody was in a towering black rage as he did his thing at the blackboard at halftime. His hand shook as he drew X's and O's on the board. He was plainly disgusted with his team's performance. Suddenly he halted in the middle of his chalk talk and let out a string of

end zone. Thus the country's No. 2 team defeated the No. 1 team, 27–10.

Minnesota fell to Purdue, 23–14, the following Saturday for its only defeat of the year but

The 1960 Minnesota squad, Big Ten co-champions, and No. 1 in AP and UPI final national polls.

With their mother in the stands, Michigan Coach Bump Elliott, left, and his brother Pete, Illinois mentor, engaged in a pregame chat; then Bump went out and won the game, 8–7, in 1960.

obscenities as though he felt he wasn't getting across to his players.

"GODDAMMIT!" he roared, and he let fly with a bare-knuckled fist at the blackboard, shattering a big hole in it. "All right, let's get back to the field!"

Mike Ingram, the big, tough linebacker, stared at the hole in the blackboard just before he left the dressing room and said to John Mummey, the quarterback, "Hell, I'm less than half Woody's age. If he can do it I can do it," and he let fly a punch at the board and barely cracked it.

"Sonofabitch Woody!" cried Ingram, howling with pain and rage, and he went out and played a whale of a game. Afterward, Mike had to wear a cast on his swollen hand and Woody thought he had hurt it legitimately in the game against Iowa.

1961

Under the spur of professional competition, college football kept showing increased vitality. Within the limits of the restrictive rules, varsity teams did more platooning and made greater use of specialists. They also put more emphasis on open play, without sacrificing the basic values that the highly skilled professionals sometimes bypass in their constant quest for the quick, easy score.

Wing T, slot T, and flanker T formations replaced the full-deck T and the split T in 1961, and the handful of teams that remained faithful to the single wing added embellishments that

gave it a bright and shiny new look. The new rule providing that the first substitute of a group entry, as well as single "wild card" entries, be unchanged gave more scope in the deployment of specialists. Die-hard platooners never will be completely satisfied with anything short of free substitution, but they made it do very well with the liberalized code. In fact, there was a well-developed trend, even in the smaller schools, toward using alternate elevens trained to play both offense and defense or organizing in three units, with specialized offensive and defensive groups in support of a two-way starting team. Paul Dietzel dramatically demonstrated once more what could be done with the three-platoon system. His famous "Chinese Bandits" at Louisiana State rolled up a 9–1–0 record during the regular season, then blasted Colorado, 25–7, in the Orange Bowl. At the end of the year, Dietzel stunned LSU supporters by suddenly resigning to accept a rebuilding assignment at Army as head coach.

Dixie produced the national champion in 1961 in unbeaten, untied Alabama, which earned No. 1 designation in both news service polls. For guiding the Crimson Tide to a perfect record and a 10 to 3 victory over Arkansas in the Sugar Bowl, Paul "Bear" Bryant was named Coach of the Year. It marked Alabama's first all-victorious season since 1945.

Syracuse's Ernie Davis became the first black athlete to win the Heisman Trophy.

College field goal specialists kicked a record 277 goals.

Ohio State swept all its six Big Ten games, but was tied by Texas Christian, 7–7, in its opening game. For the third straight season, Woody Hayes went all-out with offensive and defensive platooning. Among a flock of Buckeye honor candidates were halfbacks Paul Warfield and Matt Snell, fullback Bob Ferguson, tackles Bob Vogel and Daryl Sanders, ends Chuck Bryant and Tom Perdue, and fiery center Billy Joe Armstrong. Runner-passer John Mummey was the quarterback. Coach Hayes rated them one of his finest teams. The big conflict, however, came at the end of the season. The way with that was this. The Rose Bowl pact between the Big Ten and the PAC-8 had run out and everyone expected a new contract would be signed to go on with the series, but for 1961 there was no formal agreement

One of the greatest backfields in Ohio State history consisted of halfback Paul Warfield, shown here slipping a UCLA tackle in 1961 as the Buckeyes won, 13–3, and halfback Matt Snell, fullback Bob Ferguson, and quarterback John Mummey.

binding the Big Ten champions to appear at Pasadena. Of course, it was taken for granted that the latter would be invited on an individual basis. Sure enough, the Rose Bowl selection committee asked the Buckeyes to come, subject to approval by the Ohio State administration, naturally.

Woody Hayes was in Cleveland to address an alumni bash when the news reached him. The Ohio State faculty council had just voted 28–25 refusing his team permission to play UCLA in the Rose Bowl. Woody was in the middle of his dinner when a messenger slipped him the paper note. Those who were there said his face suddenly turned grey, stunned. "They're kidding," he whispered incredulously. The reason given was "overemphasis." The faculty representatives felt that the Ohio State players' best interests could not be served by going to California.

While badly shaken by the news, Woody did not lose his sanity. The first thing he did was to leave the banquet room and start walking, trying to understand what had gone wrong down at Columbus and what to do about it. He walked around the streets for a half-hour and got back just in time to give his speech. To the great surprise of his assistant coaches, he delivered one of the finest speeches of his career. He told the stunned audience what had happened, then went on to explain why a great

bunch of boys were being cheated out of a valued experience they had worked hard for and rightfully deserved.

"I'm bitter," he said. "The vote deeply disturbs and dismays me. But I cannot question the faculty's sincerity or their right to act." He then concluded his remarks by adding, "But I do seriously question their judgment." Then he sat down to an ovation that shook the rafters.

While Woody Hayes accepted the decision philosophically, all hell broke loose back in Columbus. The faculty veto had whipped the Ohio State students into a lather. They marched by the thousands to try to get to the governor. He was out. They thronged back to the campus in an ugly mood. It could have gotten out of hand, except for the quick-thinking of Mike Ingram, co-captain of the football team. Mike braced himself in front of the horde and raised his hand for quiet.

"Listen," he shouted, "no one is more disappointed in the faculty vote than the players—and they're all back in their dorms learning to live with that decision. If they can, then you can!" The crowd broke up.

Woody beamed when he heard how Mike Ingram had handled the mob scene.

"How proud I am that one of my football players was able to show them the way," he said.

Under the circumstances, the Rose Bowl invitation then went to second-place Minnesota and the Gophers promptly accepted. The Maroon and Gold, losers to Missouri and Wisconsin during the regular campaign, put it all together on New Year's Day. With Sandy Stephens, the flashy quarterback, directing the attack, boldly supported by runners Bill Munsey and Judge Dickson, and lineman Carl Eller, Jim Wheeler, Julian Hook, Robin Tellor, Dick Enga, and Bob Deegan, the Gophers smashed UCLA, 21–3, to hold up the honor of the Big Ten.

Individual stars of the Conference in 1961 were Sandy Stephens (MVP), and All-Americans Bob Ferguson, Ohio State's pile-driving fullback, Bill Van Buren, the super center from Iowa, Pat Richter, Wisconsin's league-leading end, and Dave Berhman, Michigan State's powerful guard.

In its annual winter meeting, the NCAA rules committee, with an eye on 1962, let things stand pretty much as they were. The most publicized change for the next season was a clarification that retroactively made legal the added-chance, last-play field goal try, after a penalty, that created such a rumpus in the 1961 Notre Dame vs. Syracuse game. Under the old rules, the Fighting Irish weren't entitled to the second kick with which they beat the Orange, 17–15, after time had run out and a roughing penalty had been imposed. But the argument that this was inconsistent and inequitable prevailed and the basic rule was extended to cover this rare specified case.

More significant, actually, was the voiding of the old rule that touching down a punt inside the rival team's 10-yard line was an automatic touchback, giving the receivers possession on their 20, instead of at the point of grounding. The revision added an element of excitement and rewarded a well-kicked, well-placed punt.

As for the final national rankings, three members of the Big Ten Conference finished in the Top Ten in 1961: Ohio State (No. 2), Minnesota (No. 6), and Michigan State (No. 7).

After eight complete seasons in the Big Ten, Duffy Daugherty, by now, was just about the most popular coach in America. Yet when his Spartans lost he had his critics. As a matter of fact, he was hanged locally in effigy after losing to Minnesota and Purdue this season on successive Saturdays, which was like burning Smokey the Bear at the stake. Duffy possessed a normal Irish-Scotch temper and sensitiveness, and he publicly reproved his executioners by asking what was wrong with a 7–2 record.

It was a good question.

1962

Everything pointed toward another banner season, with Ohio State, defending champions of the Big Ten, and Alabama, Michigan State, Louisiana State, Mississippi, Duke, Penn State, Navy, Texas, Washington, and Oregon picked by the preseason experts as the most prominent candidates to wage a wide-open scramble for national leadership.

No one paid serious attention to Southern California, a 4–5–1 also-ran in 1961. Developments, however, quickly proved the Trojans to be the class of this year's intercollegiate crop. Undefeated for the first time since the

coaching heydays of Howard Jones, USC polished off a tough 10-game schedule with a 25 to 0 victory over Notre Dame to earn the No. 1 position in both the AP and UPI polls and the MacArthur Bowl. They accentuated the positive by standing off Wisconsin's brilliant passer, Ron VanderKelen, 42 to 37, in one of the most exciting scoring duels in Rose Bowl history. Wisconsin had been even more of an outsider than the Trojans in the preseason rankings.

For guiding Southern Cal to those unexpected heights, young John McKay was named Coach of the Year. The Pacific Coast also produced the Heisman Trophy winner, for the first time, in Oregon State's Terry Baker, a left-handed quarterback and honor student.

Most of the top teams were geared to operate with three platoons—a starting two-way team, backed up by specialized offensive and defensive units. If there was a trend in football, it was in the direction of leveling strength. Where years ago, there were, perhaps, a dozen dominant teams, now that number was doubled, tripled, or maybe even quadrupled. The explanation was an increase in the talent supply coming up from the high schools, better coaching in the colleges, and a general tightening of entrance requirements that kept football-minded schools from getting an edge on those who limited their concessions to deserving halfbacks.

In the Big Ten, things didn't always go so well for Ohio State, the defending champs. Once, Woody Hayes was so disgusted with his Buckeyes that when the first half ended he took them into the dressing room for just two minutes, just long enough to rip them for their sloppy execution of plays. Then he told everybody to follow him. He stomped out the door, his players and coaches following curiously. He led them through the stadium gates and onto the practice field adjacent to the stadium. Then to his players' utter astonishment, he shouted, "It appears you didn't get the game plan down pat during the week, so you're going to get it now!" And then he drove them through a 10-minute scrimmage. Unbelievable? You don't know Woody Hayes.

High-water mark for the Buckeyes (6–3–0) was a 14–7 victory over surprising Wisconsin in their fifth game of the season. It was the lone loss for Coach Milt Bruhn's Badgers, who went to the Rose Bowl on the strength of their 8–1–0 record. Individual stars of this resurgence were All-American Pat Richter at one end and Ron Carlson at the other, tackles Roger Pillath and Roger Jacobazzi, guards Steve Schenck and Steve Underwood, and center Ken Bowman. Lou Holland and Gary Kronek were the halfbacks, Ralph Kurek was the fullback, and quarterback Ron Vander-Kelen, a third-stringer the year before, popped up as the Cinderella Story of the Year to win the Conference MVP. He led the league in total offense (1,237 yards), while left halfback Holland scored 11 touchdowns to lead the Big Ten in that department. Pat Richter repeated as the Conference's No. 1 pass-receiver with 33 catches and 440 yards.

On their way to Pasadena, the Badgers romped over Iowa, 42–14; Michigan, 34–12; Illinois, 35–6; and Notre Dame, 17–8.

In what has since been described as "one of

One of the mainstays of the line for the 1962 Wisconsin team, Big Ten champions, was two-time All-American end Pat Richter.

the most famous Rose Bowl games ever played," No. 2-ranked Wisconsin faced No. 1-ranked, unbeaten, untied Southern California. The stars of the most explosive football team in Wisconsin history were the Big Ten scoring leader who doubled as a punt returner, No. 27, Lou Holland; the quarterback, whose name will always be associated with this Rose Bowl contest, No. 15, Ron VanderKelen; and the Badgers' record-breaking pass-receiver, All-American right end, No. 88, Pat Richter.

The 1962 version of Southern California's Thundering Herd was led by All-American end, Hal Bedsole; sharp-shooting quarterback Pete Beathard; the team's rushing leader, left halfback Willie Brown, who also starred on defense; and guard Damon Bame. Their coach was the young, imaginative strategist who returned the Trojans to football greatness, Coach of the Year John McKay.

The broadcaster who called the game was Tom Kelly.

"It was one of the greatest games I ever broadcast," Kelly said. "It was simply incredible. Neither team started the season very highly regarded by the pollsters. Wisconsin had a new quarterback named VanderKelen, but they did have All-American end Pat Richter, and, of course, Lou Holland. Yet they came on strong to win 8 of their 9 games—the only one they lost to was to a team a lot of people lose to, Ohio State, 14 to 7.

"As for the Trojans, Johnny McKay had what he called his '3-B offense'—Beathard, Bedsole and Brown. They really amazed the sports world across America by winning 10 straight games, and they played an extremely tough schedule, too.

"So you thus had the No. 1 team playing the No. 2 team in the Rose Bowl. Surprisingly enough, the professional odds-makers had made the Badgers 3-point favorites."

About 55,000,000 people tuned into the game on radio and on television. A great deal of the action was saved for the final 15 minutes of the contest. Until then, Southern California had things pretty much its own way, leading by as much as four touchdowns. But the Badgers refused to give up. The fourth quarter was fantastic as the Big Ten champions scored three touchdowns and a safety. VanderKelen riddled Trojan defenses so mercilessly with his pin-point passing that the PAC-8 champions were forced to freeze the ball in the last 45 seconds of play to preserve a 42 to 37 victory. All told, the VanderKelen statistics showed that he completed 33 of 48 passes for a record 419 yards, including two touchdowns. He also scrambled 17 yards for another TD.

One of the game officials, Tom Cross, of Tacoma, Washington, told me that the action grew so wild in those final minutes that they ran out of footballs.

"We used 24 and it seemed to us on the field that the game lasted 400 hours," Tom said. "Actually, it ran for about four hours and it got so dark the lights had to be turned on."

The game reminded Curt Gowdy of an old-fashioned street brawl between two pugs in which one comes out with his clothes all ripped, both eyes black, his nose bleeding, and he says, "But ya oughta see the other guy."

Elsewhere in the Big Ten, Minnesota finished second to Wisconsin in the standings. Bobby Bell, the Gophers' 6-foot-4, 219-pound tackle from Shelby, North Carolina, won the Outland Trophy and was All-American for the second year in a row.

"Bobby came to us as a quarterback and was the quickest player I ever saw," Coach Murray Warmath said. "He could play any position; in fact, out of the 22 positions on the football field, he was capable of playing 19 of them better than most. He probably had the finest understanding of football of any player I knew. He moved to the center position to make long snaps for us in punting situations. He could be counted on to force a turnover at least twice a game."

While the rules-makers continued to tinker with the structure of football, split crews seemed to be more common as the answer to the question of officiating in intersectional games. Marv Tommervik, who began officiating Big Ten–Pacific-8 contests in 1955, was on the five-man team working the Purdue vs. Washington game at Seattle in 1962.

"Two hours before the game," recalled Tommervik, a great All-American passer, himself, at tiny Pacific Lutheran University, Tacoma, Washington, in 1940–41, "we gathered for a meeting of officials in order to blend our crew. We had two officials from the Big Ten, three from the PAC-8. One of the questions that bothers a visiting coach coming from one section of the country to another—

and I can appreciate this—is whether or not his team is going to get a fair shake from the home officials. He wants everything to be neutral. In 1962, one of my responsibilities was to go to the dressing room and bring the visiting team back onto the field to begin the game. So when I went to notify Purdue it was time to go, Jack Mollenkopf, the coach, was already standing at the door waiting for me. I told him, 'We've got 5 minutes, Sir. I want your team on the field.' And he looked at me and said, 'Who have we got officiating the game today?' I quickly ran down the list for him. He said, 'I'm not interested in the whole crew. All I want to know, are there any Big Ten officials here?' And I said, 'Yes, Sir, you've got two.' And he brightened and said, 'That's fine, that's all I want to know. We'll be right out.' That seemed to relieve him of all his tension. The score, incidentally, ended in a 7–7 tie. Actually, there isn't that much difference in officiating between the two sections anymore. The mechanics are pretty much the same."

One final 1962 note: Amos Alonzo Stagg's 100th birthday was celebrated at football banquets all across America.

The old man sent me a birthday picture of himself that year, across which he had written in shaky longhand: "When you get to be my age, this is the way you look—and this is the way you write."

Ron VanderKelen's sensational second-half passing attack in the 1963 Rose Bowl left the nation's TV-viewers breathless as Wisconsin came from far behind before losing to Southern California, 42–37. The Badger quarterback completed 33 of 48 passes for a record 419 yards and two touchdowns. Wisconsin got three TDs and a safety in the fourth quarter to nearly pull the game out.

1963

The national trend in varsity football continued to be toward a leveling off of strength in 1963. The time was rapidly fading when a handful of college teams could dominate the campus scene. By now there were upwards of 120 major-rated teams. It was no exaggeration to declare that, on any given Saturday, almost any one of them could beat almost any other.

For teams unfortunate enough to have to play Texas, however, that day did not come. The Longhorns won the whole ball of wax. Darrell Royal's powerful squad swept its 10 regularly scheduled games, the only major team with a perfect record, and endorsed its No. 1 national ranking by walloping Navy, the No. 2 team, 28–6, in the Cotton Bowl. This was the first time that Texas had been recognized as national champions, and with the honor went the Coach of the Year award to Coach Royal. Meanwhile, Roger Staubach, Navy's great All-American quarterback, gained some solace despite the Texas defeat, by winning the 1963 Heisman Trophy. The Midshipmen, under Wayne Hardin, defeated Army a fifth time in a row. The game was postponed a week following the assassination of President Kennedy, as were the Harvard–Yale and Michigan–Ohio State games, and 33 other college contests.

The run for the roses in the Big Ten was a three-way fight in 1963. Illinois, Michigan State, and Ohio State went right down to the wire. The loosening of the substitution rule caused more confusion than substitutes. Players could enter rather freely on second and third downs, but their entry was restricted on first and fourth downs.

Illinois, coached by Pete Elliott, was something of a "rags to roses" story in 1963. It was not an overwhelmingly brilliant team, but it got the job done. Starting with a 10–0 win over California, the Illini were taken for real after a 10–9 upset of Northwestern in the second game of the season. After that, they lost only to a so-so Michigan eleven, 14–8, and were tied by Ohio State, 20–20. In their showdown with Michigan State at East Lansing, November 30, a week after the murder of President Kennedy, the Illini met the test successfully, 13 to 0.

A clutch team playing a clutch game, Illinois trailed Washington in the Rose Bowl, 0–7, but came on to win, 17–7. Fullback Jim Grabowski led the attack by rushing 125 yards and scored the go-ahead touchdown. In the final news service polls, the Big Ten champions finished No. 3.

The All-American Boy in the Conference was Dick Butkus. The Illinois linebacker was a special sort of brute whose peculiar talent was mashing ball-carriers into funny shapes and sizes. What he was, in fact, was a product of an era—an era that saw the position he played properly glamorized by such primates as Sam Huff and Joe Schmidt, Bill George and Ray Nitschke. It was an era that had seen the linebacker become as big a star in college as the breakaway runner because substitution

DICK BUTKUS   ARCHIE SUTTON   DON HANSEN   MIKE TALIAFERRO

Showing the way for Coach Pete Elliott's 1963 Big Ten champions at Illinois with a 5–1–1 Conference record were All-American center Dick Butkus, tackle Archie Sutton, linebacker Don Hansen, and quarterback Mike Taliaferro.

rules had fostered specialists. And Butkus the linebacker was certainly a specialist. He was the tough-looking guy with evil in his eyes who stood up noseguard to noseguard toward the opposing quarterback and looked as if he intended to mug him.

Even the casual fan could tell who Butkus was. He was the fun-lover who got to smother the runner going wide, or spear the scrambling passer drifting backward, or hit the barging plunger head-on. He was the guy who got to drop off occasionally and intercept passes, and then run in such wild-boar fashion that Pete Elliott was hard pressed to explain at the Monday Morning Quarterbacks' breakfast why he wasn't using him on offense. The linebacker was the one player who got to show most constantly that he was the *complete* athlete, very often, the best player on the squad.

Good linebackers, like Butkus, had to be. He

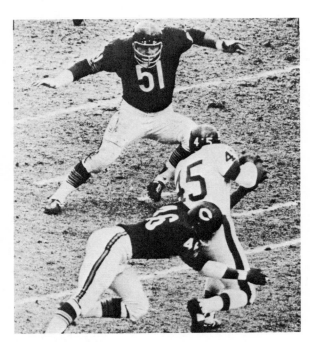

Coach Pete Elliott of Illinois said he knew from the first day Dick Butkus reported to practice that he was a great one. "He moved well and he had a sure instinct to do the right things," Elliott said of his big linebacker. "I never saw him take a loafing step." Among his college honors, Butkus was a two-time All-American, Lineman of the Year, and No. 3 in the Heisman Trophy balloting. "He plays the middle like a piranha," complained one Big Ten rival. "He gets himself so angry at you that he plays like a wild man." Butkus here is No. 51.

was the soul and heart of a defense both physically and spiritually, and just as often he was the heartthrob of the whole team. He could never *not* get up from a heap, *not* hustle to the sideline, *not* be alert enough to call the defensive signals, and *not* be enthusiastic enough to keep the steady chatter going. Dick Butkus was all of this—and more. And above everything else, he was the living, stick-'em-in-the-gizzle proof that linebackers, not blondes, have more fun.

At Champaign, no player had created such a sensation since Old 77. Coach Elliott would like to have felt that his coaching had something to do with Dick's ability, but Pete was too honest to take such credit.

"He had intuition," Elliott recalled. "On the first play of his first spring practice, before we'd even told him anything, he smelled out a screen pass and broke it up. In two seasons, Dick was only out of one screen pass. By that I mean he either diagnosed them and forced an incompletion or got there and made the tackle. He was naturally great at jamming up the middle against running plays. But somehow he managed to cover wide real good. He got there, you know, because he wanted to. Football was everything to him. When we had a workout cancelled because of bad weather or something, he got angry, almost despondent. He lived for contact."

Contact to Butkus was really only one thing: the moment of impact with the ball-carrier. All of that other business, such as people trying to block him, he ignored. He was hurrying to all the fun which, he said, consisted of "getting a good measure on a guy and stripping him down."

Butkus, in a sense, was the defensive quarterback. He prowled up and down the line behind his tackles and guards, anticipating where the daylight might occur so that he could close it off. His job was to secure all hatches. He had to know when to gamble on a blitz, which is the act of a linebacker darting through a gap in the line on the snap and trying to smash a runner for a loss or smother a passer before he throws.

Butkus, who called Illinois' defensive signals, said he liked to shoot whenever he could. Coach Elliott left it to him. On Illinois' normal defense it was reasonably safe for Butkus to put on the blitz because the tackles, 262-

pound Archie Sutton and 234-pound Bill Minor, shared the middle responsibility with him. They, too, had size, agility, and experience. Consequently, no team wore itself out running inside on Illinois. "I don't see why they would," Butkus said in 1963. "Archie and the others can take care of things pretty good—even if I guess wrong on a shoot."

The guess began as soon as an enemy had broken its huddle and the opposing quarterback had bent over to stare into Butkus small, cold, and dark eyes. "He's calling signals and I'm calling signals," said Butkus. "I look first at the formation. Then I look to see if a halfback is cheating a few inches. I look at the halfback's eyes, and then the quarterback's eyes and head. Some jokers, they throw in the first direction they look. I may decide at the last second that I'm gonna call a stunt, or that I'm gonna shoot. If I shoot, the thing I hope is that I get a good angle on the runner, or if I've played the pass that I can strip the guy down and make him drop the ball. That takes it outta guys."

One of four Big Ten stars named to the 1963 All-American team was Carl Eller, Minnesota's big, swift tackle. Other Conference players on the all-star selection were guard Mike Reilly (Iowa), halfback Sherman Lewis (Michigan State), and center-linebacker Dick Butkus (Illinois).

In three years of college football, Dick Butkus took it out of a lot of guys. The Conference rewarded him in his senior year with its coveted MVP.

The year 1963 also marked the end of Ara Parseghian in the Big Ten. After eight seasons at Northwestern, he signed on as head coach at Notre Dame. Tom Pagna, one of his aides at Evanston, later said: "I don't think anyone realized what a fantastic job he did at Northwestern," referring to Ara's 36–35–1 record. "He was 4–4–1 his first year, and 0–9–0 a year later. I noticed a change in him. He had become introspective. That losing season made him intense. That was his margin of greatness. He was now able to focus on the things he considered important. He had three key words that guided him: organization, morale and loyalty. When he left to go to Notre Dame, he gave each man on his staff a free trip to Las Vegas for him and his wife. A week's vacation free. My wife and I cashed in our plane tickets and bought a piano. We call it Ara."

When it came to football, Ara the man could also make beautiful music.

1964

There was a new dimension in college football in 1964. For the first time in a dozen years, the rules permitted the platoons to march virtually unfettered. At its January meeting, the rules committee liberalized the controversial substitution rule. Now a team could substitute any number of players when the game clock was stopped—that is, during intermissions, after a dead ball, during a legal timeout, and so forth. The lone remaining restriction was that, when the game clock was running between two successive downs, each team could send in only two substitutes. This constituted a smashing victory for the coaches, the majority of whom had campaigned incessantly for removal of the free substitution restrictions that were imposed on the varsity game in 1952. The new rule cleared the way for unhampered two-platooning, alternating specialized offensive and defensive units. Surveys indicated that practically all major teams operated with two platoons, Army and Navy starting with three and switching to two.

There were traditionalists, of course, who grieved at the disappearance of the two-way player, who could block as well as tackle, and they sounded off against depersonalized, push-button aspects of two-platoon football. Yet having the platoons march once more had its rewards. There was no disputing that specialized one-way play produced stepped-up action and a higher grade of technical football.

Under any set of rules, however, the teams with the best players will usually lead the flock, and, in 1964, they were Alabama and Arkansas, both unbeaten and untied (Arkansas for the first time in 55 years), and Notre Dame, which came within 95 seconds of finishing with a clean slate. Behind those three came Michigan, Big Ten champion for the first time since 1950, and Texas, Nebraska, Louisiana State, Oregon State, Ohio State, and Southern California. The MacArthur Bowl was awarded to Notre Dame, despite its loss to the Trojans, 20–17, after leading, 17 to 0.

For the first time in history, there was a tie for Coach of the Year honors. Ara Parseghian, in his first year at Notre Dame after leaving Northwestern, and Frank Broyles, of Arkansas, shared the award. John Huarte, quarterback of the Fighting Irish, won the Heisman Trophy.

In 1963, Michigan was fifth in the Big Ten with an inauspicious 2–3–2 record (3–4–2 overall). Bump Elliott's so-called five-year plan was running a year late, but he was not discouraged.

"The parts are beginning to fit into championship design," he said at the time. "The talent, the drive, the desire is all there."

The heart of Coach Elliott's wing T was the quarterback position, and Bob Timberlake was no ordinary quarterback. At 6–4 and 215 pounds, he was intelligent, articulate, a team leader. He could run and pass and placekick.

Potentially, the Wolverines had more speed and depth in the backfield than at any time in Elliott's six seasons at Ann Arbor. Starting halfbacks were two sophomores, Carl Ward and Jim Detwiler. Mel Anthony was the fullback. Tom Cecchini and Frank Nunley were the linebackers, and Bill Yearby on defense and Tom Mack on offense were two of the top tackles in the Conference. The ends were deep and rich, headed by Captain Jim Conley, Bill Laskey, and John Henderson. Rick Volk, a reserve quarterback, was reassigned to the defensive backfield.

With more freedom to substitute, Elliott and his staff were not lacking in material. The defense, for instance, was so deep in numbers and talent that Air Force and Navy threw 75 passes in the first two games to try to break through it. Timberlake and Anthony accounted for 250 yards in a 24–7 victory over the Air Force, and Detwiler and Ward combined for 148 yards in a 21–0 triumph over the Midshipmen, whose star, quarterback Roger Staubach, was hobbled by a bruised heel. It was only the second time the Navy had been shut out in 96 games.

The key to the season hinged on Michigan's third game against Michigan State, and the Wolverines did it the hard way, with two touchdowns in the last quarter for a 17–0 victory. The win shot Michigan to 5th place in the national polls, before the Purdue Boilermakers, or "spoilermakers," engineered one of the major upsets of the season over them, 21–20. Three Michigan fumbles, one in the end zone, were vital factors in the defeat.

With midseason injuries mounting, Michigan nearly blew a 19-point lead against Minnesota, but held on to win, 19–12, for its first victory over the Gophers in five years. Next, Northwestern was stopped cold, 35–0, and then Illinois, 21–6. Four fumble recoveries and three pass interceptions paved the way for a 34–20 win over Iowa.

The Michigan vs. Ohio State rerun was on again. The Wolverines were 5 and 1 in the Conference standings, Ohio State 5 and 0. Overall, the only team to stop the Buckeyes was Penn State—but, oh, how the Nittany Lions accentuated the positive. It was the third time that Coach Rip Engle had brought a Penn State team to Columbus to upset the mighty Bucks.

Ohio State was unbeaten (6 and 0) and ranked No. 2 in the nation's polls, but Penn State came to play. When it was all over, the Buckeyes were behind, 27–0, the most thoroughly whipped team in Ohio State's illustrious history. It was the first time in 45 games they had failed to score. Consider these figures:

Penn State held the edge in rushing, 201 yards to 33.

Penn State outpassed the Bucks, 148 yards to 30.

Total offense went to Penn State, 349 yards to 63.

Penn State controlled the ball for 79 plays to

37, and 22 first downs to 5. At the end of the first half, Ohio State had made no first downs and was minus-14 yards total offense.

Penn State played errorless football. Ohio State lost the ball four times, twice on fumbles, twice on interceptions.

Later, Woody Hayes confessed, "That's the worst beating we've ever suffered. Nothing went right. They made only one mistake and they fell on that for a touchdown. I don't know what went wrong. Either we've been masquerading as a good football team for five weeks, or Penn State is the most underrated 4–4 team in the country. I'll tell you one thing, they haven't been playing that kind of football—or they wouldn't have lost four games."

Ohio State's offense was so intimidated by the fierce Penn State line that once the Buckeyes punted on second down and twice on third down. The game was so one-sided that Rip Engle sent in his third team during the last 10 minutes. With the Nittany Lions' scrubs digging in on the Ohio State 40-yard line, the Bucks made a final attempt to cross mid-field. For the first 55 minutes they were unable to get beyond their 41.

"That's the first time I ever saw a goal-line stand on the 50-yard line," remarked one writer up in the press coop.

So the Buckeyes were fuming two weeks later when the Wolverines arrived from Ann Arbor. At stake was the Conference crown and a trip to the Rose Bowl. This was the 10th time that the two schools had played against each other with the Big Ten football championship on the line. Will Perry, who covered the game for the *Grand Rapids Press*, described the details this way:

"The first big break of the contest came late in the second quarter. Stan Kemp, with a 40-yard punting average, suddenly drove the ball 50 yards to Ohio State's Bo Rein. A sophomore sensation for Ohio, Rein had not missed a punt all season, but this one was caught in the fierce, 18-mile per hour winds shooting in from the horseshoe end of the stadium. The ball struck his hands and bounced to the turf. Henderson, sprinting downfield from his end position, dived for it and grabbed the ball on the Ohio 20. Michigan had its break and in two plays had a touchdown on a play drawn up earlier in the week.

"The 'trailer play' had been designed especially to combat Ohio's quick-reacting linebackers. Michigan unwrapped it for the first time at the Buckeyes' 17 yard line. Ben Farabee sprinted straight down from his end position as Detwiler trailed him on the play, then cut over the middle. Timberlake rifled the pass to Detwiler on the four, and the powerful halfback scored. There were just 44 seconds left in the half when Timberlake's kick made it 7 to 0.

"The Bucks tried to come back in the second half but could not dent the solid defenses of the Wolverines. Rick Volk intercepted two passes and slapped down a third to break up three drives. Ohio State gained only 180 yards in total offense. When Timberlake kicked a 27-yard field goal in the fourth period, the game was beyond Ohio State's reach. Final score: Michigan 10, Ohio State 0."

Meanwhile, on the West Coast, Oregon and Southern Cal were neck-and-neck in the race for the Rose Bowl. The Trojans topped off their regular schedule with a smashing upset of the nation's No. 1 team, Notre Dame, 20–17. That, USC felt, made them an automatic choice to represent the West at Pasadena on New Year's Day. Then came the announcement from the Tournament of Roses Committee: Oregon State, and not the Trojans, would play Michigan. Jess Hill, Director of Athletics at Southern California, typified public response in Los Angeles: "The decision is one of the rankest injustices ever perpetrated in the field of intercollegiate athletics."

The final score in the Rose Bowl seemed to support Hill's outburst: Michigan 34, Oregon State 7.

For his troubles, Bump Elliott was given the game ball.

The Big Ten contributed a record 11 players to the various All-American lists in 1964, headed by Bob Timberlake, the league's Most Valuable Player, and tackle Bill Yearby, also from Michigan. Jim Grabowski, Illinois, and Tom Nowatzke, Indiana, shared fullback votes. Two other Illini, linebacker Dick Butkus and safetyman George Donnelly, were two more choices, along with guard Don Croftcheke (Indiana), Karl Noonan (Iowa end), Harold Wells (Purdue end), and Arnie Chonko, safety, and Ike Kelley, end, both from Ohio State.

Iowa quarterback Gary Snook broke the Big Ten passing record in 1964 with 110 completions of 234 attempts and 1,544 yards. He also led the league in total offense.

In the Far West, Oregon and Oregon State officially rejoined Southern California, Washington, UCLA, Stanford, Washington State, and California to once more make it an eight-team Pacific Athletic Conference.

The Big Ten had 11 players on the various All-American selections in 1964, the most ever from one conference. Among them was Iowa end Karl Noonan, who established a new league season record of 40 catches.

Big Ten MVP award-winner Jim Grabowski, Illinois fullback, made All-American in 1964 and 1965. In 1965, he broke Red Grange's career rushing record (2,071 yards) by topping 2,500 yards, and set a new single-season rushing record (996 yards) for the Conference. He made still another league record with 201 carries in 7 games.

Even though Indiana never rose above 9th place in the three seasons he played in the Big Ten, 220-pound fullback Tom Nowatzke was an All-American choice in 1964 as he played both ways and led the Hoosiers in rushing, scoring, field goals, interceptions, and fumble recoveries. His 5-yard average on the ground was best in the league.

1965

The majority of the nation's college coaches finally attained a cherished goal in 1965. The NCAA rules committee, under relentless pressure from the coaches for more than a decade, at last lowered most of the barriers against free substitution. Each team was thus permitted to send in any number of players between periods, after any type of score, following any change of possession or when the kicking team repossessed the ball via a foul or fumble. In addition, each team could send in two substitutes at any time before the ball was put in play. This stopped short completely of free substitution but was close enough to it to permit all-out two-platooning without fear of getting into the binds that occasionally occurred in 1964, when there was no change-of-possession or repossession provision in the rule.

The final evidence was that virtually all the major schools, including those who held out in 1964, used the two platoons; that is, specialized offensive and defensive units.

On the plus side, football fans were rewarded by a higher quality of individual performance. The chief argument in favor of two-platoon football always has been that specialization allows the honing of skills to a degree that could not be attained in two-way play.

Although college football, with its young players and high degree of emotional fervor, always will retain its special rah-rah character, two-platoon football in 1965 was bringing it closer to professional football in the technical aspects of the game.

The 1965 national college champion was Alabama or Michigan State, depending on how you viewed the situation. Michigan State, which finished its regular season unbeaten and untied, as did Arkansas, Nebraska, and Dartmouth, was the No. 1 choice in both wire service polls. However, in a post-bowl poll conducted by the Associated Press, Alabama, which lost one game and tied one, was moved up from No. 4 into the top spot, on the strength of its 39–28 Orange Bowl victory over Nebraska, while Michigan State was losing to UCLA, 14–12, in the Rose Bowl, and Arkansas was bowing to Louisiana State, 14–7, in the Cotton Bowl.

The MacArthur Bowl was awarded to Michigan State, which was also the No. 1 pick by United Press International.

Mike Garrett, of Southern California, won the Heisman Trophy, and Tommy Prothro, in his first season at UCLA, was awarded the Coach of the Year plaque.

In the Big Ten, Michigan had been the favorite to repeat as champion. The Wolverines expanded their schedule to 10 games for the first time since 1945, but after the first six games, Coach Elliott could only shake his head and say, "Fate is against us." Seldom had a team been plagued by so much adversity. With 22 letterman back from the Rose Bowl squad, hopes had been high. They opened with a 31–24 victory over North Carolina, followed with a 10–7 win over California, but then lost to Georgia, 15–7, in what was their first defeat by a Southern school in 22 games. The offense just was not working, and six fumbles in the Michigan State game paved the way for another loss, 24–7. All told, Michigan was beaten six times in 1965!

The surprise team of the year was Michigan State. The Big Ten Sky-Writers, in their preseason predictions, listed the Spartans as no better than fifth place in the Conference standings. Critics of Duffy Daugherty rode him hard. They pointed out that through 1964 he had yet to win a championship. He did, however, have three runner-up teams, and his 1955 eleven beat UCLA and Red Sanders in the Rose Bowl, 17–14. Except for 1954, his first year, and 1958, all of his teams through 1962 were winners. Twice they were beaten only once; three times they dropped only two.

Duffy's personality also was used against him by the win'em-allists. He was charged with not being serious enough. Actually, nobody was more serious about his job. A severe taskmaster, with no leavening, would not have gotten as much out of MSU's type of players as Duffy did. And if he tried to be anything but himself he would have failed as a coach.

Michigan State football was well organized under Duffy, but he gave the impression of being organized in a disorganized way. Part of this was due to the staccato manner of his conversation. It was caused by an active mind, which moved so rapidly as to leave his words trying to catch up. The result was a fragmentary discourse that added to his quaint charm. On a dais or in a locker room, it was a different

Daugherty, commanding, humorous, with a professional gift for pantomime.

If he considered it worthwhile to do so, Duffy would remove himself from a prearranged work schedule. He was far more available than the average coach. He enjoyed long-distance exchanges of ideas with other coaches. "It's impossible," said his old coach and close friend Bud Wilkinson, "to have a short telephone conversation with Duffy."

Daugherty believed, and he cited history in support, that an explosive running attack was indispensable to success in the Big Ten, and Michigan State generally had a dandy. Perhaps this partly explained why the many individual stars he coached, some of them outstanding pros later, did not include distinguished passing quarterbacks. At the tail-end of his career, Duffy was putting greater emphasis on defense, after listening to Bear Bryant, Alabama's arch apostle of that style.

Duffy always took a special interest in recruiting a boy whose family, like his own, had to struggle—a boy, for example, like halfback Frank Altimore from Pittsburgh. His mother, widowed early, had to work hard to support Frank and two younger boys. With Frank in college, she had to shift her work from night to daytime, since he was no longer available to baby-sit for his two brothers. The day Altimore signed his MSU letter of intent, Duffy predicted, "He'll help us, because he has a sense of values." That's what Duffy's friends meant by saying that when Daugherty recruited he was looking for himself.

Very few players under Duffy got into academic trouble. He helped them with their school problems as he did with their personal problems. He never tried to put any pressure on the faculty if a boy was on the fence. He never tried to save a "bum." If he thought a boy was basically sound and a worker, then he would go to bat for him. He once did that for two of his players who were caught cribbing in a final examination. They worked at summer jobs in East Lansing to pay their way through the makeup course, were reinstated, and vindicated Duffy's belief in them.

In answer to all those MSU fans who believed that Duffy should win them all, Duffy often quoted Bob Zuppke: "A football coach's main problem is that he is responsible to irresponsible people."

In the years 1965–66, Duffy gave the alumni very little to complain about. The Spartans won 19 regular-season games in a row. In 1965, they crushed 10 straight opponents to become the "most decorated" team in Big Ten history. The backfield consisted of quarterback Steve Juday, Clint Jones, Dwight Lee, and Bob Apisa; Gene Washington, a great receiver and Big Ten hurdle champ, and Bob Viney, were at the ends; the tackles were Jerry West, Don Bierowicz, and Buddy Owens; John Karpinsky and Dave Techlin were the guards; and the center was Boris Dimitroff.

The 1965 preseason polls held small regard for Michigan State, but under Coach Duffy Daugherty's expert handling the Spartans came on to crush 10 straight opponents for an undefeated regular season and finish with a reputation as "the most decorated team in Big Ten history." Seven members of the squad were named on the various All-American teams; 11 on the All–Big Ten first and second platoons. Coach Daugherty is pictured in the team photo here, front row, seventh from left.

The defense was headed by 280-pound Bubba Smith at end, 265-pound middle guard Harold Lucas, linebackers Ron Goovert and Charley Thornhill, and cornerbacks George Webster and Don Jappinga.

The 1965 Spartans led the Conference in offense and defense, and led the nation defensively, limiting its opponents to rushing yardage of 45.6 per game. Against Michigan, Ohio State, and Notre Dame, MSU held the attackers to minus 51, minus 22, and minus 12 respectively. Steve Juday broke 12 school passing records.

Cleaning up in most of the Team of the Year polls, Bud Wilkinson called the Spartans "perhaps the finest team in the history of intercollegiate football."

Bubba Smith was one of seven Spartans who won All-American recognition in 1965; the others were Harold Lucas, Ron Goovert, Steve Juday, George Webster, Gene Washington, and Clint Jones.

Bubba was something special. He was listed at 6–8 and 287 pounds, but it was rumored that he weighed closer to 325. He was gargantuan, fast, and mean. The first time Jerry Kramer, of the Green Bay Packers, ever fought Bubba was in the College All-Star Game in Chicago. After watching movies of Bubba in action, Kramer said he knew he was going to be a handful.

"I knew he was strong," Jerry said, "but I didn't realize he was so fast, so quick off the ball. If he's got a weakness, it's that he doesn't seem to use his hands too well. I'll try to take advantage of that. If a man doesn't use his hands well, you can generally pop him, just drive right into him and push him back. But if he uses his hands well, he can grab you and throw you when you try to pop him, and he'll go right by you."

So much was written about Bubba's awesome strength that people could be excused if they thought of him as a monster, the subhuman type. "You don't feed him, you oil him," wrote one sports writer.

For the second straight season, Purdue finished third in Big Ten standings with another 5–2–0 record. Versatile Bob Griese was heralded as "the most complete quarterback in the league in years." Passing, running, kicking, and thinking, the All-American Boy from Evansville whooshed out the candlelight that Grantland Rice promised in the second and unremembered paragraph of his Four Horsemen story would "always gleam through the Indiana sycamores." It would, in fact, have taken all of the literary fame of Harry Stuhldreher, Don Miller, Sleepy Jim Crowley, and Elmer Layden to have kept Griese from upsetting Notre Dame, 25–21, in a grandly melodramatic 1965 afternoon of football.

All Griese did was complete 19 of 22 passes for 283 yards and three touchdowns, run nine times for an average of 5 yards per carry, punt three times high, accurately, and deliberately short to the Notre Dame 6-, 7-, and 26-yard lines, and make a touchdown-saving tackle on defense. In the face of such statistical goodies, and considering that they came against a bitter and respectable enemy, Griese left a lot of people wondering if they had ever seen a more brilliant performance by a quarterback.

The ironic twist was that Griese had wanted to attend Notre Dame, but when he was preparing to visit South Bend an alumnus of the Irish told him the school wasn't interested because he was too small.

Knute Rockne, where are you?

1966

College football's boom continued loud and clear in 1966. The collegians drew more than 25 million spectators, ranked high as a television attraction, and were in a highly vigorous state.

Notre Dame and Michigan State tied as national co-champions in the various major polls. There was no question about the Fighting Irish's worthiness of high ranking. They went through a hard schedule undefeated, but, in their big showdown game against the Spartans, who were also undefeated and untied when the teams met, November 19, in overwrought East Lansing, the Irish were held to a 10–10 tie. Obviously and admittedly, Notre Dame played for the tie, going into an offensive shell in the game's closing minutes.

"What the Fighting Irish did was, they *tied* one for the Gipper," wrote Dan Jenkins, putting a reverse twist on the "Win one for George Gipp" theme, a la Knute Rockne. "For 59 minutes out there the savages of Notre Dame and Michigan State pounded each other into enough mistakes to fill Bubba Smith's uniform but the chaotic deadlock that destiny seemed to be demanding had a strange noble quality to it. And then, horribly, it didn't have that anymore."

For the 80,000+ people stuffed into Spartan Stadium or the 33,000,000 others watching on national television, something obscene happened. It might have made sense to Ara Parseghian. It might have been percentage football. In the excitement of the moment, it might have seemed like the only sane and logical thing to do, and Coach Parseghian was willing to carry the argument that he was right for the rest of his life. But all anyone knew was that quite suddenly there at the end, the matchup that was advertised as the "Game of the Decade" suffered this enormous emptiness for which Notre Dame would be forever blamed.

Forget everything else that had happened during that afternoon, all of the fierce pounding in the trenches that created five fumbles, four interceptions, 25 other incompletions, assorted bobbles and interludes of hysteria that resulted in confusing time-outs, sideline arguments, and a total of 20 rushing plays which either lost yardage or gained none, and forget the few good plays—the passes that connected. Put the nation's No. 1 team, Notre Dame, on its own 30-yard line, first down, plenty of time-outs left, momentum going, with ample room on the clock for passing. A No. 1 team, especially Notre Dame, will try *something* to stay that way, won't it! Well, the Irish did not. For reasons all their own, they let the air out of the ball, and rode out the clock. Even as the Michigan State defenders taunted them and called the time-outs that Notre Dame should have been calling, Notre Dame ran into the line, the place where the big game had been hopelessly played all afternoon. No one really expected a scoring play in that last hectic minute, but everybody expected Notre Dame to try, as Michigan State had tried. And when the Irish gouged at the line, the Spartans were justified in considering it a minor surrender.

All-American George Webster, MSU's tough roverback, later said he couldn't believe it. "When they came up for their first play we kept hollering, 'Watch the pass, watch the pass.' But they ran," Webster said. "We knew the next one was a pass for sure. But they ran again. We were amazed. Then it dawned on us. They were settling for a *tie*."

In 1965–66, Michigan State's All-American George Webster was considered the finest corner linebacker in the nation.

The Spartans jeered at the Irish. They had their hands on their hips, and their jaws jutted out. They were plainly scornful. On the Michigan State sideline, players waved their arms in a gesture of "Get off the field if you've given up." And at the scrimmage line, the Spartans teased the Irish.

"You're going for the tie, aren't you?" Webster cried at them. "You're going for the tie."

The Notre Dame players wouldn't even look at the Spartans. They simply turned their backs and closed into a huddle.

"Come on, sissies!" seethed Bubba Smith. "You gonna quit?" And then he suddenly turned and yelled at Ara Parseghian over at the Notre Dame bench, "Quitter!" For Parseghian had made the decision to end the game this way. The Irish players had only followed instructions, some of them reluctantly.

Go inside Parseghian's head. His players had fought hard to come back from behind, 10–0 and tie the score. He didn't want to risk giving the game back to the Spartans cheaply. "One reckless pass and it could have cost us the game," Parseghian said afterward. "I wasn't going to do a jackass thing like throw it away at the last minute."

Thus ended a game that had been blown up for weeks into the biggest collegiate spectacle in 20 years. Notre Dame had won 8 games, lost none, and was rated No. 1. Michigan State had won 9 games, lost none, and was rated No. 2. In the game aftermath, everyone had something quaint to say. Parseghian still claimed No. 1 for the Irish, saying, "When you're Number One and you only get tied, you can't lose it."

Duffy Daugherty had other views.

"We ought to be No. 1 and Notre Dame ought to be No. 1-A," he said after the game.

Bear Bryant, whose Crimson Tide finished the season with an 11–0 record after demolishing Nebraska in the Sugar Bowl, refrained from coming right out and criticizing Parseghian for electing to run out the clock, but you knew he had Notre Dame in the back of his mind when he said: "I have a lot of seniors on this team. Some of them will be graduating and going on over to Vietnam, I suppose. When they get there, I just hope they don't play for a tie."

In 1976, a decade later, Duffy Daugherty admitted that his position against the Parseghian strategy had softened.

"Ara and I have since discussed it," he said. "Quite honestly, I don't think the press was fair to him. Notre Dame never had a chance of going for the score. They were back on the 30 yard line and we were in a fire defense all the time, so they couldn't do very much. If they'd put the ball in the air, we probably would have picked it off. I thought he was unjustifiably criticized. I don't know now what I might have done had the situation been reversed. Thank-

George Webster, selected by Michigan State fans as the school's "All-Time Greatest Player," shared the retirement of his old jersey No. 90 with former Spartan coaches Biggie Munn, left, and Duffy Daugherty. In the balloting for all-time honors, Webster had the distinction of being named variously as a lineman, end, and back.

fully, I didn't have to make that decision. You never know what you're going to do until the situation arises. You have to have certain rules about when you're gonna go for two, when you're gonna go for one and when you're gonna do certain things. You have to base it on time remaining in the game and whether you're going for a conference championship or a national championship. There are a lot of things involved. Sometimes a tie won't hurt you as much as a loss."

Still, for Ara Parseghian, that's *not* the way it was at East Lansing on November 19, 1966.

Michigan State was the first school in the Big Ten to win back-to-back football championships since Ohio State managed to do it in 1954 and 1955. The Spartans were pressed to prove their class in the Conference only once. In the rain against Ohio State they trailed the hopped-up Buckeyes, 2 to 0, until late in the third quarter when skittery Jimmy Raye, their quarterback, began hitting his receivers with key passes and led them 85 yards to what proved to be the only touchdown of the day. The final score was 8 to 2.

The Spartans lavished in talent. Mustacheoed Jimmy Raye, who was from South Carolina—another of the brilliant blacks who escaped Dixie—ran the attack. He shared the backfield with Clint Jones, as fine a runner as 1966 produced, and Dwight Lee and the explosive Bob Apisa. Up in the trenches, Duffy Daugherty had Gene Washington, one of the surest and fastest receivers in the country ("I can look in a man's eyes and know whether I can beat him") and Jerry West, a ferocious tackle. On defense they had "the intercontinental ballistic Bubba," as Spartan partisans referred to Bubba Smith, a creature whose play at defensive end had long ago encouraged students to wear buttons that read "Kill, Bubba, Kill"; Pat Gallinagh at tackle; and all-star linebackers Charley Thornhill and George Webster, who made 45 tackles by himself, assisted on 48 others, and was second to Bob Griese as the league's Most Valuable Player.

With Michigan State ineligible to return to the Rose Bowl a second straight time, runnerup Purdue, a sound, versatile team that had lost only to Michigan State (41–20) and to Notre Dame (26–14), got the call, and they won a thriller from Southern California, 14–13.

For Bob Griese, it was a brilliant closing of

Two-time All-American Bob Griese, winner of the Big Ten's MVP award in 1966 and runner-up in the Heisman voting, led Purdue to a 14–13 victory over Southern California on New Year's Day, 1967. The versatile quarterback passed, ran, punted, kicked off, and did all the placekicking for the Boilermakers on his way to a career total yardage league record of 4,829 yards.

his college career. Besides being the Boilermakers' punter and placekicker (extra points, field goals, and kickoffs), the two-time All-American quarterback established an all-time Big Ten record for total yardage gained in three years (4,829), and his 288 passing yards against Illinois in 1966 broke the league's single-game record. Griese was runnerup to

Florida's Steve Spurrier in the balloting for the Heisman Trophy.

"I like the unselfishness of Bob Griese," Fran Tarkenton said recently, speaking of him as a professional now. "We may never know how great he really is because he plays behind the greatest offensive line ever (Miami), and he only has to throw 10 passes a game."

1967

Indiana was the Cinderella Comeback-Team-of-the-Year in 1967. In only one year the Hoosiers, under former Yale coach Johnny Pont, improved from 1–8–1 to 9–1–0, gained a share (with Purdue and Minnesota) of the Big Ten championship for the first time since 1945, and for the first time in Bloomington history got to play in the Rose Bowl, where they lost to the No. 1 team in the nation, Southern California, 14 to 3.

But the real kick for the 1967 Hoosiers was the fun of the journey that led them to Pasadena. All around Indiana that season everybody said to keep the big red ball rolling, and handed you a little red ball. Superstition prevailed and everybody was afraid to change clothes and was looking for lucky pennies and charms and amulets and voodoo powers and shrunken skulls and soggy old tea leaves and crystal balls and magic wands. Everybody had taken to magic and sorcery and incantation and spells and was praying that their punter would—please—punt. Everybody was doing all this because a football phenomenon had overflowed the banks of the Wabash, and although there were a few undemented people who felt that reality was about to set in, it

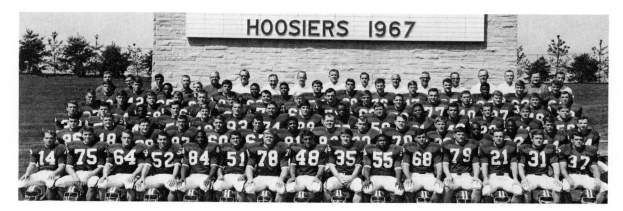

Big-Ten co-champions, 1967.

might not. For as everybody in Indiana said, God was alive and healthy and playing defensive end for Indiana.

What had happened was that the Hoosiers' flying carpet had carried them to seven victories in a row after it sneaked by Wisconsin, 14–9, and the Hoosiers did not usually win seven games in seven years. As a matter of fact, dating back to 1960, they had won a total of only five Conference games, and their football history was so depressing that their fans had learned to look back with fondness to 1958, when the team managed to finish fifth in the Big Ten with a 3–2–1 record. But there were the Hoosiers of 1967 now, 7–0–0, right up there No. 3 in the national poll, and sure-shots for the Rose Bowl with a loony bunch of sophomores who disobeyed Coach Pont at practically every turn, and who somehow won every game in that last crazy, bewildering moment.

What was their secret?

"All I know," said Pont, shaking his head, "is that we're uninhibited and unexpected. I ask my players what they're going to do to us next, and they just grin. I'm sure they don't know, themselves."

"What Indiana probably needs is Alfred Hitchcock," wrote Dan Jenkins of *Sports Illustrated*.

Indiana beat Kentucky, 12–10, when a fourth-down pass was deflected—yes—into a receiver's hands for a touchdown. It beat Kansas, 18–15, on a field goal by a substitute kicker because the regular had come up with an arthritic toe. It beat Illinois, 20–7, on a fumble. It beat Iowa, 21–17, after John Isenbarger, the punter, tried to run instead of punt on fourth down and failed, giving Iowa the ball for an easy go-ahead touchdown. A score in the last 53 seconds saved the day. It beat Michigan, 27–20, but needed a long drive in the last two minutes because Isenbarger had again tried to run instead of punt, allowing Michigan to tie the score.

"Coach, why do I *do* things like that?" Isenbarger had said.

"I don't know," Pont told him.

Neither did Isenbarger's mother, who sent the halfback a wire which read: "Dear John. Please punt for Pont."

Indiana managed to beat Wisconsin only because the Badgers were so inept (0–9–1 on the

A member of the 1967 Indiana Rose Bowl backfield, halfback John Isenbarger blossomed into a genuine All-American in 1969.

season). Trailing by only 14–9 with four minutes to play, Wisconsin proceeded to drive toward the Indiana goal. The Badgers got to midfield. They got to the Indiana 30. They got to the 25. They shoved on to the 19. By now, the Indiana defense looked about as organized as a hippie's crash pad. On the sideline, John Pont poured hot coffee on his wrist accidentally. Wisconsin got to the Indiana 10. There was time for one more play.

It was okay. John Isenbarger didn't have the ball. A Wisconsin quarterback did. And he threw it over the Indiana library, which was about a mile away. The big red ball kept rolling along.

Next to tumble was Michigan State, 14–13. But then came Minnesota, and the Gophers were primed. Before the Hoosiers knew what hit them, they were in the showers washing off the agony of defeat. Minnesota 33, Indiana 7!

The Big Ten title was on the block when Indiana and Purdue met in the final game of the regular season. A victory for the Boilermakers would make them undisputed champions; a loss would send the standings into a three-way tie between Indiana, Minnesota, and Purdue. It came up tie, as the Hoosiers won, 19–14. Their season's record of 9–1–0, as opposed to Purdue's and Minnesota's 8–2–0, earned them the ticket to Pasadena.

Gary Nicholson, trainer for the Chicago

Cubs, well remembers what the atmosphere was like at Bloomington in 1967. He was a member of the Indiana athletic training staff.

"That Indiana team was no fluke," Gary told me. "The drive for the Rose Bowl began at Spring practice. Mister Pont—we never called him Johnny—had all his athletes jogging on Tuesdays and Thursdays and lifting weights on Mondays, Wednesdays and Fridays. He ran things with precision, and was *very* well organized. What he was striving for was to turn things around. He was desperate. In his first two years at Indiana, he'd won only three games, had finished 9th in the Conference both times, and the wolves were howling. So that Spring, Mister Pont sat on this platform, bolted down to the backend of a pickup, and rode around the field observing practice. He was all over the place. He reminded me of a General of the Army, dashing around in a Jeep supervising his troops. He conducted practice by the clock. So many minutes for this, so many for that. Remember what Knute Rockne used to tell his players? 'Take out your watch and remember that when that second-hand moves from 60 to 60, that minute is gone,' Rock used to say. 'If you have wasted it, it will do you no good, because it is gone, never to come back. But if you have taken advantage of it, you can say you've made the best of your time.' Mister Pont, like Rockne, was a no-nonsense man; focused, concentrated, dedicated, a disciplinarian whose credo was excellence. And to be excellent was to *win*, and not go on losing. All he asked of his players was for them to live up to their capabilities. So when he blew that whistle of his, everybody jumped. The party was over. It was time to give Indiana fans something to cheer about.

"The big stars on the team were John Isenbarger, Harry Gonso, Gary Cassells, Ken Kaczmarek and Jim Sniadecki. Mister Pont, himself, was named Coach of the Year. Gonso was terribly short for a quarterback. Everybody said he'd need a stepladder to pass over his line. But he was a scrambler, he ran well, and he handled the ball like a magician—totally different from what the public had come to expect of Indiana quarterbacks. He brought style, flair to the attack.

"Right from the start, the Hoosiers quickly became known as the 'Cardiac Kids,' because of the last-ditch measures they took to win ball games. Practically overnight they were the sensations of the whole state. Now you saw Indiana students with sleeping bags lining up in front of football ticket booths on *Wednesdays*, waiting to get their tickets for Saturday's game. Every home game now was like World Series week in Boston. This was the first time in 22 years Indiana fans had anything to get excited about. I lived about two blocks from the stadium and on game-day the fans would start queuing up at the gates at 9 o'clock in the morning. The stadium held about 50,000 and it'd be full by noon, two hours before the kick-off. Oh, I tell you, those Indiana rooters were something.

"Even when Indiana played an away-game, the fans back in Bloomington, about 10,000 of them, would pay $2.00 apiece to watch the game on a giant screen on closed-circuit television in the Indiana gym—and the place would be jammed. Fantastic, their enthusiasm. Whenever Gonso ran or passed, the folks in that gym would stomp and cheer and rise to their feet and go bananas, just as though they were right at the game. One game, I recall, Indiana was in a dogfight at Minnesota and the Gophers were burying them. The Minnesota cheer section was so loud that Gonso couldn't make his linemen hear his signals. So he put up his hands in an appeal to the crowd to quiet down—and hundreds of miles away everybody in the Indiana gym suddenly went dead quiet, responding exactly the way they'd have reacted had they been at the stadium. When one big oaf kept talking this little old lady, about 70, told him to shut up, that the players couldn't hear Gonzo's signals, and he just ignored her. So she climbed up on her chair and hammered him over the head with her umbrella. Everybody cheered."

A record 26.4 million tickets were sold to 2,764 college football games by 610 four-year schools in 1967. This marked the 14th straight year that attendance in college football was up, following a four-year down cycle, which ended in 1953. Ohio State, Michigan, and Michigan State were the top three in attendance.

So much for the positive side. At the other end, Illinois got caught with its hands in the cookie jar in 1967. Mel Brewer, assistant athletic director, blew the whistle on the existence of an athletic slush fund at Champaign that clearly violated Big Ten Rules. Sums of money up to $50 a month beyond the legitimate athletic scholarship of tuition, books, and room and board had been given to several Illinois athletes, many of them still in school. One halfback had also received illegally several hundred dollars in travel expenses between his Florida home and the campus. The slush fund had been founded by alumni and businessmen.

When Dr. David D. Henry, the university president, heard about the under-the-table payments, he immediately went to William R. Reed, the Commissioner of the Big Ten. This resulted in the suspension of seven athletes from further competition in 1967, five of them permanently.

Commissioner Reed imposed even harsher penalties on the University of Illinois when he learned that the Illini coaches had known about the slush fund. Pete Elliott, the head football coach and basketball coach Harry Combes and his assistant, Howard Braun, were forced to walk the plank. The furor among Illini alumni, the press, and even the state legislature was intense. One faction wanted the university to stand behind its coaches and withdraw from the Big Ten Conference. But rather than force the school to act in an impossible situation, the three coaches resigned instead.

Thus the Big Ten weathered its most serious crisis of modern times.

1968

College football had an undisputed national champion once more in 1968, something that doesn't happen too often in an era of leveling competition on the higher echelons. Ohio State swept its 9-game regular-season schedule clean and went on to place No. 1 in the polls by decisively trouncing O. J. Simpson and Southern California, the 1967 champion and early 1968 stalking horse, 27 to 16, in the Rose Bowl.

The year 1968 was something more in the way of evidence that the heretofore Big Ten was now on the brink of becoming the Big Two in football. Ohio State and Michigan started playing keep-away with the Conference crown. In the first eight years of the decade, every school in the league except Northwestern won or shared at least one champi-

onship. But now the balance of power was gone, maybe forever. Now, beginning in 1968, historians could record it this way: Ohio State, Michigan–Ohio State (tie), Ohio State, Michigan, Ohio State–Michigan (tie), Michigan–Ohio State (tie), Ohio State–Michigan (tie), Ohio State.

When Woody Hayes gathered his players around him in the first week of fall practice 1968, there was an air of great expectancy and unfettered excitement in Columbus. Was it true, as Woody had been hinting, that this crop of sophomores was going to be the greatest in Buckeye history? The names did not mean anything then; youngsters like Rex Kern, John Brockington, Jack Tatum, Jan White, Larry Zelina, Leo Hayden, Tim Anderson, Mike Sensibaugh, Jim Stillwagon and a cavalry of others. As history could very well record, it was probably the most imposing single class ever recruited in college football, but the true verdict would have to be withheld until they took a crack at a real live enemy.

An even dozen sophomores were in the starting lineup as Ohio State opened the season with an impressive win over Jerry Levias and Southern Methodist, 35 to 14. They also looked pretty good beating Oregon, 21–6, the following Saturday. But then came undefeated Purdue, victors over Virginia (44–6), Notre Dame (37–22), and Northwestern (43–6), led by quarterback Mike Phipps and tailback Leroy Keyes. The Boilermakers were being touted as a possible national champion.

The Buckeyes had their work cut out for them. If they were for real they would have to beat Purdue, a very physical team. The line averaged 250 pounds, including two huge tackles who scaled out at 275.

Ohio State took the opening kickoff and marched straight down the field to the Purdue 4-yard line, where they finally gave up the ball after missing a field goal. For the rest of the first half, first one team and then the other threatened to break open the contest, but when they went to the dressing rooms it was still a scoreless tie.

Woody Hayes was deeply concerned about his players' tightness. He spent a lot of time at halftime going from player to player, easing the tension with some calm words of advice here, a pat on the back there. This uncharacteristic human side of the Ohio State martinet seemed to have a comforting effect on his young troops.

Purdue took the second half kickoff and were stopped on their own 18. Phipps passed to Leroy Keyes on the 27. A blast into the line got the first down. Now Phipps went to the air, but Jack Tatum, in the Ohio State defensive secondary, came up fast and broke up a pass intended for Keyes. On the next play, Phipps passed into the flat—right into the arms of Ohio State's lanky Ted Provost, who ran the ball back 34 yards for the first score of the game.

Then came high drama. Late in the third quarter, Bill Long, senior quarterback, who had lost the starting job to Rex Kern, the sensational sophomore, got his chance to star when Kern was injured and was forced to sit out the rest of the game. With the ball resting on the Purdue 14, Long called for a pass to right end Jan White on a delay pattern. But White was unable to get open. No one, in fact, was in the clear. So Long, spotting a hole in the middle of the line, set sail. He caught the startled Purdue secondary off-guard, swerved around a linebacker, and dashed into the end zone without a hand touching him. Ohio State now led, 13–0, and that was the end of the scoring for the day.

The odds-makers called it an upset.

"What do you mean, *upset*?" Woody Hayes wanted to know. "It's never an upset if the so-called underdog has all along considered itself the better team."

With a sophomore-studded team, Ohio State had merely held the vaunted Purdue rushing game to 69 yards. Keyes managed to carve out only 19 yards on the ground, while Phipps, the other half of the Boilermakers' super passing-running game, was charged with minus-4 yards for the day.

On their way to an undefeated season and No. 1 in the polls, the Buckeyes rolled up a total of 227 points in their next six wins, including a 50 to 14 shellacking of Michigan. But there were still doubters who wondered if Woody's Kiddie Corps could handle Southern California, No. 2 in the nation, in the Rose Bowl on New Year's Day. The Trojans were spearheaded by two-time All-American O. J. Simpson, one of the most exciting broken-field runners in the history of football.

For the first time in bowl-game annals, America's No. 1 and No. 2 teams were matched up in the same bowl. Despite Ohio State's impressive record, a surprising number of professional bettors were going with Southern Cal. One factor that influenced them was an injury in practice to the brilliant Rex Kern, which left him less than 100 percent. This was it for Woody and his peach-fuzzed prodigies.

The game started off as though it was going to be a Trojan runaway. At the end of the first quarter, USC led 10–0 on a field goal and an 80-yard run by Simpson.

Early in the second quarter, Quarterback Kern bawled at his teammates to stop messing around and get down to work. The Bucks responded by driving to the USC 31 in the next 10 plays. Then Kern faded back, faked a pass, and handed off to Leo Hayden on the draw play, good for 13 yards. Two plays later, it was third down on the 13. A fantastic headlong diving catch by Ray Gillian put the ball on the 3. Seconds later, Jim Otis bulled into the end zone to score. The try-for-point was good and now, with 1:45 left in the half, the scoreboard read 10–7, Southern California.

After the kickoff, Steve Sogge, USC's brilliant quarterback, was trapped for a 13-yard loss. The Trojans punted and the Buckeyes still had 60 seconds left in the half.

Kern switched his tactics and went to the air. He hit Jan White for 17, and Gillian for another 19. Now Ohio State had a first down on the Southern Cal 16. Jim Otis smashed the middle of the line for 6 more. After a time out and then an incompleted pass, Jim Roman set up to attempt a field goal with 3 seconds showing on the clock. The kick was good and now it was 10–10 as the half ended.

In the dressing room, Woody Hayes charged up his players.

"You've got 'em on the run now, " he told them. "If you make no mistakes there's just no way you can lose."

The Buckeye tacklers spent most of the third quarter in the Trojan backfield. Sogge and Simpson kept dropping the ball. On his own 21, Sogge finally fumbled it once too often and Ohio State recovered. That was the break Rex Kern was waiting for. On the first down, he tucked the ball in his belly and ran for 14 yards. With first-and-goal on the 7, the Trojans braced for another run, but Kern lofted a pass

Coach John Pont and 1969 Indiana tri-captains, Karl Pankratz, left, Harry Gonso, and Steve Applegate.

to Leo Hayden in the end zone, giving Ohio State the lead, 17–10.

Moments later, the great O. J. Simpson bobbled the ball on his own 16, and the Buckeyes recovered again. Kern kept up the pressure. On first down he hit Gillian on another scoring play to make it 24–10.

Ohio State kicked another field goal to fatten its lead to 17 points. The Trojans managed to score a touchdown with 45 seconds left in the game, but by then the contest was out of reach. With their 27–16 Rose Bowl victory, the Buckeyes returned to Columbus clearly the No. 1 college team in the land.

Unanimity ended with the Buckeyes, however. Behind them in the national polls, Penn State and USC were conflicting second choices. And in varying order, Texas, Georgia, Notre Dame, Arkansas, Kansas, Oklahoma, Purdue, and Tennessee were rated on the merit scale.

The Coach-of-the-Year award went to Joe Paterno of Penn State, and O. J. Simpson won the Heisman Trophy. All-Americans from the Big Ten were Dave Foley, Ohio State tackle; Leroy Keyes, Purdue halfback; Chuck Kyle,

Purdue middle guard; and Al Brenner, Michigan State defensive back.

While Ohio State dominated the major polls, the Game-of-the-Year went to Yale–Harvard. Both schools were 8–0–1 for the season and shared the Ivy League title. Going into their ancient series with both unbeaten and untied for the first time since 1909, they played one of the most sensational games in all football history. Harvard trailed 22–0 in the second quarter and 29–13 with 42 seconds remaining in the game—and still gained a *tie* by scoring two touchdowns and a pair of 2-point conversions before the final gun.

1969

The big preseason news out of Ann Arbor in 1969 was that Michigan had a new football coach, the 13th since Mike Murphy was first hired in 1891. The name was Bo Schembechler and in his first year at Michigan, he matched Bump Elliott's 1968 record of 6–1–0 in the Conference and 8–2–0 overall.

"Bo was hired in 15 minutes," Will Perry said. "It took Don Canham, in his first year as athletic director, just that long to make up his

Former Woody Hayes athlete and assistant Bo Schembechler won Big Ten championship at Michigan in his very first year as head coach in 1969. At the 1975 Heisman Trophy dinner in New York, Bo sat next to two-time winner Archie Griffin and with tongue in cheek, cracked: "Archie and I have a lot in common. We both played for Woody Hayes. He brags about it and I can't live it down."

mind. Actually, the search for a new coach began before the 1968 season had even ended. Canham asked Bump if he was interested in becoming the associate athletic director, and when Bump said yes, Don acted quickly. He asked Bump and other football people to give him a list of names they felt were good prospects to fill the vacancy. Bo Schembechler's name kept popping up on every list. Bo, a builder of mid-American football powers at Miami of Ohio and line coach for Woody Hayes at Ohio State, jumped at the chance when Bump Elliott phoned him and asked him if he'd be interested in coming to Michigan.

"'Hell, yes!' Bo told him. And, later, to me, he said, 'It isn't every day that you get a call to come to Michigan and talk about the football coaching job. I hoped at the time Bump didn't notice the excitement in my voice.'

"Bo arrived in Ann Arbor a few days later and he and Canham talked for two hours in the coffee room at the athletic administration building. Marc Plant, the faculty representative, was also there. When the meeting broke up, Bo asked Canham, 'Okay, what happens now?' And Canham told him, 'I'll call you in a day or two,' but he had already made up his mind that Bo was the man for the job. He confessed that he knew it was going to be Bo only 15 minutes after meeting him. Canham told me, 'He had great enthusiasm, charisma. He knew what he wanted, and I could see he wanted the job badly.' So Canham phoned him a day afterward and said the job was his. All Bo said was, 'Good.' Nothing else, just good. 'Fine,' Canham told him. 'The salary is $21,000.' That was about $1,000 more than Bo would have earned at Miami. 'How soon can you get back here?' Canham wanted to know. And Bo told him, 'Is tomorrow night soon enough?' He arrived the next afternoon."

Glenn E. (Bo) Schembechler, Jr., was born to football. He always dreamed of being a big-time college coach, even during his playing days at Miami of Ohio, where he was a pudgy, 190-pound offensive tackle for Woody Hayes. Bo said he will never forget the first time he saw Woody.

"It was in my junior year," Bo recalled, "and Woody had come over from little Denison University to replace Sid Gillman, a great coach and a great guy who'd left to take over at Cincinnati. We all loved Sid and here was this grim-looking guy taking his place. Woody said he wanted to meet all the players so we all lined up his first day at Miami and he came right down the line shaking hands with everybody, looking each of us smack in the eye, with something to say to each one. He seemed direct and honest as hell. I had a hunch right then and there he was something special. And on the practice field he was special, too—a shouting, screaming fireball who was bodily grabbing guys all over the place, spinning them around while showing them what he wanted, all the while yelling at them. The players were sore as hell and cussed him behind his back. They couldn't believe it. We had a 5–4 year and the more we lost the more Woody drove us. It wasn't his fault that we lost those four games. When Sid Gillman left Miami for Cincinnati he took a lot of our best talent with him as transfers. Woody never forgave Sid for that. But Woody rebuilt the team and whipped us into the kind of team he wanted, and, in 1950, we won eight out of nine games, including a biggie over Arizona State in the Salad Bowl in Phoenix. The season included a 28–0 smasher over Cincinnati. I never saw a man who got as much pleasure out of revenge as Woody did when we beat Sid Gillman's team. A lot of people were surprised a few weeks later when Woody became a candidate for the Ohio State job, but I wasn't one of them. I wasn't surprised at all."

Bo later served as a graduate student assistant under Hayes at Columbus, coached football in the Army, and then in 1954 got his first full-time job as line coach at Presbyterian College. The salary was $3,400 a year "and cafeteria rights."

The Schembechler trail led next to Bowling Green, then to Northwestern on the staff of Ara Parseghian, and back to Ohio State for five years. Bo's first head coaching position was in 1963 at Miami, where in six seasons he won two championships, twice was named Coach of the Year, and finished with a 40–17–3 record.

Bo brought his own coaching staff to Ann Arbor, but agreed to retain George Mans and Frank Maloney as assistants from the Bump Elliott administration. Bo also brought with him a new concept of football defense, the five-man angle. And he brought a passion for hard work.

Schembechler was honest with Don Canham.

"There's no way I'm going to be a winner right off the bat," he said. "You may as well know that right now."

"I know it," Canham said.

"Then how long do I have to build a winner?" Bo asked.

"Five years," Canham told him. "Take my word for it."

"Well," Bo said, "be patient with me because anything can happen."

Impulsive, quick-tempered, Bo Schembechler was never one to hide his frustrations. He liked things in the open. As for defeat, he was uncompromising. Once, when Woody Hayes threw a chair at him, Schembechler fired it right back.

Bo was not too unhappy with the material that Bump Elliott left him. "Bump has given me a good football team," he told the press in early September. "I don't know if we can win the championship, but we're going to make a run at it."

Schembechler was particularly impressed by his crop of incoming sophomores: Reggie

McKenzie, Guy Murdock, Paul Seymour along the offensive line: Glenn Doughty, Billy Taylor, and Fritz Seyferth in the backfield; Tom Darden, Fred Grambau, Mike Taylor, Mike Keller, Tom Beckman, and Bruce Elliott on defense. Team captain Jim Mandich was an outstanding tight end, and Tom Curtis was an All-American prospect at safety.

Michigan began the 1969 campaign with lopsided wins over Vanderbilt and Washington, fumbled a 40–17 game away to the opportunistic Missouri Tigers, trounced Purdue, 31–20, and went into the traditional Michigan State contest with a 3–1 record. Here again mistakes cost the young Wolverines the ball game. A fumble and a safety broke the game wide open for the Spartans. After the 23–12 defeat, Bo said, "I thought we were 3-and-2 for the season, but our alumni tell me we are 3-and-3. I didn't know that the Michigan State game counts as two."

The Wolverines were a battered team the following Saturday against Minnesota in the annual battle for the Little Brown Jug. The Gophers quickly took the lead, 9–7, but Michigan smashed back in the second half to score four more touchdowns on drives of 75 yards, 66, then 41, and finally 21. Billy Taylor, subbing for the injured Glenn Doughty, was the star with 151 yards on the ground. The final score was 35–9.

Taylor, a stubby, quick runner, also rambled 142 yards in just 15 carries as Michigan crushed Wisconsin, 35–7, the next Saturday. The week after that, they romped over Illinois, 57–0, with Garvie Craw scoring four of the touchdowns. It was the worst defeat for the Illini by Michigan in 55 years.

The next opponent was Iowa, and the Hawkeyes fell, 51–6. Billy Taylor was once more the young man of the hour, gaining 225 yards from scrimmage.

The Wolverines were 7–2–0 coming down to the final game against 8–0–0 Ohio State, the No. 1 team in the national polls. Down at Columbus, they were calling the Buckeyes "the best college team of all time." And who was to argue, for two years later, in an AP poll, Woody's 1968 team would be voted the Team of the Decade. Now his 1968 sophomores were juniors, a year older, toughened by experience. Names like Rex Kern, Jim Otis, Jack Tatum, and Jim Stillwagon headed the greatest collection of All-Americans ever assembled on one team. They were undefeated and favored to stay that way by 20 points or more over poor old Michigan. So what happened? Well, in a game played at Ann Arbor, the Wolverines did nothing wrong and the Buckeyes didn't do a lot of things right, and if you were an Ohio State fan, never mind the bloody details. Michigan 24, Ohio State 12.

Oh, how Woody seethed. There would be Revenge in 1970. Put that in large type, like this: REVENGE. Adding coal to Woody's fire was an unsympathetic carpet-maker in Columbus who shipped him a rug into which had been woven:

1969: MICHIGAN 24, OHIO STATE 12
1970. . . ?

Woody laid that damned rug at the door leading to the football practice field so that every player had to tromp on it on the way to practice every day the following year.

Ed Ferkany can tell you how much Woody hates Michigan. He once served as Woody's line coach at Ohio State, and he drove the boss up to Michigan on a recruiting trip. On the way back through southern Michigan, Ferkany noticed the gas gauge was running dangerously low.

"Woody," he said, "I think we'd better stop for gas at the next station."

Woody was in a hurry to get home.

"Naagh," he said, "keep going. We can make it."

So Ferkany passed the next station by.

A half-hour down the road, Ferkany glanced nervously at the gas gauge again. The needle rested almost on the big E. Up ahead loomed the lights of another filling station.

"Uh, Woody," Ferkany said tentatively. "There's another gas station up ahead. I really think we'd better stop this time and fill up."

"No, goddammit!" Woody growled. "We do *not* pull in and fill up."

"But why? The tank's empty."

"I'll tell you exactly why!" Woody said. "I don't buy one goddam drop of gas in the state of Michigan!"

There was a brief pause, then, "We'll coast and *push* this goddam car to the Ohio line before I give this state a penny of *my* money!"

Jerry Brondfield, Woody's biographer, testified that the Ohio State coach's dislike of anything relevant to the state of Michigan is so pronounced he will not even mention the Wolverine's by name. They are only "that team up north." Whatever he calls them, his record against Michigan during the years 1951–1975 was 16 wins, 8 losses, and 1 tie.

The 1969 Rose Bowl game, on New Year's Day, 1970, matched the nation's No. 5 team, Southern California, against No. 6 Michigan. The smart money favored the Trojans even more when Glenn Doughty injured his knee in practice and underwent emergency surgery, forcing the great Michigan running back to miss the Rose Bowl.

Then two days before the contest, Bo Schembechler failed to appear at the 5 o'clock nightly news conference at Pasadena's Huntington Hotel. Members of the press waited 20 minutes, but he never showed up. Finally, Jim Young, Bo's defensive coordinator, strolled into the room and rapped for attention.

Speaking in a soft, controlled voice, Jim said, "Bo won't be here tonight. He's got an upset stomach. If you have any questions about the game, I'll try to answer them for you."

That evening, Drs. Jerry O'Connor and Bob Anderson, the Michigan physicians, committed Bo to a Pasadena clinic for a checkup. An EKG test revealed no abnormalities, and Bo was allowed to accompany Captain Jim Mandich, his star end, to the annual kickoff luncheon the following day. Later that night, all the Michigan players and coaches were lodged in a monastery in the mountains on the edge of Pasadena, a custom practiced by most Big Ten teams in order to escape the noise and disturbances on New Year's Eve. The next morning, while the Michigan athletes were being taped prior to their short bus trip over to the Rose Bowl, Jim Young walked into the room and quietly announced to the team that Bo had just been taken to the hospital with chest pains. The doctors feared it might be a heart attack. The players listened glumly, but said nothing. When Jim Young finished talking, some of the athletes went to a nearby chapel and prayed.

"My immediate reaction was that we'd kick the hell out of Southern Cal and win it for Bo," later confessed Frank Gusich, the defensive back. "But that's a lot of bull. It wasn't what I felt at all. Deep down I felt terribly cold, like all the fire had suddenly gone out of me."

So there was no Bo Schembechler leading the Wolverines when they dashed onto the field to warm up for the game.

"Where's Bo?" somebody up in the press box wanted to know.

"I hear he's sick," he was told. "Virus or something. He won't be here."

Those close to Bo knew it was a flat lie. It would take more than a mere virus to keep him away from the Rose Bowl. Obviously he was a very sick man.

For the Michigan players, the glamour, the thrill of the Rose Bowl was gone, and they went down to defeat, 10–3. It was the first time the Big Ten had lost to the PAC-8 in the Rose

Bowl in four years. The contest, itself, was unspectacular. Six points were scored in the first half as the teams traded field goals, and then in the third quarter, Jimmy Jones found Bob Chandler in the clear and flipped the ball to him for what became a 33-yard scoring play. That ended the points for the day. Michigan had an edge in first downs, but USC had more total yards—and 7 more points.

In their postgame stories, the Pacific Coast press corps attached very little significance to Schembechler's heart attack. Most of their space was reserved for the victorious Trojans. The real story, however, lay in that hospital bed in Pasadena. When the Michigan team flew back to Ann Arbor on January 2, Bo remained behind. With him were the prayers of everyone on that plane.

The Big Two?

The 1970s

1970

The big Five of 1969—Texas, Ohio State, Michigan, Southern California, and Penn State—figured to be in the thick of the fight again for the national championship, along with Mississippi, Notre Dame, Arkansas, Stanford, LSU, Nebraska, and Houston, and who knew what other teams.

Each year, the competition was getting stiffer because, more and more, there were an increasing number of teams capable of beating any rival on any given day.

Under the stimulus of this leveling competition on an ever-widening scale, college football's officially reported attendance rose approximately 35 percent over the previous decade, from 20,403,409 in 1960 to a high of 27,626,160 in 1969. Continued gains were in prospect.

Thankfully, the NCAA Rules Committee left the football code alone again. Aside from minor technical corrections and language clarification, there were no significant rules changes in 1970. So all was set for the kickoff to another big season.

Ohio State, which had the national No. 1 spot wrapped up in 1969 until it came a final-game cropper against Michigan, was determined to go to the top, sectionally at least, with no slip-ups this time. They had lost a lot of good players through graduation but also retained many. Heading Ohio State's starry cast

was quarterback Rex Kern and cornerback Jack Tatum. The slick Kern gave the Buckeye offense one of the finest passing games in the Big Ten, if not the nation, because he was not only a sharp, pin-point passer but also a superb runner on the option. Averaging 16 to 20 passes a game, the Kern game plan called for flexibility.

Within the Big Ten, Michigan, Purdue, Minnesota, and Michigan State loomed as the chief threats to the Buckeyes. The Wolverines were strong again on defense, but not much was known about their offense, where losses had been heavy.

The Boilermakers had good personnel overall, but needed a quarterback to replace the departed Mike Phipps. They rated as a strong contender, however, with star performers in halfback Stan Brown, end Ashley Bell, fullback John Bullock, and guard Tom Luken. Minnesota had been a fast finisher in 1969 and now were a title threat. Michigan State looked to be on the rise, and were counting on a strong defense and offensive backfield. Indiana was inexperienced in spots but prospects were good overall. Iowa needed a quarterback to be a factor in the race. Twenty-nine lettermen were back at Northwestern, giving the Wildcats their most experienced squad in years. They figured to be versatile on attack. Alan Thompson, a 210-pound junior fullback, and junior quarterback Neil Graff were being

150

counted on to carry the offensive load at Wisconsin. And Illinois, winless in 1969, looked for much better things. They evaluated their 1970 squad as "deeper, faster, more talented."

When the Wolverines reported to Bo Schembechler on August 20th, he weighed 175 pounds, down 45 pounds since recovering from his heart attack. He was ready to go after another Conference championship. Most of the key members of the Rose Bowl team were back. The biggest losses were Tom Curtis and All-American end Jim Mandich. Don Moorhead, and Henry Hill, the little middle guard, were elected co-captains. The attack was set with Billy Taylor and Glenn Doughty. Schembechler was not expected to start very many sophomores. Still, the title race figured to be another Michigan–Ohio State showdown on November 21 in Columbus—and that is precisely the way it developed.

The Wolverines and Buckeyes came up to that final Saturday undefeated. If they had to pick a winner, the dopesters said, they would go with Ohio State.

Sparks flew from the start. The Bucks kicked off, Lance Scheffler fumbled, and Ohio State recovered. Michigan's big line stiffened, forcing the Buckeyes to settle for a 28-yard field goal. But the tone of the game had been established. "Breaks will decide the game," Schembechler told his players, and he was right.

Michigan tied the contest on Coin's 31-yard field goal, before it ran into trouble. Backed up against his own goal, Paul Staroba lifted a 73-yard punt downfield, only to have it called back when one of his linemen, Reggie McKenzie, was penalized for a face-mask infringement while charging down to cover the kick. Ohio State gained field position when Staroba's second punt traveled only 42 yards. The opportunistic Bucks scored a touchdown minutes later. Then quarterback Don Moorhead got hot and fired a 13-yard touchdown pass to Staroba, but Dana Coin missed the extra point and Michigan still trailed, 10–9, in the third quarter. That's as close as the Wolverines got. Ohio roared back with 10 more points in the last 15 minutes to close the door on the Maize and Blue. For the second time in three years, the Bucks represented the Big Ten in the Rose Bowl.

Ohio State was favored by 10 points over Stanford, despite the Indians' explosive attack, headed by Jim Plunkett, whom Bud Wilkinson

Don Moorhead smashed most of Michigan's passing records in 1969 and 1970 as the Wolverines won 17 out of 20 games.

It was bombs away as Stanford All-American quarterback Jim Plunkett pitched to his favorite target, Randy (The Rabbit) Vataha, to shock Ohio State in the Rose Bowl, 27–17, on New Year's Day, 1971. Plunkett completed 20 of 30 passes for 265 yards.

called "the best college quarterback I ever saw." As a senior, Plunkett passed for 2,715 yards and 18 touchdowns, both PAC-8 records, and won both the Heisman and Maxwell Trophies. His career performance at Palo Alto included 7,544 yards and 52 touchdowns through the air, which were NCAA records. After redshirting one season, he could have left school for a fat pro contract prior to his senior season, but he chose to stay with his team and college. His major was political science and he had good grades.

Plunkett's favorite target was Randy (The Rabbit) Vataha. Their coach was John Ralston, who had brought Stanford its first conference championship in 20 years. After defeating Washington to clinch the title, the Indians let down and lost their last two games. The Rose Bowl bettors cruelly called them a second-rate football team. "They can never beat Ohio State," the doubters said. "Ralston is a recruiter, not a coach. He wins the little ones, not the big ones."

The New Year's Day, 1971, Rose Bowl Game boiled down to a few vital plays in the final quarter. The first was a fourth-and-one play by Ohio State on the Stanford 20, the first play of the quarter. The Buckeyes, ahead 17–13, had driven 74 yards, and another touchdown would almost lock it up, judging by the way they had been controlling the ball.

Rex Kern handed off to John Brockington, his fullback, who had already rushed for 99 yards. Brockington headed for the left end, saw Chuck McCloud, the sophomore cornerback, racing in fast, turned inside to miss him and was nailed by linebacker Ron Kadziel for no gain.

Taking over the ball at that point, Stanford drove 80 yards in 13 plays—Plunkett throwing five-for-five—to score the touchdown that put Stanford in front, 20-17.

On the next series of Ohio State downs, Kern dumped a short pass into the hands of Jack Schultz, the Stanford co-captain, on the Buckeye 25. Four plays and 57 seconds later Stanford had a 27–17 lead, then turned the game over to its defense. When the game ended, this set of statistics pretty much told the story:"Plunkett—completed 20 of 30 passes for 265 yards."

"You have to play a full 60 minutes," Woody Hayes said after the game. "We played well at

some points, moved the ball well, but football is a 60-minute game. When they stopped us at the 20, that was the ball game."

1971

It was estimated that college football would be hard-pressed in 1971 to top the chain of events which ushered in the year back on January 1st.

On that day, from coast to coast and in between, the nation watched in amazement as first Texas' defending national champions and then mighty Ohio State forfeited their claim to be the No. 1 team in the country. When the shooting and shouting was over, the Cornhuskers of Nebraska ruled the roost, followed by Notre Dame and Texas. The results of the New Year's Day dramatics went like this: Notre Dame 24, Texas 11 in the Cotton Bowl at Dallas; Nebraska 17, Louisiana State 12 in the Orange Bowl at Miami; and, of course, Stanford 27, Ohio State 17 in the Rose Bowl at Pasadena.

Although Nebraska felt it had enough strength to retain its national championship and might be even better than the previous season, 1971 could well be the year that Notre Dame returned to the top. The Fighting Irish finished second in the 1970 polls after upsetting Texas in the Cotton Bowl and Coach Ara Parseghian's only real problem was replacing quarterback Joe Theismann. He had 17 of his 22 Cotton Bowl starters returning.

With 1970's leaders in total offense (Pat Sullivan, Auburn), passing (Sonny Sixkiller, Washington), and rushing (Ed Marinaro, Cornell) all returning, college football's 102nd season was almost certain to be another explosive one.

In the Big Ten, Ohio State had lost heavily from three straight super teams and was expected to give way to Michigan. But the Buckeyes had another great freshman contingent and could be a factor again, along with Northwestern, Michigan State, Wisconsin, and Illinois.

Michigan came down to opening day with two untested sophomores, Kevin Casey and Tom Slade, battling to be the No. 1 quarterback. The rest of the team was firmly established. Seldom had the Wolverines been so deep in reserves. There were 5 starters back from the 1970 squad—all the running backs, four offensive and four defensive linemen, and three of the defensive secondary. Guard Reggie McKenzie, linebacker Mike Taylor, cornerback-safety Tom Darden, and tailback Billy Taylor were all prime All-American candidates. As an added sidelight, once more there were two Elliotts on the Michigan squad. Bump and Pete had played together in 1946–47, and now the latter's older son, Bruce, was a starting wideside halfback, while Dave, Pete's younger son, was a defensive halfback.

Most major college schedules were increased to 11 games in 1971 as schools frantically sought new revenue. The Big Ten, moving toward a roundrobin, ordered that the extra contest be played with a team from the Conference. It was spotted as the opening game of the season, and Michigan drew Northwestern. The Wildcats had tied for second in 1970 and were destined to place right up there by themselves in 1971. Coach Alex Agase got along well with his players, and the alumni. "If you really want to advise me," he told Old Grads, "do it on Saturday afternoon between one and four o'clock. And you've got 25 seconds to do it, between plays. Not on Monday. I know the right thing to do on Monday."

It appeared he knew the right thing to do on Saturday, too. The Wildcats had Michigan in deep trouble and seemed headed for a major upset, until Dana Coin went back to try a field goal from the 42. Northwestern placed a defender in front of the crossbar. Coin's placekick appeared to fall short, and the defender tipped it with his fingers as it went over his head. With the ball bouncing erratically in the end zone, Bo Rather, with sprinter's speed, got to it first and fell on it for a touchdown.

"Weirdest play in my football career," Bo Schembechler said after the game. "A three-point field goal attempt turns into seven points."

That break turned the game completely around. Michigan won, 21–6. For the next three weekends, Michigan stomped Virginia (56–0), UCLA (38–0), and Navy (46–0). Virginia never gained a yard passing, UCLA was held to 39 yards on the ground, and Navy got a mere 34 rushing.

The Michigan juggernaut pushed on: 24–13 over Michigan State, 35–6 over Illinois, 35–7 over Minnesota, 61–7 over Indiana, 63–7 over Iowa, 20–17 over Purdue, right up to the Ohio

As the former President of the American Football Coaches Association, Bob Blackman boasts broad coaching background. In 16 years at Dartmouth, his teams had a 104–37–3 record. Illinois, with a lowly 2–19 Big Ten record, hired him in 1971 and immediately finished third in the Conference with a 5–3 record.

State game at Ann Arbor. The victory over Purdue clinched the 23rd Big Ten title for the Wolverines. Dana Coin, whose NCAA extrapoint record was intact at 53 straight, kicked a 25-yard field goal with only 26 seconds left to beat the Boilermakers.

Ohio State, meanwhile, had lost three times. For the first time in four games, the title was not at stake in a Michigan–Ohio State game. No matter. The Buckeyes had been severely beset with injuries all season—at least six starters were on the sidelines—and they traveled to Michigan to salvage the season against the No. 3 team in the nation.

Woody had done the best patch-up job of his life. He had his boys believing they actually had a chance. They nearly pulled it off, too. They went into the fourth quarter leading, 7–3. Then late in the game the defense let down just long enough for Bill Taylor to get loose on a 22-yard run and suddenly Michigan had forged ahead, 10–7.

In a final, desperate drive, Ohio fought back and looked as if it might pull off the greatest upset of Woody Hayes' career. Don Lamka pitched a long floater to Dick Wakefield on the Michigan 32. Both Wakefield and defender Tom Darden went up for the ball at the same time. They collided in mid-air and crashed to the ground. Somehow, Darden got his hands on the ball and held on to it. The officials ruled it an interception.

"Interference!" screamed Woody Hayes. A decision in his favor meant an automatic first down with excellent field position for Ohio State. With a minute left to play, they could win the game or at least tie. But the official nearest the collision refused to drop his flag. Hayes stormed onto the field in violent protest. He got nowhere with the officials—except a 15-yard penalty for storming onto the playing field. Several of the Ohio assistant coaches tried to pull Woody back to the sidelines. Woody pushed them off and grabbed one of the sideline cloth down markers off its post and tore it to shreds. Then, as an official stared in astonishment, he flung the bits like confetti on the ground. The official's response was to march off another 15 yards against Ohio State. Michigan ran out the clock, saving its 10–7 victory.

A lot of Americans were talking about Woody the Terrible's conduct the next day. In case anybody missed his performance, ABC-TV repeated it on the NCAA weekly highlight show. Newspaper editorialists were aghast. They demanded a public apology from Woody. "First it was ludicrous, then revolting," wrote the Cleveland *Plain Dealer*. "It's one thing to be a fierce competitor—quite another to be a horse's rear end, which he was at Ann Arbor."

Don Canham, Michigan's athletic director, enjoyed the show. He said he was willing to buy all the sideline markers Woody wanted to rip up.

"When Ohio State comes to Michigan," Don pointed out, "who do you think our fans come to see—the players? No sir, they come to see Woody Hayes. He's worth an extra 30,000 tickets. The men take their children down by the field and point him out. I've seen it."

After all the fumin' died down, Woody explained his deportment at Ann Arbor in these words: "I did it for my players. I owed it to them. I'd have been derelict in my duty to them if I'd done less."

Michigan opposed Stanford in the Rose Bowl on New Year's Day. The game was dominated by the defenses. Michigan's power attack chopped out a total of 264 yards, but it took a 30-yard field goal by Dana Coin to go ahead in the second quarter, 3–0. Then, in the third quarter, Stanford tied the score on a 42-yard placekick by Rod Garcia. The Wolverines went ahead in the fourth quarter when Fritz Seyferth blasted into the end zone from the one. That set the stage for one of the most dramatic climaxes in the history of the Tournament of Roses.

Facing a fourth-down situation on its 33-yard line, Stanford faked a punt and Jackie Brown broke up the field for 31 yards. Then, on the next play, he cut off tackle for another 36 yards and the touchdown. Garcia's placekick was good and now it was 10–10.

Soon after, a Michigan drive stalled in Stanford territory, and Coin failed to cash in on another field-goal attempt from the 42. The ball went to Jim Ferguson who took it on the 3-yard line, retreated a few steps, and was nailed behind his own goal line. Michigan was awarded a safety and now led, 12–10.

Forced to free kick, the Stanford defense stopped three straight running plays and got the ball back on a punt. Time was of the essence now as they started their drive from their own 22. Quarterback Don Bunce took to the air. He hit on two passes, missed another, and rifled three more receptions. Two running plays netted another three yards and excellent field position. With only 16 seconds left on the clock, Stanford quickly took a time out.

Bunce looked over to the sidelines. John Ralston had his arm around little Rod Garcia, his nifty soccer-style placekicker who had already booted one field goal.

"Be big out there," Ralston told him. "Go ahead and kick it."

"Kick!" screamed the crowd.

The ball rested on the 31. A soft breeze blew in Garcia's face, but he was game. He was confident. The crowd was hushed now. Everybody was standing, their hearts pounding, as they watched little Rod line up his kick. Now he waited for the snap-back. Several minutes ago all the pressure had been on Don Bunce, now it was on Garcia.

The ball came back. The holder set it up nice and pretty. Garcia stepped forward and put the full weight of his body into the ball.

The kick was perfect. The referee flung his arms upward like a man with a gun in his back. For the first time in the game, Stanford led. And for the second year in a row, they won the Rose Bowl in a major upset. The victory not only spoiled Michigan's first perfect season in a generation, but it also avenged Stanford's 49–0 humiliation at the hands of Michigan in that first Rose Bowl game in 1902.

The final scoreboard numbers had extra meaning for Stanford. For the second time that season, the Cardinals were caught in a 13–12 ball game. San Jose State defeated them in the first one, in the next to last game of the regular schedule. The tiny Chilean, Rod Garcia, was on center stage in that one, too: *He missed five field goals and an extra point!*

1972

The big question in college football in the fall of 1972 was : Could Nebraska make it three in a row?

The Cornhuskers had captured the last two national championships and no team had ever won three straight. Nebraska, however, was loaded again and had a real shot at it. They entered the 1972 campaign with streaks of 23 consecutive victories and 32 games without defeat and they had three superstars in wide receiver Johnny Rogers, middle guard Rich Glover, and defensive end Willie Harper. In addition, this was the final season for Bob Devaney, who had never won Coach of the Year honors, although he had the best record in football, giving Nebraska a little extra incentive.

The Cornhuskers, however, would find it no easy matter to repeat in the powerful Big Eight Conference, which posted an unprecedented 1-2-3 sweep in the final 1971 national rankings with Oklahoma and Colorado trailing Nebraska.

The preseason experts said this about the Big Ten: "The winner should come from among Ohio State, Illinois, Michigan, Purdue, and Michigan State." But in a national poll, they picked only the Buckeyes to finish in the Top Ten.

Woody had had another good recruiting year. One of his prize plums was sophomore Harold (Champ) Henson, a 6–4, 228-pound farm boy from Teays Valley High School, just 17 miles down the road from Columbus. Teays Valley was so tiny that the big-time recruiters seldom bothered to scout it. But they had heard about Champ Henson, and Notre Dame, Purdue, and Michigan already were parked on his doorstep by the time Woody Hayes got there.

Henson met him with cool indifference. He said he had just about decided to enroll at Michigan. *Michigan!* Woody could accept about any school but that institution to the north.

Woody turned on the charm.

"Son," he said, "I've seen your game film and you're a great prospect for fullback. You know, of course, that we're a fullback school. I admit we goofed by not coming to you sooner, and we've hurt your pride. I don't blame you. Pride is a great asset. No real football player should be without it."

Woody let that sink in for a moment, then, "But if I were you, I wouldn't let pride get in the way of making the right decision. This is one of those times when pride isn't the priority. You're from Ohio and you belong at Ohio State."

P.S. As a sophomore in 1972, Champ Henson scored 20 touchdowns for the Buckeyes to lead the nation.

That same fall, Rudy Hubbard, one of Woody's backfield coaches, had a tough time proving to Woody that he should be playing one of his freshmen halfbacks more. In practice, Woody ignored the advice, but in the season opener he did let the boy go into the game for several plays. Hubbard didn't like it. He was certain the boy should be seeing more action. Even starting. But in the second game, against North Carolina, Woody insisted on starting another tailback. Finally, halfway into the first quarter, Woody let Hubbard send the boy into the game.

Which was how Archie Griffin got into his first big college game and rushed 239 yards for a new Ohio State record.

Meanwhile, up at Ann Arbor, Bo Schembechler was counting on another batch of extraordinary sophomores to bolster a nucleus of only nine starters from the 1971 team. Bo did not look for any help from a corps of incoming freshmen, although the Big Ten's new rule allowed frosh to play varsity ball now. While the Wolverines had plenty of experience in their offensive line, the backfield and most of the defense had to be reconstructed.

Dennis Franklin, a willowy, All-State quarterback from Massillon, Ohio, was one of the sophomores Schembechler was counting on. He had a strong arm and he knew football. When the coach announced to the press that young Franklin was his starting quarterback, one of the writers asked the boy if playing at Ann Arbor in front of 100,000 people would make him nervous.

"I don't know," Franklin said, honestly. "Down home, the biggest crowd I ever played before was 20,000."

Franklin was the third sophomore within a year to start at quarterback for the Wolverines when they opened the season against Northwestern. His 21-yard pass to Bo Rather won the game, 7–0. They won their next nine games in a row with ease, while Ohio State rolled over Iowa, North Carolina, California, Illinois, Indiana, Wisconsin, and Minnesota, before losing a shocker to Michigan State, 19–12. So the Buckeyes were fighting for their lives when they came up to the finale against Michigan. The Wolverines could win the title outright with a victory; the best the Bucks could hope for was a co-championship. To the

Three-time All–Big Ten quarterback Dennis Franklin ran, passed, and triggered the Michigan option in 1972–73–74.

victor, however, would go the Rose Bowl invitation—and pride, prestige, blood. Michigan, 10–0–0, was favored. It had not lost in the Big Ten since this match in 1970. The final scene:

Ohio State was leading Michigan, 14–11, with only 13 seconds showing on the clock in the last quarter. Michigan had the ball on Ohio's 41-yard line, fourth down and 10 coming up. Buckeye fans were beside themselves. They could hold back their enthusiasm no longer. Suddenly they swooped down onto the field and began attacking the goal posts and splintering them. The uprights in Ohio State's end zone came down. Michigan was nearly in field goal range. From the sideline, Woody Hayes could envision a penalty, a forfeit, something dismantling this big upset his team was so close to pulling off. He charged the mob and shooed them back like an old lady shooing chickens out of her garden. Then he swatted some kid across the head and pushed him off the field.

Mercifully, security guards finally moved in, restored order, and the game was finished—minus goal posts.

The figures were all Michigan's, 20 first downs, 344 yards, balance in 184 yards rushing and 160 passing. Ohio State compiled 192 total yards, nearly all on the ground, but when it was all over the numbers on the big scoreboard read: Ohio State 14, Michigan 11.

The two teams had become terribly decent about Rose Bowl trips. They were taking turns. This was Ohio State's turn, but it left Bo Schembechler unwell. "I am just sick about not getting into the end zone more often," he said after the game.

When Woody Hayes and his Buckeyes arrived in Los Angeles to play Southern California in the Rose Bowl, they were rated No. 4 on all the better polls and there was some thought they should have enrolled in the NFL, not the Big Ten. When they left the West Coast, Harvard was trying to get on their schedule. The Trojans won big, 42–17, causing Woody to point out solemnly, "Football polls are a joke."

So was Woody's attack.

"I think USC could have beaten them with the faculty," gibed Jim Murray in the *Los Angeles Times* the next morning. "In fact, coach John McKay did everything but suit up an English Lit class to hold down the score.

And when Tom Lupo intercepted a pass and ran it into the end zone, John was eyeing the gal cheerleaders. The tipoff on Ohio State came when the water boy beat them to the bench—carrying two pails full. He could have had a hod on his back, too, it turned out. These guys couldn't catch a standing bus. Women move faster getting ready to go to a party. You could lay sidewalks faster than they could move the ball. Watching them, you kept hoping they could do bird imitations. They acted as if they had a five-year contract to make a touchdown. They put 17 passes in the air. Their players caught three of them and USC caught four of them. Meanwhile, back at Ohio State, Wayne Woodrow Hayes is going to have to do some reevaluating on the relative importance of brute strength. Unless they start handing out the Grantland Rice award for overturning street-cars, his teams ain't going to win any for a while."

Los Angeles writers, who had had to stand by tongue-tied as the Big Ten won 12 of the first 13 Rose Bowls during the years 1947–1959, were having their fun now. The Trojans' 42–17 triumph made it five out of six for the Pacific Coast since Purdue beat Southern California, 14–13, on New Year's Day, 1967.

1973

Through the previous 11 years, Southern California had won three national championships, made six bowl appearances, produced two Heisman Trophy winners, and John McKay twice was named Coach of the Year. No major college team had ever earned all four honors the same season. On two occasions, Southern Cal had everything but the Heisman Trophy. Now, in 1973, there was a good chance 49-year-old McKay and his defending National Champions could reach this first-time football "grand slam."

Like his 12–0 Trojans of 1972, McKay's 1973 edition was big, fast, and deep in talent at almost every position. "We're capable of winning every game," McKay said. "We have more proven players on this team than we did last year."

Waiting in the wings to make McKay eat those words was—Woody Hayes. He had a Rose Bowl score to settle.

Meanwhile, new coaches took over at four of the Big Ten schools: Dennis Stoltz replaced Duffy Daugherty at Michigan State; Lee Corso, formerly at Louisville, now was at Indiana: John Pont switched from Indiana to Northwestern; and Alex Agase went from Northwestern to Purdue.

Before the first game, Woody Hayes defended his irascible personality: "I never want to get to the point where people start calling me 'Good old Woody.' You know, I used to look at Bud Wilkinson at Oklahoma and wonder how it was he could be such a nice guy and win. There are coaches who can be nice and still win, guys like John McKay. Me, I can't be nice and win. It's not my way."

Doug France, Woody's star offensive lineman, told what it was like to play for Hayes. "You leave his practices with scars on your helmets," he said. "There are always wars. The helmets are proof of that. You leave practice and you want to get as far away as possible from Woody and football. Really, we hate him. But we don't let that hatred get in the way of winning football games. What he happens to be is a very successful football coach."

Cornelius Greene, the Ohio State quarterback, was asked why he spent so much time reading the Bible.

"When you play quarterback for Woody," Greene explained, "You need all the faith you can get."

The Ohio State–Michigan winning streak was unparalleled in the 77-year history of the Big Ten. For five straight years the winner of their game had been the Conference champion or co-champion and Rose Bowl representative. The Buckeyes won two undisputed titles, the Wolverines one, and they shared the other two. Michigan's five-year record was 33–4–0, Ohio State's 32–5–0. In the five games between the two schools, the home team won. The 1973 matchup was scheduled for Ann Arbor, but it was difficult to predict a winner. Both teams were stocked deep in veterans.

The Michigan story was rosy. The Wolverines retained their starting offensive backfield, which included Ed Shuttlesworth, a powerful runner; Dennis Franklin, all-Conference quarterback; tailback Chuck Heater; and wingback Clint Haslerig. Dave Brown and Gil Chapman were also dangerous runners. All told, Bo Schembechler had 37 lettermen back, led by tackle Dave Gallagher and five other starting defensemen.

Woody Hayes, with the highest winning percentage in the Big Ten since he arrived in 1951, was building his team around Archie Griffin and eight starters from his 1972 offense and eight from his defense. All 16 opened in the Rose Bowl. All-American tackle John Hicks headed up the offensive line, and linebackers Randy Gradishar, Vic Koegel, and Rick Middleton stuck out on defense.

The Big Ten had its work cut out. The Conference was 12–16 against non-league teams in 1972.

One of the biggest changes in Big Ten policy was the banning of personal scouting of league opponents. Prior to 1973 each school was allowed to send two scouts to two games of each rival. Now the teams were limited to the mere exchange of films—two game films of each team to be played.

It came as no great surprise when both Michigan and Ohio State lined up against each other at Ann Arbor undefeated. The Wolverines were 10–0–0, the Buckeyes 9–0–0. The odds-makers made the latter slight favorites.

For the sixth straight year, all the rest of the league could do was watch. Tempers were so raw down at Bloomington that Coach Lee Corso refused to open a fruitcake sent anonymously to him toward the end of the season. "When you've won two games and lost eight," Corso said, "you don't mess around with any unsigned fruitcake."

More than 105,000 tickets were sold to Michigan Stadium to watch the Buckeyes vs. Wolverines in what one writer said represented "the Conference championship, the Rose Bowl, and a possible National Championship." Ohio State was ranked No. 2 in the polls, Michigan No. 6.

Bruising defenses dominated the first quarter. Ohio ran three plays and punted. Michigan ran one play, then fumbled. The Buckeyes gained nine yards in three plays, and punted. This was the tempo of the first 15 minutes. Ohio State did not make a first down.

The Bucks started to move early in the second quarter. Archie Griffin broke loose for 38 yards. The drive got as far as the 14, then bogged down. Woody Hayes settled for a field goal.

Gil Chapman picked up 71 yards on the kickoff return and suddenly Michigan was at the Ohio 29—but wait! Michigan was caught clipping. The runback was nullified. Michigan was unable to move the ball, was forced to punt. Now Ohio had excellent field position. Pete Johnson and Griffin took turns hammering the line eight straight times. From the 5-yard line, Johnson finally muscled his way into the end zone. The half ended with Ohio State in front, 10–0.

The Bucks held the Wolverines scoreless until the second play of the last quarter, when Mike Lantry, left-footed, kicked a 30-yard field goal. The momentum had swung around now. The Wolverines were charged. Forcing Ohio State to punt, they started another drive from their own 49. Ed Shuttlesworth gained 5, then Franklin passed 27 yards to Paul Seal. Several plays later they were down to the 10, where Franklin, on fourth down and one, faked the ball to Shuttlesworth and rolled off his right end to score the touchdown. Lantry's extra point tied the score, 10–10.

Minutes later, Michigan was on the march once more. Franklin hit his receivers on three consecutive passes. The last reception was costly. Franklin was tackled so hard just as he released the ball that he broke his collar bone. Without their quarterback, the Wolverines put the burden back on Lantry. From the Ohio 48, Mike's placekick missed by only six inches.

Only 60 seconds remained, Woody Hayes went for victory, but Tom Drake intercepted a pass by Greg Hare and ran it back to the Ohio 44. Lantry up again—and once more wide to the right. Final score: Michigan 10, Ohio State 10.

In the final 1973 Conference standings, the two teams were tied with 7–0–1 records. This necessitated another vote of the 10 athletic directors to decide which school would represent the Conference in the Rose Bowl. An even 5–5 split in the balloting was all Michigan needed, but it came out 6–4—*Ohio State*.

For pure, utter frustration, consider the Michigan record for 1971, 1972, 1973: 31 wins, 1 loss, 1 tie; 1 title outright, 2 co-titles. Trips to the Rose Bowl: 0.

Bo Schembechler always did hate tie scores. Now he hated them even more.

In the Rose Bowl, Woody Hayes enjoyed sweet revenge as the Buckeyes blasted Southern California, 42–21. The victory was of particular satisfaction for Woody. Playing tackle in the Trojan line was big Gary Jeter, a 6–5,

On the way to a season record of 10–0–1 in 1973 and a tie with Ohio State for the Big Ten title, the Wolverines here blasted arch-rival Michigan State, 31–0. That's Steve Strinko (59), Carl Russ (33) and All-American Dave Brown (6) converging on the Spartan ball-carrier.

250-pound All-Ohio freshman from Cleveland who had originally declared his allegiance to Woody and Ohio State. But John McKay stole him away to Los Angeles. So in the Rose Bowl, Woody sent most of his classic runners right over Jeter's position.

1974

Once again, the Big Ten figured to be a two-team race between Ohio State and Michigan. A preseason national poll picked the Buckeyes to finish No. 2, behind Oklahoma, and Michigan No. 5, behind No. 3 Southern California and No. 4 Notre Dame.

Although he was only a junior, Ohio State's Archie Griffin, the 1973 Big Ten rushing champion with 2,444 yards gained on the ground in just two seasons, was the leading candidate for Heisman honors.

Iowa, which didn't win a game (0–11–0) in 1973, had a new football coach, Bob Commings. After signing his contract, Coach Commings told the press he would be calling all plays during the season. "I'm on a one-year

renewal," he said, "and I'm not trusting my paycheck to someone on a four-year scholarship."

Down at Alabama, Paul (Bear) Bryant had some words of advice for young coaches like Commings:

"Don't over-coach the players, let them play some.

"Don't get beat on penalties. If you get penalties, you're only admitting you can't play the game.

"Don't get beat on broken assignments. Keep things simple. Just execute.

"Don't give up on ability. I used to be stupid. I'd let some guys go just because we weren't getting along. Find a way to get the talent into the game.

Up in the trenches, this is what Archie Griffin, one of the most decorated college football players in history, looked like to opposing linemen. The Ohio State running back set three NCAA records while helping the Buckeyes to an 11–0 regular season before being upset by UCLA, 23–10, on New Year's Day, 1976. Griffin capped his college career by being named for a second Heisman Trophy and a Maxwell Club award, both as Outstanding Player of the Year, by the Sporting News as Man of the Year for 1975, as Big Ten Most Valuable Player, and as Sporting News College Player of the Year. He also was voted All-American for the third time.

"If you're angry, don't take it out on the players.

"Plan for everything. Don't be caught flat-footed.

"Don't talk too much or too soon.

"Don't hide behind anybody or anything in a crisis. They're going to find you anyway."

At Columbus, in early September, Woody Hayes was saying that Ohio State would be national champion. "We're not shooting for anything less," he told his players on the first day of practice. "We've come close a couple of times lately but we haven't done it. This time we will."

The Big Buckeye having spoken, all the Little Bucks clamored in agreement. "I'm kind of dying for it," spoke up Bruce Elia. "We ain't going to miss it this year." To which fellow linebacker Ken Kuhn added, "We're going to kill people while we're doing it."

The prospect of a national championship stirred even low-keyed, high-powered super-back Archie Griffin. "It would be cool," said Archie, who in 1973 became the only sophomore in half a century to be named the Big Ten's Most Valuable Player.

Football official Marv Tommervik, here shown, worked in a total of 22 intersectional games between Big Ten and PAC-8 teams, including two Rose Bowl contests involving Ohio State. "It was a delight to officiate for the Buckeyes," Tommervik said. "They seldom argued over decisions, were knowledgeable of the rules—Woody Hayes had taught them well."

Archie was only one of 16 returning starters. The depth and breadth of Ohio State's talent was so great that tackle John Hicks, the Outland and Lombardi trophies winner, and All-American linebacker Randy Gradishar would be hardly missed. "We don't need them," said Pete Cusick, defensive tackle.

This preponderance of talent had mellowed Woody Hayes.

"I'm getting to be a grandfather figure to these guys," Woody grumbled. "I think sometimes we get along too well, that maybe I'm too nice to them."

Some of his players did see a crumbling at the edges of his brick-and-mortar exterior.

"He's not yelling at us as much," one player said, "because he doesn't have to."

The Ohio State offense appeared to be better even than the one that placed fourth nationally in rushing in 1973 and fifth in scoring. The rapid development of sophomore Pete Johnson at fullback hastened Elia's return to linebacker and kept Champ Henson frustrated as the No. 2 man. Elia scored 14 touchdowns after Henson injured his knee early in 1973. But Johnson scored three TDs in the 42–21 Rose Bowl romp over Southern California. "He's the strongest running and best blocking fullback I've ever had," Hayes said.

Pete Johnson was a devastating addition to a backfield that already included Griffin, the quicksilver Cornelius Greene, and versatile wingback Brian Baschnagel. Although Hicks was gone, the blocking front remained strong with All-Big Ten tackle Kurt Schumacher and center Steve Myers. In 1973, the defense was fourth overall and first against scoring. Elia and Arnie Jones headed up a corps of hard-nosed linebackers.

The Ohio State defenders were downright physical.

"There's nothing I enjoy more than hitting a halfback," said Pete Cusick, defensive tackle, "especially when he doesn't see me coming. It feels the best when he hits the ground and you have your helmet stuck in him."

Striking power like that made Ohio State the No. 1 team for most of 1973 as it pulverized the opposition by more than five touchdowns a game before its celebrated 10–10 tie with Michigan. In the final ballot, Oklahoma edged the Buckeyes in the race for No. 1.

"They picked a team that hadn't lost, and we

Coach of the Year in 1957, Woody Hayes became a two-time recipient of the Football Writers Association of America award in 1975.

had a tie," Hayes said afterward. "But I'll say this, there wasn't anybody better than us."

Woody felt much the same about Archie Griffin, "the best back we've ever had," he said, putting to rest any comparison with Jim Otis or Hopalong Cassady. "Archie was the best in America last year and he'll be the best this season."

With his 4.5 speed, bullish upper torso, and slithery moves, Griffin made a genuine expert out of his coach by walking off with the Heisman Trophy at the end of the season. Ironically, in his first two years at Ohio State, he scored only 12 touchdowns.

"That's because of our button shoe offense," Hayes explained. "When we get inside an opponent's 10, we invariably let our fullback carry."

Because they finally added an 11th regular-season game, the Buckeyes were thinking about having their winningest season ever.

In the years 1969–73, Michigan was the only college team to be ranked in the final Top Ten each year. Not Nebraska. Not Ohio State. Not Alabama or Penn State or Notre Dame. But Michigan. Under Bo Schembechler the Wolverines went 48–6–1 through those five years.

In Bo's "worst" season, 1969, Michigan won 8 of 11 and upset Ohio State, while Schembechler was named Coach of the Year.

Four of Bo's six losses, and the tie, came in season finales, three in scheduled games, two in the Rose Bowl. And even the tie could be counted as a loss. Michigan lost its 1973 finale not on the scoreboard but to the Big Ten athletic directors.

In 1974, quarterback Dennis Franklin, who had 959 yards of total offense in 1973, was healthy again after a shoulder injury, but fullback Ed Shuttlesworth, third leading rusher in Michigan history, and wingback Clint Haslerig had graduated. To compensate, Schembechler took a trio of tailbacks—who together in 1973 ran for 1,672 yards—and scattered them to three positions. He moved Gil Chapman, the heart of Michigan's running attack, to wingback, 205-pound Chuck Heater to fullback, and kept Gordon Bell at tailback. That gave the 1974 Wolverines their all-time fastest backfield. Which was good. Franklin could throw 60-yard lightning bolts, but his excellent receivers sometimes dropped them—occasionally from sheer surprise that Bo allowed the team to pass.

The front line had great size and depth, most particularly on defense. In the four years since 1970 the Wolverines yielded only 6.62 points per game. That made winning easier. Behind the line, enemy passers stood in such awe of safety Dave Brown that most of his tackles in 1973 were on running plays. Linebacker Steve Strinko was in on 137 tackles, a record, and Carl Russ had 94 stops. Altogether, Michigan and Ohio State had the rest of the country referring to the Big Ten as "the Big Two plus Medium-Sized Eight."

"Our league hasn't changed a bit," said Michigan State Coach Denny Stolz before the seasoned opened. "It's Ohio State and Michigan on top again. Below that, I don't know of anybody with an outstanding football team."

By the third Saturday in October, one headline read: "Ohio State May Be No. 1. . . But Don't Tell Michigan." The Buckeyes had just destroyed Wisconsin, 52–7, to reinforce the argument that they were the best college team in the country. On the other hand, the Wolverines countered with a 21–7 triumph over Michigan State and refused to settle for No. 2.

"They were awesome," said Wisconsin Coach John Jardine of Ohio State. "They're a great football team, there's no other way to say it. Since I've been here this is the best football team we've ever met." And so forth. One writer who saw them said the Buckeyes looked perfectly capable of marching down to Cincinnati the next day and taking on the pro Bengals. "Rate it even," he said.

"I just want to keep winning," Woody Hayes said. "I just love to win. I just love to win."

And the Buckeyes did keep winning: Indiana, 49–9; Northwestern, 55–7; Illinois, 49–7; but then the miracle of miracles—Michigan State 16, Ohio State 13.

Michigan and Ohio State came down to November 23 as they had before in recent years, with everything hinging on the outcome of their game. The Wolverines were 7–0–0, the Buckeyes 6–1–0. In three of the last five seasons, they had tied for the Big Ten title. An Ohio State victory in 1974 would make it four for six.

Tom Klaban was the hero of the game. Ohio State's most successful extra point specialist made 52 of 53 conversions and 9 of 12 field goals in 1973, but nothing he ever did was as important as what he did to Michigan at Columbus. The 6-foot-1, 184-pound soccer-style placekicker from Cincinnati, by way of Czechoslovakia, merely kicked the Buckeyes into the Rose Bowl as he scored all of Ohio's points with field goals of 47, 25, 43, and 45 yards to earn his team a dramatic, come-from-behind victory. The final score was Tom Klaban 12, Michigan 10.

For the third straight year Ohio State and Southern California were matched up in the Rose Bowl. John McKay was asked if he saw anything wrong with the same teams appearing in the Rose Bowl year after year—since 1966, his Trojans played in the game seven times, and Ohio State five—and McKay replied: "Yes, I do. I don't think Ohio State should come every year." The Bucks held a 3–2 edge over the Trojans in Rose Bowl competition.

At a pregame luncheon, Woody Hayes wowed the Los Angeles press with his homespun Midwestern wit. He exhibited none of the arrogance that had infuriated McKay in 1973 when Woody walked out of the luncheon just as the USC coach was being introduced to the audience. Woody spent 20 minutes at the podium answering questions good-naturedly.

"Woody," one writer said, "you've been more cooperative with everybody the last several years. Are you changing your personal image with the press?"

"Helllll, no!" smiled Woody mischievously.

"What are your thoughts on recruiting?" he was asked.

"Some people accuse me of buying football players at Ohio State. Hell, I don't buy football players. I *sell* 'em!"

On college football: "We are in direct competition with the pros, make no mistake about that. We have a better game than they've got—and we don't stand around kicking shins all summer the way they do, either." (Applause)

On financing: "We allot four seats to each faculty member, and that's too damned many."

On USC: "They've got the psychological edge because we beat them last year, and they've got the physiological edge because of all those people pulling for them in the stands. That's a two-touchdown advantage, as I see it."

Mostly, the program belonged to Woody, just as it did in 1973 when he delivered an eloquent, impromptu eulogy to Harry Truman, who had died that morning.

"I know people are saying football has passed me up, and all that sort of thing," Woody told the 1974 audience. "But we don't do too damned bad yet!"

Ohio State's 18–17 loss to Southern California could be blamed on two key plays. The first one took its place in Rose Bowl lore along with the legendary wrong-way run of California's Roy Riegels in the 1929 Rose Bowl. It happened in the second quarter, when Jim Lucas poised to punt for the Trojans—and almost whiffed the ball.

"In 25 years of officiating, I never before saw anything like that," said Charles Moffett, the Rose Bowl referee.

The USC punter's kicking foot barely grazed the ball. It plopped to earth a yard ahead of him and bounced—almost directly into the startled Lucas' hands. He scooped it up and ran, for 16 yards and a vital first down.

Directly behind Lucas when the ball was snapped, Moffett looked on in amazement.

"I was watching to make sure he caught the

ball," Moffett said. "Then I focused on the Ohio State men rushing in. Lucas appeared to glance up—and then I saw the ball slither off his foot. Oh, boy, the rule book flashed before my eyes! What was it—a punt or a fumble? Whichever it was, what he did was legal. If it was a punt, he could run the ball, because it didn't cross the line of scrimmage. Same on a fumble. As an offensive player he could advance his own fumble."

What it was, according to Charles Weinstock, the game's official statistician, was neither a punt nor a fumble. It was a rushing play from scrimmage. "We finally agreed to put it down as a straight running play," Weinstock said after the game. So in the game's official statistical summary, Lucas was credited with carrying the ball once for a rushing gain of 16 yards.

Though Lucas went back to punt three times, he was charged technically with only one punt. Four plays after the "foot-fumble," or near-whiff, Lucas was back again to punt. This time, the Bucks blocked it. In college statistics, a blocked punt is not charged against the kicker, though it is recorded numerically as a "team punt." Minus yardage is not charged on a blocked punt.

Lucas' third and last effort finally cleared the line of scrimmage and bounced out of bounds—a 29-yard kick. So, the Trojans as a team were charged with only two punts.

"Gentlemen," John McKay said afterward, "we've got the worst punting game in the history of college football. I've decided to change our punter into a running back. The way he moved with the one he missed was our best run of the day."

It wasn't really that. But Lucas' average of 16 yards per carry was better than his team's punting average of 14.5 yards.

That never happened before.

Another oddball incident in the game was a "spiking" penalty against Ohio State's Neal Colzie, after he intercepted a pass in the third quarter. It may have cost the Buckeyes a winning touchdown. Colzie, a 202-pound defensive back, galloped 21 yards with the stolen ball and, when he was halted at the Trojans' 9-yard line, he slammed it to earth—all contrary to sportsmanlike conduct as spelled out in the rule book. The book says a player in possession of the ball must let it lie or "return

the ball to an official immediately." The 15-yard penalty gave the ball to the Buckeyes with a first down and goal to go—24 yards away. Two plays later, USC intercepted a pass.

Woody Hayes called it "a stupid penalty."

"Have you ever seen that called before?" Woody asked. "I know it's a rule, but it's not lived up to 99 percent of the time. I've *never* seen it called!"

After the game, Hayes declined to steam up over the "stupid penalty."

"I'm not going to criticize the officials," he said. "If I do, I won't be able to coach our first game next Fall."

1975

For the last three seasons, Michigan's record had been a glittering 30–2–1. In that period it shared three Big Ten titles, didn't finish lower than sixth in the national rankings—and didn't go to a single Rose Bowl game. In 1975, however, the Wolverines were practically a shoo-in to find themselves in a postseason game somewhere if only because a revision in the Rose Bowl contract allowed the Big Ten runner-up to accept an invitation to another bowl, if offered. But Coach Bo Schembechler had his sights aimed higher even though he found something in September to worry about.

"This year our offense may be so weak we could field a pro defense and still be in trouble," Bo said. "In some areas, we may need immediate help from our freshmen."

He was right, of course. One of the freshmen was quarterback Rick Leach, an 18-year-old All-Stater in football, baseball, and basketball from Southwestern High in Flint, Michigan, and a member of the 1974 national champion Connie Mack baseball team. His father and uncle played on the Wolverines' first national championship baseball team in 1953.

"This kid was just born to compete," Schembechler said. "It's something inside him. He always wants a little tougher challenge."

Leach demonstrated uncommon poise the third Saturday of the 1975 campaign against No. 5 Missouri, upset conquerors of touted Alabama. Michigan got off to a shaky start with two straight home-field ties by Stanford and Baylor and had been booed by its fickle fans. It was not propitious that the last invader to win at Michigan Stadium—back in 1969—was Missouri. So when the Wolverines got ready to face the 104,578 people packed into the stadium, Coach Schembechler decided to deliver a commandment to Leach and the rest of his young team. "I told them that the only person they have to please is Bo Schembechler," he said later. "If they please me, I don't care a bit what anybody in the stands says."

Please Bo is just what they did. Michigan 31, Missouri 7.

"We're not a great team yet," Bo said. "We're a young, struggling team. We'll get better as the season goes along. We just need time to do it."

It was Schembechler's 100th head-coaching victory. The numbers would come up 106 before the showdown with Ohio State in late November.

Ohio State was a vast departure from its "three yards and a cloud of dust" tradition. Woody Hayes had fashioned a much more versatile and wide-open attack in 1975. The squad had lost 13 starters, 8 of them defensive players, but as in other recent seasons, Woody made liberal use of freshmen, counting on them to mature rapidly.

While the 1975 Buckeyes were extremely young, Columbus fans had little trouble recognizing the offensive backfield. Headed by Heisman Trophy winner Archie Griffin, who had already rushed for 4,139 yards and 22 touchdowns, it included fellow seniors Cornelius Greene at quarterback and Brian Baschnagel on the wing, with junior Pete Johnson ensconced at fullback. Griffin's brother Ray, a sophomore who was faster than Archie and too valuable to play behind him, had been moved to safety.

Best bet to unseat the two leaders was Michigan State. The Spartans beat the Buckeyes, 16–13, in 1974 at East Lansing. What was generally overlooked in the postgame furor was that MSU was a very good young team, one that was to finish 7–3–1 and be ranked 12th in the nation at season's end.

In Coach Denny Stolz' first two seasons as head coach at East Lansing, his big worry was a weak offense. Now, despite a dearth of wide receivers, the Spartans figured to be able to move the ball. His attack was built around quarterback Charlie Baggett, whom Stolz rated "one of the best in America," and running

backs Levi Jackson and Rich Baes, fast and experienced juniors.

"We don't know if we've got great runners or just a lot of good ones," Stolz said, "but we might move a running back to receiver or to defensive back."

The Spartans played respectable defense, and with eight starters back, the nucleus was there.

Michigan State found out a lot about itself the very first Saturday against revenge-filled Ohio State. During the summer the NCAA had taken a close look at MSU recruiting policies and for a time it seemed as if the school might be placed on probation. The feeling around East Lansing was that it was Woody Hayes who blew the whistle. All of which added fuel to the Ohio State game.

"We are well aware of whom we open with," Stolz said. "At every staff meeting there is some reference to Ohio State. The constant pressure in the back of our minds and in the back of our players' minds is that we face Ohio State in the opener."

That sort of pressure produced an abject collapse: Ohio State 21, Michigan State 0.

Three weeks later, however, the Spartans gained some sort of solace by knocking off Notre Dame, 10–3.

Though Indiana again finished in the cellar (1–6–1), Coach Lee Corso readily gained the reputation as the league's court jester, the worthy successor to the retired Duffy Daugherty. Sample: "When speaking to alumni groups, I feel just like the head of a big company that lost all its money last year trying to explain it to the stockholders." And, "We get no respect. Everybody we play on the road has made us their homecoming game." Finally, commenting on the school's alumni sending basketball Coach Bobby Knight on a European vacation: "They wanted to send me over there, too, but with a one-way ticket."

At Iowa (3–8–0), life got no better. From 1970 through 1975, the Hawkeyes won only 13 of 65 games. This prompted Michigan's Athletic Director Don Canham to wonder aloud: "How much money is it going to take to bring Iowa football up to par with Michigan football? Given population, facilities, size, tradition, publicity, there is just no way to bridge the gap. Oh, sure, every blue moon Iowa will win a game; what the heck, Baylor won the

Southwest Conference in 1974." And in 1975, tied *Michigan*.

Such talk angered Iowa fans.

"Iowa fans are the best in the country," they point out. "Crowds of 57,200, and 52,780, and 54,600, and 59,160 were on hand for each of the first four Hawkeye home games in 1975. In 1974, Iowa ranked 21st nationally in attendance, averaging 48,683 per game. It's easy to be a fan of a winning football program; it takes dedication and character to be an Iowa fan."

And a sense of humor to be an Iowa football player. Brandt Yocum (no relation to Li'l Abner) spent the summer of 1975 training to compete in a big marathon race.

"Only trouble is," said the 210-pound Iowa football end, "we don't have any pass patterns where you run out 26 miles, cut 385 yards to your left and wait for the ball."

The big change in college football in 1975 was that placekickers made more and longer three-pointers than ever before. Stanford, for example, managed to tie Michigan on Mike Langford's 33-yarder with nine seconds to go, and Vince Lamia's 40-yarder lifted Wisconsin over Purdue with nine seconds to play.

Reasons given for so many dangerous kickers in recent years are (1) the emergence of the soccer-style kicker, (2) the proliferation of artificial turf, which affords consistent footing, uniform placement of the ball, etc., (3) more thoughtful athletes, (4) the balls are livelier (not proved).

Despite the fact that he had an excellent placekicker in Frank Stavroff, from Yugoslavia, Lee Corso was not sold on field goals.

"You better not kick a field goal if you have a lousy defense," Corso said. "I made a survey one year and eight of the 10 times we made a field goal early in the game the other team came back and scored a touchdown. I'd gain a field goal and be behind, 7-3."

Tom Klaban, of course, kicked Michigan out of the Rose Bowl in 1974 with four field goals. A walk-on, Klaban was spindly and splay-footed and could be seen almost daily making solitary trips up and down the steps of 100-foot-high Ohio Stadium, hopping on one leg, then the other. Klaban's best buddy was his sister Jane, with whom he escaped to Canada from Prague, then came to America in 1967. He prepped for Woody Hayes by starring as a high school swimmer in Cincinnati. When he needed coaching, Klaban didn't go to Hayes, he went to sister Jane.

"Nobody can coach 'em, those soccer kickers," said Indiana's Corso. His advice to his own Frank Stavroff when he used him was "go in there and kick it."

How do you get a soccer kicker out of a slump? Answer: you don't. If you're, say, Woody Hayes, you relieve him. Klaban kicked all those extra points and field goals in 1974, but when he was laid up with an injury in 1975 and then scuffed his first extra-point try against North Carolina, Woody yanked him. In came Klaban's roomie, team punter Tom Skladany. When Skladany missed *his* extra-point try, Hayes didn't fool around trying to tell him to keep his head down or anything like that. He returned Klaban to the first chair. Against UCLA, during the regular season, Klaban boomed two long field goals and five extra points in a 41-20 Ohio State victory.

In the 1975 Big Ten championship finale, Ohio State and Michigan surprised just about everyone by playing an exquisitely exciting, breathtakingly imperfect football game. Ohio State won, but the score was not two field goals to one, it was 21–14. Not since 1970 had the winner needed more than two touchdowns in this game. And if Ohio State–Michigan was always three yards and a spray of dust, what were they doing making 40-yard runs? Well, underdog Michigan was making 40-yard runs, while No. 1 Ohio State was mostly recovering Michigan fumbles. And what were they doing throwing long, arcing devil-may-care passes? And completing them? What were they doing committing eight turnovers and pitching the ball around so hairily? Thirty-seven passes are not a lot by ordinary standards, but when it's Michigan–Ohio State it's worth noting. By comparison, the 20 they threw in 1974 made one feel as if the ball were flying around all day.

"We will pass," said Hayes the day before the game, "because that is where they are vulnerable."

"I really wouldn't be surprised if it came down to passing," agreed Bo Schembechler. "I'll play it from the start like we were behind in the fourth quarter."

Not since he was a freshman did Archie

Griffin, just three weeks away from becoming the first collegian in history to win the Heisman for a second time, have such a terrible game. Michigan's line played straight-on when Ohio State expected it to slant; it slanted when the Bucks did not expect it to at all; dropped to a three-man front with filling linebackers; and swarmed all over the field. Everywhere that Archie went the blue shirts followed.

Griffin had gone 31 regular-season games without making fewer than 100 yards; in his last two against Michigan he made 163 yards and 111 yards. But on this day he got only 46 yards in 19 bruising carries. His average against Michigan was a meager 2.4 a carry.

Coach Hayes called the Ohio State comeback—they had been down by 7 points—the "greatest in my 25 years of coaching."

In seven possessions, from their second play of the second quarter until only seven minutes remained in the fourth, the Buckeyes were unable to move the ball. They didn't get a first down in more than 30 minutes. Michigan dominated. During that period the Wolverines got six yards for every one they gave up. Gordon Bell and fullback Rob Lytle ripped into the Ohio State defense with startling success, and Rick Leach refused to accept the opportunity to choke.

Just before the half, freshman Leach cranked up his Michigan machine and drove it 80 yards to a tying touchdown. Then, after sparring fitfully through the third quarter, he took Michigan 43 yards to a 14–7 lead, setting it up with two passes to wingback Jim Smith and getting the touchdown himself on a one-yard keep off the left side. Now there was only 7:11 to play, and time to turn Cornelius Greene loose for Ohio State.

On the first play, Greene wound up and pitched downfield, badly overshooting his receiver. On the second down he was rushed into his end zone by blitzing Wolverines. He barely got rid of the ball, incomplete again.

On third and 10, he called for a desperation play-action pass off a fake to Griffin. But the side he wanted to throw to was covered, so he threw to wingback Brian Baschnagel for 17 yards—Ohio State's first first down since the second quarter.

Just like that it became Ohio State's game.

On the next four plays Greene got four more first downs—two passes to split end Len Willis, an 11-yard Griffin run and a 12-yard keeper to the Michigan 8. Then, in four stabs at the middle, fullback Pete Johnson, whom North Carolina Coach Bill Dooley once described as "a big tackle playing fullback," scored the tying touchdown.

The Buckeyes smelled blood now. Michigan got the ball on their 20 after the kickoff and Leach was sacked for a 9-yard loss to his 11. Then he tried to hit Jim Smith and it hung dangerously high in the air over Smith's head—and straight into the arms of Raymond Griffin, Archie's younger brother. Raymond caught the ball going at full speed on the Michigan 32 and ran it down to the 3-yard line before Leach blocked him out of bounds. On first down Johnson once more banged into the end zone and Ohio State was ahead, 21–14.

With an interception by open-side defensive halfback Craig Cassady (son of Hopalong) to seal it, Woody Hayes was back in the Rose Bowl for the eighth time. And Michigan? It got to play powerful Oklahoma in the Orange Bowl as a consolation prize.

Leave it to good Ol' Woody to take care of "that team to the north."

1976

Nothing beat the ironic absurdity surrounding the Rose and Orange Bowls, on New Year's Day. The entangling postseason alliance of the Big Ten and the Pacific-8 forced Woody Hayes to take his No. 1-ranked Buckeyes back to replay 14th-ranked UCLA, a team he had poured it on, 41 to 20, in the third game of the season. This gave Bo Schembechler the privilege of taking his fifth-ranked Wolverines to Miami to play third-ranked Oklahoma.

Judging by the outcomes, the bowl scores could have been aptly titled, "The Rise and Fall of the Big Ten." Michigan was singed, 14 to 6, and UCLA embarrassed the truculent Hayes so much (23 to 10) that he refused to talk to the press after the game. The only member of his staff to comment was defensive coordinator George Hill, who said tersely: "They just kicked hell out of us." UCLA trailed the Buckeyes 3 to 0 at halftime, but lost none of their confidence. "We knew we could beat them all the time. We were not discouraged at halftime. It was just a matter of getting our offense opened," said UCLA quarterback John

Sciarra, the game's Most Valuable Player whose two second-half touchdown passes to Wally Henry ignited the big upset.

After the bitter loss, Hayes slipped onto a team bus and hid from newsmen. He also ordered his players not to say anything. Back home, a week later, Co-captain and linebacker Ken Kuhn chided his coach for his refusal to stand up like a man and comment on the loss to UCLA.

"I simply cannot go along with his copout toward the public, fans and even his own players," Kuhn said. "Coach Hayes has always been a humble winner. When we lose, however, he must also be a humble loser. Why should we be subjected to the Hayes' silence when we have so many questions that must be answered?"

The Ohio State *Lantern,* the student newspaper, also went public with criticism of its coach. In fact, it went so far as to ask for Hayes' resignation. "He is embarrassing because his fans have made him a god, and he has begun to believe it," the *Lantern* reported, in a long editorial.

Actually, the editorial was the inspiration of senior journalism major Karen Doyle, who was one of two editorial page editors on *The Lantern.*

"The general feeling, at least on *The Lantern,* is that Hayes can do whatever he wants to do and he doesn't have to answer to anyone," Ms. Doyle said afterward. "The president of our University usually spends half his time defending him. It really makes me angry and it makes everybody else on the paper angry, too. So I went to my typewriter and fired away. What sort of reaction did the editorial get? By a margin of roughly 2 to 1, alums wrote back suggesting that I, rather than Woody, be forced to resign. Woody, himself, said that he didn't try to run our editorial page and I shouldn't try to run the football team. I also got some feedback from some of his players. They really love him, some of them; a few don't.

"We also took a poll of the student body. What the survey showed was that if Woody ever announced for president, he'd carry Ohio State University hands down. Only 35 percent of the students who responded to the poll agreed with my editorial. Only 5 to 7 percent were undecided. And the rest, nearly 60 percent, were behind Woody all the way. Many of them asked me, 'How can you do this to this poor man?' One man even called long distance from Westerville, Ohio and spent nearly 90 minutes questioning my judgment and attempting to show me the error of my ways for writing the editorial."

"Who was the man?" she was asked.

"My father," she said.

John R. Hudson, of Anaheim, California, did not see UCLA's victory over Ohio State in the Rose Bowl as anything so unusual.

"The next time the Big Ten loses at Pasadena maybe it will occur to the press to describe it as something besides an upset," he said. "Each year we see the same old thing: Michigan and Ohio State take turns pummeling weak Big Ten teams, soar to the top of the polls, then play each other in their annual one-game season, which Michigan invariably loses. We then see Ohio State coming out to the Coast, ranked just above Attila the Hun and the Afrika Korps, where they are 'upset' by a PAC-8 team that wasn't supposed to show up without the Red Cross. Pay attention, now. The Big Ten has lost in six of its last seven Rose Bowl appearances. Ohio State has lost in four of its last five visits. In fact, the Big Ten has lost 11 of the last 17 Rose Bowl games played. Do you spot a trend?"

Hot on the heels of the New Year's Day 1976 defeats of Ohio State and Michigan in the bowls came scandal. Michigan State was charged by the NCAA for 34 recruiting violations and placed on a three-year probation. The penalty was one of the severest ever handed down by the NCAA:

1. The Spartans cannot play in a bowl game for three years.

2. The football team cannot appear in a TV game or receive any TV revenue over the same period of time.

3. The school was allowed to grant only 20 football scholarships to incoming freshmen in 1976. (All other Big Ten schools could recruit 30.)

4. Seven members of the 1975 football team, including four starters, were declared ineligible.

5. One assistant was fired for recruiting excesses, and head coach Denny Stolz resigned.

6. Another football assistant, Andy MacDonald, resigned his job to become offensive

backfield coach on the staff of Jack Patera, head coach for the Seattle Seahawks of the National Football League. An obviously relieved MacDonald confessed: "These days my young daughter begins her prayers by reciting, 'God bless Mama, God bless Daddy, and God bless the Seattle Seahawks.'"

Michigan State officials considered the punishment so harsh that they even toyed with the idea of going to court. They claimed that the charges came from four Ohio State players whom they had tried to recruit. All four went to Columbus, but none made the team.

"Michigan State's stand is that it was their word against the word of those four players," said Joe Falls, the Detroit sports columnist. "The MSU fact-finding committee was able to entirely discredit the testimony of one of those players so that all of his charges were thrown out. They were able to discredit the others to the point of cutting the charges from 80 to 34. But—and this was what the MSU folks didn't seem to understand—even if they were guilty of one infraction, they were guilty. What is so hard to accept was MSU trying to minimize the whole thing. You don't get slapped with 34 infractions without some cheating going on."

John B. Fullen, who spent 40 years (1928-1967) as executive director of The Ohio State University Alumni Association and editor of the alumni monthly magazine, saw something foreboding about the Michigan State scandal.

"We may be on the verge of witnessing a grand crackup of major college football as we know it," he said. "The Western Conference is no longer the Big Ten. In football, it's the Big Two and the Little Eight. The Big Two not only dominate their brethren, they also murder them. So now you have to win, you have to win *big* to get those national rankings and keep the turnstiles clicking. The rich get richer while the poor drain off legitimate scholastic revenues to try to hang in there. All of which is why Big Time college football bears as much relation to higher education as the Mafia does to legitimate business."

John Fullen was once hanged in effigy at Columbus.

Why?

"For saying things like this," he said.

Hall of Famers
From
the Big Ten

The Foundation honors men who honor the game. You have to demonstrate good citizenship, love of community, love of country. It's a question of what you give back to the game. Citizenship is very important. If we're just going to pick all the All-Americans every year, there's no sense to having a National Football Hall of Fame

> James L. McDowell,
> Executive Director
> National Football Foundation and
> Hall of Fame, explaining how
> college football players are
> elected to the Hall of Fame.

Players

NATIONAL FOOTBALL HALL OF FAME
PLAYERS FROM THE BIG TEN

Name	College	Position	Years Played	Year Of Election
Agase, Alex	Purdue	Guard	1943	1963
	Illinois	Guard	1942–46	
Ameche, Alan (The Horse)	Wisconsin	Fullback	1951–54	1975
Baston, Bert	Minnesota	End	1914–16	1954
Benbrook, Albert	Michigan	Guard	1908–10	1971
Berwanger, John Jacob	Chicago	Quarterback	1933–35	1954
Butler, Bob (Butts)	Wisconsin	Tackle	1911–13	1972
Carney, Charles R. (Chuck)	Illinois	End	1918–21	1966
Clevenger, Zora G.	Indiana	Halfback	1900–03	1968
Coleman, Donald E.	Michigan State	Tackle	1949–51	1975
Des Jardiens, Paul R. (Shorty)	Chicago	Center	1912–14	1955
Devine, Aubrey	Iowa	Quarterback	1919–21	1973
Driscoll, John Leo (Paddy)	Northwestern	Quarterback	1915–17	1974
Eckersall, Walter H.	Chicago	Quarterback	1904–06	1951
Fesler, Wesley E.	Ohio State	End	1928–30	1954
Friedman, Benjamin	Michigan	Quarterback	1924–26	1951
Giel, Paul	Minnesota	Halfback	1951–53	1975
Graham, Otto	Northwestern	Halfback	1941–43	1956
Grange, Harold (Red)	Illinois	Halfback	1923–25	1951
Harley, Charles Wesley (Chick)	Ohio State	Fullback	1916–19	1951
Harmon, Thomas Dudley	Michigan	Halfback	1938–40	1954
Herschberger, Clarence	Chicago	Fullback	1895–98	1970
Heston, William Martin (Willie)	Michigan	Halfback	1901–04	1954
Hirsch, Elroy (Crazy Legs)	Wisconsin-Michigan	Halfback	1942–43	1974
Horvath, Leslie	Ohio State	Halfback/ Quarterback	1940–44	1969
Isbell, Cecil F. (Cece)	Purdue	Halfback	1935–37	1967
Joesting, Herb W.	Minnesota	Fullback	1925–27	1954
Kinnick, Nile	Iowa	Halfback	1937–39	1951
Kipke, Harry	Michigan	Halfback	1921–23	1958
Locke, Gordon C.	Iowa	Fullback	1920–22	1960
Lund, Francis L. (Pug)	Minnesota	Halfback	1932–34	1958

Maulbetsch, John	Michigan	Halfback	1912–14	1973
Marshall, Bobby	Minnesota	End	1905–06	1971
McGovern, John Francis	Minnesota	Quarterback	1908–10	1966
Macomber, Bart	Illinois	Halfback	1914–16	1972
Nagurski, Bronislav (Bronko)	Minnesota	Tackle	1927–29	1951
Newman, Harry	Michigan	Quarterback	1929–32	1975
O'Dea, Patrick John	Wisconsin	Fullback	1897–99	1962
Oliphant, Elmer Quillen	Purdue	Halfback	1911–13	
(Ollie)	Army	Halfback	1915–17	1955
Oosterbaan, Benjamin G.	Michigan	End	1925–27	1954
Parker, Jim	Ohio State	Guard	1954–56	1973
Pihos, Pete	Indiana	End/Fullback	1942–43, 1945–46	1966
Pingel, John Spencer	Michigan State	Halfback	1936–38	1968
Rogers, Edward L.	Carlisle	End	1896–1900	
	Minnesota	End	1901–1903	1968
Schreiner, David N.	Wisconsin	End	1940–42	1955
Schulz, Adolph (Germany)	Michigan	Center	1905–08	1951
Slater, F. F. (Duke)	Iowa	Tackle	1918–21	1951
Smith, Bruce Philip	Minnesota	Halfback	1939–41	1972
Snow, Neil Worthington	Michigan	Halfback	1898–1901	1960
Steffen, Walter Peter (Wally)	Chicago	Quarterback	1907–08	1969
Stinchcomb, Gaylord (Pete)	Ohio State	Halfback	1918–20	1973
Widseth, Edwin	Minnesota	Tackle	1934–36	1954
Wildung, Richard Kay	Minnesota	Tackle	1940–42	1957
Willis, William (Bill)	Ohio State	Tackle	1942–44	1971
Wistert, Albert (Ox)	Michigan	Tackle	1940–42	1968
Wistert, Francis M. (Whitey)	Michigan	Tackle	1931–33	1967
Wyant, Andrew Robert Elmer (Polyphemus)	Bucknell	Center	1888–91	
	Chicago	Guard	1892–94	1962
Young, Claude H. (Buddy)	Illinois	Halfback	1944–46	1968
Zarnas, Gust	Ohio State	Guard	1935–37	1975

On December 9, 1975, four of nine new inductees into the National Football Hall of Fame were from the Big Ten. Those pictured at the banquet were, front row, left: Gust Zarnas, Ohio State; Coach Alonzo Gaither, Florida A&M; Don Coleman, Michigan State; and Averell Daniell, Pittsburgh. Back row, left: Paul Giel, Minnesota; Alan Ameche, Wisconsin; Pete Dawkins, Army; Chet Gladchuk, Jr. (accepting award for his late father), Boston College; and Frank Gifford, Southern California.

Big Ten Players in The Football Hall of Fame

AGASE, ALEX, in a game against Minnesota in 1942, made Big Ten history when he became the only guard of record to score two touchdowns in a single game. The Illinois whiz made the first one on a steal of the ball from Bill Daley to go 35 yards to score and the second one when he fell on a Gopher fumble in the end zone to break a 13–13 tie to win the game, 20–13.

Agase stood only 5' 10" and weighed 205 pounds yet distinguished himself in college football by being an All-American at two different schools. He first made All-American as a civilian at Illinois in 1942 and then as a V-12 training student at Purdue in 1943. After serving with the U.S. Marines in the Pacific Theater in World War II, he returned to Illinois in 1946 to earn All-American honors for a third time. He is on the all-time teams of both Illinois and Purdue, the only player ever to achieve this honor.

A model lineman, Agase did everything well as a superb team player. He was one of the stars of the 1947 Rose Bowl game as the Fighting Illini embarrassed UCLA, 45 to 14, and that season (1946) earned the Most Valuable Player award of the Big Ten.

Agase divided seven seasons in professional football between the Los Angeles Dons, Chicago Rockets, Cleveland Browns, and Baltimore Colts. He was named line coach at Iowa State in 1954, joined Ara Parseghian at Northwestern in 1956, and then took over as head coach there in 1964 when Ara moved to Notre Dame. In nine seasons at Evanston, Alex won 32 games, lost 58, tied one. After finishing 3–7 in 1969, he turned his luck around with a 6–4 record the next year, picking up the Coach of the Year award in the process. This earned him a transfer to Purdue as head coach in 1973, where in his first two seasons the Boilermakers won only 8 of their first 22 games. Asked why he doesn't recruit in talent-rich California to

Alex Agase, now head coach at Purdue, remains the only Big Ten man ever to make All-American at two schools. He did it first at Illinois as "wandering guard" in 1942, then at Purdue during World War II, and finally at Illinois again in 1946.

bolster his program at Purdue, Coach Agase candidly replied: "Any kid who would leave that wonderful weather is too dumb to play for us."

AMECHE, ALAN (*The Horse*), was a grade-A example of a star who should have won the Heisman Trophy in his sophomore or junior year, but had to wait until he was a senior to get it. "The Horse," 6-foot, 215-pound pile-driving fullback who played 55 minutes a game most games, played four years on the Wisconsin varsity, 1951–1954, during which time the Badgers were a good but not great team, winning 26, losing seven, and tying three.

Ameche ran for more than 800 yards each of his freshman and sophomore years and for more than 900 yards as a junior, but, hampered by an injury, for less than 700 yards as a senior when he won the Heisman. He did rush for 3,212 yards, a national record at the time, in his four-year career at Madison, almost a 5-yard average, and he did score 25 touchdowns. "His Heisman was clearly a career reward," Dan Jenkins said later.

Six times The Horse ran for 100 yards or more in games. Once, against Minnesota, he carved out more than 200 yards, including a run of 42 yards. He also had runs of 41, 43, 47, 54, and 64 yards in his college career, sometimes running right over tacklers. He went a long way toward receiving the Heisman at the end of his junior season when he shook up Southern California for 133 yards, including the 54-yarder, in the nationally televised Rose Bowl showdown, although the Trojans won, 7 to 0. A linebacker on defense, he had 14 unassisted tackles against Penn State, which helped.

After the 1954 season, Baltimore had two choices in the first round of the pro draft, and one of them was Ameche. At the beginning of a pro career spanning six seasons, Alan slashed off tackle for 12 yards against the Bears the very first chance he had to display his peculiar running style: running almost straight up, the way he always had in college—something of an upright galloping stride with knees pumping, arms flailing, and nothing but moving muscle to grab. With his head up and his neck straight, he looked as if he would be easy to

hit. In fact, one pro scout who had watched him run at Wisconsin, said, "He'd get killed if he ever tried that with the pros."

It didn't happen because, strong and unexpectedly quick, Ameche could cut away, move in hard, change direction, and take punishment. Style had nothing to do with any of this. Ameche's running reminded many football people of Frankie Sinkwich, the Georgia All-American. Alan had that same duck-walk running motion, that wide-braced footing that kept him from getting knocked over easily. And he could "run up," that is, gather himself at the last moment before crunching into the line or jarring against a linebacker. Where most fullbacks barrel into a defense head first, Ameche put his body behind one of his good-sized shoulders and rammed. In slow motion, it looked like a fellow pushing against a jammed door.

Alan Ameche touched all the yard stripes on his way to football immortality—two-time All-American (1953–1954), three-time All-Conference (1952–53–54), candidate for the Big Ten Trophy (1954), combatant in the Chicago Tribune All-Star Game (1955), and All-Pro—but his proudest achievement reads: "All-American *Academic* Team, 1953–1954, Alan Ameche, Wisconsin."

The Horse could also crack those books.

BASTON, BERT, the first University of Minnesota football player to score an All-American double (1915 and again in 1916), was the catching half of the renowned Arnold (Pudge) Wyman-to-Baston aerial duo in 1915, heralded by experts as the slickest bombing brigade in Minneapolis before World War I. The pair sparked the Golden Gophers' vaunted "Perfect Team" in 1915–16, which went 12–1–1 and averaged 49 points a game. The 1916 bunch piled up a total of 348 points to 28 in seven games, including 67–0 over Iowa, 54–0 over Wisconsin, and 49–0 over Chicago.

From 1932 to 1950, Baston served as Bernie Bierman's assistant in Minnesota.

While Bert Baston was the first, nine other Gophers have made All-American twice in succession: George Hauser (1916–17), Herb Joesting (1926–27), Butch Larson (1933–34), Pug Lund (1933–34), Ed Widseth (1934–35–

Bert Baston distinguished himself in 1915 and 1916 by twice making the All-American team, the first in a line of 10 Gophers to score an All-American double. Baston later served as Coach Bernie Bierman's assistant at Minnesota from 1932 to 1950.

36), Dick Wildung (1941–42), Leo Nomellini (1948–49), Paul Giel (1952–53), and Bobby Bell (1961–62).

BENBROOK, ALBERT, distinguished himself at Michigan as the first lineman from the Western Conference to make All-American two years in a row (1909–1910). A cat-like giant at 6–5 and 265 pounds, the Michigan guard was the star lineman of what Hurry-Up Yost called "the finest football game I ever saw," the November 20, 1910, clash with Minnesota, unbeaten and unscored upon. With two minutes left in the contest, the Wolverines drove to the Gopher 3-yard line. Michigan sent Stanfield Wells into the huge Minnesota line twice, but didn't gain a foot. In the huddle, Benbrook said to quarterback Shorty McMillan, "Run Wells over me this time." At the snap, Benbrook cleared a hole big enough to drive a truck through and Michigan had its victory, 6 to 0.

Years later, Yost insisted that the forward pass came into its own that day. The passing combination of Wells to Stan Borleske was the impetus behind the final Michigan drive.

A footnote for history was that sitting on the Minnesota bench that afternoon was a third-string substitute, Clark Shaughnessy, who 30 years later became known at Stanford as "the father of the Modern T formation." The 1910 Michigan–Minnesota game also marked the Wolverines' break from the Western Conference until 1917.

BERWANGER, JOHN JACOB, was the first athlete to win the coveted Heisman Trophy (1935).

Thirty-four years later, the Football Writers Association of America named him on its All-Time All-American Team for the post-1920 era.

Jay Berwanger stood 6-foot and weighed 200 pounds. He won All-State honors at Dubuque, Iowa, High School and decided to enroll at University of Chicago instead of Minnesota, Purdue, or Iowa. Football fans nicknamed him "The Man in the Iron Mask," after he broke his nose in his freshman year and was forced to wear a face protector, sort of a half baseball catcher's mask, made of spring steel bars covered with leather. In three varsity seasons, he never went into a game without the mask.

Though Chicago never had a winning season during the Berwanger years, Jay piled up some impressive statistics: As a sophomore, he played 60 minutes per game of all of Chicago's five Conference games, averaging four yards per carry, scored eight touchdowns, and was the team's leading punter. He carried the ball 37 times against Illinois—or as many times as the entire Illini backfield combined. He won the Maroon's MVP award that season, the only sophomore in the Big Ten ever to be so honored.

As a junior, Jay averaged nearly five yards per carry in 119 attempts, passed, punted, returned punts, scored eight touchdowns, and played defense—against Minnesota he made 14 tackles in the first half alone. His two touchdowns helped to beat Michigan, 27–0, in 1934.

Bob Zuppke called Berwanger "the best all-around halfback in college football" as Jay brought the first All-American certificate to the University of Chicago in 11 years.

"Berwanger is the most brilliant backfield man of the lot," added Grantland Rice in naming his 1934 All-American team, despite the preponderance of super halfbacks that season: Lund of Minnesota, Howell of Alabama, Borries of Navy, Purvis of Purdue, Mickal of Louisiana State, Leemans of George Washington, Williams of California, Wilson of Southern Methodist, Cardwell of Nebraska, and Nicksick of Pittsburgh.

Berwanger lived up to his reputation in 1935 by earning All-American honors again—the last of the Maroon to make All-American—and then capped off his college career with the Heisman Trophy.

Versatile Jay also competed in track and finished fourth in the Decathlon at the Kansas Relays as a sophomore—in his first attempt at the grueling event. He later played on the Chicago Rugby team.

BUTLER, BOB (*Butts*) was a powerful tackle and, Pat O'Dea notwithstanding, Wisconsin's first authentic All-American. A bruising blocker and crushing tackler, Butts Butler was something of a one-man gang on his side of the line as the Badgers scored 246 points against 29 in seven games on their way to an unbeaten season and the 1912 Big Ten championship. Walter Eckersall, then a leading football authority for the Chicago *Tribune,* went overboard for the Wisconsin eleven, naming nine of them to his All-Conference Team. The Badgers were coached by Bill Juneau, a former kicking star at the school. There was an attempt to match Wisconsin against undefeated Harvard in a postseason "national championship" game, but the Wisconsin faculty nixed the proposal.

In winning the Conference title in 1912, the Badgers beat Minnesota, 14 to 0, with 11 men—that is, without a single substitution. Butler, a junior, was the only one among them, however, who made Walter Camp's All-American selection, though Tubby Keeler, a guard, was chosen the next year.

Butts Butler rounded out his athletic career in professional football with the Canton, Ohio, Bulldogs.

CARNEY, CHARLES R. *(Chuck),* was the first Big Ten athlete to be named All-American in two sports. He won a total of seven letters in football and basketball. His basketball scoring record (188 points) topped the Big Ten for 20 years.

Carney was Coach Zuppke's choice for football's all-time All-American end. Zup had so much confidence in his big flanker that in the final game of the 1919 season against Ohio State for the Conference championship, he told his quarterback in the last minute of the game to throw every pass to Carney. With the Buckeyes leading, 7–6, Walquist, the Illini passer, hit Carney repeatedly to move the ball down within field goal range. Then, from the 22-yard line and with time running out, Bobby Fletcher, who had never tried a college placekick in his life, booted it through for a 9 to 7 victory.

Carney was so good he made the Illinois

Bob (Butts) Butler, powerful tackle, became Wisconsin's first All-American in 1912.

First two-sport All-American in Big Ten history was Hall of Famer Chuck Carney. The Illinois star was an All-American football end in 1920, and basketball All-American in 1922, when he led the Conference in scoring.

starting eleven in his freshman year. Walter Camp named him All-American in 1920. In basketball, he led the Big Ten in scoring in his sophomore and senior seasons, and was named All-American center in 1922, thus giving him the All-American double in football and basketball.

As a sophomore, Carney merely beat out the No. 1 basketball center at Illinois—Kenneth L. (Tug) Wilson, later Commissioner of the Big Ten Conference.

After graduation, he coached the ends at Northwestern, Wisconsin, and Harvard, and later went into the investment banking business in New York.

CLEVENGER, ZORA G., was a super all-around athlete at Indiana in football, basketball, and baseball. Lean and wiry, he was a brilliant halfback and football captain at Bloomington from 1900 through 1903. He later coached the Hoosier baseball team (1905) and basketball squad (1905–06) and then continued his coaching and athletic executive career at Nebraska Wesleyan, Tennessee, Kansas State, and Missouri, before returning to Indiana in 1923 to spend 23 years as Athletic Director.

Clevenger was football coach at Tennessee in 1914 and led the Vols to their first undefeated season. At both Missouri and Kansas State, he served as Director of Athletics.

The Zora Clevenger record is one of superior contribution to college sports: Basketball Rules Committee, Conference and NCAA administrative duties, as well as his earlier coaching. He helped to establish the East-West Shrine Game. Indiana also awarded him its highest honor, the Distinguished Alumni Service Award. He is in the University of Tennessee Football Hall of Fame, and he had year books dedicated to him at three colleges where he coached.

Zora G. Clevenger, the original Hoosier Hotshot, left his mark on college athletics.

COLEMAN, DONALD E., made opponents think they were seeing double. He was one of the last of the two-way 60-minute men. Benny Oosterbaan ranked Michigan State's first unanimous football All-American in the same class with the legendary Bronko Nagurski—this despite the fact that Coleman stood only

5–10 and averaged 180 pounds. "Pound for pound," Oosterbaan said, "there never has been a better tackle in the Big Ten than Don."

Born at Ponca City, Oklahoma, and raised at Flint, Michigan, Don Coleman never played football until his senior year in high school at Flint Central. Two brothers had died in boyhood and because he was the only son left, his mother kept him out of football. So Don played trumpet in the high school band. In 1947, he exchanged his band uniform for football togs and won All-State honors as Central High smashed its way to the state championship.

At Michigan State, Coleman was a modern lad with old-fashioned ideas about how to play raw-meat football. "Compared to Coleman," reported one talent scout, "Paul Bunyan was a bum."

Don's spectacular blocking ability led to an important modification of the MSU offense in 1949–50–51. On straight-ahead blocking he did so many improbable things that Coach Duffy Daugherty adopted plays never before attempted. "Don was largely responsible for what was known as the Michigan State offense," Duffy said later. "After the system became established, we looked for a lineman who could play what we called the 'Coleman tackle,' because he played the position as it was never played before, and started us experimenting with light, quick men at the other line positions."

Coleman played both offense and defense for three years. Daugherty estimated that he got the key blocks in about 80 percent of the Spartan plays. It was not unusual for him to take out two and three opponents on each play. Ed Prell, the Chicago sports writer, covered MSU in 1951, when the Spartans were 9–0 and ranked No. 2 in the national poll, and he figured that Coleman saved as many as four games with timely blocks and tackles. That fall, Coach Frank Leahy of Notre Dame picked Don as "the best lineman we've faced all year," repeating what he said the year before. The Irish named Coleman on their All-Opponent team three years in a row. Against Penn State in 1951, Coleman made *every* tackle on the Michigan State kickoffs and punts. In the 25–0 victory over Michigan, he was credited with eight key blocks.

Coleman capped his varsity career by being named on every major All-American selection and winning his own team's Most Valuable Player award. His jersey number (78) was the first to be retired at MSU.

After a brief career with the Chicago Cardinals of the NFL, Coleman taught school and coached at Flint Central, then switched to elementary education. He earned his Ph.D. at Michigan State and today Dr. Donald E. Coleman is a member of the MSU administrative staff.

DES JARDIENS, PAUL R. *(Shorty)*, was Amos Alonzo Stagg's key lineman in an era— 1912, 1913, and 1914—when the Maroon of Chicago won 18 Western Conference games in a row.

Shorty Des Jardiens was easy to spot. He towered nearly 6-foot-5, weighed only 182, and was All-American center in 1913 on Walter Camp's first team. An all-around athlete, he lettered 12 times in four sports—football, basketball, baseball, and track.

Des Jardiens once told what it was like to play for Coach Stagg: "The old man was a stickler for clean training habits. He was always after us to watch our eating habits. He'd say, 'Keep the hot dogs up in the stands where they belong. I never ate one in my life.' On road trips he allowed us just enough meal money, and if we charged more to the team bill, he came around and collected the difference. He'd say, 'I'm stoic, not an epicure.' Coach Stagg never smoked and frowned on those who did. All old C Men quickly stamped out their cigarettes when they saw him coming."

Born in Coffeyville, Kansas, in 1893, Des Jardiens was an outstanding three-sport prospect at Wendell Phillips High, in Chicago, where Stagg recruited him for the University of Chicago. After three seasons with the Maroon football varsity, he switched to baseball and played a season with the Cleveland Indians of the American League, then went into private business.

DEVINE, AUBREY, 5-foot-10 and 175 pounds of pure triple-threat quarterback, was the first truly nationally recognized football star in Iowa history. He was one of only four athletes in Hawkeye annals to win nine major letters—football, basketball, and track.

Aubrey Devine put it all together in 1921,

his senior year, leading Iowa to its first Big Ten title and a vigorous claim to the national championship. En route to unanimous All-American choice, Captain Devine dropkicked the Hawkeyes to a 10–7 triumph over Notre Dame, smashing a 20-game Irish win streak, and then masterminded Iowa to a combined total of 123 points to 15 as they smacked Illinois, Purdue, Minnesota, Indiana, and Northwestern to win the Conference crown.

In a game played at Minneapolis, Devine had his grandest hour. Against Minnesota, he merely scored four touchdowns, dropkicked five extra points, passed to end Les Belding for two more touchdowns, carried the ball from scrimmage 175 yards, passed for 125 more, and returned punts and kickoffs and intercepted passes 200 yards for a total of 500 yards. The 29 points he personally scored remain a modern Big Ten high for most points scored by an individual in one game. Devine played 50 minutes of the game, and when Coach Howard Jones finally took him out, the Minnesota fans gave the Iowa quarterback a standing ovation. Even in defeat, the Gophers knew a Hall of Famer when they saw one.

DRISCOLL, JOHN LEO *(Paddy)*, a 145-pound all-everything quarterback, gave Northwestern fans something to cheer about in the years 1915–16–17. Styled along the lines of the great Walter Eckersall, Paddy Driscoll was the team leader, ran, passed, punted, and dropkicked the Wildcats to an overall record of 13–8–0 during his varsity career. His 90-yard kickoff return against Iowa in 1915 is still listed among the longest kickoff runs in Northwestern history; ditto his 43-yard field goal against Chicago in 1916.

Driscoll captained the Wildcats in 1916, when they won 6 of 7 games, losing only to Ohio State, 23–3, in their final game of the season for the Western Conference championship.

ECKERSALL, WALTER H., was the All-American Boy of his day. The brilliant little 145-pound quarterback was the brains and heart of the 1905 University of Chicago eleven that smashed mighty Michigan's 55-game victory string, 2 to 0. "The greatest team that ever wore the C," said Coach Amos Alonzo Stagg afterward. The sensational upset of the Wolverines made Chicago the New Big Nine champion.

Eckersall began as University of Chicago's waterboy in 1897. He went on to enroll at the university in 1903 and led it to a record of 32 wins, 4 losses and 2 ties in 4 seasons. Walter Camp named him All-American in 1904, 1905 and 1906.

In the days when a field goal was worth five points, "Eckie" booted three dropkicks against Wisconsin to win, 15–6; he kicked five against Illinois and five against Nebraska. Against the Badgers, he once ran a kickoff back 106 yards for a touchdown. A 9.8-second hundred-yard-dash man, he was a whale of a player on defense. Walter Camp called him "the greatest quarterback of all time."

In 1906, the forward pass was legalized, and Coach Stagg asked Walter, "Do you think you can throw the ball with any accuracy?"

"Just make sure you have someone who can catch it," Eckie told him.

Against Illinois, in the fourth game of the season, Eckie threw the first pass of his college career—a 75-yard touchdown play to Wally Steffen, later coach of Carnegie Tech and prominent judge on the federal bench. Chicago smashed Illinois that afternoon, 63–0, and Eckie completed every pass he threw.

One of Eckersall's biggest fans was Knute Rockne.

"The first time I learned a football was not only something to kick, but something to think with, was when I saw a great football player in action for the first time," Rockne once recalled. "A sandlot youngster, who regarded football as a pleasantly rough recreation, I had no hero-worship for any player and no interest in any team. But when the Eastern high school champions (Brooklyn Poly Prep) of 1900 challenged the Western champions (Chicago's Hyde Park High), the meeting of the two teams in Chicago was a great event. Crashing the gate—a habit of mine as a youngster—I sat spellbound through the game. It was one-sided: the final score was 105 to 0 in favor of the Chicago team. But the clearest picture remaining from that slaughter was not the overpowering might of the Western lads, who had among them the famous Hammond brothers, later Michigan stars. The striking feature was the brilliant, heady play of Hyde Park's quarterback—a lad named Walter Eckersall.

He played prairie football, mainly wide sweeps around ends; but by instinctive timing he hit the heavier Brooklyn linemen until they were dizzy. With no more than four fundamental plays he worked so quickly and coolly that he made his offense bewildering. Eckersall's sharp, staccato calling of signals; his keen, handsome face, and the smooth precision with which he drove and countered and drove again, handling his players with the rhythm of an orchestra leader—all this gave football a new meaning to me. After the game was over and the Western boys went cheering from the field, shouting the name Eckersall like a slogan over the defeated Easterners, I tried to get close to the hero of the day. Two or three thousand other youngsters were trying to do the same thing, so I had to go home without a handshake—yet, for the first time in my life, I went home with a hero."

Walter Eckersall later became an eminent college football official and analyst for the Chicago *Tribune*.

FESLER, WESLEY E., is regarded by many as the greatest all-around athlete in the history of Ohio State. In football, 1928–29–30, he played center, end, quarterback, and fullback. In the 1930 Navy game, he was used at three positions. He threw a touchdown pass in the Pittsburgh game, and played both quarterback and fullback in a 12–7 victory over Illinois. Playing alongside him in his senior season was Dick Larkins, who was named Athletic Director at OSU in 1947, and Stu Holcomb, who went on to become head football coach at Purdue and Northwestern.

A Phi Beta Kappa student, the 6-foot, 180-pound Fesler was a talented enough first baseman to attract numerous baseball offers from big league teams. Against Illinois, in 1929, he established a Big Ten baseball record that probably will never be broken: In an 11–6 Buckeye win, he hit for 16 total bases and drove in all the Ohio State runs on two doubles and three home runs (two of them grand slams).

Fesler was thrice named All-American end in football, and three times All-Big Ten in basketball. The New York *Sun* picked him at end on its all-time Midwest team, along with the great Benny Oosterbaan.

Fesler captained the 1930 football Buck-

Greatest all-around athlete in Ohio State history was Wes Fesler, an All–Big Ten basketball star for the three years (1928–1930) he was All-American in football. He was also talented enough to receive big league baseball offers—he once drove in 11 runs against Illinois with two grand slam home runs, another homer, and two doubles.

eyes. Their overall record during his three varsity seasons was 14–7–3.

After college, he coached at Harvard (end coach, 1933–41), Connecticut Wesleyan (head coach, 1942–43), Princeton (end coach, 1945), Pittsburgh (head coach, 1946), Ohio State (head coach, 1947–50), and University of Minnesota (1951–1953). His Bucks whipped California in the 1950 Rose Bowl, 17–14.

FRIEDMAN, BENJAMIN, 5–10 and 175 pounds, was the finest passer of the Golden Twenties. He and his star catcher, Benny Oosterbaan, remain the only aerial duo in college football history to be named All-American two years in a row (1925–26). They were the stalwarts of what Hurry-Up Yost picked as his greatest Michigan team—1925—greater, even, than his famous Point-a-Minute bunch. Losing only to Northwestern by a 3–2 baseball score, the 1925 Wolverines rolled up 227 points to 3.

A promising runner, passer, and kicker in high school in Cleveland, Friedman enrolled at Ann Arbor in 1923 and found his frosh year a trial. He even considered transferring to Dartmouth. But after working all summer he went back to Michigan for the 1924 season. After warming the bench for the first two games, Benny was sent in as quarterback and threw two touchdown passes to beat Wisconsin and launch a five-game winning streak.

In 1925, Friedman, one of the best place-kickers in America, kicked the field goal that beat Illinois, 3–0, in Red Grange's last season in the Big Ten. (This was virtually the same Illini eleven that had scorched Michigan, 39–14, the year before.)

"In Benny Friedman, I have one of the greatest passers and smartest quarterbacks in history," Coach Yost remarked one time. "He never makes a mistake, and as for football brains, it's like having a coach on the field when Benny is out there calling signals."

Friedman possessed tremendous fighting spirit. In 1926, against Ohio State, he teamed up with Oosterbaan in a dramatic garrison finish. The Buckeyes had jumped off to a 10-point lead, when the two Michigan Bennies started clicking. With Oosterbaan making circus catches of Friedman's defeat-cheating pitches, Michigan faced up to the challenge brilliantly by coming from behind to win, 17–16.

Friedman and Oosterbaan had great confidence in each other. "That was the key, confidence," Friedman said. "Benny would tell me where he'd be and I knew he'd be there—and he knew I'd get the ball to him.

All-American passing great Benny Friedman proved his versatility on defense as he went high here to intercept a Minnesota pass in 1926.

That's how we beat Ohio State in 1926 for the championship. Benny said he'd go to the extreme corner of the end zone and for me to hit him on the outside of him. That's where I put the ball and we won the old ball game."

Friedman threw a then "unbelievable" 14 touchdown passes in 1925—five of them against Indiana in a 63–0 rout.

As a New York Giant, Benny Friedman went on to become the first truly great quarterback in professional football. Red Grange rated him the best quarterback he ever played against. "I saw Benny take terrible beatings in pro ball," Grange recalled, "yet I never heard him cry about it. In my opinion, the big ends and tackles have always tried harder to discourage a great passer in pro football than in the college game, but they never discouraged Benny."

In all his career as a player, Friedman was never injured. He suffered his bumps and bruises, of course, but he was always suited up and ready for the next game.

GIEL, PAUL, can build a good case as the greatest Golden Gopher of them all. "Paul was the greatest football player Minnesota ever had," declared Dale Warner, one of his teammates. "Even more remarkable, he had no team to help him. He did it all practically on his own, whereas Bruce Smith had a super bunch behind him."

Not particularly swift, Giel's biggest assets were his ability to change direction without loss of balance, finesse at stepping over tacklers, and a sixth sense which warned him of trouble.

"Paul couldn't beat anybody in a hundred-yard dash," said Otis Dypwick, who served 31 years as Minnesota Sports Information Director, "but try and tackle him. He had eyes in the back of his head."

Giel was a Hugh McElhenny-type runner. It was like trying to grab hold of a gaggle of eels to tackle him. He was also a fine passer.

In his sophomore season, 1951, Paul ran up a total offense record of 1,079 yards, then a Gopher record. "And most of the time he was playing on a varsity that was forced to use eight or nine freshmen," Coach Wes Fesler pointed out. "At times we were so hopeless it was embarrassing. About the only time we got the football was when the other team scored and then kicked off to us."

Giel picks the 22–0 victory over Michigan in 1953 as his shining hour. All he did was handle the ball 53 times (a Big Ten record at the time), gained 112 yards on the ground, completed 13 of 18 passes for another 169 yards, scored two touchdowns, and passed for a third. Giel called the signals for Minnesota, even from halfback.

In his senior season, 1953, he averaged more than 100 yards per game. He still holds Minnesota's total offense record for most rush-pass plays (869) and most yards gained (4,117) for a career. In 1952 and 1953, he earned All-American first-team honors both seasons and won the Chicago Tribune Trophy as the Big Ten's Most Valuable Player, the last one to win it twice in a row. He was also one of the first recipients of the Williams Scholarship Fund, named after the Gophers' famous football coach of earlier years.

Giel topped off his collegiate career by earning All-American honors in both football and baseball in his senior year. In a doubleheader against Michigan State that spring, he pitched 16 consecutive innings. Later, he was drafted by the Chicago Bears, but turned down George Halas' offer and signed with the New York baseball Giants; he later pitched for the Pittsburgh Pirates, Minnesota Twins, and Kansas City.

Professional baseball or football—did he make the right choice? "I still think I made the wisest move for me," said Paul Giel, now Director of Athletics at his Alma Mater.

GRAHAM, OTTO, possessed a natural gift that most great quarterbacks have had—incredible peripheral vision, the ability to spot moving figures and to gauge speed and distances without looking directly at the target. His passing was his trademark. He came from a musical family in Waukegan, Illinois, where his father was the high school band director for 22 years; his mother was a grammar school music teacher; his older brother, Gene, was an oboe player and soloist with the U.S. Marine Band. Otto, himself, played the piano, violin, cornet, and French horn, and majored in music at Northwestern.

"This early background in music gave me the perfect rhythm needed for football," Otto said. A passer with perfect pitch!

Graham actually went to Northwestern on a basketball scholarship. He did not play freshman football. But before he graduated in 1943, he was being compared favorably with Bennie Oosterbaan, Wes Fesler, and Branch McCracken (Indiana) as most versatile athlete of star quality in Big Ten annals. A three-sport star, Otto was All-American in football and basketball and a better-than-average baseball player.

Owing to Graham's natural physical gifts of size (6–1, 190 pounds), strength, and toughness, Coach Lynn Waldorf installed him as his triple-threat tailback in the Northwestern single wing attack. "Otto was the ideal running-passing threat," Waldorf said. "He had a terrific sense of timing, and fantastic peripheral vision. He was one of the best pure running-passing combinations the league has ever seen."

In his first Big Ten varsity game, Otto scored two touchdowns against Wisconsin, added a touchdown and a 6-yard-per-carry average in a losing cause against Michigan, and threw two touchdown passes against Ohio State to hand Paul Brown (later his coach with the Cleveland Browns) his only defeat in 1941. Otto set a Big Ten passing record in 1942 with 89 completions out of 182 attempts for 1,092 yards. In 1943, he had his biggest day in college football, scoring four touchdowns, passing for another, and kicking three extra points in a 40–0 romp over Wisconsin. He was chosen All-American in both football and basketball in 1943, and closed out his college career by leading the College All-Stars to a 27–7 victory over the Washington Redskins in the annual Chicago Classic, personally scoring one of the touchdowns on a 97-yard run.

In three varsity seasons, Graham completed 157 of 334 passes for a total of 2,163 yards. He led the Big Ten in passing and total offense in his junior year, and was the No. 1 passer as a senior. The Conference named him its Most Valuable Player in 1943. Otto finished behind Angelo Bertelli of Notre Dame and Penn's Bob Odell in the Heisman Trophy balloting in his junior year. He threw for more than 1,000 yards, but Northwestern won only 1 of 10 games in 1942 and that weighed against him.

Graham's real reputation stems from his pro career with Cleveland, which followed after the war. Coach Paul Brown converted him into a T quarterback, and he became the worthy successor to Sammy Baugh and Sid Luckman.

Brown's hunch paid off as "Automatic Otto," so-named because of the incredible precision with which he hit his targets, sparked Cleveland to the 1950 and 1954 world titles.

In an age of specialists, Otto Graham was a marvel. Big as a fullback, fast as an end, and light-footed as a prizefighter, Otto was often used at Cleveland even on defense. There was no man on the team better as a safetyman. He did more than pass on offense, too, for he excelled at the quarterback draw, the most devastating play in football. His last game of football for the Browns was against the Los Angeles Rams for the 1955 NFL championship. He won it for them, too, 38–14, scoring two touchdowns himself and passing for two more.

George Blanda, who came into the NFL in 1949 with the Chicago Bears and at 48 was still playing pro ball in 1975, has seen a lot of great quarterbacks, but he picks Otto Graham as the greatest of them all.

"He was simply super," Blanda said recently. "I have to pick Otto even ahead of the great Sammy Baugh."

GRANGE, HAROLD (*Red*), Old No. 77, put college football ahead of Jack Dempsey and boxing as the Golden Age of Sport picked up momentum in 1923, 1924, and 1925. His name and his pseudonyms—The Galloping Ghost and The Wheaton Iceman—became household names at the University of Illinois, where he was the most sensational, the most publicized, and, certainly, one of the most gifted broken-field runners of all time. In high school at Wheaton, Illinois, he averaged five touchdowns a game. In 20 games for Illinois he scored 31 touchdowns and ran for 3,637 yards or, as it was translated at the time, 2 miles and 117 yards. All told—high school, college, and pro—Grange carried the ball 4,013 times for 19¼ miles (8.4 yards per carry) and scored 2,366 points in 247 games.

In 1969, he was named to the backfield of college football's first All-Century team. He was an All-American halfback in 1923 and 1924, then switched to quarterback in 1925 and made All-American at that position.

The Grange style was not to waste motion and he had a freedom of movement. He would start wide, cut back, then cut back again, carving a big S on the field. "In my mind I tried to

In high school, college, and pro, Red Grange carried the ball a total of 4,013 times for 19¼ miles and scored 2,366 points in 247 games.

envision where by blockers were and what they were doing as I ran, and I'd somehow use them," Grange explained. "Actually, I can't take much credit for what I did running with a football, because I don't know what I did. Nobody ever taught me, and I can't teach anyone. You can teach a man how to block or tackle or kick or pass. The ability to run with a ball is something you have or you haven't. If you can't explain it, how can you take any credit for it?"

Grange had good speed—9.8 hundred-yard dash—a fast start, excellent balance, change-of-pace, and the uncanny ability to see tacklers coming from the sides.

Harold Edward Grange was born on June 13, 1903, in Forksville, Pennsylvania, the third of four children. His mother died when he was five. His father was the foreman of three lumber camps near Forksville, but after the death of his wife moved the family to Wheaton, Illinois, where he had relatives.

At Wheaton High School, Grange won 16 letters in football, basketball, baseball, and

track. In track he competed in the 100, 220, low and high hurdles, broad jump and high jump, and often won all six events. In one stretch he won 19 straight events. In his sophomore year he scored 15 touchdowns, in his junior year 36 (8 in one game), and in his last year 23.

Grange said he went to the University of Illinois because some of his friends from Wheaton went there and all the kids in the state wanted to play for Bob Zuppke, and because there weren't any athletic scholarships in those days and that was the cheapest place for him to enroll. His brother, Garland, two-and-a-half years younger than Red, followed him to Illinois. He was a 165-pound freshman end and was later with the Chicago Bears.

"Football did everything for me," Grange once admitted, "but what people don't understand is that it hasn't been my whole life. When I was a freshman at Illinois I wasn't even going to go out for football. My fraternity brothers made me do it."

In seven varsity games as a sophomore, Red scored 12 touchdowns and led the nation in yards gained with 1,260. Except for two games when he was hobbled by injuries, he was the star of every game he played. In 1924, at Urbana, he scored four touchdowns against Michigan in 12 minutes. It was after that performance that sports writers christened Grange the "Galloping Ghost." In 1925, in his first appearance in the East, he ran for touchdowns of 60, 55, and 15 yards in a 24–2 rout of Pennsylvania on a muddy field.

Grange's weight in college rose from 172 to 180 on a 6-foot frame. He spent his summers delivering ice in Wheaton for $37.50 a week, thus his nickname, "The Wheaton Ice Man."

"There was so much written about my job on the ice wagon, and so many pictures were taken of me lugging ice, that people thought it was a publicity stunt," Grange said. "It wasn't. I did it for eight summers, starting at 5 a.m. every day, for two reasons. The pay was good and I needed the money. I didn't even have any decent clothes until my junior year. Also, it kept me in shape. Carrying those blocks of ice up and down stairs six days a week, my legs were always in shape when football season started."

Following the 1925 college season, Grange signed with the Chicago Bears, and the "Red

Grange Football Tour" earned him more than $250,000 in two months of barnstorming. He played pro ball from 1925 through 1934, with the Bears, the New York Yankees in a rival league, and then with the Bears again. Despite arm and knee injuries, he made the first All-Pro team, and during his professional career he scored 162 touchdowns and kicked 86 conversions for a total of 1,058 points. In one 10-day period in 1925, he played five games. He is generally credited with having done more than any other single player to focus public attention and approval on the professional game.

Grange was once asked to compare pro football with the college game. "Who pulls the roughest stuff?" a reporter wanted to know.

"The dirtiest experience I ever had was in a Big Ten game," Red replied "I won't mention the team, but in that game, not one but several members of the rival team, while screened by the pile-up of players, gnawed away at my hands, arms and bare legs. At the end of the game, my whole body was dented and chewed up with teeth marks."

HARLEY, CHARLES WESLEY (*Chick*), the first three-time All-American from the Big Ten, was practically a one-man gang. In his three varsity seasons at Ohio State, the Buckeyes won 21 games, tied 1, and lost 1; they won two Big Ten championships. They still hold the Conference record for most points (726) scored in three seasons.

An all-around fullback? Dr. John W. Wilce, the Ohio State coach, was once asked what the 5–9, 165-pound Chick could do best.

"Probably run," Dr. Wilce replied. There was a pause. "No," he added, "he's possibly a better punter." Another pause. "Could be his passing." A final hesitation. "But, then, you should see him dropkick."

In his sophomore season, Harley's dropkicks beat Illinois, 7–6, and Wisconsin, 14–13. He went on in 1916 to lead Ohio State to its first Conference championship and become the Buckeyes' first All-American. In three years—he served in the Army in 1918—Chick scored more than half of Ohio State's points, did virtually all the extra point and field goal kicking, all the punting, and most of the passing. Until he came along, never had a single player so dominated the Conference.

Chick Harley was a good-natured, self-conscious boy with a lopsided grin, and was speedy enough to break high school sprint records at East High School in Columbus. Until his last high school game, against Columbus North High, the football teams that Chick played on never lost. He went into Ohio State University bent on keeping up that unblemished record, and he did, except for a 9–7 loss to Illinois in his final college game in 1919 on a field goal with eight seconds remaining.

Harley was the workhorse in a backfield that featured such household names as Pete Stinchcomb, Roy Hurm, and Frank Willaman. A heads-up, alert, fast-thinking ballhawk, Harley was a constant scoring threat. Against Wisconsin, he grabbed the ball from a Badger runner's arms, as the latter was racing downfield, and, without breaking stride, dashed toward the Wisconsin goal for a touchdown.

Harley better than Grange? Some experts said so, claiming Chick could do more things well. Whatever the case, he gave the farming community of Columbus, Ohio an emotional release second to none whenever he carried the ball.

HARMON, THOMAS DUDLEY, "Old No. 98," teamed with Forest Evashevski, the great blocking quarterback, to bring Michigan out of a long football drought in 1938–39–40. In his final college game, before his number was retired, Harmon scored three touchdowns against Ohio State to bring his career total at Michigan to 33, or two more than Red Grange who played in four fewer games.

In 1939 and 1940, Harmon led the nation in passing and running and rewrote Grange's Big Ten records as he swept all of the important honors in his senior season, including the Heisman Trophy and Associated Press Athlete of the Year award. As tailback in Fritz Crisler's vaunted single wing, Tommy twice scored four touchdowns in a game, against California and Iowa. Against the Golden Bears, he scored on runs of 94, 72, 86, and 80 yards. Like Grange, he specialized in long, slashing runs and rarely allowed tacklers to get more than their fingers on him. Time and again his jersey was ripped from his back. He broke into the clear most often on cutbacks through tackle. In his junior year, he scored all of Michigan's 27 points against Iowa.

In his senior season, 1940, Tommy Harmon led the nation in passing and running and rewrote Red Grange's Big Ten records as he swept all of the important honors for Michigan, including the Heisman Trophy and Associated Press Athlete of the Year award. As tailback in Fritz Crisler's powerful single wing, Harmon twice (1939–40) was named All-American.

Two-time All-American (1939–40), Harmon's credentials included a powerful stiff-arm and high-driving leg action; he was an excellent blocker, defender, passer, punter, placekicker, kickoff specialist, and quick kicker. He scored 237 points for three seasons (24 games) on 33 touchdowns, 33 extra points and two field goals. He completed 101 of 233 passes for 16 touchdowns and 1,396 yards and averaged nearly 6-yards per carry on 398 attempts, and 38 yards on punts.

Amos Alonzo Stagg claimed that Harmon was superior to Red Grange in everything but running. "I'll take Tommy on my all-time team and you can have all the rest," Stagg said.

Harmon won 14 letters in athletics at Horace Mann High School, Gary, Indiana. In track, he won the state title in the 100-yard dash and 220-yard low hurdles. The son of a policeman, Tommy had three older brothers who had been college stars: Lou and Harold in basketball and track at Purdue and brother Gene, a basketball captain at Tulane. Two of his uncles, Leo and Doyle, played football at Wisconsin.

At 6-feet and 195 pounds, Tommy Harmon had the look and strut of an All-American. Once, when he strolled into the Michigan dressing room, Captain Forest Evashevski piped up, "Here comes the Michigan football team, men. We can begin practice, now." One newspaper headline read: "Harmon A One-Man Team." The publicity did not set too well with Tommy's teammates, and they let him know it. A team meeting finally was called to clear the air.

"Fellows," Harmon told them, "nobody knows better than I what a great job you're all doing. I'd be just another back without you."

Actually, Captain Evashevski won almost as much fame as did Harmon as the team's great blocker. "Without the 'Ape' to clear the way," Harmon admitted, referring to Evashevski's nickname, "I never would have gotten all that publicity."

In a poll of football experts in 1969, Tommy Harmon was picked as one of the 11 top players of the 1930's.

HERSCHBERGER, CLARENCE, University of Chicago's great fullback in 1898, made history for the Western Conference that season along with Bill Cunningham, the Michigan center, by cracking through the Eastern monopoly on All-American team voting. They were the first to make Walter Camp's all-star selections. Until they were chosen, Yale, Harvard, Princeton, and Pennsylvania athletes dominated the ballots.

Herschberger was regarded as one of college football's leading punters, placekickers and dropkickers in the years 1895–98. Amos Alonzo Stagg, his coach, credited him with being the first to use the Statue of Liberty play, and the first to quick kick.

"In 1896, I had Herschberger drop back quickly from his position at left half and receive a direct pass from center, from about five or six yards back of the line of scrimmage," Stagg recalled. "Ordinarily, the quarterback received the ball from center, in a position low down under center, and passed the ball back with an underhand pass to a punter 10 or 11 yards back of center. So when Herschberger made his quick kicks, the quarterback stepped aside and became a blocking back."

Stagg recollected that the Statue of Liberty play came about in the 1898 Chicago–

Michigan game, when Herschberger faked a kick and handed the ball to his quarterback, Walter Kennedy, who circled 35 yards around end. The principle of the fake punt and a man's coming behind the kicker and receiving the ball from him was applied to the fake pass when the forward pass became legal in 1906.

"The same principle of faking was involved in the fake punt as in the Statue of Liberty play," Stagg explained. "The Statue of Liberty developed as a result of the forward pass rule adopted in 1906, when the passer could pose with extended arm and the ball being taken out of his hand."

During the Herschberger years, Chicago won 48 out of 60 games. When Walter Camp broke Ivy League tradition and named him All-American in 1898, the "Father of Football" wrote: "Against Penn this year, Herschberger exhibited the best all-around kicking of the season, punting, place-kicking and dropkicking with equal accuracy and facility. Barring Pat O'Dea of Wisconsin, he is the longest kicker in the country. He is also a fine runner. Herschberger demonstrated in actual contest with first-class teams, notably in the match with Pennsylvania, and under trying conditions, that it is not safe to give him a kick from a fair catch anywhere from 45 to 55 yards of the opponent's goal. Owing to his superiority in punting, it must devolve upon the opponents to kick out, and there are very few backs who can send the ball beyond the middle of the field."

Herschberger also had an important role in football's first fake kickoff—a dribble kick which traveled slowly for 10 yards and gave the kicker's own side time to overtake and recover the ball.

"We first worked it against Michigan," remembered Stagg, its inventor. "The rules, as now, prescribed that the ball had to travel at least 10 yards on the kickoff. Warhorse Allen was stationed alongside the ball. The pretended kicker charged forward as if to drive the ball straight ahead as usual, but just before he reached it Allen kicked it gently, at an angle. Herschberger recovered it on the bound about 12 yards ahead and near the sideline, and dodged his way through to Michigan's 20-yard line. Four years later we worked a variation of the same joker on Penn, with Herschberger kicking the top of the ball

lightly and recovering it himself after it had travelled 10 yards forward. Walter Camp saw the game and put Herschie on his All-American Team."

HESTON, WILLIAM MARTIN (*Willie*), the most famous star of the crushing Michigan "Point-a-Minute" teams at the turn of the century, distinguished himself as the first Wolverine football player to be named on Walter Camp's All-American team. On Michigan teams that scored 2,326 points in 40 games, while holding opponents to a total of only 40, Heston personally scored 71 touchdowns from his left halfback position. Though once tied (6–6, by Minnesota, in 1903), Michigan never lost a game during the Heston era.

Willie the Wonder stood 5-feet-8 and weighed 184 pounds, and ran the 100-yard dash in 10 seconds flat. Several times he ran against Michigan's Olympic sprint champion, Archie Hahn, and Heston beat him at 40 yards every time. Willie combined this swiftness with power. Against Ohio State, for example, only Clarence Foss, the safety man, stood between him and the goal line. With the ball tucked under his left arm, Willie picked Foss up with his right arm and carried him the last 15 yards into the end zone for a touchdown.

Heston's speed led Fielding Yost to devise football's first tailback formation, in 1901, thus allowing Willie to run either right or left on a direct snap from center or on a handoff.

Willie Heston came from Grants Pass, Oregon, and first met Coach Yost when Hurry-Up coached at San Jose Normal. That happened this way. Heston was a guard and captain of the San Jose eleven, which tied with Chico State for the conference championship. A playoff game was set and Heston and quarterback Billy Messe traveled 18 miles to Palo Alto and asked Yost, who was coaching at Stanford at the time, to coach them in the championship game. Yost agreed, and Heston, switching to halfback, led San Jose to a 46–0 victory. The following summer, Yost signed a three-year contract to coach at Michigan and, in 1901, sent for Heston.

Heston launched his football career at Ann Arbor by leading the Maize and Blue to 11 straight victories. The Wolverines scored 550 points to 0 and earned a tie with Harvard and Wisconsin for the 1901 national championship.

Against Stanford in the first Rose Bowl pairing, January 1, 1902, Heston averaged 9.4 yards per carry in 18 attempts in a 49 to 0 victory.

Willie led Michigan to such lopsided victories as 130–0 over West Virginia, 128–0 over Buffalo, 107–0 over Iowa, 86–0 over Ohio State, and 89-0 over Michigan State.

In 1928, Grantland Rice wrote of Heston: "Heston, thick-set, solid and fast, was as hard a man to stop as football has ever known. He was off like a flash, starting at top speed and driving through with terrific force. He could break through a line, run an end, or hold his own in any broken field. For combined speed and power, Heston has never been surpassed. Against Chicago, breaking through into an open field, Heston jumped clean over Walter Eckersall, who had come forward to meet him. That shows something of his all-around activity. Heston was a four-year star, and a star in every game he played."

Hurry-Up Yost once said that Heston, had he played in the days of the forward pass, would have been one of the greatest receivers of all time. "Willie had the quickest break of any football player I ever saw," Yost explained. "He could get away much faster than any other man. Willie receiving a forward pass would have broken away from any defenseman and scored any number of touchdowns with a passer like Benny Friedman throwing the ball. Why, he'd have scored touchdowns on forward passes all day."

After college, Heston signed for $600 to play professional football for the Canton Bulldogs. He broke his leg in his first game and withdrew from football forever. Officiating in that game, in 1905, was the great Christy Mathewson of New York Giants pitching fame, and the legendary Arthur Poe of Princeton.

But the name Heston was not through at Michigan. Willie's son later came along and played football for the Wolverines.

HIRSCH, ELROY (*Crazy Legs*), had everything: extraordinary speed, tricky moves, hands like a glue pot, and eyes in the back of his head. He had only one weakness: he should have been *twins*.

Hirsch split his college career between two Big Ten schools, first as a slim-hipped, wild-running sophomore halfback at Wisconsin in 1942, and then as a four-sport star at Michigan

in 1943. Later, he starred in the National Football League as an All-Pro end for the Los Angeles Rams. He is in both the college and professional Football Halls of Fame.

Blond, crew-cut, and with a hitch in his stride, Hirsch led Wisconsin to a No. 3 ranking in the nation with an 8–1–1 record in 1942. Coach Harry Stuhldreher called him "one of the best athletes I ever saw—fast, smart, dead game, and hard to bring down." The next time Stuhldreher saw Hirsch, he was wearing the Maize and Blue of Michigan. As a matter of fact, when Michigan played Wisconsin in 1943, the latter faced 10 former Badgers, due to the Navy V-12 and V-5 programs. Crazy Legs and Bill Daley, the All-American from Minnesota, teamed up to pace the Wolverines to a 27–0 victory. Five weeks earlier, the pair scored three touchdowns in seven plays to bust Northwestern, 21–7. Michigan won the Big Ten title and No. 3 position in the national rankings, losing only to No. 2 Notre Dame.

At Michigan, Hirsch earned four varsity letters during the 1943–44 school year—in football, basketball, baseball, and track—the only athlete in modern Michigan history to earn four "Big Ms" in a single nine-month period.

Perhaps Tex Maule, of *Sports Illustrated*, summed up the Elroy Hirsch football magic best. Hanging up his typewriter in 1975 after 26 years in and around the NFL, Maule wrote: "One of the most pleasant memories I have of pro football is Elroy Hirsch going down the sideline, and 60 yards downfield taking a pass over his head from Bob Waterfield or Norm Van Brocklin, a couple of steps ahead of the defensive back, the ball dropping in on a dime, the back well beaten and Hirsch gone for the touchdown."

And at only an $18,000-a-year salary, too.

HORVATH, LESLIE who was at Ohio State five years and played football for four of them, beat out Army's super sophomores, Glenn Davis and Doc Blanchard, to win the 1944 Heisman Trophy, the first Buckeye in history to receive it.

Les Horvath first appeared in an Ohio State varsity uniform in 1940, when, as a freshman substitute, he tackled All-American Tommy Harmon, who was on his way to a touchdown. Then, in 1942, he sparked the Buckeyes to the Big Ten championship. "I think I played my best in 1942 when we had, I think, our finest team, although my play did not show so much in the statistics. I had my best statistics and we had our best team record (9–0) in my fourth season when I won the Heisman award. I guess voters can only go on what they can see."

Horvath had to lay off football in 1943 to concentrate on a specialized Army training program in dentistry, but he came back as a dental school senior in 1944 for his finest season. The team was so surprisingly successful that its coach, Carroll Widdoes, was voted Coach of the Year. Behind the blocking of Bill Willis, the tremendous tackle, Horvath was the workhorse. Although he was only 5–10 and 170 pounds, he played 50 to 60 minutes of every game. He was not particularly fast and seldom made a long run, but he gained 905 yards rushing, scored 12 touchdowns, passed, punted, and was the inspirational leader of the Big Ten champions, Ohio State's first unbeaten season in 24 years. The nation's polls were unanimous in voting Les the Heisman Trophy, Chicago *Tribune* Trophy, Nile Kinnick Trophy, and Christy Walsh Trophy.

Player of the Year Horvath excelled in all departments as wingback, left halfback and quarterback. He picked the last game of his college career as his greatest triumph, when the Buckeyes beat Michigan for the conference championship, 18–14. "I carried the ball 33 times," Horvath recalled. "My longest run was about 12 yards. I averaged less than four yards. But I was in the thick of things all the way."

Horvath admits he never expected to win the Heisman Trophy. "When I won," he says, "it was a good feeling. I've learned you're always remembered when you win it."

Graduating from dental school in 1945, he was assigned to Great Lakes Naval Base, where he assisted his first coach at Ohio State, Paul Brown, with the base football team. Then he went to Hawaii, where he coached a Marine team. He was discharged in 1947, played three years of professional football with the Los Angeles Rams and Cleveland Browns as a defensive back, was injured, and then opened a dental office in Los Angeles.

Dan Jenkins, the author, will never forget the story of when Horvath and his wife moved to L.A. and set up housekeeping. On the day their things arrived, she noticed this ugly statue being unpacked and placed on the living room mantel.

"What's that thing?" she wanted to know. "Out. Get it out of here."

"But it's among my most precious possessions," Les told her. "It's my Heisman Trophy." He went on to explain to her what he had done at Ohio State to win it. Couldn't he just leave it there for the time being? "If you really disapprove, I'll move it to another room," he added. "Fine," she said.

Several nights later Dr. and Mrs. Horvath happened to have dinner at the home of the Tom Harmons, and Horvath's wife noticed that a Heisman Trophy adorned Harmon's mantel. And two nights later they happened to have dinner with the Glenn Davises, and Horvath's wife noticed that another Heisman Trophy had adorned that mantel as well.

"You know that thing you want to keep in the living room?" she said as they drove home from the Davises. "I wish you'd tell me what's so special about it? Everybody we *know* has one."

ISBELL, CECIL F. (*Cece*), is down in the football record book as the holder of the shortest touchdown pass in history. The 1937 Purdue All-American was playing for the Green Bay Packers at the time, and, knocking on the enemy's goal line, hit Don Hutson with a four-inch pass to score.

As a collegian, the pass-punt-run halfback starred for the Boilermakers in 1935–36–37. He made his biggest mark as a passer. He threw bullets, and could hit his target from almost any range. His best season was 1936, when he led Purdue to a 6–2 won-lost record; overall, the team won 13, lost 9, and tied 2 during his varsity career. As a junior, Isbell figured in 15 of 23 Purdue touchdowns, and did the bulk of the punting. He culminated the intercollegiate phase of his career by pitching the College All-Stars to a 28–16 victory over the Washington Redskins in 1938, and earned the first All-Star Trophy as the game's outstanding college player.

During the years 1938–1942, Isbell starred in the Packers' backfield, leading the National Football League in passing in 1941–42, and establishing records in completions and total yards gained. He returned to Purdue in 1943 as backfield coach, and head coach in 1944. In three years at Lafayette as chief, he won 14, lost 14, and tied 1. He rounded out his coaching career with the Baltimore Colts, Chicago Cardinals, and Louisiana State University.

JOESTING, HERB W., in 1926–1927, followed the great Bert Baston as the second Minnesota stalwart within 10 years to earn All-American recognition two years in succession. The "Owatonna Thunderbolt," so nicknamed because of his tank-like power smashes at the line, was the first of a long string of bulldozing fullbacks at Minnesota. He was the workhorse of the 1925–26–27 Gopher elevens that piled up a total of 654 points to 206 for a 16–5–3 overall record.

Dr. Clarence W. Spears inherited a live one in Herb Joesting when he took over the Gophers from Dr. William H. Spaulding in 1926. The big fullback was just what the doctor ordered, and Doc Spears went right to work molding his attack around the swift sophomore.

Joesting was an unselfish athlete, an excellent team man. "I don't believe he ever had any desire to be All-American or anything like that," Coach Spears said. "As long as we won, he was satisfied."

Joesting summed up his credo of the gridiron this way: "I played each game for all it

Two-time All-American Herb Joesting (1926–27) was the first of a long line of bulldozing fullbacks at Minnesota.

was worth. No more could be asked of an athlete than that he goes all-out in every situation."

How good was Herb Joesting? Well, in 1927, he was this good: not even Bronko Nagurski was able to move him out at fullback that year.

KINNICK, NILE, was so highly regarded at the University of Iowa that they named the football stadium after him.

The grandson of a former governor of Iowa, Nile was reared in Omaha, Nebraska, but returned to Des Moines to attend the University of Iowa. He was a brilliant basketball star as a sophomore and junior—the second highest scorer on the team in 1938—but gave it up to spend more time on his studies and earned Phi Beta Kappa in 1939.

Iowa was at its lowest ebb in football when Kinnick joined the varsity in 1937. Attendance averaged less than 20,000. In his first two seasons, the Hawkeyes won a total of only two games, yet Kinnick led the nation in punting with a 43-yard average as a sophomore and was named All-Big Ten quarterback both years.

In 1939, Iowa hired Dr. Eddie Anderson as new head coach. Under Coach Anderson, Kinnick had his greatest season. On the No. 9 team in the national polls, he played full 60-minute games on successive Saturdays against Indiana, Michigan, Wisconsin, Purdue, Notre Dame, and Minnesota. He was personally involved in 107 of the Hawkeyes' 135 points that fall. He threw three touchdown passes against Indiana and three against Wisconsin, scored three touchdowns against South Dakota, passed for two TDs in the fourth quarter to beat Minnesota, 13–9, and scored the winning touchdown to nip Notre Dame, 7–6. All told, Kinnick threw 11 touchdown passes in 1939, dropkicked 11 extra points, led the nation in kickoff returns with 377 yards and in pass interceptions with 8. He was the prime mover in 197 plays (104 rushing and 93 passes), a modern season record for an eight-game schedule, as was his 998 yards gained.

Three of his statistics are still listed as school records at Iowa: 201 yards gained on 9 punt returns (vs. Indiana, 1939); 16 punts for 731 yards (vs. Notre Dame, 1939); 8 interceptions (for a season, 1939); and 18 interceptions (for a career, 1937–38–39).

Five of Iowa's six victories in 1939 were decided in the fourth quarter. "Nile was the leader, the inspiration," Coach Anderson said later. "Because of his spirit, we had as many as eight players who would go the full 60 minutes with him in a tough game."

An Iron Man from the old school, Kinnick played 402 of a possible 420 minutes of football in 1939, running, passing, punting, and dropkicking. This all-around yeoman performance did not go unnoticed: He won the Heisman Trophy, Maxwell, and Walter Camp Trophies as the No. 1 college player in the U.S., was unanimous All-American, and beat out Joe DiMaggio as the "No. 1 Athlete of the Year." Dr. Eddie Anderson was named Coach of the Year.

Of the three Heisman Trophy winners who have died, none did so more tragically than Nile Kinnick.

In 1940, he entered law school, but his studies were interrupted when he was called into training as a naval aviation cadet in December 1941, the month Japan bombed Pearl Harbor and brought the United States into World War II. Only 18 months later, on June 2, 1943, Ensign Nile Kinnick, not yet 24, was killed. Returning from a mission with oil leaking badly from the engine of his fighter plane, he was unable to land on his carrier because the deck was crowded. He crashed four miles away into the waters of the Gulf of Paria in the Caribbean Sea. His motionless body was sighted in the sea, apart from the sinking plane. Another pilot directed an oncoming rescue boat to the spot, but when it got there, eight minutes after the crash, Kinnick was gone.

Years afterward, Max S. Hawkins, a teammate on that 1939 Iowa eleven, talked about Kinnick. "Nile's greatest single contribution was his quality of leadership. He set the pattern of hard work on the practice field as he was always striving for perfection. Though he stood only 5–10 and weighed 167 pounds, I would say that he is probably the best football player I have ever seen."

KIPKE, HARRY, is regarded by oldtimers as the greatest spot kicker in Big Ten history. He led the Conference in punting three years in a row. He was a master of the art of "coffin corner" punting, and placekicked field goals from distances of 40 yards and more.

A high school whiz at Lansing High School, Kipke stood only 5–9 and weighed 158, yet Walter Camp called him "the greatest punter in football history," after watching Harry deftly place 9 of his 11 punts out of bounds inside the Ohio State 8-yard line. His kicks that day averaged 47 yards. He also scored two touchdowns.

In 1922, Camp put Kipke on his All-American team, and, along with Paul Goebel and Bernie Kirk, Harry led Michigan to its first Big Ten championship since 1906. He was also named on a lot of the All-American ballots in 1923.

While Kipke's booming punts overshadowed his other assets, Conference coaches fully recognized him as an excellent ball-carrier, passer, blocker, dropkicker, and a fine defensive player. As captain of the Wolverines in 1923, he led them to an 8–0–0 record; in his three varsity seasons, they were 19–1–2, scoring a total of 520 points to their opponents' 46.

Kipke earned nine varsity letters in three major sports: football (halfback), basketball (guard), and baseball (outfielder).

He was an assistant football coach at Missouri in 1924, head coach at Michigan State in 1928, and then football chief at his alma mater, 1929–1937. He also served as President of the American Football Coaches Association.

LOCKE, GORDON C., was a first-team All-American quarterback in a Walter Camp backfield comprised of such 1922 headliners as Eddie Kaw (Cornell), Harry Kipke (Michigan), and John Thomas (Chicago). Under the great Howard Jones, Locke played both quarterback and fullback on Iowa's Big Ten champions of 1921 and 1922—certainly the two best Iowa elevens until the Nile Kinnick team of 1939. During those two years, the Hawkeyes won 14 straight games, including a 10–7 victory over Notre Dame to break an Irish 20-game winning streak.

In 1921, Locke scored 12 touchdowns for a new Big Ten scoring record; he was again the Conference scoring leader in 1922. He was named All-Big Ten both seasons, and unanimous All-American in 1922, when he also captained the Hawkeyes. He is listed on Iowa's All-Time team.

Locke weighed only 165, yet he crashed

head-on with the force of a tank. In the big upset of Notre Dame, he battered his head against the Irish line so hard that he became slightly confused and wanted to whip the whole Notre Dame team.

"This was in the last part of the third quarter after Gordy had scored our only touchdown and had given Notre Dame a lesson in line plunging they still remember," recalled Aubrey Devine, one of the Iowa stars of that game.

The 1921 Hawkeyes rolled up 185 points against only 36 on a rugged schedule that included the Irish, Illinois, Purdue, Minnesota, Indiana, and Northwestern. With Locke and Devine running and Glenn Devine and Craven Shuttleworth serving as twin blocking backs, Coach Howard Jones introduced his system of a two-runner, two-blocker backfield. The quarterback (sometimes Locke, sometimes Aubrey Devine) was the tailback, and he had to be a triple-threater. The other carrier was the fullback (sometimes the pile-driving Locke). Howard Jones' box differed from Knute Rockne's in that the latter stressed the off-tackle play and Jones specialized in sweeps at Iowa.

In the three varsity seasons that Locke played at Iowa, the Old Gold and Black won 19 games, lost only 2. A graduate in Law, he later became an attorney in Washington, D.C.

LUND, FRANCIS L. (*Pug*), a Wisconsin boy, loved the tradition of Minnesota football. Even though he had offers from other schools, including the University of Wisconsin, it was inevitable he would end up in Minneapolis.

"It only cost $500 to $600 a school year at Minnesota in the Thirties," Pug told me recently. "Even as an out-of-state student, I had to pay only an extra $10 a semester. So I went to U.M. as a walk-on. While my primary purpose for going there was to get an education, I said, what the heck, I'll go out for football and see what happens. I had no delusions about myself. What would be, would be. I was plenty raw in my frosh year. The coach sent me in at guard and on the first play I tackled the lineman opposite me. 'No, no, no!' cried the coach. 'You are supposed to tackle the man with the *ball!*' That's how little I knew about football."

Switched to the backfield, Pug Lund began his varsity career in 1932 strictly as a ball-

Hall of Fame tailback Francis L. (Pug) Lund came off the Minnesota bench as a sophomore in 1932 and quickly developed into the Gophers' do-all, be-everywhere halfback. He captained, passed, ran, blocked, and punted Minnesota to the national championship in 1934, and was named the Big Ten's MVP.

carrier, and with no other duties. He was suspected of no other talent, and coach Bernie Bierman was depending on him for considerable ground gaining. Then Myron Ubl was injured, and the frantic search began for someone to pass and punt. Just 10 days before the Purdue game, Bierman chose Lund as the best of the candidates, although Pug had never handled those assignments before. Bierman was reluctant to burden an untried sophomore with such vital extra duties, but there was no alternative. So Pug Lund became the Gophers' new do-all, be-everywhere halfback. Purdue came along, and Pug lugged the ball on anywhere from two to five successive plays, passed, blocked, and held Paul Moss, the great Boilermaker kicker, dead even in a punting duel.

Once Pug started the task of being a "backfield within a backfield," he never stopped. All through his sophomore season against Northwestern, Nebraska, Iowa, Wisconsin, Mississippi, and Michigan, he was the handy man in the Gopher backfield. Whatever he was asked to do he did well. He was a badly bruised young man when the season ended, but there was never a word of complaint from him.

Lund was All-American in 1933 and 1934. He was named the Big Ten's Most Valuable Player in 1934. He played in both the East-West Game and the College All-Stars vs. Green Bay Packers in Chicago. On the same team with him against the pro champions was a tough, heady center from Michigan—Jerry Ford.

Lund was captain of the 1934 national champions, the team's accelerator, sparkplug, and dynamo. "Pug was the boy who made Minnesota go," was the way Indiana coach Bo McMillin described him. He threw the touchdown pass to Bob Tenner which won the Pittsburgh game, 13–7, and with it the national title. He led the slashing attack which smothered Iowa, 48–12, gaining 102 yards in 15 attempts. After Michigan had held the Gophers scoreless in the first half, Lund, with two broken ribs, started the second-half drive which rolled up 34 points. Then Pug finished his career by leading Minnesota to a 35–7 victory over Chicago, and 34–0 over Wisconsin. All he did against the Badgers was gain 132 yards in 12 carries, and score the first two touchdowns in eight minutes.

Bob Zuppke was mighty high on the 1934 Golden Gophers.

"They could have beaten the Chicago Bears or the New York Giants every time they played," declared the Illinois coach.

At his peak, Pug Lund could be brushed aside about as lightly as a ten-ton tractor. "He was just about the greatest competitor I ever saw," Bierman said. "You see lots of football players come and go during a coaching career. Some of these are blockers and little more. They couldn't take a ball for a gain if it meant their graduation. Others are blockers and, in addition, everything required to make an all-around star. Pug was like that. He was our sparkplug. As a ball carrier, passer, kicker, blocker, and tackler, he carried out every heavy assignment we gave him. He was battered and butted and broken up—teeth knocked out, finger amputated, thumb broken, ribs broken—but through all that blasting barrage he carried on. Our opponents might break him in two, but they couldn't stop him."

In 1934, Lund gained 657 yards in 8 games, an average of nearly 7 yards per carry. Several of his longest punts in important games rolled out of bounds inside the 5 yard line. His long-gainers on offense earned him All-American honors, but not to be ignored was his blocking ability. He had the rhythmic sense that makes blocking easy and he loved to smack people.

Pug Lund was the ideal football player—and he lived up to his nickname in every way.

MAULBETSCH, JOHN, fast, stocky (5–7, 153 pounds) and so strong it usually took three or four tacklers to bring him down, symbolized power football of 60 years ago. "With knees churning up to his chin, and head crouched low, using one arm as an extra leg, Johnny had to be tackled from the top to be stopped," recalled Homer Post, who was born in 1888 and played against Maulbetsch in high school. "Tackling him was like tackling a hod-carrier carrying a hod full of bricks. His thighs were a mass of muscle. He was unbelievably strong. They list him among the smaller halfbacks, but he could hit like a wild bronco. I still carry a scar where he ran over me."

Johnny Maulbetsch was a young man in a hurry. He made the All-American team in 1914, his sophomore season, when he scored 12 touchdowns. Against Harvard that season, he gained more yardage (133 yards) in 30 rushes than the entire Crimson backfield. "After this," wrote Ring Lardner, "if any Easterner tells you that the game played back East is superior to that played in the Midwest, try not to laugh yourself to death. Johnny Maulbetsch of Michigan shot that theory full of holes."

A week later, Maulbetsch scored two touchdowns and accounted for 120 of the 127 yards Michigan gained against Pennsylvania, to lead the Wolverines to a 34–3 victory.

Desire was a Maulbetsch trademark and his peculiar running style was an extension of it. In 1916, he captained Michigan to a 7–2 won-loss record. So highly regarded is the name Johnny Maulbetsch by Michigan men that they have named a football award after him, given to the freshman who exhibits the most character, leadership, and spirit.

You get some notion of how they felt about him around Ann Arbor in this poem by Fred Lawton, written after the 1914 Harvard game:

> He didn't make the touchdown,
>   and we didn't win the game,
> But little Johnny Maulbetsch
>   led the Wolverines to fame.

For, in those glorious minutes,
   when young "Mauly" gave his all,
We learned of Michigan spirit
   from his words, "Gimme da ball!"
His spirit burst into a flame
   when victory hopes were slim
The "Victors" and the "Varsity"
   became a part of him!
You ask the meaning of this
   Michigan spirit—yours and mine?
Just think of Johnny Maulbetsch
   when he hit that Harvard line!

MARSHALL, BOBBY, Minnesota end, was so durable he never sustained a major injury in 20 years of football, college and pro. A second-team All-American in 1905 and 1906, perhaps his finest hour was against Chicago in the 1906 thriller, when he kicked a last-gasp, 42-yard field goal to win the game, 4 to 2, and earn the Gophers a tie for the Conference championship (a field goal counted four points then).

Bobby Marshall was the first black star to play in the Western Conference. Born in Milwaukee, he grew up in Minneapolis where he attended Central High School and was a three-sport star (football, baseball, and track). He also lettered in all three sports at Minnesota, was first baseman on the Gophers' Big Ten champions in 1907, his senior year. Marshall was so versatile that he also played semi-pro baseball, was an excellent boxer, signed to play professional hockey with a team in Hillsdale, Pennsylvania—and after graduation served as assistant to Dr. Henry L. Williams, the Minnesota coach.

Bobby Marshall was still playing football in the Minneapolis area when he was in his 50s.

The old man was a veritable Paul Bunyon with a varsity "M" on his chest.

McGOVERN, JOHN FRANCIS, an all-around football player—captain, runner, placekicker, blocker—is down in history as the first University of Minnesota man to make Walter Camp's All-American team. The honor came to him in 1909, the year he quarterbacked the Gophers to the Western Conference championship.

In the three years McGovern played in Minneapolis, 1909, 1910, and 1911, Minnesota lost only two games, both to Michigan, 15–6 and 6–0. Since the Wolverines dropped out of the Western Conference in 1910, the Gophers thus won or shared the championship all three seasons that McGovern was at quarterback.

Lucius Smith, father of the great Bruce Smith, played one season with McGovern, and remembers him as small but stocky (5–5, 148 pounds), with big legs. "He was one of the shortest All-Americans ever chosen," Smith, Sr. recalled, "but he was hard to bring down. Tough as nails. Why, he played the whole game against Wisconsin with a broken collar bone."

Team captain McGovern fitted in beautifully with Coach Dr. Henry L. Williams' successful "Minnesota shift" offense. A two-way, 60-minute player, he missed only one game in three years of varsity competition. A leg injury kept him out of the Chicago game.

McGovern was a master of the dropkick, a scoring maneuver you never see anymore. Against Amos Alonzo Stagg's powerhouse in 1909, he dropkicked three field goals to spark the Gophers to a 20–6 victory.

As a senior, he received his school's "Outstanding Achievement Award," and after graduation they named him "The Most Outstanding Alumnus." He first worked as sports editor of a Minneapolis newspaper, then turned to the legal profession and practiced law in Washington, D.C. for many years.

MACOMBER, BART, was a vital factor in the Illinois success story on the gridiron in 1914, 1915, and 1916, when the Orange and Blue won a total of 15 games, tied 3, and lost 3, on the way to winning the Western Conference title (1914) and sharing it (1915). Macomber capped his varsity career by earning a place on Walter Camp's 1916 All-American team, the third Illini in history to be so named.

Halfback Macomber is best remembered as one of the eleven Iron Men who played the entire 60 minutes to beat powerful Minnesota, 14–9, in 1916. Averaging 59 points per game and having given up only 14 points in their first four games, the Gophers needed the victory to edge out Ohio State for the conference championship. But with Macomber scoring the first touchdown and kicking the extra point, Illinois worked many plays from punt formation with Macomber back to go ahead 14–0. Sometimes kicking, sometimes running,

Macomber tore through Minnesota for substantial gains to hang on to win. The late Harry Grayson, long-time NEA Sports Editor, called it "the greatest football upset of all time."

This was the game before which Bob Zuppke made his famous speech: "I am Louis the Fourteenth and after us the deluge!"

Zup was half right. After the upset, a torrential rain flooded Minneapolis!

NAGURSKI, BRONISLAV *(Bronko)*, was truly an all-around football player at Minnesota. He was a fullback, tackle, and end, and, if you listen to old Gopher fans, he would have beaten out any man at any position. However, the experts pretty much agree that Nagurski, powerful, numb to pain, durable and inspired, played his best football at tackle.

Bronko—he got the nickname in the first grade when a school official had trouble with Bronislav—was considered a physical brute at 6–2 and 217 pounds in the Big Ten, and his bravery was often displayed when he would hunker into the line to stop every play, then shift to fullback to lug the ball repeatedly. One way or another, he made the big play.

In his three varsity seasons at Minnesota, the Gophers had an 18–4–2 record and outscored opponents, 572 to 126. They lost those four games by a combined total of five points.

"When it comes to the matter of the best all-around player," wrote Grantland Rice in 1947, "I'll have to string along with Bronko Nagurski of Minnesota. He was big and powerful and could really move. First of all, he was a great tackle, one of the best. He was an All-American. Then he became a brilliant end. Later he was one of the most devastating fullbacks in football history. Steve Owen of the New York Giants told me that Bronk was the only player who ran his own interference. In my opinion, the final answer seems to lie in this question: Who would you pick to win a football game—11 Glenn Davises—11 Jim Thorpes—11 Ken Strongs—or 11 Bronko Nagurskis? I honestly don't think it would be a contest. The 11 Nagurskis would mop up any other one-name team. Seven Bronks up front would be too good a line to run against."

Otis Dypwick, who spent 31 years at Minnesota as Sports Information Director until his retirement in 1975, remembers that Nagurski came to Minneapolis from International Falls, Minnesota. "People still think of him as a great big massive brute of a man, but as a 20-year-old senior in college he stood only a little over 6-feet and weighed about 215," Otis told me. "He didn't develop into giant-size until he joined the Chicago Bears."

Red Grange was asked recently to describe Nagurski in terms of today's stars. "He played offense like Larry Csonka and defense like Dick Butkus," Old 77 said.

For nine years, Bronko starred as a fullback for the Chicago Bears and tore NFL lines apart with all the thunder of a runaway tank. Pudge Heffelfinger said he reminded him of a wise old mule in a pasture with a bunch of horses. "Mule may look dumb," Pudge told me once, "but he sees everything out of the corner of his eye. Bronk could play any position up to the hilt. They used him at fullback a lot because of his line-smashing power, but I think he was even greater at tackle. He was bigger and stronger than I ever was. There probably has never been a football player any stronger than Nagurski or any who could develop so much horsepower from a standing start. Even his own teammates marveled at his strength."

Nagurski once was asked where he got all that power and muscle. "I owe it to plowing in the fields back home when I was a kid," he said.

"But plowing is commonplace exercise among all country boys," it was pointed out to him. "In the old days, every farmer's son did his share of plowing."

"Yes," Bronko agreed, "but without horses?"

NEWMAN, HARRY, was the unforgettable quarterback and passing star of Michigan's 1932 undefeated national champions. Called "the most dazzling quarterback in the Big Ten since Benny Friedman," the squat (5–8, 170 pounds) Newman was the leading passer in America in 1932 and a deceptive runner and safety man. He was named the Most Valuable Player in intercollegiate football that season.

"Harry came to us with no starting record behind him," Harry Kipke, his coach, recalled once. "But we discovered early that he could throw a football more accurately than anyone in the freshman class and even more accurately than anyone on the varsity. In his sophomore year, 1930, he either passed for an actual touchdown or else hurled passes that carried the ball inside the 3-yard line against Purdue, Ohio State, Illinois, and Harvard. In 1932, he either passed for an actual touchdown or else placed the ball within the 3-yard line against Michigan State, Northwestern, Illinois, Princeton, Indiana, and Ohio State. In the Chicago and Minnesota games he failed, but he ran 78 yards and 25 yards against Chicago for touchdowns, and he kicked the only 3 points scored in the Minnesota game. He was heaven's own passing, twisting, squirming, fighting answer to a coach's prayer."

A two-way Iron Man, little Harry Newman played a total of 437 minutes out of a possible 480 in 1932.

A flash in the pan? Hardly. Two years later, he led the New York Giants to the NFL championship.

O'DEA, PATRICK JOHN, enrolled at the University of Wisconsin in 1896 from Australia because his brother, Andy, was the Badgers' crew coach. For the next four years, the Big "W" featured a ravishing, kicking, smothering brand of football that America never knew before and may never know again.

The "Human Kangaroo" was a phenomenally expert punter and dropkicker. Without exaggeration, he could curve a long punted football as a pitcher curves a baseball. He could punt 85 yards against your "great" 60-yarders of today. The record books testify that he once lifted the football 110 yards in the wind. In an impossible 20-mile cross-field gale against Illinois, in 1899, he placedkicked half the length of the playing field, straight through the uprights.

Pat O'Dea specialized in rugby tricks, and could boot the ball on the dead run. Against Minnesota, in 1899, he caught a punt at midfield, eluded Gil Dobie's flying tackle, and, instead of running the ball, kicked it back over the Gopher crossbar 60 yards away. This highly irregular stunt broke the hearts of the Gophers, and they were never in the game after that. Final score: Wisconsin 19, Minnesota 0.

Before the 1898 Yale game, O'Dea put on an incredible exhibition of dropkicking ability, putting one ball after another over the crossbar from mid-field.

There never has been another football

player quite like the Human Kangaroo. In the 1897 Chicago game, he dropkicked two 40-yard field goals and punted the Maroons to submission, 28–0. In the 1899 Beloit game, he dropkicked four field goals and returned a kickoff 90 yards to the goal. In the 1899 Michigan game, he played most of the contest with a broken bone piercing the skin of a finger on his right hand. He was finally forced to the bench, the only time in his college career when he did not last the entire 60 minutes.

Once, in a tight spot, Paul Trat, his little halfback, had the ball and was in a tangle when a score was needed. O'Dea, 6-feet tall and 170 pounds, picked Trat up out of the jam and carried him, football and all, across the goal line.

Pat O'Dea had a personality around which legends clustered. Once, he was almost cut to pieces by sharks, when he saved a small girl from drowning. He almost burned to death in hot water when he once stunned his head in a bathtub fall. In 1917, when the Australian army passed through San Francisco, where by this time O'Dea was practicing law, he joined the Anzacs without even telling his family, thus leaving America as unostentatiously as he had come. For the next 17 years he was not heard from. Andy O'Dea, his brother, was certain that Pat was an unknown soldier. Then one day, in 1934, he was found living with his wife in the little California town of Westwood, up in the timber corner of the state, working under the name of "Charles J. Mitchell" as a statistician. For 15 years, no one knew of his football fame. He simply moved in as a stranger, became a prominent citizen, and served the Chamber of Commerce. When his true identity was finally revealed, he told the press: "Probably I was wrong, changing my name and all. My wife always thought it was crazy. But I had had it up to here with my football reputation. I wanted to forget the past. As Pat O'Dea, I seemed very much just an ex-Wisconsin football player."

But *what* a football player. One of his most colorful stunts was a 65-yard dropkick against Northwestern in 1898. It was the last game of the season, November 24th, and Coach Phil King had promised his players "all the champagne you can drink if you score in the first two minutes." The Badgers were sure of victory—they had won 8 of 9 games—but they had doubts of how quickly they could get on the scoreboard.

Northwestern kicked off. Wisconsin returned the ball to their own 32. On the first play, Norsky Larson gained 3 yards. Then O'Dea called the 9-10 signal, meaning a kick. Slam Anderson and Eddie Cochems were playing end for the Badgers and they looked at O'Dea in amazement.

"But Pat didn't bat an eye," Cochems said later. "He calmly went back and dropkicked the ball for the points—and we got the champagne. The ball went between the goal posts two stories high and over a fence 10 yards behind the goal posts. From where he stood, it traveled about 72 yards in the air."

After graduating, Pat O'Dea coached the kickers at Notre Dame. One of his pupils was Red Salmon.

"Red learned quickly," O'Dea said. "He got so good that opponents sometimes insisted that it was really I who was doing the kicking for Notre Dame, not Red, and they wanted to examine him. He had red hair and they even tried to tear it off, figuring to expose me wearing a wig. They were wrong, of course. Red Salmon kicked as well as I could."

OLIPHANT, ELMER QUILLEN (*Ollie***)** was right out of the pages of Frank Merriwell. Born at Bloomfield, Indiana, he started his college career at Purdue, where he earned a total of 17 varsity letters and sweaters from 1911 through 1913: three each in football, basketball, baseball, and track. On one wall of the trophy room at Purdue hang four life-size pictures of Ollie, togged out for each of these sports. He also did some hitch-kick high diving. During his career at Lafayette, Purdue never lost a football game to Indiana, their arch rival. And against Illinois, Ollie suffered a broken ankle, yet went back into the game and kicked a field goal to win the game, 3 to 0. Knocked down in the closing seconds of a basketball game against Wisconsin, with Purdue trailing, 20–21, Ollie shot the winning basket—while seated on the floor!

No one so much as raised an eyebrow when Oliphant bobbed up at West Point in 1914, for those were the days of a free-wheeling athletic policy and Army football teams were loaded with huskies who had played previously on major college teams. There Ollie became a

Elmer Oliphant stood only 5–7 and weighed 174, but he starred at Purdue (1911–12–13) in football, basketball, track, and baseball, and then went on to even greater renown for four years at West Point.

legend. He still holds the Army records for most points scored in a single game (45 against Villanova in 1916), most touchdowns in one game (6 vs. Villanova in 1916), and most points scored in a season (125 in 1917).

Ollie, 5–7 and 174 pounds, was an indestructible bull of a halfback and all-around athlete. At West Point, a special act of the Athletic Council was necessary to design a suitable varsity letter for him. Until he joined the Corps, only two cadets, George Patton and George Beavers, had ever won letters in three major sports. Their sweaters were graced by an "A" with one gold stripe on the crossbar, one above it and one below. Then Ollie came along and won four major letters in baseball, three in football, three in basketball, and one in track, plus monograms in boxing, hockey, and swimming. Along the way he smashed the world's record for the 220-yard low hurdles *on grass* at 25 seconds. He wore no heel spikes, and it is estimated that racing on cinders is three seconds faster.

When it was brought to the attention of the West Point Athletic Council that Ollie had won letters in four major sports, the council voted that he could wear a gold star on the letter to take care of the fourth major sport— the only letter sweater of its kind.

Elmer Oliphant, football All-American in 1916–1917, could just about do it all: run, pass, kick, tackle, and block. He was indeed one of the truly great "little men" in college football history. He had a neck and ankles of steel, a compact torso. He ran the inside plays without compromise; he attacked the tackler. He also ran well to the outside, and used the stiff-arm to perfection. He was hard to bring down. He made good use of the rule which permitted him to roll to his feet and keep running, if he could, after he had been knocked down.

Oliphant was named on both Walter Camp's and Knute Rockne's All-American teams, linking him with Pat O'Dea, Jim Thorpe, and Charley Brickley as the greatest dropkickers. Years afterward, he was unanimously chosen as "the best amateur athlete ever born in Indiana." In 1969, during the celebration of college football's first 100 years, the Football Writers Association of America voted him a member of the All-Time All-America team's backfield, alongside Walter Eckersall, Jim Thorpe, and Willie Heston (three of the four from the Big Ten).

Biff Jones, Oliphant's teammate at Army and then head football coach there, picked Ollie as the greatest football player of all time. "Ollie was a stubby, hard-twisted blond boy," Jones recalled. "When you first saw him his rugged build suggested that of a blocker. Yet under Coach Charlie Daly's polishing he became an unstoppable ballcarrier who could hit with tremendous impact off the tailback position from the single wing formation Daly used. I played with Ollie at Army for two years and our line always worked hard for him. We knew if we didn't move he would run right up our backs. He had supreme confidence in himself. Despite the fact that he was always in the glare of the spotlight he never ducked the drudgery of practice, nor did he ever cease trying to improve himself in the fundamentals of the game."

While at Purdue, Oliphant was a member of Kappa Sigma fraternity and for years after he graduated freshman pledges were obliged to bow before his picture, which hung in a prominent space.

Navy once worked itself into fever pitch trying to psych the Midshipmen into getting up for the Army game. Orders of the day at Annapolis read: "6 a.m.—rise. Stop Oliphant. 7 a.m.—breakfast. Stop Oliphant. 8 a.m.—go to classes. Stop Oliphant. . . ."

Ollie actually won his varsity football letter at Army only three times. How come? "Very few people knew it," Oliphant recalled shortly before his death in 1975 at the age of 82, "but I did not make my letter as a plebe. You had to get into six regular-season games or complete one play in the Army-Navy game before you made your letter. I got in five games and was warming up on the sideline all afternoon at the Navy game, but Coach Daly would not put me in."

OOSTERBAAN, BENJAMIN G., is remembered by Big Ten fans as the most complete end who ever played football. The brilliant Michigan pass-catcher was three-time All-American (1925–26–27), the only Wolverine to earn such distinction. Only Don Hutson, who came along in the next decade at Alabama, ever compared with him as a receiver, and both hold down the wings on the first All-Century team.

No matter where Benny Friedman threw the ball, Oosterbaan the acrobat was there to dive and scoop it up or one-hand it in midair. He was equally as tenacious on defense, and it is said that in three years of varsity competition no runner ever gained around his end, including the great Red Grange.

Bennie Oosterbaan stood 6–2 and weighed 198 pounds. A Dutch boy from Muskegon, where he starred in football, basketball, baseball, and track, he has been described as "the greatest schoolboy athlete in Michigan history." He did pretty well at Ann Arbor, too, where he won a total of nine varsity letters. A big league prospect in baseball (he led the Big Ten in hitting), a superb discus thrower, an All-American in basketball, Oosterbaan chose to make football his life. In 1927, he captained the football team to its first undisputed Conference championship.

During his four-sport varsity career at Michigan, Bennie led the Big Ten in touchdowns, baskets, and hits, the only athlete to do it. At graduation, he turned down professional football and baseball offers to remain at Michigan. Bennie Oosterbaan was a Wolverine all the way. After arriving on the campus as a freshman in 1924, he never again left it. He spent a total of 42 years at Ann Arbor, as coaching assistant, head basketball coach, head football coach, and finally assistant athletic director.

Oosterbaan served as head football coach for 11 years—1948–1958—and compiled a

63–33–4 record. The 1948 bunch won the mythical national championship. His 1950 team won the famous snow bowl game against Ohio State and went on to beat California in the Rose Bowl, 14–6. All told, his teams won the Big Ten title three times and his 1948 success earned him the Coach of the Year award.

On the field, Coach Oosterbaan was something of a contrast with his old coach, Fritz Crisler, who was a martinet and demanded cold efficiency. Bennie, on the other hand, was easy-going and liked to mix with his players, wearing a baseball cap and an old jersey. Sometimes he even got into a scrimmage himself and gave them a go.

Bennie Oosterbaan might have been a headache for the newspaper headline writers, but he was the most splendid thing Michigan has seen in a long, long time.

PARKER, JIM, was a two-time All-American guard at Ohio State in an era of magnificent college linemen. Playing on both offense and defense on championship teams in 1954 and 1955 coached by Woody Hayes, Parker became the most famous college lineman in the country in the mid-1950s. In listing superior guards of that period, Jim Parker is the name that generally comes quickest to mind. At 250 pounds, his strength, agility, and perception made the end and tackle on his side of the line seem superfluous. He rolled across the scrimmage line like a cannonball, piling blockers and ball-carrier into one heaping mess. On offense, his speed and power made him an awesome blocker.

Of the 64 football All-Americans who have come from Ohio State, Parker is one of only 15 who have been picked more than once. He was chosen for the first time as a junior in 1955, then again in 1956, when he also won the Outland Trophy as the best interior lineman in the nation.

In Parker's sophomore year, the Buckeyes were described as "Howard Cassady and a supporting cast of 40 other All-Americans." They were deep, talented, and sure Big Ten champions. They finished the season with a 10–0–0 record, the national title in the polls, the Conference championship, and the first undefeated Ohio State team in 10 years. In the three seasons Parker was on the varsity, the

Buckeyes were 23–5–0. They demolished Southern California, 21–7, in the January Rose Bowl in 1955, and captured a second straight Big Ten championship the following fall. The 1954 and 1955 Bucks were superb on defense and led the Big Ten in defense against rushing. The defense saved the 1954 Iowa and Michigan games, and held Pittsburgh to five first downs and USC to six. Beating Michigan, of course, was the 11th Commandment at Columbus, losing to Michigan the cardinal sin. During the Jim Parker years, the Buckeyes drubbed the Wolverines two out of three times.

Woody Hayes rates Parker as one of the greatest linemen he ever had, certainly the strongest. A lot of All-Americans flop as professionals, but when Parker's name came up in 1956 as a pro prospect, Woody simply stated that Jim couldn't miss, and looking in Woody's face and from the way he said it, you just knew Jim was going to make it big. He did, too, becoming a perennial All-Pro with the Baltimore Colts.

PIHOS, PETE, can be classified as one of the truly remarkable football players of modern times. He was a first-rate tackle, a glue-fingered, two-time All-American end, and a powerful fullback at Indiana.

In college, Bo McMillin picked Pihos as the greatest end in Hoosier history. Because of Pete's versatility and running power, Coach McMillin moved him to fullback, prompting Bernie Bierman of Minnesota to observe: "I haven't seen Doc Blanchard, but I have seen Pihos, and he's a genuine All-American if I ever saw one."

Pete Pihos gained the attention of All-American selectors as early as his sophomore season, 1943, when he played end. "He's the best pass-receiver of the year," wrote Grantland Rice. "Pihos helped set a season's offensive record beside handling his job defensively." Hall of Famer Bennie Oosterbaan called him "the pick of Big Ten ends."

In 1945, after winning a chestful of medals as a paratroop war hero, the "Glamorous Greek" was shifted to fullback when the regular Indiana fullback was hurt in the Michigan game. After that, only Ohio State's Ollie Cline outgained him. Pihos led the Hoosiers in scoring on the way to the 1945 Big Ten champi-

At Indiana in 1943 and after the war, Pete Pihos was a first-rate tackle, a two-time All-American end, and a star fullback.

onship. The following year, his teammates voted him Most Valuable Player, after he smashed all Indiana career records for touchdowns (23), pass receiving, and total points.

"Pete gave the team greatness," Bo McMillin said later. "Greatness in terms of guts, leadership, maturity and fight. He is a great football player in any position."

Pete Pihos was so superb he wound up in two Football Halls of Fame: college and pro. After graduation, he joined the Philadelphia Eagles as a two-way end and was an immediate star for Greasy Neale's NFL division champions. Pete played nine years with the Eagles and led the league in pass receptions three years in a row. In 1952, he was an All-Pro defensive specialist, and a league-leading pass-catcher in his last three seasons. When he retired in 1955 he claimed 373 receptions and a total of 378 points.

PINGEL, JOHN SPENCER, in an era when the triple-threat man was the glamour boy of college football, ran, passed, and punted Michigan State opponents silly. He led the Spartans to 20 victories and never missed a varsity game in three seasons, 1936, 1937, and 1938. He was named on the 1937 All-American second team and the first team in 1938. He won the Spartan Award for top athletic-academic excellence. His postseason action included the 1938 Orange Bowl (Auburn 6, Michigan State 0), the 1939 East-West Shrine Game (West 14, East 0), and the 1939 College All-Star Game (N.Y. Giants 9, All-Stars 0). Well, you can't win them all!

Statistically, Johnny Pingel's rushing average in college was 5.2 yards per carry, he completed better than 50 percent of his passes, he led the nation in punting in 1937, was second in 1938, and still holds two major single-season college records: most punts (99) and most yards punted (4,138), both made in 1938.

The durable Pingel played 451 minutes of football for Michigan State out of a possible 540 in three seasons. Among his college highlights: he completed 13 of 26 passes and had a 54-yard punting average in a 0–14 loss to Michigan in 1938; he ran for two touchdowns and passed for another in knocking Syracuse out of the unbeaten ranks, 19–12, in 1938; he passed for three touchdowns to beat Marquette, 20–14, in 1938; he beat Michigan in 1937 with two touchdown passes to win, 19–14, and two TD passes to edge Carnegie Tech, 13–6. In six years of high school and college football, he never had a punt blocked.

Pingel made a successful transition from college to pro football in 1939 as the Detroit Lions quarterback and led the NFL in punting. World War II cut short his professional career, but he captained and quarterbacked Brigadier General Robert Neyland's East Army All-Stars in 1942. He spent five years in the Army, finally leaving as a Lieutenant Colonel with the Bronze Star and Purple Heart.

ROGERS, EDWARD L., was born at Libby, Minnesota, to a pioneer lumberman of Scotch-Irish ancestry and a Chippewa Indian mother. He moved to Minneapolis when he was eight and completed the first eight grades of school in six years.

Ed Rogers helped put Carlisle on the football map. Under Vance McCormick, who was recruited from Yale as Carlisle's first football coach, he was a regular end on the 1896 team, and reached full stardom the next three years. He was captain in 1900, after the great Pop Warner took over as head coach.

During the Rogers years, Carlisle trounced heavily favored Wisconsin, 18–8, in 1887 in a night game at Chicago Coliseum, and managed a 2–0 victory over California for the East-West Championship in San Francisco, on Christmas Day, 1899.

Pop Warner picked Rogers at end on his All-Time team at Carlisle.

Since there were no technical eligibility rules to prevent Rogers from playing, he continued to perform on the gridiron at Carlisle after graduating in 1897, even though he was enrolled at nearby Dickinson College studying Pre-Law. "They weren't so strict about those things in the old days," he said, years later.

In 1901, Rogers enrolled at Minnesota to complete his law studies, and, under Coach Doc Williams, played three more years of varsity football as a star left end, while living in Williams' attic in southeast Minneapolis.

Rogers was captain of the 1903 Gophers, an underdog eleven which held mighty Michigan to a 6–6 tie and snapped Hurry-Up Yost's dominance of Midwest football. That was the contest that gave birth to the historic Little Brown Jug Trophy.

SCHREINER, DAVID N., in the words of his coach, Harry Stuhldreher, "had no peer as an end. Even though we had such stars as Elroy Hirsch and Pat Harder, the greatest of all was Dave Schreiner."

In 1942, co-captain Schreiner led the Wisconsin Badgers to national eminence with an 8–1–1 record. Only a 7–7 tie with Notre Dame and a 6–0 loss to tough Iowa marred an otherwise perfect season. Both Schreiner and Harder were unanimous All-Americans that season as Wisconsin ranked No. 3 in the national polls.

"Not satisfied with All-American honors in 1941, his junior year, Schreiner took daily workouts during the next Summer," the reporter from the Chicago *Tribune* wrote. "No wonder he became Wisconsin's finest football player of recent times. He was tremendous defensively because of his power and intuitiveness, and on offense he was a fine blocker and one of the best pass-catchers. The mark of his true greatness, however, was not so much those specific talents. It was his uncanny ability to come up with big clutch plays when nothing less than superior effort would get the job done."

Schreiner played both ways, offense and defense, was the Conference's choice for MVP in 1942, and the first lineman to win the award since Biggie Munn of Minnesota got it in 1931.

Dave Schreiner, All-American, was still going for all the marbles when the end came. He was killed in action on Okinawa in World War II.

SCHULZ, ADOLPH (*Germany*), had the strength of a blacksmith. He stood 6–4, weighed 245, and had hands the size of hams. As an All-American center at Michigan in 1907, some experts still insist he was "the best center of all time." He could snap the ball with one hand and block with the other. On defense, he dropped two yards behind the line. The first time Coach Yost saw him do it, he yelled from the sideline: "Dutchman, what are you doing? You're supposed to be *on* the line."

Shulz shouted back: "I think it's better to play back of the line."

"They'll run right over us," Yost screamed.

"But I can see better from here," Schulz said. "If anybody gets past me I'll move back into the line and stay there."

Rustic as the maneuver was, Germany Schulz thus became the forerunner of what today is known as "linebacker."

Schulz anchored one of the best lines of the Yost era. When an opposing team went up against it, that team generally collapsed. Minnesota, a great team, tried it, but, after the first five minutes of play it was evident that Schulz and his fellow linemen were masters of the situation in every way.

Germany Schulz belongs in that exclusive club of Iron Men. He missed only 10 minutes of play in four seasons. He was the first to pull out of the line to help the tackle or end pull down a back at the flank, the first roving center. A sure passer from center, he was among the first to use the spiral snapback, though he often insisted that the end-over-end pass was more accurate.

Grantland Rice picked Schulz on his all-time team.

"There have been great centers through every year of American football," Granny told me, "but the greatest I ever personally saw was Germany Schulz, one of the fastest big men on any field. In one game against a strong Pennsylvania team Schulz alone held Penn at bay for 45 minutes. He backed up the line and supported the ends. When he was carried from the field Penn ran up some 30 points, all in the final minutes of the game after Schulz was out of there.''

SLATER, F. F. (*Duke*), was so strong that opposing teams frequently assigned two linemen against him to block him out of a play—but the maneuver seldom worked.

Fast for a big man, Duke was usually the first man downfield under Iowa punts. He was so good that he made the Old Gold and Black varsity as a freshman in 1918. Durable and self-confident, he never lost a minute of play due to injury. "I never had a lineman who made so few mistakes," Howard Jones once said. "He was seldom out of position, was never fooled by a fake, always sensed where the opposing ball carrier was going, and he never was late on his offensive charge."

Aubrey Devine, a first-class All-American quarterback on the 1921 Iowa team, supported Coach Jones' assessment of Slater. "Duke's powerful offensive charge at right tackle has not been equalled in the history of the game," Devine said.

Slater was dynamite on offense and could hold up one side of the Hawkeye line on defense. His exceptional leg drive and quick-charging style was unstoppable. In today's game, Duke might have played fullback, he was so rangy and fast. But he would have been required to wear a helmet now. In his best days at Iowa, 1920 and 1921, he and two of his white teammates, Leo Kriz, right guard, and Craven Shuttleworth, halfback, preferred to play bareheaded—and none of them was ever removed from a game because of injuries!

Duke Slater was a black man in an era of racial barriers in college sports, but he was accepted as an equal in both college and pro football (Chicago Cardinals) by all his teammates, who found it easy to forget in the heat of battle that there is a difference in skin color. He was one of the early black stars of professional football.

Slater returned to the University of Iowa after his retirement from football and earned a degree in law. He served for many years as a judge of the Superior Court of Cook County (Chicago). He died in 1966.

SMITH, BRUCE PHILIP, made up one-half of the most famous myth in the history of Minnesota football. The story actually centered around his father, Lucius, who was a tackle on the Gopher squads of 1910 and 1911. Forced to play guard against Michigan, due to an injury to a teammate, Lucius Smith accepted the blame for the 6–0 loss to Michigan in 1910 because of his inexperience at the new position. After the contest, he was supposed to have said, "Someday I'm going to have a son who will show up Michigan."

Thirty years later, Bruce Smith ran 80 yards for the touchdown that won the Michigan game and national championship for Minnesota, 7 to 6. It made a great story—Smith Sr.'s revenge. The only thing wrong with it was that Lucius never said anything after losing to Michigan in 1910. "All that stuff about raising a son to beat Michigan was pure romanticism," Lucius said many years afterward. "I never even thought such a thing, yet over the years the myth grew. It makes a good story, though."

Minnesota went undefeated and was considered the national champion in both 1940 and 1941. Bruce Smith had a 6.38-yard rushing average in 1940, and captained the Gophers in 1941, when he also beat out such stars as Angelo Bertelli (Notre Dame), Frank Albert (Stanford), and Frank Sinkwich (Georgia) in the Heisman Trophy balloting. With Smith living up to his reputation as the "Game Breaker," the 1939–40–41 Minnesota teams ran up a 20–3–0 won-lost record. Bruce also captained the East in the annual East-West Shrine Game in San Francisco, and was named Most Valuable Player in the College All-Stars vs. Chicago Bears game the following summer. In 1942–43, he was a member of the All-Service team after starring for Great Lakes Naval Air Station and St. Mary's Pre-Flight School. After the war, he played for the Green Bay Packers.

An extraordinarily handsome young man, Bruce Smith was an even 6-feet tall and 200 pounds. He really wasn't fast. In one college contest matching 16 players in a footrace, he finished 15th. But he had a quick start, instinctive movement, and ran resourcefully. He never ran for as much as 500 yards in a season, totaling only 1,203 in his career, and he passed infrequently, yet he was one of the last of the great triple-threat tailbacks and he made the big play game after game.

The wire services, newspapers, and magazines had a lot of All-American teams in the 1930s and 1940s, a total of 15, and Smith made them all in 1941.

Judd Ringer, a teammate of Smith's on the 1941 squad, once told Dan Jenkins why he thought Bruce was a great captain. "It was not only the fact that he was an athlete with remarkable physical skills and mental toughness," Judd said, "but that he led quite simply by showing us how to win when the going was the roughest."

Against Iowa in 1941, Smith was recovering from injuries and did not start the game. The Gophers were behind, having been held to minus yards and no first downs when Bruce went into the game late in the first half. He was used on only 7 plays, but he ran or passed for all 5 touchdowns as Minnesota went on to win, 34–13. One of Minnesota's rare passes was thrown by Smith for a 70-yard score.

"Four days before Bruce's final game against Wisconsin he was walking the practice field sidelines on crutches," Judd Ringer recalled. "But we needed that game and he played that game and we won it and with it the national championship. The whole thing symbolized Bruce Smith to me. He didn't do it theatrically. He just did it and we won."

Another teammate, Fred Hull, said he rarely saw a football player to whom things came so easily, but Smith never loafed. Hull singled Bruce out as the kind of great college player whose presence his teammates were not really conscious of—in the locker room or sometimes on the field—until the Gophers needed a big play.

"Bruce was a true All-American in every sense of the word, not only as a football player, but in all that he did both on and off the field," said Dick Wildung, the Hall of Fame tackle who cleared the way for Smith's great runs. "He had our complete admiration and faith."

Tommy Harmon once described Smith as "a magnificent physical specimen and a magnificent man—a champion in every way."

In 1975, only weeks before he retired as Minnesota's Sports Information Director after 31 years, Otis Dypwick talked to me about Smith: "Bernie Bierman picked Bruce as the greatest all-around football player he coached in all his years at Minnesota. That's quite a tribute, because Bernie coached a lot of All-Americans. Bruce could do it all—run, punt, pass, and though he was not as elusive, he was stronger than Red Grange. You don't hear of triple threat backs anymore, but Bruce was one. Ask a kid today what a triple-threater is and he can't tell you. In pro football, the Green Bay Packers made Bruce a defensive back, which brings out the point that Bierman always said he was a great defensive player.

"Self-effacing, handsome, Bruce played his own part in the Hollywood movie, 'Smith of Minnesota.' He was a very devout Catholic, a model for young boys. He was truly the All-American Boy."

In the mid-1960s, Smith was stricken with cancer and was in and out of the hospital for a year. Despite the fact he knew he was dying—he was only 47 and his weight had fallen from 235 to 90 pounds—he met his fate without self-pity, without weeping, without abondoning hope. He kidded the nuns at the hospital about getting him a beer. He liked nothing better than to split a beer with a friend and talk Minnesota football. Three days before his death he invited Dick Cullum, the Minneapolis sports writer, to his room for a beer and little football talk. Even after he received the last rites, he insisted on applying again for his season tickets to the Gopher games that fall.

Perhaps one mark of a man is how well he is remembered by the people he leaves behind. When they buried Bruce Smith, August 31, 1967, some 25 of his old teammates were there to pay their last respects.

SNOW, NEIL WORTHINGTON, was the first of a long line of All-Americans from Michigan. A fullback and end in 1898–1901, he still holds the record for most touchdowns scored in the Rose Bowl (5 vs. Stanford, January 1, 1902). In 1901, Snow was the only player outside the East to be named on Caspar Whitney's All-American team.

"Snow had all the tools: good speed, a keen eye, toughness, and was not easily fooled by trick plays, delayed passes or end sweeps," Walter Camp once observed. "To be fast, to break interference, and to be wise about the time of going in, make up the requisites of an end rusher, and all these Neil Snow possessed in a marked degree. His tackling was hard and clean."

It was no coincidence that the arrival of Neil Snow started Michigan and Hurry-Up Yost off on a great football era. In two of his four varsity seasons of play (1898 and 1901) the Wolverines won the national championship. In 1901, Michigan rolled up 501 points while holding 10 opposing teams scoreless.

Snow went out in a blaze of glory as he and his teammates pounded Stanford into the Pasadena turf, 49 to 0. Rose Bowl officials were so embarrassed that they substituted chariot racing for football for the next 14 years as part of their Tournament of Roses festival.

A 10-letter man at Michigan, Snow was only 34 when he died unexpectedly of a heart attack.

STEFFEN, WALTER PETER, the first player to use the forward pass as a fake, resulting in a sprint through a hole in the line, was rated by Amos Alonzo Stagg a superior runner even to the great Walter Eckersall. "Steffen had more finesse in his ball-carrying than Eckie," the Chicago coach said, "because Eckie ran mostly to his right, whereas Steffen ran right or left equally well."

In all his years in coaching, Stagg said, never had he seen a more clever, resourceful, or quicker runner than his 5–10, 170-pound halfback-quarterback. He was a shifty, dodging ball-carrier, and a keen, accurate passer. He was a solid tackler, and could catch and return punts. He was also a good punter, dropkicker, a smart playmaker, and an inspiring team leader. "Add to all that his straight-arm ability and you had a whale of an all-around football player," Stagg said.

In 1906, his sophomore season, Steffen was a 158-pound halfback but was moved to quarterback the following year when Eckersall graduated. He was a second-team All-American in 1907, and first team in 1908, when he captained Chicago to an undefeated season. In three varsity seasons, the Maroon compiled a 13–2–1 record, with Steffen scoring 156 points. Along the way they whipped such Western Conference teams as Illinois (63–0 and 42–6), Purdue (39–0, 56–0, and 39–0), Indiana (33–8, 27–6, and 29–6), Minnesota (29–0), and Wisconsin (18–12).

During the years 1909–1912, Wally Steffen went to law school and served as Stagg's assistant coach. From 1914–1921, he was head football coach at Carnegie Tech. In 1932, he was elected to the Illinois Supreme Court.

STINCHCOMB, GAYLORD (*Pete*), served an omen on Big Ten opponents in his very first college game when he scored three touchdowns against Northwestern. The Ohio State halfback was the catcher in one of college football's finest passing combinations, Harry Workman to Pete Stinchcomb. Workman was the first of the scrambling quarterbacks, retreating 10 or 15 yards behind the line of scrimmage and dodging around before setting up to throw. In 1920, he hit Stinchcomb with a 47-yard bomb with 20 seconds to play to beat Wisconsin, 13–7.

Playing in the shadow of the great Chick Harley in 1917, when the Buckeyes won the Conference title, and again in 1919, Pete was a full-blown All-American as a senior and led the Scarlet and Grey to the Rose Bowl, where California smacked them down, 28–0.

Despite his size, 165 pounds, Stinchcomb was a powerful runner. John Heisman, who had an enthusiastic failing for football runts, ranked Pete up among such famous football names as Hinkey, Poe, Weekes, Eckersall, Maulbetsch, Casey, and Stuhldreher on his all-time list of little men.

The versatile Pete Stinchcomb capped off a brilliant career at Columbus by winning the NCAA broad jump championship, the first All-American football player to win an NCAA track title.

WIDSETH, EDWIN, was generally picked as the best college tackle in the Midwest in 1935 and 1936. He was All-Conference in 1935 and unanimous All-American and was voted by his teammates as Minnesota's Most Valuable Player in 1936. The Gophers were national champions all three years that Widseth was on the varsity. Opponents called him "the strength of the Gopher line and the fifth man in our backfield." Minnesota lost only one game during the Widseth years.

With speed, range, power, and intuitiveness spread over a 6-foot-2, 220-pound frame, Ed Widseth was too busy helping his Norweigian father on the family farm at Gonvick, Min-

Minnesota lost only one game during the years Ed Widseth was on the team. The 6-foot-2, 220-pound tackle was All-Conference in 1935 and unanimous All-American in 1936. Opponents called Widseth "the strength of the Gopher line and the fifth man in our backfield."

nesota, to enter high school at the normal age. He was 19 before enrolling at Northwest School of Agriculture in Crookston, where he starred as a fullback. When he finally arrived at the University of Minnesota in 1933, Biggie Munn, then an assistant to Bernie Bierman, told him: "You'll be a lineman." And what a lineman! He earned three letters in football and two in baseball. He was co-captain of the 1936 Gophers, one of the greatest college teams in history. He played part of his last season with a splint strapped to his injured elbow, making it difficult to straighten the arm—and still he made All-American that year.

Widseth was a starter on the East team in the January 1, 1937, East-West Game in San Francisco, and later started for the College All-Stars against the Green Bay Packers in Chicago that summer.

After college, Widseth played for the New York Giants for four years. He was named the National Football League's Most Valuable Player in 1938, and was All-Pro all four seasons.

Big Ed Widseth was simply a lot of football player.

WILDUNG, RICHARD KAY, grew up in the tradition of all super linemen at Minnesota. Bernie Bierman, his coach and master of hard-nosed power football, picked the 6-foot, 214-pound tackle as the best sophomore tackle he ever coached. Together with the great Ed Widseth, Wildung ranks as one of the two finest tackles in the history of Minnesota football. A starter for three straight seasons, 1940, 1941, and 1942, the first two of which Minnesota was national champion, Dick was born in St. Paul and lettered in football, basketball, and track at Luverne High School. He was All-American at Minnesota in 1941 and 1942.

Wildung served in World War II as a lieutenant in the Navy, then played pro football for the Green Bay Packers, 1946–1953. He spent the off-season selling insurance and as the owner of a hardware store.

WILLIS, WILLIAMS (*Bill*), was a star tackle at Ohio State during the war years of 1942, 1943, and 1944 under Paul Brown and Carroll Widdoes. The 1942 Buckeyes were ranked No. 1 in the nation, and the 1944 squad, comprised of 17-year-olds, 4-F's and medical dischargees, won all its games, finishing second to vaunted Army, with Mr. Inside and Mr. Outside, Doc Blanchard and Glenn Davis, in the national polls. Carroll Widdoes was the Ohio State coach in 1944, and earned Coach of the Year honors, while Les Horvath walked off with the Heisman Trophy.

Bill Willis was the steadying influence in the Ohio State line, an All-American in 1944. In fact, he was one of four Buckeyes to gain a place on the All-American team that season. Horvath, Jack Dugger, and Bill Hackett were the others.

At 6-feet-4 and 210 pounds, Willis was a big, crushing blocker and tackler with speed to burn. He went on to pro fame with the Cleveland Browns.

THE WISTERT BROTHERS, FRANCIS M. AND ALBERT (*Ox*), make up two-thirds of college football's most famous brother trio (Alvin is the other)—and the only such family combination in gridiron history to win All-American honors.

Francis M. (Whitey) Wistert set the pace for "The Wisterts of Michigan." The oldest of the

Michigan's All-American Wistert brothers, left to right: Alvin (1948–49), Albert (1942), and Francis (1933). They all wore No. 11 jersey, which has since been permanently retired.

brothers to make concensus All-American, the 6–2, 210-pound tackle was also the first of the Wisterts to be tapped by the National Football Hall of Fame. He did it the hard way, too. That is, he enrolled at Ann Arbor minus any high school football experience. As a matter of fact, none of the Wisterts played football in high school. All three were tackles, and all wore jersey No. 11. The number was retired in 1949 after Alvin made All-American.

Despite his inexperience, Whitey was a regular at Michigan in 1931, 1932, and 1933. He was the mainstay of the undefeated Wolverines as a senior. "Whitey was a unanimous choice on my 1933 All-American Team, the best tackle in the Midwest and the key to Michigan's defensive line play," recalled Grantland Rice years ago. "He was keen, quick and accurate in diagnosing plays; a sure tackler and next to impossible to fool on trick maneuvers. He was also called upon to forward pass, and could throw the ball as far as any back in football."

Whitey gave his younger brothers quite a personal goal to shoot at. He was a three-year letterman in baseball, winning the MVP award in the Big Ten Conference in 1934. He played for five years in pro baseball, and spent the fall seasons of 1934–38 as assistant football coach at Michigan. He later practiced law in New York, and then became a business executive in Toledo, Ohio.

Albert (Ox) Wistert was the second of the brothers to carry the Maize and Blue into the college football Hall of Fame. Whitey, six years older, beat him in by a year.

Ox was one of a cluster of five Wolverines in 1940 destined for All-American fame. In 1940,

1941, and 1942 they ganged up to win 21 out of 26 games (one tie) for Coach Fritz Crisler. One of their biggest triumphs was a 32–20 shocker over Notre Dame in 1942, in which Ox was superb. His teammates named him the Most Valuable Player on the squad that season.

But Ox Wistert was just warming up. He starred in the 1943 East-West Game, and was co-captain of the College All-Stars, victors over the pro champion Washington Redskins, 27–7, the following summer. Ox joined the Philadelphia Eagles in the fall of 1943. He captained the Eagles from 1946 through 1950 and was All-Pro tackle for five years (1944–1948). He was a big reason why the Eagles won three Eastern Division titles and were world champions in 1948 and 1949. He started every game for the Eagles for nine seasons (1944–1952), except the 1950 opener against Cleveland when he was injured. The Eagles thought so highly of Ox as a player and leader that they retired his jersey number (70) permanently when he left the game. He is a member of the Eagles' All-Time All-Star team.

There were six Wistert children. Their father, a Chicago policeman, was killed by a holdup man when the boys were still young.

Ox credits Greasy Neale, his old coach on the Eagles, with much of his success in professional football. "It was a privilege to play for him," Ox says. "After losing our father, I always wondered what I would have wanted him to be like. Now I know. Just like Greasy. During the nine years I played for him, I never dared tell him how I felt about him because I always wanted to be sure in my mind that if ever I slipped, sentiment wouldn't make Greasy keep me in the starting lineup."

Alvin, the youngest, was the only one of the three Wisterts to make All-American twice (1948–1949). With two of them already in the college Hall of Fame, Whitey and Ox must be asking themselves, "What's keepin' Alvin?"

WYANT, ANDREW ROBERT ELMER (*Polyphemus*), compiled a playing record on the gridiron almost as long as his name. It started at Bucknell University while he was still a student at a local prep school, Bucknell Academy, in 1887, and finished at University of Chicago in 1894. All told, Andy Wyant, a 6-foot-3, 180-pound center and guard, played four seasons of varsity ball at Bucknell and three more for Amos Alonzo Stagg at Chicago. In seven seasons and 98 games at the college level, he never missed a minute of action.

Before his death at the age of 97, Wyant, a Baptist minister, said, "My playing record can never be equalled under the modern collegiate football rules."

Wyant was a star in the raw-meat days of football, when an athlete was expected to play both offense and defense, equipment was skimpy, and the schedule was heavy. He was a 60-minute performer in 46 straight games spread over three years at Chicago. In 1894, for example, the University of Chicago played a 20-game schedule and won 13.

Teacher, minister, physician, author-lecturer and financier, Dr. Polyphemus Wyant earned five degrees: B.A., M.A., B.D., Ph.D., and M.D. The old lineman was proof positive that he used his head for more than to block with.

YOUNG, CLAUDE H. (*Buddy*), a black, is the first to admit that the worst discrimination in the world isn't color. "I could never stop proving myself," the old Illinois halfback said recently. "I had to work harder, play better, block better than bigger guys. When I first reported to the squad I was 5–5 and 165. At my first practice they acted like I was some kind of sideshow, like I was supposed to go out with the band at halftime."

Buddy Young showed them. With blinding speed and guile to burn, he made Big Ten fans think of Red Grange. A record-breaking runner who tied the world's indoor 60-yard dash record (6.1) and covered the 100-yard dash in 9.5, Buddy scored 13 touchdowns for Illinois in 1944 to tie Grange's 20-year-old mark, as the Illini rolled up 273 points and a 5–3–1 record. Seven of those touchdowns came on sprints of 82, 93, 92, 74, 63, 40, and 31 yards. His 78 points in 1944 placed him sixth among the nation's leading college scorers, and his 8.94-yard rushing average was second best in the country.

After a year in the wartime Navy, Buddy resumed his college football career in 1946 and led Coach Ray Eliot's Fighting Illini to the Big Ten championship. In the initial meeting of the new Big Ten–Pacific Coast Conference

Rose Bowl pact, he gained 110 yards from scrimmage and scored two touchdowns as Illinois blasted UCLA, 45 to 14.

In the two years that Buddy played at the University of Illinois, he scored 18 touchdowns and gained 1,308 yards for a 6.6 average. In nine seasons in the pros—New York Yankees, New York Yanks, Dallas, and Baltimore Colts—he scored a total of 44 touchdowns and gained 9,419 yards. The former Illinois All-American (1944) scored on the ground, on pass catches, on punts, and on kickoff returns. As the Illinois opponents could have told the professionals, it was never safe to let Buddy Young get his hands on the football.

ZARNAS, GUST, followed in the footsteps of the great Iolas Huffman, Ed Hess, Joe Gailus, Regis Monahan, and Inwood Smith by becoming the sixth guard in Ohio State football history to be named first-team All-American (1937). The powerful, hard-charging Zarnas was the workhorse of Scarlet and Grey elevens that compiled winning seasons in 1935 (7–1–0, Big Ten co-champions), 1936 (5–3–0), and 1937 (6–2–0). During the Zarnas years, Ohio State shut out 13 opponents in 24 games, yielding only 27 points in 1936, and 23 in 1937, while the offense was running up 285 points.

Zarnas, at guard, and Ray King, Minnesota end, were the only two linemen from the Big Ten to make the 1937 All-American first team. He stood with Chick Harley, Gaylord Stinchcomb, Wes Fesler, Bill Willis, Les Horvath, and Jim Parker as the only Ohio State players elected to the Football Hall of Fame through 1976.

A rugged tackler, a punishing blocker, and a tenacious and durable combatant, he led the 1937 Buckeye defense in shutting out six of eight teams. Only Southern Cal with 13 points and Indiana with 10 were able to dent the OSU end zone. Unfortunately, the Bucks themselves were shut out by the Hoosiers as Corby Davis, a great kicker, blocker, and defensive star, practically single-handedly knocked Francis A. Schmidt and his boys out of the Conference co-championship—the first Indiana victory over Ohio State since 1924.

Coaches

NATIONAL FOOTBALL HALL OF FAME
COACHES FROM THE BIG TEN

Name	Alma Mater	Big Ten School Where Coached	Years in Big Ten	Year Elected
Anderson, Dr. Edward N.	Notre Dame, 1921	Iowa	1938–49	1971
Bierman, Bernard William (Bernie)	Minnesota, 1916	Minnesota	1932–41 1945–50	1955
Crisler, Herbert Orin (Fritz)	Chicago, 1922	Minnesota Michigan	1930–31 1938–47	1954
Godrey, Ernest R.	Ohio State, 1914	Ohio State (Assistant Coach)	1929–62	1972
Hall, Edward K.	Dartmouth, 1890	Illinois	1892–95	1951
Ingram, William A.		Indiana	1923–25	1973
Jones, Howard Harding	Yale, 1908	Ohio State Iowa	1910 1916–23	1951
Little, George E.	Ohio Wesleyan, 1912	Michigan Wisconsin	1924 1925–26	1955
Munn, Clarence (Biggie)	Minnesota, 1931	Michigan State	1947–53	1959
Schmidt, Francis A.	Nebraska	Ohio State	1934–40	1971
Shaughnessy, Clark Daniel	Minnesota, 1914	Chicago	1933–39	1968
Smith, Andrew L.	Pennsylvania, 1904	Purdue	1913–15	1951
Stagg, Amos Alonzo	Yale, 1888	Chicago	1892–32	1951
Waldorf, Lynn Osbert (Pappy)	Syracuse, 1925	Northwestern	1935–46	1966
Wieman, Elton E. (Tad)	Michigan, 1919	Michigan	1927–28	1956
Wilce, John W.	Wisconsin, 1910	Ohio State	1913–28	1954
Williams, Dr. Henry L.	Yale, 1891	Minnesota	1900–21	1951
Woodruff, George W.	Yale, 1889	Illinois	1903	1963
Yost, Fielding H. (Hurry-Up)	Lafayette, 1897	Michigan	1901–23 1925–26	1951
Zuppke, Robert Carl	Wisconsin, 1905	Illinois	1913–41	1951

Big Ten Coaches in The Football Hall of Fame

ANDERSON, DR. EDWARD N., a member of Knute Rockne's first Notre Dame team in 1918, and captain and All-American end of the 1921 Irish, distinguished himself even more as coach and practicing physician.

In 39 years of football coaching—starting at little Loras College in 1922, to De Paul University to Holy Cross to Iowa and back to Holy Cross again—Dr. Anderson's teams won 201 games, lost 128, and tied 15. His Holy Cross and Iowa teams were particularly outstanding. In his first six seasons at Holy Cross, before resigning after the 1938 campaign to go to Iowa City, the Crusaders won 47, lost 7, and tied four.

Dr. Anderson hit the jackpot with the 1939 Hawkeyes. He was voted Coach of the Year and Nile Kinnick was Player of the Year as Iowa beat Notre Dame and lost only to Michigan. After years of inferior play in the second division, the Old Gold and Black was in the race for the Big Ten crown until Northwestern tied them in the final game of the season.

Dr. Anderson remained at Iowa through 1942, took time out from coaching during the war, and then resumed his post at Iowa City in 1946. After the 1949 season he went back to Holy Cross, where he doubled as head football coach and private physician once more, and finally retired from coaching at the end of the 1964 season.

BIERMAN, BERNARD WILLIAM (Bernie), never had much to say to his athletes, but their performances on the gridiron spoke loudly for him. From 1932 through 1941, the Golden Gophers won 64, lost 11, tied 5. They were undefeated five times; won six Big Ten titles—1934, 1935, 1937, 1938, 1940, 1941; were national champs four times—1934, 1936, 1940, 1941. A 28-game defeatless streak, the last 21 of them triumphs, was broken, 6 to 0, on Northwestern's muddy field in 1936. A 15-yard roughness penalty on Ed Widseth, Minnesota's All-American left tackle, set up a 1-yard scoring plunge by fullback Steve Toth. That defeat cost the Gophers the Big Ten championship, but they were still ranked No. 1 nationally at the end of the season.

Bierman called his 1934 Minnesota squad the best he ever coached. "It had great spirit and poise," he said. "It was two deep and in some spots three deep without falloff. It was very well coordinated and this came to some extent from uniform speed. We had no real fast man in the backfield and no real slow one in the line."

Pug Lund, captain and All-American left half, gave the 1934 Gophers great leadership and spirit. Recently, in Minneapolis, Pug gave me his reasons why Minnesota teams were so successful under Bierman.

"One of the prime reasons was that we were

208

just plain hungry. We were like Jack Dempsey in the prize ring," Pug said. "We had no chance to be spoiled. Inside the dressing room, Bernie was not the fire-and-brimstone type—certainly not a Rockne or a Ray Eliot. He was firm, reserved; it was not easy for him to show pent-up emotion. He never shouted, raged, or shed a tear. He let his assistants, Sig Harris and Bert Baston, get us up before a game or at halftime.

"At practice, Bernie was the boss. He never swore, but when he laced into you, you knew you'd been reprimanded. He expected you to play up to your potential every game. In week-day practice, we spent most of the time on offense, polishing our timing. We ran a lot of dummy scrimmage. I remember the first time I reported to freshman football. There were 250 candidates, but that number dropped pretty fast as soon as there was physical contact work. I think a lot of the scrubs just wanted to be able to say for the rest of their lives that they'd played football at Minnesota. I remember when I reported to the field, the frosh coach asked me my name and where I was from—that doesn't happen today! Now you don't even have to bother to suit up if they don't invite you.

"Bierman was a no-nonsense coach. He prepared us so well that we had utmost faith in his preparation. Maybe I was naive, but I believed everything he told us. In workouts, when we fouled up, he'd tell us, 'All right, take a trip around the field and think about that last play, then come back and run it right.' The *whole* squad would be punished. He'd ride us for not running hard enough in scrimmage. I can hear him yet: 'Why don't you *run* hard—*run!*' He was always telling us to get the lead out. At the end of each practice, he'd line us up at the 20-yard line and he'd stand on the goal line, and we'd have to run 20 plays to *his* satisfaction as fast, and without a mistake, as we could before he'd let us go in. If we got to the 14th play and fouled up—boom!—we had to start over again. Some nights he kept us out there till 7 o'clock. That's the way Bernie ran the show, and we responded to it. I've always maintained that your level of performance can always be higher if somebody forces you. There was a lot of the Prussian general in the Bierman style, and it paid off in national championships. Remember, his teams won 23 out of 24 games in one span (1934–35–36). How can you argue with success?"

Another Bierman halfback, Dale Warner, who played in the late 1940's, remembers Bernie as "the most organized man I've ever been around—and that's how he coached. Every minute was organized. Every day of practice, he gave us a sheet of paper outlining exactly what we were going to do. And after every game we played, he showed us what we did on *every* play, position by position. He and his staff spent all day Sunday reviewing each game, so that by Monday afternoon practice they were ready for us. The worst part of the year was late August and early September, during those preseason workouts, when everybody was trying to make the squad. We'd start each practice in the morning and the lights had to be turned on before we finished. No one knew who was going to make the team and Bernie drove us hard. We were awed by him, respectful. Many of the guys were walkons. I was a walk-on from St. Paul. They issued me a uniform and I worked my way up to the traveling squad from there. But that system's all gone now. You rarely hear of walk-ons today. It's very professional now. Too bad. I think they overlook some good prospects. Bierman had a lot of the Knute Rockne in his methods. That is, during the summer he kept in touch with each of us by mail regularly. He encouraged us to run a lot, play touch football, and lots of soccer. He especially wanted to know about our weight, what our last-semester grades were, things like that. Without good grades, we couldn't play in the Big Ten. The Conference lost a lot of athletes because of poor marks—and they'd go play in the Big Eight. The Big Eight took a lot of the academic castoffs!"

Like Frank Leahy of Notre Dame, Bierman usually took a dim view of Minnesota fortunes for preseason publication. He doted over the underdog role. One year, Otis Dypwick was in Chicago attending a summer conference of Big Ten officials. Otis was asked to get up and say a few words about the Minnesota football prospects. Before rising, the bespectacled Sports Information Director wrote down on two pieces of paper the good and bad things about the Gophers. The bad far outnumbered the good. Jerry Liska, the AP man in Chicago, picked up Dypwick's remarks and sent them out on the national wire.

"Well, Bierman always maintained that he never read the sports pages," Dypwick recalled recently. "In those days, his office was on the opposite side of Cook Hall from my office, a good walk apart. As a matter of fact, he'd never been in my office before, even though I'd been at the school for several years by that time. Suddenly, here he came into my office, holding up a copy of *The St. Paul Pioneer Press*. Across the top of the sports section screamed an 8-column headline: GOPHERS FACING DIFFICULTY FIELDING ELEVEN ABLE-BODIED MEN. Bernie looked at the headline, and then at me, and said, 'Dypwick, that's the best damn publicity I've ever had out of you!' Then he went on and finished first in the nation."

Bernie Bierman was a Spartan of what Pudge Heffelfinger called "raw-meat" football. Uncompromising, austere, aloof, relentless, dedicated, were some of the adjectives used to describe the stocky, silver-haired martinet whose 16-year record at Minnesota was 93–35–6. He was also highly inventive. The origin of the buck-lateral sequence, which had been used successfully by many teams, has been attributed to Bierman. He was at least one of the first to use it, as head coach at Montana, as early as 1921.

For those who played under him, Bierman made football a stern, challenging task. As a player and coach he gave the game everything. Under his arctic exterior, he harbored an attitude toward his alma mater, Minnesota, that was almost reverence. To him, it was inconceivable that any player wouldn't be willing to sacrifice anything, take anything, to work and win for Minnesota.

"When I have to beg a kid of 16 or 17 to go out for football," he'd say, "then I'll quit."

Born at Waseca, Minnesota, on March 11, 1894, Bierman was captain and halfback of Minnesota's 1915 conference champions, and his approach to football was deeply influenced by Dr. Henry L. Williams, who coached the Gophers from 1900 through 1921. In 1916, the fall after his graduation, Bernie began coaching at Butte High School in Montana, and showed the winning touch immediately with a 7–0 season. Then he enlisted in the Marine

Corps for World War 1, came out a captain in 1919, and coached the University of Montana from 1919 through 1921. Clark Shaughnessy, who had been a teammate of his under Williams, was now coaching Tulane, and he took Bernie on as an assistant. Next, Bierman coached the Mississippi Aggies (now Mississippi State) for two years and came back to upset Tulane, 14–0, in 1926. When Shaughnessy resigned to coach Loyola of New Orleans in 1927, Bierman replaced him. That's where he was when the University of Minnesota brought him back to Minneapolis in 1932. All told, his teams at Montana, Mississippi Aggies, Tulane, and Minnesota combined to win 161 games, lose 61, and tie 11.

Five years after Bierman quit coaching, his name was brought up to Bud Wilkinson, then on his way at Oklahoma to the modern all-winning record of 47 straight games.

"Bernie might have been frigid and forthright," admitted the old Minnesota lineman and quarterback, "but he didn't talk out of both sides of his mouth. He had integrity. He was completely fair, honest, and the most thorough, hard-working individual I have ever known. His 10-year record at Minnesota prior to the war is unequaled."

Stories growing around Bernie Bierman were rare. And when one did spring up, it had to do with some bit of psychology he had practiced. Always a driver, Bierman was extra tough with his 1938 squad the week before the final game with Wisconsin. He picked fullback Larry Buhler as his particular target, downgrading Buhler and boosting Howie Weiss, his opponent. By the end of the week the Gophers were so mad at Bierman that they took it out on Wisconsin, 21–0.

"I'm lucky," Bierman said after the game. "I'm lucky somebody didn't shoot me this last week."

Outwardly, Bierman displayed little emotion, but you knew the tension was there by the way he lit and discarded one cigarette after another on the sideline during a game. But he was not capable of showing sentiment and he admitted it.

"Even when he visited injured halfback Julie Alphonse in the hospital, his conversation began and ended with 'hello' and 'how are you?'" recalled Tim Cohane one time. Alphonse had to make most of the conversation.

Bierman was obviously ill at ease. And yet the star halfback knew the coach was concerned about him.

"I don't think I'd be able to make a sentimental dressing room talk," Bierman later confessed. "I'm afraid I would end up laughing at myself."

Nobody laughed at Bernie Bierman.

CRISLER, HERBERT ORIN *(Fritz)*, football's supersalesman and father of two-platoon football, had the ability to dramatize himself while organizing victorious gridiron empires at Princeton and Michigan. His 1947 Michigan squad won the national championship, tore Southern California apart in the Rose Bowl, 49 to 0, and earned Crisler the Coach of the Year award. That was the high water mark in a coaching career that in 116 games lost only 32 and tied 9 at Minnesota (1930–1931), Princeton (1932–1937), and Michigan (1938–1947).

A cool, unruffled, self-possessed man, Fritz directed his football forces in the quietly controlled drama of a General MacArthur. Anti, pro, or neutral, he had the respect of everyone. His buck lateral and spinner-cycle offense was one of the most eye-catching in football history. It necessitated meticulous execution, with hair-breadth timing and flawless faking.

Born at Earlville, Illinois, on January 12, 1899, Crisler was an end and backfield star at the University of Chicago in 1919–1921; was later an assistant coach there under Amos Alonzo Stagg, in 1922–1929; was athletic director as well as head football coach at Minnesota; and three years later was handed his head-coaching spurs at Princeton. Three times in nine years he waded into situations at Minnesota, Princeton, and Michigan which had been snarled by losing teams, lagging alumni support, and free-for-all intramural backbiting. In each instance his appointment was opposed strenuously—almost frantically—by factions of influential alumni. Within two seasons, each school regained all its lost prestige. He gave Princeton two undefeated teams (1933 and 1935) and he was the chief political power among his colleagues as the No. 1 personality kid and high-pressure executive in the coaching profession while at Michigan. In 1945 he was able to afford the luxury of refusing the cushy job of Athletic Commissioner of the Western Conference.

H. O. (Fritz) Crisler's 1938–1947 coaching record at Michigan was 71 wins, 16 losses, and 3 ties for a fat .816 percentage. In 10 seasons as head coach there, Crisler won 2 league titles and was runner-up 6 times.

Crisler never fell for the T craze. The single wing remained his bread-and-butter formation to the end, and he neatly divided his offense into five sections: Direct drives; spinners; sweeps, reverses, multiple-pass plays; lateral passes; and forward passes. "I used only five or six T-formation plays," he explained. "We called that part of the offense the Alumni-T, just to show the Old Grads that we were keeping up with the times."

A full professor—in college he missed Phi Beta Kappa on a technicality—Crisler was more a salesman than a coach. The special service he performed at Michigan was selling renewed loyalty to the glorious destiny and traditions of the old school, and when he donned his evangelical robes and really wound up, he sounded like the guy who founded the campus at Ann Arbor and invented its cherished traditions.

Beneath his urbanity, Crisler was a very tough-minded gent who knew exactly what he wanted and was in the habit of getting his way. He had special talents to sell to Michigan in 1938. He knew there was no other candidate in coaching with the qualifications the Wolverines needed and he made certain the setup at Ann Arbor was foolproof. He asked for more money than any coach ever made in the Middle West (an estimated $15,000 a year), and there was to be no check on his selection of assistant coaches. And he demanded, and got, a firm hand free of Fielding H. Yost's interference in football, as well as the promise that he would be appointed athletic director when Yost reached the retirement age of 70 in 1942.

Crisler operated a unique correspondence school for high school coaches in need of big league advice. The coach who wanted a new play to win a big game, didn't know what defense to use against a certain offense, had a morale problem with the kids, needed pointers in conditioning a squad, or wanted a once-over-lightly in general strategy, could have his questions solved by writing to Crisler. He corresponded with more than 200 coaches in Michigan and the surrounding area, and the pay-off was obvious. In return for services rendered, coaches were expected to steer likely prospects to Ann Arbor.

Each year, at the end of spring practice, all high school coaches and players were invited to attend Professor Crisler's clinic, in which he freely demonstrated his plays and methods. Between 1,200 and 1,500 attended the clinics, and Crisler kept no secrets from his audience.

"The coach who draws diagrams full of confusing X's and arrows, and who spouts a lot of double-talk, is a phoney," Crisler said. "There's no harm in telling coaches everything you've got as long as you don't let them know when you're going to use it."

Over the 10 years he was head coach, Michigan was the team to beat in the Western Conference. The Wolverines tied with Purdue for the title in 1943, won it outright in 1947, and finished second six times. Crisler's No. 1 motto was, "Offense is poise, defense is frenzy." Since opponents were invariably pointing for Michigan, he was in the habit of assuring his squads, "Our plan is simple, theirs, one of desperation."

Crisler was also superstitious. He kept a lucky penny he'd found, and had a lucky pair of socks, tie, and suit. At all home games he and his staff rode in a certain car over a certain route to the stadium.

Away from the gridiron or the council table, Fritz was a sociable soul, who liked to stay up late with old friends, and unlike his old coach and mentor, Amos Alonzo Stagg, favored a stronger beverage than milk.

Affable and optimistic, Herbert Orin Crisler did not object to his nickname, which dated back to his playing days at Chicago. Even though he made Walter Eckersall's first All-American team and Walter Camp's third team in 1921, his advancement as a gridder had not been rapid. After he had repeatedly flubbed the same play one afternoon, Coach Stagg said to him:

"Crisler, there's a celebrated violinist in this country. The name sounds like yours but it is spelled differently—K-r-e-i-s-l-e-r. He's world-famous because he has certain attributes and knows how to use them. He has genius, skill, coordination. From now on, Crisler, I'm going to call you Fritz, too, just to remind myself that you are absolutely his opposite."

The nickname stuck.

GODFREY, ERNEST R., was once described by Knute Rockne as "the best line coach in America." In the 33 years he coached at Ohio State, Godfrey helped to develop 23 first-team All-American linemen. Lou (The Toe) Groza, who played under Ernie at Columbus before starring as an All-Pro place-kicker for the Cleveland Browns, declared that Godfrey was "the best kicking coach in football."

Ernest R. Godfrey rivaled the great Amos Alonzo Stagg and Pudge Heffelfinger for football longevity. He was connected with the college game for more than 50 years. He enrolled at Ohio State in 1911, was a star center for two years, and was still a line coach at Columbus until 1962. In between, he coached at Wooster, Ohio, High School in 1915, and then served 13 seasons as head coach at Wittenberg College, where his overall won-lost-tied record was 63–26–6.

In 1929, Godfrey was called back to his alma mater to work as head line coach and professor of physical education. He served seven different football coaches—Sam Willaman, Francis Schmidt, Paul Brown, Carroll Widdoes, Paul Bixler, Wes Fesler, and Woody Hayes—during which time the Buckeyes rolled up a record of 196–78–18, finished first in the Big Ten nine times, second six times, and were three-for-three in the Rose Bowl.

(NOTE: Two members of the coaches' section of the National Football Hall of Fame, Edward K. Hall and William A. Ingram, had brief careers in the Western Conference. Hall was Director of Physical Education and head football coach at Illinois for four years (1892–1895). His won-lost-tied record was 20–10–5. He later served as secretary of the Intercollegiate Football Rules Committee, and from 1911 through 1932 was Chairman of the Rules Committee. He was the author of the first Football Code for players published in the *Official Football Guide.* Hall held a degree in law.

Bill Ingram was better known for his successful teams at Navy and California. Certainly his coaching record at Indiana did not qualify him for the National Football Hall of Fame. In three seasons (1923–24–25) at Bloomington, his overall record was 10–12–1. The Hoosiers finished 5th, 7th, and 9th under his guidance in the Western Conference.)

JONES, HOWARD HARDING, a prodigious competitor and relentless advocate of clean play whose strongest language was "gol-dang" and "ye-gods" and "pshaw," considered his 10 to 7 triumph over Knute Rockne and Notre Dame in 1921 at Iowa as the highlight of his 29 years in coaching. That was the first loss for the Irish in 21 games.

The Hawkeyes, undefeated in 1921 and 1922, and with a solid claim on the 1922 national crown, featured three All-Americans: tackle Duke Slater, quarterback Aubrey Devine, and halfback Gordon Locke. Devine, whom Jones once rated as the best all-purpose back he ever coached, dropkicked the winning field goal against Notre Dame from the 38-yard line. The victory was No. 5 in a 20-game defeatless string that began with the fifth game in 1920 and extended to the fourth game in 1923. There was a rumor, and not without foundation, that when Jones left Iowa after the 1923 season, to coach one year at Duke before going to Southern California, Rockne seriously considered accepting the Iowa job.

Howard Jones made the line his specialty and usually formed it of men who had previously played in the backfield. His halfbacks rarely carried the ball; they were for interference. His fullback usually lined up just in front of the quarterback, who did most of the ball carrying, and had to pass, run, and kick.

Jones's deception was less a matter of complicated ball-handling, in spinners and reverse plays, than in varying formations. The Jones shift was used purely for disguising formations instead of for gaining momentum. The shift frequently led into an unbalanced line with both guards playing on the right of the center, the inside one for running.

Jones had certain peculiarities. He never swore and would not tolerate his players doing so. He also spoke out, while he was at Iowa, even against dancing, and his indictment was specific:

"The athlete does not have to participate in order to keep up his social prestige. The objections I have against dancing are: first, it breaks in upon sleeping and eating; second, it is a different form of exercise than the boy is used to and is tiring; three, there is the danger of getting heated up and then cooling off too quickly; fourth, a midnight lunch is usually eaten, mostly because of the obligations to the girl; fifth, the boy usually doesn't feel like getting up for breakfast."

Jones believed, however, that music was a good thing for a player.

"I like to hear a squad singing popular songs after a hard practice and while dressing," he said. "I know then that most of the men will leave in good spirits, that they will have forgotten the unpleasant, unimportant occurrences of the practice by the time they are dressed."

Before a big game, Jones made no emotional orations. In a soothing voice he reviewed what he wanted the team to remember, reminded them what their opponents were likely to do and how to retaliate. He insisted, to an almost eccentric degree, upon "clean" football. He also disliked athletes who dramatized injuries on the field. When one of his men was hurt Jones seldom expressed sympathy till after the game.

"When a player is injured," he'd say, "he should say so but not until then. *Nothing* is more harmful to the morale of the squad while scrimmaging than the agonizing cry of an injured man. A good rule to follow is to keep still until one is sure he's hurt, and then not yell the information from the housetops, but to report quietly to the physician in charge."

While he was severe with his players, he bred in them a superb team spirit. Although he was not given to patting a player on the back coming off the field, he would go around the dressing room after the game and talk one by one to those who had played, thanking them for a good effort, and look into possible injuries.

A star end at Yale in 1905–1907 and the Bulldogs' first paid football coach (he was hired for $2,500 a year in 1913), Jones coached at Syracuse, Ohio State, Duke, and Southern California, besides Iowa and Yale. A composite of his lifetime record shows 193 victories, 63 defeats, and 20 ties. He coached 19 All-Americans, including 3 at Iowa and 13 at USC, and was the author of two books on football.

Jones learned at Iowa that the first law of coaching is to get good material. The Hawkeyes reflected his fierce, steely concentration. His mind was centered so deeply in football that he ignored traffic signals, lost socks and keys, forgot his appointments, left members of his family stranded, and even forgot his way home.

Although highly respected by most coaches of the profession, Jimmy Phelan, an old Notre Dame man, had no love for Jones. This was evident by the way Phelan's Washington teams manhandled the Trojans after Jones moved to Southern California. In 10 years on the Coast together, Phelan beat Jones six times—five in a row, 1934, 1935, 1936, 1937 and 1938. What did Phelan have against Jones?

"It goes back to 1922, my first year as head coach at Purdue," Phelan told me one time. "Jones was coaching Iowa and they beat us, 56 to 0. We had a kid on the sidelines with a concussion. I was trying to help him, and Jones was still pouring it on. After the game, he didn't come over to say anything to me, and then later that night we were having dinner at a hotel in Iowa City. Jones walked in with his party and didn't even nod to me. The next season, Iowa beat us only 7 to 0, and Jones came over to shake hands with me. I told him to go to hell. I've never really held any grudge against anyone in my life—except Howard Jones—and whenever I played against him, I played with hate. I think my record at Washington shows how I felt about Howard Harding Jones!"

When the football season was over, Jones led a quiet life. He was a partner and stockholder in his father's paper firm of Harding, Jones & Co., but took no active part in its affairs. He fished, played golf and bridge, and gave talks at business men's meetings. He died at Toluca Lake, California, on July 27, 1941. He was only 56 years old.

LITTLE, GEORGE E., who was head coach at both Michigan and Wisconsin in the mid-1920s, had the unique experience of watching the great Benny Friedman star for and against his teams. George always claimed he left Ann Arbor for Madison a year too soon.

"I should have waited until Benny graduated before making the change," George once told me.

A graduate of Ohio Wesleyan University, George Little began his football coaching career in 1914 at Cincinnati University. Two years later he moved to Miami University of Ohio and led the Redskins to their first football championship in history. After World War I, he returned to Miami and won another title in football and one in track. In three postwar seasons at Miami, his record was 20–3–1. That caught the eye of Fielding H. Yost, who hired him away from Oxford to serve as assistant at Michigan. With Hurry-Up at the helm and Little as top sergeant, the Wolverines won the Western Conference championship in 1922 and 1923. The following year, Yost stepped aside and made Little top dog, and George lost only to Illinois and Iowa on the way to a 6–2 record. His star was quarterback Friedman.

"Benny was terrific," George said. "He threw what I called a *soft* pass. Any man on the team could handle it. Benny was also a great team man, an excellent student, and he brought this keen intelligence to football."

Little served only one year as head coach at Michigan. In 1925, he went to Wisconsin as Director of Athletics and head football coach, a dual role he held for two seasons. Under George, the Badgers won 11 games, lost 3, with 2 ties.

Wisconsin lost only one game in 1925—to Michigan, 21–0. "And Benny figured in all of the touchdowns," Little recalled. "He was unstoppable that day. On the very first running play of the game he passed to Bruce Gregory for a score. We then made the decision to kick off instead of to receive and Benny caught it and ran it back 85 yards for a second touchdown. Michigan thus had two touchdowns on two kickoffs and one play from scrimmage and the game wasn't even two minutes old yet. Later in the game, Benny passed for a third touchdown to complete the scoring for the day."

Friedman or no Friedman, George Little was a sound football coach. His style had imagination, though he relied on the power game when he had the horses. Defensively, his teams were always tough. During the two seasons he handled the line for Yost at Michigan, opponents scored only 25 points in 15 games. At Miami, in 1921, his unbeaten Red and White champions gave up only 12 points while scoring 238 themselves. Along the way, Little helped to develop three Michigan All-Americans—Harry Kipke, Johnny Blott, and Edliff Slaughter.

George Little wound up his college career as Director of Athletics at Rutgers, then was appointed Executive Secretary of The National Football Foundation and Hall of Fame, where he was one of the prime movers back in the early 1950s.

MUNN, CLARENCE *(Biggie)*, will always be remembered at East Lansing as the genius who built Michigan State into a football powerhouse. The "Big Man" put the Spartans on the map.

Hired by then MSU President John Hannah in 1947 to help the school overcome its "cow college" image, Biggie Munn's first Michigan State team suffered a 55–0 drubbing from Big Ten rival Michigan in the opening game that fall, but the Green and White settled down and managed a respectable 7–2 season the rest of the way. After that, Munn rallied, recruited his "brawn trust," and trained them so skillfully in what he termed "my convoluted offense and rock-ribbed defense," that by the middle of the 1950 season, Michigan State started a 28-game winning streak—the longest string in Spartan history. He capped his coaching career with a 28–20 victory over UCLA in the Rose Bowl, on January 1, 1954, then replaced Ralph Young as Michigan State's athletic director. He retired from the post following a stroke in 1971.

In his seven years as head football coach at MSU, Munn put together a 54–9–2 record with the help of a staff that included Dan Devine,

Bob Devaney, Forest Evashevski, and his successor as head coach, Duffy Daugherty. His Spartans finished in the national Top Ten in 1950 (8th), 1951 (2nd), 1952 (1st), and 1953 (3rd). Eleven of his players were first-team All-Americans. In 1952, Michigan State won the national championship, and Biggie was named Coach of the Year. His 1953 team shared the Big Ten title and went to the Rose Bowl.

Biggie Munn was a whale of a lot of football player. Captain of the 1931 Minnesota Gophers and an All-American who played both fullback and guard at 215 pounds and 6-feet tall, the Grow Township, Minnesota, boy was the Most Valuable Player in the Conference that year. He appeared anything but a sprinter and yet he could run the hundred in nearly 10 seconds flat.

"Biggie was a one-man track team at North High School in Minneapolis," Otis Dypwick recalled. "As a senior, he won the state track title for North. He won the hundred-yard dash, despite that bulky build he had, the 220, the javelin, the discus, and the shotput. As a football player at Minnesota, I remember they used to drop him back on punt formation and

Clarence (Biggie) Munn built Michigan State into a football powerhouse. In his seven years as head football coach, he put together a 54–9–2 record with the help of a staff that included Dan Devine, Bob Devaney, Forest Evashevski, and his successor as head coach, Duffy Daugherty.

run him from there. He was an All-American guard who had the build of Nagurski—and to think he had so much speed to go with his size was beyond imagination."

Heralded as a punishing lineman with the getaway and speed of a sprint champion, Munn's other talents were easily overlooked. He was also one of the best punters and the slickest ball-carrying guard in Gopher history, piling up numerous yards for Minnesota from the punt formation.

Biggie Munn died at 66 of a stroke in 1975, but myriad athletic facilities and Michigan State's self-respect as a collegiate sports giant remain as a living monument to the 24 years he gave the Spartans as football coach and athletic director.

Biggie Munn was indeed a Big Man.

SCHMIDT, FRANCIS A., was nicknamed "Shut-the-Gates-of-Mercy" because of the lopsided scores his Ohio State teams rolled up on opponents. During the Schmidt years, 1934–1940, the Buckeyes swamped Western Reserve, 76–0; Drake, 85–0; New York University, 60–0; Chicago, 44–0; Iowa, 40–7; Michigan, 34–0; and Indiana, 33–0. In seven seasons at Columbus, Schmidt had a 39–16–1 record, and finished, in order, 2nd, 1st, 2nd, 2nd, 6th, 1st, and 4th in the Conference standings. He developed seven Ohio State All-Americans: Merle Wendt, Esco Sarkkinen, Regis Monahan, Inwood Smith, Gust Zarnas, Gomer Jones, and Don Scott.

Schmidt's coaching career began at Tulsa, after he finished his playing career at Nebraska. His tenure at Tulsa was interrupted by World War I, in which he was an army bayonet instructor and attained the rank of infantry captain. He returned to coach at Tulsa, 1919 to 1921, before going to Arkansas, where he won 42, lost 20, and tied 3.

Schmidt coached next at Texas Christian, from 1929 to 1934. He won the Southwest Conference championship his very first season, the first in Horned Frogs history. His 1932 team also won the title, and finished in a tie for first place the following year. In all, TCU won 46, lost 6, and tied 5 under Schmidt.

At Ohio State, Schmidt won 14 out of his first 16 games. The Bucks tied for the Western Conference crown in 1935 and won it outright in 1939.

Schmidt was renowned for the infinite variety of his attack: a tandem formation which 30 years later would be called an "I" formation. Any three men who lined up in a straight front-to-back formation behind the quarterback could and did carry the ball. He used forward passes after laterals, laterals after forwards, laterals after laterals, and his reverses flowed from all points of the backfield compass. Stan Pincura, Dick Heekin, Buzz Wetzel, and Jack Smith were prodigious runners who operated behind such great blockers in the line as Merle Wendt, Charlie Hamrick, Inwood Smith, team captain Regis Monahan, and Gomer Jones. The result was one of the wildest, most intricate scoring machines of the 1930s.

Few college coaches in history ever were more excitable during the heat of battle than Schmidt. On one occasion, he had his two first-string tackles resting on the bench. Suddenly, Schmidt commanded, "Oxman, go in for Nitro!"

"Coach," said tackle Nitro, "I'm right here on the bench."

"Good," said Schmidt, "then you go in for Oxman!"

Another time, Schmidt roared, "Look at Daniell out there, being knocked on his ass!"

Daniell, who happened to be out of the game and sitting on the bench, heard Schmidt. "You were wrong that time, Coach," he said. "I'm not even in the game."

"What's the difference?" replied the salty Schmidt. "That's where you'd be, if you were out there!"

SHAUGHNESSY, CLARK DANIEL, was the first college coach to stake his reputation and career on a revolutionary idea—the T formation. As the instigator of the *modern* T, he was the first, however, to say that the T was really the oldest offense in football. "What I did was simply to rejuvenate it, dust it off and counter-attack the general single and double-wing maneuvers," he said.

It was during his 1933–1939 coaching years at the University of Chicago that Clark Shaughnessy studied the T under George Halas of the Chicago Bears and Ralph Jones of obscure Lake Forest, Illinois, College. In 1940, the University of Chicago gave up football and Shaughnessy was hired by Stanford. In a page right out of the Cinderella Story, he took a team of much the same personnel that had won only one game in 1939 and led it to the Rose Bowl, where it defeated Nebraska, 21–13. They gave Shaughnessy the Coach of the Year award after that season.

Shaughnessy considered his Stanford backfield of quarterback Frankie Albert, wingback Pete Kmetovic, left half Hugh Gallarneau, and fullback Norm Standlee as "one of the 12 greatest backfields of all time. They were the perfect backfield."

"A lesser man would have been afraid to present a formation so startling as the T," spoke All-American Frankie Albert of Shaughnessy. "He alone deserves credit for creating many formations from the basic T while with George Halas in Chicago."

Skeptics, including the great Pop Warner, were sure Shaughnessy had lost his mind when he initiated the pro-type T at Stanford, spotlighting a flanker and man-in-motion. "If Stanford wins a single game with that crazy formation, you can throw all the football I ever knew into the Pacific Ocean," Warner declared. "What they're doing is absolutely ridiculous."

Shaughnessy had his reasons, of course. "Always in the past," he elaborated, "the offense tried to coil up power in a ball, then explode it, splitting the defense. The effort was made to stretch the defense thin, then penetrate it. That was the idea of Pop Warner's single wing and Rockne's shift. Our approach is different. We coil up the defense in as small an area as possible, then run around it or throw over it. We shuttle tackles and ends back and forth along the line laterally, shifting the guards sometimes in an unbalanced line and sometimes in a balanced line. Shuttling tackles and ends, shifting guards, and setting a man in motion—away from the play—force the defense out of a set position. It makes old set defenses obsolete."

Hugh Gallarneau didn't know what to think of Shaughnessy.

"We were skeptical," Hugh said later. "At our first meeting with him, Shaughnessy reminded us that his name wasn't Shag and advised us to call him coach or mister. He sounded like a professor. But he had enthusiasm. He would diagram a play on the blackboard and say, 'This play will score fifty touchdowns.' That sounded great to me, but when he said we'd be going into the line without blockers, I thought he was crazy."

The old fundamentalists of power football—Brigadier General Robert Neyland of Tennessee and Bernie Bierman of Minnesota, to name two—scoffed at the brush blocking, the deception, the flankers. But Shaughnessy's huge success at Palo Alto started the rush to the T in 1941. By 1950, there were only a half-dozen schools still using the single wing, Notre Dame box, or anything else. And as the defense began catching up with the Shaughnessy T, the offense evolved into the split T, on to the wing T, the slot T, and such.

Clark Shaughnessy was born at St. Cloud, Minnesota, on March 6, 1892. He was an end, fullback, and two-way tackle at Minnesota in 1911–12–13. Dr. Harry Williams, his coach, called him "the finest forward passer Minnesota ever had, and, in my opinion, the best ever developed in the Western Conference." After graduation, Shaughnessy served as coaching assistant to Dr. Williams. At 23, he was hired by Tulane to head the football staff, where, from 1915 through 1926, he compiled a record of 58 wins, 27 losses, and 6 ties. His 1925 Green Wave were 9–0–1 and received a Rose Bowl bid to play Washington, but the president of Tulane sent a telegram to the Tournament of Roses Committee declining the invitation without even first talking to Shaughnessy.

After leaving Tulane, Shaughnessy moved around considerably. He coached at Loyola of New Orleans, Chicago, Stanford, Maryland, and Pittsburgh. His total college record for 31 years was 149–106–14. Thirty-three of those defeats were at Chicago, where he won only 18 and tied 4. In 1939, the handwriting was on the wall when Chicago lost to Harvard, 61–0, Michigan, 85–0, Virginia, 47–0, and Ohio State, 61–0. It was time for the Maroon to toss in the towel—and time for Clark Shaughnessy to follow the advice of Horace Greeley and go West.

SMITH, ANDREW L., with an ability to inspire a team in a few words, knew football so thoroughly and his rival coaches so completely that, in his blackboard chalk talks and lectures before a game, he was able to tell his players precisely what to expect. And he seldom was wrong.

Lee Cranmer, who played for Andy Smith in 1919 at California, confirmed the coach's genius. "He sized up everything that was ever sprung on us by another team and warned us about it in advance," Cranmer said. "He seemed to have analyzed the character of the other coach and knew exactly how much and what kind of football he would use. In 1920, we listened to everything Andy told us. In 1921, we were so good and knew we were so good that Andy had his troubles. For years you have heard the story that Andy in the tough spots would signal his team from the bench. According to the story, Andy, who, in the nervous excitement of the game, drank so much water that he kept a tin dipper in almost continuous motion ladling up sips from the waterbuckets, had an elaborate system of signs, depending on what bucket he dipped water from. There was no truth to the story at all. In the three years I played under Andy I never once saw him signal from the bench. He was too smart for that. He left the signal-calling in the hands of Charley Erb. Charley called every play. One reason he was such a great quarterback was that Andy Smith, after the game started, left him absolutely alone."

One of the most remarkable coaching records football has known was compiled by Andy Smith from 1920 through 1924, when his California "Wonder Teams" did not suffer a single defeat in 48 games. They won 44 and tied 4. In 10 years at Berkeley, the Golden Bears under Smith won 74 games, lost 16, tied 7. His 1920 and 1921 squads represented the old Pacific Coast Conference in the Rose Bowl.

Andy Smith was an All-American fullback at Pennsylvania in 1904. The Quakers were co-national champions that season, undefeated in 12 games, a powerhouse that scored 222 points to 4. Smith was the workhorse of the backfield. He later coached at Penn (1909–1912), winning 30, losing 10, and tying 3.

The Western Conference phase of the Andy Smith Story happened at Purdue during the years 1913–1915. His overall record in the league was 12–6–3. Even that early in his coaching career he was able to inspire his boys and put points on the scoreboard. The 1913 Boilermakers piled up 171 points to 20, and the 1914 edition scored a total of 157 to 63.

Dr. John Wilce, whose Ohio State Big Ten champions lost to Smith's California Bears in the 1921 Rose Bowl, 28–0, summed up Wonder Coach Andy Smith in 1954: "Andy brought to a rugby-steeped West Coast, then relatively backward in American football, a brilliance of all-around coaching know-how, which, combined with the great Coast material, left an indelible record in the total annals of football."

STAGG, AMOS ALONZO, didn't invent football. It just seemed that way. Walter Camp, his coach at Yale, was the inventor. At the rules conventions of 1881 and 1882, Camp put through his two brain-children, the scrimmage line and yards-in-downs, the individuating notes that first distinguished the game from rugby. There was not much else, though, that was not thought up by Stagg. He was one of the first coaches to use the forward pass on the end of a double reverse; he pioneered double and triple passes behind the line, split back, end-around runs, laterals, and line shifts. Knute Rockne used to say, "All football comes from Stagg."

Stagg's numerous innovations included: the huddle (1896); direct pass from center (1896); wind sprints (1896); man in motion (1899); unbalanced offensive line (1900); backfield shift (1904); numbering players (1913); cross-blocking (1918); 6-2-1-2 defense (1932); double flanker with twin backs and blocking back (1947).

Stagg also played a pioneer role in the exploitation of the forward pass. In 1952 he recalled: "I have read statements giving credit to certain people originating the pass. The fact is many coaches were working on it long before it was even legal. As far back as 1894, two years before the forward pass was legalized by

Two of the greatest names in college football coaching in the 1920s were Chicago's Amos Alonzo Stagg, left, and Knute Rockne of Notre Dame.

the Rules Committee, I had a quarterback at Chicago, Frank Hering, who threw the football like a baseball pitcher. I used him to make a long lateral pass to an end on certain plays when he received a kick. Hering was the first man I ever saw throw a football that way. The normal method was to curl the ball against the forearm and throw it out with a sidearm pass. The first season the forward pass was legal, 1906, I personally had 64 different passing patterns. Part of them were duplicated with six-man and seven-man lines. Against Illinois, Eckersall went to the pass to defeat them, 63 to 0; and we won the Western Conference championship with it in 1907 and 1908."

Stagg also blazed trails in other sports. In baseball, he invented the indoor batting cage and pioneered the headlong slide. He conducted the first tour of Japan by American ballplayers, and from 1906 to 1933 served on the Olympic track committee. In swimming, he invented troughs for overflows in pools.

Amos Alonzo Stagg was a head football coach for 57 seasons: 2 at Springfield College, 41 at the University of Chicago, and 14 at College of the Pacific. He began in 1890 at 28, finished in 1946 at 84. He won a total of 314 games, one more than Pop Warner. He brought Chicago football to national championship stature. He coached seven Big Ten champs: 1896, 1899, 1905, 1907, 1908, 1913, 1924, and all but 1896, 1907, and 1924 were unbeaten. His teams from 1902 through 1909 lost a total of only seven games. Under Stagg, Chicago won 256 games, lost 108, tied 29.

When Stagg coached at Springfield, his center was a tough little gamecock who weighed only 160 pounds. One day, the boy asked Stagg why he had been put at center.

"Jim," Stagg told him seriously, "I play you there because you can do the meanest things in the most gentlemanly way."

"Jim" was James Naismith, who two years later invented the game of basketball.

Stagg was a 27-year-old divinity school student when he played end on the great 1889 Yale eleven, the bunch that rolled up a total of 698 points to 0 in 13 games. His pudgy look was deceptive; he was very strong, always well conditioned. At no time did his 5-feet-7 carry more than 166 pounds. He was still scrimmaging with his players at Chicago when he was 40; he was jogging a mile a day at 70;

he was taking walk-and-run hikes at 80. He never wore glasses until he was 50, and he kept all his hair for life. He never smoked, drank, or used profanity. "Jackass" was the closest he would allow himself to cussing. "Like all forms of over-statement," he said, "swearing is an opiate, and progressively increasing doses are necessary for effect. Too, cursing is likely to leave a personal wound on the object, no matter how impersonally it is delivered."

For all his Biblical precepts, Stagg was the foxiest of gridiron tacticians. He thought two plays ahead of the other fellow, like a master surveying a chessboard. Early in his coaching career, one of his pet plays was the "dead man." When the ball was snapped, the whole team would run toward the left flank, as though on an end run, except the man who took the pass from center. He flopped on his stomach with the ball concealed beneath him—and played dead. When the rival tacklers rushed over to stop the fake end sweep, the "corpse" leaped to his feet and was off to the races. "It's a rather unchristian trick," griped one opponent.

Coach Stagg was ageless. When the University of Chicago tried to pension him in 1932 at the age of 70, he demurred. "I refuse to be idle and a nuisance," he told the university's Board of Trustees after they had voted to force him to obey a school rule. "No man has the right to retire as long as his work benefits humanity." He waited until the end of the 1932 season before relinquishing the football coaching reins to Clark Shaughnessy.

In 1951, at the age of 88, Old Man Stagg was still at it. By this time his list of coaching firsts included the onside kick, the quick kick, the short-punt formation, the handoff from a fake kick, practice under the lights with a white football, padded goalposts, and the charging sled.

Down the years, Stagg hadn't overlooked much. The modern T formation, for example, features four distinct Stagg contributions: the stand-up quarterback behind center, the split buck, the man-in-motion, and the quarterback keeper, although that maneuver and its companion, the pitchout, are inherited from rugby. In sum, any time a modern coach thinks he has come up with something new, he soon learns it is probably a mere reclamation with modification of something probably first used by Stagg 75 years ago.

In 1941, at the age of 78, old Double-A brought his College of the Pacific eleven to play Pacific Lutheran in Tacoma, Washington. Stagg called it one of the most satisfying experiences of his 60 years as a player and a coach. "What a relief to play against a team of A and B students," he sighed. "This is the way I like it. The Lutherans seem to enjoy the game more, and they certainly play just as intelligently and as hard as any I've seen."

The final score was Pacific Lutheran 13, College of the Pacific 7. One of the Lutheran stars was Little All-American tailback Marv Tommervik, who later became a prominent football official and worked in 22 PAC-8 vs. Big Ten games, including the Rose Bowl.

"When I was a kid," Tommervik told me recently, "I remember hearing the name Amos Alonzo Stagg on network radio when the Chicago games were broadcast. Then, in 1941, when we played his Pacific team in Tacoma, I got to meet the old gentleman finally. He was now 78 and still coaching—and he'd go on coaching for another 10 years or so. So after the game, I climbed that long, steep hill up the side of Stadium Bowl to the Pacific dressing room, still in my muddy uniform, to get his autograph. I guess there's some of the small boy in all of us. Mr. Stagg not only gave me his autograph—but he signed the game ball and gave that to me, too. He completely reverted my impromptu visit around. He made me feel it was *his* honor to meet me, instead of vice versa.

"Later, after I went into the Navy, I served with one of Stagg's former players, and he said that if the Old Man caught any of them swearing during practice, they had to do five laps around the field before being banished to the showers. There was no argument about it, either—it was standard procedure. Mr. Stagg tolerated no funny business. Those who played for him really respected him."

In 1943, after Pacific logged a 7–2–0 record and scared the Billy Blazes out of Southern California's Rose Bowl team before losing, 6–0, the 80-year-old Stagg was still winning Coach of the Year and Man of the Year awards.

Eight years later, NEA sent me up to Susquehanna College in the Pennsylvania hills to do a story on Stagg. By now he was the 88-

August 16, 1961

Dear Friend:

Thank you very much for remembering me. At 99, one looks like this -- and writes like this.

Gratefully,

Amos Alonzo Stagg

Amos Alonzo Stagg, Old Double-A, seemed to go on forever. In 1961, at the age of 99, he still showed his sense of humor in this card he sent to all those who remembered him on his birthday.

year-old assistant to his son, the head football coach. He was still spry, still attending daily practice.

The varsity was scrimmaging the scrubs the day I was there and old Double-A took his position in the defensive secondary to take notes. The quarterback called for a line smash, handed the ball to the fullback, who skimmed off a linebacker, plowed over a halfback, flattened the safety man—and crashed into the Old Man with every ounce of strength. His 220 pounds caught Mr. Stagg by surprise, drove him three feet in the air. The Old Man came down thump. Flat on his back. He groped for breath, his face pale. The fullback was sure he had injured the famous Amos Alonzo Stagg. I was already thinking about a lead for the obituary. The players hovered over the Old Man anxiously.

"Coach . . . coach!" one of them whispered, kneeling alongside him. "Are you all right?"

Color returned to the wrinkled face, and he grinned sheepishly at the fullback.

"Nice running," he said, climbing back on his feet. "Now, *that's* the way you're supposed to hit that line!"

Later, back in New York at NEA, I told Harry Grayson, our hard-bitten Sports Editor from the old school, about the incident. Harry was unimpressed.

"Hell!" he snorted. "If he *dies* yuh got yourself the scoop."

WALDORF, LYNN OSBERT *(Pappy),* knew the value of blocking, tackling and the other bread-and-butter fundamentals of football.

Rotund, chain-cigar-smoking Pappy Waldorf put some much-needed punch into Northwestern football in 1935. Taking over a Wildcat squad that won only three games in 1934, he brought a New Look to Evanston after winning the Big Seven championship at Kansas State with a 7–2–1 record. The Wildcats responded with big wins over DePaul, Illinois, Notre Dame, Wisconsin, and a tie with Iowa. This turn-around earned Waldorf the Coach of the Year award.

In 1936, Northwestern won 7 out of 8 games (only Notre Dame beat them) to claim their first and only outright Big Ten championship. On his way to coaching 8 All-Americans in 12 seasons at Evanston—Paul Tangora, Steve Reid, Bob Voigts, John Haman, Alf Bauman, the incomparable Otto Graham, Herb Hein, and Max Morris—Pappy won 50 games, lost 46, and tied 6. Twenty-three of his Wildcats graduated to pro ball.

The Waldorf magic moved on to University of California in 1947, and two years later he led the Bears to Pasadena in the first of three straight Rose Bowl appearances, 1949, 1950 and 1951. Ironically, the 1949 matchup was a 20–14 loss to—Northwestern.

As a student, Pappy Waldorf had been a second-team All-American tackle at Syracuse in 1922 and again in 1924. He was a 5-foot-11, 210-pound reason why Coach John F. (Chick) Meehan's Orangemen compiled a 22–4–3 record during Pappy's varsity career.

Waldorf began his coaching career at Oklahoma A & M, where he won 34, lost 10, and tied 6 during the years 1929–1933, before switching to Kansas State, and then Northwestern. He completed his college football coaching career at Berkeley, 1947–1956, with an overall record in the old Pacific Coast Conference of 62–32–4.

In 31 seasons as a head coach, Pappy Waldorf won 175, lost 99, tied 10. He later became Personnel Director of the San Francisco 49ers.

WIEMAN, ELTON E. *(Tad)*, Phi Beta Kappa captain of the undefeated 1918 Michigan football team, looked like a professor of anthropology rather than a profound student of line play. Once a hard-boiled driver, time and maturity later mellowed the Wolverine (1927–28) and Princeton (1938–42) head coach. He was methodical, painstaking, thorough,

dogged. A steadying influence, he was not susceptible to jinxes, hexes, or pregame jitters. He had few equals at tutoring guards and tackles—this in an era when linemen had to play both ways, tackle as well as block.

As successor to the domineering Fielding H. Yost in 1927, Tad Wieman's Maize and Blue, with All-American captain Bennie Oosterbaan anchoring one end, ran up a combined total of 137 points to a mere 39 in posting a 6–2 record in his first season. Despite a third-place finish in Conference standings, rumors persisted that Athletic Director Yost and Wieman were not hitting it off. Fielding waited until October 4, the day before the 1928 opener, to announce "officially" that Tad would remain as coach. Even though the Wolverines beat Illinois, the conference champions, 3–0, their record fell to 3–4–1 and Tad got the boot. Harry Kipke replaced him at the helm, and Wieman spent 1929 at Minnesota as chief assistant to Fritz Crisler.

Wieman's two-year record at Michigan was 9–6–1; at Princeton, 20–18–3. His bright spot at Old Nassau was in beating Yale four out of five years.

WILCE, JOHN W., spent all of his college coaching career at one school—Ohio State, 1913 through 1928. As the Buckeyes' seventh head coach since they took up football in 1892, the Scarlet and Grey had never won a Western Conference championship until he came along.

John Wilce gave Buckeye fans something to cheer about. He caught the pennant fever, and drove Ohio State to titles in 1916, 1917, and 1918. In 16 seasons at Columbus, he won a total of 80 games, lost 31, tied 7. After sweeping to the Conference crown in 1920 with seven straight victories, he took his team to Pasadena, where it ran into a red-hot California eleven and was derailed, 28–0. He had another fine team in 1926, losing only to Michigan in a 17–16 heart-stopper for the Western Conference championship.

Wilce was a solid football coach. His teams were well-balanced. They could score and they could defend. With Chick Harley in the backfield, the 1916 Buckeyes smashed Oberlin, 128–0, and then finished out an unbeaten season with triumphs over Illinois, Wisconsin, Indiana, Case, and Northwestern; and Wilce's

1917 juggernaut romped through an 8-game schedule with a perfect record, running up a total of 291 points to 6. In 1919, with halfback Harley back from the war, OSU was once more off to the races, scoring 169 points to 3 in six straight victories.

Wilce turned out nine genuine All-Americans: Chuck Bolen, Wes Fesler, Bob Karch, Iolas Huffman, Leo Roskowski, Ed Hess, Chick Harley, Gaylord Stinchcomb, and Martin Karow.

John W. Wilce knew how to get the most out of his athletes.

WILLIAMS, DR. HENRY L., had few contemporaries surpass him as an inventor of football tactics in the years 1900 to 1921 at Minnesota. Old Eli ranked right up there alongside two other Yale men, Lonnie Stagg and George Woodruff.

Dr. Henry Williams, Yale class of 1891, was a right halfback on Billy Rhodes' 1890 Bulldog eleven and a champion hurdler in track. Upon graduation, he got a job as a teacher at Siglar's Academy in Newburgh, New York, located only a mashie shot above West Point. In the autumn of 1891, he traveled down to the Point twice weekly to coach the first Army team ever to defeat Navy. He later enrolled in the School of Medicine at the University of Pennsylvania and helped pay for his medical education by coaching football and track at the William

Dr. Henry L. Williams, inventor of the famous "Minnesota shift," was the first full-time salaried ($2,500 a year) coach in Gopher history. He practiced medicine on the side. In 21 years at Minnesota, the former Yale halfback won or shared eight Western Conference titles, with an overall record of 136–33–9.

Penn Charter School. He then moved to Minneapolis and started building a football dynasty at Minnesota, originating such new offensive twists as the Minnesota shift, forerunner of the famed Notre Dame shift. But his biggest tactical contribution was born at Penn Charter School, in 1895. He devised a formation in which he pulled back only one lineman, normally the left tackle, into the backfield. In this formation, he could place any of his five backs as close to the line as he wanted. The result was a violently powerful formation. The good doctor was very enthusiastic over his new offense. He wanted his alma mater, Yale, to benefit from it, and wrote to Coach Walter Camp, but the Father of Football rejected the formation. So Dr. Williams took the plan to West Point and the Cadets blasted Navy with it, 17 to 5. The next season, Yale installed the tackle-back formation into its system.

At a salary of $2,500 a year, Dr. Williams was the first full-time salaried coach in Gopher history. The pact also granted him permission to practice medicine as well. The two professions complemented one another in those raw-meat days of football. In 21 years at Minneapolis, Dr. Williams posted a 136–33–9 record, and won or shared eight Western Conference championships, in 1900, 1903, 1904, 1906, 1909, 1910, 1911, and 1915.

In additon to devising the "Minnesota shift," Dr. Williams invented the revolving wedge in 1892 and the tackle-back formation seven years later. He was one of those largely responsible for persuading the Football Rules Committee to legalize the forward pass and was a member of the committee. John Heisman credited him with originating criss-cross plays (1891) in which the halfbacks and ends, while going in opposite directions, passed the ball back to each other, and also, in 1892, the on-side quarterback kick.

Dr. Williams never devoted the time to football fundamentals—blocking, charging, tackling—to anywhere near the extent that such successful coaches as Knute Rockne or Bernie Bierman did. He was first and foremost a tactician, a deviser of offensive plays, equally expert at setting up a defense for any type of attack.

Born at Hartford, Connecticut, June 26, 1869, Dr. Henry L. Williams died on June 14, 1931.

WOODRUFF, GEORGE W., is nothing more than a "footnote" in Western Conference records. He had already reached his zenith at the University of Pennsylvania (1892–1901) long before rounding out his career at Illinois in 1903. His record at Penn was 124–15–2, including a share of the national championship in 1894–95–97. From 1894 through 1897, the Quakers won 56 out of 57 contests, and scored 1,777 points to 88!

Like so many other great coaches of the era, George Woodruff played his football at Yale, 1885–1888, at right guard. The night before the MIT game at Boston in his frosh year, Woodruff had his beard shaved off and walked up to team captain Peters in the lobby of the Tremont House, team headquarters. He stared at Peters, but Peters didn't recognize him. Frowning, Peters asked him, "What do you want, sir?" Woodruff did not reply, just kept staring at him. Gradually, an incredulous look stole over Peters. "Gad!" he said. "Woodruff! So *that's* what you look like!"

George Woodruff had no trouble being identified as head coach at Lehigh and Penn. He became known far and wide as one of the game's leading strategists of power football. As a matter of fact, he invented the running guard play while he was still playing at Yale; later, he pioneered the guards-back offense, forerunner of tackle-back, and the principle of smashing ends on defense.

In his only season at Champaign, Coach Woodruff had a schedule of 14 games. The Illini won their first 8, romping over a bunch of nondescript teams with names like "Osteopaths," "Physicians & Surgeons," and "Chicago Dentists," and then opened the conference competition with a 24–0 victory over Purdue. After that—disaster. Illinois then lost 6 straight games, scoring only 17 points against a total of 107. Woodruff's Western Conference record shows only that one triumph over Purdue.

YOST, FIELDING H. *(Hurry-Up)*, was always in a hurry, but always knew where he was going. Hurry-up was his battle cry, and Hurry-Up his nickname. He pronounced Michigan wrong, but coached it right. Few football teams could stop his "Mee-chigan" Wolverines.

In a quarter-century at Ann Arbor, he had eight unbeaten teams, and eight Western Con-

ference champions. His first five Michigan teams, 1901 through 1905, played 56 straight games without a loss until beaten at Chicago in 1905, 2–0. On the way to winning lasting fame as the "point-a-minute" teams, they outscored opponents, 2,821 to 56.

Fielding Harris Yost was born at Fairview, West Virginia, in 1871, six months before the Chicago fire. While still in his teens he served as a deputy marshal in rowdy mining towns. A robust 200-pounder, he played in the first football game he ever saw, and later was a regular for three teams at one time. At 24, he entered West Virginia Law School—and then returned in 1904 with his "Mee-chigan" eleven to rout WVU, 130 to 0.

If Hurry-Up Yost was not playing, sleeping, or talking football, he was coaching it. In 1900, he coached four teams successfully; Stanford Freshman, Lowell High of San Francisco, the California Ukiah team, and San Jose Teachers.

Yost was a gray-haired man with bushy eyebrows and beady, black eyes, when George Trevor, sports reporter for *The New York Sun* and a Yale man, accompanied the 1929 Harvard team to Ann Arbor. Yost had retired from coaching in 1926 but was still the power behind the throne, as Harry Kipke, the nominal head coach, learned to his sorrow. When the Wolverines won, Yost was there to take the bows, and when they lost good old Harry made a convenient scapegoat.

As Trevor waited in the ante-room of the fieldhouse, which Yost himself had designed, strange thumping sounds came from Athletic Director Yost's office—crashes and grunting noises as though a pack of house movers were doing their thing inside.

"Don't worry, Mr. Trevor," smiled a pretty secretary, "that's only Mr. Yost talking to a newspaperman. I hope you brought your helmet and shoulder pads with you. Mr. Yost can get quite animated."

Nobody escaped unscathed from an interview with Hurry-Up Yost, as Trevor soon found out. Yost believed in personal demonstration and took delight in flinging chairs and tables around his office as he illustrated a particular football play.

"When the noise gets real loud," the secretary told George, "we know from out here that he's explaining Old 83, his best play."

Finally, Trevor got the signal to go in. What followed was a liberal education in the art of football science as Yost fired away with his patented blend of philosophy.

"At Mee-chigan," Yost told George, "we believe that position is more important than possession. In other words, we hold our fire till we are fairly deep in enemy territory. Not till then do we spring our scoring plays. Football games are usually *lost* rather than *won*. That's why we prefer to let the enemy gamble with passes and trick plays in his own territory. When they misfire, we seize our opportunity and strike hard."

Here he grabbed George by the collar and shook him vigorously.

"Why do you suppose we beat physically superior Minnesota teams year after year?" he demanded. "Because we let them pile up the first downs while we bided our time and went for touchdowns. Don't repeat this stuff to my old friend Pop Warner. Pop wants to hang onto that ball all the time. He tried to get the Rules Committee to make first downs count in the scoring."

Cynics called Yost's offense "a punt, a pass, and a prayer." Hurry-Up ignored the criticism. "Control kicking has won many games for us when we seem out-classed in manpower," he told Trevor. "By kicking the ball into the coffin corner, we keep the pressure on our opponents and sooner or later they blunder. An enemy fumble is as good as a 50-yard run. In Benny Friedman, I had one of the greatest passers and smartest quarterbacks in football history, but I did my share of praying, too. And don't think we couldn't run that ball when necessary. Here, let me show you how Old 83 worked. That was our pay-off goal-line getter, a double reverse with an end-around tacked on."

Yost reached for the chairs, and George guessed what was coming. The two of them wound up in a tangled heap under a pile of broken lumber. "Mee-chigan" had scored again.

Yost was one of the first of the big-time coaches who believed in a training table for his athletes. He was an advocate of *controlled* dietary habits, of designating a regular place where his players could properly eat together and talk football.

Nobody ever interrupted a Yost monologue. He talked you to death. He would talk football with anyone. He once blocked traffic in the middle of a busy downtown Ann Arbor street while he calmly diagrammed a new play with a piece of chalk on the pavement for Bottle Thompson, his big fullback.

Grantland Rice once asked Ring Lardner if he ever had a conversation with Yost.

"No," sports writer Lardner replied. "My parents taught me never to interrupt."

For all his talking, Yost surpassed it with his doing. Of those coaches who survived the business 25 years or more, none matches his record of 198–38–13. When he started at Michigan as a 30-year-old coach, he already had a national reputation. He had developed a state championship team in his first coaching job, Ohio Wesleyan in 1897; it tied Michigan and beat Ohio State, 6–0, for the only time in history it beat the Buckeyes. He won Missouri Valley titles at Nebraska and Kansas, and a California state championship at Stanford.

Hurry-Up Yost stands today as a legend at Ann Arbor. He had the foresight to build the present Michigan stadium with a double foundation so that it could be enlarged to its present capacity of 101,701. He also insisted upon the rectangular shape of Michigan Stadium, which hugs the gridiron snugly at the corners so that the spectators would be closer to midfield. A tough, shrewd businessman, Yost also built the Yost Field House, Women's Athletic Building, the Indoor Sports Building, the Ice Rink, and the 18-hole golf course. As an intercollegiate athletic plant, it is unsurpassed. His chief objective was to make sports as available to as many students as possible, and he succeeded.

Except for self-centeredness and incessant maceration of cigars, Yost had no bad habits. His personal life was exemplary, a reflection of his upbringing. He never told an off-color story, and used *damn* and *hell* only for "medicinal purposes." In demonstrating a forward pass in a hotel room, he inadvertently threw a Gideon Bible in his excitement, and apologized afterwards. Alcohol was taboo with him, yet he allowed his players to have a tankard of ale before Friday night dinner to unwind them—under his strict supervision.

"Some folks can drink and it doesn't harm them," he told his athletes. "But it doesn't do them any good. And ye want to be good, don't ye?"

Born and reared in a cabin, Yost later became comfortably fixed financially by augmenting his salary as a coach; he was part owner of a hydroelectric plant and a credit company, and also served as a bank official. He was careful of his money.

Because its strategy and tactics bear a certain similarity to football, Yost found a fascination in military history, and eventually became an authentic expert. He visited Little Big Horn to study the layout and decide whether Custer should be blamed for what happened to the Seventh Cavalry; he never did decide. He spent many hours retracing the Battle of Gettysburg, and he visited the Waterloo battlefield and discussed it at every opportunity. Andy Baker, his secretary for years, said that whenever they drove by a piece of landscape that resembled the site of the Wellington-Napoleon confrontation, Yost would stop the car, back up, and shout, "There it is! There's Hougoumont Farm! There's the sunken road! Over there's where Napoleon sat on his white horse, y'know."

Willie Heston felt his old coach would have made a good military general.

"During World War I," Heston recalled in 1952, "I met Coach Yost frequently in his office. He would have maps and diagrams on the table and would prognosticate the next moves of the opposing armies. Usually he was right.

"Coach Yost was a strong believer in physical condition. Our practice sessions were long and hard, but he always kept in close touch with the trainer to find out if everybody was standing up under the grind. We used every running play that is being used today. That meant every player must learn at least 50 plays and know what his assignment would be in every play. The coach did not have any time for a player who would not give his all in every play and would not tolerate a boy who showed any signs of physical fear.

"His pep talks just before gametime were all classics," Heston continued. "Ten or 15 minutes before kickoff, he'd have the squad form a semicircle in front of him. He'd first tell us what he'd learned about our opponents, their strong points and their weak points. He'd then pull from his pocket a list on which he had jotted down mistakes that were made during the week's practices. Then he would tell us that the entire Michigan alumni—in fact, the

whole football world—were awaiting the final result of the game. He would finally wind up by telling us to always be alert, be 'ball hounds,' and would sometimes say, 'Ye know what Willie Heston says, *Use your searchlights and jump the dead ones*,' an expression I made while talking to the team in 1902. Whenever the squad left the dressing room to go onto the field, Coach Yost would say, 'Who are they to beat a Mee-chigan team? They're only human.' By now every player was in a state of mind to eat raw meat."

In all history, few coaches have taken football more seriously than Yost. Hollywood once hired him as technical adviser to a movie called "The Quarterback," and after he returned to Ann Arbor, he shook his head sadly. "You should have seen the actors they gave me for football players—a bunch of Ping-Pong players and dancing boys. They couldn't even catch a football in a butterfly net."

ZUPPKE, ROBERT CARL, is listed second only to Amos Alonzo Stagg for unbroken job longevity at one college. Stagg put in 41 straight seasons at Chicago, while Zup coached at Champaign-Urbana for 29.

Bob Zuppke was the toughest of all college coaches to beat when he pointed for a certain game, especially if he could find some psychological advantage to use against the opposition. He coached at Illinois from 1913 until 1941, winning 131 games, losing 81, tying 12. The Fighting Illini won or shared the Big Ten title seven times, were runners-up twice. The 1914, 1915, 1923, and 1927 teams were unbeaten; in 1914, 1923, and 1927 they had a good claim on the national championship.

Zup called his 1914 team the best. He said that its diversification in talent enabled him to give it a more complex offense than any of his later teams. Next to Red Grange, he considered quarterback Potsy Clark and halfback Harold Pogue of the 1914 eleven as his greatest players.

Born in Berlin, Germany, on July 2, 1879, moved to Milwaukee, Wisconsin, when he was two, Bob Zuppke coached the Illini until he was 62. Over the years, he was one of football's master innovators: He originated the modern *outdoor* huddle in 1921 (Stagg was the first to use it *indoors,* in 1896). "I started using the huddle outdoors because too often it was impossible to hear the signals, and the other team would often shout to make the signals even more difficult to understand," Zuppke explained one time. "The huddle was not very popular at first, and the Rules Committee even considered barring its use. Our 1923 team with Grange made it stick, and after Red's great day against Michigan in 1924 the huddle became widely accepted."

Other Zuppke football contributions included the spiral pass from center 10 years before it was popular, pulling back guards to protect the passer, the screen pass, and "strategy maps" for quarterbacks. He was also the first coach to use the 5–4–2 defense.

Zup had an astonishingly agile brain. An Illinois official once said of him: "On the street, during the season, he walks with his head down, thinking football. He is grim. He is in a mental state which he wishes to encourage in his men." Yet, he did not take football home with him. His wife, Fannie, was not forced to listen to shoptalk. They seldom discussed football, they had so many other interests and diversions. She kept a scrapbook of all Illinois games, but pasted only the newspaper accounts of the contests which the Illini won. When they lost, she could not understand why they scheduled such people.

Most of the plays Zuppke used at Illinois he had earlier put on successfully in his three seasons as coach of Oak Park High, where he turned out two national championship teams, and before that at Muskegon High. One of those going out for his squad at Oak Park was Ernest Hemingway. "I was no good at football, but does that make an unhappy boyhood?" Hemingway once confessed. "Zuppke put me at center but I never knew what a digit was, so I couldn't figure out the plays. I used to look at my teammates' faces and guess who looked like they expected the ball. I was called Drag-Ass when they put me at guard. I wanted to play backfield but they knew better. There was one guy on the team beat me up in the locker room every day for two years, but then I grew up to him and I beat the be-Jesus out of him and that was the end of that."

Author Hemingway played for Zuppke a year before George Huff, Illinois' famous athletic director, hired Zup to coach the Illini Blue and Gold. "Scrimmaging against Zup's first team was tougher than shooting lions in Africa," Hemingway recalled later.

For coaching genius and personal color, not even Knute Rockne surpassed Zuppke. Zuppke the coach was the compendium of Zuppke the man: philosopher, psychologist, dreamer, doer, driver, artist, strategist, tactician, leader. As a painter of oils, he was no mere dabbler. In galleries as well as stadia, he had his exhibitions.

As a public speaker, only Frank Cavanaugh and Rockne of his time were in his class. His wit was enhanced by the smidgen of stutter and a German accent. The droll Zup trained some of his warmest wit on fellow coaches. "It's true that Stagg never swears at his men—because he doesn't have any men," he used to say. "He calls this man a jackass, then that man a jackass, then another. By the end of the workout there are no men playing—just jackasses grazing."

Zuppke and Rockne shared a wide range of interests beyond football. Both were interested in science, literature, and art. Coming upon them suddenly, one might discover to his surprise that the subject under discussion was not a new method of applying power off tackle, but eurythmics, the art of harmonious and expressive bodily movement. Eurythmics, they agreed, was something the ballet virtuoso and the classic open-field runner had in common.

During the years he coached at Illinois, football crowds rose from 4,500 to 70,000. Zup

Knute Rockne, left, and Bob Zuppke shared a wide range of interests beyond football. Both the Notre Dame and Illinois coaches were interested in science, literature, and art.

was their man. He had a prodigious wit and is identified with more funny stories than any other character in football history, except, perhaps, his old friend, Rockne.

Rockne's teams of the early 1920s provoked much argument about whether they came to the full-second stop required by the rules after shifting from the T to the box. Zuppke used the controversy as background for a story about a visit he made to Notre Dame.

"When I got on the campus," he said, "three freshmen came out of a building hollering, 'One-two-three shift!' From another building farther along, two young priests came out, lifted their cassocks, and shouted, 'One-two-three-hike!' Then I visited the office of the president of Notre Dame. He rose to greet me and advanced yelling, 'One-two-three-hike!' But he's getting old and can't move as fast as the others. In fact, he was the only one I saw on the campus whose shift was legal."

Zuppke also had an especial fondness for Howard Jones, one who never took a drink in his life. In January, 1935, Grantland Rice was in Los Angeles and Zup and Jones dropped over to his hotel to visit him. Midway through the conversation, Zup turned to Howard and said, "You are a great coach, Howard, but you'd be even greater if you'd take a drink once in a while. You'd have more imagination."

"I never heard yet where booze figured out a play," Howard responded.

"You never did?" Zup said. "Well, I've just had two drinks and I have doped out three new plays. They are the Flea Flicker, the Whoa Back, and the Double Jump. Here, let me diagram them for you. I'm going to use them next season when we come out here to play you."

All three were brand new plays, including the Flea Flicker—a predetermined lateral off a forward pass, getting its name from the finger flick used by the receiver in executing the lateral (still functional today).

Final score: Illinois 19, Southern California 0.

P.S. Each touchdown was scored with one of the three plays.

When Bob Zuppke had something to say, it was usually worth hearing. "It is foolish," he said, "to claim that football is all good. There are both good and bad in the game, as there are in all human beings. A thing that is all good is no good. We wouldn't learn anything, if everything was good." That was Zuppke the serious philosopher. Some other memorable Zuppke aphorisms, all original with him, but frequently quoted by many:

"All quitters are good losers."

"No athletic director holds his job longer than two unsuccessful football coaches."

"The hero of a thousand plays becomes a bum after one error."

"The undefeated team is not always the strongest team. It might be the luckiest."

"My definition of an All-American is a player who has weak opposition and a poet in the press box."

"On the first two downs, play for a touchdown; on third down, play for a first down."

"The sheik may be God's gift to women, but the second guess is God's gift to the football coach."

The Records

Big Ten Claimants to
The National Championship

Year	Team, Record	Coach	Other Claimants To National Championship
1901	Michigan, 11–0	Fielding H. Yost	Harvard
1902	Michigan, 11–0	Fielding H. Yost	Yale
1905	Chicago, 11–0	Amos Alonzo Stagg	Yale
1913	Chicago, 7–0	Amos Alonzo Stagg	Harvard
1914	Illinois, 7–0	Bob Zuppke	Army
1919	Illinois, 6–1	Bob Zuppke	Harvard, Notre Dame
1921	Iowa, 7–0	Howard Jones	Cornell
1923	Illinois, 8–0	Bob Zuppke	
1927	Illinois, 7–0–1	Bob Zuppke	
1931	Purdue, 9–1	Noble Kizer	Pittsburgh
1932	Michigan, 8–0	Harry Kipke	Southern California, Colgate
1933	Michigan, 7–0–1	Harry Kipke	Southern California, Princeton
1934	Minnesota, 8–0	Bernie Bierman	Alabama
1935	Minnesota, 8–0	Bernie Bierman	Southern Methodist, Princeton, Louisiana State
1936	Minnesota, 7–1	Bernie Bierman	Pittsburgh, Louisiana State
1940	Minnesota, 8–0	Bernie Bierman	Tennessee, Stanford
1941	Minnesota, 8–0	Bernie Bierman	
1942	Ohio State, 9–1	Paul Brown	Wisconsin, Georgia
1947	Michigan, 10–0	Fritz Crisler	Notre Dame
1948	Michigan, 9–0	Bennie Oosterbaan	
1951	Michigan St., 9–0	Biggie Munn	Tennessee, Maryland, Georgia Tech
1952	Michigan St., 9–0	Biggie Munn	Georgia Tech
1954	Ohio State, 10–0	Woody Hayes	UCLA
1957	Ohio State, 9–1	Woody Hayes	Michigan State, Auburn
1958	Iowa, 8–1–1	Forest Evashevski	Louisiana State
1960	Minnesota, 8–2	Murray Warmath	Washington, Mississippi
1961	Ohio State, 9–0–1	Woody Hayes	Alabama
1965	Michigan St., 10–1	Duffy Daugherty	Alabama
1966	Michigan St., 9–0–1	Duffy Daugherty	
1968	Ohio State, 10–1	Woody Hayes	

Minnesota's 1941 champions.

BIG TEN CHAMPIONS

(Since Ohio State entered the conference in 1913)

	Outright Titles	Shared Titles	Total
Michigan	8	12	20
Ohio State	12	6	18
Illinois	7	3	10
Minnesota	6	3	9
Purdue	1	5	6
Iowa	3	2	5
Northwestern	1	3	4
Wisconsin	2	1	3
Michigan State	2	1	3
Chicago	2	0	2
Indiana	1	1	2

TOURNAMENT OF ROSES

Big Ten vs. PAC-8

1902 *Michigan* 49, Stanford 0
1921 California 28, *Ohio State 0*
1947 *Illinois* 45, UCLA 14
1948 *Michigan* 49, Southern California 0
1949 *Northwestern* 20, California 14
1950 *Ohio State* 17, California 14
1951 *Michigan* 14, California 6
1952 *Illinois* 40, Stanford 7
1953 Southern California 7, *Wisconsin* 0
1954 *Michigan State* 28, UCLA 20
1955 *Ohio State* 20, Southern California 7
1956 *Michigan State* 17, UCLA 14
1957 *Iowa* 35, Oregon State 19
1958 *Ohio State* 10, Oregon 7
1959 *Iowa* 38, California 12

1960 Washington 44, *Wisconsin* 8
1961 Washington 17, *Minnesota* 7
1962 *Minnesota* 21, UCLA 3
1963 Southern California 42, *Wisconsin* 37
1964 *Illinois* 17, Washington 7
1965 *Michigan* 34, Oregon State 7
1966 UCLA 14, *Michigan* 12
1967 *Purdue* 14, Southern California 13
1968 Southern California 14, *Indiana* 3
1969 *Ohio State* 27, Southern California 16
1970 Southern California 10, *Michigan* 3
1971 Stanford 27, *Ohio State* 17

Quarterback Don Burson passed the 1948 Northwestern Wildcats into the Rose Bowl and a 20–14 victory over California.

Michigan State played in the Rose Bowl for the first time in 1954 and beat UCLA, 28–20. The key play was this blocked Paul Cameron punt by Ellis Duckett, who scooped up the ball and scored.

1972	Stanford 13, *Michigan* 12
1973	Southern California 42, *Ohio State* 17
1974	*Ohio State,* 42, Southern California 21
1975	Southern California 18, *Ohio State* 17
1976	UCLA 23, *Ohio State* 10

BIG TEN HEISMAN TROPHY WINNERS

1935	Jay Berwanger	Quarterback	Chicago
1939	Nile Kinnick	Halfback	Iowa
1940	Tom Harmon	Halfback	Michigan
1941	Bruce Smith	Halfback	Minnesota
1944	Les Horvath	Halfback	Ohio State
1950	Vic Janowicz	Halfback	Ohio State
1954	Alan Ameche	Halfback	Wisconsin
1955	Howard Cassady	Halfback	Ohio State
1974	Archie Griffin	Halfback	Ohio State
1975	Archie Griffin	Halfback	Ohio State

BIG TEN NATIONAL COACHES OF THE YEAR

Year	Name	School	Record
1935	Lynn (Pappy) Waldorf	Northwestern	4–3–1
1939	Eddie Anderson	Iowa	6–1–1
1944	Carroll Widdoes	Ohio State	9–0–0
1945	Alvin (Bo) McMillin	Indiana	9–0–1
1947	H. O. (Fritz) Crisler	Michigan	10–0–0
1948	Bennie Oosterbaan	Michigan	9–0–0
1952	Clarence (Biggie) Munn	Michigan State	9–0–0
1955	Hugh (Duffy) Daugherty	Michigan State	8–1–0
1957	Woody Hayes	Ohio State	8–1–0
1960	Murray Warmath	Minnesota	8–1–0
1967	John Pont	Indiana	9–1–0
1969	Glenn (Bo) Schembechler	Michigan	8–2–0
1975	Woody Hayes	Ohio State	11–0–0

(NOTE: The Coach of the Year is named by the American Football Coaches Association.)

The gentleman from Indiana, Bo McMillan, accepts the Coach of the Year award after winning the Big Ten championship in 1945.

SEATING CAPACITY OF BIG TEN STADIUMS

School	Name of Stadium	Year Built	Capacity
Michigan	Michigan	1927	101,701
Ohio State	Ohio	1922	83,112
Wisconsin	Camp Randall	1917	77,280
Michigan State	Spartan	1923	76,000
Illinois	Memorial	1923	71,227
Purdue	Ross-Ade	1924	69,200
Iowa	Iowa	1929	60,000
Minnesota	Memorial	1924	56,652
Northwestern	Dyche	1926	55,000
Indiana	Memorial	1960	52,354

(NOTE: All but Ross-Ade Stadium have artificial turf.)

Where the Michigan State Spartans play their home games—Spartan Stadium (capacity, 76,000), East Lansing, Michigan.

Where the Michigan Wolverines play their home games—Michigan Stadium (capacity, 101,001), Ann Arbor, Michigan. (Crisler Arena—capacity, 13,609—is shown in background.)

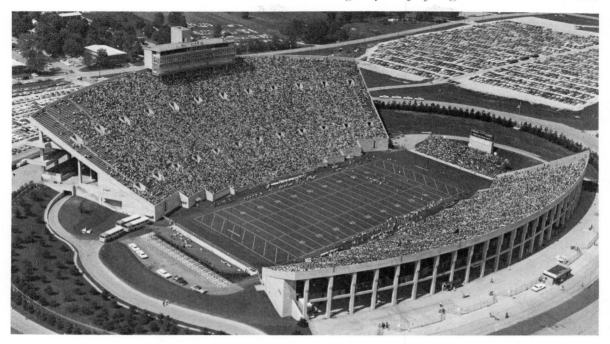

Home in Indiana for the football Hoosiers is Memorial Stadium at Bloomington. Despite the fact that the Hoosiers own the worst percentage of wins-losses-ties in the Big Ten—228–382–40—their loyal fans continue to fill the stadium to near capacity (52,354).

Where the Northwestern Wildcats play their home games—Dyche Stadium (capacity, 55,000), Evanston, Illinois.

WESTERN CONFERENCE CHAMPIONS
SINCE 1896

1896	Wisconsin	1936	Northwestern
1897	Wisconsin	1937	Minnesota
1898	Michigan	1938	Minnesota
1899	Chicago	1939	Ohio State
1900	Iowa, Minnesota	1940	Minnesota
1901	Michigan, Wisconsin	1941	Minnesota
1902	Michigan	1942	Ohio State
1903	Michigan, Minnesota, Northwestern	1943	Michigan, Purdue
1904	Michigan, Minnesota	1944	Ohio State
1905	Chicago	1945	Indiana
1906	Michigan, Minnesota, Wisconsin	1946	Illinois
1907	Chicago	1947	Michigan
1908	Chicago	1948	Michigan
1909	Minnesota	1949	Michigan, Ohio State
1910	Illinois, Minnesota	1950	Michigan
1911	Minnesota	1951	Illinois
1912	Wisconsin	1952	Purdue, Wisconsin
1913	Chicago	1953	Illinois, Michigan State
1914	Illinois	1954	Ohio State
1915	Illinois	1955	Ohio State
1916	Ohio State	1956	Iowa
1917	Ohio State	1957	Ohio State
1918	Illinois, Michigan, Purdue	1958	Iowa
1919	Illinois	1959	Wisconsin
1920	Ohio State	1960	Iowa, Minnesota
1921	Iowa	1961	Ohio State
1922	Iowa, Michigan	1962	Wisconsin
1923	Illinois, Michigan	1963	Illinois
1924	Chicago	1964	Michigan
1925	Michigan	1965	Michigan State
1926	Michigan, Northwestern	1966	Michigan State
1927	Illinois	1967	Indiana, Minnesota, Purdue
1928	Illinois	1968	Ohio State
1929	Purdue	1969	Michigan, Ohio State
1930	Michigan, Northwestern	1970	Ohio State
1931	Michigan, Northwestern, Purdue	1971	Michigan
1932	Michigan	1972	Michigan, Ohio State
1933	Michigan	1973	Michigan, Ohio State
1934	Minnesota	1974	Michigan, Ohio State
1935	Minnesota, Ohio State	1975	Ohio State

BIG TEN COMPOSITE STANDINGS

Big Ten Conference Totals

Team	Year Joined Conference	Conference Wins	Conference Losses	Conference Ties
Ohio State	1913	248	101	20
Michigan	1896	255	116	14
Michigan State	1953	90	60	4
Minnesota	1896	226	171	25
Chicago	1896*	120	99	14
Illinois	1896	209	224	23
Purdue	1896	184	201	26
Wisconsin	1896	193	213	35
Northwestern	1896	166	255	19
Iowa	1900	134	229	20
Indiana	1900	102	252	22

*Discontinued play after 1939.

ALL GAMES THROUGH 1975 SEASON

Team	Years in Football	No. of Games	Won	Lost	Tied
Michigan	96	801	576	194	31
Ohio State	89	762	508	208	46
Minnesota	91	801	460	302	38
Michigan State	79	689	420	231	37
Wisconsin	87	722	391	285	46
Purdue	88	719	383	294	42
Illinois	86	747	396	309	42
Iowa	86	720	343	345	32
Northwestern	85	720	330	351	39
Indiana	88	710	288	382	40

BIG TEN CONFERENCE STANDINGS
1925–1975

(Note: Until mid-1920s, conference records were only loosely published. Here shown are only *league* totals for wins, losses, ties and do not include non-conference results; for all games, please see game-by-game scores for years 1925-1941 listed under each school's record further back in this section.)

1927 Conference Games Only

	W	L	T
Illinois	5	0	0
Minnesota	3	0	1
Michigan	3	2	0
Chicago	3	3	0
Purdue	2	2	0
Northwestern	2	3	0
Ohio State	2	3	0
Indiana	1	2	1
Iowa	1	4	0
Wisconsin	1	4	0

1925 Conference Games Only

	W	L	T
Michigan	6	1	0
Northwestern	3	1	0
Wisconsin	3	1	1
Minnesota	1	1	1
Iowa	2	2	0
Illinois	2	2	0
Chicago	2	2	1
Ohio State	1	3	1
Purdue	0	3	1
Indiana	0	3	1

1928 Conference Games Only

	W	L	T
Illinois	4	1	0
Wisconsin	3	1	1
Minnesota	4	2	0
Ohio State	3	2	0
Iowa	3	2	0
Purdue	2	2	1
Northwestern	2	3	0
Michigan	2	3	0
Indiana	2	4	0
Chicago	0	5	0

1926 Conference Games Only

	W	L	T
Northwestern	5	0	0
Michigan	5	0	0
Ohio State	3	1	0
Purdue	2	1	1
Wisconsin	3	2	1
Minnesota	2	2	0
Illinois	2	2	0
Indiana	0	4	0
Chicago	0	5	0
Iowa	0	5	0

1929 Conference Games Only

	W	L	T
Purdue	4	0	0
Illinois	2	1	1
Ohio State	2	1	1
Minnesota	3	2	0
Northwestern	3	2	0
Iowa	3	2	0
Indiana	1	2	1
Michigan	1	3	0
Chicago	1	3	0
Wisconsin	1	4	0

1930 Conference Games Only

	W	L	T
Northwestern	5	0	0
Michigan	5	0	0
Purdue	4	2	0
Wisconsin	2	2	1
Ohio State	2	2	1
Minnesota	1	3	0
Indiana	1	3	0
Illinois	1	4	0
Iowa	0	1	0
Chicago	0	4	0

1932 Conference Games Only

	W	L	T
Michigan	6	0	0
Purdue	5	0	1
Wisconsin	4	1	1
Ohio State	2	1	2
Northwestern	2	3	1
Minnesota	2	3	0
Illinois	1	4	1
Indiana	1	4	1
Chicago	1	4	0
Iowa	0	5	0

1933 Conference Games Only

	W	L	T
Michigan	5	0	1
Ohio State	4	1	0
Purdue	3	1	1
Minnesota	2	0	4
Iowa	3	2	0
Illinois	3	2	0
Northwestern	1	4	1
Indiana	0	3	2
Chicago	0	3	2
Wisconsin	0	5	1

1934 Conference Games Only

	W	L	T
Minnesota	5	0	0
Ohio State	5	1	0
Illinois	4	1	0
Purdue	3	1	0
Wisconsin	2	3	0
Northwestern	2	3	0
Chicago	2	4	0
Iowa	1	3	1
Indiana	1	3	1
Michigan	0	6	0

A stalwart in the middle of the line for the 1931 Purdue champions was All-American center Chuck Miller.

1931 Conference Games Only

	W	L	T
Purdue	5	1	0
Northwestern	5	1	0
Michigan	5	1	0
Ohio State	4	2	0
Minnesota	3	2	0
Wisconsin	3	3	0
Indiana	1	4	1
Chicago	1	4	0
Iowa	0	3	1
Illinois	0	6	0

1935 Conference Games Only

	W	L	T
Minnesota	5	0	0
Ohio State	5	0	0
Purdue	3	3	0
Indiana	2	2	1
Northwestern	2	3	1
Chicago	2	3	0
Michigan	2	3	0
Iowa	1	2	2
Illinois	1	4	0
Wisconsin	1	4	0

1936 Conference Games Only

	W	L	T
Northwestern	6	0	0
Ohio State	4	1	0
Minnesota	4	1	0
Purdue	3	1	1
Indiana	3	1	1
Illinois	2	2	1
Chicago	1	4	0
Iowa	0	4	1
Wisconsin	0	4	0
Michigan	0	5	0

1940 Conference Games Only

	W	L	T
Minnesota	6	0	0
Michigan	3	1	0
Northwestern	4	2	0
Ohio State	3	3	0
Wisconsin	3	3	0
Iowa	2	3	0
Indiana	2	3	0
Purdue	1	4	0
Illinois	0	5	0

1937 Conference Games Only

	W	L	T
Minnesota	5	0	0
Ohio State	5	1	0
Indiana	3	2	0
Northwestern	3	3	0
Michigan	3	3	0
Purdue	2	2	1
Wisconsin	2	2	1
Illinois	2	3	0
Chicago	0	5	0
Iowa	0	5	0

1941 Conference Games Only

	W	L	T
Minnesota	5	0	0
Michigan	3	1	1
Ohio State	3	1	1
Northwestern	4	2	0
Wisconsin	3	3	0
Purdue	1	3	1
Indiana	1	3	0
Iowa	1	5	0
Illinois	1	5	0

1938 Conference Games Only

	W	L	T
Minnesota	4	1	0
Purdue	3	1	1
Michigan	3	1	1
Northwestern	2	1	2
Wisconsin	3	2	0
Ohio State	3	2	1
Illinois	2	3	0
Iowa	1	3	1
Indiana	1	4	0
Chicago	0	4	0

1942

	Conference Games			All Games		
	W	L	T	W	L	T
Ohio State	5	1	0	9	1	0
Wisconsin	4	1	0	8	1	1
Illinois	3	2	0	6	4	0
Michigan	3	2	0	7	3	0
Indiana	2	2	0	7	3	0
Iowa	3	3	0	6	4	0
Minnesota	3	3	0	5	4	0
Purdue	1	4	0	1	8	0
Northwestern	0	6	0	1	9	0

1939 Conference Games Only

	W	L	T
Ohio State	5	1	0
Iowa	4	1	1
Purdue	2	1	2
Northwestern	3	2	1
Michigan	3	2	0
Illinois	3	3	0
Indiana	2	3	0
Minnesota	2	3	1
Chicago*	0	3	0
Wisconsin	0	5	1

(*Chicago discontinued football)

1943

	Conference Games			All Games		
	W	L	T	W	L	T
Michigan	6	0	0	8	1	0
Purdue	6	0	0	9	0	0
Northwestern	5	1	0	6	2	0
Indiana	2	3	1	4	4	2
Minnesota	2	3	0	5	4	0
Illinois	2	4	0	3	7	0
Ohio State	1	4	0	3	5	0
Wisconsin	1	6	0	1	9	0
Iowa	0	4	1	1	6	1

1944	Conference Games W	L	T	All Games W	L	T
Ohio State	6	0	0	9	0	0
Michigan	5	2	0	8	2	0
Purdue	4	2	0	5	5	0
Minnesota	3	2	1	5	3	1
Indiana	4	3	0	7	3	0
Illinois	3	3	0	5	4	1
Wisconsin	2	4	0	3	6	0
Northwestern	0	5	1	1	7	1
Iowa	0	6	0	1	7	0

1948	Conference Games W	L	T	All Games W	L	T
Michigan	6	0	0	9	0	0
Northwestern	5	1	0	7	2	0
Minnesota	5	2	0	7	2	0
Ohio State	3	3	0	6	3	0
Iowa	2	4	0	4	5	0
Purdue	2	4	0	4	5	0
Indiana	2	4	0	2	7	0
Illinois	2	5	0	3	6	0
Wisconsin	1	5	0	2	7	0

1945	Conference Games W	L	T	All Games W	L	T
Indiana	5	0	1	9	0	1
Michigan	5	1	0	7	3	0
Ohio State	5	2	0	7	2	0
Northwestern	3	3	1	4	4	1
Purdue	3	3	0	7	3	0
Wisconsin	2	3	1	3	4	2
Illinois	1	4	1	2	6	1
Minnesota	1	5	0	4	5	0
Iowa	1	5	0	2	7	0

1949	Conference Games W	L	T	All Games W	L	T
Ohio State	4	1	1	6	1	2
Michigan	4	1	1	6	2	1
Minnesota	4	2	0	7	2	0
Wisconsin	3	2	1	5	3	1
Illinois	3	3	1	3	4	2
Iowa	3	3	0	4	5	0
Northwestern	3	4	0	4	5	0
Purdue	2	4	0	4	5	0
Indiana	0	6	0	1	8	0

1946	Conference Games W	L	T	All Games W	L	T
Illinois	6	1	0	*8	2	0
Michigan	5	1	1	6	2	1
Indiana	4	2	0	6	3	0
Iowa	3	3	0	5	4	0
Minnesota	3	4	0	5	4	0
Northwestern	2	3	1	4	4	1
Ohio State	2	3	1	4	3	2
Wisconsin	2	5	0	4	5	0
Purdue	0	5	1	2	6	1

*Includes Illinois victory over UCLA, 45–14, in Rose Bowl game.

1950	Conference Games W	L	T	All Games W	L	T
Michigan	4	1	1	5	3	1
Ohio State	5	2	0	6	3	0
Wisconsin	5	2	0	6	3	0
Illinois	4	2	0	7	2	0
Northwestern	3	3	0	6	3	0
Iowa	2	4	0	3	5	1
Minnesota	1	4	1	1	7	1
Indiana	1	4	0	3	5	1
Purdue	1	4	0	2	7	0

1947	Conference Games W	L	T	All Games W	L	T
Michigan	6	0	0	9	0	0
Wisconsin	3	2	1	5	3	1
Minnesota	3	3	0	6	3	0
Purdue	3	3	0	5	4	0
Indiana	2	3	1	5	3	1
Iowa	2	3	1	3	5	1
Northwestern	2	4	0	3	6	0
Ohio State	1	4	1	2	6	1

1951	Conference Games W	L	T	All Games W	L	T
Illinois	5	0	1	8	0	1
Purdue	4	1	0	5	4	0
Wisconsin	5	1	1	7	1	1
Michigan	4	2	0	4	5	0
Ohio State	2	2	2	4	3	2
Northwestern	2	4	0	5	4	0
Minnesota	1	4	1	2	6	1
Indiana	1	5	0	2	7	0
Iowa	0	5	1	2	5	2

1952	Conference Games			All Games		
	W	L	T	W	L	T
Wisconsin	4	1	1	6	2	1
Purdue	4	1	1	4	3	2
Ohio State	5	2	0	6	3	0
Michigan	4	2	0	5	4	0
Minnesota	3	1	2	4	3	2
Illinois	2	5	0	4	5	0
Northwestern	2	5	0	2	6	1
Iowa	2	5	0	2	7	0
Indiana	1	5	0	2	7	0

1956	Conference Games			All Games		
	W	L	T	W	L	T
Iowa	5	1	0	8	1	0
Michigan	5	2	0	7	2	0
Minnesota	4	1	2	6	1	2
Michigan State	4	2	0	7	2	0
Ohio State	4	2	0	6	3	0
Northwestern	3	3	1	4	4	1
Purdue	1	4	2	3	4	2
Illinois	1	4	2	2	5	2
Wisconsin	0	4	3	1	5	3
Indiana	1	5	0	3	6	0

1953	Conference Games			All Games		
	W	L	T	W	L	T
Michigan State	5	1	0	8	1	0
Illinois	5	1	0	7	1	1
Wisconsin	4	1	1	6	2	1
Ohio State	4	3	0	6	3	0
Minnesota	3	3	1	4	4	1
Iowa	3	3	0	5	3	1
Michigan	3	3	0	6	3	0
Purdue	2	4	0	2	7	0
Indiana	1	5	0	2	7	0
Northwestern	0	6	0	3	6	0

1957	Conference Games			All Games		
	W	L	T	W	L	T
Ohio State	7	0	0	8	1	0
Michigan State	5	1	0	8	1	0
Iowa	4	1	1	7	1	1
Wisconsin	4	3	0	6	3	0
Purdue	4	3	0	5	4	0
Michigan	3	3	1	5	3	1
Illinois	3	4	0	4	5	0
Minnesota	3	5	0	4	5	0
Indiana	0	6	0	1	8	0
Northwestern	0	7	0	0	9	0

1954	Conference Games			All Games		
	W	L	T	W	L	T
Ohio State	7	0	0	9	0	0
Wisconsin	5	2	0	7	2	0
Michigan	5	2	0	6	3	0
Minnesota	4	2	0	7	2	0
Iowa	4	3	0	5	4	0
Purdue	3	3	0	5	3	1
Indiana	2	4	0	3	6	0
Michigan State	1	5	0	3	6	0
Northwestern	1	5	0	2	7	0
Illinois	0	6	0	1	8	0

1958	Conference Games			All Games		
	W	L	T	W	L	T
Iowa	5	1	0	7	1	1
Wisconsin	5	1	1	7	1	1
Ohio State	4	1	2	6	1	2
Purdue	3	1	2	6	1	2
Indiana	3	2	1	5	3	1
Illinois	4	3	0	4	5	0
Northwestern	3	4	0	5	4	0
Michigan	1	5	1	2	6	1
Minnesota	1	6	0	1	8	0
Michigan State	0	5	1	3	5	1

1955	Conference Games			All Games		
	W	L	T	W	L	T
Ohio State	6	0	0	7	2	0
Michigan State	5	1	0	8	1	0
Michigan	5	2	0	7	2	0
Purdue	4	2	1	5	3	1
Illinois	3	3	1	5	3	1
Wisconsin	3	4	0	4	5	0
Iowa	2	3	1	3	5	1
Minnesota	2	5	0	3	6	0
Indiana	1	5	0	3	6	0
Northwestern	0	6	1	0	8	1

1959	Conference Games			All Games		
	W	L	T	W	L	T
Wisconsin	5	2	0	7	2	0
Michigan State	4	2	0	5	4	0
Illinois	4	2	1	5	3	1
Purdue	4	2	1	5	2	2
Northwestern	4	3	0	6	3	0
Iowa	3	3	0	5	4	0
Michigan	3	4	0	4	5	0
Indiana	2	4	1	4	4	1
Ohio State	2	4	1	3	5	1
Minnesota	1	6	0	2	7	0

1960	Conference Games			All Games		
	W	L	T	W	L	T
Iowa	5	1	0	8	1	0
Minnesota	5	1	0	8	1	0
Ohio State	4	2	0	7	2	0
Michigan State	3	2	0	6	2	1
Illinois	2	4	0	5	4	0
Michigan	2	4	0	5	4	0
Northwestern	2	4	0	5	4	0
Purdue	2	4	0	4	4	1
Wisconsin	2	5	0	4	5	0
*Indiana	0	0	0	1	8	0

*Ineligible for title.

1964	Conference Games			All Games		
	W	L	T	W	L	T
Michigan	6	1	0	8	1	0
Ohio State	5	1	0	7	2	0
Purdue	5	2	0	6	3	0
Illinois	4	3	0	6	3	0
Minnesota	4	3	0	5	4	0
Michigan State	3	3	0	4	5	0
Wisconsin	2	5	0	3	6	0
Northwestern	2	5	0	3	6	0
Iowa	1	5	0	3	6	0
Indiana	1	5	0	2	7	0

1961	Conference Games			All Games		
	W	L	T	W	L	T
Ohio State	6	0	0	8	0	1
Minnesota	6	1	0	7	2	0
Michigan State	5	2	0	7	2	0
Purdue	4	2	0	6	3	0
Wisconsin	4	3	0	6	3	0
Michigan	3	3	0	6	3	0
Iowa	2	4	0	5	4	0
Northwestern	2	4	0	4	5	0
Indiana	0	6	0	2	7	0
Illinois	0	7	0	0	9	0

1965	Conference Games			All Games		
	W	L	T	W	L	T
Michigan State	7	0	0	10	0	0
Ohio State	6	1	0	7	2	0
Purdue	5	2	0	7	2	1
Minnesota	5	2	0	5	4	1
Illinois	4	3	0	6	4	0
Northwestern	3	4	0	4	6	0
Michigan	2	5	0	4	6	0
Wisconsin	2	5	0	2	7	1
Indiana	1	6	0	2	8	0
Iowa	0	7	0	1	9	0

1962	Conference Games			All Games		
	W	L	T	W	L	T
Wisconsin	6	1	0	8	1	0
Minnesota	5	2	0	6	2	1
Northwestern	4	2	0	7	2	0
Ohio State	4	2	0	6	3	0
Purdue	3	3	0	4	4	1
Michigan State	3	3	0	5	4	0
Iowa	3	3	0	4	5	0
Illinois	2	5	0	2	7	0
Indiana	1	5	0	3	6	0
Michigan	1	6	0	2	7	0

1966	Conference Games			All Games		
	W	L	T	W	L	T
Michigan State	7	0	0	9	0	1
Purdue	6	1	0	8	2	0
Michigan	4	3	0	6	4	0
Illinois	4	3	0	4	6	0
Minnesota	3	3	1	4	5	1
Ohio State	3	4	0	4	5	0
Northwestern	2	4	1	3	6	1
Wisconsin	2	4	1	3	6	1
Indiana	1	5	1	1	8	1
Iowa	1	6	0	2	8	0

1963	Conference Games			All Games		
	W	L	T	W	L	T
Illinois	5	1	1	7	1	1
Michigan State	4	1	1	6	2	1
Ohio State	4	1	1	5	3	1
Purdue	4	3	0	5	4	0
Michigan	2	3	2	3	4	2
Northwestern	3	4	0	5	4	0
Wisconsin	3	4	0	5	4	0
Iowa	2	3	1	3	3	2
Minnesota	2	5	0	3	6	0
Indiana	1	5	0	3	6	0

1967	Conference Games			All Games		
	W	L	T	W	L	T
Indiana	6	1	0	9	1	0
Purdue	6	1	0	8	2	0
Minnesota	6	1	0	8	2	0
Ohio State	5	2	0	6	3	0
Michigan State	3	4	0	3	7	0
Illinois	3	4	0	4	6	0
Michigan	3	4	0	4	6	0
Northwestern	2	5	0	3	7	0
Iowa	0	6	1	1	8	1
Wisconsin	0	6	1	0	9	1

1968	Conference Games			All Games		
	W	L	T	W	L	T
Ohio State	7	0	0	9	0	0
Michigan	6	1	0	8	2	0
Purdue	5	2	0	8	2	0
Minnesota	5	2	0	6	4	0
Indiana	4	3	0	6	4	0
Iowa	4	3	0	5	5	0
Michigan State	2	5	0	5	5	0
Northwestern	1	6	0	1	9	0
Illinois	1	6	0	1	9	0
Wisconsin	0	7	0	0	10	0

1972	Conference Games			All Games		
	W	L	T	W	L	T
Michigan	7	1	0	10	1	0
Ohio State	7	1	0	9	2	0
Purdue	6	2	0	6	5	0
Michigan State	5	2	1	5	5	1
Minnesota	4	4	0	4	7	0
Indiana	3	5	0	5	6	0
Illinois	3	5	0	3	8	0
Iowa	2	6	1	3	7	1
Wisconsin	2	6	0	4	7	0
Northwestern	1	8	0	2	9	0

1969	Conference Games			All Games		
	W	L	T	W	L	T
Michigan	6	1	0	8	2	0
Ohio State	6	1	0	8	1	0
Purdue	5	2	0	8	2	0
Minnesota	4	3	0	4	5	1
Indiana	3	4	0	4	6	0
Iowa	3	4	0	5	5	0
Northwestern	3	4	0	3	7	0
Wisconsin	3	4	0	3	7	0
Michigan State	2	5	0	4	6	0
Illinois	0	7	0	0	10	0

1973	Conference Games			All Games		
	W	L	T	W	L	T
Ohio State	7	0	1	9	0	1
Michigan	7	0	1	10	0	1
Minnesota	6	2	0	7	4	0
Northwestern	4	4	0	4	7	0
Illinois	4	4	0	5	6	0
Purdue	4	4	0	5	6	0
Michigan State	4	4	0	5	6	0
Wisconsin	3	5	0	3	8	0
Indiana	0	8	0	2	9	0
Iowa	0	8	0	0	11	0

1970	Conference Games			All Games		
	W	L	T	W	L	T
Ohio State	7	0	0	9	0	0
Michigan	6	1	0	9	1	0
Northwestern	6	1	0	6	4	0
Iowa	3	3	1	3	6	1
Michigan State	3	4	0	4	6	0
Wisconsin	3	4	0	4	5	1
Minnesota	2	4	1	3	6	1
Purdue	2	5	0	4	6	0
Illinois	1	6	0	3	7	0
Indiana	1	6	0	1	9	0

1974	Conference Games			All Games		
	W	L	T	W	L	T
Ohio State	7	1	0	10	1	0
Michigan	7	1	0	10	1	0
Michigan State	6	1	1	7	3	1
Wisconsin	5	3	0	7	4	0
Illinois	4	3	1	6	4	1
Purdue	3	5	0	4	6	1
Minnesota	2	6	0	4	7	0
Iowa	2	6	0	3	8	0
Northwestern	2	6	0	3	8	0
Indiana	1	7	0	1	10	0

1971	Conference Games			All Games		
	W	L	T	W	L	T
Michigan	8	0	0	11	1*	0
Northwestern	6	3	0	7	4	0
Ohio State	5	3	0	6	4	0
Illinois	5	3	0			
Michigan State	5	3	0	6	5	0
Purdue	3	5	0	4	6	0
Wisconsin	3	5	0	4	6	1
Minnesota	3	5	0	4	7	0
Indiana	1	6	0	1	9	0
Iowa	1	8	0	1	10	0

(*Michigan lost to Stanford in Rose Bowl.)

1975	Conference Games			All Games		
	W	L	T	W	L	T
Ohio State	8	0	0	11	1*	0
Michigan	7	1	0	8	1	2
Illinois	4	4	0	5	6	0
Michigan State	4	4	0	7	4	0
Purdue	4	4	0	4	7	0
Wisconsin	3	4	1	4	6	1
Iowa	3	5	0	3	8	0
Minnesota	3	5	0	6	5	0
Northwestern	2	6	0	3	8	0
Indiana	1	6	1	2	8	1

(*Ohio State lost to UCLA in Rose Bowl.)

Big Ten All-Americans
1896–1975

There are still riddles aplenty as to who originated the idea of selecting an All-American football team, but the strong probabilities are these:

Either Caspar Whitney, manager of *The Week's Sport* and the reigning sports writer of his day, or Walter Camp, or both in concert, hit upon the idea of picking a mythical All-American college football team. The popular theory is that the idea probably started with Whitney and he came to Camp with it. Because Whitney leaned heavily on Camp's inside information and acknowledged judgment on football, the leading authorities on the subject seem to favor the argument that Whitney and Camp together selected the All-American teams of 1889 and 1890 for *The Week's Sport*. Pudge Heffelfinger, all-time All-American from Yale, told me in 1953, shortly before his death, that "the All-America idea was originated in 1889 by Caspar Whitney." Pudge was on that first All-American team, so take your pick.

Documentary evidence establishes the fact that from 1891 through 1896, Whitney selected the All-American teams for *Harper's Weekly*. Tim Cohane, Yale football historian and for years sports editor of *Look* magazine, researched the question extensively and concluded: "In 1891 and in 1894, Whitney mentioned and listed in *Harper's* the All-American teams that had been chosen in 1889 and 1890.

However, neither in 1891 nor in 1894 did Whitney mention that the '89 and '90 selections had appeared in *The Week's Sport*. Nor did he mention Camp as a collaborator. The implication is clear enough, that he, Whitney, claimed authorship of the 1889 and 1890 All-American teams."

Whitney left on a world's tour in 1897, and in his absence, his friend Walter Camp picked the '97 team for *Harper's* and started the custom of choosing a second and third team as well as a first team. Camp brought the All-American team idea to *Collier's Weekly*, in 1898, and his selections for that season appeared in the January 7, 1899, issue of the magazine. From that time on, Camp picked the All-American team for *Collier's*, missing only the war year of 1917.

After Walter Camp's death in 1925, Grantland Rice took up the task of selecting the All-American team for *Collier's*. This led to the magazine's All-American Board. For Camp, a great part of the time, had worked in a far smaller football world. His territory had been limited to the East. His first 22 All-American players had been strictly all Harvard, Yale, and Princeton. Then, in 1891, John Adams of Pennsylvania crashed the sacred circle, followed by teammate Harry Thayer in 1892.

It was not until 1898—10 years after the All-American business began—that Chicago's incomparable kicker, Clarence Herschberger,

244

became the first recognized All-American from the Middle West. Football started in the East and for the next 30 years, until Michigan's vaunted point-a-minute team, the Ivy League was in the driver's seat. Later, football supremacy rolled overland from the East to the Midwest, then to the Far West—later to the South and Southwest—until it finally became an all-nation blend as the victory pendulum swung back and forth. Football, after much dragging of feet, finally became All-American.

By 1925, the spread of football skill, material, and coaching had covered the entire country. There no longer was any leading section. There were glittering stars from New Hampshire to Alabama, from New Jersey to Washington, from Texas to Michigan, from Nebraska to California, and from Arkansas to Minnesota and Ohio.

It was soon after this that Grantland Rice, realizing no one man could possibly cover millions of square miles of football territory, decided to expand his staff of college observers. These were selected from well-known football writers from each section of the nation, men who not only knew their stuff but who, in addi-

tion, were close to the leading coaches and officials who regularly gave out their confidential opinions of the year's finest players. Each coach was asked to name not only the best players on his squad, but also the best on each team he had played against. As there were hundreds of coaches involved, this check was as reliable as any that could be devised.

Since *Collier's* suspended publication some years ago, *Look* magazine took over the All-American sweepstakes, following a formula similar to *Collier's*. And when *Look* suspended publication, the American Football Coaches Association filled the gap.

Today, there are a number of recognized groups that pick All-American teams: Associated Press (AP), United Press International (UPI), Newspaper Enterprise Association (NEA), Football Writers Association of America, Newsweek Magazine, The Sporting News, and on and on and on. Between the years 1898 and 1975, there have been a total of 379 players from the Big Ten who were first-team selections on the various accredited All-American teams. Their names are listed in the following pages.

Team Records

UNIVERSITY OF CHICAGO

Chicago, Illinois
Established 1891
Color, Maroon
Football discontinued after 1939 season

Head Coaches

Amos Alonzo Stagg, 1892–1933
Clark Shaughnessy, 1933–1939

All-American Players

Clarence Herschberger, fullback, 1898
Fred Speik, end, 1904
Walter Eckersall, quarterback, 1904–05–06
Mark Catlin, end, 1905
Walter Steffen, quarterback, 1908
Paul Des Jardiens, center, 1913

Charles Higgins, guard, 1917
Chuck McGuire, 1920–21
John Thomas, fullback, 1922
Franklin Gowdy, tackle, 1924
Joe Pondelik, guard, 1924
Elmore Patterson, center, 1934

Jay Berwanger, quarterback, 1934–35

Scores
1892–1939

1892			1893			1894		
12	HPHS	0	0	Lake Forest	10	32	EHS	0
12	Englewood HS	6	12	Northwestern	6	22	EHS	0
16	HPHS	10	10	Michigan	6	46	Manual Training	0
18	YMCA	4	10	Purdue	20	4	Chicago AA	12
26	HPHS	0	28	Cincinnati	0	46	Northwestern	0
18	YMCA	12	12	Oberlin	33	14	Rush	6
0	Northwestern	0	18	Armour	6	16	Beloit	0
4	Northwestern	6	6	Northwestern	6	20	Chicago AA 2nds.	0
18	Lake Forest	18	14	Lake Forest	14	0	Wisconsin	30
10	Michigan	18	10	Michigan	28	0	Chicago AA	30
10	Illinois	4	22	Northwestern	14	18	Iowa	18
0	Purdue	38	8	Notre Dame	0	26	Prairie AC	0
12	Illinois	28	52	"The Reserves"	0	6	Purdue	10

Throughout records section, scores in lefthand column are those of the Big Ten team; opposing team scores appear in righthand column.

4	Eng. YMCA	0
28	Lake Forest	0
36	Northwestern	0
4	Michigan	6
24	Stanford	4
0	Stanford	12
0	Reliance AC	6
52	Salt Lake YMCA	

1895

28	Englewood HS	0
42	Englewood YMCA	6
24	HPHS	0
28	Eureka	0
8	CAA	0
52	Lake Forest	0
6	Northwestern	22
24	Armour	4
6	Minnesota	10
22	Wisconsin	12
16	Western Res.	0
6	Northwestern	0
0	Michigan	12

1896

24	Englewood HS	0
24	HPHS	0
12	Englewood HS	0
43	Wheaton	0
48	Eureka	0
43	Monmouth	0
34	Hahneman Medical	0
6	Iowa	0
18	Notre Dame	0
30	Oberlin	0
36	Armour	0
6	Northwestern	46
12	Illinois	0
0	Wisconsin	24
0	Lake Forest	0
18	Northwestern	6
7	Michigan	6

1897

22	HPHS	0
11	HPHS	0
21	Englewood HS	0
31	Monmouth	4
71	Lake Forest	0
24	Armour	0
39	Beloit	6
21	Northwestern	6
18	Illinois	12
34	Notre Dame	5
8	Wisconsin	23
21	Michigan	12

1898

22	Knox	0
8	Rush	0
24	Monmouth	0
22	P. and Surg.	0

38	Iowa	0
21	Beloit	0
34	Northwestern	5
11	Pennsylvania	23
17	Purdue	0
6	Wisconsin	0
11	Michigan	12

1899

40	Knox	0
12	P. and Surg.	0
23	Notre Dame	6
5	Iowa	5
29	Dixon	0
17	Cornell	6
58	Oberlin	0
5	Pennsylvania	5
44	Purdue	0
76	Northwestern	0
35	Beloit	0
29	Minnesota	0
17	Brown	6
17	Wisconsin	0

1900

24	Lombard	0
29	Monmouth	0
16	Knox	0
23	Dixon	5
17	Purdue	5
40	Rush	0
6	Minnesota	6
6	Brown	11
0	Pennsylvania	41
0	Iowa	17
0	Northwestern	5
5	Wisconsin	39
15	Michigan	6

1901

38	Lombard	0
23	Monmouth	0
12	Milwaukee Medical	0
6	Knox	0
22	Illinois Wesleyan	0
5	Purdue	5
0	Illinois	24
0	Pennsylvania	11
17	Beloit	17
5	Northwestern	6
0	Michigan	22
0	Wisconsin	35

1902

27	Lombard	6
24	Monmouth	0
53	Ft. Sheridan	0
5	Knox	0
21	Cornell College	0
33	Purdue	0
12	Northwestern	0
6	Illinois	0

18	Beloit	0
39	Indiana	0
0	Michigan	21
11	Wisconsin	0

1903

34	Lombard	0
23	Lawrence	0
108	Monmouth	0
34	Indiana	0
23	Cornell College	0
22	Purdue	0
40	Rush	0
0	Northwestern	0
18	Illinois	6
15	Wisconsin	6
17	Haskell	11
6	West Point	10
0	Michigan	28

1904

29	Lawrence	0
40	Lombard	5
56	Indiana	0
20	Purdue	0
39	Iowa	0
32	Northwestern	0
6	Illinois	6
68	Texas	0
12	Michigan	22
18	Wisconsin	11

1905

15	Wabash	0
38	Beloit	0
42	Iowa	0
16	Indiana	5
4	Wisconsin	0
32	Northwestern	0
19	Purdue	0
44	Illinois	0
2	Michigan	0

1906

39	Purdue	0
33	Indiana	8
2	Minnesota	4
63	Illinois	0
38	Nebraska	5

1907

27	Indiana	6
42	Illinois	6
18	Minnesota	12
56	Purdue	0
4	Carlisle	18

1908

39	Purdue	0
29	Indiana	6
11	Illinois	6

29	Minnesota	0
6	Cornell	6
18	Wisconsin	12

1909

40	Purdue	0
21	Indiana	0
14	Illinois	8
6	Minnesota	20
34	Northwestern	0
6	Cornell	6
6	Wisconsin	6

1910

0	Indiana	6
0	Illinois	3
10	Northwestern	0
0	Minnesota	24
14	Purdue	5
0	Cornell	18
0	Wisconsin	0

1911

23	Indiana	6
11	Purdue	3
24	Illinois	0
0	Minnesota	30
9	Northwestern	3
6	Cornell	0
5	Wisconsin	0

1912

13	Indiana	0
34	Iowa	14
7	Purdue	0
12	Wisconsin	30
3	Northwestern	0
10	Illinois	0
7	Minnesota	0

1913

21	Indiana	7
23	Iowa	6
6	Purdue	0
28	Illinois	7
14	Northwestern	0
13	Minnesota	7
19	Wisconsin	0

1914

34	Indiana	0
28	Northwestern	0
7	Iowa	0
21	Purdue	0
0	Wisconsin	0
7	Illinois	21
7	Minnesota	13

1915

7	Northwestern	0
13	Indiana	7

7	Purdue	0
14	Wisconsin	13
35	Haskell	0
7	Minnesota	20
0	Illinois	10

1916

0	Carleton	7
22	Indiana	0
0	Northwestern	10
7	Wisconsin	30
16	Purdue	7
20	Illinois	7
0	Minnesota	49

1917

48	Vanderbilt	0
27	Purdue	0
7	Northwestern	0
0	Illinois	0
0	Minnesota	33
0	Wisconsin	18

1918

7	Naval Reserve	14
3	Purdue	7
0	Michigan	13
6	Northwestern	21
0	Illinois	29
0	Minnesota	7

1919

123	Great Lakes	0
16	Purdue	0
41	Northwestern	0
0	Illinois	10
13	Michigan	0
9	Iowa	6
3	Wisconsin	10

1920

20	Purdue	0
41	Wabash	0
10	Iowa	0
6	Ohio State	7
0	Illinois	3
0	Michigan	14
0	Wisconsin	3

1921

41	Northwestern	0
9	Purdue	0
9	Princeton	0
35	Colorado	0
0	Ohio State	7
14	Illinois	6
3	Wisconsin	0

1922

20	Georgia	0
15	Northwestern	7

12	Purdue	0
18	Princeton	21
14	Ohio State	9
9	Illinois	0
0	Wisconsin	0

1923

34	Michigan Ag.	0
10	Colorado Ag.	0
13	Northwestern	0
20	Purdue	6
0	Illinois	7
27	Indiana	0
17	Ohio State	3
13	Wisconsin	6

1924

0	Missouri	3
3	Ohio State	3
19	Brown	7
23	Indiana	0
19	Purdue	6
0	Wisconsin	0
21	Illinois	21
3	Northwestern	0

1925

7	Dartmouth	33
9	Kentucky	0
3	Ohio State	3
0	Pennsylvania	7
6	Purdue	0
7	Wisconsin	20
6	Illinois	13
6	Northwestern	0

1926

21	Maryland	0
12	Florida	6
0	Ohio State	18
0	Pennsylvania	27
0	Purdue	6
7	Wisconsin	14
0	Illinois	7
7	Northwestern	38

1927

7	Oklahoma	13
13	Indiana	0
7	Purdue	6
13	Pennsylvania	7
7	Ohio	13
0	Michigan	14
6	Illinois	15
12	Wisconsin	0

1928

0	South Carolina	6
0	Ripon (Res.)	12
47	Wyoming	0
3	Lake Forest	0

0	Iowa	13
7	Minnesota	33
0	Purdue	40
13	Pennsylvania	20
0	Wisconsin	25
0	Illinois	40

1929

27	Beloit	0
9	Lake Forest	6
13	Indiana	7
10	Ripon	0
18	Terre Haute	0
0	Purdue	26
15	Princeton	7
6	Wisconsin	20
6	Illinois	20
26	Washington	6

1930

19	Ripon	0
7	Hillsdale Res.	6
0	Wisconsin	34
0	Florida	19
0	Mississippi	0
0	Princeton	0
7	Purdue	26
0	Illinois	28
0	Michigan	16

1931

12	Cornell College	0
0	Hillsdale Res.	7
7	Michigan	13
0	Yale	27
6	Indiana	32
6	Purdue	14
13	Arkansas	13
13	Illinois	6
7	Wisconsin	12
7	Iowa	0
0	Indiana	6

1932

41	Monmouth College	0
7	Yale	7
20	Knox College	0
13	Indiana	7
7	Illinois	13
0	Purdue	37
0	Michigan	12
7	Wisconsin	18

1933

32	Cornell College	0
40	Washington	0
0	Purdue	14
0	Michigan	28
0	Wisconsin	0
7	Indiana	7
0	Illinois	7
39	Dartmouth	0

1934

19	Carroll	0
27	Michigan	0
21	Indiana	0
19	Missouri	6
20	Purdue	26
0	Ohio State	33
7	Minnesota	35
0	Illinois	6

1935

7	Nebraska	28
31	Carroll	0
31	West State Teachers	6
0	Purdue	19
13	Wisconsin	7
13	Ohio State	20
0	Indiana	24
7	Illinois	6

1936

34	Lawrence	0
0	Vanderbilt	37
6	Butler	6
7	Purdue	35
7	Wisconsin	6
0	Ohio State	44
7	Indiana	20
7	Illinois	18

1937

0	Vanderbilt	18
0	Wisconsin	27
7	Princeton	16
0	Ohio State	39
12	Michigan	13
26	Beloit	9
0	Illinois	21

1938

0	Bradley	0
7	Michigan	45
14	Iowa	27
7	Ohio State	42
34	DePauw	14
13	Harvard	47
0	College of Pacific	32
0	Illinois	34

1939

0	Beloit	6
12	Wabash	2
0	Harvard	61
0	Michigan	85
0	Virginia	47
0	Ohio State	61
25	Oberlin	0
0	Illinois	46

UNIVERSITY OF ILLINOIS

Champaign, Illinois
Established 1867
Colors, Orange and Blue
Nickname, Fighting Illini

Head Coaches

George A. Huff, 1895–1899
Fred L. Smith, 1900
Edgar G. Holt, 1901–1902
George Woodruff, 1903
George A. Huff, 1904–1905
J. M. Lindgren, 1906
A. R. Hall, 1907–1911

Fred Lowenthal,
E. A. White, 1912
Bob Zuppke, 1913–1941
Ray Eliot, 1942–1959
Pete Elliott, 1960–1966
Jim Valek, 1967–1970
Bob Blackman, 1971–

All-American Players

Ralph Chapman, guard, 1914
Perry Graves, end, 1914
Bart Macomber, halfback, 1915
John Depler, center, 1918
Charles Carney, end, 1920
Jim McMillen, guard, 1923
Red Grange, halfback, 1923–24–25
Bernie Shively, guard, 1926
Russ Crane, guard, 1927
Bob Reitsch, center, 1927
Leroy Wietz, guard, 1928
Al (Butch) Nowack, tackle, 1928
Lou Gordon, tackle, 1929
Jim Reeder, tackle, 1939

Alex Agase, guard, 1942, 1946
Buddy Young, halfback, 1944
Ralph Serpico, guard, 1944
Eddelman, Dwight, back, 1949
Albert Tate, tackle, 1950
Bill Vohaska, center, 1950
John Karras, halfback, 1951
Al Brosky, safety, 1951
Charles Boerio, center-linebacker, 1951
J. C. Caroline, halfback, 1953
Bill Burrell, guard, 1959
Dick Butkus, linebacker, 1963–64
George Donnelly, safety, 1964
Jim Grabowski, fullback, 1964–65

Scores
1890–1975

1890

0	Illinois Wesleyan	16
0	Purdue	62
12	Illinois Wesleyan	6

1891

0	Lake Forest	8
	Forfeited later to Illinois	
26	Bloomington	0
40	Eureka	0
44	Illinois Wesleyan	4
12	Knox	0
20	Bloomington	12

1892

6	Purdue	12
16	Northwestern	16
22	Washington	0
20	Doane College	0
0	Nebraska	6
26	Baker	10
4	Kansas	26
42	Kansas City AC	0
	Wisconsin (Forfeit to Illinois)	
38	Englewood HS	0
4	Chicago	4
	Beloit (Forfeit to Illinois)	
34	DePauw	0
28	Chicago	12

1893

60	Wabash	6
14	DePauw	4
0	Northwestern	0
4	Chicago AA	10
24	Oberlin	34
18	Pastime AC	16
26	Purdue	26
10	Lake Forest	10

1894

36	Wabash	6
0	Chicago AC	14
54	Lake Forest	6
66	Northwestern	0
2	Purdue	22
6	Chicago (Forfeit)	0
14	Indianapolis LA	18
10	Pastime AC	0

1895

48	Wabash	0
0	Chicago AC	8
79	Illinois College	0
10	Wisconsin	10
38	Rush-Lake For.	0
38	Northwestern	4
2	Purdue	6

1896

38	Lake Forest	0
70	Knox	4
10	Missouri	0
22	Oberlin	6
0	Chicago	12
4	Northwestern	10
4	Purdue	4

1897

26	Eureka	0
6	Phys. & Surg.	0
36	Lake Forest	0
34	Purdue	4
12	Chicago	18
74	Knox	0
6	Carlisle Indians	23

1898

18	Illinois Wesleyan	0
6	Phys. & Surg.	11
0	Notre Dame	5
16	DePauw	0
10	Alumni	6
17	Alumni	23
5	Michigan	12
0	Carlisle Indians	11
11	Minnesota	10

1899

6	Illinois Wesleyan	0
5	Knox	0
0	Indiana	5
0	Michigan	5
0	Alumni	0
0	Wisconsin	23
0	Purdue	5
29	St. Louis	0
0	Iowa	58

1900

26	Rose Poly	0
63	DePauw	0
21	Illinois Wesleyan	0
6	Phys. & Surg.	0
16	Knox	0
35	Lombard	0
0	Northwestern	0
0	Michigan	12
17	Purdue	5
0	Minnesota	23
0	Indiana	0
0	Wisconsin	27

1901

39	Englewood HS	0
52	Marion Sims	0
23	Phys. & Surg.	0
21	Washington	0
24	Chicago	0
11	Northwestern	17
18	Indiana	0

27	Iowa	0
28	Purdue	6
0	Minnesota	16

1902

34	North Division	6
45	Englewood	0
22	Osteopaths	0
33	Monmouth	0
24	Haskell	10
44	Washington	0
29	Purdue	5
0	Chicago	6
47	Indiana	0
5	Minnesota	17
0	Ohio State	0
17	Northwestern	0
80	Iowa	0

1903

45	Englewood	5
43	Lombard	0
36	Osteopaths	0
29	Knox	5
40	Phys. & Surg.	0
64	Rush	0
54	Chi. Dents.	0
24	Purdue	0
6	Chicago	18
14	Northwestern	12
0	Indiana	17
0	Minnesota	32
0	Iowa	12
0	Nebraska	16

1904

10	Northwestern Col.	0
23	Wabash	2
11	Knox	0
26	Phys. & Surg.	0
31	Washington U.	0
10	Indiana	0
24	Purdue	6
6	Chicago	6
46	Ohio State	0
6	Northwestern	12
29	Iowa	0
10	Nebraska	16

1905

6	Knox	0
6	Wabash	0
24	Northwestern	0
12	St. Louis	6
0	Purdue	29
30	Phys. & Surg.	0
0	Michigan	33
0	Chicago	44
6	Nebraska	24

1906

0	Wabash	0

9	Michigan	28
6	Wisconsin	16
0	Chicago	63
5	Purdue	0

1907

6	Chicago	42
15	Wisconsin	4
21	Purdue	4
12	Iowa	25
10	Indiana	6

1908

17	Monmouth	6
6	Marquette	6
6	Chicago	11
10	Indiana	0
22	Iowa	0
15	Purdue	6
64	Northwestern	8

1909

23	Millikin	0
2	Kentucky	6
8	Chicago	14
24	Purdue	6
6	Indiana	5
35	Northwestern	0
17	Syracuse	8

1910

13	Millikin	0
29	Drake	0
3	Chicago	0
11	Purdue	0
3	Indiana	0
27	Northwestern	0
3	Syracuse	0

1911

33	Millikin	0
9	St. Louis	0
0	Chicago	24
12	Purdue	3
0	Indiana	0
27	Northwestern	13
0	Minnesota	11

1912

87	Illinois Wesleyan	3
13	Washington U.	0
13	Indiana	7
0	Minnesota	13
9	Purdue	9
0	Chicago	10
0	Northwestern	6

1913

21	Kentucky	0
24	Missouri	7

37	Northwestern	0
10	Indiana	0
7	Chicago	28
0	Purdue	0
9	Minnesota	19

1914

37	Chris. Bros.	0
51	Indiana	0
37	Ohio State	0
33	Northwestern	0
21	Minnesota	6
21	Chicago	7
24	Wisconsin	9

1915

36	Haskell Indians	0
75	Rolla Mines	7
3	Ohio State	3
36	Northwestern	6
6	Minnesota	6
17	Wisconsin	3
10	Chicago	0

1916

30	Kansas	0
3	Colgate	15
6	Ohio State	7
14	Purdue	7
14	Minnesota	9
7	Chicago	20
0	Wisconsin	0

1917

22	Kansas	0
44	Oklahoma	0
7	Wisconsin	0
27	Purdue	0
0	Chicago	0
0	Ohio State	13
6	Minnesota	27
28	Camp Funston	0

1918

3	Chanute	0
0	Great Lakes	7
0	Muni. Pier	7
19	Iowa	0
22	Wisconsin	0
13	Ohio State	0
29	Chicago	0

1919

14	Purdue	7
9	Iowa	7
10	Wisconsin	14
10	Chicago	0
10	Minnesota	6
29	Michigan	7
9	Ohio State	7

1920

41	Drake	0
20	Iowa	3
7	Michigan	6
17	Minnesota	7
3	Chicago	0
9	Wisconsin	14
0	Ohio State	7

1921

52	South Dakota	0
2	Iowa	14
0	Wisconsin	20
0	Michigan	3
21	DePauw	0
6	Chicago	14
7	Ohio State	0

1922

7	Butler	10
7	Iowa	8
0	Michigan	24
6	Northwestern	3
3	Wisconsin	0
0	Chicago	9
3	Ohio State	6

1923

24	Nebraska	7
21	Butler	7
9	Iowa	6
29	Northwestern	0
7	Chicago	0
10	Wisconsin	0
27	Mississippi A & M	0
9	Ohio State	0

1924

9	Nebraska	6
40	Butler	10
39	Michigan	14
45	DePauw	0
36	Iowa	0
21	Chicago	21
7	Minnesota	20
7	Ohio State	0

1925

0	Nebraska	14
16	Butler	13
10	Iowa	12
0	Michigan	3
24	Pennsylvania	2
13	Chicago	6
21	Wabash	0
14	Ohio State	9

1926

27	Coe	0
38	Butler	7
13	Iowa	6
0	Michigan	13
3	Pennsylvania	0
7	Chicago	0
27	Wabash	13
6	Ohio State	7

1927

19	Bradley	0
58	Butler	0
12	Iowa State	12
7	Northwestern	6
14	Michigan	0
14	Iowa	0
15	Chicago	6
13	Ohio State	0

1928

33	Bradley	6
31	Coe	0
13	Indiana	7
6	Northwestern	0
0	Michigan	3
14	Butler	0
40	Chicago	0
8	Ohio State	0

1929

25	Kansas	0
45	Bradley	0
7	Iowa	7
14	Michigan	0
0	Northwestern	7
17	Army	7
20	Chicago	6
27	Ohio State	0

1930

7	Iowa State	0
27	Butler	0
0	Northwestern	32
0	Purdue	25
9	Ohio State	12
7	Michigan	15
28	Chicago	0
0	Army	13

1931

20	St. Louis	6
0	Purdue	7
20	Bradley	0
0	Michigan	35
6	Northwestern	32
6	Wisconsin	7
6	Chicago	13
0	Ohio State	40

1932

13	Coe	0
20	Miami	7
20	Bradley	0
0	Northwestern	26
0	Michigan	32
13	Chicago	7
12	Wisconsin	20
18	Indiana	6
0	Ohio State	3

1933

13	Drake	0
21	Washington	6
21	Wisconsin	0
0	Army	6
6	Michigan	7
3	Northwestern	0
7	Chicago	0
6	Ohio State	0

1934

40	Bradley	7
12	Washington	7
14	Ohio State	13
7	Michigan	6
7	Army	0
14	Northwestern	3
3	Wisconsin	7
6	Chicago	0

1935

0	Ohio	6
28	Washington	6
19	Southern California	0
0	Iowa	19
3	Northwestern	10
3	Michigan	0
0	Ohio State	6
6	Chicago	7

1936

9	DePaul	6
13	Washington	7
6	Southern California	24
0	Iowa	0
2	Northwestern	13
9	Michigan	6
0	Ohio State	13
18	Chicago	7

1937

20	Ohio	6
0	DePaul	0
0	Notre Dame	0
6	Indiana	13
6	Michigan	7
6	Northwestern	0
0	Ohio State	19
21	Chicago	0

1938

0	Ohio	6

Except for a heartbreaking 7–3 loss to Wisconsin in the next-to-the-last game of 1934, Illinois came just this far from an unbeaten record and a tie for the Big Ten title. The team was led by its brilliant quarterback, captain Jack Beynon, shown here with coach Zuppke. A highlight of the 1934 season was the Illini victory over powerful Ohio State, 14–13. "When Illinois came out onto the field they looked like a bunch of high school kids dressed up in their older brothers' football suits," said Red Grange. "The experts didn't give them a chance."

44	DePaul	7
12	Indiana	2
6	Notre Dame	14
0	Northwestern	13
0	Michigan	14
14	Ohio State	32
34	Chicago	0

1939

0	Bradley	0
0	California	26
6	Indiana	7
0	Northwestern	13
16	Michigan	7
7	Wisconsin	0
0	Ohio State	21
46	Chicago	0

1940

31	Bradley	0
7	Southern California	13
0	Michigan	28
0	Notre Dame	26
6	Wisconsin	13
14	Northwestern	32
6	Ohio State	14
7	Iowa	18

1941

45	Miami	0
6	Minnesota	34
40	Drake	0
14	Notre Dame	49
0	Michigan	20
0	Iowa	21
7	Ohio State	12
0	Northwestern	27

1942

46	South Dakota	6
67	Butler	0
20	Minnesota	13
12	Iowa	7
14	Notre Dame	21
14	Michigan	28
14	Northwestern	7
20	Ohio State	44
0	Great Lakes	6
20	Camp Grant	0

1943

0	Camp Grant	23
18	Iowa Seahawks	32
21	Purdue	40
25	Wisconsin	7
33	Pittsburgh	25
0	Notre Dame	47
6	Michigan	42
19	Iowa	10
26	Ohio State	29
6	Northwestern	53

1944

79	Illinois State Normal	0
26	Indiana	18
26	Great Lakes	26
19	Purdue	35
40	Iowa	6
39	Pittsburgh	5
7	Notre Dame	13
12	Ohio State	26
25	Northwestern	6

1945

23	Pittsburgh	6
0	Notre Dame	7
0	Indiana	6
7	Wisconsin	7
0	Michigan	19
6	Great Lakes	12
48	Iowa	7
2	Ohio State	27
7	Northwestern	13

1946

33	Pittsburgh	7
6	Notre Dame	26
7	Michigan	14
43	Purdue	7
7	Indiana	14
27	Wisconsin	21
13	Michigan	9
7	Iowa	0
16	Ohio State	7
20	Northwestern	0

1947

14	Pittsburgh	0
35	Iowa	12
0	Army	0
40	Minnesota	13
7	Purdue	14
60	Western Michigan	14
28	Ohio State	7
13	Northwestern	28

1948

40	Kansas State	0
16	Wisconsin	20

Dwight (Dyke) Eddleman, an 11-letter star at Illinois and Conference Medal winner, culminated a brilliant intercollegiate career with a 43.3-yard punting average and All-American selection in 1949.

21	Army	26
0	Minnesota	6
10	Purdue	6
20	Michigan	28
14	Iowa	0
7	Iowa State	34
7	Northwestern	20

1949

20	Iowa State	20
13	Wisconsin	13
20	Iowa	14
20	Missouri	27
19	Purdue	0
0	Michigan	13
33	Indiana	14
17	Ohio State	30
7	Northwestern	9

1950

28	Ohio U.	2
6	Wisconsin	7
14	UCLA	6
20	Washington	13
20	Indiana	0
7	Michigan	0
21	Iowa	7
14	Ohio State	7
7	Northwestern	14

1951

27	UCLA	13

14	Wisconsin	10
41	Syracuse	20
27	Washington	20
21	Indiana	0
7	Michigan	0
40	Iowa	13
0	Ohio State	0
3	Northwestern	0
40	*Stanford	7
	*Rose Bowl	

1952

33	Iowa State	7
6	Wisconsin	20
48	Washington	14
7	Minnesota	13
12	Purdue	40
22	Michigan	13
33	Iowa	13
7	Ohio State	27
26	Northwestern	28

1953

21	Nebraska	21
33	Stanford	21
41	Ohio State	20
27	Minnesota	7
20	Syracuse	13
21	Purdue	0
19	Michigan	3
7	Wisconsin	34
39	Northwestern	14

1954

12	Penn. State	14
2	Stanford	12
7	Ohio State	40
6	Minnesota	19
34	Syracuse	6
14	Purdue	28
7	Michigan	14
14	Wisconsin	27
7	Northwestern	20

1955

20	California	13
40	Iowa State	0
12	Ohio State	27
21	Minnesota	13
7	Michigan State	21
0	Purdue	13
25	Michigan	6
17	Wisconsin	14
7	Northwestern	7

1956

32	California	20
13	Washington	28
6	Ohio State	26
13	Minnesota	16
20	Michigan State	13
7	Purdue	7
7	Michigan	17
13	Wisconsin	13
13	Northwestern	14

1957

6	UCLA	16
40	Colgate	0
7	Ohio State	21
34	Minnesota	13
14	Michigan State	19
6	Purdue	21
20	Michigan	19
13	Wisconsin	24
27	Northwestern	0

1958

14	UCLA	18
13	Duke	15
13	Ohio State	19
20	Minnesota	8
16	Michigan State	0
8	Purdue	31
21	Michigan	8
12	Wisconsin	31
27	Northwestern	20

1959

0	Indiana	20
20	Army	14
9	Ohio State	0
14	Minnesota	6
9	Penn State	20
7	Purdue	7
15	Michigan	20
9	Wisconsin	6
28	Northwestern	0

1960

17	Indiana	6
33	West Virginia	0
7	Ohio State	34
10	Minnesota	21
10	Penn State	8
14	Purdue	12
7	Michigan	8
35	Wisconsin	14
7	Northwestern	14

1961

7	Washington	20
7	Northwestern	28
0	Ohio State	44
0	Minnesota	33
10	Southern California	14
9	Purdue	23
6	Michigan	38
7	Wisconsin	55
7	Michigan State	34

1962

7	Washington	28
0	Northwestern	45
15	Ohio State	51
0	Minnesota	17
16	Southern California	28
14	Purdue	10
10	Michigan	14
6	Wisconsin	35
7	Michigan State	6

1963

10	California	0
10	Northwestern	9
20	Ohio State	20
16	Minnesota	6
18	UCLA	12
41	Purdue	21
8	Michigan	14
17	Wisconsin	7
13	Michigan State	0
17	*Washington	7

*Rose Bowl

1964

20	California	14
17	Northwestern	6
0	Ohio State	26
14	Minnesota	0
26	UCLA	7
14	Purdue	26
6	Michigan	21
29	Wisconsin	0
16	Michigan State	0

1965

10	Oregon State	12
41	Southern Methodist	0
12	Michigan State	22
14	Ohio State	28
34	Indiana	13
28	Duke	14
21	Purdue	0
3	Michigan	23
51	Wisconsin	0
20	Northwestern	6

1966

7	Southern Methodist	26
14	Missouri	21
10	Michigan State	26
10	Ohio State	9
24	Indiana	10
3	Stanford	6
21	Purdue	25
28	Michigan	21
49	Wisconsin	14
7	Northwestern	35

1967

0	Florida	14
34	Pittsburgh	6
7	Indiana	20
7	Minnesota	10
7	Notre Dame	47
17	Ohio State	13
9	Purdue	42
14	Michigan	21
27	Northwestern	21
21	Iowa	19

1968

7	Kansas	47
10	Missouri	44
14	Indiana	28
10	Minnesota	17
8	Notre Dame	51
24	Ohio State	31
17	Purdue	35
0	Michigan	36
14	Northwestern	0
13	Iowa	37

1969

18	Washington	19
6	Missouri	37
20	Iowa State	47
6	Northwestern	10
20	Indiana	41
0	Ohio State	41
22	Purdue	49
0	Michigan	57
14	Wisconsin	55
0	Iowa	40

1970

20	Oregon	16
9	Tulane	23
27	Syracuse	0
0	Northwestern	48
25	Indiana	30
29	Ohio State	48
23	Purdue	21
0	Michigan	42
17	Wisconsin	29
16	Iowa	22

1971

0	Michigan State	10
0	North Carolina	27
0	Southern California	28
14	Washington	52
10	Ohio State	24
6	Michigan	35
21	Purdue	7
24	Northwestern	7
22	Indiana	21
35	Wisconsin	27
31	Iowa	0

1972

0	Michigan State	24
20	Southern California	55
11	Washington	31

17	Penn State	35
7	Ohio State	26
7	Michigan	31
14	Purdue	20
43	Northwestern	13
37	Indiana	20
27	Wisconsin	7
14	Iowa	15

1973

28	Indiana	14
27	California	7
10	West Virginia	17
0	Stanford	24
15	Purdue	13
6	Michigan State	3

50	Iowa	0
0	Ohio State	30
6	Michigan	21
16	Minnesota	19
6	Northwestern	9

1974

16	Indiana	0
41	Stanford	7
21	Washington State	19
14	California	31
27	Purdue	23
21	Michigan State	21
12	Iowa	14
7	Ohio State	49
6	Michigan	14

17	Minnesota	14
28	Northwestern	14

1975

27	Iowa	12
20	Missouri	30
13	Texas A & M	43
27	Washington State	21
42	Minnesota	23
24	Purdue	26
21	Michigan State	19
9	Wisconsin	18
3	Ohio State	40
15	Michigan	21
28	Northwestern	7

INDIANA UNIVERSITY

Bloomington, Indiana
Established 1820
Colors, Cream and Crimson
Nickname, Hoosiers

Head Coaches

Billy Herod, 1891
(no established coach, 1892–93)
Ferbert and Huddleston, 1894
Dana Osgood & Wren, 1895
Madison Gonterman, 1896–1897
James Horne, 1898–1904
James Sheldon, 1905–1913
Clarence Childs, 1914–1915
Ewald Stiehm, 1916–1921
Jim Herron, 1922

William Ingram, 1923–1925
Harlan Page, 1926–1930
Earle Hayes, 1931–1933
A. N. (Bo) McMillin, 1934–1947
Clyde Smith, 1948–1951
Bernie Crimmins, 1952–1956
Bob Hicks, 1957
Phil Dickens, 1958–1964
John Pont, 1965–1972
Lee Corso, 1973

All-American Players

Clare Randolph, center, 1928
Chuck Bennett, halfback, 1928
Vern Huffman, quarterback, 1936
Corby Davis, fullback, 1937
Bill Hillenbrand, halfback, 1941–42
Pete Pihos, end, 1943, 1945
Bob Hoernschemeyer, quarterback, 1943
John Tavener, center, 1944
Bob Ravensberg, end, 1945
George Taliaferro, halfback, 1945–47–48
Howard Brown, guard, 1945
Russ Deal, tackle, 1945
Ben Raimondi, quarterback, 1946
John Cannady, center, 1946

In 1928, chunky, hard-running Chuck Bennett earned a niche in the Indiana Hall of Fame by becoming the Hoosiers' first All-American football player.

Brad Bomba, end, 1956
Mike Rabold, tackle, 1958
Ted Aucreman, end, 1958
Earl Faison, end, 1960
Marv Woodson, halfback, 1963
Tom Nowatzke, fullback, 1964
Don Croftcheck, guard, 1964

Gary Cassells, guard, 1967
John Isenbarger, halfback, 1967, 1969
Doug Crusan, defensive tackle, 1967
Ken Kaczmarek, linebacker, 1967
Jim Sniadecki, linebacker, 1968
Jade Butcher, fullback, 1969
Chris Gartner, field goal kicker, 1972

Scores
1891–1975

1891

30	Louisville AC	0
6	Butler	52
4	DePauw	62
0	Purdue	60
6	Butler	26
0	Wabash	25

1892

11	Butler	10
0	Purdue	68
36	Wabash	24
	Forfeit to DePauw	

1893

0	Butler	38
18	Danville AC	0
0	DePauw	34
24	Kentucky	24
0	Purdue	64
12	Wabash	24

1894

0	Butler	58
10	DePauw	20
0	Louisville AC	0
0	Wabash	46
	Forfeit to Purdue	

1895

36	Louisville AC	0
8	Indianapolis	16
30	Noblesville AC	0
0	DePauw	14
14	DePauw	14
2	Butler	34
8	Rose Poly Tech	4
12	Wabash	10

1896

4	DePauw	22
6	Noblesville	8
50	Knightstown	0
22	Butler	6
16	Cincinnati	0
38	Wabash	0
38	Louisville	24
12	DePauw	0

1897

6	Rose Poly	6
12	Rose Poly	0
40	Bedford	0
30	Manual Training	0
6	Purdue	20
18	DePauw	0
22	Miami	6
14	DePauw	0

1898

16	Rose Polytechnic	0
20	Indiana	0
0	Cincinnati	0
11	Notre Dame	5
32	DePauw	0
0	Purdue	14
11	Cincinnati	11

1899

16	Rose Polytechnic	0
6	Illinois	0
0	Notre Dame	17
20	Vanderbilt	0
35	Cincinnati	0
34	DePauw	0
6	Northwestern	11
17	Purdue	5

1900

0	Alumni	0
18	Earlham	0
0	Northwestern	12
62	Vincennes	0
6	Notre Dame	0
0	Michigan	12
0	Illinois	0
24	Purdue	5

1901

24	Wabash	6
56	Rose Polytechnic	0
0	Michigan	33
76	Franklin	0
11	Purdue	6
0	Illinois	18
5	Notre Dame	18
18	Ohio State	6
24	DePauw	0

1902

34	Wabash	0
0	Michigan	60
16	DePauw	5
5	Notre Dame	11
0	Illinois	47
0	Chicago	39
0	Purdue	39
33	Vincennes	0
6	Ohio State	6

1903

0	Wabash	5
0	Chicago	34
39	Earlham	0
0	Michigan	51
17	Illinois	0
70	DePauw	0
5	Kentucky	18
17	Ohio State	16

1904

11	Alumni	5
12	Indiana Medics	0
0	Chicago	56
0	Kentucky State	12
0	Illinois	10
22	Washington University	6
8	Ohio State	0
4	Wabash	0
0	Purdue	27
27	Kent	0

1905

5	Alumni	0
31	Butler	0
29	Kentucky	0
5	Chicago	16
39	Washington University	0
11	Purdue	11
47	Cincinnati	6
22	Notre Dame	5
40	Wabash	0
11	Ohio State	0

1906

16	Alumni	0
12	Wabash	5
8	Chicago	33

55	DePauw	0
12	Notre Dame	0
6	Minnesota	8

1907

25	DePauw	9
6	Chicago	27
40	Alumni	0
0	Notre Dame	0
8	Wisconsin	11
6	Illinois	10

1908

11	Alumni–Freshmen	0
16	DePauw	0
6	Chicago	29
0	Wisconsin	16
0	Illinois	10
0	Notre Dame	11
10	Purdue	4

1909

28	DePauw	5
0	Chicago	28
27	Lake Forest	5
3	Wisconsin	6
30	St. Louis	0
5	Illinois	6
36	Purdue	3

1910

12	DePauw	0
6	Chicago	0
33	Millikin	0
12	Wisconsin	3
33	Butler	0
0	Illinois	3
15	Purdue	0

1911

9	DePauw	6
6	Chicago	23
42	Franklin	0
0	Northwestern	5
12	Washington University	0
0	Illinois	0
5	Purdue	12

1912

20	DePauw	0
0	Chicago	13
7	Illinois	13
33	Earlham	7
6	Iowa	13
6	Northwestern	21
7	Purdue	34

1913

48	DePauw	3
7	Chicago	21

0	Illinois	10
7	Ohio State	6
0	Iowa	60
21	Northwestern	20
7	Purdue	42

1914

13	DePauw	6
0	Chicago	34
0	Illinois	52
27	Northwestern	0
48	Miami	3
3	Ohio State	13
13	Purdue	23

1915

7	DePauw	0
41	Miami	0
7	Chicago	13
7	Washington & Lee	7
9	Ohio State	10
14	Northwestern	6
0	Purdue	7

1916

20	DePauw	0
0	Chicago	22
10	Tufts	12
0	Northwestern	7
7	Ohio State	46
14	Florida	3
0	Purdue	0

1917

50	Franklin	0
51	Wabash	0
40	St. Louis	0
9	Minnesota	33
3	Ohio State	26
35	DePauw	0
37	Purdue	0

1918

7	Kentucky State	24
3	Camp Taylor	7
41	Fort Harrison	0
13	DePauw	0

1919

20	Wabash	7
3	Centre	12
24	Kentucky State	0
6	Minnesota	20
3	Notre Dame	16
2	Northwestern	3
12	Syracuse	6

1920

47	Franklin	0
7	Iowa	14

24	Mississippi Aggies	0
21	Minnesota	7
10	Northwestern	7
10	Purdue	7
10	Notre Dame	13

1921

47	Franklin	0
29	Kalamazoo	0
0	Harvard	19
0	Minnesota	6
7	Notre Dame	28
0	Iowa	41
3	Purdue	0

1922

0	DePauw	0
0	Minnesota	20
0	Wisconsin	20
14	MAC	6
0	Notre Dame	27
0	West Virginia	33
7	Purdue	7

1923

0	DePauw	3
7	Northwestern	6
0	Wisconsin	52
32	Hanover	0
0	Chicago	27
6	Wabash	29
3	Purdue	0

1924

65	Rose Poly	0
21	DePauw	0
14	Louisiana	20
0	Chicago	23
7	Northwestern	17
12	Ohio State	7
21	Wabash	7
7	Purdue	26

1925

31	Indiana Normal	0
0	Michigan	63
0	Syracuse	14
14	Northwestern	17
0	Ohio State	7
32	Rose Poly	7
0	Purdue	0
25	Miami	7

1926

31	DePauw	7
14	Kentucky	6
0	Northwestern	20
2	Wisconsin	27
0	Northwestern	21
0	Notre Dame	26

19	Mississippi Aggies	6
14	Purdue	24

1927

21	Kentucky	0
14	Minnesota	14
6	Harvard	26
18	Northwestern	7
0	Chicago	13
6	Notre Dame	19
33	Michigan State	7
6	Purdue	21

1928

14	Wabash	0
10	Oklahoma	7
6	Michigan	0
7	Illinois	13
0	Ohio State	13
12	Minnesota	21
6	Northwestern	0
0	Purdue	14

1929

19	Wabash	2
0	Ohio University	18
0	Notre Dame	14
7	Chicago	13
0	Ohio State	0
6	Colgate	21
7	Minnesota	19
19	Northwestern	14
0	Purdue	32

1930

14	Miami	0
0	Ohio State	23
7	Oklahoma A & M	7
0	Minnesota	6
0	Southern Methodist	27
0	Notre Dame	27
0	Northwestern	25
7	Purdue	6

1931

7	Ohio University	6
0	Notre Dame	25
0	Iowa	0
32	Chicago	6
6	Ohio State	13
0	Michigan	22
6	Northwestern	7
0	Purdue	19

1932

7	Ohio University	6
7	Ohio State	7
12	Iowa	0
7	Chicago	13
19	Mississippi	0

0	Michigan	7
6	Illinois	18
7	Purdue	25

1933

6	Miami	0
6	Minnesota	6
2	Notre Dame	12
0	Northwestern	25
0	Ohio State	21
7	Chicago	7
0	Xavier	6
3	Purdue	19

1934

27	Ohio University	0
0	Ohio State	33
6	Temple	6
0	Chicago	21
0	Iowa	0
0	Minnesota	30
17	Maryland	14
17	Purdue	6

1935

14	Centre	0
0	Michigan	7
0	Cincinnati	7
6	Ohio State	28
6	Iowa	6
13	Maryland	6
24	Chicago	0
7	Purdue	0

1936

38	Centre	0
14	Michigan	3
9	Nebraska	13
0	Ohio State	7
13	Iowa	6
9	Syracuse	7
20	Chicago	7
20	Purdue	20

1937

12	Centre	0
0	Minnesota	6
13	Illinois	6
27	Cincinnati	0
0	Nebraska	7
10	Ohio State	0
3	Iowa	0
7	Purdue	13

1938

0	Ohio State	6
2	Illinois	12
0	Nebraska	0
6	Kansas State	13
0	Wisconsin	6

0	Boston College	14
7	Iowa	3
6	Purdue	13

1939

7	Nebraska	7
29	Iowa	32
14	Wisconsin	0
7	Illinois	6
0	Ohio State	24
0	Fordham	13
7	Michigan State	7
6	Purdue	7

1940

6	Texas	13
7	Nebraska	13
10	Iowa	6
7	Northwestern	20
6	Ohio State	21
20	Michigan State	0
10	Wisconsin	27
3	Purdue	0

1941

7	Detroit	14
6	Notre Dame	19
14	TCU	20
21	Nebraska	13
25	Wisconsin	27
7	Iowa	13
14	Northwestern	20
7	Purdue	0

1942

53	Butler	0
21	Ohio State	32
12	Nebraska	0
19	Pittsburgh	7
13	Iowa	14
6	Iowa Cadets	26
7	Minnesota	0
54	Kansas State	0
20	Purdue	0
51	Ft. Knox	0

1943

7	Miami (Ohio)	7
6	Northwestern	14
52	Wabash	0
54	Nebraska	13
7	Iowa	7
34	Wisconsin	0
20	Ohio State	14
6	Michigan	23
7	Great Lakes	21
0	Purdue	7

1944

72	Ft. Knox	0

Billy Hillenbrand, 6-foot, 190 pounds and 1942 All-American triple-threater, was one of the greatest halfbacks in Indiana history.

18	Illinois	26	
20	Michigan	0	
54	Nebraska	0	
14	Northwestern	7	
32	Iowa	0	
7	Ohio State	21	
14	Minnesota	19	
47	Pittsburgh	0	
14	Purdue	6	

1945

13	Michigan	7
7	Northwestern	7
6	Illinois	0
54	Nebraska	14
52	Iowa	20
7	Tulsa	2
46	Cornell	6
49	Minnesota	0
19	Pittsburgh	0
26	Purdue	0

1946

6	Cincinnati	15
0	Michigan	21
21	Minnesota	0
14	Illinois	7
0	Iowa	13
27	Nebraska	7
20	Pittsburgh	6
7	Northwestern	6
34	Purdue	20

1947

17	Nebraska	0
7	Wisconsin	7
14	Iowa	27
41	Pittsburgh	6
6	Northwestern	7
7	Ohio State	0
0	Michigan	35
48	Marquette	6
16	Purdue	14

1948

35	Wisconsin	7
7	Iowa	0
6	TCU	7
0	Ohio State	17
14	Pittsburgh	21
7	Minnesota	30
6	Notre Dame	42
0	Michigan	54
0	Purdue	39

1949

6	Notre Dame	49
7	Ohio State	46
6	TCU	13
9	Iowa	35
48	Pittsburgh	14
14	Wisconsin	30
14	Illinois	33
7	Michigan	20
6	Purdue	14

1950

20	Nebraska	20
20	Iowa	7
14	Ohio State	26
20	Notre Dame	7
0	Illinois	20
0	Michigan State	35
7	Michigan	20
18	Marquette	7
0	Purdue	13

1951

6	Notre Dame	48
13	Pittsburgh	6
14	Michigan	33
32	Ohio State	10
0	Illinois	21
0	Wisconsin	6
14	Minnesota	16
26	Michigan State	30
13	Purdue	21

1952

13	Ohio State	33
20	Iowa	13
13	Michigan	28
33	Temple	0
13	Northwestern	23
7	Pittsburgh	28
14	Michigan State	41
14	Wisconsin	37
16	Purdue	21

1953

12	Ohio State	36
14	Southern California	27
21	Marquette	20
18	Michigan State	47
13	Iowa	19
7	Missouri	14
20	Minnesota	28
14	Northwestern	6
0	Purdue	30

1954

0	Ohio State	28
34	College of Pacific	6
14	Michigan State	21
14	Missouri	20
14	Iowa	27
13	Michigan	9
0	Miami (Ohio)	6
7	Purdue	13

1955

13	Michigan State	20
0	Notre Dame	19
6	Iowa	20
14	Villanova	7
20	Northwestern	14
21	Ohio University	14
13	Ohio State	20
0	Michigan	30
4	Purdue	6

1956

0	Iowa	27
6	Notre Dame	20
6	Michigan State	53
19	Nebraska	14
19	Northwestern	13
19	Marquette	13
14	Ohio State	35
26	Michigan	49
20	Purdue	39

1957

0	Michigan State	54
0	Notre Dame	26
7	Iowa	47
0	Ohio State	56
14	Villanova	7
0	Minnesota	34
0	Cincinnati	21
13	Michigan	27
13	Purdue	35

1958

0	Notre Dame	18
13	West Virginia	12
13	Iowa	34
8	Ohio State	49
12	Miami (Ohio)	7
6	Minnesota	0
6	Michigan State	0
8	Michigan	6
15	Purdue	15

1959

20	Illinois	0
14	Minnesota	24
33	Marquette	13
23	Nebraska	7
6	Michigan State	14
13	Northwestern	30
0	Ohio State	0
26	Michigan	7
7	Purdue	10

1960

6	Illinois	17
0	Minnesota	42
6	Oregon State	20
34	Marquette	8
0	Michigan State	35
3	Northwestern	21
7	Ohio State	36
7	Michigan	29
6	Purdue	35

1961

8	Kansas State	14
3	Wisconsin	6
8	Iowa	27
33	Washington State	7
0	Michigan State	35
8	Northwestern	14
7	Ohio State	16
17	West Virginia	9
12	Purdue	34

1962

21	Kansas State	0
26	Cincinnati	6
6	Wisconsin	30
10	Iowa	14
15	Washington State	21
8	Michigan State	26
21	Northwestern	26
7	Ohio State	10
12	Purdue	7

1963

21	Northwestern	34
0	Ohio State	21
26	Iowa	37
3	Michigan State	20
20	Cincinnati	6
24	Minnesota	6
20	Oregon State	15
22	Oregon	28
15	Purdue	21

1964

13	Northwestern	14
9	Ohio State	17
20	Iowa	21
27	Michigan State	20
28	Miami (Florida)	14
0	Minnesota	21
14	Oregon State	24
21	Oregon	29
22	Purdue	28

1965

19	Kansas State	7
0	Northwestern	20
12	Texas	27
18	Minnesota	42
13	Illinois	34
7	Washington State	8
21	Iowa	17
10	Ohio State	17
13	Michigan State	27
21	Purdue	26

1966

10	Miami (Ohio)	20
26	Northwestern	14
0	Texas	35
7	Minnesota	7
10	Illinois	24
7	Miami (Florida)	14
19	Iowa	20
0	Ohio State	7
19	Michigan State	37
6	Purdue	51

1967

12	Kentucky	10
18	Kansas	15
20	Illinois	7
21	Iowa	17
27	Michigan	20
42	Arizona	7
14	Wisconsin	9
14	Michigan State	13
7	Minnesota	33
19	Purdue	14
3	*Southern California	14
	*Rose Bowl	

1968

40	Baylor	36
20	Kansas	38
28	Illinois	14
38	Iowa	34
22	Michigan	27
16	Arizona	13
21	Wisconsin	20
24	Michigan State	22
6	Minnesota	20
35	Purdue	38

1969

58	Kentucky	30
14	California	17
7	Colorado	30
17	Minnesota	7
41	Illinois	20
34	Wisconsin	36
16	Michigan State	0
17	Iowa	28
27	Northwestern	30
21	Purdue	44

1970

9	Colorado	16
14	California	56
10	West Virginia	16
0	Minnesota	23
30	Illinois	24
12	Wisconsin	30
7	Michigan State	32
13	Iowa	42
7	Northwestern	21
0	Purdue	40

1971

0	Minnesota	28
26	Kentucky	8
0	Baylor	10
0	Syracuse	7
29	Wisconsin	35
7	Ohio State	27
10	Northwestern	24
7	Michigan	61
21	Illinois	22
14	Iowa	7
38	Purdue	31

1972

27	Minnesota	23
28	TCU	31
35	Kentucky	34
10	Syracuse	2
33	Wisconsin	7
7	Ohio State	44
14	Northwestern	23
7	Michigan	21
20	Illinois	37
16	Iowa	8
7	Purdue	42

1973

14	Illinois	28
10	Arizona	26
17	Kentucky	3
28	West Virginia	14
3	Minnesota	24
7	Ohio State	37
7	Wisconsin	31
13	Michigan	49
20	Northwestern	21
9	Michigan State	10
23	Purdue	28

1974

0	Illinois	16
20	Arizona	35
22	Kentucky	28
0	West Virginia	24
34	Minnesota	3
0	Ohio State	49
25	Wisconsin	35
7	Michigan	21
22	Northwestern	24
10	Michigan State	19
17	Purdue	38

1975

20	Minnesota	14
0	Nebraska	45
31	Utah	7
0	North Carolina State	27
0	Northwestern	30
10	Iowa	20
7	Michigan	55
14	Ohio State	24
6	Michigan State	14
9	Wisconsin	9
7	Purdue	9

UNIVERSITY OF IOWA

Iowa City, Iowa
Established 1847
Colors, Old Gold and Black
Nickname, Hawkeyes

Head Coaches

A. E. Ball, 1896
T. Wagonhurst, 1897
A. A. Knipe, 1898–1901
S. W. Hobbs, 1902
J. G. Chalmers, 1903–1905
Mark Catlin, 1906–1908
J. G. Griffith, 1909
Jesse Hawley, 1910–1915
Howard Jones, 1916–1923
Burt Ingwersen, 1924–1931
Ossie Solem, 1932–1936

Irl Tubbs, 1937–1938
Dr. Eddie Anderson, 1939–1942
Slip Madigan, 1943–1944
Clem Crowe, 1945
Dr. E. Anderson, 1946–1949
Leonard Raffensperger, 1950–1951
Forest Evashevski, 1952–1960
Jerry Burns, 1961–1965
Ray Nagel, 1966–1970
Frank Lauterbur, 1971–1973
Bob Commings, 1974–

All-American Players

Fred Becker, tackle, 1916
Les Belding, end, 1919
Duke Slater, tackle, 1921
Aubrey Devine, quarterback, 1921
Gordon Locke, quarterback, 1921–1922
Dick Romey, end, 1925
Emerson Nelson, tackle, 1926

Peter Westra, tackle, 1928
Willis Glassgow, halfback, 1929
Francis Schammel, guard, 1933
Ozzie Simmons, halfback, 1935
Nile Kinnick, halfback, 1939
Mike Enich, tackle, 1940
Jerry Hilgenberg, center, 1953

Calvin Jones, guard, 1953–54–55
Alex Karras, tackle, 1956–57
Ken Ploen, quarterback, 1956
Jim Gibbons, end, 1957
Randy Duncan, quarterback, 1958
Curt Merz, end, 1958
Don Norton, end, 1959

Larry Ferguson, halfback, 1960
Mark Manders, guard, 1960
Bill Van Buren, center, 1961
Mike Reilly, guard, 1963
Karl Noonan, flanker, 1964
John Niland, offensive guard, 1965
Dave Long, defensive end, 1965

Craig Clemons, cornerback, 1971

Scores
1889–1975

1889

0	Grinnell	24

1890

| 6 | Grinnell | 11 |
| 91 | Iowa Wesleyan | 0 |

1891

64	Cornell	6
4	Minnesota	42
4	Grinnell	6
22	Nebraska	0
18	Kansas	14

1892

44	Knox	0
48	Coe	0
4	Kansas	24
0	Missouri	22
10	Nebraska	10
18	Grinnell	12

1893

56	Coe	0
0	Denver AC	58
32	Luther	0
24	Kansas	35
14	Grinnell	36
34	Missouri	12
18	Nebraska	20

1894

8	Iowa State	16
60	Cornell	0
34	Augustana	0
18	Chicago	18
0	Wisconsin	44
14	Kansas	12
6	Grinnell	0
6	Missouri	32
0	Nebraska	36

1895

0	Doane	10
28	Parsons	0
0	Ames	24

| 0 | Kansas | 52 |
| 0 | Missouri | 34 |

1896

32	Drake	0
0	Chicago	6
6	Kansas	0
27	Wilton	0
12	Missouri	0
15	Grinnell	6
0	Nebraska	0

1897

12	Northwestern	6
0	P & S	14
0	Kansas	56
0	Ames	6
16	Drake	0
16	Grinnell	12

1898

0	Knox	0
0	Chicago	38
5	Drake	18
23	UIU	5
11	Rush	15
5	Normal	11
5	Grinnell	5
12	Simpson	0
6	Nebraska	5

1899

22	Normal	0
5	Chicago	5
35	Penn	0
17	Rush	0
5	Ames	0
30	Nebraska	0
16	Grinnell	0
33	Knox	0
58	Illinois	0

1900

57	Upper Iowa	0
68	Normal	0
47	Simpson	0
26	Drake	0

17	Chicago	0
28	Michigan	5
63	Grinnell	2
5	Northwestern	5

1901

16	Normal	0
6	Drake	5
12	Ames	0
0	Minnesota	16
23	Knox	6
0	Illinois	27
17	Grinnell	11
0	Michigan	50

1902

26	Normal	5
12	Drake	0
10	Simpson	0
0	Minnesota	34
10	Ames	6
0	Michigan	107
61	Washington, Mo.	0
0	Missouri	6
0	Illinois	80

1903

6	Cornell	0
16	Coe	0
29	Normal	0
22	Drake	6
0	Minnesota	75
17	Grinnell	0
6	Nebraska	17
35	Simpson	2
16	Missouri	0
12	Illinois	0
12	Washington, Mo.	2

1904

16	Coe	0
33	Augustana	5
88	Cornell	2
11	Drake	0
0	Chicago	20
11	Ames	0
11	Normal	6

12	Nebraska	17
69	Grinnell	9
0	Illinois	29
0	Minnesota	11

1905

27	Coe	0
40	Monmouth	0
0	Chicago	42
0	Alumni	4
0	Minnesota	39
41	Normal	5
46	Grinnell	0
72	Des Moines	0
44	Drake	0
8	Ames	0
31	St. Louis	0

1906

27	Missouri	4
15	Coe	12
4	Wisconsin	18
11	Alumni	0
0	Ames	2
0	St. Louis	39

1907

21	Missouri	6
5	Wisconsin	6
25	Illinois	12
14	Ames	20
25	Drake	4

1908

92	Coe	0
5	Missouri	10
16	Morningside	0
8	Nebraska	11
0	Illinois	22
6	Drake	12
5	Kansas	10

1909

0	Minnesota	41
3	Cornell	0
6	Nebraska	6
12	Missouri	13
14	Drake	17
16	Ames	0
7	Kansas	20

1910

12	Morningside	0
5	Northwestern	10
0	Missouri	5
16	Purdue	0
2	Ames	0
21	Drake	0
38	Washington, Mo.	0

1911

11	Morningside	5
0	Cornell	3
6	Minnesota	24
0	Wisconsin	12
11	Purdue	0
0	Ames	9
6	Northwestern	0

1912

35	Normal	7
31	Cornell	0
14	Chicago	34
7	Minnesota	56
13	Indiana	6
20	Ames	7
10	Wisconsin	28

1913

45	Normal	0
76	Cornell	0
6	Chicago	23
60	Indiana	0
78	Northwestern	6
45	Ames	7
0	Nebraska	12

1914

95	Normal	0
49	Cornell	0
0	Chicago	7
0	Minnesota	7
27	Northwestern	0
26	Ames	6
7	Nebraska	16

1915

33	Cornell	0
17	Morningside	6
9	Northwestern	6
13	Minnesota	51
13	Purdue	19
0	Ames	16
7	Nebraska	51

1916

31	Cornell	6
17	Grinnell	7
24	Purdue	6
0	Minnesota	67
13	Northwestern	20
19	Ames	16
17	Nebraska	34

1917

22	Cornell	13
0	Nebraska	47
0	Grinnell	10
0	Wisconsin	20

14	Great Lakes	23
35	South Dakota	0
14	Northwestern	25
6	Ames	3
0	Alumni	19

1918

0	Great Lakes	10
12	Nebraska	0
27	Coe	0
34	Cornell	0
0	Illinois	19
6	Minnesota	0
21	Ames	0
23	Northwestern	7
0	Camp Dodge	0

1919

18	Nebraska	0
7	Illinois	9
9	Minnesota	6
26	South Dakota	13
14	Northwestern	7
6	Chicago	9
10	Ames	0

1920

14	Indiana	7
63	Cornell	0
3	Illinois	20
0	Chicago	10
20	Northwestern	0
28	Minnesota	7
14	Ames	10

1921

52	Knox	14
10	Notre Dame	7
14	Illinois	2
13	Purdue	6
41	Minnesota	7
41	Indiana	0
14	Northwestern	0

1922

61	Knox	0
6	Yale	0
8	Illinois	7
56	Purdue	0
28	Minnesota	14
12	Ohio State	9
37	Northwestern	3

1923

20	Oklahoma A & M	0
7	Purdue	0
20	Ohio State	0
6	Illinois	9
3	Michigan	9

7	Minnesota	20
17	Northwestern	14

1924

43	S. East T.	0
0	Ohio State	0
13	Lawrence	5
13	Minnesota	0
0	Illinois	36
7	Butler	0
21	Wisconsin	7
9	Michigan	2

1925

25	Arkansas	0
41	St. Louis	0
12	Illinois	10
15	Ohio State	0
28	Wabash	7
0	Wisconsin	6
0	Minnesota	33
0	Southern California	13

1926

24	Colo. Tchrs.	0
40	North Dakota	7
6	Illinois	13
6	Ohio State	23
21	Carroll	0
0	Minnesota	41
10	Wisconsin	20
6	Northwestern	13

1927

32	Monmouth	6
6	Ohio State	13
38	Wabash	0
0	Minnesota	38
15	Denver	0
0	Illinois	14
16	Wisconsin	0
0	Northwestern	12

1928

26	Monmouth	0
13	Chicago	0
61	Ripon	6
7	Minnesota	6
19	South Dakota	0
14	Ohio State	7
0	Wisconsin	13
7	Michigan	10

1929

46	Carroll	0
46	Monmouth	0
6	Ohio State	7
7	Illinois	7
14	Wisconsin	0

9	Minnesota	7
0	Purdue	7
0	Michigan	0

1930

38	Bradley	12
0	Oklahoma A & M	6
12	Centenary	19
0	Purdue	20
7	Detroit	3
0	Marquette	7
19	Penn State	0
12	Nebraska	7

1931

0	Pittsburgh	20
0	Texas A & M	29
0	Indiana	0
0	Minnesota	34
7	George Washington	0
0	Nebraska	7
0	Purdue	22
0	Northwestern	19

1932

31	Bradley	7
0	Wisconsin	34
0	Indiana	12
6	Minnesota	21
6	George Washington	21
13	Nebraska	14
0	Purdue	18
6	Northwestern	44

1933

7	Northwestern	0
38	Bradley	0
26	Wisconsin	7
7	Minnesota	19
27	Iowa State	7
6	Michigan	10
14	Purdue	6
6	Nebraska	7

1934

34	South Dakota	0
20	Northwestern	7
13	Nebraska	14
6	Iowa State	31
12	Minnesota	48
0	Indiana	0
6	Purdue	13
7	Ohio State	40

1935

26	Bradley Tech	0
47	South Dakota	2
12	Colgate	6
19	Illinois	0

6	Indiana	6
6	Minnesota	13
6	Purdue	12
0	Northwestern	0

1936

14	Carleton	0
7	Northwestern	18
33	South Dakota	7
0	Illinois	0
6	Indiana	13
0	Minnesota	52
0	Purdue	13
25	Temple	0

1937

0	Washington	14
14	Bradley Tech	7
6	Wisconsin	13
6	Michigan	7
0	Purdue	13
10	Minnesota	35
0	Indiana	3
0	Nebraska	28

1938

3	UCLA	27
13	Wisconsin	31
27	Chicago	14
0	Colgate	14
0	Purdue	0
0	Minnesota	28
3	Indiana	7
0	Nebraska	14

1939

41	South Dakota	0
32	Indiana	29
7	Michigan	27
19	Wisconsin	13
4	Purdue	0
7	Notre Dame	6
13	Minnesota	9
7	Northwestern	7

1940

46	South Dakota	0
30	Wisconsin	12
6	Indiana	10
6	Minnesota	34
6	Purdue	21
6	Nebraska	14
7	Notre Dame	0
18	Illinois	7

1941

25	Drake	8
0	Michigan	6
0	Wisconsin	23

6	Purdue	7
13	Indiana	7
21	Illinois	0
13	Minnesota	34
13	Nebraska	14

1942

26	Washington	7
27	Nebraska	0
0	Great Lakes	25
33	Camp Grant	16
7	Illinois	12
14	Indiana	13
13	Purdue	7
6	Wisconsin	0
7	Minnesota	27
14	Michigan	28

1943

7	Great Lakes	21
5	Wisconsin	7
0	Iowa Pre-Flight	25
7	Indiana	7
7	Purdue	28
10	Illinois	19
14	Minnesota	33
33	Nebraska	13

1944

0	Ohio State	34
6	Illinois	40
7	Purdue	26
0	Indiana	32
27	Nebraska	6
7	Wisconsin	26
0	Minnesota	46
6	Iowa Pre-Flight	30

1945

14	Bergstrom AAF	13
0	Ohio State	42
0	Purdue	40
20	Indiana	52
0	Notre Dame	56
7	Wisconsin	27
7	Illinois	48
20	Minnesota	19
6	Nebraska	13

1946

39	North Dakota State	0
16	Purdue	0
7	Michigan	14
21	Nebraska	7
13	Indiana	0
6	Notre Dame	41
0	Illinois	7
21	Wisconsin	7
6	Minnesota	16

1947

59	North Dakota State	0
7	UCLA	22
12	Illinois	35
27	Indiana	14
13	Ohio State	13
0	Notre Dame	21
0	Purdue	21
14	Wisconsin	46
13	Minnesota	7

1948

14	Marquette	12
0	Indiana	7
14	Ohio State	7
13	Purdue	20
12	Notre Dame	27
19	Wisconsin	13
0	Illinois	14
21	Minnesota	28
34	Boston University	14

1949

25	UCLA	41
21	Purdue	7
14	Illinois	20
35	Indiana	9
28	Northwestern	21
34	Oregon U	31
7	Minnesota	55
13	Wisconsin	35
7	Notre Dame	28

1950

20	Southern California	14
7	Indiana	20
0	Wisconsin	14
33	Purdue	21
21	Ohio State	83
13	Minnesota	0
7	Illinois	21
14	Notre Dame	14
6	Miami (Fla.)	14

1951

16	Kansas State	0
30	Purdue	34
34	Pittsburgh	17
0	Michigan	21
21	Ohio State	47
20	Minnesota	20
13	Illinois	40
7	Wisconsin	34
20	Notre Dame	20

1952

14	Pittsburgh	26
13	Indiana	20

14	Purdue	41
13	Wisconsin	42
8	Ohio State	0
7	Minnesota	17
13	Illinois	33
39	Northwestern	14
0	Notre Dame	27

1953

7	Michigan State	21
54	Washington State	12
13	Michigan	14
21	Wyoming	7
19	Indiana	13
6	Wisconsin	10
26	Purdue	0
27	Minnesota	0
14	Notre Dame	14

1954

14	Michigan State	10
48	Montana	6
13	Michigan	14
14	Ohio State	20
27	Indiana	14
13	Wisconsin	7
25	Purdue	14
20	Minnesota	22
18	Notre Dame	34

1955

28	Kansas State	7
14	Wisconsin	37
20	Indiana	6
20	Purdue	20
13	UCLA	33
21	Michigan	33
26	Minnesota	0
10	Ohio State	20
14	Notre Dame	17

1956

27	Indiana	0
14	Oregon State	13
13	Wisconsin	7
34	Hawaii	0
21	Purdue	20
14	Michigan	17
7	Minnesota	0
6	Ohio State	0
48	Notre Dame	8
35	*Oregon State	19
	*Rose Bowl	

1957

70	Utah State	14
20	Washington State	13
47	Indiana	7
21	Wisconsin	7

6	Northwestern	0
21	Michigan	21
44	Minnesota	20
13	Ohio State	17
21	Notre Dame	13

1958

17	TCU	0
13	Air Force	13
34	Indiana	13
20	Wisconsin	9
26	Northwestern	20
37	Michigan	14
28	Minnesota	6
28	Ohio State	38
31	Notre Dame	21
38	*California	12
	*Rose Bowl	

1959

42	California	12
10	Northwestern	14
37	Michigan State	8
16	Wisconsin	25
7	Purdue	14
53	Kansas State	0
33	Minnesota	0
16	Ohio State	7
19	Notre Dame	20

1960

22	Oregon State	12
42	Northwestern	0
27	Michigan State	15
28	Wisconsin	21
21	Purdue	14
21	Kansas	7
10	Minnesota	27
35	Ohio State	12
28	Notre Dame	0

1961

28	California	7
35	Southern California	34
27	Indiana	8
47	Wisconsin	15
0	Purdue	9
13	Ohio State	29
9	Minnesota	16
14	Michigan	23
42	Notre Dame	21

1962

28	Oregon State	8
0	Southern California	7
14	Indiana	10
14	Wisconsin	42
3	Purdue	26
28	Ohio State	14

0	Minnesota	10
28	Michigan	14
12	Notre Dame	35

1963

14	Washington State	14
17	Washington	7
37	Indiana	26
7	Wisconsin	10
0	Purdue	14
3	Ohio State	7
27	Minnesota	13
21	Michigan	21
	Notre Dame	canceled

1964

34	Idaho	24
39	Washington	18
21	Indiana	20
21	Wisconsin	31
14	Purdue	19
19	Ohio State	21
13	Minnesota	14
20	Michigan	34
0	Notre Dame	28

1965

0	Washington State	7
27	Oregon State	7
13	Wisconsin	16
14	Purdue	17
3	Minnesota	14
0	Northwestern	9
17	Indiana	21
0	Michigan State	35
0	Ohio State	38
20	North Carolina State	28

1966

31	Arizona	20
3	Oregon State	17
0	Wisconsin	7
0	Purdue	35
0	Minnesota	17
15	Northwestern	24
20	Indiana	19
7	Michigan State	56
10	Ohio State	14
0	Miami (Fla.)	44

1967

24	TCU	9
18	Oregon State	38
6	Notre Dame	56
17	Indiana	21
21	Wisconsin	21
22	Purdue	41
0	Minnesota	10
24	Northwestern	39

10	Ohio State	21
19	Illinois	21

1968

21	Oregon State	20
17	TCU	28
28	Notre Dame	51
34	Indiana	38
41	Wisconsin	0
14	Purdue	44
35	Minnesota	28
68	Northwestern	34
27	Ohio State	33
37	Illinois	13

1969

14	Oregon State	42
61	Washington State	35
31	Arizona	19
17	Wisconsin	23
31	Purdue	35
19	Michigan State	18
8	Minnesota	35
28	Indiana	17
6	Michigan	51
40	Illinois	0

1970

14	Oregon State	21
0	Southern California	48
10	Arizona	17
24	Wisconsin	14
3	Purdue	24
0	Michigan State	37
14	Minnesota	14
22	Indiana	13
0	Michigan	55
22	Illinois	16

1971

21	Ohio State	52
19	Oregon State	33
14	Penn State	44
13	Purdue	45
3	Northwestern	28
14	Minnesota	19
3	Michigan State	34
20	Wisconsin	16
7	Michigan	63
7	Indiana	14
0	Illinois	31

1972

0	Ohio State	21
19	Oregon State	11
10	Penn State	14
0	Purdue	24
23	Northwestern	12
14	Minnesota	43

6	Michigan State	6	7	Wisconsin	35	10	Ohio State	35
14	Wisconsin	16	13	Ohio State	55	21	Michigan State	60
0	Michigan	31	6	Michigan State	15			
8	Indiana	16					**1975**	
15	Illinois	14				12	Illinois	20
				1974		7	Syracuse	10
	1973		7	Michigan	24	10	Penn State	30
7	Michigan	31	21	UCLA	10	16	Southern California	27
18	UCLA	55	0	Penn State	27	0	Ohio State	49
8	Penn State	27	3	Southern California	41	20	Indiana	10
20	Arizona	23	35	Northwestern	10	7	Minnesota	31
15	Northwestern	31	17	Minnesota	23	24	Northwestern	21
23	Minnesota	31	14	Illinois	12	45	Wisconsin	28
0	Illinois	50	14	Purdue	38	18	Purdue	19
23	Purdue	48	15	Wisconsin	28	23	Michigan State	27

UNIVERSITY OF MICHIGAN

Ann Arbor, Michigan
Established 1817
Colors, Maize and Blue
Nickname, Wolverines

Head Coaches

Charles M. Gayley, 1876–1883
Horace G. Prettyman, 1884–1890
Mike Murphy, 1891
Frank Barbour, 1892–1893
W. L. McCauley, 1894–1896
George H. Ferbert, 1897–1899
Langdon Lea, 1900
Fielding H. Yost, 1901–1923

George E. Little, 1924
Fielding H. Yost, 1925–1926
Elton E. (Tad) Wieman, 1927–1928
Harry Kipke, 1929–1937
H. O. (Fritz) Crisler, 1938–1947
Bennie Oosterbaan, 1948–1958
C. W. (Bump) Elliott, 1959–1968
Bo Schembechler, 1969–

All-American Players

William Cunningham, center, 1898
Neil Snow, end, 1901
Willie Heston, halfback, 1903–04
Adolph (Germany) Schulz, center, 1907
Albert Benbrook, guard, 1909–10
Stanfield Wells, end, 1910
Miller H. Pontius, tackle, 1913
Jim Craig, halfback, 1913
John Maulbetsch, halfback, 1914
Frank Culver, guard, 1917
Cedric Smith, fullback, 1917
Ernest Allmendinger, guard, 1917
Frank Steketee, fullback, 1918
Henry Vick, center, 1921
Paul Goebel, end, 1922
Harry Kipke, halfback, 1922
Jack Blott, center, 1923
Edliff R. Slaughter, guard, 1924
Benny Friedman, quarterback, 1925–26
Bennie Oosterbaan, end, 1925–26–27
Harry Hawkins, guard, 1925
Bob Brown, center, 1925
Otto Pommerening, tackle, 1928
Maynard Morrison, center, 1931

Ted Petoskey, end, 1932–33
Chuck Bernard, center, 1932–33
Harry Newman, quarterback, 1932
Francis Wistert, tackle, 1933
Ralph Heikkinen, guard, 1938
Tom Harmon, halfback, 1939–40
Ed Frutig, end, 1940
Bob Westfall, fullback, 1941
Albert Wistert, tackle, 1942
Julius Franks, guard, 1942
Mervin Pregulman, tackle, 1943
Bill Daley, fullback, 1943
Elmer Madar, end, 1946
Bob Chappuis, halfback, 1947
Bump Elliott, halfback, 1947
Dick Rifenburg, end, 1948
Alvin Wistert, tackle, 1948–49
Pete Elliott, quarterback, 1948
Allen Wahl, tackle, 1949–50
Lowell Perry, end, 1951
Art Walker, tackle, 1954
Ron Kramer, end, 1955–56
Jim Pace, halfback, 1957
Bob Timberlake, quarterback, 1964

Bill Yearby, tackle, 1964–65
Dick Volk, halfback, 1966
John Clancy, end, 1966
Ron Johnson, halfback, 1968
Tom Curtis, halfback, 1969
Jim Mandich, end, 1969
Marty Huff, linebacker, 1970
Dan Dierdorf, tackle, 1970

Henry Hill, guard, 1970
Reggie McKenzie, guard, 1971
Mike Taylor, linebacker, 1971
Billy Taylor, halfback, 1971
Tom Darden, halfback, 1971
Randy Logan, halfback, 1972
Paul Seymour, tackle, 1972
Dave Brown, halfback, 1973–74

Dave Gallagher, tackle, 1973

Scores
1878–1975

1878–'79 (A)

1g, 1t	Racine	0g, 0t

1879 (Fall)

0g, 0t	Toronto	0g, 0t

1880

1g, 2t	Toronto	0g, 0t

1881

0g, 0t, 0s	Harvard	0g, 1t, 0s
0g, 0t, 0s	Yale	2g, 0t, 5s
0g, 0t, 1s	Princeton	1g, 2t, 3s

1882—

No Football

1883

6	Wesleyan	14
0	Yale	64
0	Harvard	3
1	Stevens	5

1884

18	Albion	0
18	University Club (Chi.)	10

1885

(Canadian Rules)

8	Windsor Club	2
32	Windsor Club	0
42	Peninsular Club	0

1886

50	Albion	0
24	Albion	0

1887–88

32	Albion	0
8	Notre Dame	0
26	Harvard School	0
26	Notre Dame	6
10	Notre Dame	4

1888 (Fall)

14	Detroit AC	0
4	University Club (Chi.)	28

1889

33	Albion	4
0	Cornell	66
0	University Club (Chi.)	20

1890

56	Albion	10
38	Detroit AC	0
16	Albion	0
34	Purdue	6
5	Cornell	20

1891

4	Albion	10
18	Olivet	6
26	Oberlin	6
42	Butler	6
0	University Club (Chi.)	20
12	Cornell	58
4	Cleveland AA	8
0	Cornell	10

1892

74	Michigan AA	0
68	Michigan AA	0
10	Wisconsin	6
6	Minnesota	14
18	DePauw	6
0	Purdue	24
8	Northwestern	10
60	Albion	8
0	Cornell	44
18	Chicago	10
26	Oberlin	24
10	Cornell	30

1893

6	Detroit AC	0
26	Detroit AC	0
6	Chicago	10
20	Minnesota	34
18	Wisconsin	34
46	Purdue	8
34	DePauw	0
72	Northwestern	6
22	Kansas	0
28	Chicago	10

1894

12	Michigan M. A.	12
26	Albion	10
48	Olivet	0
40	Michigan M. A.	6
46	Adrian	0
18	Case	8
0	Cornell	22
22	Kansas	12
14	Oberlin	6
12	Cornell	4
6	Chicago	4

1895

34	Michigan M. A.	0
42	Detroit AC	0
64	Adelbert	0
40	Lake Forest	0
42	Oberlin	0
0	Harvard	4
12	Purdue	10
20	Minnesota	0
12	Chicago	0

1896

18	Michigan Normal	0
28	Physicians & Surgeons	0
66	Lake Forest	0
16	Purdue	0
40	Lehigh	0
6	Minnesota	4
10	Oberlin	0
28	Wittenberg	0
6	Chicago	7

1897

24	Michigan Normal	0
0	Ohio Wesleyan	0
34	Ohio State	0

16	Oberlin	6
0	Graduates	15
34	Purdue	4
14	Minnesota	0
32	Wittenberg	0
12	Chicago	21

1898

21	Michigan Normal	0
29	Kenyon	0
39	Michigan Aggies	0
18	Western Reserve	0
23	Case	5
23	Notre Dame	0
11	Graduates	2
6	Northwestern	5
12	Illinois	5
22	Beloit	0
12	Chicago	11

1899

11	Hillsdale	0
26	Albion	0
17	Western Reserve	0
12	Notre Dame	0
0	Graduates	0
5	Illinois	0
38	Virginia	0
10	Pennsylvania	11
28	Case	6
24	Kalamazoo	0
5	Wisconsin	17

1900

29	Hillsdale	0
11	Kalamazoo	0
24	Case	6
11	Purdue	6
12	Illinois	0
12	Indiana	0
5	Iowa	28
7	Notre Dame	0
0	Ohio State	0
6	Chicago	15

1901

50	Albion	0
57	Case	0
33	Indiana	0
29	Northwestern	0
128	Buffalo	0
22	Carlisle Indians	0
21	Ohio State	0
22	Chicago	0
89	Beloit	0
50	Iowa	0
49	*Stanford	0
	*Rose Bowl	

1902

88	Albion	0
48	Case	6

119	Michigan Aggies	0
60	Indiana	0
23	Notre Dame	0
86	Ohio State	0
6	Wisconsin	0
107	Iowa	0
21	Chicago	0
63	Oberlin	0
23	Minnesota	6

1903

31	Case	0
76	Albion	0
79	Beloit	0
65	Ohio Northern	0
51	Indiana	0
88	Ferris	0
47	Drake	0
6	Minnesota	6
36	Ohio State	0
16	Wisconsin	0
42	Oberlin	0
28	Chicago	0

1904

33	Case	0
48	Ohio Northern	0
95	Kalamazoo	0
72	Physicians & Surgeons	0
31	Ohio State	6
72	American Med.	0
130	West Virginia	0
28	Wisconsin	0
36	Drake	4
22	Chicago	12

1905

65	Ohio Wesleyan	0
44	Kalamazoo	0
36	Case	0
23	Ohio Northern	0
18	Vanderbilt	0
31	Nebraska	0
70	Albion	0
48	Drake	0
33	Illinois	0
40	Ohio State	0
12	Wisconsin	0
75	Oberlin	0
0	Chicago	2

1906

28	Case	0
6	Ohio State	0
28	Illinois	9
10	Vanderbilt	4
0	Pennsylvania	17

1907

9	Case	0
46	Michigan Aggies	0
22	Wabash	0

22	Ohio State	0
8	Vanderbilt	0
0	Pennsylvania	6

1908

16	Case	6
0	Michigan Aggies	0
12	Notre Dame	6
10	Ohio State	6
24	Vanderbilt	6
62	Kentucky	0
0	Pennsylvania	29
4	Syracuse	28

1909

3	Case	0
33	Ohio State	6
6	Marquette	5
44	Syracuse	0
3	Notre Dame	11
12	Pennsylvania	6
15	Minnesota	6

1910

3	Case	3
6	Michigan Aggies	3
3	Ohio State	3
11	Syracuse	0
0	Pennsylvania	0
6	Minnesota	0

1911

24	Case	0
15	Michigan Aggies	3
19	Ohio State	0
9	Vanderbilt	8
6	Syracuse	6
0	Cornell	6
11	Pennsylvania	9
6	Nebraska	6

1912

34	Case	0
55	Michigan Aggies	7
14	Ohio State	0
7	Syracuse	18
7	South Dakota	6
21	Pennsylvania	27
20	Cornell	7

1913

48	Case	0
14	Mt. Union	0
7	Michigan Aggies	12
33	Vanderbilt	2
43	Syracuse	7
17	Cornell	0
13	Pennsylvania	0

1914

58	DePauw	0

69	Case	0
27	Mt. Union	7
23	Vanderbilt	3
3	Michigan Aggies	0
6	Syracuse	20
0	Harvard	7
34	Pennsylvania	3
13	Cornell	28

1915

39	Lawrence	0
35	Mt. Union	0
28	Marietta	6
14	Case	3
0	Michigan Aggies	24
7	Syracuse	14
7	Cornell	34
0	Pennsylvania	0

1916

30	Marietta	0
19	Case	3
54	Carroll	0
26	Mt. Union	0
9	Michigan Aggies	0
14	Syracuse	13
66	Washington (Mo.)	7
20	Cornell	23
7	Pennsylvania	10

1917

41	Case	0
17	Kalamazoo Normal	13
69	Mt. Union	0
14	Detroit	3
27	Michigan Aggies	0
20	Nebraska	0
62	Kalamazoo	0
42	Cornell	0
0	Pennsylvania	16
12	Northwestern	21

1918

33	Case	0
13	Chicago	0
15	Syracuse	0
21	Michigan Aggies	6
14	Ohio State	0

1919

34	Case	0
26	Michigan Aggies	0
3	Ohio State	13
16	Northwestern	13
0	Chicago	13
7	Illinois	29
7	Minnesota	34

1920

35	Case	0
35	Michigan Aggies	0
6	Illinois	7
21	Tulane	0
7	Ohio State	14
14	Chicago	0
3	Minnesota	0

1921

44	Mt. Union	0
64	Case	0
30	Michigan Aggies	0
0	Ohio State	14
3	Illinois	0
7	Wisconsin	7
38	Minnesota	0

1922

48	Case	0
0	Vanderbilt	0
19	Ohio State	0
24	Illinois	0
63	Michigan Aggies	0
13	Wisconsin	6
16	Minnesota	7

1923

36	Case	0
3	Vanderbilt	0
23	Ohio State	0
37	Michigan Aggies	0
9	Iowa	3
26	Quantico Marines	6
6	Wisconsin	3
10	Minnesota	0

1924

55	Miami (Ohio)	0
7	Michigan Aggies	0
14	Illinois	39
21	Wisconsin	0
13	Minnesota	0
27	Northwestern	0
16	Ohio State	6
2	Iowa	9

1925

63	Indiana	0
39	Michigan State	0
21	Wisconsin	0
3	Illinois	0
54	Navy	0
2	Northwestern	3
10	Ohio State	0
35	Minnesota	0

1926

42	Oklahoma A & M	3
55	Michigan State	3
20	Minnesota	0
13	Illinois	0
0	Navy	10
37	Wisconsin	0
17	Ohio State	16
7	Minnesota	6

1927

33	Ohio Wesleyan	0
21	Michigan State	0
14	Wisconsin	0
21	Ohio State	0
0	Illinois	14
14	Chicago	0
27	Navy	12
7	Minnesota	13

1928

7	Ohio Wesleyan	17
0	Indiana	6
7	Ohio State	19
0	Wisconsin	7
3	Illinois	0
6	Navy	6
3	Michigan State	0
10	Iowa	7

1929

39	Albion	0
16	Mt. Union	6
17	Michigan State	0
16	Purdue	30
0	Ohio State	7
0	Illinois	14
14	Harvard	12
7	Minnesota	6
0	Iowa	0

1930

33	Denison	0
7	Michigan Normal	0
0	Michigan State	0
14	Purdue	13
13	Ohio State	0
15	Illinois	7
6	Harvard	3
7	Minnesota	0
16	Chicago	0

1931

27	Central Teachers	0
34	Michigan Normal	0
13	Chicago	7
7	Ohio State	20
35	Illinois	0
21	Princeton	0
22	Indiana	0
0	Michigan State	0
6	Minnesota	0
16	Wisconsin	0

1932

26	Michigan State	0
15	Northwestern	6
14	Ohio State	0

32	Illinois	0
14	Princeton	7
7	Indiana	0
12	Chicago	0
3	Minnesota	0

1933

20	Michigan State	6
40	Cornell	0
13	Ohio State	0
28	Chicago	0
7	Illinois	6
10	Iowa	6
0	Minnesota	0
13	Northwestern	0

1934

0	Michigan State	16
0	Chicago	27
9	Georgia Tech	2
6	Illinois	7
0	Minnesota	34
0	Wisconsin	10
0	Ohio State	34
6	Northwestern	13

1935

6	Michigan State	25
7	Indiana	0
20	Wisconsin	12
19	Columbia	7
16	Pennsylvania	6
0	Illinois	3
0	Minnesota	40
0	Ohio State	38

1936

7	Michigan State	21
3	Indiana	14
0	Minnesota	26
13	Columbia	0
6	Illinois	9
7	Pennsylvania	27
0	Northwestern	9
0	Ohio State	21

1937

14	Michigan State	19
0	Northwestern	7
6	Minnesota	39
7	Iowa	6
7	Illinois	6
13	Chicago	12
7	Pennsylvania	0
0	Ohio State	21

1938

14	Michigan State	0
45	Chicago	7
6	Minnesota	7
15	Yale	13

14	Illinois	0
19	Pennsylvania	13
0	Northwestern	0
18	Ohio State	0

1939

26	Michigan State	13
27	Iowa	7
85	Chicago	0
27	Yale	7
7	Illinois	16
7	Minnesota	20
19	Pennsylvania	17
21	Ohio State	14

1940

41	California	0
21	Michigan State	14
26	Harvard	0
28	Illinois	0
14	Pennsylvania	9
6	Minnesota	7
20	Northwestern	13
40	Ohio State	0

1941

19	Michigan State	7
6	Iowa	0
40	Pittsburgh	0
14	Northwestern	7
0	Minnesota	7
20	Illinois	0
28	Columbia	0
20	Ohio State	20

1942

9	Great Lakes	0
20	Michigan State	0
14	Iowa Pre-Flight	26
34	Northwestern	16
14	Minnesota	16
28	Illinois	14
35	Harvard	7
32	Notre Dame	20
7	Ohio State	21
28	Iowa	14

1943

26	Camp Grant	0
57	Western Michigan	6
21	Northwestern	7
12	Notre Dame	35
49	Minnesota	6
42	Illinois	6
23	Indiana	6
27	Wisconsin	0
45	Ohio State	7

1944

12	Iowa Pre-Flight	7
14	Marquette	0

0	Indiana	20
28	Minnesota	13
27	Northwestern	0
40	Purdue	14
41	Pennsylvania	19
14	Illinois	0
14	Wisconsin	0
14	Ohio State	18

1945

27	Great Lakes	2
7	Indiana	13
40	Michigan State	0
20	Northwestern	7
7	Army	28
19	Illinois	0
26	Minnesota	0
7	Navy	33
27	Purdue	13
7	Ohio State	3

1946

21	Indiana	0
14	Iowa	7
13	Army	20
14	Northwestern	14
9	Illinois	13
21	Minnesota	0
55	Michigan State	7
28	Wisconsin	6
58	Ohio State	6

1947

55	Michigan State	0
49	Stanford	13
69	Pittsburgh	13
49	Northwestern	21
13	Minnesota	6
14	Illinois	7
35	Indiana	0
40	Wisconsin	6
21	Ohio State	0
49	*Southern California	0
	*Rose Bowl	

1948

13	Michigan State	7
14	Oregon	0
40	Purdue	0
28	Northwestern	0
27	Minnesota	14
28	Iilinois	20
35	Navy	0
54	Indiana	0
13	Ohio State	3

1949

7	Michigan State	3
27	Stanford	7
7	Army	21
20	Northwestern	21

14	Minnesota	7
13	Illinois	0
20	Purdue	12
20	Indiana	7
7	Ohio State	7

1950

7	Michigan State	14
27	Dartmouth	7
6	Army	27
26	Wisconsin	13
7	Minnesota	7
0	Illinois	7
20	Indiana	7
34	Northwestern	23
9	Ohio State	3
14	*California	6
	*Rose Bowl	

1951

0	Michigan State	25
13	Stanford	23
33	Indiana	14
21	Iowa	0
54	Minnesota	27
0	Illinois	7
7	Cornell	20
0	Northwestern	6
7	Ohio State	0

1952

13	Michigan State	27
7	Stanford	14
28	Indiana	13
48	Northwestern	14
21	Minnesota	0
13	Illinois	22
49	Cornell	7
21	Purdue	10
7	Ohio State	27

1953

50	Washington	0
26	Tulane	7
14	Iowa	13
20	Northwestern	12
0	Minnesota	22
24	Pennsylvania	14
3	Illinois	19
6	Michigan State	14
20	Ohio State	0

1954

14	Washington	0
7	Army	26
14	Iowa	13
7	Northwestern	0
34	Minnesota	0
9	Indiana	13
14	Illinois	7
33	Michigan State	7
7	Ohio State	21

1955

42	Missouri	7
14	Michigan State	7
26	Army	2
14	Northwestern	2
14	Minnesota	13
33	Iowa	21
6	Illinois	25
30	Indiana	0
0	Ohio State	17

1956

42	UCLA	13
0	Michigan State	9
48	Army	14
34	Northwestern	20
7	Minnesota	20
17	Iowa	14
17	Illinois	7
49	Indiana	26
19	Ohio State	0

1957

16	Southern California	6
26	Georgia	0
6	Michigan State	35
34	Northwestern	14
24	Minnesota	7
21	Iowa	21
19	Illinois	20
27	Indiana	13
14	Ohio State	31

1958

20	Southern California	19
12	Michigan State	12
14	Navy	20
24	Northwestern	55
20	Minnesota	19
14	Iowa	37
8	Illinois	21
6	Indiana	8
14	Ohio State	20

1959

15	Missouri	20
8	Michigan State	34
18	Oregon State	7
7	Northwestern	20
14	Minnesota	6
10	Wisconsin	19
20	Illinois	15
7	Indiana	26
23	Ohio State	14

1960

21	Oregon	0
17	Michigan State	24
31	Duke	6
14	Northwestern	7
0	Minnesota	10
13	Wisconsin	16
8	Illinois	7
29	Indiana	7
0	Ohio State	7

1961

29	UCLA	6
38	Army	8
0	Michigan State	28
16	Purdue	14
20	Minnesota	23
28	Duke	14
38	Illinois	6
23	Iowa	14
20	Ohio State	50

1962

13	Nebraska	25
17	Army	7
0	Michigan State	28
0	Purdue	37
0	Minnesota	17
12	Wisconsin	34
14	Illinois	10
14	Iowa	28
0	Ohio State	28

1963

27	SMU	16
13	Navy	26
7	Michigan State	7
12	Purdue	23
0	Minnesota	6
27	Northwestern	6
14	Illinois	8
21	Iowa	21
10	Ohio State	14

1964

24	Air Force	7
21	Navy	0
17	Michigan State	10
20	Purdue	21
19	Minnesota	12
35	Northwestern	0
21	Illinois	6
34	Iowa	20
10	Ohio State	0
34	*Oregon State	7
	*Rose Bowl	

1965

31	North Carolina	24
10	California	7
7	Georgia	15
7	Michigan State	24
15	Purdue	17
13	Minnesota	14
50	Wisconsin	14
23	Illinois	3
22	Northwestern	34
7	Ohio State	9

1966

41	Oregon State	0
17	California	7
7	North Carolina	21
7	Michigan State	20
21	Purdue	22
49	Minnesota	0
28	Wisconsin	17
21	Illinois	28
28	Northwestern	20
17	Ohio State	3

1967

10	Duke	7
9	California	10
21	Navy	26
0	Michigan State	34
20	Indiana	27
15	Minnesota	20
7	Northwestern	3
21	Illinois	14
27	Wisconsin	14
14	Ohio State	24

1968

7	California	21
31	Duke	10
32	Navy	9
28	Michigan State	14
27	Indiana	22
33	Minnesota	20
35	Northwestern	0
36	Illinois	0
34	Wisconsin	9
14	Ohio State	50

1969

42	Vanderbilt	14
45	Washington	7
17	Missouri	40
31	Purdue	20
12	Michigan State	23
35	Minnesota	9

35	Wisconsin	7
57	Illinois	0
51	Iowa	6
24	Ohio State	12
3	*Southern California	10
	*Rose Bowl	

1970

20	Arizona	9
17	Washington	3
14	Texas A & M	12
29	Purdue	0
34	Michigan State	20
39	Minnesota	13
29	Wisconsin	15
42	Illinois	0
55	Iowa	0
9	Ohio State	20

1971

21	Northwestern	6
56	Virginia	0
38	UCLA	0
46	Navy	0
24	Michigan State	13
35	Illinois	6
35	Minnesota	7
61	Indiana	7
63	Iowa	7
20	Purdue	17
10	Ohio State	7
12	*Stanford	13
	*Rose Bowl	

1972

7	Northwestern	0
26	UCLA	9
41	Tulane	7
35	Navy	7
10	Michigan State	0
31	Illinois	7
42	Minnesota	0
21	Indiana	7

31	Iowa	0
9	Purdue	6
11	Ohio State	14

1973

31	Iowa	7
47	Stanford	10
14	Navy	0
24	Oregon	0
31	Michigan State	0
35	Wisconsin	6
34	Minnesota	7
49	Indiana	13
21	Illinois	6
34	Purdue	9
10	Ohio State	10

1974

24	Iowa	7
31	Colorado	0
52	Navy	0
27	Stanford	16
21	Michigan State	7
24	Wisconsin	20
49	Minnesota	0
21	Indiana	7
14	Illinois	6
51	Purdue	0
10	Ohio State	12

1975

23	Wisconsin	6
19	Stanford	19
14	Baylor	14
31	Missouri	7
16	Michigan State	6
69	Northwestern	0
55	Indiana	7
28	Minnesota	21
28	Purdue	0
21	Illinois	15
14	Ohio State	21

MICHIGAN STATE UNIVERSITY

East Lansing, Michigan
Established 1855
Colors, Green and White
Nickname, Spartans

Head Coaches

No established coach, 1896
Henry Keep, 1897–1898
Charles O. Bemies, 1899–1900
George Denman, 1901–1902
Chester L. Brewer, 1903–1910
John F. Macklin, 1911–1915
Frank Sommers, 1916

Chester L. Brewer, 1917
George E. Gauthier, 1918
Chester L. Brewer, 1919
George (Potsy) Clark, 1920
Albert M. Barron, 1921–1922
Ralph H. Young, 1923–1927
Harry G. Kipke, 1928

Jimmy Crowley, 1929–1932
Charles W. Bachman, 1933–1946
Clarence (Biggie) Munn, 1947–1953
Hugh (Duffy) Daugherty, 1954–1972
Dennis Stolz, 1973–1975
Darryl Rogers, 1976–

All-American Players

Neno J. DaPrato, halfback, 1915
Sidney Wagner, guard, 1935
John Pingel, halfback, 1938
Ed Bagdon, guard, 1949
Lynn Chandnois, halfback, 1949
Everett Grandelius, halfback, 1950
Dorne Dibble, end, 1950
Don Coleman, tackle, 1951
Bob Carey, end, 1951
Al Dorow, quarterback, 1951
Frank Kush, guard, 1952
Dick Tamburo, center-linebacker, 1952
Don McAuliffe, halfback, 1952
Don Dohoney, end, 1953
Earl Morrall, quarterback, 1955
Norman Masters, tackle, 1955
Dan Currie, center, 1957
Walt Kowalczyk, halfback, 1957
Sam Williams, end, 1958
Dean Look, quarterback, 1959

Dave Behrman, guard, 1961
George Saimes, fullback, 1962
Sherman Lewis, halfback, 1963
Harold Lucas, middle guard, 1965
Ron Goovert, linebacker, 1965
Steve Juday, quarterback, 1965
Charles (Bubba) Smith, end, 1965–66
George Webster, roverback, 1965–66
Gene Washington, end, 1965–66
Clinton Jones, halfback, 1965–66
Bob Apisa, fullback, 1965–66
Jerry West, tackle, 1966
Al Brenner, safety, 1968
Ronald Saul, guard, 1969
Eric B. Allen, tailback, 1971
Brad Van Pelt, safety, 1971–72
Ronald Curl, tackle, 1971
Joe DeLamielleure, guard, 1972
Billy Joe DuPree, end, 1972
William Simpson, back, 1973

Scores
1896–1975

1896

10	Lansing HS	0
0	Kalamazoo	24
0	Alma	0
16	Kalamazoo	18

1897

26	Olivet	6
0	Kalamazoo	28
18	Olivet	18
30	Alma	16
38	Alma	4
6	Notre Dame	34

1898

11	Ypsilanti	6
0	Michigan	39

0	Notre Dame	53
62	Albion	6
45	Olivet	0
24	Ypsilanti	6
0	Kalamazoo	17

1899

0	Notre Dame	40
6	Detroit AC	16
6	Kalamazoo	10
11	Alma	11
18	Ypsilanti	0
17	Olivet	18
23	DePauw	6

1900

0	Albion	23

45	Adrian	0
6	Detroit AC	21
0	Alma	23

1901

5	Alma	6
22	Hillsdale	0
11	Albion	0
0	Detroit AC	33
42	Kalamazoo	0
17	Albion	17
5	Kalamazoo	15
18	Olivet	23

1902

0	Notre Dame	32
11	Detroit	0

0	Michigan	119
35	Hillsdale	0
2	Michigan Frosh	0
12	DePauw	17
6	Olivet	11
22	Albion	11
5	Alma	16

1903

0	Notre Dame	12
11	Alma	0
11	Michigan Frosh	0
11	Kalamazoo	0
51	Detroit YMCA	6
43	Hillsdale	0
6	Albion	6

1904

47	Flint	0
28	Ohio Northern	6
29	Port Huron	0
0	Albion	4
104	Hillsdale	0
39	Michigan Frosh	0
35	Olivet	6
40	Alma	0
58	Kalamazoo	0

1905

42	Flint	0
0	Notre Dame	28
43	Port Huron	0
24	Michigan Frosh	0
30	Olivet	0
18	Hillsdale	0
18	Armour	0
30	Kalamazoo	0
46	Albion	10
11	Northwestern	37
18	Alma	0

1906

23	Olivet	0
0	Alma	0
38	Kalamazoo	0
33	DePauw	0
0	Notre Dame	5
37	Albion	0
5	Albion	0
35	Hillsdale	9
6	Olivet	8
6	Detroit AC	6

1907

17	Detroit	0
40	Flint	0
0	Michigan	46
15	Wabash	6
55	Olivet	4
0	Alma	0
0	Detroit AC	4

1908

0	Michigan	0
35	Kalamazoo	0
0	DePauw	0
6	Wabash	0
46	Olivet	2
30	Saginaw NB	6
37	Detroit AC	14

1909

51	Flint	0
27	Detroit	0
34	Alma	0
28	Wabash	0
0	Notre Dame	17
29	Culver	0
51	DePauw	0
10	Marquette	0
20	Olivet	0
34	Detroit AC	0

1910

35	Detroit	0
11	Alma	0
3	Michigan	6
37	Lake Forest	0
17	Notre Dame	0
3	Marquette	2
62	Olivet	0

1911

12	Alma	0
3	Michigan	25
29	Olivet	3
6	DePauw	0
26	Mt. Union	6
17	Wabash	6

1912

14	Alma	3
7	Michigan	55
52	Olivet	0
58	DePauw	0
46	Ohio Wesleyan	0
61	Mt. Union	21
24	Wabash	0
35	Ohio State	20

1913

26	Olivet	7
57	Alma	0
12	Michigan	7
12	Wisconsin	7
41	Bucknell	0
13	Mt. Union	7
19	South Dakota	7

1914

26	Olivet	7
60	Alma	0

0	Michigan	3
0	Nebraska	24
75	Akron	0
21	Mt. Union	14
6	Penn State	3

1915

34	Olivet	0
77	Alma	12
56	Carroll	0
24	Michigan	0
0	Oregon State	20
67	Marquette	6

1916

40	Olivet	0
20	Carroll	0
33	Alma	0
0	Michigan	9
30	North Dakota State	0
3	South Dakota	3
0	Notre Dame	14

1917

7	Alma	14
3	Kalamazoo	7
0	Michigan	27
0	Detroit	14
0	Western State	30
6	Northwestern	70
0	Notre Dame	23
7	Syracuse	21
0	Camp McArthur	30

1918

21	Albion	6
66	Hillsdale	6
16	Western State	7
6	Purdue	14
13	Notre Dame	7
6	Michigan	21
6	Wisconsin	7

1919

14	Albion	13
46	Alma	6
18	Western State	21
0	Michigan	26
27	DePauw	0
6	Purdue	13
13	South Dakota	0
0	Notre Dame	13
7	Wabash	7

1920

2	Kalamazoo	21
16	Albion	0
48	Alma	0
0	Wisconsin	27
0	Michigan	35
7	Marietta	23

108	Olivet	0
81	Chicago Y	0
7	Nebraska	35
0	Notre Dame	25

1921

28	Alma	0
7	Albion	24
0	Michigan	30
17	Western State	14
0	Marquette	7
14	South Dakota	0
2	Butler	3
0	Notre Dame	48

1922

33	Alma	0
7	Albion	7
0	Wabash	26
7	South Dakota	0
6	Indiana	14
0	Michigan	63
6	Ohio Wesleyan	9
0	Creighton	9
45	Massachusetts State	0
7	St. Louis	7

1923

0	Chicago	34
21	Lake Forest	6
0	Wisconsin	21
13	Albion	0
0	Michigan	37
14	Ohio Wesleyan	19
7	Creighton	27
2	Detroit	0

1924

59	N. W. College	0
54	Olivet	3
0	Michigan	7
34	Chicago Y	3
9	Northwestern	13
42	Lake Forest	13
3	St. Louis	9
9	South Dakota State	0

1925

16	Adrian	0
0	Michigan	39
0	Lake Forest	6
15	Centre	13
6	Penn State	13
0	Colgate	14
58	Toledo	0
10	Wisconsin	21

1926

16	Adrian	0
9	Kalamazoo	0
3	Michigan	55

14	Cornell	24
0	Lake Forest	0
6	Colgate	38
42	Centre	14
7	Haskell	40

1927

12	Kalamazoo	6
27	Ohio	0
0	Michigan	21
13	Cornell	19
7	Detroit	24
7	Indiana	33
20	Albion	6
25	Butler	0
0	North Carolina State	19

1928

103	Kalamazoo	0
0	Albion	2
37	Chicago Y	0
0	Colgate	16
6	Mississippi A & M	6
0	Detroit	39
0	Michigan	3
7	North Carolina State	0

1929

59	Alma	6
0	Michigan	17
0	Colgate	31
74	Adrian	0
40	North Carolina State	6
38	Case	0
33	Mississippi A & M	19
0	Detroit	25

1930

28	Alma	0
0	Michigan	0
32	Cincinnati	0
14	Colgate	7
45	Case	0
13	Georgetown	14
19	North Dakota State	11
0	Detroit	0

1931

74	Alma	0
47	Cornell	0
7	Army	20
34	Illinois Wesleyan	6
6	Georgetown	0
10	Syracuse	15
100	Ripon	0
0	Michigan	0
13	Detroit	20

1932

93	Alma	0
0	Michigan	26

27	Grinnell	6
27	Illinois Wesleyan	0
19	Fordham	13
27	Syracuse	13
20	South Dakota	6
7	Detroit	0

1933

14	Grinnell	0
6	Michigan	20
20	Illinois Wesleyan	12
6	Marquette	0
27	Syracuse	3
0	Kansas State	0
0	Carnegie	0
0	Detroit	14

1934

33	Grinnell	20
16	Michigan	0
13	Carnegie	0
39	Manhattan	0
13	Marquette	7
0	Syracuse	10
7	Detroit	6
6	Kansas	0
26	Texas A & M	13

1935

41	Grinnell	0
25	Michigan	6
42	Kansas	0
6	Boston College	18
47	Washington	13
12	Temple	7
7	Marquette	13
27	Loyola	0

1936

27	Wayne	0
21	Michigan	7
7	Carnegie	0
13	Missouri	0
7	Marquette	13
13	Boston College	13
7	Temple	7
41	Kansas	0
7	Arizona	0

1937

19	Wayne	0
19	Michigan	14
0	Manhattan	3
2	Missouri	0
21	Marquette	7
16	Kansas	0
13	Temple	6
13	Carnegie	6
14	San Francisco	0
0	*Auburn	6
	*Orange Bowl	

1938

34	Wayne	6
0	Michigan	14
18	Illinois Wesleyan	0
26	West Virginia	0
19	Syracuse	12
6	Santa Clara	7
0	Missouri	6
20	Marquette	14
10	Temple	0

1939

16	Wayne	0
13	Michigan	26
14	Marquette	17
7	Purdue	20
13	Illinois Wesleyan	6
14	Syracuse	3
0	Santa Clara	6
7	Indiana	7
18	Temple	7

1940

14	Michigan	21
20	Purdue	7
19	Temple	21
0	Santa Clara	0
32	Kansas State	0
0	Indiana	20
6	Marquette	7
17	West Virginia	0

1941

7	Michigan	19
13	Marquette	7
0	Santa Clara	7
39	Wayne	6
0	Missouri	19
0	Purdue	0
46	Temple	0
31	Ohio Wesleyan	7
14	West Virginia	12

1942

0	Michigan	20
46	Wayne	6
7	Marquette	28
14	Great Lakes	0
7	Temple	7
13	Washington State	25
19	Purdue	6
7	West Virginia	0
7	Oregon State	7

1943

No Football

1944

40	Scranton	12

2	Kentucky	0
45	Kansas State	6
8	Maryland	0
32	Wayne	0
7	Missouri	13
33	Maryland	0

1945

0	Michigan	40
7	Kentucky	6
12	Pittsburgh	7
27	Wayne	7
13	Marquette	13
14	Missouri	7
7	Great Lakes	27
33	Penn State	0
7	Miami	21

1946

42	Wayne	0
20	Boston College	34
0	Mississippi State	6
19	Penn State	16
7	Cincinnati	18
14	Kentucky	39
7	Michigan	55
20	Marquette	0
26	Maryland	14
26	Washington State	20

1947

0	Michigan	55
7	Mississippi State	0
21	Washington State	7
20	Iowa State	0
6	Kentucky	7
13	Marquette	7
28	Santa Clara	0
14	Temple	6
58	Hawaii	19

1948

7	Michigan	13
68	Hawaii	21
7	Notre Dame	26
61	Arizona	7
14	Penn State	14
46	Oregon State	21
47	Marquette	0
48	Iowa State	7
40	Washington State	0
21	Santa Clara	21

1949

3	Michigan	7
48	Marquette	7
14	Maryland	7
42	William & Mary	13
24	Penn State	0
62	Temple	14

21	Notre Dame	34
20	Oregon State	25
75	Arizona	0

1950

38	Oregon State	13
14	Michigan	7
7	Maryland	34
33	William & Mary	14
34	Marquette	6
36	Notre Dame	33
35	Indiana	0
27	Minnesota	0
19	Pittsburgh	0

1951

6	Oregon State	0
25	Michigan	0
24	Ohio State	20
20	Marquette	14
32	Penn State	21
53	Pittsburgh	26
35	Notre Dame	0
30	Indiana	26
45	Colorado	7

1952

27	Michigan	13
17	Oregon State	14
48	Texas A & M	6
48	Syracuse	7
34	Penn State	7
14	Purdue	7
41	Indiana	14
21	Notre Dame	3
62	Marquette	13

1953

21	Iowa	7
21	Minnesota	0
26	TCU	19
47	Indiana	18
0	Purdue	6
34	Oregon State	6
28	Ohio State	13
14	Michigan	6
21	Marquette	15
28	*UCLA	20
	*Rose Bowl	

1954

10	Iowa	14
0	Wisconsin	6
21	Indiana	14
19	Notre Dame	20
13	Purdue	27
13	Minnesota	19
54	Washington State	6
7	Michigan	33
40	Marquette	10

1955

20	Indiana	13
7	Michigan	14
38	Stanford	14
21	Notre Dame	7
21	Illinois	7
27	Wisconsin	0
27	Purdue	0
42	Minnesota	14
33	Marquette	0
17	*UCLA	14
	*Rose Bowl	

1956

21	Stanford	7
9	Michigan	0
53	Indiana	6
47	Notre Dame	14
13	Illinois	20
33	Wisconsin	0
12	Purdue	9
13	Minnesota	14
38	Kansas State	17

1957

54	Indiana	0
19	California	0
35	Michigan	6
13	Purdue	20
19	Illinois	14
21	Wisconsin	7
34	Notre Dame	6
42	Minnesota	13
27	Kansas State	9

1958

32	California	12
12	Michigan	12
22	Pittsburgh	8
6	Purdue	14
0	Illinois	16
7	Wisconsin	9
0	Indiana	6
12	Minnesota	39
26	Kansas State	7

1959

7	Texas A & M	9
34	Michigan	8
8	Iowa	37
19	Notre Dame	0
14	Indiana	6
24	Ohio State	30
15	Purdue	0
15	Northwestern	10
13	Miami (Fla.)	18

1960

7	Pittsburgh	7
24	Michigan	17
15	Iowa	27
21	Notre Dame	0
35	Indiana	0
10	Ohio State	21
17	Purdue	13
21	Northwestern	18
43	Detroit	15

1961

20	Wisconsin	0
31	Stanford	3
28	Michigan	0
17	Notre Dame	7
35	Indiana	0
0	Minnesota	13
6	Purdue	7
21	Northwestern	13
34	Illinois	7

1962

13	Stanford	16
38	North Carolina	6
28	Michigan	0
31	Notre Dame	7
26	Indiana	8
7	Minnesota	28
9	Purdue	17
31	Northwestern	7
6	Illinois	7

1963

31	North Carolina	0
10	Southern California	13
7	Michigan	7
20	Indiana	3
15	Northwestern	7
30	Wisconsin	13
23	Purdue	0
12	Notre Dame	7
0	Illinois	13

1964

15	North Carolina	21
17	Southern California	7
10	Michigan	17
20	Indiana	27
24	Northwestern	6
22	Wisconsin	6
21	Purdue	7
7	Notre Dame	34
0	Illinois	16

1965

13	UCLA	3
23	Penn State	0
22	Illinois	12
24	Michigan	7
32	Ohio State	7
14	Purdue	10
49	Northwestern	7

35	Iowa	0
27	Indiana	13
12	Notre Dame	3
12	*UCLA	14
	*Rose Bowl	

1966

28	North Carolina State	10
42	Penn State	8
26	Illinois	10
20	Michigan	7
11	Ohio State	8
41	Purdue	20
22	Northwestern	0
56	Iowa	7
37	Indiana	19
10	Notre Dame	10

1967

7	Houston	37
17	Southern California	21
35	Wisconsin	7
34	Michigan	0
0	Minnesota	21
12	Notre Dame	24
7	Ohio State	21
13	Indiana	14
7	Purdue	21
41	Northwestern	27

1968

14	Syracuse	10
28	Baylor	10
39	Wisconsin	0
14	Michigan	28
13	Minnesota	14
21	Notre Dame	17
20	Ohio State	25
22	Indiana	24
0	Purdue	9
31	Northwestern	14

1969

27	Washington	11
23	SMU	15
28	Notre Dame	42
21	Ohio State	54
23	Michigan	12
18	Iowa	19
0	Indiana	16
13	Purdue	41
10	Minnesota	14
39	Northwestern	7

1970

16	Washington	42
28	Washington State	14
0	Notre Dame	29
0	Ohio State	29
20	Michigan	34

37	Iowa	0
32	Indiana	7
24	Purdue	14
13	Minnesota	23
20	Northwestern	23

1971

10	Illinois	0
0	Georgia Tech	10
31	Oregon State	14
2	Notre Dame	14
13	Michigan	24
28	Wisconsin	31
34	Iowa	3
43	Purdue	10
17	Ohio State	10
40	Minnesota	25
7	Northwestern	28

1972

24	Illinois	0
16	Georgia Tech	21
6	Southern California	51
0	Notre Dame	16

0	Michigan	10
31	Wisconsin	0
6	Iowa	6
22	Purdue	12
19	Ohio State	12
10	Minnesota	14
24	Northwestern	14

1973

10	Northwestern	14
14	Syracuse	8
21	UCLA	34
10	Notre Dame	14
0	Michigan	31
3	Illinois	6
10	Purdue	7
21	Wisconsin	0
0	Ohio State	35
10	Indiana	9
15	Iowa	6

1974

41	Northwestern	7

19	Syracuse	0
14	UCLA	56
14	Notre Dame	19
7	Michigan	21
21	Illinois	21
31	Purdue	7
28	Wisconsin	21
16	Ohio State	13
19	Indiana	10
60	Iowa	21

1975

0	Ohio State	21
14	Miami (Ohio)	13
37	North Carolina State	15
10	Notre Dame	3
6	Michigan	16
38	Minnesota	15
19	Illinois	21
10	Purdue	20
14	Indiana	6
47	Northwestern	14
27	Iowa	23

UNIVERSITY OF MINNESOTA

Minneapolis, Minnesota
Established 1851
Colors, Maroon and Gold
Nickname, Golden Gophers

Head Coaches

Thomas Peebles, 1882–83
Fred S. Jones, 1886–89
Tom Eck, 1890
Ed (Dad) Moulton, 1891
(no coach in 1892
"Wallie" Winter, 1893
Tom Cochrane, Jr., 1894
W. W. (Pudge) Heffelfinger, 1895
Alex N. Jerrems, 1896–97
Jack Minds, 1898

Bill Leary & J. Harrison, 1899
Dr. Henry L. Williams, 1900–1921
William Spaulding, 1922–1924
Dr. Clarence W. Spears, 1925–1929
Fritz Crisler, 1930–1931
Bernie Bierman, 1932–1941
Dr. George Hauser, 1942–1944
Bernie Bierman, 1945–1950
Wes Fesler, 1951–1953
Murray Warmath, 1954–1971

Cal Stoll, 1972–

All-American Players

Johnny McGovern, quarterback, 1909
Jim Walker, tackle, 1910
Bert Baston, end, 1915–16
C. I. (Shorty) Long, quarterback, 1916
Earl Martineau, halfback, 1923
Herb Joesting, fullback, 1926–27
Harold Hanson, guard, 1927
George Gibson, guard, 1928
Ken Haycraft, end, 1928
Bronko Nagurski, tackle, 1929
Clarence (Biggie) Munn, 1931

Frank (Butch) Larson, end, 1933–34
Francis (Pug) Lund, halfback, 1934
Bill Bevan, guard, 1934
Charles (Bud) Wilkinson, guard, 1935
Dick Smith, tackle, 1935
Ed Widseth, tackle, 1936
Ray King, end, 1937
Francis Twedell, guard, 1938
Urban Odson, tackle, 1940
George Franck, halfback, 1940
Bruce Smith, halfback, 1941

Dick Wildung, halfback, 1941
Leo Nomellini, tackle-guard, 1948–49
Clayton Tonnemaker, center, 1949
Paul Giel, halfback, 1952–53
Bob McNamara, fullback-halfback, 1954
Bob Hobert, tackle, 1956
Tom Brown, guard, 1960
Sandy Stephens, quarterback, 1961
Bobby Bell, tackle, 1961–62
Carl Eller, tackle, 1963
Aaron Brown, end, 1965
Bob Stein, end, 1967
Doug Kingsriter, end, 1971

A stalwart in the defensive platoon of the 1961 Minnesota Rose Bowl team was two-time All-American Bobby Bell, one of the greatest tackles in tradition-rich Gopher history.

Scores
1882–1975

1882

4	Hamline	0

1883

2	Carleton	4
4	Hamline	2
2	Hamline	4

1884

No Games

1885

No Games

1886

5	Shattuck	9
8	Shattuck	8

1887

8	Shattuck	18
14	Shattuck	0

1888

8	Shattuck	16
14	Shattuck	0

1889

2	Ex-Collegiates	0
10	Ex-Collegiates	0
8	Shattuck	28
26	Shattuck	0

1890

63	Wisconsin	0
2	Ex-Collegiates	0
10	Ex-Collegiates	10
58	Shattuck	0

1891

26	Wisconsin	12
42	Iowa	4
0	Ex-Collegiates	4
12	Grinnell	12
22	Grinnell	14

1892

32	Wisconsin	4
14	Michigan	6
16	Northwestern	12
18	Ex-Collegiates	10
40	Grinnell	24

1893

40	Wisconsin	0
34	Michigan	20
16	Northwestern	0
36	Grinnell	0
10	Hamline	6
12	Kansas	6

1894

0	Wisconsin	6
24	Purdue	0
40	Beloit	0
10	Grinnell	2

1895

14	Wisconsin	10
0	Michigan	20
10	Chicago	6
4	Purdue	18
6	Boat Club	0
14	Ex-Collegiates	0
4	Grinnell	6
20	High Schools	0
24	Iowa State	0
40	Macalester	0

1896

0	Wisconsin	6
4	Michigan	6
14	Purdue	0
16	Carleton	6
8	Ex-Collegiates	0
12	Grinnell	0
50	High Schools	0
34	High Schools	0
18	Iowa State	6
12	Kansas	0

1897

0	Wisconsin	39
0	Michigan	14
0	Purdue	6
48	Carleton	6
6	Grinnell	0
22	High Schools	0
10	Iowa State	12
26	Macalester	0

1898

0	Wisconsin	28
10	Illinois	11
17	Northwestern	6
0	Alumni	5
32	Carleton	0
6	Grinnell	16
0	Iowa State	6
15	North Dakota State	0
12	Rush Medical College	0

1899

0	Wisconsin	19
0	Chicago	29
5	Northwestern	11
6	Alumni	5
5	Beloit	5
35	Carleton	5
5	Grinnell	5
20	High Schools	0
6	Iowa State	0
29	Macalester	0
40	Shattuck	0

1900

6	Wisconsin	5
6	Chicago	6
23	Illinois	0
21	Northwestern	0
44	Carleton	0
26	Grinnell	0
0	High Schools	0
26	High Schools	0
27	Iowa State	0
66	Macalester	0
20	Nebraska	12
34	North Dakota	0

1901

0	Wisconsin	18
16	Iowa	0
16	Illinois	0
16	Northwestern	0
35	Carleton	0
27	Chicago	0
28	Haskell	0
16	High School	0
19	Nebraska	0
10	North Dakota	0

1902

11	Wisconsin	0
34	Iowa	0
6	Michigan	23
17	Illinois	5
29	Beloit	0
33	Carleton	0
102	Grinnell	0
59	Hamline	0
28	High Schools	0
16	Iowa State	0
0	Nebraska	6

1903

17	Wisconsin	0
75	Iowa	0
6	Michigan	6
32	Illinois	0
46	Beloit	0
29	Carleton	0
39	Grinnell	0
65	Hamline	0
57	High Schools	6
37	High Schools	0
46	Iowa State	0
46	Lawrence	0
112	Mecalester	0
11	North Dakota	0

1904

28	Wisconsin	0
11	Iowa	0
17	Northwestern	0
65	Carleton	0
146	Grinnell	0
107	High Schools	0
32	Iowa State	0
69	Lawrence	0
16	Nebraska	12
35	North Dakota	0
47	St. Thomas	0
75	Shattuck	0
77	South Dakota	0

1905

12	Wisconsin	16
39	Iowa	0
72	Northwestern	6
74	High Schools	0
42	Ames	0
46	Lawrence	0
35	Nebraska	0
45	North Dakota	0
21	Pillsbury	0
42	St. Thomas	0
30	Shattuck	0
8	South Dakota	0

1906

4	Chicago	2
8	Indiana	6
0	Carlisle	17
22	Ames	4
13	Nebraska	0

1907

17	Wisconsin	17
12	Chicago	18
10	Carlisle	12
8	Ames	0
8	Nebraska	5

1908

5	Wisconsin	0
0	Chicago	29
11	Carlisle	6
15	Ames	10
6	Lawrence	0
0	Nebraska	0

1909

25	Lawrence	0
41	Iowa	0
18	Ames	0
14	Nebraska	0
20	Chicago	6
34	Wisconsin	6
6	Michigan	15

1910

34	Lawrence	0
17	South Dakota	0
49	Ames	0
27	Nebraska	0
24	Chicago	0
28	Wisconsin	0
0	Michigan	6

1911

5	Ames	0
5	South Dakota	0
21	Nebraska	3
30	Chicago	0
24	Iowa	6
6	Wisconsin	6
11	Illinois	0

1912

0	South Dakota	10
5	Ames	0
13	Nebraska	0
56	Iowa	7
13	Illinois	0
0	Wisconsin	14
0	Chicago	7

1913

14	South Dakota	0
25	Ames	0
0	Nebraska	7
30	North Dakota	0
21	Wisconsin	3
7	Chicago	13
19	Illinois	9

1914

28	North Dakota	6
26	Ames	0
29	South Dakota	7
7	Iowa	0
6	Illinois	21
14	Wisconsin	3
13	Chicago	7

1915

41	North Dakota	0
34	Ames	6
19	South Dakota	0
51	Iowa	13
6	Illinois	6
20	Chicago	7
20	Wisconsin	3

1916

41	South Dakota State	7
47	North Dakota	7
81	South Dakota	0
67	Iowa	0
9	Illinois	14
54	Wisconsin	0
49	Chicago	0

1917

64	South Dakota State	0
33	Indiana	9
7	Wisconsin	10
33	Chicago	0
27	Illinois	6

1918

0	All-Stars	0
33	Overland-Avi.	0
27	St. Thomas	6
57	Carleton	7
0	Iowa	6

6	Wisconsin	0
6	Municipal Pier (Chicago)	20
7	Chicago	0

1919

39	North Dakota	0
6	Nebraska	6
20	Indiana	6
6	Iowa	9
19	Wisconsin	7
6	Illinois	10
34	Michigan	7

1920

0	Wisconsin	3
7	Iowa	28
0	Michigan	3
7	Illinois	17
0	Northwestern	17
7	Indiana	21
41	North Dakota	3

1921

0	Wisconsin	35
7	Iowa	41
0	Michigan	38
28	Northwestern	0
6	Indiana	0
0	Ohio State	27
19	North Dakota	0

1922

0	Wisconsin	14
14	Iowa	28
7	Michigan	16
7	Northwestern	7
20	Indiana	0
0	Ohio State	0
22	North Dakota	0

1923

0	Wisconsin	0
20	Iowa	7
0	Michigan	10
34	Northwestern	14
13	Haskell	12
20	Iowa State	17
27	North Dakota	0

1924

7	Wisconsin	7
0	Iowa	13
0	Michigan	13
20	Illinois	7
20	Haskell	0
7	Iowa State	7
14	North Dakota	0
0	Vanderbilt	16

1925

12	Wisconsin	12
33	Iowa	0
0	Michigan	35
33	Butler	7
34	Grinnell	6
25	North Dakota	6
7	Notre Dame	19
32	Wabash	6

1926

16	Wisconsin	10
41	Iowa	0
0	Michigan	20
6	Michigan	7
81	Butler	0
51	North Dakota	0
7	Notre Dame	20
67	Wabash	7

1927

13	Wisconsin	7
38	Iowa	0
13	Michigan	7
14	Indiana	14
27	Drake	6
57	North Dakota	10
7	Notre Dame	7
40	Oklahoma A & M	0

1928

6	Wisconsin	0
6	Iowa	7
33	Chicago	7
9	Northwestern	10
21	Indiana	12
15	Purdue	0
40	Creighton	0
52	Haskell	0

1929

13	Wisconsin	12
7	Iowa	9
6	Michigan	7
26	Northwestern	14
19	Indiana	7
39	Coe	0
54	Ripon	0
15	Vanderbilt	6

1930

0	Wisconsin	14
0	Michigan	7
6	Northwestern	27
6	Indiana	0
59	South Dakota	0
48	South Dakota State	0
0	Stanford	0
7	Vanderbilt	33

1931

14	Wisconsin	0
34	Iowa	0
0	Michigan	6
14	Northwestern	32
19	Ohio State	7
47	Cornell (Iowa)	7
13	North Dakota State	7
20	Oklahoma A & M	0
30	Ripon	0
0	Stanford	13

1932

12	South Dakota State	0
0	Purdue	7
7	Nebraska	6
21	Iowa	6
7	Northwestern	0
26	Mississippi	0
13	Wisconsin	20
0	Michigan	3

1933

19	South Dakota State	6
6	Indiana	6
7	Purdue	7
7	Pittsburgh	3
19	Iowa	7
0	Northwestern	0
0	Michigan	0
6	Wisconsin	3

1934

56	South Dakota State	12
20	Nebraska	0
13	Pittsburgh	7
48	Iowa	12
34	Michigan	0
30	Indiana	0
35	Chicago	7
34	Wisconsin	0

1935

26	North Dakota State	6
12	Nebraska	7
20	Tulane	0
21	Northwestern	13
29	Purdue	7
13	Iowa	6
40	Michigan	0
33	Wisconsin	7

1936

14	Washington	7
7	Nebraska	0
26	Michigan	0
33	Purdue	0
0	Northwestern	6
52	Iowa	0

47	Texas	19
24	Wisconsin	0

1937

69	North Dakota State	7
9	Nebraska	14
6	Indiana	0
39	Michigan	6
6	Notre Dame	7
35	Iowa	10
7	Northwestern	0
13	Wisconsin	6

1938

15	Washington	0
16	Nebraska	7
7	Purdue	0
7	Michigan	6
3	Northwestern	6
28	Iowa	0
0	Notre Dame	19
21	Wisconsin	0

1939

62	Arizona	0
7	Nebraska	6
13	Purdue	13
20	Ohio State	23
7	Northwestern	14
20	Michigan	7
9	Iowa	13
23	Wisconsin	7

1940

19	Washington	14
13	Nebraska	7
13	Ohio State	7
34	Iowa	6
13	Northwestern	12
7	Michigan	6
33	Purdue	6
22	Wisconsin	13

1941

14	Washington	6
34	Illinois	6
39	Pittsburgh	0
7	Michigan	0
8	Northwestern	7
9	Nebraska	0
34	Iowa	13
41	Wisconsin	6

1942

50	Pittsburgh	7
6	Iowa Seahawks	7
13	Illinois	20
15	Nebraska	2
16	Michigan	14

19	Northwestern	7
0	Indiana	7
27	Iowa	7
6	Wisconsin	20

1943

26	Missouri	13
54	Nebraska	0
13	Camp Grant	7
6	Michigan	49
6	Northwestern	42
7	Purdue	14
33	Iowa	13
25	Wisconsin	13
0	Iowa Seahawks	32

1944

13	Iowa Seahawks	19
39	Nebraska	0
13	Michigan	28
39	Missouri	27
14	Ohio State	34
14	Northwestern	14
19	Indiana	14
46	Iowa	0
28	Wisconsin	26

1945

34	Missouri	0
61	Nebraska	7
14	Fort Warren	0
30	Northwestern	7
7	Ohio State	20
0	Michigan	26
0	Indiana	49
19	Iowa	20
12	Wisconsin	26

1946

33	Nebraska	6
0	Indiana	21
7	Northwestern	14
46	Wyoming	0
9	Ohio State	39
0	Michigan	21
13	Purdue	7
16	Iowa	6
6	Wisconsin	0

1947

7	Washington	6
28	Nebraska	13
37	Northwestern	21
13	Illinois	40
6	Michigan	13
29	Pittsburgh	0
26	Purdue	21
7	Iowa	13
21	Wisconsin	0

1948

20	Washington	0
39	Nebraska	13
16	Northwestern	19
6	Illinois	0
14	Michigan	27
30	Indiana	7
34	Purdue	7
28	Iowa	21
16	Wisconsin	0

1949

48	Washington	20
28	Nebraska	6
21	Northwestern	7
27	Ohio State	0
7	Michigan	14
7	Purdue	13
55	Iowa	7
24	Pittsburgh	7
14	Wisconsin	6

1950

13	Washington	28
26	Nebraska	32
6	Northwestern	13
0	Ohio State	48
7	Michigan	7
0	Iowa	13
0	Michigan State	27
27	Purdue	14
0	Wisconsin	14

1951

20	Washington	25
14	California	55
7	Northwestern	21
39	Nebraska	20
27	Michigan	54
20	Iowa	20
16	Indiana	14
13	Purdue	19
6	Wisconsin	30

1952

13	Washington	19
13	California	49
27	Northwestern	26
13	Illinois	7
0	Michigan	21
17	Iowa	7
14	Purdue	14
13	Nebraska	7
21	Wisconsin	21

1953

7	USC	17
0	Michigan State	21
30	Northwestern	13
7	Illinois	27
22	Michigan	0
35	Pittsburgh	14
28	Indiana	20
0	Iowa	27
21	Wisconsin	21

1954

19	Nebraska	7
46	Pittsburgh	7
26	Northwestern	7
19	Illinois	6
0	Michigan	34
19	Michigan State	13
44	Oregon State	6
22	Iowa	20
0	Wisconsin	27

1955

0	Washington	30
6	Purdue	7
18	Northwestern	7
13	Illinois	21
13	Michigan	14
25	USC	19
0	Iowa	26
14	Michigan State	42
21	Wisconsin	6

1956

34	Washington	14
21	Purdue	14
0	Northwestern	0
16	Illinois	13
20	Michigan	7
9	Pittsburgh	6
0	Iowa	7
14	Michigan State	13
13	Wisconsin	13

1957

46	Washington	7
21	Purdue	17
41	Northwestern	6
13	Illinois	34
7	Michigan	24
34	Indiana	0
20	Iowa	44
13	Michigan State	42
6	Wisconsin	14

1958

21	Washington	24
7	Pittsburgh	13
3	Northwestern	7
8	Illinois	20
19	Michigan	20
0	Indiana	6
6	Iowa	28

39	Michigan State	12
12	Wisconsin	27

1959

12	Nebraska	32
24	Indiana	14
0	Northwestern	6
6	Illinois	14
6	Michigan	14
20	Vanderbilt	6
0	Iowa	33
23	Purdue	29
7	Wisconsin	11

1960

26	Nebraska	14
42	Indiana	0
7	Northwestern	0
21	Illinois	10
10	Michigan	0
48	Kansas State	7
27	Iowa	10
14	Purdue	23
26	Wisconsin	7
7	*Washington	17
	*Rose Bowl	

1961

0	Missouri	6
14	Oregon	7
10	Northwestern	3
33	Illinois	0
23	Michigan	20
13	Michigan State	0
16	Iowa	9
10	Purdue	7
21	Wisconsin	23

1962

0	Missouri	0
21	Navy	0
22	Northwestern	34
17	Illinois	0
17	Michigan	0
28	Michigan State	7
10	Iowa	0
7	Purdue	6
9	Wisconsin	14

1963

7	Nebraska	14
24	Army	8
8	Northwestern	15
6	Illinois	16
6	Michigan	0
6	Indiana	24
13	Iowa	27
11	Purdue	13
14	Wisconsin	0

1964

21	Nebraska	26
26	California	20
21	Northwestern	18
0	Illinois	14
12	Michigan	19
21	Indiana	0
14	Iowa	13
14	Purdue	7
7	Wisconsin	14

1965

20	USC	20
13	Washington State	14
6	Missouri	17
42	Indiana	18
14	Iowa	3
14	Michigan	13
10	Ohio State	11
27	Northwestern	22
0	Purdue	35
42	Wisconsin	7

1966

0	Missouri	24
35	Stanford	21
14	Kansas	16
7	Indiana	7
17	Iowa	0
0	Michigan	49
17	Ohio State	7
28	Northwestern	13
0	Purdue	16
6	Wisconsin	7

1967

13	Utah	12
0	Nebraska	7
23	SMU	3
10	Illinois	7
21	Michigan State	0
20	Michigan	15
10	Iowa	0
12	Purdue	41
33	Indiana	7
21	Wisconsin	14

1968

20	USC	29

14	Nebraska	17
24	Wake Forest	19
17	Illinois	10
14	Michigan State	13
20	Michigan	33
28	Iowa	35
27	Purdue	13
20	Indiana	6
23	Wisconsin	15

1969

26	Arizona State	48
35	Ohio University	35
14	Nebraska	42
7	Indiana	17
7	Ohio State	34
9	Michigan	35
35	Iowa	7
28	Northwestern	21
14	Michigan State	10
35	Wisconsin	10

1970

12	Missouri	34
49	Ohio University	7
10	Nebraska	35
23	Indiana	0
8	Ohio State	28
13	Michigan	39
14	Iowa	14
14	Northwestern	28
23	Michigan State	13
14	Wisconsin	39

1971

28	Indiana	0
7	Nebraska	35
20	Washington State	31
38	Kansas	20
13	Purdue	27
19	Iowa	14
7	Michigan	35
12	Ohio State	14
20	Northwestern	41
25	Michigan State	40
23	Wisconsin	21

1972

23	Indiana	27

6	Colorado	38
0	Nebraska	49
28	Kansas	34
3	Purdue	28
43	Iowa	14
0	Michigan	42
19	Ohio State	27
35	Northwestern	29
14	Michigan State	10
14	Wisconsin	6

1973

7	Ohio State	56
41	North Dakota	14
19	Kansas	34
7	Nebraska	48
24	Indiana	3
31	Iowa	23
7	Michigan	34
52	Northwestern	43
34	Purdue	7
19	Illinois	16
19	Wisconsin	17

1974

19	Ohio State	34
42	North Dakota	30
9	TCU	7
0	Nebraska	54
3	Indiana	34
23	Iowa	17
0	Michigan	49
13	Northwestern	21
24	Purdue	20
14	Illinois	17
14	Wisconsin	49

1975

14	Indiana	20
38	Western Michigan	0
10	Oregon	0
21	Ohio University	0
23	Illinois	42
15	Michigan State	38
31	Iowa	7
21	Michigan	28
33	Northwestern	9
6	Ohio State	38
24	Wisconsin	3

NORTHWESTERN UNIVERSITY

Evanston, Illinois
Established 1851
Colors, Purple and White
Nickname, Wildcats

Head Coaches

No coach, 1888–1892
Paul Noyes, 1893

A. A. Ewing, 1894
Alvin Culver, 1895–1896

Jesse Van Doozer, 1897
W. H. Bannard, 1898
C. M. Hollister, 1899–1902
Walter McCornack, 1903–1905
No football, 1906–1907
Alton Johnson, 1908
1909, Bill Horr
C. E. Hammett, 1910–1912
Dennis Grady, 1913
Fred Murphy, 1914–1918
Charles Bachman, 1919
Elmer McDevitt, 1920–1921
Glen Thistlethwaite, 1922–1926
Dick Hanley, 1927–1934
Lynn (Pappy) Waldorf, 1935–1946
Bob Voigts, 1947–1954
Lou Saban, 1955
Ara Parseghian, 1956–1963
Alex Agase, 1964–1972
John Pont, 1973–

All-American Players

Alton Johnson, halfback, 1901
Tim Lowry, center, 1925
Ralph (Moon) Baker, halfback, 1926
Bob Johnson, tackle, 1926
Henry Anderson, guard, 1929
Fayette (Reb) Russell, fullback, 1930
Frank Baker, end, 1930
Wade (Red) Woodworth, guard, 1930
Ernest (Pug) Rentner, halfback, 1931
Dallas Marvil, tackle, 1931
Jack Riley, tackle, 1931
Edgar (Eggs) Manske, end, 1933
Paul Tangora, guard, 1935
Steve Reid, guard, 1936
Bob Voigts, tackle, 1938
John Haman, center, 1939
Alf Bauman, tackle, 1940
Otto Graham, halfback, 1943

Halfback Alton Johnson, in 1901, distinguished himself as the first All-American in the history of Northwestern football.

Herb Hein, end, 1943
Max Morris, end, 1945
Art Murakowski, fullback, 1948
Alex Sarkisian, center, 1948
Don Stonesifer, end, 1950
Joe Collier, end, 1952
Andy Cvercko, tackle, 1958
Ron Burton, halfback, 1959
Jim Andreotti, center, 1959
Larry Onesti, center, 1961
Jack Cvercko, guard, 1962
Tom Myers, quarterback, 1962
Mike Adamle, fullback, 1970
Eric Hutchinson, safety, 1971

Scores
1888–1975

1888

16	W. Div. HS	6
4	Lake Forest	18
12	Lake Forest	6

1889

18	Evanston HS	4
0	Notre Dame	9
0	University Grads	25
24	Chi. Wanderers	0

1890

16	Evanston HS	4
0	S. Div. HS	0
0	University Grads	24

| 22 | Wisconsin | 10 |
| 22 | Beloit | 6 |

1891

0	Lake Forest	0
0	Wisconsin	0
12	Beloit	12
6	Lake Forest	20
0	Wisconsin	40
20	Chicago YMCA	0

1892

16	Chicago YMCA	0
16	Illinois	16
36	Beloit	0

0	Chicago	0
6	Chicago	4
10	Michigan	8
12	Minnesota	18
18	Lake Forest	0
6	Wisconsin	20
6	Wisconsin	26

1893

6	Chicago	12
0	Illinois	0
12	Lake Forest	12
0	Minnesota	16
6	Chicago	6
10	Beloit	6
38	Lake Forest	22

6	Michigan	72
14	Chicago	22
0	Denver AC	8

1894

0	Chicago	46
6	Lake Forest	24
0	Beloit	42
12	Lake Forest	8
0	Illinois	66
0	Chicago	36

1895

24	Purdue	6
4	Illinois	38
6	Wisconsin	12
0	Iowa State	36
34	Beloit	6
12	Evanston HS	0
44	Armour	0
22	Chicago	6
24	Rush	0
0	Chicago	6
18	Missouri	22
24	Lake Forest	0

1896

25	Englewood HS	0
40	Armour	0
4	Chicago AC	0
46	Chicago	6
6	Chicago	18
10	Illinois	4
6	Wisconsin	6
6	Beloit	6
16	Physicians & Surgeons	6

1897

6	Beloit	0
6	Iowa	12
6	Chicago	21
6	Physicians & Surgeons	0
16	Rush	0
25	Alumni	0
0	Wisconsin	22

1898

34	N.W. Div. HS	0
22	Englewood HS	0
18	Hyde Park HS	0
57	Dixon College	0
17	Beloit	0
11	Physicians & Surgeons	2
5	Chicago	34
27	Lake Forest	0
5	Michigan	6
6	Minnesota	17
0	Wisconsin	47

1899

29	Englewood HS	0
0	Alumni	18
0	Rush	6
0	Wisconsin	38
0	Beloit	11
16	Lake Forest	0
0	Notre Dame	12
11	Minnesota	5
0	Chicago	76
11	Indiana	6
29	Purdue	0
24	N.U. Dental	0

1900

26	Naperville	0
0	Physicians & Surgeons	6
6	Rush	0
12	Indiana	0
0	Illinois	0
6	Beloit	6
11	Knox	5
5	Chicago	0
0	Minnesota	21
5	Iowa	5
23	Lake Forest	0

1901

44	Lombard	0
12	Lake Forest	0
21	Fort Sheridan	0
2	Notre Dame	0
0	Michigan	29
17	Illinois	11
6	Chicago	5
11	Beloit	11
0	Minnesota	16
10	Purdue	5
30	Naperville	0

1902

10	Naperville	5
26	Lake Forest	0
11	Rush	0
0	Chicago	12
0	Knox	15
0	Purdue	5
0	Wisconsin	51
10	Beloit	0
0	Illinois	17
0	Nebraska	12
15	Ft. Sheridan	0

1903

17	N. Div. HS	5
28	Fort Sheridan	0
35	Englewood HS	0
22	Naperville	6
5	Alumni	0
24	Lombard	0

10	Chicago Dental	11
23	Washington (Mo.)	0
0	Chicago	0
35	Cincinnati	0
0	Notre Dame	0
6	Wisconsin	6
0	Carlisle	28

1904

17	Fort Sheridan	0
34	Naperville	0
18	N. Div. HS	0
55	Lombard	0
34	Beloit	0
0	Chicago	32
45	DePauw	0
97	Oshkosh Normal	0
12	Illinois	6
0	Minnesota	17

1905

32	Evanston HS	0
11	N. Div. HS	0
41	St. Viator	0
5	Wabash	0
18	Beloit	2
0	Transylvania	0
0	Chicago	32
30	Marquette	5
34	Ohio Northern	0
37	Michigan State	11
6	Minnesota	72

1906

No intercollegiate games

1907

No intercollegiate games

1908

10	Alumni	6
44	Beloit	4
10	Purdue	16
8	Illinois	64

1909

0	Illinois Wesleyan	0
14	Purdue	5
11	Wisconsin	21
0	Chicago	34
0	Illinois	35

1910

0	Illinois Wesleyan	3
10	Iowa	5
0	Chicago	10
0	Wisconsin	0
0	Illinois	27

1911

26	Monmouth	0
10	Illinois Wesleyan	0
5	Indiana	0
3	Wisconsin	28
3	Chicago	9
13	Illinois	27
0	Iowa	6

1912

0	Lake Forest	0
0	Wisconsin	56
20	Indiana	7
6	Purdue	21
0	Chicago	3
6	Illinois	0

1913

10	Lake Forest	0
0	Purdue	34
0	Illinois	37
6	Iowa	78
0	Chicago	14
20	Indiana	21
0	Ohio State	58

1914

7	Lake Forest	0
0	Chicago	28
0	Indiana	27
0	Illinois	33
0	Iowa	27
6	Purdue	34
0	Ohio State	27

1915

27	Lake Forest	6
0	Chicago	7
6	Iowa	9
6	Illinois	36
24	Missouri	6
6	Indiana	14
0	Ohio State	34

1916

26	Lake Forest	7
10	Chicago	0
40	Drake	6
7	Indiana	0
20	Iowa	13
38	Purdue	6
3	Ohio State	23

1917

48	Lake Forest	0
0	Ohio State	40
0	Chicago	7
12	Purdue	6
39	Michigan State	6

| 25 | Iowa | 14 |
| 21 | Michigan | 12 |

1918

0	Great Lakes	0
0	Municipal Pier	25
47	Knox	7
21	Chicago	6
7	Iowa	23

1919

20	Depauw	0
6	Wisconsin	10
13	Michigan	16
0	Chicago	41
7	Iowa	14
3	Indiana	2
0	Rutgers	28

1920

14	Knox	0
17	Minnesota	0
7	Wisconsin	27
7	Indiana	10
0	Iowa	20
14	Purdue	0
7	Notre Dame	33

1921

0	Beloit	7
0	Chicago	41
0	Minnesota	28
0	Wisconsin	27
34	DePaul	0
0	Purdue	3
0	Iowa	14

1922

17	Beloit	0
7	Chicago	15
7	Minnesota	7
3	Illinois	6
24	Purdue	13
58	Monmouth	14
3	Iowa	37

1923

21	Beloit	6
6	Indiana	7
0	Chicago	13
0	Illinois	29
14	Minnesota	34
32	Lake Forest	0
3	Purdue	6
14	Iowa	17

1924

| 28 | South Dakota | 0 |
| 42 | Cincinnati | 0 |

3	Purdue	7
13	Michigan State	9
17	Indiana	7
0	Michigan	27
0	Chicago	3
6	Notre Dame	13

1925

14	South Dakota	7
17	Carleton	0
0	Chicago	6
7	Tulane	18
17	Indiana	14
3	Michigan	2
13	Purdue	9
10	Notre Dame	13

1926

34	South Dakota	0
31	Carleton	3
20	Indiana	0
0	Notre Dame	6
21	Indiana	0
22	Purdue	0
38	Chicago	7
13	Iowa	6

1927

47	South Dakota	2
13	Utah	6
19	Ohio State	13
6	Illinois	7
19	Missouri	34
6	Purdue	18
7	Indiana	18
12	Iowa	0

1928

14	Butler	0
0	Ohio State	10
7	Kentucky	0
0	Illinois	6
10	Minnesota	9
7	Purdue	6
0	Indiana	6
27	Dartmouth	6

1929

27	Cornell (Iowa)	18
13	Butler	0
7	Wisconsin	0
14	Minnesota	26
66	Wabash	0
7	Illinois	0
18	Ohio State	6
14	Indiana	19
6	Notre Dame	26

1930

| 14 | Tulane | 0 |

19	Ohio State	2
32	Illinois	0
45	Centre	7
27	Minnesota	6
25	Indiana	0
20	Wisconsin	7
0	Notre Dame	14

1931

19	Nebraska	7
0	Notre Dame	0
19	UCLA	0
10	Ohio State	0
32	Illinois	6
32	Minnesota	14
7	Indiana	6
19	Iowa	0
0	Purdue	7

1932

27	Missouri	0
6	Michigan	15
26	Illinois	0
7	Purdue	7
0	Minnesota	7
6	Ohio State	20
0	Notre Dame	21
44	Iowa	6

1933

0	Iowa	7
0	Stanford	0
25	Indiana	0
0	Ohio State	12
0	Minnesota	0
0	Illinois	3
0	Notre Dame	7
0	Michigan	13

1934

21	Marquette	12
7	Iowa	20
0	Stanford	20
6	Ohio State	28
7	Wisconsin	0
3	Illinois	14
7	Notre Dame	20
13	Michigan	6

1935

14	DePaul	0
0	Purdue	7
7	Ohio State	28
13	Minnesota	21
10	Illinois	3
14	Notre Dame	7
32	Wisconsin	13
0	Iowa	0

1936

18	Iowa	7

40	North Dakota State	7
14	Ohio State	13
13	Illinois	2
6	Minnesota	0
26	Wisconsin	18
9	Michigan	0
6	Notre Dame	26

1937

33	Iowa State	0
7	Michigan	0
14	Purdue	7
0	Ohio State	7
14	Wisconsin	6
0	Illinois	6
0	Minnesota	7
0	Notre Dame	7

1938

21	Kansas State	0
33	Drake	0
0	Ohio State	0
13	Illinois	0
6	Minnesota	3
13	Wisconsin	20
0	Michigan	0
7	Notre Dame	9

1939

0	Oklahoma	23
0	Ohio State	13
13	Wisconsin	7
13	Illinois	0
14	Minnesota	7
0	Purdue	3
0	Notre Dame	7
7	Iowa	7

1940

40	Syracuse	0
6	Ohio State	3
27	Wisconsin	7
20	Indiana	7
12	Minnesota	13
32	Illinois	14
13	Michigan	20
20	Notre Dame	0

1941

51	Kansas State	3
41	Wisconsin	14
7	Michigan	14
14	Ohio State	7
7	Minnesota	8
20	Indiana	14
6	Notre Dame	7
27	Illinois	0

1942

12	Iowa Naval Cadets	20
3	Texas	0

6	Purdue	7
16	Michigan	34
6	Ohio State	20
7	Minnesota	19
7	Illinois	14
19	Wisconsin	20
20	Notre Dame	27
0	Great Lakes	48

1943

14	Indiana	6
7	Michigan	21
13	Great Lakes	0
13	Ohio State	0
42	Minnesota	6
41	Wisconsin	0
6	Notre Dame	25
53	Illinois	6

1944

62	DePauw	0
6	Wisconsin	7
0	Great Lakes	25
0	Michigan	27
7	Indiana	14
14	Minnesota	14
7	Purdue	27
0	Notre Dame	21
6	Illinois	25

1945

18	Iowa State	6
7	Indiana	7
7	Michigan	20
7	Minnesota	30
26	Purdue	14
14	Ohio State	16
28	Wisconsin	14
7	Notre Dame	34
13	Illinois	7

1946

41	Iowa State	9
28	Wisconsin	0
14	Minnesota	7
14	Michigan	14
26	College of Pacific	13
27	Ohio State	39
6	Indiana	7
0	Notre Dame	27
0	Illinois	20

1947

0	Vanderbilt	3
27	UCLA	26
21	Minnesota	37
21	Michigan	49
7	Indiana	6
0	Wisconsin	29
6	Ohio State	7
19	Notre Dame	26
28	Illinois	13

1948

19	UCLA	0
21	Purdue	0
19	Minnesota	16
0	Michigan	28
48	Syracuse	0
21	Ohio State	7
16	Wisconsin	7
7	Notre Dame	12
20	Illinois	7
20	California	14

1949

20	Purdue	6
7	Pittsburgh	16
7	Minnesota	21
21	Michigan	20
21	Iowa	28
7	Ohio State	24
6	Wisconsin	14
39	Colgate	20
9	Illinois	7

1950

23	Iowa State	13
22	Navy	0
28	Pittsburgh	23
13	Wisconsin	14
0	Ohio State	32
19	Purdue	14
23	Michigan	34
14	Illinois	7
13	Minnesota	6

1951

35	Colorado	14
20	Army	14
21	Minnesota	7
16	Navy	7
0	Wisconsin	41
0	Ohio State	3
14	Purdue	35
6	Michigan	0
0	Illinois	3

1952

0	Southern California	31
20	Vanderbilt	20
26	Minnesota	27
14	Michigan	48
23	Indiana	13
21	Ohio State	24
20	Wisconsin	24
14	Iowa	39
28	Illinois	26

1953

35	Iowa State	0
33	Army	20
13	Minnesota	30
12	Michigan	20
27	Pittsburgh	21
13	Ohio State	27
13	Wisconsin	34
6	Indiana	14
14	Illinois	39

1954

27	Iowa State	14
7	Southern California	12
7	Minnesota	26
0	Michigan	7
7	Pittsburgh	14
7	Ohio State	14
13	Wisconsin	34
13	Indiana	14
20	Illinois	7

1955

14	Miami (Ohio)	25
0	Tulane	21
7	Minnesota	18
2	Michigan	14
14	Indiana	20
0	Ohio State	49
14	Wisconsin	41
8	Purdue	46
7	Illinois	7

1956

14	Iowa State	13
13	Tulane	20
0	Minnesota	0
20	Michigan	34
13	Indiana	19
2	Ohio State	6
17	Wisconsin	7
14	Purdue	0
14	Illinois	13

1957

6	Stanford	26
13	Oregon State	22
6	Minnesota	41
14	Michigan	34
0	Iowa	6
6	Ohio State	47
12	Wisconsin	41
0	Purdue	27
0	Illinois	27

1958

29	Washington State	28
28	Stanford	0
7	Minnesota	3
55	Michigan	24
20	Iowa	26
21	Ohio State	0
13	Wisconsin	17
6	Purdue	23
20	Illinois	27

1959

45	Oklahoma	13
14	Iowa	10
6	Minnesota	0
20	Michigan	7
30	Notre Dame	24
30	Indiana	13
19	Wisconsin	24
10	Michigan State	15
0	Illinois	28

1960

19	Oklahoma	3
0	Iowa	42
0	Minnesota	7
7	Michigan	14
7	Notre Dame	6
21	Indiana	3
21	Wisconsin	0
18	Michigan State	21
14	Illinois	7

1961

45	Boston College	0
28	Illinois	7
3	Minnesota	10
0	Ohio State	10
12	Notre Dame	10
14	Indiana	8
10	Wisconsin	29
13	Michigan State	21
6	Miami (Fla.)	10

1962

37	South Carolina	20
45	Illinois	0
34	Minnesota	22
18	Ohio State	14
35	Notre Dame	6
26	Indiana	21
6	Wisconsin	37
7	Michigan State	31
29	Miami (Fla.)	7

1963

23	Missouri	12
34	Indiana	21
9	Illinois	10
15	Minnesota	8
37	Miami (Ohio)	6
7	Michigan State	15
6	Michigan	27
14	Wisconsin	17
17	Ohio State	8

1964

7	Oregon State	3
14	Indiana	13
6	Illinois	17
18	Minnesota	21
27	Miami (Ohio)	28

6	Michigan State	24
0	Michigan	35
17	Wisconsin	13
0	Ohio State	10

1965

14	Florida	24
20	Indiana	0
7	Notre Dame	38
15	Oregon State	7
7	Wisconsin	21
9	Iowa	0
7	Michigan State	49
22	Minnesota	27
34	Michigan	22
6	Illinois	20

1966

7	Florida	43
14	Indiana	26
7	Notre Dame	35
14	Oregon State	6
3	Wisconsin	3
24	Iowa	15
0	Michigan State	22
13	Minnesota	28
20	Michigan	28
35	Illinois	7

1967

12	Miami (Fla.)	7
6	Missouri	13
16	Purdue	25
6	Rice	50
2	Ohio State	6
17	Wisconsin	13
3	Michigan	7
39	Iowa	24
21	Illinois	27
27	Michigan State	41

1968

7	Miami (Fla.)	28
7	Southern California	24
6	Purdue	43
7	Notre Dame	27
21	Ohio State	45

13	Wisconsin	10
0	Michigan	35
34	Iowa	68
0	Illinois	14
14	Michigan State	31

1969

10	Notre Dame	35
6	Southern California	48
0	UCLA	36
10	Illinois	6
27	Wisconsin	7
20	Purdue	45
6	Ohio State	35
21	Minnesota	28
30	Indiana	27
7	Michigan State	38

1970

14	Notre Dame	35
7	UCLA	12
20	SMU	21
48	Illinois	0
24	Wisconsin	14
38	Purdue	14
10	Ohio State	24
28	Minnesota	14
21	Indiana	7
23	Michigan State	20

1971

6	Michigan	21
7	Notre Dame	50
12	Syracuse	6
24	Wisconsin	11
28	Iowa	3
20	Purdue	21
24	Indiana	10
7	Illinois	24
41	Minnesota	20
14	Ohio State	10
28	Michigan State	7

1972

0	Michigan	7
0	Notre Dame	37
27	Pittsburgh	22

14	Wisconsin	21
12	Iowa	24
0	Purdue	37
23	Indiana	14
13	Illinois	43
29	Minnesota	35
14	Ohio State	27
14	Michigan State	24

1973

14	Michigan State	10
0	Notre Dame	44
14	Pittsburgh	21
12	Ohio University	14
31	Iowa	15
10	Purdue	21
0	Ohio State	60
43	Minnesota	52
21	Indiana	20
34	Wisconsin	36
9	Illinois	6

1974

7	Michigan State	41
3	Notre Dame	49
7	Nebraska	49
14	Oregon	10
10	Iowa	35
26	Purdue	31
7	Ohio State	55
21	Minnesota	13
24	Indiana	22
7	Wisconsin	52
14	Illinois	28

1975

31	Purdue	25
10	Northern Illinois	3
7	Notre Dame	31
6	Arizona	41
30	Indiana	0
0	Michigan	69
14	Wisconsin	17
21	Iowa	24
9	Minnesota	33
14	Michigan State	47
7	Illinois	28

OHIO STATE UNIVERSITY

Columbus, Ohio
Established 1870
Colors, Scarlet and Grey
Nickname, Buckeyes

Head Coaches

Alex S. Lilley, Jack Ryder, 1890–91
Jack Ryder, 1892–1895
Charles A. Hickey, 1896
Dave Edwards, 1897

Jack Ryder, 1898
John Eckstorm, 1899–1901
Perry Hale, 1902–1903
E. R. Sweetland, 1904–1905

Albert Herrnstein, 1906–1909
Howard Jones, 1910
Harry Vaughn, 1911
John R. Richards, 1912
John W. Wilce, 1913–1928
Sam S. Willaman, 1929–1933
Francis A. Schmidt, 1934–1940
Paul E. Brown, 1941–1943
Carroll C. Widdoes, 1944–1945
Paul O. Bixler, 1946
Wes Fesler, 1947–1950
Woody Hayes, 1951–

Sam Willaman never had a losing season at Ohio State (1929–1933). His total wins-losses-ties added up to 26–10–5. Willaman's last season was his best in Big Ten play (7–1–0) as the Buckeyes finished second to Michigan.

All-American Players

Robert Karch, tackle, 1916
Charles (Chick) Harley, fullback, 1916–17–19
Charles Bolen, end, 1917
Gaylord Stinchcomb, halfback, 1920
Iolas Huffman, guard, 1920–21
Edwin Hess, guard, 1925–26
Marty Karow, halfback, 1926
Leo Raskowski, tackle, 1927
Wes Fesler, end, 1928–29–30
Joe Gailus, guard, 1932
Regis Monahan, guard, 1934
Merle Wendt, end, 1934–35
Inwood Smith, guard, 1935
Gomer Jones, center, 1935
Gust Zarnas, guard, 1937
Esco Sarkkinen, end, 1939

Don Scott, halfback, 1939
Bob Shaw, end, 1942
Charles Csuri, tackle, 1942
Lindell Houston, guard, 1942
Jack Dugger, end, 1944
Bill Willis, tackle, 1944
Bill Hackett, guard, 1944
Les Horvath, halfback, 1944
Warren Amling, guard-tackle, 1945–46
Vic Janowicz, halfback, 1950
Bob Momsen, guard, 1950
Bob McCullough, center, 1950
Mike Takacs, guard, 1952
Howard Cassady, halfback, 1954–55
Dean Dugger, end, 1954
Jim Parker, guard, 1955–56
Aurelius Thomas, guard, 1957
Jim Houston, end, 1958–59
Bob White, fullback, 1958
Jim Marshall, tackle, 1958
Bob Ferguson, fullback, 1960–61
Jim Davidson, tackle, 1964
Arnold Chonko, defensive back, 1964
Dwight Kelley, linebacker, 1964–65
Doug Van Horn, guard, 1965
Ray Pryor, center, 1966
Dave Foley, tackle, 1968
Rufus Mayes, tackle, 1968
Jim Stillwagon, guard, 1969–70
Jack Tatum, linebacker, 1969–70
Rex Kern, offensive back, 1969
Jim Otis, offensive back, 1969
Ted Provost, defensive back, 1969
Jan White, end, 1970
John Brockington, offensive back, 1970
Tim Anderson, defensive back, 1970
Mike Sensibaugh, defensive back, 1970
Tom DeLeone, center, 1971
John Hicks, tackle, 1972–73

Ohio State's Bob Karch, All-American tackle in 1916 for the champion Buckeyes.

Randy Gradishar, linebacker, 1972–73
Van DeCree, end, 1973–74
Archie Griffin, offensive back, 1973–74–75
Kurt Schumacher, tackle, 1974

Pete Cusick, tackle, 1974
Steve Myers, center, 1974
Neal Colzie, defensive back, 1974
Tom Skladany, punter, 1974

Scores
1890–1975

1890

20	Ohio Wesleyan	14
0	Wooster	64
0	Denison	14
10	Kenyon	18

1891

6	Western Reserve	50
0	Kenyon	26
8	Denison	4
6	Akron	0

1892

0	Oberlin	40
62	Akron	0
80	Marietta	0
32	Denison	0
42	Dayton YMCA	4
18	Western Reserve	40
26	Kenyon	10

1893

16	Otterbein	22
36	Wittenberg	10
10	Oberlin	38
6	Kenyon	42
16	Western Reserve	30
32	Akron	18
38	Cincinnati	0
40	Marietta	8
8	Kenyon	10

1894

6	Akron	12
0	Wittenberg	6
32	Antioch	0
6	Wittenberg	18
30	Columbus Barracks	0
4	Western Reserve	24
10	Marietta	4
0	Case	38
6	Cincinnati	4
46	17th Regiment	4
20	Kenyon	4

1895

14	Akron	6
6	Otterbein	14
6	Oberlin	12
4	Denison	4
8	Ohio Wesleyan	8

4	Cincinnati	0
8	Kentucky	6
0	Central Kentucky	18
0	Marietta	24
12	Kenyon	10

1896

24	Ohio Medical	0
6	Cincinnati	8
12	Otterbein	0
0	Oberlin	16
30	Case	10
4	Ohio Wesleyan	10
10	Columbus Barracks	2
0	Ohio Medical	0
6	Wittenberg	24
12	Ohio Medical	0
18	Kenyon	34

1897

6	Ohio Medical	0
0	Case	14
0	Michigan	34
12	Otterbein	12
0	Columbus Barracks	6
0	Oberlin	44
0	West Virginia	28
0	Cincinnati	24
0	Ohio Wesleyan	6

1898

17	Heidelberg	0
0	Ohio Medical	10
34	Denison	0
0	Marietta	10
0	Western Reserve	49
5	Case	23
0	Kenyon	29
24	Ohio Wesleyan	0

1899

30	Otterbein	0
28	Wittenberg	0
5	Case	5
41	Ohio University	0
6	Oberlin	0
6	Western Reserve	0
17	Marietta	0
12	Ohio Medical	0
34	Muskingum	0
5	Kenyon	0

1900

20	Otterbein	0
20	Ohio University	0
29	Cincinnati	0
47	Ohio Wesleyan	0
17	Oberlin	0
27	West Virginia	0
24	Case	10
6	Ohio Medical	11
0	Michigan	0
23	Kenyon	5

1901

0	Otterbein	0
30	Wittenberg	0
17	Ohio University	0
24	Marietta	0
6	Western Reserve	5
0	Michigan	21
0	Oberlin	6
6	Indiana	18
11	Kenyon	6

1902

5	Otterbein	0
17	Ohio University	0
30	West Virginia	0
34	Marietta	0
0	Michigan	86
51	Kenyon	5
12	Case	23
0	Illinois	0
17	Ohio Wesleyan	16
6	Indiana	6

1903

18	Otterbein	0
28	Wittenberg	0
24	Denison	5
30	Muskingum	0
59	Kenyon	0
0	Case	12
34	West Virginia	6
0	Michigan	36
27	Oberlin	5
29	Ohio Wesleyan	6
16	Indiana	17

1904

34	Otterbein	0
80	Miami	0

24	Denison	0
46	Muskingum	0
6	Michigan	31
16	Case	6
0	Indiana	8
0	Illinois	46
2	Oberlin	4
11	Kenyon	5
0	Carlisle Indians	23

1905

6	Otterbein	6
28	Heidelberg	0
40	Muskingum	0
17	Wittenberg	0
2	Denison	0
32	DePauw	6
0	Case	0
23	Kenyon	0
0	Michigan	40
36	Oberlin	0
15	Wooster	0
0	Indiana	11

1906

41	Otterbein	0
52	Wittenberg	0
16	Muskingum	0
0	Michigan	6
6	Oberlin	0
6	Kenyon	0
9	Case	0
12	Wooster	0
11	Ohio Medical	8

1907

28	Otterbein	0
16	Muskingum	0
28	Denison	0
6	Wooster	6
0	Michigan	22
12	Kenyon	0
22	Oberlin	10
9	Case	11
23	Heidelberg	0
16	Ohio Wesleyan	0

1908

18	Otterbein	0
0	Wooster	8
16	Denison	2
0	Western Reserve	18
6	Michigan	10
20	Ohio Wesleyan	9
8	Case	18
17	Vanderbilt	6
14	Oberlin	12
19	Kenyon	9

1909

14	Otterbein	0

39	Wittenberg	0
74	Wooster	0
6	Michigan	33
29	Denison	0
21	Ohio Wesleyan	6
3	Case	11
5	Vanderbilt	0
6	Oberlin	26
22	Kenyon	0

1910

14	Otterbein	5
62	Wittenberg	0
23	Cincinnati	0
6	Western Reserve	0
3	Michigan	3
5	Denison	5
10	Case	14
6	Ohio Wesleyan	0
0	Oberlin	0
53	Kenyon	0

1911

6	Otterbein	0
3	Miami	0
0	Western Reserve	0
0	Michigan	19
3	Ohio Wesleyan	0
0	Case	9
24	Kenyon	0
0	Oberlin	0
0	Syracuse	6
11	Cincinnati	6

1912

55	Otterbein	0
34	Denison	0
0	Michigan	14
45	Cincinnati	7
31	Case	6
23	Oberlin	17
0	Penn State	37
36	Ohio Wesleyan	6
20	Michigan State	35

1913

58	Ohio Wesleyan	0
14	Western Reserve	8
0	Oberlin	0
6	Indiana	7
0	Wisconsin	12
18	Case	0
58	Northwestern	0

1914

16	Ohio Wesleyan	2
7	Case	6
0	Illinois	37
6	Wisconsin	7
13	Indiana	3

39	Oberlin	0
27	Northwestern	0

1915

19	Ohio Wesleyan	6
14	Case	0
3	Illinois	3
0	Wisconsin	21
10	Indiana	9
25	Oberlin	0
34	Northwestern	0

1916

12	Ohio Wesleyan	0
128	Oberlin	0
7	Illinois	6
14	Wisconsin	13
46	Indiana	7
28	Case	0
23	Northwestern	3

1917

49	Case	0
53	Ohio Wesleyan	0
40	Northwestern	0
67	Denison	0
26	Indiana	3
16	Wisconsin	3
13	Illinois	0
0	Auburn	0
28	Camp Sherman	0

1918

41	Ohio Wesleyan	0
34	Denison	0
0	Michigan	14
56	Case	0
0	Illinois	13
3	Wisconsin	14

1919

38	Ohio Wesleyan	0
46	Cincinnati	0
49	Kentucky	0
13	Michigan	3
20	Purdue	0
3	Wisconsin	0
7	Illinois	9

1920

55	Ohio Wesleyan	0
37	Oberlin	0
17	Purdue	0
13	Wisconsin	7
7	Chicago	6
14	Michigan	7
7	Illinois	0
0	*California	28
	*Rose Bowl	

1921

28	Ohio Wesleyan	0
6	Oberlin	7
27	Minnesota	0
14	Michigan	0
7	Chicago	0
28	Purdue	0
0	Illinois	7

1922

5	Ohio Wesleyan	0
14	Oberlin	0
0	Michigan	19
0	Minnesota	9
9	Chicago	14
9	Iowa	12
6	Illinois	3

1923

24	Ohio Wesleyan	7
23	Colgate	23
0	Michigan	23
0	Iowa	20
42	Denison	0
32	Purdue	0
3	Chicago	17
0	Illinois	9

1924

7	Purdue	0
0	Iowa	0
10	Ohio Wesleyan	0
3	Chicago	3
7	Wooster	7
7	Indiana	12
6	Michigan	16
0	Illinois	7

1925

10	Ohio Wesleyan	3
9	Columbia	0
3	Chicago	3
0	Iowa	15
17	Wooster	0
7	Indiana	0
0	Michigan	10
9	Illinois	14

1926

40	Wittenberg	0
47	Ohio Wesleyan	0
32	Columbia	7
23	Iowa	6
18	Chicago	0
13	Wilmington	7
16	Michigan	17
7	Illinois	6

1927

31	Wittenberg	0

13	Iowa	6
13	Northwestern	19
0	Michigan	21
13	Chicago	7
0	Princeton	20
61	Denison	6
0	Illinois	13

1928

41	Wittenberg	0
10	Northwestern	0
19	Michigan	7
13	Indiana	0
6	Princeton	6
7	Iowa	14
39	Muskingum	0
0	Illinois	8

1929

19	Wittenberg	0
7	Iowa	6
7	Michigan	0
0	Indiana	0
2	Pittsburgh	18
6	Northwestern	18
54	Kenyon	0
0	Illinois	27

1930

59	Mt. Union	0
23	Indiana	0
2	Northwestern	19
0	Michigan	13
0	Wisconsin	0
27	Navy	0
16	Pittsburgh	7
12	Illinois	9

1931

67	Cincinnati	6
21	Vanderbilt	26
20	Michigan	7
0	Northwestern	10
13	Indiana	0
20	Navy	0
6	Wisconsin	0
40	Illinois	0
7	Minnesota	19

1932

34	Ohio Wesleyan	7
7	Indiana	7
0	Michigan	14
0	Pittsburgh	0
7	Wisconsin	7
20	Northwestern	6
19	Pennsylvania	0
3	Illinois	0

1933

75	Virginia	0

20	Vanderbilt	0
0	Michigan	13
12	Northwestern	0
21	Indiana	0
20	Pennsylvania	7
6	Wisconsin	0
7	Illinois	6

1934

33	Indiana	0
13	Illinois	14
10	Colgate	7
28	Northwestern	6
76	Western Reserve	0
33	Chicago	0
34	Michigan	0
40	Iowa	7

1935

19	Kentucky	6
85	Drake	7
28	Northwestern	7
28	Indiana	6
13	Notre Dame	18
20	Chicago	13
6	Illinois	0
38	Michigan	0

1936

60	New York University	0
0	Pittsburgh	6
13	Northwestern	14
7	Indiana	0
2	Notre Dame	7
44	Chicago	0
13	Illinois	0
21	Michigan	0

1937

14	TCU	0
13	Purdue	0
12	Southern California	13
7	Northwestern	0
39	Chicago	0
0	Indiana	10
19	Illinois	0
21	Michigan	0

1938

6	Indiana	0
7	Southern California	14
0	Northwestern	0
42	Chicago	7
32	New York University	0
0	Purdue	12
32	Illinois	14
0	Michigan	18

1939

19	Missouri	0
13	Northwestern	0

23	Minnesota	20
14	Cornell	23
24	Indiana	0
61	Chicago	0
21	Illinois	0
14	Michigan	21

1940

30	Pittsburgh	7
17	Purdue	14
3	Northwestern	6
7	Minnesota	13
7	Cornell	21
21	Indiana	6
14	Illinois	6
0	Michigan	40

1941

12	Missouri	7
33	Southern California	0
16	Purdue	14
7	Northwestern	14
21	Pittsburgh	14
46	Wisconsin	34
12	Illinois	7
20	Michigan	20

1942

59	Fort Knox	0

32	Indiana	21
28	Southern California	12
26	Purdue	0
20	Northwestern	6
7	Wisconsin	17
59	Pittsburgh	19
44	Illinois	20
21	Michigan	7
41	Iowa Seahawks	12

1943

13	Iowa Seahawks	28
27	Missouri	6
6	Great Lakes	13
7	Purdue	30
0	Northwestern	13
14	Indiana	20
46	Pittsburgh	6
29	Illinois	26
7	Michigan	45

1944

54	Missouri	0
34	Iowa	0
20	Wisconsin	7
26	Great Lakes	6
34	Minnesota	14
21	Indiana	7
54	Pittsburgh	19

26	Illinois	12
18	Michigan	14

1945

47	Missouri	6
42	Iowa	0
12	Wisconsin	0
13	Purdue	35
20	Minnesota	7
16	Northwestern	14
14	Pittsburgh	0
27	Illinois	2
3	Michigan	7

1946

13	Missouri	13
21	Southern California	0
7	Wisconsin	20
14	Purdue	14
39	Minnesota	9
39	Northwestern	27
20	Pittsburgh	13
7	Illinois	16
6	Michigan	58

1947

13	Missouri	7
20	Purdue	24
0	Southern California	32

All-American guard Lin Houston opened up the holes that enabled Ohio State ball-carriers to average 33 points per game in 1942.

13	Iowa	13
0	Pittsburgh	12
0	Indiana	7
7	Northwestern	6
7	Illinois	28
0	Michigan	21

1948

21	Missouri	7
20	Southern California	0
7	Iowa	14
17	Indiana	0
34	Wisconsin	32
7	Northwestern	21
41	Pittsburgh	0
34	Illinois	7
3	Michigan	13

1949

35	Missouri	34
46	Indiana	7
13	Southern California	13
0	Minnesota	27
21	Wisconsin	0
24	Northwestern	7
14	Pittsburgh	10
30	Illinois	17
7	Michigan	7
17	*California	14
	*Rose Bowl	

1950

27	SMU	32
41	Pittsburgh	7
26	Indiana	14
48	Minnesota	0
83	Iowa	21
32	Northwestern	0
19	Wisconsin	14
7	Illinois	14
3	Michigan	9

1951

7	SMU	0
20	Michigan State	24
6	Wisconsin	6
10	Indiana	32
47	Iowa	21
3	Northwestern	0
16	Pittsburgh	14
0	Illinois	0
0	Michigan	7

1952

33	Indiana	13
14	Purdue	21
23	Wisconsin	14
35	Washington State	7
0	Iowa	8
24	Northwestern	21
14	Pittsburgh	21
27	Illinois	7
27	Michigan	7

1953

36	Indiana	12
33	California	19
20	Illinois	41
12	Pennsylvania	6
20	Wisconsin	19
27	Northwestern	13
13	Michigan State	28
21	Purdue	6
0	Michigan	20

1954

28	Indiana	0
21	California	13
40	Illinois	7
20	Iowa	14
31	Wisconsin	14
14	Northwestern	7
26	Pittsburgh	0
28	Purdue	6
21	Michigan	7
20	*Southern California	7
	*Rose Bowl	

1955

28	Nebraska	20
0	Stanford	6
27	Illinois	12
14	Duke	20
26	Wisconsin	16
49	Northwestern	0
20	Indiana	13
20	Iowa	10
17	Michigan	0

1956

34	Nebraska	7
32	Stanford	20
26	Illinois	6
6	Penn State	7
21	Wisconsin	0
6	Northwestern	2
35	Indiana	14
0	Iowa	6
0	Michigan	19

1957

14	Texas Christian	18
35	Washington	7
21	Illinois	7
56	Indiana	0
16	Wisconsin	13
47	Northwestern	6
20	Purdue	7
17	Iowa	13
31	Michigan	14
10	*Oregon	7
	*Rose Bowl	

1958

23	SMU	20
12	Washington	7
19	Illinois	13
49	Indiana	8
7	Wisconsin	7
0	Northwestern	21
14	Purdue	14
38	Iowa	28
20	Michigan	14

1959

14	Duke	13
0	Southern California	17
0	Illinois	9
15	Purdue	0
3	Wisconsin	12
30	Michigan State	24
0	Indiana	0
7	Iowa	16
14	Michigan	23

1960

24	SMU	0
20	Southern California	0
34	Illinois	7
21	Purdue	24
34	Wisconsin	7
21	Michigan State	10
36	Indiana	7
12	Iowa	35
7	Michigan	0

1961

7	TCU	7
13	UCLA	3
44	Illinois	0
10	Northwestern	0
30	Wisconsin	21
29	Iowa	13
16	Indiana	7
22	Oregon	12
50	Michigan	20

1962

41	North Carolina	7
7	UCLA	9
51	Illinois	15
14	Northwestern	18
14	Wisconsin	7
14	Iowa	28
10	Indiana	7
26	Oregon	7
28	Michigan	0

1963

17	Texas A & M	0
21	Indiana	0
20	Illinois	20
3	Southern California	32
13	Wisconsin	10
7	Iowa	3
7	Penn State	10
8	Northwestern	17
14	Michigan	10

1964

27	SMU	8
17	Indiana	9
26	Illinois	0
17	Southern California	0
28	Wisconsin	3
21	Iowa	19
0	Penn State	27
10	Northwestern	0
0	Michigan	10

1965

3	North Carolina	14
23	Washington	21
28	Illinois	14
7	Michigan State	32
20	Wisconsin	10
11	Minnesota	10
17	Indiana	10
38	Iowa	0
9	Michigan	7

1966

14	TCU	7
22	Washington	38
9	Illinois	10
8	Michigan State	11
24	Wisconsin	13
7	Minnesota	17
7	Indiana	0
14	Iowa	10
3	Michigan	17

1967

7	Arizona	14
30	Oregon	0
6	Purdue	41
6	Northwestern	2
13	Illinois	17
21	Michigan State	7
17	Wisconsin	15
21	Iowa	10
24	Michigan	14

1968

35	SMU	14
21	Oregon	6
13	Purdue	0
45	Northwestern	21
31	Illinois	24

25	Michigan State	20
43	Wisconsin	8
33	Iowa	27
50	Michigan	14
27	*Southern California	16
	*Rose Bowl	

1969

62	TCU	0
41	Washington	14
54	Michigan State	21
34	Minnesota	7
41	Illinois	0
35	Northwestern	6
62	Wisconsin	7
42	Purdue	14
12	Michigan	24

1970

56	Texas A & M	13
34	Duke	10
29	Michigan State	0
28	Minnesota	8
48	Illinois	29
24	Northwestern	10
24	Wisconsin	7
10	Purdue	7
20	Michigan	9
17	*Stanford	27
	*Rose Bowl	

1971

52	Iowa	21
14	Colorado	20
35	California	3
24	Illinois	10
27	Indiana	7
31	Wisconsin	6
14	Minnesota	12
10	Michigan State	17
10	Northwestern	14
7	Michigan	10

1972

21	Iowa	0
29	North Carolina	14
35	California	18
26	Illinois	7
44	Indiana	7
28	Wisconsin	20

27	Minnesota	19
12	Michigan State	19
27	Northwestern	14
14	Michigan	11
17	*Southern California	42
	*Rose Bowl	

1973

56	Minnesota	7
37	TCU	3
27	Washington State	3
24	Wisconsin	0
37	Indiana	7
60	Northwestern	0
30	Illinois	0
35	Michigan State	0
55	Iowa	13
10	Michigan	10
42	*Southern California	21
	*Rose Bowl	

1974

34	Minnesota	19
51	Oregon State	10
28	SMU	9
42	Washington State	7
52	Wisconsin	7
49	Indiana	9
55	Northwestern	7
49	Illinois	7
13	Michigan State	16
35	Iowa	10
12	Michigan	10
17	*Southern California	18
	*Rose Bowl	

1975

21	Michigan State	0
17	Penn State	9
32	North Carolina	7
41	UCLA	20
49	Iowa	0
56	Wisconsin	0
35	Purdue	6
24	Indiana	14
40	Illinois	3
38	Minnesota	6
21	Michigan	14
10	*UCLA	23
	*Rose Bowl	

PURDUE UNIVERSITY

Lafayette, Indiana
Established 1869
Colors, Old Gold and Black
Nickname, Boilermakers

Head Coaches

Albert Berg, 1887
G. A. Reisner, 1889
C. L. Hare, 1890

K. (Snake) Ames, 1891–1892
D. M. Balliet, 1893–1895
S. M. Hammond, 1896

W. S. Church, 1897
Alpha P. Jamison, 1898–1900
D. M. Balliet, 1901
C. M. Best, 1902
Oliver F. Cutts, 1903–1904
A. E. Hernstein, 1905
M. E. Witham, 1906
L. C. Turner, 1907
F. Speik, 1908–1909
M. H. Horr, 1910–1912
Andy Smith, 1913–1915

Cleo O'Donnell, 1916–1917
A. (Butch) Scanlon, 1918–1920
W. (Lone Star) Dietz, 1921
Jimmy Phelan, 1922–1929
Noble Kizer, 1930–1936
Mal Elward, 1937–1941
Elmer Burnham, 1942–1943
Cecil Isbell, 1944–1946
Stu Holcomb, 1947–1955
Jack Mollenkopf, 1956–1969
Bob DeMoss, 1970–1972

Alex Agase, 1973–

All-American Players

Elmer Oliphant, halfback, 1916 (selected
    while playing for Army following completion
    of Purdue career)
Elmer Sleight, tackle, 1929
Ralph (Pest) Welch, halfback, 1929
Charles Miller, center, 1931
Paul Moss, end, 1931
Roy Horstmann, fullback, 1932
Paul Moss, end, 1932
Duane Purvis, halfback, 1933–35
Dave Rankin, end, 1939–40
Alex Agase, guard, 1943
Tony Butkovich, fullback, 1943
Babe Dimancheff, halfback, 1944
Tom Hughes, tackle, 1945
Leo Sugar, end, 1951
Bernie Flowers, end, 1952

Tom Bettis, guard, 1954
Gene Selawski, tackle, 1958
Jerry Beabout, tackle, 1960
Donald Brumm, tackle, 1962
Harold Wells, defensive end, 1964
Bob Griese, quarterback, 1965–66
Jerry Shay, defensive tackle, 1965
Karl Singer, offensive tackle, 1965
John Charles, safety, 1966
Jim Beirne, tight end, 1966
Leroy Keyes, halfback, 1968
Chuck Kyle, middle guard, 1968
Mike Phipps, quarterback, 1969
Tim Foley, defensive halfback, 1969
Bill Yanchar, defensive tackle, 1969
Otis Armstrong, halfback, 1972
Dave Butz, defensive tackle, 1972

Larry Burton, wide receiver, 1974

Scores
1887–1975

1887

| 6 | Butler | 48 |

1888

No Football

1889

34	DePauw	10
18	Wabash	4
0	Butler	13

1890

6	Chicago University Club	10
54	Wabash	4
6	Michigan	34
32	DePauw	0
62	Illinois	0
10	Butler	12

1891

44	Wabash	0
60	Indiana	0
58	Butler	0
30	DePauw	0

1892

12	Illinois	6
72	Wabash	0
34	Wisconsin	6
24	Michigan	0
40	Butler	6
68	Indiana	0
38	Chicago	0
32	DePauw	6

1893

64	Indiana	0
96	Butler	0
20	Chicago	10
48	Wabash	8
8	Michigan	46
30	Wisconsin	36
26	Illinois	26
42	DePauw	18

1894

6	Light Artillery	4
30	Butler	0
36	Armour	0

0	Minnesota	24
10	Chicago	6
22	Illinois	2
6	Wisconsin	0
44	Wabash	0
6	Indiana	0
28	DePauw	0

1895

32	Kentucky	0
6	Missouri	16
18	Minnesota	4
6	Northwestern	24
10	Michigan	12
6	Illinois	2

1896

36	Greer	0
32	Rush	4
0	Minnesota	14
0	Michigan	16
22	DePauw	0
28	Notre Dame	26
4	Illinois	4

1897

28	Illinois Normal	0
6	Oberlin	22
8	DePauw	0
4	Illinois	34
20	Indiana	6
4	Michigan	34
30	Missouri	12
6	Minnesota	0
0	Alumni	0

1898

0	Alumni	6
5	Haskell	0
15	Haskell	0
0	Chicago	17
14	Indiana	0
0	Oberlin	10

1899

10	Alumni	5
30	Earlham	5
0	Oberlin	12
40	DePauw	0
0	Chicago	44
10	Notre Dame	10
0	Northwestern	29
5	Illinois	0
5	Indiana	17

1900

39	Wesleyan	0
6	Chicago	17
28	DePauw	5
6	Michigan	11
46	Rose Polytech	5
5	Illinois	17
38	Earlham	0
5	Indiana	24

1901

24	Franklin	0
45	Wabash	0
5	Chicago	5
19	DePauw	0
6	Indiana	11
22	Case	0
6	Notre Dame	12
6	Illinois	28
5	Northwestern	10

1902

56	Franklin	0
39	DePauw	0
0	Chicago	33
5	Illinois	29
5	Case	0
5	Northwestern	0
73	Greer	0
87	Butler	0
39	Indiana	0
6	Notre Dame	6

1903

34	Englewood HS	0
18	Wabash	0
17	Beloit	0
0	Chicago	22
0	Illinois	24
18	Oberlin	0

1904

5	North Div. HS	0
11	Beloit	0
2	Alumni	6
28	Earlham	11
0	Chicago	20
6	Wabash	0
6	Illinois	24
11	Missouri	0
34	Indiana Med.	5
27	Indiana	0
10	Culver	0
36	Notre Dame	0

1905

33	Wendell Phillips	0
36	Beloit	0
12	Wabash	0
29	Illinois	0
11	Indiana	11
24	Missouri	0
0	Chicago	19
32	Notre Dame	0

1906

0	Chicago	39
0	Wabash	11
0	Notre Dame	2
5	Wisconsin	29
0	Illinois	5

1907

0	Wabash	2
4	Illinois	21
0	Chicago	56
6	Wisconsin	12
0	Notre Dame	17

1908

0	Chicago	39
40	Earlham	0
30	Monmouth	0
28	DePauw	4
6	Illinois	15
4	Indiana	10
16	Northwestern	10

1909

0	Chicago	40
6	Northwestern	14
15	DePauw	12
6	Illinois	24
17	Wabash	18

26	Rose Poly	3
3	Indiana	36

1910

0	Wabash	3
0	Iowa	16
0	Illinois	11
5	Chicago	14
12	DePauw	0
0	Indiana	15

1911

0	Wabash	3
3	Chicago	11
5	DePauw	0
3	Illinois	12
0	Iowa	11
35	Rose Poly	6
12	Indiana	5

1912

21	DePauw	0
0	Wisconsin	41
0	Chicago	7
21	Northwestern	6
9	Illinois	9
91	Rose Polytech	0
34	Indiana	7

1913

26	Wabash	0
34	Northwestern	0
7	Wisconsin	7
0	Chicago	6
62	Rose Poly	0
0	Illinois	0
42	Indiana	7

1914

27	Wabash	3
26	Western Reserve	0
7	Wisconsin	14
0	Chicago	21
40	Kentucky	6
34	Northwestern	6
23	Indiana	13

1915

7	Wabash	7
26	Beloit	0
3	Wisconsin	28
0	Chicago	7
19	Iowa	13
0	Kentucky State	7
7	Indiana	0

1916

13	DePauw	0
28	Wabash	7
6	Iowa	24
7	Illinois	14

7	Chicago	16
6	Northwestern	14
0	Indiana	0

1917

54	Franklin	0
7	DePauw	6
0	Chicago	27
0	Illinois	27
6	Northwestern	12
28	Wabash	0
0	Indiana	37

1918

7	DePauw	9
7	Chicago	3
14	MAC	6
6	Notre Dame	26
0	Great Lakes	27

1919

7	Franklin	7
7	Illinois	14
0	Chicago	16
13	MAC	7
0	Ohio State	20
24	DePauw	0
13	Notre Dame	33

1920

10	DePauw	0
0	Chicago	20
0	Ohio State	17
19	Wabash	14
0	Northwestern	14
0	Notre Dame	28
7	Indiana	10

1921

0	Wabash	9
0	Chicago	9
0	Notre Dame	33
6	Iowa	13
3	Northwestern	0
0	Ohio State	28
0	Indiana	3

1922

10	James Milliken	0
0	Notre Dame	20
0	Chicago	12
0	Iowa	56
6	Wabash	7
13	Northwestern	24
7	Indiana	7

1923

39	Wilmington	0
0	Iowa	7
7	Wabash	7

6	Chicago	20
7	Notre Dame	34
0	Ohio State	32
6	Northwestern	3
0	Indiana	3

1924

21	Wabash	7
0	Ohio State	7
41	Rose Poly	3
7	Northwestern	3
6	Chicago	19
36	DePauw	0
26	Indiana	7

1925

0	Wabash	13
39	DePauw	0
44	Rose Poly	0
0	Wisconsin	7
0	Chicago	6
20	Franklin	0
0	Northwestern	13
0	Indiana	0

1926

13	Navy	17
21	Wabash	14
0	Wisconsin	0
6	Chicago	0
38	Indiana Normal	0
44	Franklin	0
24	Indiana	14
0	Northwestern	22

1927

19	Harvard	0
18	Northwestern	6
21	Indiana	6
6	Chicago	7
6	Wisconsin	12
15	DePauw	0
46	Franklin	0
39	Montana	7

1928

31	DePauw	0
0	Minnesota	15
19	Wisconsin	19
40	Chicago	0
19	Case	0
6	Northwestern	7
14	Wabash	0
14	Indiana	0

1929

26	Kansas Aggies	14
30	Michigan	16
26	DePauw	7
26	Chicago	0

13	Wisconsin	0
27	Mississippi	7
7	Iowa	0
32	Indiana	0

1930

20	Baylor	7
13	Michigan	14
20	Iowa	0
7	Wisconsin	6
25	Illinois	0
26	Chicago	7
33	Butler	0
6	Indiana	7

1931

28	Western Reserve	0
19	Coe	0
7	Illinois	0
14	Wisconsin	21
13	Carnegie Tech	6
14	Chicago	6
49	Centenary	6
22	Iowa	0
19	Indiana	0
7	Northwestern	0

1932

29	Kansas Aggies	13
7	Minnesota	0
7	Wisconsin	6
7	Northwestern	7
34	NYU	39
37	Chicago	0
18	Iowa	0
25	Indiana	7

1933

13	Ohio	6
7	Minnesota	7
14	Chicago	0
14	Wisconsin	0
17	Carnegie Tech	7
19	Notre Dame	0
6	Iowa	14
19	Indiana	3

1934

0	Rice	14
7	Notre Dame	18
14	Wisconsin	0
20	Carnegie Tech	0
27	Chicago	20
13	Iowa	6
7	Fordham	0
6	Indiana	17

1935

7	Northwestern	0
20	Fordham	0

19	Chicago	0
0	Carnegie Tech	7
7	Minnesota	29
0	Wisconsin	8
12	Iowa	6
0	Indiana	7

1936

47	Ohio	0
35	Wisconsin	14
35	Chicago	7
0	Minnesota	33
7	Carnegie Tech	6
0	Fordham	15
13	Iowa	0
20	Indiana	20

1937

33	Butler	7
0	Ohio State	13
7	Carnegie Tech	0
7	Northwestern	14
13	Iowa	0
3	Fordham	21
7	Wisconsin	7
13	Indiana	7

1938

19	Detroit	6
21	Butler	16
10	Minnesota	7
6	Fordham	6
13	Wisconsin	7
0	Iowa	0
12	Ohio State	0
13	Indiana	16

1939

0	Notre Dame	3
13	Minnesota	13
20	Michigan State	7
6	Santa Clara	13
0	Iowa	4
3	Northwestern	0
7	Wisconsin	7
7	Indiana	6

1940

28	Butler	0
14	Ohio State	17
7	Michigan State	20
13	Wisconsin	14
21	Iowa	6
7	Fordham	13
6	Minnesota	33
0	Indiana	3

1941

0	Vanderbilt	3
6	Pittsburgh	0

14	Ohio State	16
7	Iowa	6
0	Fordham	17
0	Michigan State	0
0	Wisconsin	13
0	Indiana	7

1942

7	Fordham	14
0	Vanderbilt	26
7	Northwestern	6
0	Ohio State	26
0	Wisconsin	13
7	Iowa	13
0	Great Lakes	42
6	Michigan State	19
0	Indiana	20

1943

23	Great Lakes	13
21	Marquette	0
40	Illinois	21
19	Camp Grant	0
30	Ohio State	7
28	Iowa	7
32	Wisconsin	0
14	Minnesota	7
7	Indiana	0

1944

18	Great Lakes	27
40	Marquette	7
35	Illinois	19
6	Iowa Pre-Flight	13
26	Iowa	7
14	Michigan	40
35	Wisconsin	0
27	Northwestern	7
0	Navy	32
6	Indiana	14

1945

14	Marquette	13
20	Great Lakes	6
13	Wisconsin	7
40	Iowa	0
35	Ohio State	13
14	Northwestern	26
28	Pittsburgh	0
21	Miami	7
13	Michigan	27
0	Indiana	26

1946

13	Miami	7
0	Iowa	16
7	Illinois	43
6	Notre Dame	49
14	Ohio State	14
10	Pittsburgh	8
20	Wisconsin	24

7	Minnesota	13
20	Indiana	34

1947

14	Wisconsin	32
24	Ohio State	20
7	Notre Dame	22
62	Boston	7
14	Illinois	7
21	Iowa	0
21	Minnesota	26
28	Pittsburgh	0
14	Indiana	16

1948

27	Notre Dame	28
0	Northwestern	21
0	Michigan	40
20	Iowa	13
6	Illinois	10
14	Marquette	9
7	Minnesota	34
13	Pittsburgh	20
39	Indiana	0

1949

6	Northwestern	20
7	Iowa	21
12	Notre Dame	35
14	Miami (Fla.)	0
0	Illinois	19
13	Minnesota	7
12	Michigan	20
41	Marquette	7
14	Indiana	6

1950

26	Texas	34
28	Notre Dame	14
14	Miami (Fla.)	20
21	Iowa	33
6	UCLA	20
7	Wisconsin	33
14	Northwestern	19
14	Minnesota	27
13	Indiana	0

1951

0	Texas	14
34	Iowa	30
0	Miami (Fla.)	7
7	Wisconsin	31
9	Notre Dame	30
28	Penn State	0
35	Northwestern	14
19	Minnesota	13
21	Indiana	13

1952

20	Penn State	20

Three-time league-leading passer Len Dawson of Purdue (1954–55–56) was the only man in history to win total offense laurels for three straight seasons in the Big Ten.

21	Ohio State	14
41	Iowa	14
14	Notre Dame	26
40	Illinois	12
7	Michigan State	14
14	Minnesota	14
10	Michigan	21
21	Indiana	16

1953

7	Missouri	14
7	Notre Dame	37
14	Duke	20
19	Wisconsin	28
6	Michigan State	0
0	Illinois	21
0	Iowa	26
6	Ohio State	21
30	Indiana	0

1954

31	Missouri	0
27	Notre Dame	14
13	Duke	13
6	Wisconsin	20
27	Michigan State	13
28	Illinois	14
14	Iowa	25
6	Ohio State	28
13	Indiana	7

1955

14	Pacific	7
7	Minnesota	6
0	Wisconsin	9
20	Iowa	20
7	Notre Dame	22
13	Illinois	0
0	Michigan State	27
46	Northwestern	8
6	Indiana	4

1956

16	Missouri	7

14	Minnesota	21
28	Notre Dame	14
6	Wisconsin	6
20	Iowa	21
7	Illinois	7
9	Michigan State	12
0	Northwestern	14
39	Indiana	20

1957

0	Notre Dame	12
17	Minnesota	21
14	Wisconsin	23
20	Michigan State	13
37	Miami (Ohio)	6
21	Illinois	6
7	Ohio State	20
27	Northwestern	0
35	Indiana	13

1958

28	Nebraska	0
24	Rice	0
6	Wisconsin	31
14	Michigan State	6
29	Notre Dame	22
31	Illinois	8
14	Ohio State	14
23	Northwestern	6
15	Indiana	15

1959

0	UCLA	0
28	Notre Dame	7
21	Wisconsin	0
0	Ohio State	15
14	Iowa	7
7	Illinois	7
0	Michigan State	15
29	Minnesota	23
10	Indiana	7

1960

27	UCLA	27

51	Notre Dame	19
13	Wisconsin	24
24	Ohio State	21
14	Iowa	21
12	Illinois	14
13	Michigan State	17
23	Minnesota	14
35	Indiana	6

1961

13	Washington	6
20	Notre Dame	22
19	Miami (Ohio)	6
14	Michigan	16
9	Iowa	0
23	Illinois	9
7	Michigan State	6
7	Minnesota	10
34	Indiana	12

1962

7	Washington	7
24	Notre Dame	6
7	Miami (Ohio)	10
37	Michigan	0
26	Iowa	3
10	Illinois	14
17	Michigan State	9
6	Minnesota	7
7	Indiana	12

1963

0	Miami (Fla.)	3
7	Notre Dame	6
20	Wisconsin	38
23	Michigan	12
14	Iowa	0
21	Illinois	41
0	Michigan State	23
13	Minnesota	11
21	Indiana	15

1964

17	Ohio University	0

15	Notre Dame	34
28	Wisconsin	7
21	Michigan	20
19	Iowa	14
26	Illinois	14
7	Michigan State	21
7	Minnesota	14
28	Indiana	22

1965

38	Miami (Ohio)	0
25	Notre Dame	21
14	SMU	14
17	Iowa	14
14	Michigan	15
10	Michigan State	14
0	Illinois	21
45	Wisconsin	7
35	Minnesota	0
26	Indiana	21

1966

42	Ohio University	3
14	Notre Dame	26
35	SMU	23
35	Iowa	0
22	Michigan	21
20	Michigan State	41
25	Illinois	21
23	Wisconsin	0
16	Minnesota	0
51	Indiana	6
14	*Southern California	13
	*Rose Bowl	

1967

24	Texas A&M	20
28	Notre Dame	21
25	Northwestern	16
41	Ohio State	6
14	Oregon State	22
41	Iowa	22
42	Illinois	9
41	Minnesota	12
21	Michigan State	7
14	Indiana	19

1968

44	Virginia	6

37	Notre Dame	22
43	Northwestern	6
0	Ohio State	13
28	Wake Forest	27
44	Iowa	14
35	Illinois	17
13	Minnesota	27
9	Michigan State	0
38	Indiana	35

1969

42	TCU	35
28	Notre Dame	14
36	Stanford	35
20	Michigan	31
35	Iowa	31
45	Northwestern	20
49	Illinois	22
41	Michigan State	13
14	Ohio State	42
44	Indiana	21

1970

15	TCU	0
0	Notre Dame	48
26	Stanford	14
0	Michigan	29
24	Iowa	3
14	Northwestern	38
21	Illinois	23
14	Michigan State	24
7	Ohio State	10
40	Indiana	0

1971

35	Washington	38
7	Notre Dame	8
45	Iowa	13
27	Minnesota	13
21	Northwestern	20
7	Illinois	21
10	Michigan State	43
10	Wisconsin	14
17	Michigan	20
31	Indiana	38

1972

14	Bowling Green	17
21	Washington	22

14	Notre Dame	35
24	Iowa	0
28	Minnesota	3
37	Northwestern	0
20	Illinois	14
12	Michigan State	22
27	Wisconsin	6
6	Michigan	9
42	Indiana	7

1973

14	Wisconsin	13
19	Miami (Ohio)	24
7	Notre Dame	20
27	Duke	7
13	Illinois	15
21	Northwestern	10
7	Michigan State	10
48	Iowa	23
7	Minnesota	34
9	Michigan	34
28	Indiana	23

1974

14	Wisconsin	28
7	Miami (Ohio)	7
21	Notre Dame	20
14	Duke	16
23	Illinois	27
31	Northwestern	26
7	Michigan State	31
38	Iowa	14
20	Minnesota	24
0	Michigan	51
38	Indiana	17

1975

25	Northwestern	31
0	Notre Dame	17
6	Southern California	19
3	Miami (Ohio)	14
14	Wisconsin	17
26	Illinois	24
6	Ohio State	35
20	Michigan State	10
0	Michigan	28
19	Iowa	18
9	Indiana	7

UNIVERSITY OF WISCONSIN

Madison, Wisconsin
Established 1884
Colors, Red and White
Nickname, Badgers

Head Coaches

Alvin Kletsch, 1889
Ted Mestre, 1890
Herb Alward, 1891

Crawford, 1892
Parke H. Davis, 1893
Hiram O. Stickney, 1894–1895

Phil King, 1896–1902
Art Curtis, 1903–1904
Phil King, 1905
Dr. C. P. Hutchins, 1906–1907
J. A. (Tom) Barry, 1908–1910
John R. Richards, 1911
William J. Juneau, 1912–1915
Paul Withington, 1916
John R. Richards, 1917
Guy Lowman, 1918

John R. Richards, 1919–1922
Jack J. Ryan, 1923–1924
George Little, 1925–1926
Glenn F. Thistlethwaite, 1927–1931
Dr. Clarence W. Spears, 1932–1935
Harry Stuhldreher, 1936–1948
Ivy Williamson, 1949–1955
Milton Bruhn, 1956–1966
John Coatta, 1967–1969
John Jardine, 1970–

All-American Players

Pat O'Dea, fullback, 1899
Robert P. (Butts) Butler, tackle, 1912
R. M. (Tubby) Keeler, guard, 1913
Arlie Mucks, guard, 1914
Howard (Cub) Buck, tackle, 1915
Charles Carpenter, center, 1919
Frank (Red) Weston, end, 1920
Ralph Scott, tackle, 1920
Marty P. Below, tackle, 1923
Milo Lubratovich, tackle, 1930
Howard Weiss, fullback, 1938

Dave Schreiner, end, 1941–42
Marlin (Pat) Harder, fullback, 1942
Earl (Jug) Girard, quarterback, 1944
Ed Withers, defensive halfback, 1950
Harold Faverty, defensive end, 1951
Pat O'Donahue, defensive end, 1951
Don Voss, defensive end, 1952
Dave Suminski, tackle, 1952
Alan Ameche, fullback, 1953–54
Dan Lanphear, tackle, 1959
Pat Richter, end, 1961–62

Scores
1889–1975

1889

| 0 | Calumet Club | 27 |
| 0 | Beloit | 4 |

1890

106	Whitewater Normal	0
0	Minnesota	63
6	Lake Forest	16
10	Northwestern	22

1891

40	Beloit	4
12	Minnesota	26
0	Northwestern	0
6	Lake Forest	4
40	Northwestern	0

1892

32	Beloit	4
6	Michigan	10
4	Purdue	32
10	Lake Forest	6
4	Minnesota	32
26	Northwestern	6
20	Northwestern	6

1893

0	Chicago Athletic Association	4
24	Lake Forest	0
18	Beloit	0
34	Michigan	18

| 0 | Minnesota | 40 |
| 36 | Purdue | 30 |

1894

22	Chicago Athletic Association	4
F	Purdue	W
30	Chicago University	0
4	Chicago Athletic Association	16
44	Iowa	0
46	Beloit	0
6	Minnesota	0

1895

12	Northwestern	6
28	Iowa State	6
32	Armour	4
26	Lake Forest	5
14	Grinnell	4
10	Illinois	10
12	Chicago	22
10	Minnesota	14

1896

34	Lake Forest	0
18	Madison High	0
50	Rush Medical	0
54	Grinnell	6
6	Beloit	0
24	Chicago	0
6	Minnesota	0

| 6 | Northwestern | 6 |
| 8 | Carlisle Indians | 18 |

1897

30	Lake Forest	0
8	Madison High	0
28	Rush Medical	0
20	Platteville Normal	0
29	Madison High	0
39	Minnesota	0
11	Beloit	0
23	Chicago	8
0	Alumni	6
22	Northwestern	0

1898

52	Ripon	0
21	Madison High	0
76	Dixon (Ill.) College	0
42	Rush Medical	0
17	Beloit	0
29	Minnesota	0
12	Alumni	11
0	Chicago	6
22	Whitewater Normal	0
47	Northwestern	0

1899

45	Lake Forest	0
36	Beloit	0
38	Northwestern	0
0	Yale	6
17	Rush	0

17	Alumni	5
23	Illinois	0
19	Minnesota	0
58	Lawrence	0
17	Michigan	5
0	Chicago	17

1900

50	Ripon	0
5	P. & S.	0
11	Beloit	0
64	Upper Iowa	0
45	Grinnell	0
5	Minnesota	6
54	Notre Dame	0
39	Chicago	5
27	Illinois	0

1901

26	Milwaukee Medical	0
62	Hyde Park HS	0
40	Beloit	0
23	Knox	5
50	Kansas	0
18	Nebraska	0
45	Ames	0
18	Minnesota	0
35	Chicago	0

1902

11	Lawrence	0
24	Hyde Park HS	5
52	Lawrence	0
52	Beloit	6
38	Kansas	0
0	Michigan	6
51	Northwestern	0
0	Minnesota	11
0	Chicago	11

1903

28	Naperville	0
40	Lawrence	7
87	Beloit	0
32	Osteopaths	0
54	Knox	6
6	Chicago	15
52	Oshkosh	0
0	Michigan	16
6	Northwestern	6
0	Minnesota	17

1904

45	Fort Sheridan	0
33	Marquette	0
82	Drake	0
0	Michigan	28
36	Beloit	0
0	Minnesota	28
11	Chicago	18
58	Notre Dame	0

1905

16	Company 10	20
49	Northwestern College	0
29	Marquette	0
34	Lawrence	0
21	Notre Dame	0
0	Chicago	4
17	Alumni	0
16	Minnesota	12
44	Beloit	0
0	Michigan	12

1906

5	Lawrence	0
10	North Dakota	0
18	Iowa	4
29	Purdue	5
16	Illinois	6

1907

4	Illinois	15
6	Iowa	5
11	Indiana	8
12	Purdue	6
17	Minnesota	17

1908

35	Lawrence	0
16	Indiana	0
24	Freshmen	15
9	Marquette	6
5	Minnesota	0
12	Chicago	18

1909

22	Lawrence	0
6	Indiana	3
21	Northwestern	11
6	Minnesota	34
6	Chicago	6

1910

6	Lawrence	6
3	Indiana	12
0	Northwestern	0
0	Minnesota	28
10	Chicago	0

1911

15	Lawrence	0
24	Ripon	0
26	Colorado	0
28	Northwestern	3
12	Iowa	0
6	Minnesota	6
0	Chicago	5

1912

13	Lawrence	0

56	Northwestern	0
41	Purdue	0
30	Chicago	12
64	Arkansas	7
14	Minnesota	0
28	Iowa	10

1913

58	Lawrence	7
13	Marquette	0
7	Purdue	7
7	MAC	12
3	Minnesota	21
12	Ohio	0
0	Chicago	19

1914

21	Lawrence	0
48	Marquette	0
14	Purdue	7
7	Ohio State	6
6	Chicago	0
3	Minnesota	14
9	Illinois	24

1915

82	Lawrence	0
85	Marquette	0
28	Purdue	3
21	Ohio State	0
13	Chicago	14
3	Illinois	17
3	Minnesota	20

1916

20	Lawrence	0
28	South Dakota	3
13	Haskell	0
30	Chicago	7
13	Ohio State	14
0	Minnesota	54
0	Illinois	0

1917

34	Beloit	0
0	Notre Dame	0
0	Illinois	7
20	Iowa	0
10	Minnesota	7
3	Ohio State	16
18	Chicago	0

1918

0	Camp Grant	7
21	Beloit	0
0	Illinois	22
0	Minnesota	6
14	Ohio State	3
7	MAC	6

1919

13	Marquette	0
10	Northwestern	6
14	Illinois	10
7	Minnesota	19
0	Ohio State	3
10	Chicago	3
37	Ripon	0

1920

60	Lawrence	0
27	MAC	0
27	Northwestern	7
7	Ohio State	13
3	Minnesota	0
14	Illinois	9
3	Chicago	0

1921

28	Lawrence	0
24	South Dakota Aggies	3
27	Northwestern	0
20	Illinois	0
35	Minnesota	0
7	Michigan	7
0	Chicago	3

1922

41	Carlton	0
20	South Dakota Aggies	6
20	Indiana	0
14	Minnesota	0
0	Illinois	3
6	Michigan	13
0	Chicago	0

1923

7	Coe	3
21	MAC	0
52	Indiana	0
0	Minnesota	0
0	Illinois	10
3	Michigan	6
6	Chicago	13

1924

25	North Dakota	0
17	Ames	0
7	Coe	7
7	Minnesota	7
0	Michigan	21
3	Notre Dame	38
7	Iowa	21
0	Chicago	0

1925

30	Ames	0
35	Franklin	0
0	Michigan	21
7	Purdue	0
12	Minnesota	12

6	Iowa	0
21	Michigan State	10
20	Chicago	7

1926

38	Cornell College	0
13	Kansas	0
0	Purdue	0
27	Indiana	7
0	Michigan	37
10	Minnesota	16
20	Iowa	10
14	Chicago	7

1927

31	Cornell	6
26	Kansas	6
0	Michigan	14
12	Purdue	6
7	Minnesota	13
20	Grinnell	2
0	Iowa	16
0	Chicago	12

1928

12	Purdue	19
22	Notre Dame	6
49	Cornell	0
7	Michigan	0
15	Alabama	0
25	Chicago	0
13	Iowa	0
0	Minnesota	6

1929

21	South Dakota	0
13	Colgate	6
0	Northwestern	7
0	Notre Dame	19
0	Iowa	14
0	Purdue	13
20	Chicago	6
12	Minnesota	13

1930

53	Lawrence	6
28	Carlton	0
34	Chicago	0
27	Pennsylvania	0
6	Purdue	7
0	Ohio State	0
58	South Dakota State	7
7	Northwestern	20
14	Minnesota	0

1931

33	Bradley	6
12	North Dakota State	7
7	Auburn	7
21	Purdue	14
13	Pennsylvania	27
0	Minnesota	14

7	Illinois	6
12	Chicago	7
0	Michigan	16
0	Ohio State	6

1932

7	Marquette	2
34	Iowa	0
6	Purdue	7
39	Coe	7
7	Ohio State	7
20	Illinois	12
20	Minnesota	13
18	Chicago	7

1933

19	Marquette	0
0	Illinois	21
7	Iowa	26
0	Purdue	14
0	Chicago	0
25	West Virginia	6
0	Ohio State	6
3	Minnesota	6

1934

3	Marquette	0
28	South Dakota State	7
0	Purdue	14
0	Notre Dame	19
0	Northwestern	7
10	Michigan	0
7	Illinois	3
0	Minnesota	34

1935

6	South Dakota	13
0	Marquette	33
0	Notre Dame	27
12	Michigan	20
7	Chicago	13
8	Purdue	0
13	Northwestern	13
7	Minnesota	33

1936

24	South Dakota	7
6	Marquette	12
14	Purdue	35
0	Notre Dame	27
6	Chicago	7
18	Northwestern	26
27	Cincinnati	6
0	Minnesota	24

1937

32	South Dakota	0
12	Marquette	0
27	Chicago	0
0	Pittsburgh	21
13	Iowa	6
6	Northwestern	14

| 7 | Purdue | 7 |
| 6 | Minnesota | 13 |

1938

27	Marquette	0
31	Iowa	13
6	Pittsburgh	26
7	Purdue	13
6	Indiana	0
20	Northwestern	13
14	UCLA	7
0	Minnesota	21

1939

14	Marquette	13
13	Iowa	19
7	Texas	17
0	Indiana	14
7	Northwestern	13
0	Illinois	7
7	Purdue	7
6	Minnesota	23

1940

33	Marquette	19
12	Iowa	30
7	Northwestern	27
14	Purdue	13
13	Illinois	6
6	Columbia	7
27	Indiana	10
13	Minnesota	22

1941

7	Marquette	28
14	Northwestern	41
23	Iowa	0
27	Indiana	25
20	Syracuse	27
34	Ohio State	46
13	Purdue	0
6	Minnesota	41

1942

7	Camp Grant	0
7	Notre Dame	7
35	Marquette	7
17	Missouri	9
13	Great Lakes	7
13	Purdue	0
17	Ohio State	7
0	Iowa	6
20	Northwestern	19
20	Minnesota	6

1943

7	Marquette	33
7	Camp Grant	10
7	Iowa	5
7	Illinois	25
0	Notre Dame	50
0	Indiana	34
0	Purdue	32
0	Northwestern	41
0	Michigan	27
13	Minnesota	25

1944

7	Northwestern	6
21	Marquette	2
7	Ohio State	20
13	Notre Dame	28
12	Great Lakes	40
0	Purdue	35
26	Iowa	7
0	Michigan	14
26	Minnesota	28

1945

0	Great Lakes	0
40	Marquette	13
0	Ohio State	12
7	Illinois	7
7	Purdue	13
27	Iowa	7

14	Northwestern	28
7	Navy	36
26	Minnesota	12

1946

34	Marquette	0
28	California	7
0	Northwestern	28
20	Ohio State	7
21	Illinois	27
24	Purdue	20
7	Iowa	21
6	Michigan	28
0	Minnesota	6

1947

32	Purdue	14
7	Indiana	7
7	California	48
9	Yale	0
35	Marquette	12
29	Northwestern	0
46	Iowa	14
6	Michigan	40
0	Minnesota	21

1948

7	Indiana	35
20	Illinois	16
14	California	40
7	Yale	17
32	Ohio State	34
13	Iowa	19
7	Northwestern	16
26	Marquette	0
0	Minnesota	16

1949

41	Marquette	0
13	Illinois	13
20	California	35
48	Navy	13

One of the Big Ten's All-American selections in 1942 was Pat Harder, Wisconsin's bulldozing fullback.

0	Ohio State	21
30	Indiana	14
14	Northwestern	6
35	Iowa	13
6	Minnesota	14

1950

28	Marquette	6
7	Illinois	6
14	Iowa	0
13	Michigan	26
14	Northwestern	13
33	Purdue	7
14	Ohio State	19
0	Pennsylvania	20
14	Minnesota	0

1951

22	Marquette	6
10	Illinois	14
6	Ohio State	6
31	Purdue	7
41	Northwestern	0
6	Indiana	0
16	Pennsylvania	7
34	Iowa	7
30	Minnesota	6

1952

42	Marquette	19
20	Illinois	6
14	Ohio State	23
42	Iowa	13
7	UCLA	20
21	Rice	7
24	Northwestern	20
37	Indiana	14
21	Minnesota	21
0	*Southern California	7
	*Rose Bowl	

1953

20	Penn State	0
13	Marquette	11
0	UCLA	13
28	Purdue	19
19	Ohio State	20
10	Iowa	6
34	Northwestern	13
34	Illinois	7
21	Minnesota	21

1954

52	Marquette	14
6	Michigan State	0
13	Rice	7
20	Purdue	6
14	Ohio State	31
7	Iowa	13
34	Northwestern	13
27	Illinois	14
27	Minnesota	0

1955

28	Marquette	14
37	Iowa	14
9	Purdue	0
21	Southern California	33
16	Ohio State	26
0	Michigan State	27
41	Northwestern	14
14	Illinois	17
6	Minnesota	21

1956

41	Marquette	0
6	Southern California	13
7	Iowa	13
6	Purdue	6
0	Ohio State	21
0	Michigan State	33
7	Northwestern	17
13	Illinois	13
13	Minnesota	13

1957

60	Marquette	6
45	West Virginia	13
23	Purdue	14
7	Iowa	21
13	Ohio State	16
7	Michigan State	21
41	Northwestern	12
24	Illinois	13
14	Minnesota	6

1958

20	Miami (Fla.)	0
50	Marquette	0
31	Purdue	6
9	Iowa	20
7	Ohio State	7
9	Michigan State	7
17	Northwestern	13
31	Illinois	12
27	Minnesota	12

1959

16	Stanford	14
44	Marquette	6
0	Purdue	21
25	Iowa	16
12	Ohio State	3
19	Michigan	10
24	Northwestern	19
6	Illinois	9
11	Minnesota	7
8	Washington	44

1960

24	Stanford	7
35	Marquette	6
24	Purdue	13
21	Iowa	28
7	Ohio State	34
16	Michigan	13
0	Northwestern	21
14	Illinois	35
7	Minnesota	26

1961

7	Utah	0
0	Michigan State	20
6	Indiana	3
23	Oregon State	20
15	Iowa	47
21	Ohio State	30
29	Northwestern	10
55	Illinois	7
23	Minnesota	21

1962

69	New Mexico State	13
30	Indiana	6
17	Notre Dame	8
42	Iowa	14
7	Ohio State	14
34	Michigan	12
37	Northwestern	6
35	Illinois	6
14	Minnesota	9
37	Southern California	42

1963

41	Western Michigan	0
14	Notre Dame	9
38	Purdue	20
10	Iowa	7
10	Ohio State	13
13	Michigan State	30
17	Northwestern	14
7	Illinois	17
0	Minnesota	14

1964

17	Kansas State	7
7	Notre Dame	31
7	Purdue	28
31	Iowa	21
3	Ohio State	28
6	Michigan State	22
13	Northwestern	17
0	Illinois	29
14	Minnesota	7

1965

0	Colorado	0
6	Southern California	26
16	Iowa	13
0	Nebraska	37
21	Northwestern	7
10	Ohio State	20
14	Michigan	50
7	Purdue	45
0	Illinois	51
7	Minnesota	42

1966

20	Iowa State	10
3	Southern California	38
7	Iowa	0
3	Nebraska	31
3	Northwestern	3
13	Ohio State	24
17	Michigan	28
0	Purdue	23
14	Illinois	49
7	Minnesota	6

1967

0	Washington	17
16	Arizona State	42
7	Michigan State	35
11	Pittsburgh	13
21	Iowa	21
13	Northwestern	17
9	Indiana	14
15	Ohio State	17
14	Michigan	27
14	Minnesota	21

1968

7	Arizona State	55
17	Washington	21
0	Michigan State	39
0	Utah State	20
0	Iowa	41
10	Northwestern	13
20	Indiana	21
8	Ohio State	43
9	Michigan	34
15	Minnesota	23

1969

21	Oklahoma	48
23	UCLA	34
7	Syracuse	43
23	Iowa	17

7	Northwestern	27
36	Indiana	34
7	Michigan	35
7	Ohio State	62
55	Illinois	14
10	Minnesota	35

1970

7	Oklahoma	21
14	TCU	14
29	Penn State	16
14	Iowa	24
14	Northwestern	24
30	Indiana	12
15	Michigan	29
7	Ohio State	24
29	Illinois	17
39	Minnesota	14

1971

31	Northern Illinois	0
20	Syracuse	20
28	LSU	38
11	Northwestern	24
35	Indiana	29
31	Michigan State	28
6	Ohio State	31
16	Iowa	20
14	Purdue	10
27	Illinois	35
21	Minnesota	23

1972

31	Northern Illinois	7
31	Syracuse	7
7	LSU	27
21	Northwestern	14
7	Indiana	33
0	Michigan State	31
20	Ohio State	28
16	Iowa	14
6	Purdue	27

7	Illinois	27
6	Minnesota	14

1973

13	Purdue	14
25	Colorado	28
16	Nebraska	20
37	Wyoming	28
0	Ohio State	24
6	Michigan	35
31	Indiana	7
0	Michigan State	21
35	Iowa	7
36	Northwestern	34
17	Minnesota	19

1974

28	Purdue	14
21	Nebraska	20
21	Colorado	24
59	Missouri	20
7	Ohio State	52
20	Michigan	24
35	Indiana	25
21	Michigan State	28
28	Iowa	15
52	Northwestern	7
49	Minnesota	14

1975

6	Michigan	23
48	South Dakota	7
21	Missouri	27
7	Kansas	41
17	Purdue	14
0	Ohio State	56
17	Northwestern	14
18	Illinois	9
28	Iowa	45
9	Indiana	9
3	Minnesota	24

Index